RECOMMENDATIONS FOR DR. MOREY'S MINISTRY

Dr. Morey's speaking and writing ministry is recommended by some of the best-known Christian leaders in this generation.

Dr. D. James Kennedy

"Dr. Robert A. Morey is an excellent speaker and writer on the subject of cults and the occult, His books are excellent resource tools on these -subjects. It is my pleasure to recommend him to churches everywhere throughout our land."

Dr. John Ankerberg

"I have known Dr. Robert Morey for a number of years and welcome this opportunity to recommend him to you. Dr. Morey is a man with an excellent understanding of the historic Christian faith and a particular skill as a defender of the Faith. I heartily recommend him to you."

Dr. Stephen Olford

"I praise the Lord that He has given you such a strategic ministry in the field of apologetics and theology. The Lord bless you richly."

Dr. Herbert Ehrenstein

"It is a genuine privilege for me to recommend Dr. Robert A. Morey as a competent Biblical scholar in the field of apologetics, Bible teaching and evangelism. I have known Dr. Morey for over 30 years and it has been a delight to me to see his developing a fantastic grasp of Biblical truth, and his unique ability to translate that exalted truth of God's Word into down-to-earth, meaningful and methodical ways his audiences can make use of it."

Dr. Kevin Johnson

"Dr. Robert Morey is one of the finest Biblical scholars in the field of comparative religious studies (apologetics) in North America. His books and presentations have been tremendously useful. I highly recommend him to you."

DEATH AND THE AFTERLIFE

Nominated as "1985 Book of the Year" by Cornerstone and chosen as "Best Reading of 1985" by Biblical Evangelist, this book quickly made it on several "Best Seller" lists. It has been featured on the John Ankerberg Show and many other radio/TV ministries. It is used in many seminaries such as Trinity Evangelical, Dallas, Southwestern, Conservative Baptist, Reformed, Gordon-Conwell, Moody Bible Institute, etc.

Dr. Roger Nicole (Reformed Seminary)

Dr. Morey's work provides an extensive examination of the biblical language related to human destiny beyond the grave. The lucid style and the very careful organization of the material make the work readily understandable to lay people as well as useful for pastors and other scholars.

Dr. Vernon Grounds (Conservative Baptist Seminary)

Since the earliest years of Christianity, the doctrine of eternal punishment has been fiercely attacked. Today that attack continues. Conditionalism and universalism are widely accepted as being biblically, logically and ethically far more acceptable than traditional theology. But Dr. Morey here presents a persuasive case with which anyone who seeks to malign or weaken the historical doctrine must reckon.

Dr. Jay Adams (Westminster Theological Seminary)

Here is a book to buy. It has been some time since a notable work on the future state of man after death has appeared. Morey's book admirably fills this gap. In addition to the Biblical data, as a plus, Morey includes a wealth of intertestamental and patristic resources.

Dr. Gleason Archer (Trinity Evangelical Divinity)

The author does everything right. His knowledge of the Jewish literature on death and the afterlife is profound. I recommend this work to one and all as the finest treatment of death, the soul, hell, and heaven.

Dr. Gary R. Habermas (Liberty University)

This volume generally exhibits a high degree of scholarship. One is repeatedly impressed by the amount of background material and research that had to be done in order to interact properly with the individual topics in Part I. This volume by Morey is a well-researched treatise on the biblical data concerning death and the afterlife. The topic of death and the afterlife is always a popular one. Accordingly, I recommend this book as a textbook for courses on cults or eschatology, whether for group studies or for personal reading. Much noteworthy data is supplied which needs to be studied and digested.

Christian Scholar's Review

Morey's book is the most comprehensive biblical study on the doctrine of death and the afterlife to appear in the last half century. He is a first-rate exegete whose command of the Hebrew and Greek languages is apparent in every chapter. He also displays a vast familiarity with the Apocrypha, Pseudepigrapha, Patristic material, Talmud, Midrash, Philo and Josephus. The author's careful scholarship and his attention to details make this volume a valuable contribution to the study of personal eschatology. <u>Death and The Afterlife</u> is a stimulating work worth reading.

Dr. Walter R. Martin (Christian Research Institute)

The first major work on the subject in this century, <u>Death And The Afterlife</u> will for many years be a standard reference work in this sorely neglected field. The scholarship of this volume will impress those who have studied the subject with any degree of thoroughness. At the same time, he communicates many great and profound truths in language that the average layman will both appreciate and profit from. It is a clear, cool breath of fresh air in the midst of a vacuum of doubt and unbelief.

John Ankerberg

A group of men have asked me to pick out what I consider to be the most important book on the market that Christians should read. The book I have chosen is Dr. Robert A. Morey's book, <u>Death And The Afterlife</u>. This is a landmark book that presents overwhelming proof for the biblical doctrine concerning death and the afterlife.

The Biblical Evangelist

The jacket of this remarkable volume calls it "a landmark work." We are willing to go even further and describe it as "a masterpiece!" This book is especially devastating to the cultists and all those who teach soul sleep, annihilation and universalism. We urge every preacher and every Bible student to obtain a copy without delay!"

Spiritual Counterfeits Project

Dr. Morey's book offers a source of order amidst the prevailing chaos of cultism, faddism, and quasi-Christian teaching about the subject of death and the afterlife. The section on exposition begins with a vitally necessary and helpful chapter "The Hermeneutics of Death." Here Dr. Morey present a brief but gutsy review of hermeneutical principles essential to a fair reading of Scripture. This chapter alone would make excellent required reading for Christian students. Students in my "Death, Dying, and Grieving" classes have also found Dr. Morey's discussion of the principle of progressive revelation significant in counseling Christians who wonder if the Old Testament presents views of death and the afterlife that contradict the New Testament. Dr. Morey's dual expertise in biblical languages and cult evangelism are combined to bring solid scholarship to bear on issues that affect not only scholars but the general populace, for as Dr. Morey insightfully notes, "the present popularity of the subject of death and the afterlife is extremely important to all of us, because the death rate is still one per person.

The Trinity: Evidence and Issues

Almost 600 pages in length, this book is the most detailed exegetical work on the Trinity ever written by an evangelical scholar. It begins with a discussion of epistemology and hermeneutics and then proceeds to deal with all the Trinitarian passages found in the Old and New Testaments, the intertestamental period Jewish literature and the writings of the early Church. It concludes with a detailed refutation of all the arguments given by anti-Trinitarians.

Dr. John Ankerberg and Dr. John Weldon

Dr. Robert Morey's new book, *The Trinity: Evidences and Issues*, is simply excellent. It will undoubtedly become the standard reference work on the subject for years to come.

This book not only offers indisputable biblical proof of the historic Christian doctrine of the Trinity, carefully evaluating the Greek and Hebrew texts, it evaluates a very large number of associated issues relating to historical theology, contemporary culture, denials of the Trinity and apologetics generally.

Among these topics are Arianism, feminism, liberal theology and the Jesus Seminar, humanism, Mormonism, contemporary philosophy, the intertestamental period, Islam, modalism, Jewish views, Unitarianism, Oneness Pentecos-talism, and much more.

We wish to give our highest recommendation to this book and to congratulate both the publisher and Dr. Morey for making it available to the larger Christian public. We pray it will have a major ongoing ministry to the layman and scholar alike. If you purchase only one book on the Trinity, this must be it.

Dr. Gleason Archer (Trinity Evangelical Divinity)

This is, without a doubt, the best defense of the Trinity ever written. It contains original research in the intertestamental literature, such as the Dead Sea Scrolls, that surprised even me.

The Islamic Invasion

This book is the first fully documented refutation of Islam in over a century. Over one hundred errors in the Qur'an are revealed. Dr. Morey proves that Allah is not God, Muhammad was not God's prophet, and the Qur'an is not the Word of God. The book deals with the "Black Muslims" as well as orthodox Islam. It has been translated into Swedish, Norwegian, Farsi, and Spanish with many more languages in preparation.

Dr. Erwin Lutzer (The Moody Church)

Here is a book that concisely tells what Islam is- and what it isn't! I found it absorbing, clear and very helpful. It is a readable expose of a major world religion that could be a threat to our basic freedoms. I wish every evangelical who is concerned about Muslim evangelism would read this book and pass it along to a friend.

The Biblical Evangelist

Morey, a careful scholar whose statements we have learned to trust, has divided his material into 5 divisions: "The Nature of Islam" (2 chapters), "The Cultural Background of Islam (2 chapters), "The God Of Islam (1 chapter, contrasting Allah with the God of the Bible; among other things he lists ten major differences), The Prophet Of Islam" (2 chapters, very telling about Muhammad, including his sex life and 21 differences between him and Jesus Christ), "The Scared Book OF Islam" (3 chapters). Most Christians, including many preachers and teachers, know that Islam is a false religion and Muhammad a false prophet, but don't know how to proceed in refutation. If you want a reliable, trustworthy study of Islam, this is the book for you. Morey consulted every book in the Library of Congress; he read widely and digested carefully. This volume is the fruit of his labors. This is good, solid intensely helpful and valuable teaching about Islam. Even if you didn't want the book to assist you in reaching Muslims, which we hope you will, you need to read it carefully in order to understand what is going on in the Middle East in our day. We urge you to get this book!

Dr. Herbert Ehrenstein (Eternity Magazine)

I received the book today---finished reading it today! Superb! Absolutely outstanding! Your book is coherent, easy to read, comprehensive, touching on every major concept of Islam---while retaining brevity. It is succinct, giving just basic information without getting bogged down with minutiae; yet having ample references for anyone who wants to check your accuracy. Best of all, it is not offensive to the

Muslim---any more than truth has to be. You will, of course be a target for their animosity; but then, I suspect you already are!

Thanks for making such a book available to Christian who may have encounters with Muslims, and to Muslims themselves who may be honest and sufficiently open-minded to face truth.

The Battle of the Gods

This book is without a doubt the most detailed biblical exposition and defense of the Christian concept of God in the 20th century. It refutes the heresy of the so-called "Open View of God" that is now being taught in many evangelical circles.

Dr. Walter Martin

Once again, Dr. Robert A. Morey methodically dissects his topic, and exhausts the relevant evidence. Morey is a "voice crying in the wilderness," crying out for God's people to be faithful to the "faith once for all delivered to the saints." His unashamed passion for the glory of God, that "God be true though every man a liar," is evident throughout. The Battle of the Gods is a resounding, painstakingly thorough, inescapable refutation of the teaching that the Christian God does not know the future.

Dr. D. James Kennedy

Today, God's character and attributes are again being called into question. Some well-known theologians have resurrected neo-pagan views of God and have tried to pass them off as Christian. Dr. Morey has written the definitive rebuttal to the "god as finite" view. May God use it to arrest this abomination before it spreads.

John Ankerberg

The proper work of Christian apologetics is to articulate fully and clearly the Truth of the Bible, and also to point out the fallacies and weaknesses of any opposing view. On those terms, The Battle of the Gods is a cogent apologetic for the Biblical doctrine of God.

The proper Biblical teachings are advanced with all the clarity and intensity of a Pastor-teacher. Passage after passage is examined in its proper contexts and then marshaled to build a comprehensive and unassailable statement of the changelessness, wisdom and sovereignty of God.

In addressing those views that teach that God is in some way finite or limited, Morey proves equally unrelenting. The pagan origins and history of the "finite God" teaching are examined and documented. The arguments for such teachings are shown to be built on flawed logic and weak foundations. In the vernacular, Morey has "dusted off the spot" on which any teachings that God is limited may be able to stand.

In a day when the correct view of God is under siege from a host of competing theologies, Dr. Morey's book will stand as a fortress for the Truth, and as a "must" reading for those concerned with safe-guarding truth.

Dr. Simon Kistemaker

I am thankful for the work Dr. Morey has done. This book is a contribution to evangelical scholarship. I hope this volume receives a wide reading, for it deserves to be read by everyone who is an evangelical. It shows the reader the dangers that surround us and lie ahead.

Dr. Robert P. Lightner

Morey has given a "definitive rebuttal of the god as finite view," as D. James Kennedy has said in his evaluation of this book. The general Christian public is not yet aware that pagan ideas about God continue to infiltrate the evangelical community. Men respected as evangelical scholars, such men as Richard Rice and Clark Pinnock, are accused of embracing dangerous aspects of process theology. Morey cites convincing evidence for his accusations.

The book is divided into four parts—the gods of the heathen, the finite God traditions, the God of the Bible, and the God of Christian theology. Each part is well documented.

Morey has built an excellent base for his contention— rejection of a totally inerrant Bible inevitably results in man instead of God becoming the measure. This book will serve well in courses on theology proper.

The Bible, Natural Law, and Natural Theology: Conflict or Compromise?

By Dr. Robert A. Morey

Copyright © 2010 by Dr. Robert A. Morey
Christian Scholars Press
P.O. Box 240,
Millerstown, PA 17062
www.faithdefenders.com
1-800-41-TRUTH

The Bible, Natural Theology and Natural Law: Conflict or Compromise?
by Dr. Robert A. Morey

Printed in the United States of America

ISBN 9781609571436

All rights reserved solely by the author. The author guarantees all contents are original and do not infringe upon the legal rights of any other person or work. No part of this book may be reproduced in any form without the permission of the author. The views expressed in this book are not necessarily those of the publisher.

Unless otherwise indicated, Bible quotations are taken from the New American Standard Version. Copyright © 1974 by The Lockman Foundation.

www.xulonpress.com

About the Author:

Dr. Robert Morey (B.A., M.Div., D. Min., Ph.D., D.D.) is an internationally recognized scholar in the fields of biblical philosophy, theology, and apologetics. He is the Executive Director of the Research and Education Foundation that seeks to define, document, and defend "the faith once for all delivered unto the saints" (Jude 3). He has also written:

A Bible Handbook on Slander and Gossip

Is Eastern Orthodoxy Christian?

The Islamic Invasion

Winning the War Against Radical Islam

The Trinity: Evidence and Issues

Death and The Afterlife

How the Old and New Testaments Relate to Each Other

The Nature and Extent of God's Knowledge

Fearing God

Studies in the Atonement

Battle of the Gods

Satan's Devices

The Encyclopedia of Practical Christianity

The Truth about Masons

How to Keep Your Faith While In College

The New Atheism and the Erosion of Freedom

An Introduction to Defending the Faith

When Is It Right To Fight?

How to Answer a Jehovah's Witness

How to Answer a Mormon

Reincarnation and Christianity

Horoscopes and the Christian

Worship Is Not Just For Sundays

How to Keep Your Kids Drug-Free

The Dooyeweerdian Concept of the Word of God

Here Is Your God

Is The Sabbath For Today?

Dedicated to Dr. Cornelius Van Til

"We cannot properly set off the Reformed faith against the Roman Catholic Faith unless natural theology be rejected as springing from the autonomous man's efforts to keep from facing the claims of his Creator Redeemer God. We cannot even set off the Protestant view of faith unless we distinguish God's clear revelation speaking to us in man and in nature and man's false response to this clear revelation in his natural theology."

-Cornelius Van Til

Special thanks to Thomas F. Smith II, Jessica and Omar Garcia, Jon Powell, John Morey, and Stephen Macasil for their help in preparing the manuscript.

Recommendation for This Book

Dr. Robert Morey's study of natural law and natural theology raises important questions that every Bible-believer will want answered. Though the subject may at first glance seem daunting, Morey's presentation seeks to clarify the issues at stake and the consequences attending various answers in this potentially divisive discussion. His careful study and explanation of various Bible passages will yield a useful orientation to the classic arguments furnished us by the Reformers and their faithful heirs. All of this should caution us not to underestimate the importance of this book!

Dr. Nelson D. Kloosterman

Professor of Ethics and New Testament Studies

Mid-America Reformed Seminary

I have known Dr. Morey for over forty years. He is one of the clearest thinkers and writers that I have ever met. His latest book on natural theology, as usual, gets to the heart of the matter, and again, as usual, gives clear and concise Biblical answers. A.W. Tozer said, "the most important thing about any person is what comes into their mind when they think of the word God." If you digest Dr. Morey's book, you will think of 'God' as the glorious One depicted in Holy Scripture.

John G. Reisinger,

Editor, Sound of Grace

Forward

Dr. Vincent Cheung

Natural theology[1] arises from man's attempt to discover reality – God, man, ethics, even salvation – with methods that exclude divine revelation. Such a project requires ultimate confidence in man's faculties and procedures. It assumes an attitude that says, "If it is there, I will find it. If it is true, I will prove it." The natural theologian trusts in himself to discover what he needs to know and what there is to know. Since the object of his trust is himself, and since his conclusions are founded on his reliance on his own abilities, his own methods, and his own premises, what this man-oriented enterprise amounts to is self-worship.

When I was asked to write the foreword to Dr. Robert Morey's new book, I thought that to mention this implication of natural theology is one way to direct the reader's attention to the grave importance of the subject. Although many of those who contend against natural theology fail to characterize the matter in this manner, I was pleased that Morey indeed stresses this point with remarkable clarity right at the beginning. He writes, "If you begin only with yourself, you will end only with yourself. The only 'god' you will find looking into the well of your own soul is a reflection of your own image." And later he adds, "When a Natural Theologian looks into the well of his mind, he thinks he is seeing God in the reflection at the bottom. But, in reality, he is only looking at his own reflection!"

This is a simple but profound way to illustrate our contention that natural theology and revealed theology are not just two ways of pursuing the same purpose and of attaining the same knowledge. And human speculation or natural theology is not to be seen as the prolegomena to divine revelation or reveal theology. Rather, these represent two divergent ways of discovery that carry their adherents in different directions. Morey notes that natural theology is not "man's search for God but man's flight from God." It is not man's earnest pursuit to know, to love, and to honor God, but it is his attempt to replace God with his own human construction, derived from his own speculation.

Scripture is rich with teachings and illustrations on the opposition between natural theology and revealed theology. Consider Paul's speech to the Areopagus in Acts 17:22-31. It is ironic that this passage is often used by natural theologians to demonstrate the concord between natural theology – even pagan theology – and the revealed theology of the Christian faith.

For example, John Sanders, whom Morey also mentions, comments on this passage as follows:

---

[1] Although Morey appropriately distinguishes between natural law, natural religion, and natural theology, for the sake of convenience, here I will use only the term natural theology.

Interestingly, Paul does not refer to the Old Testament in his speech. He quotes only from pagan poets and uses the ideas and vocabulary of Greek philosophy in his attempt to reach these people. Yet all of Paul's points can be found in the Old Testament, because there are affinities between general and special revelation.[2]

Of course there are affinities between general and special revelation, since both are from God, and God does not contradict himself.[3] But Sanders means something else. He is asserting that the Greek philosophers had derived a natural theology from general revelation, and this natural theology was in substantial agreement with special revelation, although it had been constructed entirely without its benefit.[4] However, this is the very opposite of what the passage indicates.

Although it is true that Paul cites the Greek poets in his speech, this does not automatically mean that he agrees with what they say. The fact itself proves nothing. Right now I am quoting from Sanders, but I am doing so to signal my disagreement with him. Likewise, Paul quotes the poets not to express his agreement, but for another purpose, to expose their inconsistencies. The same can be said of his using the "ideas...of Greek philosophy."

Sander writes, "Paul does not refer to the Old Testament in his speech....Yet all of Paul's points can be found in the Old Testament." That is, he thinks that instead of quoting from the Old Testament, Paul quotes from the Greek poets, but his points are found in the Old Testament; therefore, Greek philosophy agrees with the Old Testament. But is this the best explanation? All of Paul's points are *found in* the Old Testament because all of his points are *taken from* the Old Testament.

This is not the place to perform an exegesis of the passage,[5] but we can be certain that this interpretation is mistaken even without it. This is because Sanders' interpretation would make Paul's intention contradict what he writes in Romans 1:18 and 1 Corinthians 1:21, which state that unbelievers suppress general revelation, and that they did not come to know God by their own speculation. What does this mean for natural theology? It is incompatible with biblical revelation, and so as Morey points out, to maintain the viability of their premise and method, some natural theologians eventually come to reject biblical inspiration and inerrancy. Again, this illustrates the earlier statement that natural theology and revealed theology carry their adherents in different directions.

Christians need not fear that to reject natural theology is to become defenseless before the assaults of non-Christian challenges. We are not at a disadvantage, since Paul writes, "For the foolishness of God is wiser than man's wisdom, and the weakness of God is stronger than man's strength" (1 Corinthians

---

[2] John Sanders, editor; *What About Those Who Have Never Heard?*; InterVarsity Press, 1995; p. 41.
[3] However, note Morey's comments on the dichotomy between general and special revelation.
[4] Morey also draws attention to the common confusion between general revelation and natural theology.
[5] I have done that in my *Presuppositional Confrontations*. Also see Greg Bahnsen, *Always Ready*.

1:25). Full reliance on divine revelation does not make us vulnerable, but invincible. What Christians must do is to learn how to think and communicate on the basis of God's word, rather than to search for security by learning how to function apart from it. As Morey writes, "Without Special Revelation from God, man cannot even explain any aspect of reality." On the other hand, "If we begin with the biblical doctrines of Creation, Fall, and Redemption, we can understand God, man, the world and how they are relate to each other. We have final answers to all the questions of life and death."

Introduction
Dr. John M. Frame

Around 600 BC, a number of Greek thinkers in Miletus, Asia Minor, took up a new intellectual project: to describe the whole universe by reason alone. They did not want to follow earlier writers like Homer and Hesiod, who ascribed natural happenings to gods like Zeus, Hera, Apollo, and Dionysius. Rather, they intended to cast aside all religious and literary tradition and determine by reason alone what the world is *really* like. Among these were Thales, who postulated that all is water; Anaximenes, who thought rather that all reality was air; and Anaximander, who thought that the basic element of the world was an indeterminate stuff that later differentiated itself into water, air, earth, and fire. Other thinkers followed these, like Parmenides, Heraclitus, Plato, Aristotle, and the Stoics, who were far more sophisticated than the Milesians, but who agreed entirely with them that reason was our only means of understanding the world. Some of these thinkers, especially Plato, Aristotle, and the Stoics, also applied this principle to ethics, certain that human reason could discern in nature a moral order that would tell us how to live. Thus began the philosophical tradition of *natural law*.

Coincidentally, these same thinkers also used their reason to find evidence of the divine. Plato found godlike reality in his world of Forms, Aristotle in his Prime Mover, the Stoics in their pantheistic God, Plotinus in his ineffable One. Thus began the philosophical tradition of *natural theology*.

It is not surprising that pagan Greeks would try to find God and moral goodness by reason alone, for they did not believe that there was any reliable revelation from any supernatural being. Those who trusted the God of the Bible, however, found such a revelation close at hand. For them, the knowledge of God and the good was a gift, received from the hand of God himself, the God and Father of Jesus Christ. For them, neither God nor goodness were puzzlements to be resolved by sharper thinking. Rather, God himself had made known his person and his standards. More than that, God's revelation indicated that human beings were not capable of meeting God's standards by their good works. If God were to forgive their sins and save them from his own wrath, they would have to receive another gift: the righteousness of God by the sacrifice of Jesus the Son of God on the cross.

This difference between the Greeks and the Christians had philosophical, epistemological ramifications. Scripture distinguishes sharply between the wisdom of the Greeks and that of God's revelation (1 Cor. 1:22-23). Those who are saved by the blood of Christ should never presume that they can discover God or his moral standards by reason alone. They should rather subordinate their reason to God's revealed words, "not taught by human wisdom but taught by the Spirit" (1 Cor. 2:13).

This is not to deny that there is revelation of God in the created universe. Indeed, there is clear revelation there, both of God's nature (Rom. 1:19-21) and of God's moral standards (verse 32). But because human beings are fallen (Gen. 3) they inevitably misuse the revelation of God in nature: suppressing it (Rom. 1:18), exchanging it for pagan lies (verses 23, 25), refusing to worship the God revealed in his creation (verses 21, 28), refusing to obey his moral standards (24-31). The only remedy for this terrible situation is divine grace, God's salvation through Christ, revealed not in nature, but in the Gospel (Rom. 10:14-17). The implication is that we may gain no reliable knowledge of God from nature, unless we view it in the light of the Gospel, the word of grace, the message of Scripture.

So the Bible contradicts the project of the Greek philosophers. It tells us that the way to know God, right, and wrong, is not through reason alone, but through God's written word. Natural theology and natural law are blind alleys. Certainly reason is a good gift of God. We need it to understand the Scriptures and to apply them to circumstances. In the light of Scripture, indeed, we can see that the heavens declare the glory of God (Ps. 19:1). But human reason loses its way unless it is subject to what God has said in the Bible.

The Greeks did not acknowledge Scripture, and that is why they attempted to know God and the Good by reason alone. As I said, their rationalism is understandable, even though it led to confusion in their thought. But what is very difficult to understand is that many Christian theologians have sought to incorporate Greek natural theology and ethics into their teaching. From the time of the early church fathers (as Justin Martyr) to the great thinkers of the church (Augustine, Aquinas), Greek philosophy has been a huge influence on the formulations of Christian theologians. Reformers like Luther and Calvin resisted this influence. But others, Protestant, Roman Catholic, and Eastern Orthodox alike, have incorporated natural theology and natural law into their theological works, often taking pride in their ability to use these pagan traditions. In modern America, many evangelical and Reformed thinkers have sought to vindicate Christianity by reason alone, and to determine right and wrong by a rational examination of natural law.

This natural theology and natural law ethics represent compromise of Scripture, and as such they represent a great danger to the church. If the Christian worldview and morality are based in human reason, then they are of no value. Nobody should trust his eternal destiny to human speculation. Only if God has spoken can we know him with confidence as our Father, Lord, and Savior. Only if God has spoken can we stand firmly for the wisdom of God, over against the wisdom of the world.

The present volume presents a devastating critique of natural theology and natural law. I have known Dr. Robert Morey for nearly forty years, and I have long admired his gifts of scholarship and writing. He spends months in research, getting to the bottom of issues. He has studied with the top scholars in theology and apologetics, and he has been working in these fields constantly through his long ministry. While carrying on the work of the pastorate, he has written and published nearly fifty books. He has engaged in many debates and given lectures on many philosophical, historical, and theological subjects. More important, he stands boldly for God's word, against any denial or compromise of it. He puts his very life on the line. Militant Muslims have threatened to kill him because of his firm stance for biblical truth.

I'm delighted that he has stepped forward to deal with the issue of natural theology. He understands well the philosophical and theological traditions that have given rise to this compromise, and he has dug deeply into Scripture to present God's truth on this matter.

I will have to say that I have a few disagreements with Dr. Morey's statements in this book. No two theologians are likely to agree on everything, and when I read a huge book like this I inevitably find a number of assertions that I would put differently. He and I differ somewhat on his evaluations of a number of writers; in my view he is somewhat prone to overstatement. He understands my view of this; I understand likewise if he finds me prone to understatement. But he has taken up this huge and vitally important task, while I and others have held our peace. We must allow Dr. Morey to put his critique in his own way.

My disagreements with Dr. Morey are minor, however, compared to my great admiration for him and for the book as a whole. Its argument is solidly biblical, and its accumulation of biblical data is overwhelming. I hope that God prospers it so that many will read it and take heed. The greatest need of Christianity today is a renewed commitment to *sola Scriptura*, the Reformation principle that Scripture alone, not human reason, imagination, or sensation, must be our final authority. God's voice is what needs to be heard, not our speculations or feelings. Only when God's Word is preached as the ultimate and sufficient authority will our preaching bring reformation and revival.

Author's Introduction

Having worked in the retail business for many years, I learned that the best way to train cashiers to recognize counterfeit money is for them to become so familiar with *real* money (the feel of it, the look of it and even the smell of it) so that when a counterfeit bill comes along, they will recognize it instinctively.

Since there are so many different counterfeit bills, with new ones coming out all the time, studying all past ones is a waste of time. If the cashiers know the *true* currency, they will be able to detect the *false*. In the same way, the best way to train Christians to detect false theology is for them to have a good understanding of true biblical theology first. Once they know the true, they can detect the false.

It is no surprise that Natural Law and Natural Theology rise and fall in popularity in tandem with the level of sound biblical knowledge. In Roman Catholic and Orthodox countries, where biblical illiteracy is the norm, all you have is Natural Law and Theology. Wherever the *Sola Scriptura* of the Protestant Reformation gained ground, biblical preaching and Revealed Theology became dominant, and as a result Natural Law and Theology died away.

Luther thundered that "Reason was a whore" who slept with anyone, and stated that Thomas Aquinas was in hell. Calvin always spoke of Aquinas' "schoolmen" as enemies of the gospel. *Sola Scriptura* was the basis of the Reformation and the Bible was the final authority on what to believe (theology) and how to live (law). Biblical Law and Theology replaced Natural Law and Theology.

The beginning of the new millennium has witnessed new aggressive forms of *Reasonalotry* in evangelical circles. "Reasonalotry" is the enthronement of human reason in the place of God as the Origin of truth, justice, morals, meaning, and beauty. Man's faculty of reasoning is abstracted, absolutized, idealized, and romanticized into a false idol.

"Reason" is an idol because it supposedly infallibly knows all things. Everything, including God, must bow before the "Bar of Reason" for judgment. Human Reason is the "god of the gaps," who can explain all things *rationally.*

Why has Reasonalotry been revived in our day? Biblical knowledge, theology, law, and expository preaching are at an all time low. Most "mega" churches, with thousands in attendance, do not focus on Biblical Truth but on the "felt" needs of the community. "Deeds, not Creeds" and "Works, not Words" seem to be the mantra of today. The darker the religious situation, the more aggressive Reasonalotry becomes. The following illustration will help us at this point.

Imagine you became lost in a jungle where fierce and dangerous animals came out at night to hunt their prey. As the sun begins to set, you desperately try to start a fire, but darkness falls before you can get the fire going. All around you encircling eyes wink on as the predators begin to creep closer. But, the fire finally catches on, and as the brightness of the fire flares up, the encircling eyes begin to recede back into the darkness. The encircling eyes finally wink out as the fire blazes to full strength.

In the middle of the night, as the fire begins to die down, the encircling eyes reappear as the animals begin to creep near again. You awaken and see that the fire has died down and the beasts are getting closer to you. You quickly throw more fuel on the fire, and, as it blazes up, the encircling eyes withdraw once again.

All the different forms of religious humanism such as the cults, the occult, liberalism, paganism, Natural Theology, Natural Law, witchcraft, socialism, rationalism, empiricism, mysticism, fideism, Roman Catholicism, Eastern Orthodoxy, etc., are the encircling eyes that surround us. When we preach and teach sound biblical theology, the encircling eyes withdraw back into the darkness. When the fire of biblical theology and expository preaching die down, the encircling eyes return.

It is time for a New Reformation that will once again define, document, and defend the glorious Gospel of salvation by grace alone, through faith alone, in Christ alone, according to Scripture alone, for the glory of God alone. As we teach and preach the Gospel, Reasonalotry (Natural Religion, Natural Theology, and Natural Law) will once again recede back into the darkness from which it came.

In PART ONE, we will give an EXPOSITION of the Revealed worldview given in the Bible. Once you understand Biblical theology, it will be easier to detect false theologies such as Natural Theology.

In PART TWO, we will APPLY the biblical worldview to God, man, and the world. We have chosen several issues that religious humanists assume lie only within the domain of Natural Philosophy and Theology. In opposition to humanistic thought, we will apply the Lordship of Christ to all of life and claim every square inch of this world for Jesus. There is no "secular" realm where man is lord. Messiah is either Lord of all or not Lord at all.

In PART THREE, we will proceed from exposition and application to a REFUTATION of Natural Theology based upon Scripture. Natural theologians will not take kindly to the idea that we will open up the Bible and judge their views by what is revealed by God in Scripture. But, God *alone* is the Origin of truth, justice, morals, meaning, and beauty. God *alone* is the Measure of all things, including philosophy and theology. We will all stand before God alone for judgment. He *alone* is infinite in wisdom and knowledge.

This book is dedicated to a revival of Reformation theology and biblical preaching. As they increase, the encircling eyes of Reasonalotry will decrease and fade way. This has happened during every great evangelical revival in the past and will happen again as revival fires burn bright once again by God's sovereign grace.

To God alone be all the glory!

Table of Contents

PART ONE EXPOSITION

CHAPTER ONE	THE FOUNDATION OF THE CHRISTIAN WORLDVIEW	1
CHAPTER TWO	THE THREE PILLARS	59
CHAPTER THREE	CREATION EX NIHILO	81
CHAPTER FOUR	THE RADICAL FALL OF MAN INTO SIN AND GUILT	99
CHAPTER FIVE	REDEMPTION	113
CHAPTER SIX	THE BOOK OF ECCLESIASTES	123

PART TWO EXPOSITION

CHAPTER SEVEN	BIBLICAL THEISM	145
CHAPTER EIGHT	BIBLICAL ANTHROPOLOGY	209
CHAPTER NINE	A BIBLICAL PHILOSOPHY OF SCIENCE	235

PART THREE REFUTATION

CHAPTER TEN	THE FAILURE OF DEFINITION	271
CHAPTER ELEVEN	NATURAL LAW	289
CHAPTER TWELVE	NATURAL RELIGION	345
CHAPTER THIRTEEN	NATURAL THEOLOGY	369
CHAPTER FOURTEEN	NATURAL APOLOGETICS	389
CHAPTER FIFTEEN	WHAT THE WORLD NEEDS TO HEAR	399
BIBLIOGRAPHY		405
ENDNOTES		418

Chapter One

The Foundation of the Christian Worldview

Introduction

Since the radical Fall of man into sin and guilt, the "natural man" (1 Cor. 2:14) has "leaned upon his own understanding" (Pro. 3:5) to comprehend God, the world and himself on the basis of human reason, experience, feelings or faith. His "natural" understanding ended in absolute failure because he "cannot understand" these things apart from and independent of God (1Cor. 2:14). Because "all of us like sheep have gone astray, Each of us has turned to his own way," (Isa. 53:6) the natural man "did not know God" (1Cor. 1:21).

Both the Old and New Testaments clearly state "there is no one who understands" (Psa. 14:1-3; Rom. 3:10). The "natural man" produced Natural Laws, Natural Religions, and Natural Theologies on the basis of rationalism, empiricism, mysticism and fideism. All of these ended in apostasy and never did anyone any good. If you begin only with yourself, you will end only with yourself. The only "god" you will find looking into the well of your own soul is a reflection of your own image. The "gods" created through rationalism, empiricism, mysticism, and fideism are false gods; mere reflections of man's hopes, dreams, fears, and psychological problems.

The Importance of the Book of Job

In this light, the importance of the Book of Job cannot be overstated. As the oldest book in the Bible and thus the first book revealed by God and recorded in Scripture, it is the only firm foundation of the biblical worldview. It begins with God's view of the origin, nature, attributes, meaning, and purpose of evil. Any attempt to develop a distinctive "Christian" worldview without the Book of Job as its foundation will utterly fail. As Dr. J. Vernon McGee pointed out,

> This is a great philosophic work and has been acclaimed so by many. Tennyson called this book "the greatest poem, whether of ancient or modern literature." Speaking of the Book of Job, Thomas Carlyle, the Scottish philosopher said, "I call that one of the grandest ever written with pen." Martin Luther said that this book is "more magnificent and sublime than any other book of Scripture." And Dr. Moorehead said, "The Book of Job is one the noblest poems in existence."[1]

The words of Tennyson, Carlyle, Luther, and Moorehead may seem strange to many Christians today. Why did Luther esteem Job higher than Romans? The answer is that Job is the *foundation* of the rest of Scripture, including Romans.

Is it by mere chance or luck that the first biblical book ever written established the principle of *Sola Scriptura* by refuting the vaunted claims of Natural Theology, Philosophy, and Law? The friends of Job assumed the pagan dogma of human autonomy:

- Man is the origin of truth, justice, morals, meaning, and beauty.
- Man is the measure of all things, including God and evil.
- Man does not need divine revelation to figure things out.
- Man's reason, experience, feelings and faith are sufficient basis for what to believe and how to live.

Job's message concerns man's absolute need for and dependence on divine revelation to understand himself, God, and the world.

The biblical authors appealed to the Scriptures as the final authority for what to believe and how to live. They taught that God, not man, is the Source of truth and morals. As Tayler Lewis states in his classic commentary on Job,

> **Job demands a Pure Theism first as the Ground of all other Religious Ideas.**
> Among all writings, inspired or uninspired, the Book of Job stands preeminent for its lofty representations of the pure moral personality, the holiness, the unchallengeable justice, the wisdom, the Omnipotence, the absolute Sovereignty of God. Whatever may be said of its obscurities and difficulties in other respects, in the splendor of its theism it is unsurpassed. Our best modern Theology, in its most approved and philosophical symbols may be challenged to produce anything surpassing the representations which this ancient writing gives us of God as 'a Spirit, infinite, eternal and unchangeable in His being, power, holiness, justice, goodness and truth.' Nothing approaches its ideal of the ineffable purity of the divine character, before which the heavens veil their brightness, and the loftiest intelligences are represented as comparatively unholy and impure. God the Absolute, the Infinite, the Unconditioned, the Unknowable – these are the terms by which our most pretentious philosophizing would characterize Deity as something altogether beyond the ordinary theological conception. But even here this old Book of Job surpasses them in setting forth the transcending glory, the ineffable height, the measureless profundity of the Eternal. [2]

Special revelation is the "ground" or foundation for *all* religious ideas that claim to be "Christian" in the biblical sense of the word. An idea is not "Christian" just because the one asserting it *claims* to be a Christian.

The Word "Christian"

Those who have fallen into the quicksand of modern relativism apply the word "Christian" to any idea as long as the author of that idea claims to be a "Christian." They view the word "Christian" as a "rubber band" word that can be stretched and pulled out of shape to include any and all contradictory philosophies and theologies. This has led to our contemporary situation in which liberals, Roman Catholics, Eastern Orthodox, New Agers, occultists, cultists, neo-orthodox, Open View, and neo-evangelicals are all called "Christian" philosophers and theologians.[3]

What people forget today is that in order for a philosophy or Theology to be truly "Christian," it must be "biblical." Its ideas must be grounded in Holy Scripture instead of "vain speculations" (Rom. 1:21). If the word "Christian" is to mean *anything*, it cannot mean *everything*. It must have a *specific* meaning. It cannot be a "rubber band" word.

The test of whether a philosophy or Theology is truly Christian is whether it begins and ends with the Bible. If a Theology or philosophy is not biblical, then it is not "Christian" in any real sense.

This Sounds Strange Today

I know this sounds strange in a politically-correct world of relativism, compromise, and heresy. Some will claim that we are being mean and unkind when we condemn heresy as heresy. But "let God be true even if this means that all men are liars" (Rom. 3:4) and as Jesus cleansed the temple in His day, so may His church be purified of serious heretical doctrines today.

A Firm Foundation

Again, as the first revelation of Scripture, the Book of Job is the firm foundation of the Biblical worldview and, therefore, the foundation of the Christian worldview. Any so-called "Christian" philosopher or theologian who either ignores or denies the Bible, particularly the Book of Job, is engaging in another sad attempt to masquerade humanism itself as "Christian" in order to deceive the naïve.

Building a Christian Worldview is a good example of the wrong way to construct a "Christian" worldview. While it has some good material and we do not doubt the good intentions of all the authors, instead of a careful exegesis of Scripture as the Origin of truth, the editor of the book adopts the "historical approach" which focuses on an analysis of what *man* has historically said about God, not what *God* has said about man. The historical approach replaces the Bible with man's speculations. The history of man's vain ideas becomes the only proper subject of Theology. In this way it reduces theology to a history of human psychology and sociology.

The editor of the book specifically rejected the idea that we should begin solely with the Bible for our theoretical materials to construct our worldview. He wrote,

> That approach, however, would not enable us to compare and contrast biblical ideas with others that confronted Christians in earlier times and that directly affected the development of

> contemporary viewpoints. Limiting our analysis to biblical materials would also prohibit us from seeing how Christians have both defended their ideas and criticized alternate views. Since Christianity has never existed in a vacuum, its followers have always had to express and implement their faith in particular cultural environments.[4]

The "historical approach" assumes that relative and subjective "cultural environments" factors ultimately control what people believe and how they live. Christians are no different. When culture changes, they say that Christians should change their beliefs. The church must conform to the world or die.

To be sure, Eastern Orthodoxy, Roman Catholicism, and modern Protestant apostate theologies such as liberalism, neo-orthodoxy, neo-evangelicalism, Open View of God, etc. do indeed derive their beliefs and practices from the apostate "cultural environment" around them. In contrast, those who base their worldview on God's Revelation found in Scripture have escaped this problem.

First, the historical approach is a total surrender to relativism. Each individual "cultural environment" is different and changes from nation to nation and age to age. This is the fatal error of Natural Theology. Like a chameleon on a wall, it changes its beliefs to match the colors of its cultural background. This is why Natural theologians change their arguments from generation to generation.

Second, if it is true that what we believe is due to such irrational causes as one's "cultural environment," then that statement has just refuted itself! It is likewise based on irrational forces and therefore meaningless. If it is right, then it is wrong. If it is wrong, then it is wrong. Either way, it is wrong! Any view that defeats itself is doomed for the ash heap of history.

Paul warns us not to allow the cultural environment to mold our thinking.

> And do not be conformed to this age, but be transformed by the renewing of your mind, that you may prove what the will of God is, that which is good and acceptable and perfect. (Rom. 12:2)
>
> καὶ μὴ συσχηματίζεσθε τῷ αἰῶνι τούτῳ, ἀλλὰ μεταμορφοῦσθε τῇ ἀνακαινώσει τοῦ νοὸς εἰς τὸ δοκιμάζειν ὑμᾶς τί τὸ θέλημα τοῦ θεοῦ, τὸ ἀγαθὸν καὶ εὐάρεστον καὶ τέλειον.

First, Paul commands us not to allow "the present cultural environment" (τῷ αἰῶνι τούτῳ) to mold and shape our ideas, priorities, values or standards. D. A. Carson points out,

> V 2, while grammatically parallel to v 1, really explains in more detail how this giving of ourselves as sacrifices is to be carried out. What is required is nothing less than a total transformation in world-view. No longer are we to look at life in terms of *this world*, the realm of sin and death from which we have been transferred by

> God's power (see 5:12–21), but in terms of the new realm to which we belong, the realm ruled by righteousness, life and the Spirit. Living in the world, we are nevertheless no longer 'of the world' (Jn. 17:15–16). The essence of successful Christian living is the *renewing of our minds* so that we might be able to *approve what God's will is*—that is, to recognize and put into practice God's will for every situation we face. God has not given to Christians a set of detailed commandments to guide us. He has given us his Spirit, who is working to change our hearts and minds from within, so that our obedience to God might be natural and spontaneous (see 7:6; 8:5–9; Je. 31:31–34; 2 Cor. 3:6–7; Eph. 4:22–24). [5]

What our "cultural environment" has to say about truth, justice, morals, meaning, and beauty is not as important as what GOD says about truth, justice, morals, meaning, and beauty in Scripture. To the degree our "cultural environment" agrees with the Word of God is the degree it is true and good. When it disagrees with Scripture, we, like Paul, toss it aside as foolishness. And, continuing with this scripture, full surrender to the Lordship of Christ is required.

> I urge you therefore, brethren, by the mercies of God, to present your bodies a living and holy sacrifice, acceptable to God, *which is* your spiritual service of worship. (Rom. 12:1)
>
> Παρακαλῶ οὖν ὑμᾶς, ἀδελφοί, διὰ τῶν οἰκτιρμῶν τοῦ θεοῦ παραστῆσαι τὰ σώματα ὑμῶν θυσίαν ζῶσαν ἁγίαν εὐάρεστον τῷ θεῷ, τὴν λογικὴν λατρείαν ὑμῶν·

This is where the rubber meets the road. Either submit to the absolute authority of Scripture, or bow before the dung hill idols of human reason, experience, feelings, and faith.

Third, do you want to "prove" that the revealed will of God is good, acceptable, and perfect? Let God's Word "transform" your mind as you "renew" your commitment to the Lordship of Christ over all of life.

It is thus no surprise that the Book of Job is not mentioned in *Building a Christian Worldview*. No exegesis of it is even attempted. It does not do us any good to say that our ideas are "biblical" if we never bother to exegetically demonstrate that they are biblical.

Author's Note

Now, do not be distracted when we refer to people by name. The authors of Scripture such as Paul did this. Let us make this point absolutely clear: We have no interest in judging the hearts of people. Most Neo-evangelicals claim to be "saved" in some sense of the word. Maybe they are and maybe not. We don't know. God will on the Day of Judgment judge the hearts of all people (Mat. 7:21-22).

We Must Judge Doctrine

But, while we cannot judge their hearts, we can judge their theology and philosophy by Scripture to see if it is "Christian." This point must be absolutely clear. We have the biblical responsibility to critically judge whether the teachings of someone are in line with Scripture. In 1 Cor. 14:29, after Paul permitted several people to speak, he adds,

> Let the others pass judgment.
>
> καὶ οἱ ἄλλοι διακρινέτωσαν·

The word διακρίνω means to evaluate what is taught under the categories of biblical "truth" and "morals." Hendriksen comments,

> What is the standard by which the listeners judge the words of the speaker? They must evaluate the speaker's message with God's Word. As the Bereans examined the Scriptures every day to see whether Paul's teaching was in harmony with God's revelation (Acts 17:11; see also I Thess. 5:21, *Didache* 11:7 for similar instances), so they are to weigh the words of the prophet. Elsewhere Paul exhorts the believers to let the word of Christ dwell in them richly (Col. 3:16); in teaching and admonishing one another, let the Scriptures serve as the standard.[6]

In the politically correct world of liberalism, doctrine is not placed under these two categories. Doctrine is under the category of "personal preference." But Scripture does not exempt anyone from being judged on their beliefs. Even the Apostle Paul was not exempt. Furthermore, the Bereans were *praised* for using Scripture to judge Paul's teachings. They were called "noble-minded."

> Now these were *more noble-minded* than those in Thessalonica, for they received the word with great eagerness, *examining the Scriptures daily, to see whether these things were so.* (Acts 17:11)
>
> οὗτοι δὲ ἦσαν εὐγενέστεροι τῶν ἐν Θεσσαλονίκῃ, οἵτινες ἐδέξαντο τὸν λόγον μετὰ πάσης προθυμίας καθ' ἡμέραν ἀνακρίνοντες τὰς γραφὰς εἰ ἔχοι ταῦτα οὕτως.

They were described as εὐγενής. The meaning of this word is not difficult to discover. It is found in the Septuagint and in Josephus, and was also used by Greek writers such as Aristophanes. It means to act like a high-class, educated person with discernment. It is the opposite of being a gullible, low-class dunce.

> *Open–minded* translates a word which originally referred to persons of noble birth (see RSV "noble"), but which later came to be used of those qualities which were expected in a person of such birth.[7]

Whenever we judge the worldview of Neo-evangelical Natural theologians, they are insulted and often angry. They whine that we are attacking them personally. They shout and carry on that we are judging their hearts. But we are not interested in judging whether or not they are "saved." That issue is between them and God. But this does not mean that we cannot judge what they *teach*.

In the context of 1 Cor. 14:29, the word διακρίνω means to judge what is said in order to discern if it is in line with Scripture. If they judged what prophets said, how much more what Natural theologians and philosophers teach! Jesus commanded us,

> Do not judge according to appearance, but *judge with righteous judgment*. (John 7:24)
>
> μὴ κρίνετε κατ' ὄψιν, ἀλλὰ τὴν δικαίαν κρίσιν κρίνετε.

While Jesus clearly condemned hypocritical judgment (Mat. 7:1 cf. 7:5), He also said that we are to judge whether someone is a "wild dog" or a "savage pig" (Mat. 7:6, 15). He even commanded us to judge some people as "false prophets." The teachings of Jesus lead us to judge the teachings of all men.

The Example of Jesus

If we look at the example of Jesus to see if He practiced what He preached, we find that He condemned the teachings of the Pharisees, Sadducees, and others. He did not tolerate false doctrine. Thus we will not apologize for judging the worldview of anyone – including professing Christian theologians and philosophers.

Rationalists (like Moreland and Craig) promote a "philosophical foundation" of what they call "a Christian worldview." But they base it upon an idealized and romantic view of man's Natural Reason. They assume their "reason" is self-sufficient and infallible. Thus they are the ultimate origin of truth, justice, morals, meaning, and beauty.

In Moreland's and Craig book, *Philosophical Foundations*, if you look under the name index, you will find many references to Aristotle, Plato, etc. But, if you look under the Js for "Jesus," you will not find a single reference! How can you have a "Christian" worldview if the teachings of Jesus are ignored?

It is not surprising that rationalists do not see any *need* to seek a *supernatural* or *divine* Origin of truth. While having absolute confidence in the infallibility of human reason, they have serious doubts about the infallibility of divine revelation!

Most rationalists, (like Stephen Davis, Clark Pinnock, etc.), deny the inerrancy of Scripture. A few like J. P. Moreland, Norman Geisler, etc. still hold to it. For this we are thankful. They are to be commended for going against their fundamental principles and retaining their faith in the inerrancy of Scripture.

The worldview of rationalists is god-less, Christ-less, and Bible-less because they view their own depraved Reason as a sufficient basis for final answers. In reality, they are religious humanists who believe that *man* is the origin of truth, justice, morals, meaning, and beauty; that *man* is the measure of all things including God; that *man* must begin only with himself, by himself, in and of himself, rejecting any outside information from Special Revelation. They believe that *man*, not God, is, philosophically speaking, the Beginning and the End, the Alpha and Omega, the First and the Last.

James Taylor

James Taylor, following the religious existentialism of Kierkegaard, correctly saw through the sham arguments set forth by rationalists like Geisler, Moreland, and Craig. He realized that human Reason cannot justify belief in God. Instead of turning away from fallen man to God as the Origin of truth, Taylor, like all humanists, looked within himself and chose something else to idealize and romanticize as the Origin of all things.

Taylor chose his own personal experiences as the basis of his worldview. He defines his experience as the basis of the Christian worldview.

> My Christian faith is grounded primarily in my experience of God in Christ through the ministry in my life of the Holy Spirit.[8]
> Belief in God...is grounded in the right kinds of experiences.[9]

Since he chooses his own personal and subjective experience as the basis of his worldview, what does Taylor think of the Bible? Like most humanists, he assumes his own infallibility, while rejecting the infallibility of Scripture.[10]

Of course, if you accept the pagan dogma of libertarian "free will," you cannot "rationally" have an infallible Bible. This is why Natural theologians like Clark Pinnock reject the inerrancy of the Bible.

The libertarian dogma of "free will" means that man must be free at all times from God's control – *even when writing the Bible*. This means that the authors of the Bible were free to make all kinds of stupid and erroneous statements that reflected the culture and superstitions of their day. Taylor explains,

> If God allowed the authors a certain amount of freedom and creativity (and it seems reasonable to think that he did), then they were not merely God's mouthpieces. In that case, even if God does not ever say anything false, it seems possible that those he inspired to write the Scriptures did, at least about relatively unimportant matters.[11]

Because the dogma of libertarian "free will" led Taylor and Pinnock to reject the inerrancy of Scripture, they cannot "rationally" view the Bible as reliable as their own personal reason, experience, feelings, and faith. Humanists always exalt man at the expense of God.

The Inerrancy of Scripture

This is why we, without shame or embarrassment, begin with the inerrant and infallible Bible as the Origin of our worldview. Because the first biblical book written is Job, it is the biblical foundation of the Christian worldview.

An Introduction to Job

Given these facts, we will begin with a brief introduction to the Book of Job. Since we are not writing a commentary on Job *per se*, we will avoid obscure literary jargon and will be content with giving the fruit of our literary analysis of the story of Job and his friends.

First, Job and his friends were real historical characters. They were not poetic fiction drawn from ancient mythology and legend. As *The Pulpit Commentary* points out,

> The early Christian Fathers and the earlier Jewish rabbis treat it as absolutely historical, and no whisper arises to the contrary till several centuries after the Christian era.[12]

Liberals usually dismiss the historicity of Job as an "entirely antiquated" idea that no modern scholar accepts.[13] When forced to admit that there are modern scholars who argue for the historicity of Job, they reply that the issue is of no significance.[14]

The historicity of Job and his friends is assured because of later echoes in both the Old and New Testament.[15]

> Even *though* these three men, Noah, Daniel, and Job were in its midst, by their *own* righteousness they could *only* deliver themselves," declares the Lord God. (Ezekiel 14:14)
>
> Behold, we count those blessed who endured. You have heard of the endurance of Job and have seen the outcome of the Lord's dealings, that the Lord is full of compassion and *is* merciful. (James 5:11)

The context of both passages clearly demonstrates the historicity of Job, his friends, their discussions, and the book that bears his name. They are sufficient to demonstrate that Job was a real flesh and blood man who experienced the pain and suffering described in the book that bears his name. Tayler Lewis again comments,

> It shows that Job lives – and the first reporter, too, we think not only before the giving of the Mosaic Law, but at that still earlier time when there was, indeed, a most sublime theism.[16]

Liberal theologians have speculated that Job was a fictional construct that idealized pre-Mosaic religious life and thought. They dismissed the historical prologue and epilogue as "window dressing." They argued that the poetic structure of the debates between Job and his friends automatically precludes any idea of the historicity of the characters or the discussions.

The liberal hermeneutic is erroneous at this point. Just because the author of Job stylized the discussions in poetic measure does not automatically negate the fact that those debates actually took place. Just because we do not have a literal transcript of exactly who said what, when, where, and how should not disturb us. The story is substantially true and the main points of each speaker are faithfully rendered in poetic language. After all, the author is recasting "something" – not nothing – in a poetic style.

The literary genre of poetry does not preclude the historicity of what the poem describes. There are Psalms that celebrate Creation, the Exodus, and other events in redemptive history (Psa. 89; 104; 105, etc.). Are we to assume that those events did not take place because they are celebrated in poetry?

In preparation for this book, when I asked a Natural theologian why he did not at any point deal with the Book of Job, he replied, "It is poetry and therefore irrelevant." Joseph Parker comments on this dodge,

> Why do we edge the Almighty out of life by describing his supposed intervention as the suggestion of poetry? Why is this poetry supposed to be so mischievous? Is it any more mischievous than a sky? What crimes has it committed? What is the indictment against poetry…Men suppose that when they designated a saying or a suggestion as poetical, they have put it out of court. It is not so…Does he ask little questions? Are they frivolous interrogations that he propounds? Is the inquiry worthy of his name, even though that name be poetical? Is every question here on the level of the highest thinking? Judge the Theophany as a whole, and then say how far we are at liberty to excuse ourselves from the application of its argument on the trivial ground that it is but poetry.[17]

Even in the secular world, one can think of many epic poems written throughout history that celebrated real historic events. "The Charge of the Light Brigade" and the "Midnight Ride of Paul Revere" come to mind. As Rawlinson comments in <u>The Pulpit Commentary,</u>

> Nothing was more common in antiquity than to take a set of historical facts, and expand them into a poem...[18]

The author of Job structured the story of Job and his friends and stylized their discussions in poetry to highlight the focus of his message: *Man is not the origin of truth, justice, morals, meaning or beauty. God through His special revelation is the origin. Without Divine Revelation, man knows nothing.*

Second, we must make the distinction between dating the events and when the Book of Job was written. In terms of dating the events and debates described in Job, they are clearly pre-Mosaic and thus predate the rest of the Bible. This explains the absence in Job of any specific references to Old Covenant rites, ceremonies, temples, and priests. Job probably lived during the time of the Patriarchs, and may have been a contemporary of Abraham.

The discovery of ancient clay tablets from the Patriarchal Period has settled the issue for those who lust after empirical proof. As Gibson pointed out, there are clear parallels to the words found in Job (Ayab) to those found on the clay tablets.

> It is interesting to find that the very similar form Ayab is found on one of the Tel el-Amarna tablets (Winckler, no. 237).[19]

Most scholars guess the ancient clay tablets of Job were collected and translated in the days of Solomon, during which the genre of Jewish Wisdom literature was developed. Since Ezekiel specially refers to Job without explaining who he was to his readers, the book was already well-known before the time of the prophets. Thus there was no need to introduce the book for the first time.

Any standard introduction to Job will also provide a list of many additional passages in the Bible where the Book of Job is either quoted or alluded to. For example, Romans 11:35 is an echo of Job 41:11.

Third, the author is not known. Since God did not tell us, evidently it is not essential to understand the message of Job.

The rationalists of the eighteenth century assumed that Job could not have written it because there was no writing in his day. This is the same reason they gave for denying the Mosaic authorship of the Torah. Archeology exploded that liberal myth a long time ago, and we have many examples of writing before the time of Abraham.

Fourth, the text of Job remains a challenge. When you compare the Hebrew, Greek, Aramaic and Latin texts of Job, you will find a great deal of contradiction. The Greek version is shorter than the Hebrew text!

The Targums of Job do not even help us at this point because of deliberate insertions and even suppression. Céline Mangan, the translator of <u>The Targum of Job</u> comments,

> The targum of Job is one of the most enigmatic of targums: while a targum of the Book of Job was discovered among the Dead Sea Scrolls (11 Qtg Job), this bears little resemblance to the later Rabbinic targum (henceforth tg. Job) known to us from the printed editions of the Bible and which is the subject of this study. Said R. Jose: It once happened that my father, Halafta, visited R. Gamaliel Berabbi at Tiberias and found him sitting at the table of Johanan b. Nizuf with the Targum of the Book of Job in his hand which he was reading. Said he to him, 'I remember that R. Gamaliel, your grandfather, was standing on a high eminence on the Temple Mount, when the Book of Job in a targumaic version was brought before him, whereupon he said to the builder, 'Bury it under the bricks.' He (R. Gamaliel II) too gave orders and they hid it.'" <u>Shabb</u>. 115a.[20]

In this light we have given the priority to the Hebrew text and use the other translations as mere commentary.

Fifth, the place of Job in the canon of Scripture is significant. Since it is the first biblical book ever written, why is it not placed first in the Bible, i.e. before Genesis? Or, since it deals with a historic situation, why is it not in the historical narrative section of the Old Testament?

The order of the books found in the English Bible is not a product of chronology, authorship, chance, or size. We refer the reader to our course material on the Text and Canon of Scripture for the details.[21] But, to summarize that material, it is clear that the scrolls of sacred Scripture were arranged thematically or topically.

Job is in the section of the Old Testament called "Wisdom Literature." This section includes Psalms, Proverbs, Ecclesiastes, and Song of Solomon. Gibson comments,

> The place which the book of Job occupies in our English Bibles after the historical books and before the Psalms is that which it has always occupied in the Western Church, at least since the days of S. Jerome, in whose translation (The Vulgate) it is found in this position, in accordance with the arrangement of the books commonly (though not invariably) adopted in the Greek Bibles.[22]

The King James Version followed the order of Wisdom books found in the Septuagint, the Greek Old Testament used by the early church.[23] Job was placed first in the Wisdom Literature because it was foundational to the rest of the books in that section.

When compared to the other wisdom books, the following order of themes can be seen.

Job: How to cope with evil.
Psalms: How to walk with God.
Proverbs: How to walk with your neighbor.

Ecclesiastes: How to live with meaning.
Song of Solomon: How to walk with your wife.

It is significant that the first biblical book ever written deals with the issue of why evil happens to good people! The subject of evil is thus the *first* issue discussed through divine revelation.

It is important that the existence of God is *not* the first issue addressed by divine revelation, because God's existence is never treated in the Bible as a *problem* that needs solving. It is always assumed to be the *solution* to man's problems, and not as a problem itself. This is why Genesis 1:1 *begins* with God and then explains the origin and structure of the universe and the uniqueness of man on that basis. Any apologetic system that views the existence of God as the problem instead of the solution is not biblical in its foundation.

As a matter of fact, the subject of evil requires the existence of the God of the Bible. There is no "evil" to have a problem with once you take the biblical God out of the equation. Theodicy is thus both an application and implication of the existence of the biblical Creator and Ruler of the universe. Since the God of the Bible is good, all powerful, and sovereign over all things, why does evil exist? Why do evil things happen to supposedly good people – even upon those who believe in Him?

If the biblical God does not exist, then there is *no* problem with evil because the word "evil" no longer has any meaning. Any "God" not absolutely good or absolutely sovereign is a bridge broken at either end, and thus is not the God of the Bible.

This is why neo-evangelicals, Open View Deists, Processians, New Age pantheists, and other heretical theologies reject the sovereign God of the Bible and substitute in His place an idiotic androgynous god or goddess created by their depraved mind.

The Cults and the Sovereignty of God

Let the reader take note of the fact that man-made gods are *never* viewed as *sovereign over all things*. Stop and think about that for a moment. Whenever and wherever man creates his own gods, he makes them in his own image. Thus these gods are never the Sovereign Creator of the universe who predetermines and controls all things. They are always limited in the same ways as man.

The cults and the occult, heresies new and old, and all pagan religions are based upon limited deities. Only the Scripture tells us that the "God who is there" ordains and controls all that comes to pass for His glory.

But when we turn to Natural theologies past and modern that are made *by* man and *for* man, they always create weak pathetic deities who float around helplessly in a sea of chance and chaos, crying out for *man* to save them. They are powerless to save and powerless to keep. They are worthless, as far as gods are concerned.

Once they have thrown out the sovereignty of God, modern "thinkers" then strip God of His immutability, omniscience, omnipotence, etc. In the end, they whittle God down like a bar of soap until they are left with a deity unknown to the biblical authors and to church history. This god is not worthy of being worshipped as GOD.

One of the keys to determining if a view of God is biblical is to see if it generates the kinds of objections noted in Rom. 9. If your "god" escapes the objections noted by Paul, then your "god" is not the GOD of the Bible. The false god of Open Theism, Process Theology, liberalism, and Eastern thought does not generate the objections found in Rom. 9:14-23.

> And not only this, but there was Rebekah also, when she had conceived *twins* by one man, our father Isaac; for though *the twins* were not yet born, and had not done anything good or bad, in order that God's purpose according to *His* election might stand, not because of works, but because of Him who calls, it was said to her, "The older will serve the younger." Just as it is written, "Jacob I loved, but Esau I hated." (Rom. 9:10-13)

Humanists have always disagreed with this passage because their depraved "reason" tells them that God is neither fair nor just. God is unjust if He does not love both Jacob and Esau equally. He does not have the right to choose Jacob and reject Esau. He cannot love one and hate the other.

> What shall we say then? There is no injustice with God, is there? May it never be! For He says to Moses, "I will have mercy on whom I have mercy, and I will have compassion on whom I have compassion." So then it does not depend on the man who wills or the man who runs, but on God who has mercy. For the Scripture says to Pharaoh, "For this very purpose I raised you up, to demonstrate My power in you, and that My name might be proclaimed throughout the whole earth." So then He has mercy on whom He desires, and He hardens whom He desires. (Rom. 9:14-18)

The only theology that generates the same exact objections listed by Paul above is biblical Calvinism. All other forms of Christian theism are inconsistent in their concept of God; they have exalted man and reduced God in order that these objections are never raised against them. Just as Calvinism is the final destination of biblical theism, Arminianism is only a bus stop on the way to atheism.

> You will say to me then, "Why does He still find fault? For who resists His will?" On the contrary, who are you, O man, who answers back to God? The thing molded will not say to the molder, "Why did you make me like this," will it? Or does not the potter have a right over the clay, to make from the same lump one vessel for honorable use, and another for common use? What if God, although willing to demonstrate His wrath and to make His power known, endured with much patience vessels of wrath prepared for destruction? And

> He did so in order that He might make known the riches of His glory upon vessels of mercy, which He prepared beforehand for glory. (Rom. 9:9-23)

Defective views of God do not teach that God's will is irresistible. Hence they cannot generate the objections listed by Paul above. Neither would they give Paul's biblical answer that God is the sovereign Potter who has the right to make some men vessels of wrath and others vessels of mercy for His glory. This is Christianity for the tough-minded!

Humanistic theologies always view evil as the product of chance, luck, bad potty-training, ignorance, low blood sugar, defective vitamins or a bad "cultural environment." The "problem" of evil is a "problem" only if we begin by assuming that the good and omnipotent Sovereign Creator and Ruler of the universe revealed in Scripture actually exists. The moment the biblical God is pushed aside, the problem of evil evaporates.

Whatever "god" the rationalists permit to exist has been reduced to manageable size and power. This limited deity is helpless and hopeless because evil is in control of the universe, not God. The rationalists live in their own fantasy make-believe world where man is autonomous.

The German word Vergeltungslehre is an accurate description of the imaginary world in which rationalists "live and move and have their being." As Gibson put it,

> They cannot conceive that there are more things in heaven and earth than are dreamt of in their philosophy. They have their theory, and if facts do not square with it, then – so much the worse for facts.[24]

Two examples of the rationalist's Vergeltungslehre come to mind.

First, why bad things happen to bad people is never viewed by rationalists as a problem that requires solving. They do not agonize over the issue. They do not give up their belief in God because bad things happen to bad people. They do not even use it as a club to beat theists over the head. Why is this so?

The psychological phenomenon called "wish fulfillment" explains why rationalists do not get upset when bad things happen to bad people. They actually *want (i.e.* wish) bad things to happen to bad people. Why?

Humanists always assume a works-based theology in which if we do good things, good things will happen to us because *we* merited or earned it. They say,

> What goes around, comes around.

> You get what you deserve.

> It's their just deserts.

> It's their karma.

It's poetic justice.

This explains why Eastern Orthodox and Roman Catholic philosophers and theologians are *extremely* vexed over the problem of evil. They assume that God will reward their good works and punish their evil works. When bad things happen to good people, this upsets their works-based system of salvation.

This also explains why the Reformers were not bothered by the issue. They held to a grace-based system in which salvation is the free gift of God through the merits of Jesus Christ *alone*. Upon comparison, the Protestant Reformers did not spend a great deal of time on the problem of evil when compared to the amount of time spent on the issue by humanists such as Thomas Aquinas.

No "Good" People

There is a second issue that reveals the Vergeltungslehre of the rationalists. Why do the Orthodoxs, Catholics, pagans, neo-evangelicals, etc. *assume* that there are any "good" people around? The key to their angst is that bad things happen to *good* people. But, what if there are *no good people*? Their Vergeltungslehre disappears with a bang! What humanists fail to realize is that there are *no* "good" people in the sight of God according to the Bible. David declared in Psalm 14:2-3,

> YHWH looked down from heaven upon the sons of men, to see if there are any who understand, who seek after God. They have all turned aside; together they have become corrupt; There is no one who does good, not even one.

The Apostle Paul expands upon this passage by saying,

> What then? Are we better than they? Not at all; for we have already charged that both Jews and Greeks are all under sin; as it is written,
> "There is none righteous, not even one;
> There is none who understands,
> There is none who seeks for God;
> All have turned aside, together they have become useless;
> There is none who does good, There is not even one."
> "Their throat is an open grave, with their tongues they
> keep deceiving,"
> "The poison of asps is under their lips";
> "Whose mouth is full of cursing and bitterness";
> "Their feet are swift to shed blood, destruction and misery
> are in their paths, and the path of peace have they not known."
> "There is no fear of God before their eyes." (Romans 3:9-18)

The fact that bad things happen to bad people should not shock anyone. Since we are all "bad" according to Scripture, then we should expect bad things to happen to us. Eternal torment in hell is the final bad thing that may happen to us unless God intervenes on our behalf!

We cannot do enough good works to balance our evil works. Salvation is by grace alone, through faith alone, in Christ alone, according to Scripture alone.

The Vergeltungslehre of humanism is a world populated by "good" (sic) people who merit blessings through their good works. They cannot deal with such passages as Psalm 14. As Taylor Lewis stated,

> This fantastic Vergeltungslehre, as thus held by the Rationalists, is inconsistent moreover with the tone of the most important and most serious of the Psalms.[25]
>
> ...the Vergeltungslehre...Delitzsch justly estimates as "a phantom of the Rationalists..."[26]

Rationalists are modern examples of the "friends" of Job who believed that retribution and blessing are based solely upon one's performance and person. They have no concept of grace because they do not know the biblical God of grace. This is why they cannot handle biblical anthropology or soteriology.

Fifth, the author of the book of Job structured the story as a series of debates on the origin, nature, meaning, and purpose of evil. The debates are arranged in three cycles.

Naturalist	Job's Answer
Eliphaz 4-5	6-7
Bildad 8	9-10
Zophar 11	12-14
Eliphaz 15	16-17
Bildad 18	19
Zophar 20	21
Eliphaz 22	23-24
Bildad 25	26
Zophar's silence	27-31
Elihu	32-33
Elihu	34
Elihu	35
Elihu	36
Elihu	37

The politically-correct world of the liberal Vergeltungslehre condemns debates. We are all supposed to get along and go along with each other in the name of tolerance and ecumenical unity. Of course, they are never tolerant of those who disagree with their humanism and always end up in self-contradiction!

It is important that the very first divine revelation was in the context of a series of debates. ==Those who condemn the art of debate and its usefulness in education reveal that they do not know the Word or power of God.==

Sixth, the revealed solution to the problem of evil is the grand doctrine of the absolute sovereignty of God over all things, including the evil committed by devils and men. Lewis comments,

> **The Great Lesson of the Book – The Absolute Sovereignty of God**
>
> ...the great lesson...to teach the absolute moral sovereignty of God, and the unqualified duty of human submission, as to demand carrying in itself its own inherent righteousness. The theism, the theodicé of the Book is its great feature. Never were the divine personality, the divine holiness, the divine government unchallengeable, in a word, the absolute divine sovereignty, more sublimely set forth. Here there is no reserve: God most wise and good, most just and holy, to be acknowledged as such whether we can see it or not; God who 'maketh one vessel to honor and another to dishonor,' who 'setteth on high or casteth down.' Who 'bindeth up and breaketh in pieces,' who is to be regarded as having their holiest reasons for all this, yes 'giveth no account of His ways,' allowing 'no one to touch His hand, and say unto Him what does Thou?'[27]
>
> **The Absolute Divine Sovereignty before any Doctrine of Human Destiny**
>
> Thus regarded, the value of a pure theism, in which the absolute divine sovereignty holds its sovereign place, is beyond that of every other dogma. Without it, all other religious teaching may become not only vain but mischievous. It is not too much to say that even now, in this advanced age of Theology, there is arising a new need of this idea. There is something in the Naturalistic tendencies of our science, and our literature, which more and more demands a revival of the thought of a personal, holy, omnipotent, unchallengeable God, who "doeth all things according to His good pleasure," whether through nature, or against nature, or above nature. The sharpening of this would give a new edge to every other religious dogma. The ideas of sin, holiness, accountability, would receive a new impress of clearness and power. The doctrine of a future life would get a moral significance, throwing in the back-ground those Naturalistic and merely imaginative features which are now making it a matter of curious speculation, or of physical, rather than of

> ethical interest. Such a sudden sharpening of the divine idea would have a startling effect, like the actual witnessing of a miracle, in bringing so near the thought of God as to set it in a new and surprising light, resembling vision rather than theory, and calling forth something like the exclamation of Job, when 'the hearing of the ear" had become an actual beholding.
>
> **Its One Idea: The Divine Omnipotence. God 'can do All Things.**
>
> If the solution of the problem, as some call it, is to be found anywhere, it is in the address of the Almighty. That is what every reader naturally expects, and is disappointed to some extent, in not finding. No explanation, however, is given of the cause of Job's mysterious sufferings, nor any decision made in regard to the matters in debate between him and his antagonists. Instead of that, one idea, predominant and exclusive, pervades every part of that most sublime exhibition. It is that of power, omnipotent power, first as exhibited in the great works of creation, and afterwards in those greater productions of nature that seem next in rank to the creative power itself. Nothing is said of any purpose in the great trial, or of anything which should be made known to Job as preparatory to his submission. There is no hint in respect to ultimate compensation as a motive for endurance, such as is held out in the Gospel to the Christian: 'They that endure unto the end, shall be saved.' There is no allusion to any scheme of discipline, no suggestion of afflictions which are only evils apparently, since they are designed for purification, or as a preparative for a higher blessedness. The curtain is not withdrawn to disclose to us any vision of optimism as a motive for the creature's submission. Nothing of this kind appears, but only that idea of power, omnipotent power, thundered forth in tones that seem intended to silence rather than to convince.[28]

Zockler agrees in his classic German commentary on Job. He then quotes several great commentators who clearly saw the sovereignty of God as the divine answer to the problem of evil.

> **The Idea and Aim of the Book**
>
> In so far as the Book of Job seeks to harmonize the fact that men endure unmerited suffering, or at least suffering which is not directly merited, with the divine justice, it labors at the solution of a problem which falls in the category of the *theodices, i.e.* the attempt to justify the presence of sin in a world created by God."[29]
>
> Chap. Xxxviii. 4 seq. Brentius: The aim of this discourse is to show that no one has the right to accuse the Lord of injustice. The proof

of this point is that the Lord alone is the Creator of all things, which with a certain amplification is illustrated from various classes of creatures…From the history of these creatures God proves that it is permitted to no one to accuse Divine sovereignty of injustice, or to resist it; for of all creatures not one was the Lord's counselor, or rendered Him any aid in the creation of the world. He can without any injustice therefore dispose of all creatures according to His own will, and create one vessel to honor, another to dishonor, as it may please Him. Oecolampadius: No other reason can be given than His own good pleasure why God did not make the earth ten times larger. He had the power to enlarge it no less than to confine it within such narrow limits; He would have been able to make valleys, where there are mountains, and conversely, *etc.* But He is Lord, and it pleased Him to assign to things the length and depth and breadth which they now have. Von Gerlach: The fundamental thought of these representations which God here puts forth is that only He who can create and govern all things in their relation to each other, can also comprehend the connection of human destinies. Inasmuch however as feeble short-sighted man cannot understand and fathom the created things which are daily surrounding him, how can he assume to himself any part of God's agency in administering the universe?[30]

Albert Barnes in The Biblical Illustrator argues that,

The highest importance is to inculcate the duty of submitting to the will and sovereignty of God. This is a lesson which we often have to learn in life, and which almost all the trying dispensations of providence are fitted to teach us. It is not because God has no reason for what He does; it is not because He intends we shall never know the reason: but it is because it is our duty to bow with submission to His will, and to acquiesce in His right to reign even when we cannot see the reason for His doings. Could we reason it out, then submit because we saw the reason, our submission would not be to our Maker's pleasure, but to the deductions of our own minds. Hence, all along, He so deals with man, by concealing the reasons of His doings, as to bring him to submission to His authority and to humble all human pride. To this termination all the reasonings of the Almighty in this Book are conducted; and after the exhibition of His power in the tempest, after His sublime description of His own works, after His appeals to the numerous things where are, in fact, incomprehensible to man, we feel that God is great—that is presumptuous in man to sit in judgment on His world, and that the mind, no matter what it does, should bow before Him with profound veneration and silence.[31]

Modern commentaries also view the sovereignty of God as the theme of Job. Robert Alden in The New American Commentary (1993) states,

> What the believer does know, as the Book of Job teaches, is that we serve a personal God who is intimately aware of each person and his or her needs and concerns. Furthermore, the Lord has not only a cosmic plan but an individual purpose he is wisely, justly, and lovingly pursuing in each believer's life. Finally, our God is powerful enough to accomplish his will on earth as well as in heaven. Thus, the other purpose of Job is give comfort to believers of all ages who find themselves in Job's situation of suffering...the message of Job is that nothing happens to us that is not ultimately controlled by the knowledge, love, wisdom and power of our God of all comfort (2 Cor. 1:3).[32]

Max Anders, in the Holman Old Testament Commentary series, has written what is probably the best modern commentary on Job. Under the section entitled, "What is Job About?" he states,

> The most prominent theme of this book is the message of the sovereignty of God. More than being a book about Job, it is, actually, a book about *God*. In the opening chapters, the reader is allowed to see into heaven's throne room where divine decisions affecting both heaven and earth are made. God controls Satan's power and man's circumstances. The book ends with God querying Job about the nature of his own right to rule his creation. This is the primary lesson learned by Job as taught in this book. God *is* God. He will do as he pleases, when he pleases, with whom he pleases, without consulting his creatures, and he will do so for his own glory and the ultimate good of his people. Job serves as a good example to all believers as he humbly submits to the sovereign rule of God over his life. Job's reaction to the rapid-fire tragedies is one of reverent submission as he acknowledges God's divine discretion over all the possessions and persons in his life. This submission is understood by Job in the context of his own life when he says, "Though he slay me, yet I will hope in him" (Job 13:15)[33]

How different are the convoluted theories of Natural theologians. Whereas chance, luck, the "sovereignty of man," and his supposed "free will" are put forth by Natural theologians and philosophers as the only "rational" solution to the problem of evil, in His answer, God nowhere even mentions such pagan idols! The silence is thunderous, to say the least.

==Consider this, if man's supposed free will and human autonomy were true in any sense, the Book of Job would have been the perfect place to find it in Scripture==. But these humanistic solutions to evil are not mentioned. Even the so-called "argument from design" is nowhere to be found. Lewis points this out clearly.

> One might be led to think, at first view, that the great matter worthy of such a sublime book as this, would be the solution of the problem of evil – how sin came into the world, and man is held accountable. It is the question of the ages, to the settling of which not even the Critical Philosophy makes an approach. There is, however, no allusion to it in the divine allocution, except as comprehended in that awful declaration of power and sovereignty, seeming to say, as the voice said to Moses: 'I will be gracious to whom I will be gracious, forgiving iniquity, transgression, and sin – visiting iniquities onto the third and fourth generation, and showing mercy unto thousands of them that love me and keep my commandments.' Beyond this, no solution is offered...[34]

> No argument from Design. The Divine Ways Transcending and Ineffable. Eph. iii, 10; John ix, 3.

> What right have we to apply the measure of our Ethics, or our Psychology, or our Ontology, to Him 'whose ways are above our ways, and whose thinking is above our thinking, even as the heavens are high above the earth,' that is, immeasurably and inconceivably beyond us?...Here is no throwing it upon nature, as the Rationalist would have done, but a positive assertion of a Divine purpose, and yet that purpose had being of the individual sufferer. "Who art thou that repliest against God? Shall the thing formed say unto him who formed it, Why has thou made me thus?" Such is the idea that is brought to us by this voice from the thunder-cloud....especially needed in this age of Naturalism, of scientific boasting, of godless spiritualism."[35]

> The Rationalist is repelled by the supernatural everywhere. He has a most irrational, and yet an easily-explained, dislike to the very idea, in whatever part of the Scriptures he may meet with it."[36]

The Pulpit Commentary points out,

> That man can fully comprehend God is denied, and disproved by very cogent and valid reasonings (ch. xxviii. 12-28; xxxvi. 26-33; xxxvii. 1-23; xxxviii. 4-41; xxxix.; xl.; xli.). Man, therefore, must not

presume to sit in judgment upon God, who "doeth great things, which man cannot comprehend" (ch. xxxvii.5), and "whose ways are past finding out." His attitude must be one of submission, reserve, and reverence [obscured] has no faculties to g[obscured] er their relations one [obscured] eme of the universe, [obscured] of him who made it.

This is one way to fe[obscured] es the self-proclaimed "evangelical" theologian or pl[obscured] d or the sovereignty of *man* as the solution to the pr[obscured] nportant.

Seven, the heresy of [obscured] is sufficient in and of himself to be the origin of tr[obscured] ails in light of the Book of Job because humanism [obscured] or rational grounds. Furthermore, without Specia[obscured] any aspect of reality.

Eight, while there [obscured] could interest us, an epistemological analysis of the "Dialogues of Natural Theology" as recorded in the Book of Job reveal the total bankruptcy of Natural Theology.

==We spent several years at the Library of Congress researching every single book it had on Natural Theology and Natural Law, but we did not find a single writer who examined the dialogues found in Job.==

Natural theologians always assume that their chief nemesis is David Hume's <u>Dialogues and Natural History of Religion</u>. Indeed, he shot and buried the horse of Natural Theology as far as secular philosophy is concerned. This is why Natural theologians spend so much time and effort desperately trying to resurrect a dead horse.[38] But Hume's attack is mere child's play compared to the dialogues on Natural Theology found in the Book of Job.

Nine, the outline of God's speech in chapters 38-41 is instructive. The sovereignty of God is applied to all of life as God slowly paints Job and his friends into a corner. The point is that no aspect of creation is free from the Creator's sovereign control. ==Pagan concepts of chance, luck, chaos, and free will are not part of the biblical worldview.== God is in absolute control over:

- The creation of the earth: 38:4-7
- The boundaries of the oceans: 38:8-11
- The cycle of morning and evening: 38:12-15
- The hidden depths of the oceans: 38:16
- The depths of the afterlife: 38:17
- The circumference of the earth: 38:18
- The light and darkness: 38:19-21
- The snow, hail, and wind: 38:22-24

- The droughts: 38:37-38
- The lions: 38:39-40
- The ravens: 38:41

- The goats: 39:1a
- The deer: 39:1b-4
- The donkeys: 39:5-8
- The oxen: 39:9-12
- The ostriches: 39:13-18

[Handwritten note: "This is a terrible arg. Even if he did read all those books does not preclude the nature of the arg. for NT."]

- The lightning and the rain: 38:25-28
- The ice and frost: 38:29-30
- The constellations: 38:31-33
- The clouds and thunderstorms: 38:34-35
- The mind and understanding of man: 38:36
- The horses: 39:19-25
- The hawks: 39:26
- The eagles: 39:27-30
- The behemoth: 40:15-24
- The leviathan: 41:1-34

Once Job realized that God controls everything, he fell to his knees in wonder, awe, and praise and exclaimed,

> I know that you can do all things and that no purpose of yours can be thwarted. (Job 42:1)

We will now proceed to examine the epistemological worldviews represented by each friend of Job and how they failed to explain evil.

Job's friends represent every school of Natural Theology that has been spawned by the devil throughout human history. Their failure to explain the origin, nature, and meaning of the evil suffered by Job and his family is forever their Waterloo – and they didn't even know it!

Eliphaz, the Empiricist

Eliphaz represents the worldview called *empiricism*. This form of humanism believes that the five senses of man are the Origin of truth, justice, morals, meaning, and beauty. It thus abstracts, absolutizes, idealizes, and romanticizes human sensory experience, which reduces all knowledge to those experiences. McGee correctly states,

> Eliphaz is the first to speak. His is the voice of experience. The key to what he has to say is found in verse 8, "Even as I have seen." Everything he has to say rests on that.[39]

Eliphaz states his worldview in Job 4:8,

> According to what I have seen...
>
> כַּאֲשֶׁר רָאִיתִי

This is later repeated in 5:3,

> I have seen....
>
> אֲנִי־רָאִיתִי

He also states in 5:27,

Behold this, we have investigated it, thus it is [true]; Hear it, and know for yourself.

הִנֵּה־זֹאת חֲקַרְנוּהָ כֶּן־הִיא שְׁמָעֶנָּה וְאַתָּה דַּע־לָךְ: פ

In his second dialogue he argues,

I will tell you, listen to me; and what I have seen I will also declare. (15:17)

אֲחַוְךָ שְׁמַע־לִי וְזֶה־חָזִיתִי וַאֲסַפֵּרָה:

First, both the Hebrew and Greek texts are clear: Eliphaz believed that *man* is the origin and measure of all things. This is why, in Job 4:8, he said,

According to what I have seen; I will tell you; We have investigated it; what I have seen I will also declare." (Emphasis added.)

Rawlinson observes,

The "I" is emphatic. "I myself have seen," etc.[40]

Second, the word "seen" refers to physical sight. As Eliphaz looked at the world, he assumed, like all humanists, that if he started with himself, by himself, and in himself, he could understand the meaning of life, death, and all things because *man*, not God, is the Beginning and the End, the Alpha and the Omega, the First and the Last. Eliphaz assumed that he could deduce from "Nature" rational truth about God.

Third, based on his observations of "Nature," Eliphaz deduced certain rational conclusions of why evil happens to people and how evil relates to God.

Whoever perished being innocent? Or where were the upright destroyed? (4:7)

זְכָר־נָא מִי הוּא נָקִי אָבָד וְאֵיפֹה יְשָׁרִים נִכְחָדוּ:

The humanistic doctrine of retribution means that we are rewarded according to our deeds. If good things happen to us, we merited them. If bad things happen to us, we brought them upon ourselves. Thus when someone "perishes" or is "destroyed," he is not "upright" or "innocent," but wicked. Gibson comments,

"[The] theory of a strict system of retribution as carried out in the visible government of this world, underlies all their arguments. Briefly the theory amounts to this: suffering is the punishment of sin. Holding this, they are confronted with the case of Job. Here is manifestly a great sufferer: therefore, so runs the argument, he is a great sinner....They assume rather than state that Job must be guilty, and that his troubles are the consequences of his sin.[41]

Rawlinson agrees,

> Eliphaz, then, probably the oldest of the three "comforters," took the word, rebuking Job for his want of fortitude, and at suggesting (ch. iv. 7-11) - what becomes one of the main points of the controversy - that Job's calamities have come upon him from God's hand as a punishment for sins which he has committed, and of which he has not repented.[42]

A half-truth presented as the whole truth becomes a non-truth. Eliphaz said that all suffering is a punishment for sin. He assumed that man merits or demerits all things.

> Although almost everything that Eliphaz says is true, it is not the whole truth. Underlying his whole argument is the assumption that all suffering is the punishment of sin, even if designed to be corrective, and not simply vindictive.[43]

Eliphaz even drags God into the web of retribution.

> Those who plow iniquity and those who sow trouble harvest it.

כַּאֲשֶׁר רָאִיתִי חֹרְשֵׁי אָוֶן וְזֹרְעֵי עָמָל יִקְצְרֻהוּ׃

> By the breath of God they perish, and by the blast of His anger they come to an end. (4:8-9)

מִנִּשְׁמַת אֱלוֹהַּ יֹאבֵדוּ וּמֵרוּחַ אַפּוֹ יִכְלוּ

On the basis of a humanistic epistemology of empiricism, Eliphaz denies the free grace and forgiveness of God, basing his hope for divine acceptance upon his own works and character. Eliphaz thus reveals the basis of all false religion: The idea that we can gain acceptance before God based on our own person and performance.

This error is nothing more or less than works-based salvation. It is rightly condemned by Paul with a divine anathema in Gal. 1:8-9. This is why Roman Catholicism and Eastern Orthodoxy are false religions. They deny the sovereign, free grace of God and exalt the works of man.

Fourth, how did Eliphaz prove that sinners are punished for their evil? He points to the fate of animals in Nature. He deduced from their fate that God punishes evil with evil.

> The roaring of the lion and the voice of the *fierce* lion, and the teeth of the young lions are broken. The lion perishes for lack of prey, and the whelps of the lioness are scattered. (Job 4:10-11)

This is Natural Theology in all its vaunted glory. Job must be evil because evil beasts such as lions perish for the evil they do.[44]

Fifth, not only does Eliphaz argue from what he saw with his own eyes, but also from occult experience. Spirits had communicated with him through dreams and visitations.

> Now a word was brought to me stealthily, and my ear received a whisper of it. Amid disquieting thoughts from the visions of the night, when deep sleep falls on men, then a spirit passed by my face; The hair of my flesh bristled up. It stood still, but I could not discern its appearance; A form *was* before my eyes; *There was* silence, then I heard a voice. (4:12-16)

One of the problems that confronts those who base their worldview on their own personal experience is that experiences do not carry within themselves their own explanation. The interpretation comes from outside of the experience. It is *transcendent*, i.e. they come from somewhere else.

Eliphaz interpreted his experience with a spirit guide as a good thing that gave him information, but the Bible condemns it as an occult experience with lying spirits or demons (1 Tim. 4:1).

Shirley MacLaine

When a neo-evangelical bases his Natural Theology on his own personal experience, on what grounds can he deny Shirley MacLaine the right to base her New Age religion on her personal experience? Last time I checked, experience *qua* experience has no religion.

In her experience, Shirley felt that she was GOD. Without the information from special revelation (via the Bible) that man is not God and that people like MacLaine are deceived by demons, how can you deny her experience? You cannot.

Sixth, Eliphaz assumed that the God who is there is silent and has not spoken in special revelation to man. Thus Job did not have any "secret" information. All men are equal in that no one has information from God.

> Do you hear the secret counsel of God, and limit wisdom to yourself?

הַבְסוֹד אֱלוֹהַ תִּשְׁמָע וְתִגְרַע אֵלֶיךָ חָכְמָה׃

> What do you know that we do not know? What do you understand that we do not? (15:8-9)

מַה־יָּדַעְתָּ וְלֹא נֵדָע תָּבִין וְלֹא־עִמָּנוּ הוּא׃

Humanists have always been irritated by Christians who quote the Bible as if it contains revealed truth that man cannot discover on his own. The idea that God reveals things in the Bible that can only be known by divine revelation strikes at the conceit and pride of man. It destroys the heresy of human autonomy and makes man dependent upon God and His revelation in Scripture.

The point of the Book of Job is that it is only by *special* revelation from God that we could ever understand why Job suffered so many evil things. With all his empirical knowledge from his five senses, all his occult experiences, all his observations of nature, and all his rational deductions, Eliphaz could never discover anything about heaven or what took place there. Gibson comments,

> It must be remembered that the parties to the debate knew nothing whatever of the scene in heaven as described in the prologue.[45]
>
> But of [the wager in heaven] neither the friends nor Job himself were aware. They only knew what they could see with the eye of sense.[46]
>
> Perhaps the whole mystery of suffering is insoluble by us in our present condition; and whatever advances we make in knowledge, there will still be much which, as the speeches of the Almighty out of the whirlwind tell us, we cannot hope to understand unless we can comprehend the whole mind of God.[47]

Experience-based religions always collapse into the quicksand of relativism. Why should your personal subjective experience be of any greater value or authority than mine? One experience cancels out the other.

Bildad, The Rationalist

Bildad the Shuhite, represents those who believe that human reason through philosophy can discover the answers to life's great questions. He was impressed by antiquity and looked back to a philosophic golden age in which the human mind, unaided by divine revelation, was able to discern truth, justice, morals, meaning, and beauty.[48] He urges Job to look to the great thinkers of the past (Job 8:8).

> Please inquire of past generations, and consider the things searched out by their fathers,
>
> כִּי־שְׁאַל־נָא לְדֹר רִישׁוֹן וְכוֹנֵן לְחֵקֶר אֲבוֹתָם׃

He asserts that the reason why we should study the history of philosophy is that we are intellectually immature today and do not understand the issues of life and death.

> For we are only of yesterday and know nothing; because our days on earth are as a shadow. (8:9)
>
> כִּי־תְמוֹל אֲנַחְנוּ וְלֹא נֵדָע כִּי צֵל יָמֵינוּ עֲלֵי־אָרֶץ׃

The empiricist Eliphaz looked to the five physical senses of man as the origin of truth. In contrast, the rationalist Bildad looked to the mind, i.e. human reason, as the origin of truth, justice,

[Handwritten note at top: 8:10 Clearly the author links 'heart' and 'mind' as a thinking thing; man is holistic in his philosophy, both heart and mind.]

Chapter One The Foundation of the Christian Worldview

morals, meaning, and beauty. He believed that the great philosophers of the past will teach us and tell us the truth about evil through their *minds*.

> Will they not teach you and tell you, And being words *from their minds*? (8:10)
>
> הֲלֹא־הֵם יוֹרוּךָ יֹאמְרוּ לָךְ וּמִלִּבָּם יוֹצִאוּ מִלִּים׃

[Handwritten: Error = 'bring']
[Handwritten: AV translates 'mind' as 'heart,' ESV = 'understanding,' NASB = 'minds']

Bildad refers to past philosophers as his "fathers" because they discovered the truth through their "minds," i.e. their superior intellects. The Hebrew word לֵב translated as "mind" in Job 8:10 is elsewhere translated in Job as "intelligence" (12:24), "understanding" (36:5), and "heart" (33:3). *[Handwritten: See notes]*

> [Bildad] had appealed to the wisdom of the ancients, and had quoted various proverbial maxims and pithy sayings.[49]
>
> Books of advice and instruction embodied in proverbs, or moral precepts, were among the earliest, in Egypt certainly.[50]
>
> Bildad appeals to the wisdom of the ancients, from whom He quotes maxims.[51]

In Deut. 29:4 לֵב is the faculty by which we know or understand things. In 1 Kings 3:9 the mind or intellect is the means by which we discern good from evil. Pro. 28:26 gives us this solemn warning,

> He who trusts in his own intellect is stupid, But he who walks wisely will be delivered.
>
> בּוֹטֵחַ בְּלִבּוֹ הוּא כְסִיל וְהוֹלֵךְ בְּחָכְמָה הוּא יִמָּלֵט׃

The word כְסִיל refers to someone who is stupid, and thus a fool. The irony could not be greater. Bildad wants Job to trust in something that divine revelation tells us *not* to trust.

> Trust in Yahweh with all your heart,
> And do not lean on your own understanding.
>
> בְּטַח אֶל־יְהוָה בְּכָל־לִבֶּךָ
> וְאֶל־בִּינָתְךָ אַל־תִּשָּׁעֵן׃

In terms of the syntax of the text, the Hebrew parallelism is clear. The word לֵב and the word בִּינָה are equivalents. We are commanded not to lean on our own reason or intellect, but instead to rest upon divine revelation.

The Prophet Jeremiah warned us that the mind, intellect, and reason of man are depraved and cannot be trusted.

> The mind [לֵב] is more deceitful than all else and is desperately sick; Who can understand it? (Jer. 17:9)
>
> עָקֹב הַלֵּב מִכֹּל וְאָנֻשׁ הוּא מִי יֵדָעֶנּוּ׃

Because our reason is deceitful, it may tell us that good is evil and evil is good. We may rationalize sin and turn it into a virtue. Thus the only one who understands the depravity of our minds is YHWH.

> I, Yahweh, search the mind [לֵב], I test the feelings [כִּלְיָה], Even to give to each man according to his ways, According to the results of his deeds.
>
> אֲנִי יְהוָה חֹקֵר לֵב בֹּחֵן כְּלָיוֹת וְלָתֵת
> לְאִישׁ (כְּדַרְכּוֹ) [כִּדְרָכָיו] כִּפְרִי מַעֲלָלָיו: ס

Jeremiah uses the word כִּלְיָה (lit. kidneys) to refer to feelings or emotions. In contrast, he uses לֵב to refer to that part of man that thinks, reasons, and comes to conclusions (Pro. 16:9).

> The mind [לֵב] of man plans [יְחַשֵּׁב] his way, But Yahweh directs his steps.
>
> לֵב אָדָם יְחַשֵּׁב דַּרְכּוֹ וַיהוָה יָכִין צַעֲדוֹ:

Bildad does not trust in YHWH with his entire mind. Instead, he "leans upon the understanding" of the philosophers. This is why he quotes the pagan philosophers of Egypt in verses 11-22. Gibson comments,

> These proverbial sayings are evidently Egyptian in their origin. The rush (a rare word, possible Coptic in origin) is really the papyrus of the Nile.[52]

What did he learn from pagan philosophers? They believed in the principle of retribution in which good people are rewarded with good things and evil people with evil things. Thus, Bildad believed that Job's sons died because of their sins.[53]

> If your sons sinned against Him, then He delivered them into the power of their transgression. (8:4)
>
> אִם־בָּנֶיךָ חָטְאוּ־לוֹ וַיְשַׁלְּחֵם בְּיַד־פִּשְׁעָם:

Bildad represents those who with hushed tones and reverent sighs invoke the names of Plato, Aristotle, or Aquinas. But, without special revelation, these sinners knew nothing. They used their minds to invent false religions and false gods according to Rom. 1. The judgment of God is thus manifest:

> For it is written,
> "I will destroy the philosophy of the philosopher,
> And the cleverness of the clever I will set aside."
> Where is the philosopher?
> Where is the scribe?
> Where is the debater of this age?

*para. 6, Morey is guilty of 'poisoning the well.'

Chapter One   The Foundation of the Christian Worldview

> Has not God made foolish the philosophy of the world?
> For since in the philosophy of God *the world through
> its philosophy did not know God,*
> God was well-pleased through the foolishness
> of the message preached to save those who believe.
> (1 Cor. 1:19-21, emphasis added.)

In his second attack on Job (chapters 18-19), Bildad appeals to Natural Law as found in Nature.

> Bildad had declared that a moral principle might be discerned in the government of this world, that the good were rewarded and the wicked punished.[54]

Bildad assumed that the great pagan philosophers of the past were able to understand everything. Thus we should study philosophy in order to find the answers to the riddles of life. This is the motto of neo-evangelicals like Geisler, Moreland, Craig, etc. ==They stress that knowledge of pagan philosophy is the *most* important preparation for the ministry, and that it is even more important than knowledge of the Bible.==

A Modern Protestant-Basher

The starting point of Moreland and Craig in <u>Philosophical Foundations</u> is human reason, not Scripture (p.1). In particular, they begin with a quote from a Lebanese Roman Catholic scholar named Charles Malik. He was a politician, theologian, philosopher, and international diplomat. Dr. Malik "was Honorary Rector of the University of Dubuque, Fellow of the Institute for Advanced Religious Studies at University of Notre Dame, and Jacques Maritain Distinguished Professor of Moral and Political Philosophy at the Catholic University of America."

As a Catholic theologian, Malik was a strong believer in "Natural Law," the pagan Greek philosophic idea that human reason is the <u>O</u>rigin of truth, justice, morals, meaning, and beauty apart from and independent of the Bible. Man is the measure of all things, not God.

It is clear from his writings that Malik was ignorant of the Bible and of the Gospel of justification by grace alone, through faith alone, in Christ alone, according to Scripture alone. He died trusting in Mary, the saints, and his works for his salvation. He was not a "Christian" in the *biblical* sense of the word. He was well-known for being a Protestant-basher.

==Moreland and Craig quote Malik on page two of <u>Philosophical Foundations</u> that those who are going into the ministry should spend their time studying Greek philosophy instead of the Bible!== [LIE!] Malik viewed the Reformation as guilty of "anti-intellectualism" because of its doctrine of *Sola Scriptura*. Instead of going to the Bible for truth and morals, we should trust in our own reason, experience, feelings, and faith. Humanism has always been hostile to the study of Scripture.

From the outset of their book, it is clear that Moreland and Craig have rejected the Reformation and fallen into the quagmire of Roman Catholic Natural Theology and Natural Law. If you were to ask them if Malik was a "Christian," they would be shocked with such a question. They have a higher regard for him than for the Reformers!

Has Natural Theology Ever Done Any Good?
What *good* has Natural Theology done for the Catholic Church? Nothing! It has led the Church of Rome to deny the Gospel, kill millions of Protestants, and burn tons of Bibles. It led them to such heresies as papal infallibility, Immaculate Conception, Marian worship, saint worship, the sacrifice of the Mass, and its spiritual cannibalism. Thomas Aquinas did not Christianize Aristotle, he paganized Christianity!

Eastern Orthodoxy followed the same road of apostasy as Rome, but they did it through Plato instead of Aristotle. The mysticism of Plato infected Eastern Orthodoxy just as the rationalism of Aristotle infected the Western Church.

What good has Platonic Natural Theology ever done for Eastern Orthodoxy? It seduced Orthodoxy to also deny the gospel, kill Protestants, ban the Bible, and replace it with the original lie of the Devil in the Garden: the pernicious doctrine of human deification. Instead of seeking to be justified before God, they think they can become God!

Natural Theology is the mother of heresy and the fountain of error. When the Jesuits introduced it into Protestant circles, it became a cancer that ate away at the gospel of free grace. It produced such heresies as Arminianism, Socinianism, Unitarianism, liberalism, neo-orthodoxy, and neo-evangelicalism.

Protestant Coverts to Popery
Natural Theology has always led some Protestants to convert to Roman Catholicism or Eastern Orthodoxy. A perfect example is Joshua Hochschild. After being educated by the Jesuits in Natural Theology at Notre Dame, he was hired by the well-known evangelical school Wheaton College to teach students a course on Aquinas' theology.

According to the article on the front page of the "Wall Street Journal" (Jan. 7/8, 2006), when Hochschild announced his conversion to Catholicism, this put Wheaton into a bind. Its official statement of faith was written back in the days when Bible-believing Christians built the school. Even though it is now liberal and allows professors to attack the Bible and teach heresy, Wheaton was forced to fire Hochschild.

Wheaton is to be commended for firing him, and Hochschild is to be commended for being honest about his conversion. Most so-called "evangelical" schools who hire Jesuit-trained Natural theologians and philosophers see students betraying Christ, renouncing the gospel, and converting to popery or Orthodoxy all the time but do nothing to stop it.

Other Jesuit-trained Natural theologians and philosophers have taken a different path and denied the inspiration and inerrancy of Scripture, the deity of Christ, His bodily resurrection, the virgin birth, the miracles of the Bible, the Trinity, the immortality of the soul, a conscious afterlife, eternal conscious punishment, the lost condition of the heathen, etc. They became liberal instead of converting to Roman Catholicism.

The Arminian Wesley

Moreland and Craig not only quote the Catholic Malik, they go on to quote the Arminian hymn writer Wesley who voiced the same sentiment as Malik. Wesley's dependence on pagan philosophy, combined with his profound ignorance of the Bible, led him to preach heretical doctrines such as sinless perfectionism!

Wesley's Arminianism was due to his dependence on Greek philosophy instead of Scripture. The Methodist Church he founded was the first major denomination to fall into apostasy and today accepts homosexuality, goddess worship, witchcraft, and other abominations. The seeds of this apostasy were sown by Wesley's attachment to humanism via Natural Theology.

Bildad represents theological rationalists who pretend that *man* starting from himself, by himself, within himself, rejecting all divine revelation, can understand God, man, the world, and all things. God's rebuke of Bildad is their rebuke.

Zophar, The Mystic

Mysticism, like empiricism or rationalism, is a form of humanism that looks within man and then absolutizes and idealizes some aspect of man into the origin of truth, justice, morals, meaning, and beauty. Zophar represents those who choose human feelings or emotions as the Origin instead of man's reason or experience. Their heart actually tells them right from wrong. They trust their feelings to lead them through life.

Most mystics love mysterious sayings that stir the emotions even if they do not inform the intellect. Today, many mystics love Zen Haikus and Eastern proverbs. In Job 11:12, Zophar quotes a mystical Egyptian proverb.

> An idiot will become intelligent when the foal of a wild donkey is
> born a man.
> וְאִישׁ נָבוּב יִלָּבֵב וְעַיִר פֶּרֶא אָדָם יִוָּלֵד

Fortune cookie philosophy sounds "deep" but is quite meaningless. The purpose of such proverbs is to stir the emotion, not to inform the mind.

When Zophar looked at the world around him, he did not see what empiricists like Eliphaz claimed to see. He did not see Natural Law operating in the world. What he saw was not always what he got. He heeded the proverb, "All that glitters is not gold." Life is far more complicated, mysterious, wonderful, and full of bright colors than the grey world of empiricism.

When Zophar looked within himself, he did not see that human reason is able to understand everything. It is not as omniscient, omnipotent, and omnipresent as Bildad claimed. One man's "reason" is another man's idiocy.

Zophar did not see the possibility of divine revelation. Like most humanists, he assumed that God has *not* spoken and thus we do *not* know the "secrets" of life. According to mysticism, the answers to life, love, and death are "secrets" that cannot be rationally or empirically discovered.

> But would that God might speak, And open his lips against you, And show you the secrets [תַּעֲלֻמוֹת] of wisdom. (Job 11:5-6a)

Since he believes that there is no special revelation from God that gives us secret answers [תַּעֲלֻמוֹת] to solve the ultimate questions, Job cannot have a rational knowledge of God. Zophar, like all mystics, actually believed that God is ultimately unknowable. He is an agnostic at this point, and stresses that we can't really know anything objective about God.

> Can you discover the depths of God?
>
> Can you discover the limits of the Almighty? (v. 7)
>
> הַחֵקֶר אֱלוֹהַ תִּמְצָא אִם
> עַד־תַּכְלִית שַׁדַּי תִּמְצָא׃
>
> *They are* high as the heavens, what can you do?
>
> Deeper than Sheol, what can you know? (v. 8)
>
> גָּבְהֵי שָׁמַיִם מַה־תִּפְעָל
> עֲמֻקָּה מִשְּׁאוֹל מַה־תֵּדָע׃

He abandoned the way of reason and challenged the rationalists,

> What can *you* really discover?
>
> What can *you* really know?
>
> *Nothing*!
>
> Finite reason cannot comprehend the Infinite!

Zophar turned inward to his feelings. He was motivated by "disquieting thoughts" and "inward agitations" (Job 20:2). He begins to answer Job by saying, "the spirit of my understanding makes me answer" (Job 20:3).

His approach to Job is summed up in an "If…then" equation in Job 11:13, 15.

> If you would direct your heart right…
>
> אִם־אַתָּה הֲכִינוֹתָ לִבֶּךָ
>
> Then you could lift up your face
>
> כִּי־אָז תִּשָּׂא פָנֶיךָ מִמּוּם

In Job 11:15-20 Zophar challenged Job to get his "heart in the right place." If he did, there would be touchy-feely psychological benefits. Reading Zophar is like reading a Yoga advertisement.

You will be emotionally stable.

You will no longer be afraid.

You will forget your troubles.

Your life will be brighter than noonday.

Your darkness will be like the morning.

You be able to trust others because you have hope.

You will look around and rest securely.

You will lie down and no one will disturb you.

Many will ask you for favors.

Zophar is an ancient parallel to modern New Age gurus who promise "inner peace." His path was that of a mystic whose heart could tell right from wrong, good from evil.

Why did Zophar quit after his second speech while Eliphaz and Bildad spoke three times? This question has puzzled both Jewish and Christian commentators for centuries. Since the Bible does not tell us the answer in Job or elsewhere, all we can do is guess.

Most commentators say that Zophar stopped talking when he saw that he was getting nowhere. His feelings were hurt and he withdrew from the conversation.

Although there is no clear answer to this question, if Job were a fictional account (as liberals claim), Zophar would have been given a third speech to balance out the three debates. The fact that he does not speak again is clear evidence that the Book of Job is a real historical record, not a literary construct.

The Heart of Man: The Heart of the Issue

Mystics assume that we can trust our heart to tell us truth and morals. But the Bible has a lot to say about the "heart" of man. The heart is so corrupt that it has always led to divine judgment.

> **Genesis 6:5** Then YHWH saw that the wickedness of man was great on the earth, and that every intent of the thoughts of his heart was only evil continually.

> **Genesis 8:21** And YHWH smelled the soothing aroma; and YHWH said to Himself, "I will never again curse the ground on account of man, for the intent of man's heart is evil from his youth; and I will never again destroy every living thing, as I have done.

The heart of man is more deceitful than we can imagine.

> **Jeremiah 17:9** The heart is more deceitful than all else
> And is desperately sick; Who can understand it?

Do truth, justice, morals, meaning, and beauty come out of the heart of man? In order for Natural Theology and Natural Law to work, man's heart must be the Origin of truth and morals. But what did Jesus say comes out of the heart of man?

> **Matthew 15:18-19** "But the things that proceed out of the mouth come from the heart, and those defile the man. For out of the heart come evil thoughts, murders, adulteries, fornications, thefts, false witness, slanders."

Is man's heart foolish and darkened by sin?

> **Romans 1:21** For even though they knew God, they did not honor Him as God, or give thanks; but they became futile in their speculations, and their foolish heart was darkened.

Since your heart is evil, foolish, darkened, deceitful, and desperately sick, should you trust your heart to tell you right from wrong, truth from error?

> **Proverbs 28:26** He who trusts in his own heart is a fool.

But what if what your "heart" tells you is in direct conflict with what the Bible tells you? Who has greater authority? God or your heart?

> **1 John 3:20** God is greater than our heart, and He knows all things.

But what if your own understanding of something contradicts God's Revelation? Which one should you choose?

> **Proverbs 3:5-6** Trust in YHWH with all your heart, And do not lean on your own understanding. In all your ways acknowledge Him, And He will make your paths straight.
>
> **And do not rely on your own insight: Rely** renders a word meaning to lean or support oneself. It is used in 2 Sam 1.6 of Saul leaning on his spear and in 2 Kgs 5.18 of the king of Syria leaning on Naaman's

arm. It takes on the extended sense of trusting (the Lord) in Isa 10.20. **Insight** translates the same word as used in 1.2 and 2.3, and refers to comprehension, understanding, or intelligence. In some languages the contrast between the two commands in this verse is more naturally stated by placing the negative command (line 2) before the positive command (line 1). For example, FRCL says:
- Do not trust in your own intelligence, but rather put your entire confidence in the Lord.

Some languages express this as
- Don't think that your own understanding is enough to help you. You must trust God with all your thinking. [55]

Mystical movements have always ended in heresy. Pietism always starts out by claiming it opposes liberalism but, in the end, it only prepares the way for it. The "Jesus Movement" of the 1960s produced many cults. Once you look to your feelings to tell you truth, justice, morals, meaning, and beauty, your depravity will become your god.

Elihu, The Fideist

Humanists agree that *man* is the origin and measure of all things, not the God of the Bible. Where they disagree is on what part of man should be deified and exalted as the origin and measure. Fideists view their faith as the Archimedean point. Therefore, something is true because they believe it. They do not believe something because it is true.

Elihu represents fideism. He believed something purely because he *believed* it. This is why he was angry and impatient with Job and his friends.

> the anger of Elihu burned (32:2a)
>
> his anger burned (32:2b)
>
> his anger burned against his three friends (32:3)
>
> his anger burned (32:5)

What was he so angry about? Job and his three friends wasted his time. All their "arguments" [אִמְרָה] (32:14) and "reasonings" [תְּבוּנָה] (32:11) were worthless because they never answered Job.

> They had found no answer and yet they condemned Job (32:3)
>
> There was no answer in the mouth of the three friends (32:5)
>
> There was no one who refuted Job, not one of you who answered his words (32:12)

they are dismayed, they no longer answer; words have failed them. (32:15)

Elihu dismissed Bildad's rational appeal to philosophy because antiquity does not guarantee truth.

> The abundance in years may not be wise, Nor may elders understand justice. (32:9)

Eliphaz's attempt to empirically derive answers from the world of animals and nature is a failure. You cannot find God through "Nature."

> Behold, God is exalted, and *we do not know Him*. The number of his years is *unsearchable*. (34:26)

> *Can anyone understand* the spreading of the clouds, the thundering of His pavilion? (34:29)

> God thunders with His voice wondrously, doing great things which *we cannot comprehend*. (37:5)

> The Almighty – *we cannot find Him*. (37:23)

Elihu does not even accept the mysticism of Zophar. He can match his own mystical experiences to Zophar's, making all experience relative.

> Indeed, God speaks...in a dream, a vision of the night; When sound sleep falls on men, While they slumber in their beds. (33:14-15)

The arguments and reasoning of Job and his friends did not establish why evil came upon Job. Thus it was time for them to hear the voice of faith. Elihu was a "positive thinker" before Norman Vincent Peale and a "possibility thinker" before Robert Schuller.

> Listen to me, I too will tell what I think. (32:10)

> I also will tell my opinion. (32:17)

> Pay attention, O Job, listen to me; And let me speak. (32:31)

> Listen to me; keep silent, and I will teach you wisdom. (33:33)

As a humanist, Elihu is committed to the dogma of human autonomy.

> Let us choose for ourselves what is right; Let us know among ourselves what is good. (34:4)

Chapter One   The Foundation of the Christian Worldview

מִשְׁפָּט נִבְחֲרָה־לָּנוּ נֵדְעָה בֵינֵינוּ מַה־טּוֹב׃

According to Elihu, man – not God – is the origin of right and wrong, good and evil. This was the lie that the Devil used to deceive Eve in the Garden, and he has used it since then. Man chooses for himself what is right and wrong, good and evil. God is not part of the equation.

What guarantee do we have that Elihu is going to tell us the truth when all others failed?

My words are from the uprightness of my heart;

And my lips speak knowledge sincerely. (Job 33:3)

In other words, "You must believe in me because I would not lie to you. Have faith in me and my sincerity. Take a leap of faith and trust me and all will be well." This is why Rowley describes Elihu as "verbose and self-opinionated,"[56] whose "self-importance and pomposity" made him so obnoxious that even God ignored him.[57]

Elihu assumed the same approach as the three friends. They all assumed the doctrine of retribution, i.e. "we get what we deserve." Since great evil had come upon Job, he must have been a great sinner.

Elihu promises against this charge that he will justify, i.e. declare righteous, both Job and God.

I desire to justify you. (33:34)

כִּי־חָפַצְתִּי צַדְּקֶךָּ׃

Far be it from God to do wickedness, And from the Almighty to do wrong. (34:10)

שִׁמְעוּ לִי חָלִלָה לָאֵל מֵרֶשַׁע וְשַׁדַּי מֵעָוֶל׃

Like Elihu, Natural theologians claim that they can solve the problem of evil. It comes upon man not as punitive, but as *corrective*. Job's pain and suffering are *remedial* in that they are a form of *chastisement* that will bring him back to the right path (33:17-30). Elihu's contribution to the debate is that *evil* is not necessarily *evil.* It can actually be a "good." Gibson comments,

Elihu does add what is practically a new thought, viz. that suffering is designed for moral discipline and improvement.[58]

Some [trials], as the prologue to Job reminds us, are permitted by God to test us.[59]

Zockler agrees.

Two things are implied in what is here said to Job: that his suffering is founded on a plan of God's, and that he by his perverse speeches is guilty of distorting and mistaking this plan (in representing it as caprice, without a plan).[60]

The four humanists who debated why evil things happened to Job only had two answers. First, the three friends argued that Job was not really good, but evil. Thus, he got what he deserved. In contrast, Elihu argued that the evil Job suffered was not really "evil," but actually a disguised good that would ultimately benefit him. God uses evil to test our character and chastise us.

One trick used by humanists is to pretend that the issue before us is the relationship between "faith" and "reason." They argue:

- Faith versus reason,
- Faith and reason
- Faith or reason
- Faith beyond reason
- Etc.

When someone frames the issue in terms of "faith or reason," that person is a humanist. Why? Whose "faith" are they talking about? *Man*'s faith. Whose "reason" are they talking about? *Man*'s reason. God is nowhere to be seen.

Imagine a restaurant with only one item on the menu. In this case, all the items are different cuts of beef. You can choose steaks or roasts or hamburgers, but, in the end, beef is your only choice.

In the same way, humanists have only one item on their menu: *man*. The only choice they give to you is different cuts of man. You can choose between man's reason, man's experience, man's feelings or man's faith as the origin of truth, justice, morals, meaning, and beauty, but in the end, the only choice they give you is an aspect of man as the origin.

I called a radio program, which describes itself as "Faith or Reason," and asked the host, "To whose faith and reason are you referring?" He admitted that he was talking about *man's* faith and *man's* reason. Man was the Alpha and Omega of his faith! I pointed out that the real issue is:

- God versus man
- Divine revelation versus human reason
- Divine revelation versus human experience
- Divine revelation versus human feelings
- Divine revelation versus human faith

I was rushed off the program as if I had committed the unpardonable sin because I had exposed that the host was humanistic in the way he approached truth. The same problem is found in most apologetic ministries that appeal to fallible human reason instead of Scripture alone.

The God Who Interrupts and Disrupts

Finally, God rebuked Job and his three friends. Note the following points.

First, God's appearance was a *surprise* because no one *asked* Him for answers. Job's friends never prayed to God at any time during the debates. As humanists, they assumed that they did not *need* God as much as He needed them.

For over forty years I have attended hundreds of conferences, seminars, and classes on apologetics held by Natural theologians, and it has always bothered me that they usually begin and end without any prayer. I mentioned this to Francis Schaeffer one day and he had seen the same problem. He stated that the lack of true spirituality at these meetings was indicative of humanism. Since humanists do not *need* God to find truth, justice, morals, meaning or beauty, *why pray*? Schaeffer was right.

Second, God's appearance was *unmerited*. Job and his friends did not merit, deserve or earn the favor of God's presence.

Third, God's appearance was due 100% to His unmerited grace and mercy. Despite their lies and wickedness, God mercifully paid them a visit.

Fourth, God's appearance was *startling*. He did not come as a dove, but as a lion. He did not speak in a still quiet voice, but with thunder. There was a sudden windstorm that broke upon them.

The KJV incorrectly translated the word הַסְּעָרָה as "whirlwind" in Job 38:1. This translation gives people the mental image of the kind of tornado seen in the movie <u>The Wizard of Oz</u>, but this is not the meaning of the word.

The word הַסְּעָרָה is from the Akkadian root of sarum. It refers to a violent wind storm that suddenly breaks without warning, and is so strong that it blows away whatever is in its path. The tents fly away and the animals run away. It usually referred to the sudden wind storms that came rushing out of the Arabian Desert.

When הַסְּעָרָה is used for the activity of God, it refers to His burning anger and wrath (Psa. 83:16; Isa. 66:15; Jer. 23:19: 25:32; 30:23; Amos 1:14). This explains why God chose to appear as a violent הַסְּעָרָה that shook the tent where Job and his friends were seated. To put it bluntly, Job and his friends made God angry.

Fifth, God's speech began with a rebuke. He immediately dismissed everything they had said (38:2).

> Who is this that darkens counsel
>
> זֶה מַחְשִׁיךְ עֵצָה
>
> by words without knowledge?
>
> מִי בְמִלִּין בְּלִי־דָעַת:

Joseph Parker observes that God began by condemning all the speeches as "absolute ignorance."[61] Job's friends represented all four schools of Natural Theology: rationalism, empiricism, mysticism, and fideism. Despite their discussion, their words were absolutely worthless. The Lord of the Universe declared Natural Theology, Natural Law, and Natural philosophy to be failures. Delitzsch comments,

> [God] surprises him with questions which are intended to bring him indirectly to the consciousness of the wrong and absurdity of his challenge – questions among which "there are many which the Natural philosophy of the present day can frame more scientifically, but cannot satisfactorily solve."[62]

First, instead of giving counsel to Job that enlightened the issue of why evil came upon him, all they did was *darken* the issue.

The word חֹשֶׁךְ originally referred to total darkness found in deep mines. It means total absence of light, i.e. pitch black. This is why "darkness" is used throughout Scripture as the description of the intellectual state of the Gentiles, i.e. those without the light of Scripture. Gentiles "sit in darkness" and "have no light" (Isa. 8:20; 42:6-7; Lk. 1:79).

Note that God Almighty passed judgment on the intellectual worth of Natural Theology, Natural Law, and Natural Philosophy, declaring them "pitch black darkness." This means that Socrates, Plato, Aristotle, Kant, Hegel, and all other non-Christian thinkers were "in the dark" and cannot give us any light on ultimate questions. In stark contrast to God's opinion, unfortunately, Natural theologians, and philosophers speak of pagan philosophy in such glowing terms as "enlightening." As Delitzsch pointed out, Job and his friends were guilty "of self-delusion, as though they were in possession of the key to the mystery of the divine government of the world."[63]

The Mind of Man

The darkness of the mind of man is not just intellectual. The word "darkness" also refers to man's moral problem, namely, his hatred of and aversion to God and the light revealed in Christ and in Scripture. Because man is totally depraved in his fallen state, his thoughts, words, and deeds are morally averse to and antagonistic toward the God of the Bible. Scripture declares that we are by nature "God-haters" ,θεοστυγεῖς. (Rom. 1:30). Thus we naturally "hate the light" and will not seek it.

> And this is the judgment, that the light is come into the world, but men loved the darkness rather than the light; for their deeds were evil. For everyone who does evil hates the light, and does not come to the light, lest his deeds should be exposed. (John 3:19-21)

Natural Theology assumes that people are seeking the light because they really want the truth. But Jesus said the exact opposite. People are running from God as fast as they can. Why? The Natural mind of man,

Chapter One   The Foundation of the Christian Worldview

> Is hostile toward God; for it does not subject itself to the Law of God, for it is not even able to do so. (Rom. 8:7).

The Natural hostility of man's mind toward God dooms Natural Law to failure. People would not accept God's Law if they could somehow find it in "Nature" by human reason alone.

Not only is the mind naturally hostile and hateful toward God, it is filled with darkness (Rom. 1:21; Eph. 4:18). The Bible denies the silly idea that the "light of reason shines forth in all mankind." Man's mind is naturally filled with darkness, not light. Even worse is the fact that man's mind has been blinded by Satan.

> the god of this world has blinded the minds of the unbelieving, that they might not see the light of the gospel of the glory of Christ, who is the image of God. (2 Cor. 4:4)
>
> ὁ θεὸς τοῦ αἰῶνος τούτου ἐτύφλωσεν τὰ νοήματα τῶν ἀπίστων εἰς τὸ μὴ αὐγάσαι τὸν φωτισμὸν τοῦ εὐαγγελίου τῆς δόξης τοῦ Χριστοῦ, ὅς ἐστιν εἰκὼν τοῦ θεοῦ.

People do not "see" the truthfulness of the Gospel because of some defect in it. No, the defect is in man's mind and not in the Revelation of God.

Since the mind of man is naturally evil, wicked, hostile, blind, and full of hate against God, it is described in Scripture as "depraved."

> 2 Tim. 3:8:   men of depraved mind:
> ἄνθρωποι κατεφθαρμένοι τὸν νοῦν,
>
> 1 Tim. 6:5:   men of depraved mind:
> διεφθαρμένων ἀνθρώπων τὸν νοῦν;

The words κατεφθαρμένοι and διεφθαρμένων are emphatic. The mind of man has been utterly ruined and morally corrupted by sin and Satan.

Natural theologians and philosophers do not believe that man's mind is totally depraved, blinded by Satan or filled with darkness. They have a romantic notion that the mind is perfect, infallible, and untainted by sin. Thus it can be the Origin of truth, justice, morals, meaning, and beauty.

This is why humanists "dream the impossible dream" that man, apart from and independent of God's revelation in Scripture, can understand and explain God, man, and the world around him. But, just as "you can lead a horse to water but cannot make him drink," you may give the gospel to rebel sinners, but they will not accept it because they love darkness and hate the light. They would rather believe the stupidest lies than submit to the Lordship of Christ. It takes the regenerating work of the Spirit of God to enable rebel sinners to repent and believe.

> No one has the ability (lit. Gk. "power" (δύναται) to say, "Jesus is Lord," except by the Holy Spirit. (1 Corinthians 12:3)
>
> οὐδεὶς δύναται εἰπεῖν· Κύριος Ἰησοῦς, εἰ μὴ ἐν πνεύματι ἁγίῳ.

While the unbelieving world "sits in total darkness," the Bible is "the light" that enables us to discover truth, justice, morals, meaning, and beauty (Psa. 36:9; 118:27; 119:105). Those studying for the ministry should spend most of their time studying the Light of Scripture instead of the darkness of Natural Theology and Philosophy. If you do not know the Bible, the theologians and philosophers will deceive you with "smooth and flattering speech" that seems reasonable (Rom. 16:18).

Job and his friends had confused and complicated the issue of evil to such an extent that truth became impossible. All the philosophers in the world with all their learning and education have only darkened the issues, and have not given us any light at all. The judgment of God stands firm that, "they never knew God" (1 Cor. 1:21).

Second, instead of speaking words of knowledge, Job and his friends spoke words that were "without knowledge" [בְּלִי־דָעַת]. All the eloquent speeches given by Job and his friends were devoid of knowledge, i.e. sheer ignorance. What a rebuke to the pride of these humanists.

In Job 35:16, Elihu had condemned Job's words as "without knowledge." Now God condemns all his words as "without knowledge." This will shock Natural theologians who assume that philosophers are the only ones with any knowledge to give on these issues.

Third, we must appreciate the divine sarcasm and ridicule that now commences.[64] In Psa. 2:1-5, God uses sarcasm and ridicule when dealing with rebel sinners.

> Why are the Gentiles in an uproar, And the peoples devising a vain thing? The kings of the earth take their stand, And the rulers take counsel together Against Yahweh and against His Messiah. "Let us tear their fetters apart, And cast away their cords from us!" He who sits in the heavens laughs, The Lord scoffs at them. Then He will speak to them in His anger And terrify them in His fury:

God laughs at and ridicules man's puny attempt to throw off His sovereign control. Their rebellion will not succeed, and is worthy only of scoffing.

If you do not understand God's sarcasm to Job and his friends or that He mocked their pride and self-sufficiency, you misunderstand His speech. God humbles and humiliates their pride and conceit. He showed them that they were pompous orators who distressed Job instead of comforting him. With "friends" like these, Job did not need any enemies! They added to the problem of evil with their own words and deeds.

With dripping sarcasm and irony, God challenges Job. It was time to see if they really knew everything.

Chapter One   *The Foundation of the Christian Worldview*

Now gird up your loins like a man,

אֱזָר־נָא כְגֶבֶר חֲלָצֶיךָ

He did not use the normal Hebrew words for "man," but a special word that refers to virile, masculine manhood.[65] In effect, God said,

> It is time for you to assert your manhood. Don't be a girly man but a manly man [גֶבֶר]. Don't wimp out on me now. Lift up robes and get ready to run.

Habel points out that the Targums and Syriac have *gibbor* instead of *geber*. *Gibbor* means "warrior, hero," which means that God challenged Job's manhood.[66]

God now challenged them with an amazing command.

And I will ask you,

וְאֶשְׁאָלְךָ

And you will instruct Me.

וְהוֹדִיעֵנִי׃

God said, "I am really excited at the prospect of you teaching me right from wrong and good from evil. You are so smart and intelligent that I am in awe of you and your high IQ. This is the moment you have been waiting for. You can instruct Me and teach Me where I went wrong running the universe. I need your help."

Humanists assume that they know how to run the universe better than God. Their conceit manifests itself when they say,

"Let me tell you what I think…"

"Listen to my opinion…"

"My reason tells me…"

"My heart tells me…"

"My experience tells me…"

"I believe that…"

They ignore the Bible as a relic of ancient prejudices and superstitions, and do not know that He is there and has not been silent. They have yet to learn what Scripture says,

> Oh, the depth of the riches both of the wisdom and knowledge of God! How unsearchable are His judgments and unfathomable His ways! (Rom. 11:33)

> Ὦ βάθος πλούτου καὶ σοφίας καὶ γνώσεως θεοῦ· ὡς ἀνεξεραύνητα
> τὰ κρίματα αὐτοῦ καὶ ἀνεξιχνίαστοι αἱ ὁδοὶ αὐτοῦ.

Paul emphatically states that when man tries to rationally "search out" [ἀνεξεραύνητα] and "fathom" [ἀνεξιχνίαστοι] the judgments and ways of God, he meets with total defeat. Why are Natural Theology, Natural Law, and Natural philosophy doomed to fail?

> For who has known the mind of the Lord, or who became His
> counselor? (Rom. 11:34)
>
> τίς γὰρ ἔγνω νοῦν κυρίου; ἢ τίς σύμβουλος αὐτοῦ ἐγένετο;

Humanists claim that they can know the mind of the Lord through human reason, experience, feelings, or faith. They can "figure out" His judgments and "get to the bottom" of His ways. Delitzsch comments,

> God is able to put everything into operation, and that the plans according to which He acts are beyond the reach of human comprehension.[67]

Because humanists think they can rationally figure out why God does what He does, they try to "counsel" Him on what He should and should not do.

> Or who has first given to Him that it might be paid back to him
> again? (Rom. 11:35)
>
> ἢ τίς προέδωκεν αὐτῷ, καὶ ἀνταποδοθήσεται αὐτῷ;

Humanists honestly believe that God "owes" man. As an example, they believe that the heathen who never hear the Gospel will not go to hell because God "owes" them a chance. God "owes" all people salvation, happiness, health, and wealth. Some humanists even claim that man must have a free will because God owes it to man.

Those who think that God owes them are ignorant of Job 4:11 and Rom. 11:35. Both passages state that God does not owe man anything.

> Who has given to Me that I should repay *him*? (Job 41:11)
>
> מִי הִקְדִּימַנִי וַאֲשַׁלֵּם

The only thing that God owes people is *eternal damnation*. Hell is the only thing we have all merited (Rom. 6:23)! Salvation is not something God owes us because of our good deeds. It is a free gift merited through the atoning work of the Messiah, Jesus of Nazareth. He is YHWH (Phil. 2:11).

In chapters 38-42 of Job, God now proceeds with marvelous sarcasm to ask Job and his friends a series of questions. His interrogations reveal that when man attempts to figure out the meaning of life beginning only with himself, in himself, and by himself, rejecting or ignoring divine revelation, he is doomed to become a babbling idiot. This is what Paul calls the futile exercise of philosophy in Col[...]

God used [...] questions that revealed the finite limitations of ma[...]ent, immutable or omnipresent, he cannot be the ab[...]e, morals, meaning and beauty. He is only a finite pa[...]n him. Parker observes that,

[...] ...man's power is

In order [...] theologians and philosophers, God sarcastically tau[...] claim to know and understand everything apart [...] be able to answer simple questions about the origin, [...] oseph Exell in the Biblical Illustrator reminds us that,

> There is mystery regarding the why of God's working, and there is mystery regarding the how. We cannot explain the one or the other. The path is invisible to us; but the path is there. There is mystery everywhere. There are three things which it is well always to bear in mind when thinking of the ways of God. First, God may interfere in the affairs of the world without men knowing it; second, God may influence motives without men knowing it; third, God may touch the secret and subtle spring of nature without men knowing it.[69]

According to Habel, the "ironic nuances" of the questions reveal the "cosmic irony" of the total ignorance and inability of man to come up with final answers on his own.[70] Frank Gaebelein in *The Expositor's Bible Commentary* correctly sees Job's need to "get rid of his ignorant fantasies."[71]

> The irony in the Lord's words "Surely you know" (v.5; cf. v.21) is sharp and purposeful. Job had dared criticize God's management of the universe. Had he been present at the Creation (an obvious absurdity), he might have known something about God's management of its vast expanses (vv.4-6).[72]

God confronts the pride of man with questions that reveal how little man knows.

Tell me, since you understand [everything] (Job 38:4) and

since you know [everything] (Job 38:5):

[Note: The unknowable nature or why — we do not know why or how God works.]

- Is it by your understanding that the hawk soars? (Job 39:26)
- Have you understood the expanse of the earth? Tell *Me*, if you know all this. (Job 38:18)
- You know, for you were born then, and the number of your days is great! (Job 38:12)
- Do you know the ordinances of the heavens, Or fix their rule over the earth? (Job 38:33)
- Do you know the time the mountain goats give birth? (Job 39:1)

In order to fully appreciate the sarcastic humor of God displayed in His interrogation of autonomous man, we will cast it into a comical dialogue.

God: Since you are so smart that you can figure everything out all by yourself, I have a few questions to ask you. I am ready to be instructed.

Man: Yes, we can figure everything out on the sole basis of our own reason, experience, feelings, and faith. You don't have to say a word. We can discover truth by ourselves.

God: Let us begin with the origin and existence of the universe. According to your reason, experience, feelings, and faith, is the universe eternal or did it have a beginning?

Man: For most of history, mankind believed the world was eternal. Western philosophers such as Aristotle believed that the world was eternal. Eastern Philosophers agreed as well. Hindus and Buddhists don't even believe that the universe exists, and may be an illusion. But Western Europeans are the smartest people in the world, and through reason alone they discovered that the universe is not eternal, but had a beginning. This is a self-evident, intuitive, and universal truth.

God: I thought you said that it has not been self-evident nor intuitive to the vast majority of mankind. How is it universal?

Man: As long as it is self-evident and intuitive to **us**, then it is universal to **us**. Stop being so picky. Just accept what we say as a philosophical *absolute*. The rest of the world is culturally inferior to the West and not philosophically advanced.

God: Since you speak with such confidence about the creation of the universe, were you *there* when it came into being? You must be really old!

Chapter One The Foundation of the Christian Worldview

Man: No, man was not in existence when the universe came into being.

God: Are you saying that no human being *experienced* it? No one *saw* it happen? No one has any firsthand knowledge about it? Are you merely guessing, speculating, extrapolating or shooting the breeze? If you weren't *there*, how do you know so much about it?

Man: Our reason, experience, feelings and faith tell us that the universe has to have a beginning. It cannot be eternal.

God: But didn't you admit that almost all of mankind through reason, experience, feelings and faith believed that the world was eternal?

Man: Yes, *their* reason, experience, feelings, and faith led them in the opposite conclusion of *our* reason, experience, feelings, and faith. As we said, *we* are racially and culturally superior. What they believe doesn't matter.

God: If according to your reason, experience, feelings and faith, you know that the world was not eternal and that it had a beginning, can you tell me how long it took for the universe to come into existence?

Man: According to our best western philosophers and scientists, it took 15 to 25 billion years. This is a self-evident, intuitive, and universal truth.

God: What if I told you that it only took six days to create the universe and everything in it?

Man: Nonsense! That cannot be true, rationally speaking. It would contradict modern western science and philosophy. The idea of a literal six day creation is simply impossible. If this were true, it would mean that we would have to revise our theories once again. It would reduce most of our science and philosophy to idiocy. We cannot accept the idea of a literal six day creation.

God: What if I *revealed* in the Bible that I only took six days to create the universe?

Man: Then we would have to reinterpret the Bible until it conformed to what *we* say. For example, each "day" represents two billion years. Man is the measure of *all* things, including the Bible. Thus we are free to interpret the Bible any way we want.

God: Let us go on. Since you are so smart, you can surely tell me how the universe works. I will now ask you how nature works and why animals do what they do.

Man: I am capable of explaining all things.

49

> God: Tell me about the foundations of the world, the limits of the ocean, the ways of animals like the eagle, the hippo, the crocodile, etc. Why do bees buzz and birds sing?
>
> (God at this point asked Job and his friends many probing questions that revealed their ignorance. When the "rubber met the road," they did not know as much as they claimed.)
>
> God: You haven't answered any of my questions. Maybe you are sovereign over what you cannot understand. Can you control the weather? Surely you control lightning?
>
> Man: No, we cannot control the weather or lightning.
>
> God: Surely you can control animals such as the crocodile or the hippo?
>
> Man: No.
>
> God: Do you mean you are **not** eternal, omniscient, omnipotent, and sovereign? Then how can you be the Origin, source, infinite, and absolute measure of truth, justice, morals, meaning, and beauty?

Job's friends could not answer any of God's questions. Their pretentious human autonomy and self-sufficient reason, experience, feelings, and faith did not enable them to come up with any answers. They could not understand themselves, the world around them or God.

This is why the Bible emphasizes over and over again that if God does not *reveal* to us the truth about the existence, origin, form, and meaning of the universe, we will remain in bondage to the darkness of our depraved reason. In Rom. 1:21, Paul comments,

> They became futile in their speculations, and their foolish mind was darkened.
>
> ἐματαιώθησαν ἐν τοῖς διαλογισμοῖς αὐτῶν καὶ ἐσκοτίσθη ἡ ἀσύνετος αὐτῶν καρδία.

All philosophic and theological speculations of Natural philosophy and Natural Theology are described by Scripture as "futile" (ἐματαιώθησαν). The word is derived from ματαιότης, which means their ideas are not only devoid of truth, but are pure nonsense and sheer foolishness. They are *worthless* because they come not from enlightened minds, but from darkened hearts.

Note that while humanists refer to the Renaissance as the "Age of Enlightenment," God calls it the "Age of Darkness." The Renaissance was not the dawning of the light of Reason, but the darkening of the mind and heart of Western man.

Job's Response

Chapter One The Foundation of the Christian Worldview

After God exposes him as an ignorant fool, Job responds to this revelation. He acknowledges that only God is sovereign over all things and that whatever He decrees shall infallibly happen. Thus the future is certain and fixed in concrete. Job expresses the omnipotence of God in its positive and negative forms.

First, he states in the positive that the omnipotence of God guarantees that He has infinite power to do whatever He decides to do:

> I know that You can do all things. (Job 42:2)
>
> יָדַעְתָּ כִּי־כֹל תּוּכָל
>
> אֲסָאנָךְ אתנאָף תע אד׃
>
> סתף אנמ אק צס

Once God decides that something shall be done, it shall be done.

> Calling a bird of prey from the east, The man of My purpose from a far country. Truly I have spoken; truly I will bring it to pass. I have planned *it*, Surely I will do it. (Isaiah 46:11)

Second, he states in the negative that the omnipotence of God guarantees that no one can hinder or frustrate God's will.

> And that no purpose of Yours can be thwarted. (Job 42:1-2).
>
> וְלֹא־יִבָּצֵר מִמְּךָ מְזִמָּה׃
> (יָדַעְתָּ) וְיָדַעְתִּי כִּי־כֹל תּוּכָל
> וְלֹא־יִבָּצֵר מִמְּךָ מְזִמָּה׃

The Hebrew, Greek, and Latin texts could not be clearer. On the basis of the revelation of God in the wind storm, Job now "knew" (יָדַעְתָּ) that only God is omnipotent (omnia potes) because only He has the power (תּוּכָל) to do whatever He wants. Since God is sovereign over all things, no purpose or plan of His can be blocked or rendered powerless by man or devil.

The Septuagint has a beautiful play upon the word for power ($δύναμις$). It reads $δύνασαι$ $ἀδυνατεῖ$, i.e. "No one has the power to render God powerless." The Pulpit Commentary rightly observes,

> The fact of God's supremacy: This is what Job now comes to see. God is supreme both in power and in wisdom...There is no resisting his might. He does as he wills with the children of men...All rebellion against God's will must be futile. It can be no better than dashing one's self against a granite cliff.[73]

51

Any so-called "Christian" worldview claiming that God is powerless in a chance-based universe does not have the God of the Bible in view. Anders comments,

> Job confessed, "I know that you can do all things." He saw, at last, that God's purposes are supreme. God will do as he pleases, when he pleases, how he pleases, with whom he pleases. Furthermore, no plan of his can be thwarted. Job realized that all his sovereign purposes will be fully carried. He came back to the single, most fundamental truth of Theology that God rules over all. Implied in this strong declaration by Job was a new submission to the God whose eternal purposes cannot be resisted or altered. Thus, it was insane for Job to question the Lord's verdicts or oppose his decrees. God is supreme, not Job.[74]

Having acknowledged the absolute sovereignty of God, Job repents.

> Therefore I retract [all my bitter accusations], And I repent in dust and ashes. (Job 42:6)

Job acknowledges that he and his friends did not give sound counsel and did not convey any knowledge.

> Who is this that hides counsel without knowledge? Therefore I have declared that which I did not understand (Job 42:3).

Job now states that the reason why evil fell upon him was an issue,

> too wonderful for me
> וְלֹא אָבִין נִפְלָאוֹת מִמֶּנִּי

The word פָּלָא translated "wonderful" literally means "incomprehensible." The issue of evil goes *beyond* man's finite capacity to understand it. The German commentator Delitzsch notes that,

> the plans according to which he acts are beyond the reach of human comprehension.[75]

Because the ultimate questions of the universe are ultimately "incomprehensible, "Natural Theology, Philosophy, and Law cannot and will not work. Thus Job concludes in Job 42:3,

> I did not understand (42:3)

Chapter One   The Foundation of the Christian Worldview

וְלֹא אָבִין

I did not know. (42:3)

וְלֹא אֵדָע

Instead of man being the origin of truth, justice, morals, meaning, and beauty, Job now looks to God as the origin. Instead of instructing God, he now asks God to instruct him.

I will ask You, and You will instruct me (Job 42:4)

וְאָנֹכִי אֲדַבֵּר אֶשְׁאָלְךָ וְהוֹדִיעֵנִי׃

Humanists assume that their knowledge is greater and better than God's. Clark Pinnock is a perfect example of this. He denies that eternal conscious punishment awaits sinners in the future. He is absolutely certain that there is no eternal hell waiting for him or others like him. However, he also claims that God cannot know the future because the future is not fixed, i.e. it is open to an infinite number of chance-based possibilities. Evidently Pinnock knows *more* than his pathetic god, because while his god does not know the future, he does! He knows that there is no eternal hell!

God's Condemnation

Job's friends had pooled their ignorance, and represented all schools of Natural Theology. They spoke with absolute confidence and certainty that they knew the truth. Now God gives His opinion of their "rational" theories.

> YHWH said to Eliphaz the Temanite, "My wrath is kindled against you and against Your two friends, because you have not spoken of Me what is true." (Job 42:7)

Humanists cannot stand the idea that God is angry with them. They declare that "God hates the sin but loves the sinner," and quote other meaningless cliches. The text plainly states that God was angry with Eliphaz and his two friends. The Bible teaches that God hates unrepentant sinners and will cast them into hell forever (Psa. 11:5).

God told Eliphaz that he and his friends did not speak the truth (שֶׁהִקְהִלְשָׁא כּוּן). Rationalism, empiricism, mysticism, and fideism are all lies. They failed to discover the true explanation of evil.

The main point of the Book of Job is that there was absolutely no way for man to discover the true purpose behind Job's pain and suffering. Their reason, experience, feelings, and faith utterly failed them. Natural Theology, Law, and Philosophy are failures, incapable of discovering real truth.

The futility of Natural Theology and philosophy reminds me of a scene in Shakespeare's Macbeth:

> To-morrow, and to-morrow, and to-morrow, Creeps in this petty pace from day to day to the last syllable of recorded time, And all our yesterdays have lighted fools the way to dusty death. Out, out,

brief candle! Life's but a walking shadow, a poor player that struts and frets his hour upon the stage And then is heard no more: it is a tale told by an idiot, full of sound and fury, Signifying nothing. (Macbeth, Act V, scene 5)

The Way of Sacrifice

God now offers a way of forgiveness for Job's friends. It is the ancient way of sacrifice established in the Garden of Eden, practiced by man from the beginning of human history (Gen. 4:3-4).

> Now therefore, take for yourselves seven bulls and seven rams, and go to My servant Job, and offer up a burnt offering for yourselves, and My servant Job will pray for you. For I will accept him so that I may not do with you according to your senseless foolishness, because you have not spoken of Me what is right, as My servant Job has. (Job 42:8)

וְעַתָּ֡ה קְחֽוּ־לָכֶ֣ם שִׁבְעָֽה־פָרִים֩ וְשִׁבְעָ֨ה אֵילִ֜ים וּלְכ֣וּ ׀ אֶל־עַבְדִּ֣י אִיּ֗וֹב וְהַעֲלִיתֶ֤ם עוֹלָה֙ בַּֽעַדְכֶ֔ם וְאִיּ֣וֹב עַבְדִּ֔י יִתְפַּלֵּ֖ל עֲלֵיכֶ֑ם כִּ֧י אִם־פָּנָ֣יו אֶשָּׂ֗א לְבִלְתִּ֞י עֲשׂ֤וֹת עִמָּכֶם֙ נְבָלָ֔ה כִּ֠י לֹ֣א דִבַּרְתֶּ֥ם אֵלַ֛י נְכוֹנָ֖ה כְּעַבְדִּ֥י אִיּֽוֹב׃

Imagine the shock of Job's friends when God demanded that they provide a very expensive sacrifice to cover *their* sins. These pompous self-righteous Natural theologians assumed that *they* were not the problem, Job was. They thought they had figured everything out. They were smarter than Job. However, God rebuked *them* for "folly!"

Can you imagine their chagrin when God dismissed all their philosophical reasoning as "senseless foolishness" (נְבָלָה)? They did not get anything right!

The Hebrew word is elsewhere translated as "folly," "foolishness," and "senselessness." In its noun form, it is the regular word for "fool." In Psa. 14:1-3 we read,

> The fool (נָבָל) has said in his heart, "There is no God." They are corrupt, they have committed abominable deeds; There is no one who does good. YHWH looked down from heaven upon the sons of men, To see if there are any who understand, Who seek after God. They have all turned aside; together they have become corrupt; There is no one who does good, not even one.

The word נָבָל is quite strong. It was a sharp rebuke to their intellectual pride. The word did not just indicate an error of judgment, it indicated that an evil heart lay behind their errors.

Chapter One The Foundation of the Christian Worldview

It is combined twice in Isaiah 32:6 in the phrase "a senseless fool speaks nonsense" (נְבָלָה נָבָל).

> For a senseless fool speaks nonsense, And his heart inclines toward wickedness, To practice ungodliness And to speak error against YHWH, To keep the hungry person unsatisfied And to withhold drink from the thirsty. (Isaiah 32:6)
>
> כִּי נָבָל נְבָלָה יְדַבֵּר וְלִבּוֹ יַעֲשֶׂה־אָוֶן לַעֲשׂוֹת
> חֹנֶף וּלְדַבֵּר אֶל־יְהוָה תּוֹעָה לְהָרִיק נֶפֶשׁ
> רָעֵב וּמַשְׁקֶה צָמֵא יַחְסִיר׃

Natural Theology, Natural Philosophy, and Natural Law are utter nonsense, and are the products of rebellion against God. Those who are, according to Scripture, deceived by them are fools. God crushed their smug attitudes by demanding that they beg Job to intercede on their behalf. Imagine the irony. They tried to make Job humble himself before them. Now they had to humble themselves before Job! Divine sarcasm is brilliant.

Note that Natural theologians are not just intellectually wrong because they do not speak the truth. Their erroneous truth claims have a *moral* dimension. They sin when they speak lies!

Notice also that the way to God and truth was not through more education. Humanists assume that if we know better, we will live better, but this is not true. Nazi Germany was the most educated country of its day, and it used its knowledge to start World War II and murder millions of people.

Would Eliphaz, Bildad, Zophar, and Elihu humble themselves before Job, admit they were wrong, ask his forgiveness, and beg him to intercede on their behalf before God?

> So Eliphaz the Temanite and Bildad the Shuhite *and* Zophar the Naamathite went and did as YHWH told them; and YHWH accepted Job. (Job 42:9)
>
> וַיֵּלְכוּ אֱלִיפַז הַתֵּימָנִי וּבִלְדַּד הַשּׁוּחִי צֹפַר
> הַנַּעֲמָתִי וַיַּעֲשׂוּ כַּאֲשֶׁר דִּבֶּר אֲלֵיהֶם יְהוָה
> וַיִּשָּׂא יְהוָה אֶת־פְּנֵי אִיּוֹב׃

The first three friends did as God demanded and God forgave them on the basis of Job's intercessory sacrifice. However, they never learned why Job suffered so terribly. They died without ever knowing that what happened on earth was the result of what happened in heaven.

What about Elihu? He had monopolized the conversation with his pompous and inflated speeches. Why was he now ignored? Rabbinic tradition says that, unlike Job's other three friends, Elihu did not repent. He was not willing to humble himself before Job and admit his sin. He did not offer a sacrifice, and as a result died in his sins.

All's Well That Ends Well

Now that God had vindicated Job, it would only be natural for him to be angry and bitter at his so-called friends. They had said harsh, unkind, and terrible things against him and his family. He could now "stick it to them" and refuse to forgive them or intercede for them before God. He could not bring flowers to their funerals or dance on their graves.

However, since God was merciful to Job, Job had to be merciful to his friends. Once he "prayed for his friends," God restored his wealth and health. God then gave him more children, and he was better off in the end than at the beginning.

> And YHWH restored the fortunes of Job when he prayed for his friends, and YHWH increased all that Job had twofold. (Job 42:10)
>
> וַיהוָה שָׁב אֶת־(שְׁבִית) [שְׁבוּת] אִיּוֹב
> בְּהִתְפַּלְלוֹ בְּעַד רֵעֵהוּ וַיֹּסֶף יְהוָה
> אֶת־כָּל־אֲשֶׁר לְאִיּוֹב לְמִשְׁנֶה׃

> And YHWH blessed the latter *days* of Job more than his beginning, and he had 14,000 sheep, and 6,000 camels, and 1,000 yoke of oxen, and 1,000 female donkeys. (Job 42:12)
>
> וַיהוָה בֵּרַךְ אֶת־אַחֲרִית אִיּוֹב מֵרֵאשִׁתוֹ וַיְהִי־לוֹ
> אַרְבָּעָה עָשָׂר אֶלֶף צֹאן וְשֵׁשֶׁת אֲלָפִים
> גְּמַלִּים וְאֶלֶף־צֶמֶד בָּקָר וְאֶלֶף אֲתוֹנוֹת׃

Those who find fault with God for taking *away* Job's creature comforts never have any problems with God *giving* them back. Why is this? They assume that God *owed* Job and all men long life free from pain and suffering. There is no moral outrage concerning the blessings conferred upon Job.

God does not owe us anything but His just wrath and indignation. It was God's grace and mercy that restored Job. Job's use of sacrifice to absolve the sins of his friends and their need for a mediator to intercede on their behalf prefigures the person and work of King Messiah.

This is remarkable. Even though it was the first biblical book ever written (long before Moses), it takes us to the foot of the Cross and shows us that salvation is by blood atonement.

Delitzsch's conclusion is worth repeating.

> The comfort which this theologically and artistically incomparable book presents to us is substantially none other than that of the New Testament. For the final consolation of every sufferer is not dependent upon the working of good genii in the heavens, but has its seat in God's love, without which even heaven would become a very hell. Therefore the book of Job is also a book of consolation for the New Testament Church. From it we learn that we have not only to fight with flesh and blood, but with the prince of this world, and to accomplish our part in the conquest of evil, to which, from Gen. iii.15 onwards, the history of the world tends; that faith and

avenging justice are absolutely distinct opposites; that the right kind of faith clings to divine love in the midst of the feeling of wrath; that the incomprehensible ways of God always lead to a glorious issue; and that the suffering of the present time is far outweighed by the future glory- a glory not always revealed in this life and visibly future but the final glory above. The nature of faith, the mystery of the cross, the right practice of the care of souls, - this and much besides, the church learns from this book, the whole teaching of which can never be thoroughly learned and completely exhausted.[76]

Conclusion

The Book of Job infallibly demonstrates that unless God reveals the final answers to the riddles of life and death, we will wander forever in the mists of darkness. Man cannot find truth or morals within himself. He was created to be a truth-receiver, not a truth-maker.

Chapter Two

The Three Pillars

Creation, Fall, Redemption

The Book of Job reveals the absolute sovereignty of God over all things - *including evil*. This Divine Special Revelation is the foundation of the biblical worldview and the granite bedrock on which the rest of Scripture rests.

The sovereignty of God is thus the biblical context or framework within which all the other ideas in the Bible are understandable. For example, the doctrine of the inspiration, infallibility, and inerrancy of Scripture is possible only within the context of God's absolute sovereignty over the mind and will of man.

What if you reject the doctrine of the sovereignty of God and instead believe in the heathen idea that the universe is based upon chaos, contingency, chance, luck, and free will?

Once you deny the sovereignty of God, a domino effect begins in which, one by one, all the doctrines of the Bible are rejected as irrational and even repugnant. One way to find out if you are dealing with liberals is to test them with the biblical doctrine that the heathen must hear of and believe in Christ and His gospel in order to make it to heaven. They will go ballistic if you dare speak of the eternal conscious punishment of those who never heard the gospel.

The Link between Scripture and Divine Sovereignty

Why have so many "evangelical" Natural theologians ultimately rejected the inerrancy of the Bible? It became *unintelligible* to them. Their fanatical commitment to the old Greek idol of "free will" led them to deny the inerrancy of the Bible.

In forty years of theological research I have never met anyone who believed in the absolute sovereignty of God over all things, including the mind and will of man, and who rejected the inerrancy of Scripture at the same time. Those who reject the inerrancy of Scripture begin by rejecting the sovereignty of God.

Back in the 1960's, Clark Pinnock had no problem with the inerrancy of Scripture. He even wrote a book defending it. Why? He was under the influence of the Reformed apologist Francis Schaeffer, who believed in the sovereignty of God. But, while he was a professor at Trinity Evangelical Divinity School, Pinnock fell under the influence of those who rejected the sovereignty of God.

I was speaking at Trinity Evangelical Divinity School at the time and was amazed to hear Clark openly attack the sovereignty of God. I warned people that he would ultimately reject all evangelical doctrines because they all depend upon the sovereignty of God for their rationale. Sadly, he no longer believes in the inerrancy of the Bible.

The Root Causes of Liberalism

The root causes of such liberalism have always been rebellion against the sovereignty of God and the vain attempt to establish the sovereignty of man in its place. Psalm 2:1-5 points this out in bold poetic imagery.

> Why are the heathen nations in an uproar, And why are the masses imagining an empty delusion? The kings of the earth set themselves, and the rulers take counsel together, against YHWH, and against his Messiah, saying, "Let us break their leg shackles asunder, and cast away their handcuffs from us. "But He who sits enthroned in the heavens laughs, The Lord scoffs at them. Then He will speak to them in His anger, And terrify them in His fury.

The futility of attempting to cast off the leg shackles and handcuffs of the sovereignty of God over all things leads to divine ridicule as well as judgment. The revolt against the sovereignty of God is an empty delusion that leads only to eternal perdition.

The Book of Genesis

We now proceed to the next written record of Special Revelation, the Book of Genesis. And we are delighted to find that God continued to give us the theological keys to unlock the mysteries of life.

A Perfect Man in a Perfect World

The pre-fall condition of man is the key to a biblical view of epistemology. Adam and Eve were perfect in every respect. They lived in a perfect world. Their five senses were perfect. Their brains and minds were perfect. Their feelings were prefect. Everything about man and around man was perfect.

If there was ever a perfect time for Natural Law and Natural Theology, i.e. rationalism, empiricism, mysticism, and fideism, to shine, it is with a perfect humanity in a perfect world. But what do we find?

Man's own reason, experience, feelings or faith could not tell him who he was, why he existed, what was his purpose in life, what is right and wrong, etc. The pre-fall perfection of the Garden of Eden proves that man is not the Origin of truth, justice, morals, meaning, and beauty.

How Did Adam Know Right from Wrong?

How did Adam know which trees to eat from and which tree not to eat from? This is an important question. If Natural theology is valid, then we would expect to find that Adam was able to discover which tree to avoid by his reason, experience, feelings, and faith, apart from and independent of special revelation.

Did Adam's perfect "reason" tell him not to eat from a particular tree? No. Did he know not to eat from that tree through his perfect intuition? No. Was it self-evident and universal not to eat from that tree? No. Did his five perfect empirical senses of sight, smell, taste, touch, or hearing tell him not to eat from it? No. Did his perfect feelings warn him not to eat from it? No. Did a perfect "Nature" reveal to him not to eat from that tree? No.

There was simply no humanistic way for man to know not to eat of that tree any more than he could know that he was obligated to name the animals or rake the leaves. His perfect reason, experience, feelings, and faith were not the Origin of truth, justice, morals, meaning, and beauty. How then did Adam know which trees he could eat of and which tree was forbidden?

> And YHWH Elohim commanded the man, saying, "From any tree of
> the garden you may eat freely; but from the tree of the knowledge
> of good and evil you shall not eat, for in the day that you eat from it
> you shall surely die." (Gen. 2:16-17)

It was by Special Revelation **alone** (*Sola Scriptura*) that man understood right from wrong. In fact, *Sola Scriptura* was the basis of everything man knew in the Garden. God walked with man in the Garden and revealed truth, justice, morals, meaning, and beauty to him.

No Other Source

Let the Catholics and the Orthodox also take note of the fact that Adam had none of the things that they depend upon for truth. Were there any: Traditions? No. Councils? No. Creeds? No. Fathers? No. Popes? No. The *only* Source of information by which Adam could understand God, the world, man, sin, and salvation was through Divine Propositional Revelation. *Sola Scriptura* was the rule in the Garden of Eden. Why should we abandon perfect and infallible Revelation for imperfect and fallible human traditions, councils, creeds, fathers, and clergymen?

The Creator Talked with Man

The Lord came down to man in human form and walked and talked with them in the cool of the day.

> And they heard the sound of YHWH Elohim walking in the garden in the cool of the day. (Genesis 3:8)

אֱלֹהִים מִתְהַלֵּךְ בַּגָּן לְרוּחַ הַיּוֹם וַיִּשְׁמְעוּ אֶת־קוֹל יְהוָה

God told Adam what he was and was not to do. He told man how to worship and how not to worship. God explained to man the purpose of life and right from wrong. Left only to himself, man could not get anything right. In Gen. 3, Eve tried to understand the tree by her reason (rationalism), experience (empiricism), and feelings (mysticism), and faith (fideism).

> When the woman saw that the tree was good for food, and that it
> was a delight to the eyes, and that the tree was desirable to make
> her wise, she took from its fruit and ate. (Genesis 3:6)

Eve's physical senses told her that the fruit looked good for food. Her feelings felt that the fruit was beautiful to eat. And her reason concluded that eating it would make her wise. Then by faith she reached out, took the fruit, bit a chunk out of it, and swallowed. When she did not die, she handed it to Adam and told him to eat it. Adam ate the fruit on the basis of faith in his wife.

Eve beginning only with herself, by herself, rejecting any revelation from God, chose to believe the lie of Satan that she was the Origin of truth, justice, morals, meaning, and beauty; that she could judge God; that she could determine good and evil. Thus Eve ate the forbidden fruit and fell into sin and guilt.

Stop and Let These Facts Sink In.

If, when man was a perfect being in a perfect world, God's Word was the Origin of truth, justice, morals, meaning and beauty (*Sola Scriptura*), why would anyone in their mind think that *fallen* man in a *fallen* world no longer needs God's Revelation? Have things become worse or better since Eden? Is sinful man *less* capable or more capable of finding truth? How can fallen man in a fallen world, apart from and independent of Special Revelation, be self-sufficient and autonomous to be the Origin of truth, justice, morals, meaning, and beauty, when he was not sufficient for these things when he was a perfect being living in a perfect world? This is why Natural Theology is delusional. If it did not work in the Garden of Eden, why would any sane man or woman think that it can work now?

The Three Pillars of Biblical Revelation

Genesis reveals three concepts that form the pillars upon which the biblical worldview rest. They are so essential to each other that they stand or fall together. To deny one is to deny the others.

(1.) Creation *ex nihilo*. (God made all things out of nothing.)
(2.) The Radical Fall of man into sin and guilt. (Man blew it.)
(3.) Redemption by grace alone through faith alone. (God alone can provide salvation by grace.)

Genesis is essential to establish the Christian worldview on anything and everything. Without its special revelation, it is impossible to be "Christian" in your thinking. The famous English expositor Dr. G. Campbell Morgan comments:

> To deny the accuracy of these fundamental statements is to lose the meaning of all subsequent teaching. If God is not Creator, King, and Redeemer, there is no resting place for man other than the restlessness of agnosticism. On the way to agnosticism, human speculations may retain the name of religion; but the logical outcome of the denial of these fundamental assertions concerning God is denial of the existence of God. To deny what this book teaches concerning the origin of the universe is to be compelled to attempt to account for the teachings seen by some undefined action and interaction within the universe, which has behind it no personality...To deny that man is a mysterious mingling of dust and Deity by the will and act of God is necessarily to be compelled to think of him as the last product of animal evolution; and therefore as himself an animal, and nothing more.[77]

The Sovereignty of God as revealed in Job is the only theoretical context or framework within which these three concepts can and must be understood. God is completely sovereign over Creation, Fall, and Redemption.

Keeping in mind that the absolute sovereignty of God is the biblical context or theoretical framework for Creation, Fall, and Redemption, we find that these three key concepts are used by the authors of Scripture to understand God, man, and the world and their relationships to each other.

From Genesis to Revelation, Creation, Fall, and Redemption are the interpretive principles by means of which the biblical worldview is applied to all of life. They are like trifocal glasses that enable the wearer to see with crystal clear vision what is really there. Let me illustrate what I mean.

The Trees Have Leaves!

I was born with defective vision and did not clearly see the world around me. But since my defective vision was all I knew, I did not know that I had defective vision. But a kind teacher noticed my difficulty seeing the blackboard and sent me to an eye doctor.

I will never forget the day I put on glasses for the first time and looked out the window of the doctor's office. I exclaimed, "Leaves! I see individual leaves on the tree." Up to that point trees looked like green cotton candy because my eyes were nearsighted. But when I put on the glasses that corrected my poor vision, I could see that trees had individual leaves.

In the same way, we are all born with defective intellectual eyesight. We can't see reality as it really is. But when we put on the biblical glasses of Creation, Fall, and Redemption, we can clearly see God, man, and the world as they really are and how they relate to each other.

The Biblical Authors

This point is important. Creation, Fall, and Redemption are utilized as interpretive principles by the prophets, apostles, and the Lord Jesus Himself. They looked at life and all it entails and interpreted everything through the lens of Creation, Fall, and Redemption. Sometimes they invoked all three principles, other times just two, or even one.

Under both the Old and New Covenants, two or three witnesses were sufficient to establish the truthfulness of a claim (Deut. 19:15; 1 Tim. 5:19). Thus I will now give three exegetical witnesses that the authors of Scripture used Creation, Fall, Redemption as interpretive principles by which they understood the world.

Witness #1

In Matthew 19:3 the Pharisees challenged Jesus to answer a question.

> Is it lawful for a man to divorce his wife for any cause at all?
>
> Εἰ ἔξεστιν ἀνθρώπῳ ἀπολῦσαι τὴν γυναῖκα αὐτοῦ κατὰ πᾶσαν αἰτίαν;

The question was a contemporary controversy between two dominant schools of Judaism at that time. They disagreed as to the meaning of Deut. 24:1. The Shammai believed that the Torah allowed divorce only upon immorality. The Hillel believed that a man could divorce his wife for any reason. How did Jesus answer the question? By framing it in terms of the Creation account in Genesis.

> And He answered and said, "Have you not read, that He who created them from the Beginning made them male and female, and said, "For

> this cause a man shall leave his father and mother, and shall cleave to
> his wife; and the two shall become one flesh?" Consequently, they are
> no longer two, but one flesh. What therefore God has joined together,
> let no man separate. (Matt. 19:4-6)

Instead of beginning with Deut. 24:1, Jesus begins with the Genesis account of Creation as the interpretive principle or Archimedean point by which we understand the origin, nature, structure, dignity, and purpose of marriage.

Let all Natural Theologians take note of the fact that Jesus did *not* appeal to common sense, human reason, experience, feelings, faith, Plato, Aristotle, etc. as the Origin of the truth about marriage. As a matter of fact, Jesus *never* argued from a humanistic base as if man were the measure of all things. He *always* appealed to the authority of Scripture ("as it is written"). As we shall demonstrate later, *Sola Scriptura* was His clear *modus operandi*.

The institution of marriage is not a meaningless fluke of an equally meaningless evolutionary process spawn out of pure chance. It cannot be twisted into same sex marriages or a marriage between animals and human beings. According to Genesis 1-2, it is a Creation Ordinance between a man and a woman and was created and instituted by God at the dawn of human history.

Where Did Divorce Originate?

What about divorce? Where did it come from? Creation does not explain divorce as it was not part of the original divine design for man. Divorce came into existence as a result of man's radical Fall into sin and guilt. Jesus said to them,

> Because of your hardness of heart, Moses permitted you to divorce
> your wives; but from the Beginning it has not been this way.
> (Matthew 19:8)

ὅτι Μωϋσῆς πρὸς τὴν σκληροκαρδίαν ὑμῶν ἐπέτρεψεν ὑμῖν ἀπολῦσαι τὰς γυναῖκας ὑμῶν, ἀπ' ἀρχῆς δὲ οὐ γέγονεν οὕτως.

The Fall of man into sin resulted in the total depravity of the heart. Jesus describes this depravity as "hardness of heart." The Greek word sklhrokardi,an is a combination of two words: sklhro,j (extreme hardness) and kardi,a (heart.)

The combination of the two words means that Jesus is describing not what man *does* but what man *is* in terms of his fallen condition. Because his mind or heart is hardened by sin, divorce was invented by man.

The "heart" in Scripture is the seat of the intellect and not just a sloppy metaphor for feelings or emotion. Humanistic Christian apologists usually assume the Western philosophic dichotomy between "mind" and "heart." They assume that "heart" is a metaphor for the emotions of man.

Natural theologians, true to form, never bother to pick up a Bible to see how the word "heart" was understood and used by the biblical authors. They just assume that Plato or Kant or some other pagan philosopher was correct in the "heart versus mind" motif.

One way to ferret out humanists is to ask, "Is it possible to read the Bible in a devotional way with your heart as opposed to reading it in an intellectual way with your mind?" Humanists love to talk about reading the Bible in a "devotional" way, which means that they read the Bible with their mind in neutral gear. They can feel all warm and fuzzy about the Bible as long as they don't have to exegete it. Since this issue touches on the subject of Biblical Anthropology, we will wait until we reach that section of the book to offer an exegetical answer to that issue.

God said, "I hate divorce" (Mal. 2:16). God is nowhere in Scripture said to create divorce. Fallen man created it. This is why Jesus is careful to say that Moses only allowed it because of the fallen nature of man. Jesus clearly uses Creation and Fall as the interpretive principles for marriage and divorce.

Witness #2

We now turn to the Book of Acts for our second witness. In Acts 17 Paul confronted the Greek philosophers with three shocking ideas that had never crossed their minds:

a. Creation *ex nihilo* (v. 24-28),
b. The Fall of man into sin and guilt (v. 30),
c. Redemption through a resurrected Savior called Jesus (v. 18 cf. v. 31).

Paul pointed out that the "unknown God" - whom they admit they knew absolutely nothing about – happened to be the Creator of the universe, the only God that actually existed!

I know this is going to be quite a shock to Natural theologians and philosophers. Plato, Aristotle and all other philosophers never found the true God through their reason (rationalism), experience (empiricism), feelings (mysticism), faith (fideism) or common sense, or intuition. Paul confronted the philosophers on Mars Hill with this truth and then explained it in detail to the Corinthians (1 Cor. 1:21).

the world through its philosophy did not know God!

οὐκ ἔγνω ὁ κόσμος διὰ τῆς σοφίας τὸν θεόν

Morey claims it is emphatic due to word placement.

Chapter Two   The Three Pillars: Creation, Fall and Redemption

The Greek syntax of the verse is emphatic for two reasons. First, the word οὐκ ("not") is taken out of its normal word order and placed first for emphasis sake. This means when you read the verse out loud, you emphasize the word "not."

the world through its philosophy did NOT know God!

Second, the verb ἔγνω is emphatic. The world *utterly failed* to know God. All the greatest philosophers and theologians never found the true God. All their philosophic wisdom ended with idolatry in which they "worshiped and served the creature rather than the Creator" (Rom. 1:25). A. T. Robertson comments,

> Failed to know, second aorist (effective) active indicative of γινωσκω [ginǎskǎ], solemn dirge of doom on both Greek philosophy and Jewish theology that failed to know God. Has modern philosophy done better? There is today even a godless theology (Humanism). "Now that God's wisdom has reduced the self-wise world to ignorance" (Findlay).[78]

The Natural theologians and philosophers of Greece had erected great temples to the gods and goddesses created by human reason, experience, feelings, and faith. Yet, Paul dismisses these natural gods created by Natural theology and philosophy as depraved figments of vain speculations. The Greeks wasted their time and money erecting the temples on the Parthenon to worship the false gods and goddesses housed inside!

Some of the Natural philosophers understood that they were being insulted by Paul's revealed religion and "sneered" at Paul (v. 18). They attacked him with such *ad hominem* slurs as "babbling idiot" (v. 18 cf. 32) and dismissed his message as irrational. Notice that Paul ignored the personal slander just as Jesus ignored it. My recent book, *A Bible Handbook on Slander and Gossip*, documents this point.

When Paul preached the biblical concept of God to these Natural philosophers, he did so in two moves. First, he established the absolute sovereignty of God.

Seeing He is Lord of heaven and earth

οὗτος οὐρανοῦ καὶ γῆς ὑπάρχων κύριος

Paul first stressed the dynamic sovereignty of God over all things by the using the present active participle ὑπάρχων (from ὑπάρχω). God is pictured as being in active control of the universe NOW and even determining when and where we are born (v. 26). This is why God is described as the sovereign "Maker" of heaven and earth throughout the Book of Job (Job 4:17; 10:8,9; 31:15; 32:22; 33:4; 35:10; 36:3; 40:15,19). His Creatorship is an application and extension of His divine sovereignty.

Divine Predestination

Paul goes on to alarm the heathen philosophers by stating that God has predetermined the future by fixing a Day of Judgment on which He will judge all men through Jesus the Messiah (v.31).

He had already shocked them by saying that GOD determined where and when they would be born. They always assumed that chance determined such things. Now he tells them that the future is "fixed" i.e. predetermined by the Creator God. This was shocking news to the pagans. They always thought that free will, chance and luck guaranteed that the future was open to an infinite number of possible outcomes.

The future according to Paul is "fixed," (ἔστησεν) in concrete and is not open to change through chance and luck. Man with his vaunted "free will" cannot alter or escape the future that is already "fixed" by the Sovereign Lord of the Universe.

> because <u>He has fixed a day</u> in which He will judge the world in righteousness through a Man whom He has appointed, having furnished proof to all men by raising Him from the dead." (Acts 17:31)

> καθότι <u>ἔστησεν ἡμέραν</u> ἐν ᾗ μέλλει κρίνειν τὴν οἰκουμένην ἐν δικαιοσύνῃ, ἐν ἀνδρὶ ᾧ ὥρισεν, πίστιν παρασχὼν πᾶσιν ἀναστήσας αὐτὸν ἐκ νεκρῶν.

Since the God of the Bible is sovereign over all things, including space/time history, any view of God that limits His knowledge of or control over the future is anti-biblical, anti-Christian, and heretical. This is why Process theologians and the so-called "Open View" theologians are not Christians, but heretics.

Paul then proceeded to state that the Sovereign Lord of heaven and earth is,

> the God who made the world and all things in it. (Acts 17:24)

> ὁ θεὸς ὁ ποιήσας τὸν κόσμον καὶ πάντα τὰ ἐν αὐτῷ,

It is important to see that Paul places Creation in the framework or context of the absolute sovereignty of God. That is why ou-toj is translated as "since" or "seeing" or "because."

Paul goes on to state other revealed truths from the doctrine of Creation, which we will exegete later in this book. What is germane at this moment is to see that *Paul used the sovereignty of God as the interpretive principle and theoretical framework for the doctrine of Creation.*

This point is so important because the sovereignty of God answers all the questions that are provoked by the biblical concept of Creation. The whys, whats, wheres, whens, hows, and whos of

Creation are answered by the sovereignty of God. This is exactly how Paul dealt with the question, "*Why* did you make me this way?" (τί με ἐποίησας οὕτως).

> Doesn't the potter have a right over the clay, to make from the same lump one vessel for honorable use, and another for common use? (Rom. 9:21)
>
> ἢ οὐκ ἔχει ἐξουσίαν ὁ κεραμεὺς τοῦ πηλοῦ ἐκ τοῦ αὐτοῦ φυράματος ποιῆσαι ὃ μὲν εἰς τιμὴν σκεῦος ὃ δὲ εἰς ἀτιμίαν;

A human potter is sovereign over what he makes, when he makes it, where he makes it, how he makes it, and why he makes it. He has the sovereign right to do whatever he wants with what he makes. A pot has no right to challenge the decisions of the potter.

Paul is clearly paraphrasing Jer. 18:1-6.

> The word which came to Jeremiah from Yahweh saying, "Arise and go down to the potter's house, and there I shall announce My words to you."Then I went down to the potter's house, and there he was, making something on the wheel. But the vessel that he was making of clay was spoiled in the hand of the potter; so he remade it into another vessel, as it pleased the potter to make. Then the word of Yahweh came to me saying, "Can I not, O house of Israel, deal with you as this potter *does*?" declares Yahweh. Behold, like the clay in the potter's hand, so are you in My hand, O house of Israel."

If we admit that a human potter has the right to do whatever he wants with what he makes, how can we think *less* of the Sovereign Lord of the universe? When He makes some people "vessels of wrath" and others "vessels of mercy," He has the sovereign right to do so! Christians will read what both Jeremiah and Paul said and then say to themselves,

> God said it,
> That settles it,
> I believe it!
> Let God be true and
> Every man a liar!

This biblical truth is found in both the OT (Jeremiah) and in the NT (Romans). Natural theologians have given up trying to escape these clear passages. So, they simply ignore them and hope you do not bring them up.

The biblical truth that the God who made you can do with you whatever He wants, is the line drawn in the sand between true and false Christianity. If you rebel against the biblical idea that

God has the right to do with you whatever pleases Him, then you are a heathen and no Christian at all.

Witness #3

In the Book of Romans, the Apostle first interpreted the world through the glasses of Creation. In Rom. 1:20, the universe is described as the "Creation" of God.

> For since the Creation of the world His invisible attributes, His eternal power and divine nature, have been clearly seen, being understood through what has been made, so that they are without excuse.
>
> τὰ γὰρ ἀόρατα αὐτοῦ ἀπὸ κτίσεως κόσμου τοῖς ποιήμασιν νοούμενα καθορᾶται, ἥ τε ἀΐδιος αὐτοῦ δύναμις καὶ θειότης, εἰς τὸ εἶναι αὐτοὺς ἀναπολογήτους

The Word "Nature"

The word "Creation" is not a term that is near or dear to Natural Theologians. They prefer the word "Nature," which is the secular vacuum left once you remove God from the world. This is why the Bible *never* describes the world as "Nature." The word is never found in Scripture as a description of the universe. Instead of the heathen word "Nature," the biblical authors used the word "Creation."

This is why I personally avoid using the word "Nature" in the place of "Creation." While I can speak of the "nature" of God or the world in the sense of giving a Western philosophic definition of what God and man are in term of "being," I do not reduce the entire universe to "Nature." The moment you capitalize "nature" to "Nature" you have moved from definition to idolatry.

A Good Test

This is why these three foundational biblical truths are a good litmus test of salvation and fellowship. If someone in your church denies Creation *ex nihilo*, the radical Fall of man into sin and guilt, and Redemption by grace alone through faith alone in Christ alone, he or she should be excommunicated and be "delivered unto Satan" in a public service.

If a professor at a so-called "Christian" college, university, or seminary, denies Creation, the Fall or Redemption, he or she should be fired. This action is necessitated by the liberal takeover of Evangelical churches and schools. Liberal pastors and professors are malignant cancerous tumors on the visible Body of Christ, and should be surgically removed by church discipline.

As we warned you, this book is for the tough-minded, who honestly believe in and obey the Bible, who do not want to play at religion, who want the truth, the whole truth and nothing but the truth, and who want the real thing and not a fraud or a sham. ==Liberals are exposed whenever church discipline is applied to heretics.==

In Romans, after speaking of Creation in chapter one, Paul moves on to contrast the Fall of Adam to the Atonement of Christ in chapter five. Then in chapter eight he applies both the Fall and Redemption to the Creation itself.

While Creation was subjected to ruination by the Fall of Adam, it will be set free from ruination by Second Coming of Christ.

> For the Creation was subjected to futility, not of its own will, but because of Him who subjected it, in hope that the Creation itself also will be set free from its slavery to corruption into the freedom of the glory of the children of God. (Romans 8:20-21)
>
> τῇ γὰρ ματαιότητι ἡ κτίσις ὑπετάγη, οὐχ ἑκοῦσα ἀλλὰ ιὰ τὸν ὑποτάξαντα, ἐφ' ἐλπίδι ὅτι καὶ αὐτὴ ἡ κτίσις 'λευθερωθήσεται ἀπὸ τῆς δουλείας τῆς φθορᾶς εἰς τὴν ἐλευθερίαν τῆς δόξης τῶν τέκνων τοῦ θεοῦ.

Did Paul in Romans use Creation, Fall, and Redemption to explain the world around him? Yes. Did he appeal to these three concepts as the basis by which we can understand how evil came into the world and why it became part of man's very constitution? Yes. Then our position is established by this third witness and anyone who dares to deny it will receive the just condemnation of Almighty God.

Having established the biblical validity of using Creation, Fall, Redemption as the biblical worldview through which we understand all things, we now conclude our discussion of the three-fold basis of the biblical worldview by asking a question. Why should you adopt the biblical worldview? Why not just "go along" and "get along" with the liberals and humanists?

Why Should We Care?

When I asked myself these questions, I concluded the following reasons why I had to adopt the biblical worldview.

First, my Master and my God has commanded us in Scripture to apply the Lordship of Christ to all of life.

> ==sanctify Christ as Lord in your hearts==, always *being* ready to make a defense to everyone who asks you to give an account for the hope that is in you...(1 Peter 3:15)

> κύριον δὲ τὸν Χριστὸν ἁγιάσατε ἐν ταῖς καρδίαις ὑμῶν, ἕτοιμοι
> ἀεὶ πρὸς ἀπολογίαν παντὶ τῷ αἰτοῦντι ὑμᾶς λόγον περὶ τῆς ἐν
> ὑμῖν ἐλπίδος

The word "Lord" (κύριον) is taken out of its normal word order in the sentence and is placed first to emphasize it. The Messiah is to be set aside (ἁγιάσατε) on the throne of your life as your LORD!

The Lordship of the Messiah over all things means that He must have the preeminence in theology, philosophy, science, psychology, biology, mathematics, politics, etc.

> in order that He Himself might come to have first place
> in everything.
>
> ἵνα γένηται ἐν πᾶσιν αὐτὸς πρωτεύων, (Col. 1:18)

Those who give the preeminence to man, to human reason, experience, feelings or faith, to Barth, Brunner, Darwin, Marx, Freud, Whitehead, Pinnock, Boyd, Shepherd, Wilson, etc, have betrayed Christ as Lord.

I was invited to give a chapel talk at Messiah College in PA. In my sermon I emphasized the Christ alone should be given the preeminence in all academic departments. Christ over Freud, Darwin, Marx, etc. While the students were excited to hear this biblical truth, the faculty had an emergency meeting and declared that I would never be invited to speak there again for daring to say Christ alone had preeminence!

Second, the biblical worldview is actually *true* and all the other views are *false*. It is not just my personal subjective preference. It is for *real*. There really is a heaven to gain and a hell to shun. It is *not* a myth, a legend, a fairy tale or a rip off. If you reject it, you are rejecting your only hope of salvation.

Third, the biblical worldview is the *only way* of salvation. There is only *one God*, only *one way* to gain acceptance before that God, and only *one name* under heaven whereby we must be saved. You must hear of and believe in Jesus Christ and His gospel in order to be saved from eternal perdition.

→ I gave a chapel talk at Eastern Baptist Theological Seminary in Philadelphia and when I declared that Christ was the only way of salvation, several faculty members got up in protest and marched out! I was surrounded by an angry mob of students and teachers who could not believe that I actually said in their presence that there was hell to shun and a heaven to gain. I was later told that I would never be invited to speak there again.

Fourth, you should adopt the biblical worldview because it is *good*. All the other worldviews are *evil*. Man's problem is moral and not metaphysical. His depravity is the real issue, not his finiteness. It is sin to believe and teach a lie.

Fifth, you should accept the biblical worldview because it is *superior* to all other views. It is *better* than the other views because they utterly fail to provide a sufficient basis for truth, justice, morals, meaning, and beauty. They cannot provide any valid answers to the final questions of life. Only the biblical worldview can give us dignity and freedom; significance and meaning; light and immortality; hope and truth. The other views are hopelessly mired in relativism and are self-refuting.

Sixth, the biblical worldview is superior because it is *unique*. *No one* in the history of the world through human reason, experience, feelings or faith even discovered Creation *ex nihilo*, the Radical Fall of man into sin and guilt, and Redemption by grace alone, through faith alone, in Christ alone. No natural religion ever developed the three pillars of the biblical worldview. No natural philosopher or theologian ever discovered these beliefs by human reason, experience, feelings or faith.

While all the other worldviews share the same basic humanistic ideals, concepts, dogmas, and fictions such as free will, human autonomy, the sufficiency of human reason, etc., the biblical worldview stands totally unique in the history of ideas. This is why humanists have spent centuries desperately trying to find an ancient pre-biblical natural religion or philosophy that contained the core beliefs of the biblical worldview. But, in the end, they have utterly failed.

Failed Pagan Origins For Biblical Religion

Each time they announced the discovery of some ancient pagan religion that predates the Bible, which they claim is the true origin of the biblical ideas of Creation, Fall, and Redemption, upon closer examination, the claim falls to pieces.

First, some liberals knowingly perpetrated deliberate fraud. They used trickery and deception as a ruse to attack the uniqueness and superiority of the Bible. But this should not surprise us as those who believe that everything is relative - including truth, will have no problem lying to achieve what they feel is a worthy goal.

The term "Scripture" is a good example of how liberals play word games. The Biblical idea of an "inspired, infallible, inerrant Scripture" involves several key concepts:

- The God of the Bible is the personal and infinite Creator of the universe. He is there and is not silent.
- He made man in His own image and can speak to him in human language. This is a totally unique view of God that was unknown in pagan religions and cultures.

- The God of the Bible is sovereign over all things and all things happen in accordance with his eternal decrees. Any god that is not quite sovereign, thus limited in His omni-attributes, cannot give us an inspired, infallible, inerrant Scripture.
- God so completely controlled the authors of Scripture that they wrote only what He wanted them to write. They had absolutely no freedom to write the opposite of what they wrote.
- The God of the Bible is the only theoretical context that makes an "inspired infallible Scripture" possible. A different god cannot generate the biblical concept of scripture.

The concept of a libertarian "free will" is incompatible with the biblical worldview of an inerrant and infallible inspired Scripture. They are mutually exclusive. Those who claim that the Bible is the product of chance are heretics.

The "Open View" Heresy

Why do the "Open View of God" heretics deny the full inspiration of the Bible? They have a false god that is incapable of producing an inspired, inerrant, infallible Bible. Their pathetic limited finite deity is helpless and hopeless in the face of a chance-based universe that is out of control.

Not Dictation - But Inspiration

The biblical concept of inspiration should be confused with some kind of crude "dictation" theory in which the authors merely recorded what God spoke. Each author of Scripture wrote using his own unique personality, vocabulary, cultural background, etc. Yet, through God's mysterious sovereignty over their hearts, minds, and wills, what they wrote was only what He wanted them to write. What they wrote down was the very words, thoughts, and commands of God. Hence these sacred writings are called the "Word of God."

Since it is the infallible "Word" of God, Jesus proclaimed that the "Scripture cannot be broken" (John 10:35). As a product of the absolute sovereignty of God, the Bible is free from any errors on anything. The concept of chance or luck is incompatible with the infallibility and inerrancy of Scripture.

Since the Bible is both infallible and inerrant, it is the Origin of truth, justice, morals, meaning, and beauty. Thus it is the final authority (*sola scriptura*) on what to believe and how to live.

No Pagan "Scripture"

Ancient Pagan religions such as Animism, Hinduism, Buddhism, Taoism, etc. do not have any concept of God that allows for the kind of "inspiration" that approaches the biblical idea, and neither do they have any "Scripture" in the biblical sense of the word.

Since Buddhism is atheistic in its foundation, it denies the existence of the kind of God who could inspire an infallible Scripture. Yet, this fact did not stop the liberals from referring to the "Buddhist Scriptures" or the "Hindu Scriptures," to give the erroneous impression that there is nothing *unique* about the "Hebrew Scriptures." They do their best to deceive people into thinking that all religions have their own "Scriptures." This reduces the Bible to just one more sacred book among many. But this is a bold face lie from beginning to end.

Liberals use the same ruse when describing the Muslim Qur'an. Islam claims that the archangel Gabriel brought down the Qur'an on a huge stone tablet. As Muhammad recited it, those around him wrote down what was recited by Muhammad on whatever writing material was available: palm leaves, clothing, tree bark, bones, and tree bark. The Qur'an is supposedly 100% the words of Allah and does not contain anything from Muhammad. Liberals pretend that this Muslim concept of inspiration is the same as the biblical view. Thus the Qur'an is the Muslim "Scripture." Is this true? No.

Islam has no concept of inspiration that approaches the biblical concept. Muhammad would fall on the ground, and during an epileptic seizure would dictate a Surah. The Qur'an does not have any human authors. It only took 23 years to produce. In contrast, no biblical authors fell on the ground with brain seizures. The Bible was not produced during a trance. The Bible was written by over forty different human authors during a period of almost two thousand years. At no point does its inspiration have anything in common with the supposed inspiration of the Qur'an, the Vedas, the Book of Mormon or a thousand other false books. The moon-god Allah is incapable of producing an inspired Scripture like the Bible because he is a false god, a figment of a diseased mind. See my books, *Islamic Invasion* and *Winning the War Against Radical Islam*.

No Pagan Atonement Theories

Second, the biblical concept of a vicarious and substitutionary blood atonement by the incarnate Son of God on the cross for the sins of His people and His bodily resurrection from the dead is another unique concept.

Natural theologians have tried for over two centuries to refute it by tracing it back to a pagan myth of a "dying and rising savior." This myth was supposed to be part of ancient Persian and Egyptian religions and the biblical authors "borrowed" (i.e. stole) the idea of the atonement of Christ from those sources.

Of course, the pagan source theory of the biblical doctrine of the atonement fell apart when it was tested by scholars such as Machen, Yamuchi, and Kim. They pointed out that, in order to be a source of the biblical doctrine, two things had to be true. (See my book, *The Trinity*, for the documentation).

First, the liberals had to demonstrate that the biblical doctrine of a vicarious, substitutionary blood atonement by the incarnate Son of God on the cross for the sins of His people and His bodily resurrection from the dead is found in an ancient pagan Middle Eastern religion. If they cannot find a pagan religion in the Middle East that had this concept as part of their doctrine in pre-biblical times, then the issue is dead on arrival. This is where deception is quite common.

Liberal: "The authors of the Bible stole the idea of a dying and rising savior from pagan religions that pre-date the Bible. The Persians, the Egyptians, and many other religions all taught that concept, so the Bible is false." Christian: "I have several problems with your argument. First, that a biblical author used previously existing ideas does not mean imply that such ideas are wrong. They quoted those who went before them. Second, factually speaking, no one has ever found any ancient religion in the Middle East who taught Creation ex nihilo, the radical Fall of man into sin and guilt, and salvation by a vicarious, substitutionary, blood atonement by incarnate deity."

Liberal: "But didn't the Adonis myth picture him as a dying and rising Savior? Didn't the Persian speak of a dying and rising Savior?" Christian: "No. You are confusing the natural cycle of vegetation dying in the winter and returning in the Spring. The supposed "dying and rising savior" only referred to the weather cycle of vegetation in which trees lose their leaves in the Fall and then grow them back in the Spring. What possible connection is there between the death of God the Son for the sins of His people and a tree that sprouts leaves in the Spring? There is no connection. What does that have to do with Jesus dying on the cross for my sins? Nothing. You are also confusing reincarnation with incarnation and you are mixing up the pagan idea of a man becoming a god with the biblical doctrine of God becoming a man. Jesus did not become a demigod like pharaoh or Caesar. He was God incarnate. The Persian argument was exposed fifty years as a deliberate fraud. It is no more valid than the Piltdown man. Did any of these religions teach monotheism? No. Did any of them teach the biblical concept of sin? No. Day of Judgment? No. Did any of them teach that the Creator so loved us that He sent His only Son to die in our place? No. The biblical doctrines of Creation *ex nihilo*, the Fall, and Redemption are unique to the Bible. Second, the pagan myth had to *predate* the Bible. But none of the written records of a dying-rising savior are pre-biblical or even pre-Christian for that matter! They were written long after Christian missionaries had arrived and challenged pagans with the gospel. Thus there is no hard evidence that the Persians, the Gnostics or the Hindus or any other pagans had any concept of the biblical idea of the atonement of Christ before Christianity arrived. Gresham Machen and many other NT scholars have so demolished the pagan source theory that only among the uneducated does this argument against the Bible still arise."

Supposed Greek Origins

The same holds true for claims that the Bible obtained many concepts such as "Creation" from Greek philosophy. While this claim is still asserted in junior colleges around the country, the truth is that pagan philosophers such as Aristotle believed that the world was eternal and had no beginning! The unavoidable fact is that no one has ever found one Greek philosopher who taught the biblical idea of creation *ex nihilo*. Ronald Nash has done an excellent job of refuting the old liberal idea of supposed Greek philosophic origins of biblical concepts.

This is the shame that Natural theologians and philosophers must bear. They tried to defend the Bible by denying its uniqueness! They sought to find historical pagan sources for biblical ideas such as the atonement. In trying to save Christianity, they destroyed it!

They also removed any reason to claim that the biblical world was superior to the pagan worldviews. By pretending that the Bible only repeats what pagans discovered through their own reason, experience, feelings, and faith, they destroyed any reason to accept the gospel. The uniqueness of the biblical worldview is the basis of its superiority. You can't have one without the other!

The Golden Bough

This was the goal of the *The Golden Bough*. James Frazer thought he was defending Christianity by proving that it did not have any unique ideas. Thus the Bible was in line with pagan religions that predated it. He tried to trace biblical concepts back to pagan sources, but his work was based on hearsay evidence found in newspaper clippings. Frazer never actually did any firsthand research. It thus became a laughingstock in its own day.

Sad to say, the *Golden Bough* is still being printed today for no other reason than it gives liberals an easy way to dismiss the Bible. It does not matter to them that it was exposed a hundred years ago as a fraud. There is no hard historical evidence for the supposed pagan sources of biblical ideas. The whole enterprise is a vast "shell and pea game," and not worth the paper it is printed on.

Dr. Robert Candlish

There is a big difference between believing something on the basis of the authority of someone you trust and guessing that something is true on the basis of what you can figure out on your own.

Dr. Robert Candlish was one of the great lights in the heyday of 19th Century Scottish Theology. His commentary on Genesis is still considered a classic today. His comments are instructive and should be remembered by all thoughtful Christians.

> There is the widest possible difference between our believing certain truths as the result of reasoning or discovery, and our believing them on the direct assertion of a credible witness whom we see and hear,—especially if the witness be the very individual to whom the truths relate, and indeed himself their author. The truths themselves may be identically the same; but how essentially

> different is the state of the mind in accepting them; and how different the impression made by them on the mind when accepted.[79]

Candlish viewed the popularity of Roman Catholic Natural Theology in Protestant circles with alarm. In the previous century, William Paley had argued that he was so smart that he could start with "intelligent design" in Nature to the Intelligent Designer of Nature; from a watch to the Watch Maker.

> In the deeply interesting and beautiful work of Paley on natural Theology…the author, in stating the argument for the being of a God, derived from the proofs of intelligence and design in nature, makes admirable use of an imaginary case respecting a watch.
> You gather much of his character from the obvious character of his handiwork; you search in that handiwork for traces of his mind and his heart; you speculate concerning his plans and purposes; your fancy represents him to your eye; you think you understand all about him; you find the exercise of reasoning and discovery delightful, and you rejoice in the new views which it unfolds.[80]

Like John the Baptist, Candlish was a "voice crying in the wilderness" that Natural Theology was not in line with Scripture, Reformation Theology, or even science.

When a Natural Theologian looks into the well of his mind, he thinks he is seeing God in the reflection at the bottom. But, in reality, he is only looking at his own reflection! He has actually created a "god" in his own image. Thus a rationalist creates a "rational" god, a mystic a "mystical" god, an existentialist an "existential" god, and so on. Candlish comments,

> When I draw inferences for myself concerning the Author of creation,—when I reason out from his works the fact of his existence, and the chief attributes of his character,—I am conscious of a certain feeling of superiority. The Deity becomes almost, in a certain sense, my creature,—the product of my own elaborated process of thought. I am occupied more with my own reasonings that with the transcendent excellences of him of whom I reason. The whole is very much an exercise of intellect, attended, certainly, with those emotions of beauty and sublimity which the exercise of the intellect on matters of taste calls forth,—but with scarcely anything more of the real apprehension of an unseen Being, in my conclusions respecting the author of
> nature, than in my premises respecting nature itself. The God whom I discover is like the dead abstract truth to which a train of demonstration leads. I myself alone have a distinct personality,—all

else is little more than the working of my brain on its own imaginations. [81]

The Natural theologians of his day sought to justify them enterprise by claiming that the Bible in many passages started with Nature and from there ascended to Nature's God, but Candlish did not accept such claims.

> We are all of us familiar with this idea, that in contemplating the works of creation, we should ascend from nature to nature's God. It is apparent, however, even in these and similar passages, that related things are mentioned, not as arguments, but rather as illustrations; not as suggesting the idea of God, the Creator, but as unfolding and expanding that idea, otherwise obtained. [82]

Of course, the Natural theologians pointed to Rom. 1 as the place where the Bible justifies their existence, but Candlish pointed out,

> Here it is expressly said, that from the things that are made might be understood the invisible things of God, even his eternal power and Godhead; so that atheists, idolaters, and worshippers of the creature, are without excuse. But why are they without excuse? Not because they failed to discover God, in this way, from his works, but because, when they knew God otherwise, they did not glorify him, as these very works might have continually taught them to do;—not because they did not in this way acquire, but because they did not like in this way to retain, the knowledge of God. For the fact of the creation is regarded in the Bible as a fact revealed; and, as such, it is commended to our faith. Thus the scriptural method on this subject is exactly the reverse of what is called the natural. It is not to ascend from nature up to nature's God, but to descend, if we may so speak, from God to God's nature, or his works of nature; not to hear the creation speaking of the Creator, but to hear the Creator speaking of the creation. We have not in the bible an examination and enumeration of the wonders to be observed among the works of nature, and an argument founded upon these that there must be a God, and that he must be of a certain character, and must have had certain views in making what he has made. God himself appears, and tells us authoritatively who he is, and what he has done, and why he did it. Thus, "through faith we understand that the worlds were made by the word of God; so that things which are seen were not made of things which do appear." We understand and believe this, not as a deduction of reasoning, but as a matter of fact, declared and revealed to us. [83]

As a matter of fact, the Natural theologians have everything backward. The existence of God explains the existence of the world and man. But the Bible reverses the order. Candlish explains.

> But, in our habit of mind, let this order be just reversed. Let us conceive of God as telling us concerning them as his works. While they reveal and interpret him, let him reveal and interpret them. And whenever we meet with anything that pleases our eye, and affects our heart, let us consider God himself, our God and our Father, as informing us respecting that very thing; I made it,—I made it what it is, —I made it what it is for you. [84]

> Your position, in fact, is now precisely reversed. Instead of questioning the watch concerning its maker, you now question the maker concerning his watch. You hear, not what the mechanism has to say of the mechanic, but what the mechanic has to say of the mechanism. [85]

Candlish stated that to find the truth we must begin with God and then proceed to the world.

> The truth is, when we got to the works and creatures of God, we go, not to discover him, but as having already discovered and known him. [86]

Dr. Candlish concludes,

> Thus, then, in a spiritual view, and for spiritual purposes, the truth concerning God as the Creator must be received, not as a discovery of our own reason, following a train of thought, but as a direct communication from a real person, even from the living and present God. [87]

We conclude by adopting Prof. Candlish's conclusion as our own. Creation, Fall, and Redemption are revealed truths that never crossed the mind of the natural man. You cannot put your ear to a rock or cast your eyes on a star and derive by some kind of circuitous reasoning the grand truths of Creation *ex nihilo*, the radical Fall of man into sin and guilt, and divine Redemption by grace alone through faith alone.

Chapter Three

Creation Ex Nihilo

The Apostle's Creed begins with the first foundational concept of the biblical worldview when it identifies God as "Maker of heaven and earth."

The Creed is not only right, but brilliant. It begins with the doctrine of Creation *ex nihilo* because Creation not only defines the nature of God, the world, and man but it also explains God's relationship to the world and to man. Indeed, everything that exists must be understood through the biblical idea of Creation *ex nihilo*. Trees are a good example.

How Humanists View Trees

When a humanist looks at a tree, he sees a chance-produced evolutionary tree to which man gives relative meaning because he thinks he is the Origin of truth, justice, morals, meaning, and beauty.

Humanists assume that meaning, like beauty, is in the eye of the beholder, i.e. man, because they believe that man is the measure of all things. Thus trees, like everything else, have no intrinsic meaning, worth or significance.

Because human autonomy always collapses into relativism, each man is free to define things according to his own subjective and personal prejudices, formed and influenced by his environment and upbringing. Thus a tree in and of itself is actually quite meaningless.

You can worship the tree or chop it into firewood. It doesn't really matter. The tree is a fluke, i.e. an accident, spawned out of a chance-driven meaningless evolutionary process with no rhyme or reason.

We must remember that evolution is not progressing or regressing; it is not going up or down; it is not moving toward anything, but it lurches through time according to chaotic luck and chance. This is why species become extinct.

This means that Humanism can never provide a sufficient basis for environmentalism. Nothing has absolute value or meaning. Everything is relative. In the end, man can either destroy the world or save it – either way it does not mean anything.

How a Christian Views Trees

When a Christian looks at a tree, he sees a Creator-produced tree that God has given absolute meaning because He is the Origin of truth, justice, morals, meaning, and beauty. Meaning, like beauty, is in the eye of the Beholder, God. He is the measure of all things, including trees. Thus trees have intrinsic meaning and worth.

The difference between the theist and the humanist could not be greater. For example, a typical humanist professor might ask his students, "If a tree falls to the ground in a forest, when there is no one around to hear it fall, does it make a sound? If a flower blooms in a desert, where no man will see it, is it beautiful?" The humanist's answer is obvious. Since *man* is the Measure of all things, then the tree makes no sound and the flower is not beautiful. If man is absent, meaning is absent as well.

The theist has an entirely different view. Since God is Omnipresent, He hears the tree fall to the ground and He sees the desert flower bloom. This is why David could play his harp and sing when he was alone. He knew that YHWH was listening (Psa. 55:17).

The Owner

Who owns the trees? Humanists believe that no one really owns the trees *per se*. Those inclined toward socialism would assert that trees belong to the state. But the state "owns" trees only by the power of the gun. Since man is the measure of all things, trees can be used by man as he sees fit.

Theists point out that since God created the trees, He is the Owner. This is why the Bible refers to them as "the trees of YHWH" (Psa. 104: 16). Trees exist to glorify the God who created them (Psa. 96:12; 148:9-13).

> The earth is Yahweh's, and everything it contains, the world, and those who dwell in it. (Psalm 24:1)

לְדָוִד מִזְמוֹר לַיהוָה הָאָרֶץ וּמְלוֹאָהּ תֵּבֵל וְיֹשְׁבֵי בָהּ׃

God, not man, is the Creator and Owner of all things – including trees. Thus He is the only one who has the right to determine their meaning and how they are to be treated.

In the early chapters of Genesis, God tells man how to treat trees.

Then Yahweh Elohim took the man And put him into the Garden of

Eden to cultivate it and protect it. (Gen. 2:15)

וַיִּקַּח יְהוָה אֱלֹהִים אֶת־הָאָדָם
וַיַּנִּחֵהוּ בְגַן־עֵדֶן לְעָבְדָהּ וּלְשָׁמְרָהּ׃

The two words לְעָבְדָהּ (cultivate) and וּלְשָׁמְרָהּ (protect) summarize the original Creation Mandate that God gave to man in the Garden of Eden. Since the first word is used in Scripture to refer to *herding* domesticating animals as well as *cultivating* vegetation (ex. Deut. 15:19), the word "cultivate" is not a good translation. It should be translated "manage."

Adam's naming the animals was part of this original Creation Mandate (Gen. 2:19). In Hebrew thought, the act of naming the animals meant that he took dominion over them.

The second word usually meant "to protect" or "to guard." It is used for tending sheep in Gen. 30:31. These two Hebrew words must be taken together as a literary unit. Together they indicate that God gave man the stewardship to protect, guard, cultivate, shepherd, and manage the Garden of Eden. This involved physical labor as well as intellectual activity.

We have to remember that the word "Garden" means that Adam and Eve were placed in a protected animal and plant preserve surrounded by high walls. Fausset defines "garden" as,

> an enclosure in the suburbs, fenced with a hedge or wall (Isa. 5:5; Prov. 24:31), planted with flowers, shrubs, and trees, guarded (from whence comes "garden").[88]

God planted the Garden with an orchard of nut trees and fruit trees for man's food and then placed harmless domesticated animals in it for man's companionship. *The International Standard Bible Encyclopedia* comments:

> The Arabic jannah (diminutive, jannainah), Like the Hebrew Heb: gannah, literally, "a covered or hidden place," denotes in the mind of the dweller in the East something more than the ordinary garden. Gardens in Biblical times, such as are frequently referred to in Semitic literature, were usually walled enclosures, as the name indicates (Lam 2:6 the American Revised Version, margin), in which there were paths winding in and out among shade and fruit trees, canals of running water, fountains, sweet-smelling herbs, aromatic blossoms and convenient arbors in which to sit and enjoy the effect. These gardens are mentioned in Gen 2 and 3; 13:10; Song 4:12-16; Eccl 2:5,6; Ezek 28:13; 31:8,9; 36:35; Joel 2:3. Ancient Babylonian, Assyrian and Egyptian records show the fondness of the rulers of these countries for gardens laid out on a grand scale and planted with the rarest trees and plants. The drawings made by the ancients of their gardens leave no doubt about their general features and

their correspondence with Biblical gardens. [89]

Too often Christians assume that the Garden of Eden encompassed the entire planet and that man had to deal with dangerous animals and dinosaurs. The reason why Moses used the word "Garden" was to point out that man was placed in a protected zoological park surrounded by walls on all sides.

This explains how man was able to name the animals in a few hours. If Adam had to name *all* the animals, fish, and insects on the planet, including all the ones in the oceans, it would have taken *many, many* years! Since Eve was not created until *after* he finished naming the animals, he would have been so old that he could not have procreated the human race!

Once Adam finished naming all the animals in the Garden, it became apparent to him that he, unlike the animals, was alone, i.e. without a mate. Once he realized this, Eve was created to be his mate.

All of this happened in the course of a single Creation day because Adam named the animals only in the Garden, not all the animals outside of it. The animals in the Garden were domesticated barnyard animals such as chickens, cows and dogs. T Rex, the tigers, lions, bears, etc. were outside the walls of the Garden.

The Basis of True Environmentalism

God commands man to take dominion over the planet by exercising stewardship over the Garden, including the trees. On the Day of Judgment, man will be judged by God concerning his stewardship of the planet and its natural resources. The mismanagement of the planet and the abuse of its resources is a violation of the divine Creation Mandate and will result in divine judgment.

As Francis Schaeffer pointed out in his insightful book, *Pollution and the Death of Man*, the only sufficient basis for environmentalism is the biblical doctrine of Creation *ex nihilo*. The humanist, regardless of whether he is Eastern or Western in worldview, has no mandate to protect, take care or rule over nature. There is no basis for human accountability except within the biblical worldview.

Who Says What?

God tells man which trees he may eat from and which trees he is forbidden to eat from. Since God owned all the trees, He had the right to dictate to man what to do and not to do with His trees. But, under the influence of the first Natural theologian, Satan, man chose to give his own meaning to the trees and to decide which trees he can eat from. He rejected the Divine Revelation of the meaning of the tree of knowledge and substituted Satan's meaning in its place.

God warned man that if he ate of the tree of the knowledge of good and evil, he would die. But Satan convinced man that the tree was not a threat of death but a promise of life; it was not the end but the beginning; it meant his deification, not his destruction.

The Fall of man revolved around the issue of who is the Origin of truth, justice, morals, meaning, and beauty:

> God or Man?
> Revelation or reason?
> Revelation or experience?
> Revelation or feelings?
> Revelation or faith?

This is why the first sin was broken down into different components.

> When the woman saw,
> (*She had adopted Satan's worldview*)
> the tree was good for food,
> (*lust of the flesh*)
> and that it was a delight to the eyes,
> (*lust of the eye*)
> and that the tree was desirable to
> make one wise,
> (*pride of life*)
> she took from its fruit and ate;
> (*open rebellion*)
> and she gave also to her husband with her,
> (*tempting others to sin*)
> and he ate.
> (*Adam joined her in rebellion*)

(Genesis 3:6)

Dr. Carl F. Henry, one of the most important and influential Evangelical thinkers of the 20th century, pointed out that the original sin was not the physical act of eating the forbidden fruit but the intellectual shift from a theistic view of life revealed by God to a humanist view of life derived from human reason through the deceit of Satan.

> The arch-liar begins by calling into question the truth of God's word.
> He skillfully leads the woman to question the goodness of God. Such
> questioning is mistrust and doubt, the opposite of faith. The very

> moment the woman began to mistrust God the Fall took place; the act of taking forbidden fruit was merely evidence that the Fall had occurred. The woman apparently used the same approach upon Adam when "she gave some to her husband, and he ate." [90]

This is why conversion begins with God opening the mind or heart of man to understand the biblical worldview.

> And a certain woman named Lydia, from the city of Thyatira, a seller of purple fabrics, a worshiper of God, was listening; and <u>the Lord opened her heart</u> to respond to the things spoken by Paul. (Acts 16:14)
>
> καί τις γυνὴ ὀνόματι Λυδία, πορφυρόπωλις πόλεως Θυατείρων σεβομένη τὸν θεόν, ἤκουεν, ἧς ὁ κύριος διήνοιξεν τὴν καρδίαν προσέχειν τοῖς λαλουμένοις ὑπὸ τοῦ Παύλου.

It is also interesting to note that while sin entered the world through a tree, salvation entered the world through another tree (Gal. 3:13; 1 Pet. 2:24). God has a great sense of humor!

In the Beginning

The very first concept that God wants you to understand when you open the Bible is that the space/time universe is not eternal, but had a Beginning. We translate the first two verses of Genesis as follows in order to emphasize its dynamic character.

> When the Beginning began,
> Out of nothing,
> God created the heavens and the earth,
> And the earth was devoid of life and a desert,
> And darkness covered the surface of the sea,
> And the Spirit of God was brooding over
> the surface of the waters.
>
> בְּרֵאשִׁית
> בָּרָא
> אֱלֹהִים אֵת הַשָּׁמַיִם וְאֵת הָאָרֶץ׃
> וְהָאָרֶץ הָיְתָה תֹהוּ וָבֹהוּ
> וְחֹשֶׁךְ עַל־פְּנֵי תְהוֹם
> וְרוּחַ אֱלֹהִים מְרַחֶפֶת
> עַל־פְּנֵי הַמָּיִם׃

We must remember that the punctuation found in our English Bibles is not part of the Hebrew text, but is a modern interpretation, not a translation.

The Hebrew text has a series of vav וַ consecutives that reveal that verses one and two are actually one sentence in terms of the grammar of the Hebrew syntax, not two sentences as found in the KJV. The description of the earth as it came forth from the hand of the Creator is given by three vav consecutives.

> And וַ the earth was devoid of life and a desert,
> And וַ darkness covered the surface of the sea,
> And וַ the Spirit of God was brooding over the
> surface of the waters.

The KJV made the mistake of putting a period at the end of verse one, thus giving the false impression that verse one was a title.

Because of this error, verse one was cut loose or separated from the verses that followed. This is the root error of such obnoxious doctrines as the "gap theory" and all the vain attempts by "theistic" evolutionists to insert billions of years between Gen. 1:1 and 1:2. As Keil and Delitzsch pointed out,

> Heaven and earth have not existed from all eternity, but had a beginning; nor did they arise by emanation from an absolute substance, but were created by God. This sentence, which stands at the head of the records of revelation, is not a mere heading, nor a summary of the history of the Creation, but a declaration of the primeval act of God, by which the universe was called into being. That this verse is not a heading merely, is evident from the fact that the following account of the course of the Creation commences with w> (and), which connects the different acts of the Creation with the fact expressed in ver. 1, as the primary foundation upon which they rest.[91]

All pagan thought is built on the assumption that the space/time universe is eternal.

> What is
> Has always been,
> And shall always be
> What it is.

It does not matter if you look to the East or to the West, the eternity of the space/time universe is the foundational concept of all Natural philosophies and religions, and it forms and shapes all their other concepts. Mathew Henry, the most famous of all English preachers, commented on Gen. 1:1,

> The foundation of all religion being laid in our relation to God as our Creator, it was fit that the book of divine revelations which was intended to be the guide, support, and rule, of religion in the world, should begin, as it does, with a plain and full account of the Creation of the world—in answer to that first enquiry of a good conscience, "Where is God my Maker?" (Job 35:10). Concerning this the pagan philosophers wretchedly blundered, and became vain in their imaginations, some asserting the world's eternity and self-existence, others ascribing it to a fortuitous concourse of atoms: thus "the world by wisdom knew not God," but took a great deal of pains to lose him.[92]

Rationalism, empiricism, mysticism, and fideism never produced or discovered the doctrine of Creation *ex nihilo*. It never crossed the mind of any pagan philosopher or religious sage that the space/time universe was created out of nothing by an infinite and personal God.

This is why the biblical concept of Creation *ex nihilo* is maligned and hated by both secular and religious humanists. The famous German commentator, Peter Lange, comments,

> By faith we understand that the world was made (prepared) by the word of God, so that the things which are seen were not made of things which do appear. The record of Creation is therefore a record of the very first act of faith, and then the very first act of revelation, which, as such, lies at the foundation of all the following, and in its result reproduces itself in the region of faith, from the beginning on to the end of days. It is the monotheistic Christian creative word, the special watchword of the pure believing view of the world. *Ex ungue leonem.* The first leaf of scripture goes at a single step across the great abyss of materialism into which the entire heathen view of the world has fallen, and which no philosophic system has know how to avoid, until perfected by this. **Pantheism** here meets its refutation in the word of the eternal personal God of Creation, who established the world by his almighty word; **abstract theism**, in the production of the world out of the living word of God; **dualism**, in the doctrine that God has created matter itself; **naturalism**, in the clear evidence of this positive divine foundation of the world, in the origin of every new step in nature. With the pure idea of God, we win at the same place
> with the pure idea of the world, and with the pure idea if Creation, the pure idea of nature.[93]

Humanists are always offended when you tell them that God created the world. Lange goes on to state,

> **The Pantheist** often takes offense here, because the record speaks

> of an eternally present God, and, in opposition to his view, of a temporal world which the eternal God has called into being through his word; **the dualist** stumbles at the assumption that even matter itself, the original substance of the world, has sprung from the creative power of God; **the deist**, on the contrary, finds in the assumption that God, after the day's works were completed, had then rested, a childish dream, which ignores the idea of omnipotence; **the naturalist** believes that with the co-working of omnipotence from moment to moment the idea of the natural orderly development of things is destroyed; philosophy generally thinks that it is here dealing with a myth, which is arranged partly through its orthodox positiveness, and partly through its sensuous pictures or images; the modern skeptical natural philosopher makes it a matter of ridicule that the sun, moon, and stars should first be formed in the fourth creative day, and indeed that the whole universe is viewed as rendering a service to this little world; that the heavenly light should have existed before the heavenly lights, but especially that the original world should have arisen only 6000 years ago, and that its present form, for which millions of years are requisite, should have been attained in the brief period of six ordinary days. But the opponents who differ most widely agree in this, that it is fabulous, that the Bible should make an entirely new report of pre-historical things, with the most perfect assurance. [94]

In his classic commentary on Genesis, H. C. Leupold surveys all the ancient cosmologies and demonstrated that *none* of them taught the concept of Creation *ex nihilo*. [95]

This poses a tremendous problem for those professing Christians who believe in Natural Theology and Natural Law instead of revealed truth. All the Greek philosophers, such as Aristotle, believed that the world was eternal.

Aquinas usually followed Aristotle. But even he could see that Aristotle's eternal world contradicted Scripture. This was a problem also for the Muslim philosophers who likewise followed Aristotle.

To solve this problem, Muslim philosophers set up a false dichotomy between faith and reason. Their "reason" told them that the world was eternal, but their "faith" told them it was created. They could accept both "truths" at the same time if they assumed a false dichotomy between "reason and faith."

They argued that *knowledge* came only from human reason. Faith did not give man any knowledge *per se,* but referred to the disposition of the heart or emotions. It is a humanistic trap in which the only option you are given is, which aspect of man should be absolutized into the Origin. You could choose man's reason, experience, feelings or faith. God had nothing to do with the issue.

Many professing "Christians" today have adopted humanism as the basis of their worldview. They often claim that evolution is a "fact" of reason while Creation is a statement of "faith." They "know" evolution is true, while they "believe" in Creation.

They foolishly think that they can have their cake and eat it too! While they like to think of themselves as smarter than other people, they are, according to God, quite stupid (Jer. 10:8, 14, 21). They know neither the power of God nor the Scriptures (Mat. 22:29).

It is either one way or the other. Either the Bible is true or it isn't. Either one of the various conflicting theories of evolution is true or it is false. There is no middle ground.

Dear Reader, you must make up your mind about who will you believe: Moses or Marx; Jesus or Socrates; Paul or Plato; the Bible or the philosophers; David or Darwin. Your eternal destiny hangs on your choice. Choose wisely.

Out of Nothing

When we read the Hebrew text of Gen 1-2, what do we find?

First, the word בָּרָא "created" in Gen. 1:1, means that the universe was created by God without using any pre-existing eternal materials whatsoever.

The universe was not even made out of God's being. The world is not divine, but created; it is finite, not infinite; temporal, not eternal; particular, not universal; dependent being, not independent being.

Liberals in the 19th and 20th century tried to twist בָּרָא into meaning that God only formed or molded pre-existing materials. They were guilty of trying to reduce the God of the Bible to Plato's Demiurge! But their assertion was not based on sound linguistic principles of Hebrew grammar. It was actually philosophic in nature. Why?

Humanists *assume* that the Jews had to borrow their ideas from the surrounding pagan religions. Since no ancient pagan religion or philosophy taught Creation *ex nihilo*, how could the Jews teach something that was totally unique and out of step with the surrounding religions?

If they admitted that the Jews had a unique idea of Creation *ex nihilo*, this might lead to the abhorrent idea that their religion was actually *revealed* by their God as they claimed. This cannot be tolerated!

This is why liberals are both deceitful and foolish when they claim that the Genesis Creation account was "borrowed" from the Babylonian Gilgamesh or another ancient pagan mythology. The Gilgamesh poem and other pagan mythologies all teach an eternal universe! They do not teach Creation *ex nihilo*.

Chapter Three   Creation Ex Nihilo

The average professor of religion usually delights in telling his Christians students, "The Bible got its ideas of Creation from older pagan stories such as the Gilgamesh myth. Thus the Bible is not the Word of God."

The Christian student should be trained how to deal with such nonsense by asking the question: "Are you saying that the Gilgamesh poem or some other ancient pagan mythology spoke of Creation *ex nihilo*? Are you prepared to stake your academic credentials on it? The truth is that no ancient religion ever taught Creation *ex nihilo*. They all believed that the world was eternal."

Second, the tenses of the Hebrew verbs used in the Genesis account of Creation describe God's acts of Creation as taking place at once, i.e. *instantaneously*. They were not slowly done over a long period of time and the process was not a long drawn out affair.

An analysis of the tenses of the Hebrew verbs used in Genesis chapter one, reveals that Creation was a fast, instantaneous, series of divine fiats. Three illustrations are sufficient to establish this grammatical fact.

> Then God said [וַיֹּאמֶר], "Let there be light";
> and there was light [וַיְהִי־אוֹר]. (Gen. 1:3)
>
> Then God said [וַיֹּאמֶר], "Let the waters below
> the heavens be gathered [יִקָּווּ] into one place,
> and let the dry land appear [וְתֵרָאֶה]";
> and it was so [וַיְהִי־כֵן]. (Gen. 1:9)
>
> Then God said [וַיֹּאמֶר], "Let the earth sprout
> [aveÛd>T;(] sprouts, plants yielding seed, *and* fruit
> trees bearing fruit after their kind, with seed in
> them, on the earth"; and it was so [וַיְהִי־כֵן]. (Gen. 1:11)

The Hebrew grammar refutes the liberal interpretation that sees billions of years transpiring in Genesis one. The verbs are dynamic and instantaneous in nature. God commanded and it came into existence at once.

The pernicious theory of theistic evolution requires billions or millions of years between God's divine command and the event taking place. But this is not grammatically possible.

God created the world by speaking it into being. In Psa. 33:9 we read,

> For He spoke-
> כִּי הוּא אָמַר
> and it was done;

וַיְהִי
He commanded-
הוּא־צִוָּה
and it stood fast.
וַֽיַּעֲמֹד

Notice the tenses of the verbs.

אָמַר	qal perfect
וַיְהִי	qal imperfect
הוּא־צִוָּה	piel perfect
וַֽיַּעֲמֹד	qal imperfect

The Hebrew text pictures God's creative acts as instantaneous in nature, not drawn out and protracted over billions of years. Nowhere in Scripture is it ever taught that Creation took billions or even millions of years. Thus the "old earth" people are fideists in that they make blind leaps of faith to believe that evolutionists are more reliable than the inspired authors of the Bible.

The only example of man's creative word has to do with legal declarations. When a judge pronounces you "guilty" or "innocent," his words render you instantaneously guilty or innocent before the law.

When a minister or Justice of the Peace or pronounces a man and a woman "husband and wife," their marriage is created by his speaking the words.

The "old earth" theory of Creation is championed by humanistic Christians who want to accommodate the heathen idea of evolution. But it is simply not biblical. The billions of years required by the heresy of evolution cannot be reconciled with the dynamic tenses of the Hebrew verbs used in Genesis.

God commanded,
"Let there be light,"
and instantaneously
"there was light!"
God commanded,
"Let the earth sprout sprouts,"
and instantaneously it happened.

There is simply no way that you can squeeze billions of years out of these texts. In the end, they must choose between God and man. Oh that they, like the Apostle Paul, would proclaim,

Let God be true even if it
means that all men are liars!

(Rom. 3:4)

Third, Adam and Eve were both instantaneously created. God did not take an ape and transform him into Adam. The text says, "man became a living being" (יְהִי הָאָדָם לְנֶפֶשׁ חַיָּה), not "a living being became man." Any theory that entails the existence of pre-Adamic humanoids that became man is a very serious heresy. It should be rebuked as such.

Fourth, the days of Genesis were literal 24 hour days. It is so amusing to see humanists dancing around the six days of Creation, trying desperately to magically transform each day into billions of years.

I once debated a liberal theologian on the "days" of Genesis. I took a different approach by asking, "Since we are dealing with a biblical text, the first issue to debate is hermeneutics. A biblical text must be interpreted in the light of its cultural context as well as its literary context. A text taken out of context becomes a pretext for false teaching. Do you agree with the hermeneutical principle that the context rules the interpretation?"

The "Christian" evolutionist was not prepared to discuss the hermeneutical principles that he had to follow when attempting to interpret the days of Genesis. But I would not let him off the hook until he promised to submit to the historical grammatical hermeneutic that all Bible-believing Christians utilize when interpreting Scripture. Once this was established, I then asked him, "The second issue we need to debate is the hermeneutical principle that we must not read back into the Bible modern concepts that could not, in principle, be found in biblical times because those ideas did not exist at that time. For example, if you tried to convince me that the authors of the Bible ate "Kentucky Fried Chicken," you would be wasting your breath. Do you agree that the attempt to insert modern ideas into ancient biblical texts is a false hermeneutic?" I could tell he did not like where we were going, but I made him admit that it would be wrong to take modern ideas and insert them into the Bible.

My next point was his "Waterloo." "The most important aspect of this debate is *the history of numbers and mathematics*. According to what you have written on the "days" of Genesis, your position is that Moses and the people of his day understood that the "days" of Genesis represented billions of years and not literal twenty four days? Yes? Ok. Then it is crucial to your position that the abstract mathematical concept of "billion" be present in the culture of the age in which Genesis was written."

The evolutionist could see that I had just placed a hood over his head, a noose around his neck, and my hand was on the lever of the trapdoor under his feet. Of course, I pulled the lever and let him swing in the breeze. I pointed out:

> I have in front of me various histories of numbers and mathematics.[96] The abstract concept of "billions" of years is a

Western European idea of recent origin and was not known in biblical times. The authors of Scripture, such as Moses, knew only concrete numbers and the very idea of "millions" or "billions" of years or anything else for that matters was simply not possible in that time frame. What we call "Arabic numbers" (1,2,3, etc,) were unknown to the authors of the Bible. If you asked Abraham, "What does 2+2 equal?" he would not have a clue what you were talking about. The authors of the Bible used concrete items to correspond to things. For example, the number of stones in a bag corresponded to how many sheep were in their flock. The highest Hebrew word with numeric value was ten thousand. The ancient Egyptians, Babylonians, Assyrians, etc., did not have any abstract numbers either. How were amounts of items recorded in Scripture? They wrote out the words that indicated the amounts in view. For example, they wrote out the three words "one hundred thousand" because "100,000" did not exist at that time. I submit that it was impossible for Moses and his readers, in their cultural context, to teach or even to understand the modern abstract mathematical concept of "billion" that is essential to your view.

The debate began to fall apart at that point, as he did not want to discuss the history of mathematics. Instead, he tried to change the subject to modern Western European interpretations of Genesis such as the framework theory. Of course, I dismissed all modern interpretations as logically and hermeneutically irrelevant to the issue of what Moses and his readers understood the "days" of Creation meant. It was at this point that he made an astounding admission: "Ok. But what if I admitted that Moses and his readers understood the days of Creation to mean 24 hour days? It doesn't matter. They were ignorant and were in error. They also believed that the world was flat and had four corners. Surely you don't defend them on this issue, do you?"

Now the truth finally came out. After claiming all along that he was a fellow born-again Christian and "Evangelical" theologian who believed in the full inspiration of the Bible, he revealed that he was actually an apostate liberal masquerading as an Evangelical. He had thrown off his sheep skin and now we could all see that he was a vicious wolf!

In my reply, I pointed out that his response was a flat denial of the inerrancy of Scripture. If the authors of Scripture wrote things that were in fact not true, who was the pope to tell us which verses to believe and which verses to ignore?

He went on to assert that the Hebrew word "yom" could mean an indefinite number of years. When I pointed out that when the word "yom" was modified by a number, for example, "*first* day, *second* day, etc.," it always meant a literal day. He responded that in Hosea 6:2 yom was modified by a numeral, but it clearly did not mean a literal day. But, when I pressed him, he admitted that he had not bothered to look up the Hebrew text. But I had already done so and found that he was 100% in error. The passage is as follows.

> He will revive us after *two* days;
> יְחַיֵּנוּ מִיֹּמָיִם
> He will raise us up on the third day
> בַּיּוֹם הַשְּׁלִישִׁי יְקִמֵנוּ
> That we may live before Him.
> וְנִחְיֶה לְפָנָיו׃

In the first occurrence of "yom," it is a simple dual absolute and it is *not* modified by a numeral. The English word "two" was added by the translator and is *not* in the Hebrew text *per se*.

In the next occurrence of "yom," it is indeed modified by the numeral "third" (הַשְּׁלִישִׁי) as in "third day." But the question still remains whether the word "yom" modified by a numeral in this passage refers to a literal 24 hour day or an indefinite period of time.

Under the inspiration of the Holy Spirit, the apostle Paul in 1 Cor. 15:4 interpreted Hosea 6:2 as prophesying the resurrection of Messiah "on the third day" after His death.

> For I delivered to you as of first importance what I also received, that Messiah died for our sins according to the Scriptures, and that He was buried, and that He was *raised on the third day according to the Scriptures*.

If the professor would have bothered to read the Hebrew text on Hosea or exegete 1 Cor. 15:4, he would have seen that Hosea was prophesying about the *literal* three 24 hour days between the death and resurrection of the Messiah.

Jesus had promised that on the "third day" after his death He would be resurrected.

> From that time Jesus Christ began to show His disciples that He must go to Jerusalem, and suffer many things from the elders and chief priests and scribes, and be killed, and be *raised up on the third day*. (Matt. 16:21)

Matthew Henry pointed out that Hosea 6:2

> seems to have a further reference to the resurrection of Jesus Christ; and the time limited is expressed by *two days* and the *third day,* that it may be a type and figure of Christ's rising the *third day,* which he is said to do *according to the scriptures,* according to this scripture; for all the prophets testified of *the sufferings of Christ and the glory that should follow.*[97]

> By Old-Testament predictions. He died for our sins, according to the scriptures; he was buried, and rose from the dead, according to the scriptures, according to the scripture - prophecies, and scripture-types. Such prophecies as Ps. 16:10; Isa. 53:4-6; Dan. 9:26, 27; **Hos. 6:2**…Note, It is a great confirmation of our faith of the gospel to see how it corresponds with ancient types and prophecies.[98]

The classic commentaries agree:

> The burial was a single act; the Resurrection is permanent and eternal in its issues. According to the Scriptures (Ps. 16:10; Isa. 53:10; Hos. 6:2; Jonah 2:10; comp. Matt. 12:40; 16:4; Acts 2:31; 13:34).[99]

> It is impossible for the Christian to read this text and not wonder if it foreshadows Christ's resurrection on the third day. Wolff attempts to eliminate the idea of resurrection here, which he casts in a pagan light, and asserts that this text only describes recovery from illness. The language Hosea employs, however, renders this view impossible. Besides that, recovery after a two-day illness, as opposed to two days in the grave, is hardly significant. The New Testament does not explicitly cite this verse, but 1 Cor 15:4 asserts that Christ arose on the third day "in accordance with the Scriptures," and no other text speaks of the third day in the fashion that Hos 6:2 does. It is clear that in its original context this passage describes the restoration of Israel, the people of God; and for many interpreters this is proof enough that the resurrection of Christ is not in view here. Such interpretation, however, understands messianic prophecy too narrowly as simple, direct predictions by the prophets of what the Messiah would do. In fact, the prophets almost never prophesied in that manner. Instead, they couched prophecy in typological patterns in which the works of God proceed along identifiable themes. Furthermore, Christ in his life and ministry embodied Israel or recapitulated the sojourn of Israel. Thus, for example, Christ's forty days in the wilderness paralleled Israel's forty years of wandering, and his giving of his Torah on a mountain (Matt 5–7) paralleled the Sinai experience.[100]

I have waited over forty years for those who believe that the days of Genesis refer to billions of years to show me just one clear verse in the original text where yom modified by a numeral meant anything other than a literal 24 hour day. Hosea 6:2 is the only text they tried to twist, but it actually proves our position.

Since this is not a book on the days of Genesis *per se*, we will leave the issue at this point. Enough has been said to establish that any attempt to insert modern abstract ideas of billions of years into the Genesis Creation account is hermeneutically fallacious.

Conclusion

One last word is needed. Should we make the length of Creation days of Genesis a test of salvation? Of course not! There are many true Christians today who have never studied the issue and naively follow their humanistic pastors and teachers on this point. They don't know any better.

Our evangelical colleges, seminaries, and universities today are dominated by ignorant professors who are incapable of exegeting the original text of Scripture. They are now controlled by Boards who are only interested in studying "market driven" techniques for hyper-church growth. "Buildings, numbers, and money" are the new "holy trinity" of the church growth movement, not Hebrew, Greek, and Latin. The bottom line is not knowledge but sales.

The ignorant professor I debated is just one example of thousands of teachers who are leading their students astray. He did not even bother to check the Hebrew text because he was philosophically committed to a humanistic view of God, the world, man, and the long days of Creation. It really did not make any difference to him what the Bible actually taught. His mind was already made up before he picked up his Bible.

True Christians can and do disagree over the days of Genesis. But, if someone honestly believes that Moses was in *error* in his understanding of the days of Genesis, that is a serious issue. Anyone who denies the inerrancy of Scripture is not a fellow Christian. He is a "false brother" who is preaching a "false gospel" and is under the divine anathema of Gal. 1:8.

The biblical doctrine of Creation is the first pillar of divine revelation. Everything in life must be interpreted and understood in its light. No philosophy or theology deserves to be called "Christian" if it does not begin where the Bible begins.

Chapter Four

The Radical Fall of Man into Sin and Guilt

Most theological errors begin with the failure to take seriously the radical nature of man's Fall into sin and guilt. Eastern Orthodoxy, Roman Catholicism, Arminianism, liberalism, Open View heretics, New Agers, Natural theologians, and Natural Law advocates all begin their descent down "the highway to hell" by denying that man was radically affected by the Fall.

They all admit that man was weakened somewhat by the Fall and is no doubt sick to some extent today, but they do not really believe that man died in a spiritual sense. He only needs a little help to find the truth and earn his salvation for himself and from himself.

They believe that man still has a free will and his mind is still capable of being the Origin of truth, justice, morals, meaning, and beauty. Man can still figu[re out truth apart] from God via special revelation. Human reason, feelings, expe[rience, etc. are] self-sufficient to find the truth. Man does not really need God [...]

Father Adam

Most Christians understand that Adam is the "Father" of th[e human race,] the first human being from which all others originated. For [Adam is called the first] man in such places as I Cor. 15:45.

What most modern Christians do not seem to understand [is that Adam is our father in more] ways than DNA. In Rom. 5 and I Cor. 15, the Apostle Paul dra[ws a parallel between Adam and] Christ. Jesus is described as the "last Adam" just as Adam i[s called the first Adam (I Cor.] 15:45).

Adam and the Messiah

[Handwritten note: Man is currently in Covenant relationship with God in either Adam or Christ. This is inescapable.]

In both passages it is clear that Adam's fall into sin was substitutionary and vicarious in nature. His sin was our sin. His Fall was our Fall too. We "sinned" in Adam and "died" in Adam.

In the same way with the same language, the work of the Messiah is described as substitutionary and vicarious in nature. We died when He died and rose when He rose.

In fact, as we shall see, Rom. 5 says that we are condemned by virtue of Adam's disobedience just as surely as we are justified by virtue of Christ's obedience. While the imputation of Adam's sin is the problem confronting all men (Rom. 5:12), the imputation of Christ's righteousness is the remedy to that problem (Rom. 5:17).

Bound Together

Our participation in Adam's disobedience and our participation in Christ's obedience are linked together in such a way that if one rejects the doctrine of the imputation of Adam's sin—the basis of the doctrine of original sin—he must also reject the imputation of Christ's righteousness -- the basis of the doctrine of forensic justification.

Throughout church history, intelligent heretics have always seen that the doctrines of original sin, substitutionary atonement, and forensic justification stand or fall together. This is why Socinus, the father of Unitarianism, and Charles Finney, the father of revivalism, felt compelled to deny all three doctrines.

The Same Terms

Our relationship to Adam is spoken of in the same terms that are used to speak of our relationship to Christ. For example, we are described as being "in Adam" just as we are "in Christ." Thus, union with Adam and union with Christ are two realities that share mutual meanings.

All those "in Adam," i.e. in union with Adam, receive certain things by virtue of that union just as all those "in Christ," i.e. in union with Christ, receive certain things by virtue of that union.

Part I
Inconsistent Denials

Because the Evangelical world is filled with teachers, pastors, and evangelists who have very little theological knowledge, no grasp of church history, and absolutely no training in logic, it is not surprising to find some people objecting to the doctrine of original sin on the grounds that it would be "unjust" if God punishes us on the basis of evil done by someone else. According to them, the very idea that God would view and treat us on the basis of what someone else did or did not do is "absurd."

Yet, at the same time, these same people when pressed will admit that God viewed and treated Jesus on the basis of their sin! *If "Jesus died for our sins according to the Scriptures" (I Cor. 15:4), then how can it be unjust for us to die for Adam's sin?*

What Church History Reveals

Church history demonstrates that a rejection of the doctrine of original sin will in time lead to a rejection of the vicarious atonement and forensic justification. This is exactly what happened in 18th Century Liberal Theology.

Liberal theologians began with a rejection of the doctrine of original sin and its resulting depravity. This led them to reject the doctrine of Christ's substitutionary atonement.

On the basis of "Reason," they then concluded that if it is unjust to be condemned on the basis of the work of another, then it is equally unjust to be saved on the basis of the work of another. Their rationalism eventually led them to deny the blood atonement of Christ.

This is why the doctrine of original sin is absolutely essential to Christian theology and why the Christian Church has always condemned as heretical all Pelagian and semi-Pelagian views of man, which in some way deny or weaken the doctrine of original sin and its resulting depravity. The validity of a substitutionary atonement and forensic justification is based on the validity of the imputation of Adam's sin to us.

Three Essential Concepts

There are three essential concepts that form the basis of the doctrines of original sin, vicarious atonement, and forensic justification:

#1 Solidarity

The Bible teaches a concept of solidarity in which an individual is viewed and treated in terms of his relationship to a group, whether it is a tribe, a nation or mankind as a whole, while the "group" is viewed and treated in terms of its relationship to its original head.

Man as Image Bearer

This is why the Bible can speak of each individual human being as having dignity and worth by virtue of his or her participation in the solidarity of the human race. Each individual person is important because mankind as a whole is important. We can view each person we meet as being in the image of God by virtue of mankind's relationship to Adam who was created in the image of God (Gen. 1:26-27; James 3:9).

Corporate and Individual Election

An individual Jew was viewed as "chosen" by virtue of his participation in the solidarity of the "chosen" nation. Yet, at the same time, the nation was viewed as "chosen" because of its relationship to Abraham who was individually chosen by God (Gen. 12:1-7).

The Levitical Priesthood

An individual could be blessed by virtue of his participation in the solidarity of his tribe. For example, an individual Levite could be a priest by virtue his participation in the solidarity of the Tribe of Levi while the Tribe of Levi was viewed as the priesthood by virtue of its relationship to Levi who was individually chosen to be the high priest (Num. 18:6-24).

The Ninevites

Each individual Ninevite was delivered from judgment by virtue of his participation in the solidarity of the nation of Nineveh whose King repented before God (Jonah 3; 4:11). He could just as easily have been punished for the corporate guilt he bore. But the nation as a whole was delivered on a corporate basis when its head repented in sackcloth and ashes. It did not matter if he, as an individual, had sinned or repented. The destiny of his nation was his destiny.

Corporate Guilt and Punishment

The suffering experienced by individual Egyptians during the plagues; by individual Canaanites, Philistines, Amorites, Hittites, etc., during the Conquest; by individual Jews in the Assyrian and Babylonian captivities; and all the other judgments sent against nations, were justified by God on the basis of their participation in the solidarity of their nation.

For example, even though a certain individual Egyptian may not have harmed or mistreated the Jews in any way, yet, because he was an Egyptian, he suffered under the ten plagues. His individual actions did not negate his corporate guilt which arose out of his participation in the solidarity of the nation of Egypt.

Even the Righteous

A righteous man can view himself guilty in a corporate sense by virtue of the solidarity of his tribe's or nation's sin. Thus Nehemiah confessed the corporate sins of his nation (Neh. 1:5-11).

In the passage above, it is clear that an individual can be viewed and treated by God as being guilty of sins for which his nation was guilty. The fact that he himself had not committed the particular sins in question did not negate the corporate guilt he bore.

It is on this basis that punishment for certain sins was visited on entire cities like Sodom or entire nations such as Egypt. Because of the solidarity of the family unit, the punishment for certain sins could rest on several generations (Exo. 20:5; Josh. 7:24-26; Jer. 22:28-30; 36:31).

God's corporate blessing or judgment on tribes, cities, nations, and mankind as a whole are possible only on the basis of the concept of solidarity. Such judgments as the Flood or the Conquest can only be understood and justified in this way.

In Our Secular life

The concept of solidarity is also an essential aspect of politics as well as a Biblical principle. When the leadership of a nation declares war on another nation, each individual citizen is at war whether he knows or agrees with it. He can be killed or his goods seized simply on the basis of being a part of his nation. He must bear corporate guilt and punishment due to the sins of his nation. Thus, human government itself is based on the concept of solidarity. If we condemn the biblical principle of solidarity, then human government must be rejected as well.

#2 Representation

The Bible teaches a concept of representation in which the acts and decisions of one's representative is viewed and treated as one's own acts and decisions.

In its secular sense, this concept serves as the basis for representative government. If our representatives in Congress declare war, it means that we are viewed and treated as having declared war.

If our representatives vote in a new tax, we have to pay it because we are viewed and treated as if we voted it into law. It does not matter if you disagree with or are ignorant of the actions of your representative. You are legally and morally responsible for the acts and decisions of your representatives.

Examples in Scripture

We find this same principle at work in Scripture. Individuals are viewed and treated by God according to the actions and decisions of their representatives. This worked for either cursing or for blessing.

For Cursing

In terms of cursing, Pharaoh's stubbornness led to God's judgment on the entire nation of Egypt (Exo. 7-11). Those who followed Korah, Dathan, Abiram, and On suffered their fate (Num. 16). Each evil king of Israel or Judah brought judgment on the entire nation. For example, Israel had no rain because of the evil deeds of King Ahab (I Kings 17f).

For Blessing

In its positive sense, the actions and decisions of good kings brought blessing to the entire nation. For example, the nation was delivered because godly King Hezekiah sought the Lord (II Kings 19).

The Atonement

The greatest illustration of the principle of representation is the substitutionary and vicarious atonement of Christ (I Cor. 15:3-4).

We are saved on the basis of the actions and decisions of Christ our representative. He is our mediator, advocate, and great high priest (I Tim. 2:5; I John 2:1; Heb. 2:17). Atonement, justification, and original sin are all based on the principle of representation.

#3 Imputation

The Bible teaches a concept of imputation in which God takes the life and works of someone and applies them to the record of another who is then treated on that basis.

Christian theology has always taught that there are three great acts of imputation:

  1. Adam's sin was imputed to us at conception.
  2. Our sin was imputed to Christ in the atonement.
  3. Christ's righteousness is imputed to us in justification.

The imputation of Adam's sin to us should not bother us any more than the fact that our sins were imputed to Christ. That we should suffer for Adam's sin is just as acceptable as Christ suffering for our sins. The fact that death came to us through Adam is just as acceptable as life coming to us through Christ.

Divine justice is as equally satisfied with the imputation of Adam's sin as it is with the imputation of Christ's righteousness. The justice of all three acts of imputation rises or falls together.

Biblical Examples

The fact that God can choose to "impute" sin or not to "impute" sin is clear from Psa. 32:2 and Rom. 4:6. That it is God who determines what sins are to be placed on one's record is clear from the usage of the word in Scripture: Lev. 7:18; 17:3-4; I Sam. 22:15; Rom. 4:8, 11, 22, 23, 24; 5:13; II Cor. 5:19; James 2:23.

That Christ suffered and died for our sins, which were imputed to His account by the Father, is the very heart and soul of the Christian Gospel (I Cor. 15:3-4). Our sins were imputed to Christ, and He was viewed and treated by God accordingly.

Such passages as Isa. 53:4-6; John 1:29; I Cor. 15:3-4; II Cor. 5:21; I Pet. 2:24, etc., are so clear that only a deranged mind could miss this point.

Once a person accepts the justice of Christ bearing his sin, guilt, and punishment, then he cannot reject the justice of bearing the sin, guilt, and punishment of Adam.

Forensic Justification

In the Biblical doctrine of justification, the righteousness of Christ is "imputed" to us, i.e., God places it on our record and then views and treats us in terms of that righteousness (Rom. 5:1-21; Phil. 3:9).

Righteousness can be imputed to us because Christ is our representative (Heb. 9:11-28) and because of the solidarity of His people for whom He came (Matt. 1:21). Justification is based on the concept of imputation just as much as the doctrines of original sin and the atonement.

It is no surprise that those who deny the imputation of Adam's sin also deny the imputation of Christ's righteousness.

The modern heresy called the "New Perspective on Paul" popularized by apostates such as E. P. Sanders, N. T. Wright, James Dunn, Norman Shepherd, etc. always leads to a denial of original sin. They work backward from a denial of the imputation of Christ's righteousness to a denial of the imputation of Adam's sin.

Part II
Our Relationship to Adam

In what ways are we related to Adam according to the Bible?

#1. We are related to Adam in terms of genetic solidarity.

In Scripture, genetic solidarity in and of itself can serve as a sufficient basis for moral and spiritual implications. Thus the superiority of Christ's priesthood over against the Levitical priesthood is based solely on the fact that Abraham, the *genetic* source of Levi, paid tithes to Melchizedek (Heb. 5:6; 7:4-10).

The fact that all men participate in a genetic solidarity with Adam is the basis for the doctrine that all men are created in the image of God. Thus if you deny the justice of genetic solidarity when it comes to original sin, you have also in principle denied that mankind is God's image bearer.

Ideas are not like taxi cabs in which you can get out of whenever you want. You have to ride in that cab until you get to the end of your journey. The attempt to deny the principle of solidarity when it comes to the Fall but accept it when it comes to Creation, is sheer hypocrisy.

#2. We are related to Adam in terms of spiritual solidarity.

Adam procreated his descendants "in his own image," which had been corrupted by his fall into sin and guilt (Gen. 5:3). That Adam's depravity was passed on to his children is manifested by the universality and inevitability of man's sinfulness, which reveals itself "from the womb" and even "in the womb" (Gen. 6:5; 8:21; 25:22-26; Psa. 14:1-6; 51:5; 58:3; Rom. 3:23; Eph. 2:1-3).
 Cain's murder of Abel is sufficient evidence that Adam's depravity was passed down to this children.

#3. We are related to Adam in terms of representation.

In Rom 5:12-21, Paul clearly draws several parallels between the representative nature of Christ's actions and the representative nature of Adam's actions.
In I Cor. 15, Paul tells us that by virtue of our being "in Adam," i.e. in union with Adam as our head and representative, we are all spiritually dead. He sets forth a parallel between being "in Adam" and being "in Christ."
What Adam or Christ did is viewed by God as what we did. When Adam sinned, we sinned (Rom. 5:12). When he died spiritually, we died spiritually (I Cor.15:22).
In the same way, when Christ was crucified, we were crucified with Him (Gal. 2:20). We died, were buried, and rose when Christ our Head and Representative died, was buried, and rose from the dead (Rom. 6:1-6; Eph. 2:6).
It does not matter to me if you whine about this reality and complain that "it isn't fair." What is "fair" according to your limited, subjective, and culturally conditioned ideas means nothing. What is "fair" is what God decides to be fair.

#4. We are related to Adam by imputation.

Rom. 5 clearly teaches that Adam's sin and condemnation were imputed to his descendants. Thus the universality of death is traced to the solidarity of mankind's participation in the sin of Adam (v.12-17).
The universality of condemnation is also traced back to man's solidarity in Adam (v.18). Paul also tells us that all men are "constituted" or "made" sinners by virtue of their union with Adam (v.19).
Again, if you don't like this truth, there is really nothing you can do about it. You can deny total depravity, but in doing so you are only illustrating the truth of it!

Part III
Eden and Calvary

What Christ did on Mt. Calvary is viewed in Scripture as the remedy to what Adam did in the Garden. Thus, as our legal representative and substitute, Christ lived and died in our place.

In other words, what He did was credited to our account as if we did it. His life and death were substitutionary in the same way that Adam's life and death was substitutionary.

> For if while we were enemies, we were reconciled to God through the death of His Son, much more, having been reconciled, we shall be saved by His life. (Rom. 5:10)

> εἰ γὰρ ἐχθροὶ ὄντες κατηλλάγημεν τῷ θεῷ διὰ τοῦ θανάτου τοῦ υἱοῦ αὐτοῦ, πολλῷ μᾶλλον καταλλαγέντες σωθησόμεθα ἐν τῇ ζωῇ αὐτοῦ·

Christ's atoning work is the answer or remedy to the consequences of Adam's Fall into sin and guilt. Thus God designed forensic justification to remove the forensic imputation of Adam's guilt, while progressive sanctification is designed to remove the impartation of Adam's depravity.

The atonement of Christ is structured to be the parallel remedy to the imputation and impartation of Adam's sin and guilt. To claim that it is unjust for us to share in Adam's sin and, yet, at the same time, to claim that it is just to share in Christ's righteousness is anti-scriptural. You cannot have your cake and eat it too! This is why the "New Perspective on Paul" will only populate hell.

The Temptation

The obvious parallel between Christ's temptation in the wilderness (Matt. 4) and Adam's temptation in the Garden (Gen. 3:1-7) cannot be ignored. But, whereas Adam was defeated by the devil, Christ was now victorious over Satan.

Did the Messiah have to go through the Temptation? Yes. Jesus had to endure the same trial that Adam endured. But the second Adam had to pass the same trial that foiled the first Adam.

The Parallels

The following chart reveals some of the parallels between Adam and Christ

The First Adam	The Second Adam
The Son of God (Lk. 3:38)	The Son of God (Mk. 1:1)
Temptation (Gen. 3)	Temptation (Matt. 4)
Disobedience (Gen. 3)	Obedience (Matt. 4)
Condemnation (Rom. 5)	Justification (Rom. 5)
Death (Rom. 5:1 Cor. 15)	Life (Rom. 5:1 Cor. 15)

Obedience Vs Disobedience

The chart above reveals that it is the "obedience" of Christ which removes the "disobedience" of Adam (Rom. 5:19; Phil. 2:5-11; Heb. 5:8). We are saved by His active and passive obedience, not just by His death on the cross alone. This is why the "New Perspective" heresy is exegetically impossible.

Creation

Chapter Four   The Radical Fall of Men Into Sin and Guilt

All men are viewed as being in the image of God because of their solidarity with Adam, who as their representative was created in the image of God. Although this image is marred by sin, man is still the image-bearer of God and has intrinsic worth and dignity (Gen. 1:26-27 cf. James 3:9).

The Creation Mandate

Because of man's solidarity with Adam, when he was given the task of taking dominion over the earth, all his descendants were given the responsibility to be good stewards of the earth and its resources. Thus mankind as a whole was given the Creation Mandate through Adam their representative (Gen. 1:27-30; 2:1-17).

The Radical Fall

The imputation of Adam's sin, guilt, and condemnation to his descendants and the resulting universality of death and totality of depravity are clearly revealed in Scripture.

In Rom. 5:12-21, we are said to receive the following things from our solidarity with Adam our representative:

>sin (v. 12a) -legal and personal
>physical death (v.12b) -consequence
>spiritual death (v.15) -depravity
>judgment/condemnation (v.16) -guilt
>the reign of death (v.17) -bondage
>condemnation for all (v.18) -guilt
>all made sinners (v.19) -depravity

In I Cor. 15, our union with Adam means:

1. death (v.21) -consequence
2. all "in Adam" died when he spiritually died (v.22) – consequence
3. we bear his image and likeness which is sinful, mortal and corrupt (v.45-49) -nature

Redemption

The results of Adam's disobedience and Christ's obedience are paralleled to each other in Scripture.

Adam	Christ
condemnation (position)	justification (position)
depravity (condition)	sanctification (condition)
death (future)	life (future)

The doctrine of original sin is based on the same biblical principles which underlie the doctrines of man as the image bearer of God, the atonement of Christ, and forensic justification. We are viewed and treated by God as sinners on the basis of the imputation of Adam's sin, guilt, and condemnation to our account and the impartation of Adam's depravity and death to our natures.

In short, we sin because we are sinners by nature from conception. Thus it is no surprise that sin and death are universal, total, and inevitable.

All of humanity is in solidarity with Adam in his Creation and his Fall. Just as man's dignity is based on his solidarity with Adam in his Creation, man's depravity is based on his solidarity with Adam in his Fall. Both begin at conception. To reject one is to reject the other.

Christ's work of atonement is based on the same kind of solidarity and representation that are found in our relationship to Adam. They are both substitutionary and vicarious in nature. To reject one is to reject the other.

The imputation of Christ's righteousness in justification is structured in Scripture to be the remedy to the imputation of Adam's unrighteousness in original sin. To reject the one is to reject the other.

The impartation of Christ's righteousness to our natures in sanctification is structured in Scripture to be the remedy to the impartation of Adam's depravity and death to our natures. To reject the one is to reject the other.

In short, the decisions and actions of Adam and Christ are so intertwined in Scripture that they cannot be separated. To deny one is to deny the other. Thus any denial of the doctrines of original sin, substitutionary atonement, and forensic justification must be deemed as serious heresy and sufficient grounds for excommunication.

Part Three
Implications of the Radical Fall

The implications of the Fall penetrate every aspect of how Christians view the world, man, and society. Since we have already developed this in previous books, we will only give a brief overview.

The Way We See the World

When a humanist sees a tree, he does not think anything about it. After all, he assumes that man is the Origin of truth, justice, morals, meaning, and beauty and thus trees, dead or alive, have no intrinsic value or meaning. A tree has no meaning apart from what he gives to it.

When a Christian sees a tree, he understands that the entire Creation is under the curse of Adam's Fall into sin. But when Jesus comes back to this old world of sin and death, the trees and all creation will be delivered from that curse.

> For the anxious longing of the Creation waits eagerly for the revealing of the sons of God. For the Creation was subjected to futility, not of its own will, but because of Him who subjected it, in hope that the Creation itself also will be set free from its slavery to corruption into the freedom of the glory of the children of God. (Rom. 8:19-21)

The storms, earthquakes, forest fires, tidal waves, droughts, floods, etc, that disrupt and destroy the planet are the result of man's sin. Thus the ecological crisis we face today is rooted in the moral issue of man's sin. Pollution is a moral issue, not just a financial problem.

Pollution and the rape of the planet will continue until Jesus comes back to raise the dead and to judge all mankind. Until then, Christians have a divine mandate to be good stewards of the planet.

The Way We Treat Animals

How animals should be treated is another good example. The righteous are kind to animals, but the wicked are cruel.

> A righteous man understands for the life of his animal, But the compassion of the wicked is cruel. (Pro. 12:10)
> יוֹדֵעַ צַדִּיק נֶפֶשׁ בְּהֶמְתּוֹ
> וְרַחֲמֵי רְשָׁעִים אַכְזָרִי׃

A righteous man will יָדַע (i.e., understand) the needs and proper care of his animals. His treatment of them will be kind. In contrast, a wicked man does not bother to understand his animals. Even his acts of רַחֲמִים (i.e. lit. compassions) lead to all kinds of cruel abuse. Solomon points out that what unbelievers think is "compassion" for animals is actually cruel if judged by the Law of God. The "green" humanists can pretend to care about the planet but, in the end, since they reject the Creator and the Fall of man into sin and guilt, they have no intellectual basis for understanding or solving the ecological problems that face us.

How We View Marriage and Divorce

We have already seen that Jesus in Mat. 19:3-10 interpreted marriage and divorce in terms of Creation and the Fall. The pain and suffering of a failed marriage is the result of Adam's Fall into sin and guilt.

How We View Prisons

Humanists live in a fantasy world in which people are viewed as intrinsically good. People are not really "sinners" *per se*. Man's problems are not rooted in what he *is*. They are rooted in what he *does* due to a lack of *education*. Thus man does bad things because he doesn't understand that they are bad. Since his problems are rooted in ignorance, public education is the solution to all the problems man creates.

The humanist perspective has changed prisons from being a place where criminals are punished to "correctional institution" where the "inmates" can be transformed by education. It is hoped that if they can earn a high school or college degree while in prison and have plastic surgery to better their looks, they will go straight when they get out. All the statistics reveal that the ugly truth that the "bleeding heart liberals" have not delivered the goods. All they have managed to produce are better-looking well-educated criminals!

Their failure to view man in the light of the Fall has resulted in rewarding criminals with free education to make them smarter and free plastic surgery to make them better looking. They have only made the situation worse, not better.

Christians understand that people sin because they *are* sinners by nature. Jesus said that people are intrinsically bad, not good. What we *are* determines what we do. Man's problem is not educational but moral. His sin is his problem, not a lack of knowledge. Prisons should be a place of punishment for crimes committed, not a resort with tennis courts.

Liberals can throw all the money in the world into public education but it will not change society one iota. Education is not the final answer because man's real problem is not his ignorance, but his sinful depravity. Salvation by grace alone through faith alone in Christ alone is the only hope for a sinful mankind.

Conclusion

Christians must apply the biblical truth of the radical Fall of man to all of life. Only from that perspective can they deal with the evils that plague our society. Any attempt to develop a "Christian view" of psychology, anthropology, sociology, law, medicine, science, politics, etc. that is not based upon Creation, Fall, and Redemption is not "Christian." Be not deceived. God is not mocked.

Chapter Five

Redemption

The marvelous surprise in Genesis is the promise of Divine Redemption given in Gen. 3:15. It has been called the "proto-evangelium," i.e. the first preaching of the Gospel.

> And I will put enmity between you and the woman, and between your seed and her seed; He shall crush you on the head, and you shall crush him on the heel.

תְּשׁוּפֶנּוּ עָקֵב׃ ס אָשִׁית בֵּינְךָ וּבֵין הָאִשָּׁה וּבֵין זַרְעֲךָ וּבֵין זַרְעָהּ הוּא יְשׁוּפְךָ רֹאשׁ וְאַתָּה וְאֵיבָה

Dr. D. A. Carson comments,

> It has, therefore, traditionally been seen by Jews and Christians, as the first hint of a saviour for mankind, and 3:15 is often called the *protevangelion* the 'first gospel'. Allusions to it in the NT include Rom. 16:20; Heb. 2:14; Rev. 12.[101]

To Whom the Promise Was Given

It is important to note that the promise of salvation was not announced to Adam or Eve when God placed His curse upon them. It was announced to the devil when God cursed the serpent! Why?

The greatest curse that could ever be placed upon Satan for his role in the Fall of man was the announcement that God would *undo* what Satan had done to man. A Redeemer called the "Seed of the woman," identified in the Aramaic Targums as the Messiah, would "crush the head of the serpent," i.e. defeat him.

The Meaning of "Crush"

The same Hebrew word "crush" [שׁוּף] is used to describe what the Seed would do to the serpent and what the serpent would do to the Seed. The defeat of Satan is illustrated by crushing a snake's head under a heel and killing it. But before the snake died, he would manage to bite the heel of the one killing him.

The difference between crushing the "head" and crushing the "heel" of someone is important. Once the head of a snake is crushed, there is no hope that he will recover, but one can recover from a bite on the heel. This is the first indication that the Messiah would be resurrected after His defeat of Satan on the cross. This is why the head of the Seed was not crushed.

> The same word is used in connection with both head and heel, to show that on both sides the intention is to destroy the opponent; at the same time, the expressions head and heel denote a *majus* and *minus,* or, as *Calvin* says, *superius et inferius.* This contrast arises from the nature of the foes. The serpent can only seize the heel of the man, who walks upright; whereas the man can crush the head of the serpent, that crawls in the dust. But this difference is itself the result of the curse pronounced upon the serpent, and its crawling in the dust is a sign that it will be defeated in its conflict with man. However pernicious may be the bite of a serpent in the heel when the poison circulates throughout the body (Gen. 49:17), it is not immediately fatal and utterly incurable, like the crushing of a serpent's head.[102]

Surprised by Grace

First, the idea that God would provide salvation for lost and fallen sinners comes as a complete surprise. After all, why in the world would God redeem the very rebel sinners who had trampled His Law under their feet, rebelled against His Word, questioned His motives, condemned Him as a liar, and chosen Satan over Him, etc.? Grace is truly amazing!

Second, no pagan religion ever conceived of salvation by grace alone through faith alone. Works-based salvation has always been the pagan way, not the biblical way.

Heathen religions assume that the only way to gain acceptance before offended spirits, devils, and deities is to merit or earn it on the basis of man's person and performance.

Third, God could have justly left man in his sin and guilt because He did not *owe* man anything but hell and destruction. In one debate with an Arminian, he challenged me as follows: "Are you saying that God chose to save only *some* of mankind? That's not fair!" I responded, "Why do you assume that God has an obligation to save *anyone*? That God chose to save any sinners at all is the mystery of grace!"

Grace is Found - Not Earned

Throughout the history of Redemption, sinners *"found* grace" in the eyes of the Lord, not earned it!

Noah "found grace": Gen. 6:8
Abraham "found grace": Gen. 18:3

> Lot "found grace": Gen. 19:19
> Moses "found grace": Exo. 33:12-33, 16-17; 34:9
> Mary "found grace": Lk. 1:30
> David "found grace": Acts 7:46

The Hebrew word מָצָא, translated "found," means that grace was something that they *discovered as a complete surprise*. It is like finding a twenty dollar bill on the street. You find it - not earn it.

> **Gen. 6:8 But Noah found grace.** *Hēn;* the same letters as in Noah, but reversed (cf. ch. 18:3; 39:4; 1 Kings 11:19). The present is the first occurrence of the word in Scripture. "Now for the first time *grace* finds a tongue to express its name" (Murphy); and it clearly signifies the same thing as in Rom. 4, 5, Ephes. 2, Gal 2, the gratuitous favour of God to sinful men. [103]

This is why salvation in the Bible is a free act of God 100% and not something that man has earned or merited. This is the point that Paul emphasized in his Epistle to the Romans.

> What then shall we say that Abraham, our forefather according to the flesh, has found? For if Abraham was justified by works, he has something to boast about; <u>but not before God.</u> For what does the Scripture say? "And Abraham believed God, and it was reckoned to him as righteousness." <u>Now to the one who works, his wage is not reckoned as a favor, but as what is due.</u> But to the one who does not work, but believes in Him who justifies the ungodly, his faith is reckoned as righteousness, (Rom. 4:1-5)
>
> Τί οὖν ἐροῦμεν εὑρηκέναι Ἀβραὰμ τὸν προπάτορα ἡμῶν κατὰ σάρκα; εἰ γὰρ Ἀβραὰμ ἐξ ἔργων ἐδικαιώθη, ἔχει καύχημα, ἀλλ' οὐ πρὸς θεόν. τί γὰρ ἡ γραφὴ λέγει; Ἐπίστευσεν δὲ Ἀβραὰμ τῷ θεῷ καὶ ἐλογίσθη αὐτῷ εἰς δικαιοσύνην. τῷ δὲ ἐργαζομένῳ ὁ μισθὸς οὐ λογίζεται κατὰ χάριν ἀλλὰ κατὰ ὀφείλημα, τῷ δὲ μὴ ἐργαζομένῳ πιστεύοντι δὲ ἐπὶ τὸν δικαιοῦντα τὸν ἀσεβῆ λογίζεται ἡ πίστις αὐτοῦ εἰς δικαιοσύνην·

Salvation, A Gift, Not a Wage

In the passage above, Paul argues that salvation must not be viewed as "wages" that we have earned or merited, and thus God owes us. The word μισθὸς is the normal everyday word for remuneration for work done.

> the laborer is worthy of his wages. (Luke 10:7)

> ὁ ἐργάτης τοῦ μισθοῦ αὐτοῦ.

The moment we think that God owes man anything other than divine wrath and judgment, we have denied that salvation is by grace alone. The classic commentaries concur that Paul uses,

> an illustration of the workman (ἐργαζομενῳ [*ergazomenōi*]) who gets his wages due him, "not as of grace" (οὐ κατα χαριν) [ou kata charin]).[104]

> Not grace but debt is the regulative standard according to which his compensation is awarded. The workman for hire represents the legal method of salvation; he who does not work for hire, the gospel method; *wages* cannot be tendered as a *gift*. Grace is out of the question when wages is in question.[105]

> He pointed out that a worker's **wages are** what are owed him because he earned them, and are **not** graciously given **to him as a gift**. Conversely, a person **who** is not working but is believing on (these participles are in the pres. tense) **God who justifies the wicked** (asebē, "the ungodly, impious"; cf. 5:6), **his faith is credited as righteousness** (cf. 4:3).[106]

> The idea is the same in all cultures:
> "Wage" implies a transaction involving an exchange of services for money or something of value. Paul insists that God does not relate to us as an employer, "paying" us with salvation in exchange for some service we render by doing what is right and good. Since we have all sinned, the only wage we have "earned" is death! (Rom. 6:23) Instead, God relates to us through promise and freely gives us righteousness (salvation) if we have faith in Him. Since "wages" and "gift" are contradictory concepts, "law" and "promise" can never be mixed in relating to God. We must choose to relate to either by faith, or by works. We can't have it both ways.[107]

> Salvation is either a reward for works or a gift through grace; it cannot be both. Verse 5 states that God justifies the ungodly (not the righteous) through faith and not works. The Jews thought that God justified religious people on the basis of their works; yet Paul has proved that "Father Abraham" was saved simply on the basis of faith. Then Paul refers to David and quotes Ps. 32:1–2, proving that Israel's great king taught justification by faith, apart from works. God does not impute sin to our account, because that was charged to Christ's account (2 Cor. 5:21, and see Phile. 18). Rather, He imputes Christ's righteousness to our account purely on the basis of grace! What a wonderful salvation we have![108]

Chapter Five Redemption

God Does Not Have To Save Anyone

Salvation is not something that God does because He *has* to. It is not something that is *required* of Him. Salvation is not a *necessary* act of God, but a *free* act of a sovereign God.

> He who did not spare His own Son, but delivered Him up for us all, how will He not also with Him *freely give* us all things?
> (Romans 8:32)

ὅς γε τοῦ ἰδίου υἱοῦ οὐκ ἐφείσατο ἀλλὰ ὑπὲρ ἡμῶν πάντων παρέδωκεν αὐτόν, πῶς οὐχὶ καὶ σὺν αὐτῷ τὰ πάντα ἡμῖν χαρίσεται;

> Now we have received, not the spirit of the world, but the Spirit who is from God, that we might know the things *freely given* to us by God, (1 Cor. 2:12)

ἡμεῖς δὲ οὐ τὸ πνεῦμα τοῦ κόσμου ἐλάβομεν ἀλλὰ τὸ πνεῦμα τὸ ἐκ τοῦ θεοῦ, ἵνα εἰδῶμεν τὰ ὑπὸ τοῦ θεοῦ χαρισθέντα ἡμῖν·

> to the praise of the glory of His grace, which He *freely bestowed* on us in the Beloved. (Eph. 1:6)

εἰς ἔπαινον δόξης τῆς χάριτος αὐτοῦ ἧς ἐχαρίτωσεν ἡμᾶς ἐν τῷ ἠγαπημένῳ.

The word χαρίζομαι, translated "freely given or bestowed," literally means that God was under *no necessity* to save us. It was His *free* act to redeem us.

No One Deserves a Chance To Be Saved

This is in sharp contrast to Natural Theology, which is based on the erroneous idea that God *owes* man salvation. This is the rotten foundation of the heresy that the heathen "deserve" the chance of salvation. Thus they cannot be denied heaven simply because they never heard of or believed in Jesus.

While the Bible describes those who die without faith in Jesus as having "no hope" (1 Thess. 4:13) and "perishing" (Rom. 2:12), heretics always teach a "wideness to God's mercy" in which there is always "hope" for anyone who is good, regardless of what they believed. This "wider hope" heresy is based on a works-based salvation, and is antithetical to the gospel, evangelism, and missions.

The Basis of Orthodoxy and Catholicism

The works-for-salvation foundation of both Eastern Orthodoxy and Roman Catholicism is based on the "wage model" in which God owes salvation to good people who do good works. The "fly in the ointment" is that, from God's perspective, there are no good people!

> as it is written, "There is none righteous, not even one; There is none who understands, There is none who seeks for God;
> All have turned aside, together they have become useless; There is none who does good, There is not even one." (Rom.3:10-12)

> καθὼς γέγραπται ὅτι Οὐκ ἔστιν δίκαιος οὐδὲ εἷς, οὐκ ἔστιν ὁ συνίων, οὐκ ἔστιν ὁ ἐκζητῶν τὸν θεόν. πάντες ἐξέκλιναν ἅμα ἠχρεώθησαν· οὐκ ἔστιν ὁ ποιῶν χρηστότητα, [οὐκ ἔστιν] ἕως ἑνός.

Paul is simply echoing what was taught in the Psalms.

> The fool has said in his heart, "There is no God." They are corrupt, They have committed abominable deeds; There is no one who does good. YHWH has looked down from heaven upon the sons of men, To see if there are any who understand, Who seek after God. They have all turned aside; Together they have become corrupt; There is no one who does good, not even one. (Psa. 14:1-3)

> לְדָוִד אָמַר נָבָל בְּלִבּוֹ אֵין אֱלֹהִים הִשְׁחִיתוּ הִתְעִיבוּ עֲלִילָה אֵין עֹשֵׂה־טוֹב׃
> יְהוָה מִשָּׁמַיִם הִשְׁקִיף עַל־בְּנֵי־אָדָם לִרְאוֹת הֲיֵשׁ מַשְׂכִּיל דֹּרֵשׁ אֶת־אֱלֹהִים׃
> לַמְנַצֵּחַ הַכֹּל סָר יַחְדָּו נֶאֱלָחוּ אֵין עֹשֵׂה־טוֹב אֵין גַּם־אֶחָד׃

Salvation is not something we earn or merit. Works and grace cannot be mixed together as they are diametrically opposed to each other.

Unconditional Election

For example, divine predestination is not based upon our works. God does not choose sinners on the basis of what they have done or what they will do in the future, but election is based on sovereign grace alone. Election is thus either by grace alone or by works alone. It is either one or the other, not both. This is argued by Paul in Rom. 11:5-6,

> In the same way then, there has also come to be at the present time a remnant according to <u>election by grace. But if it is by grace, it is no longer on the basis of works, otherwise grace is no longer grace.</u>

> οὕτως οὖν καὶ ἐν τῷ νῦν καιρῷ λεῖμμα κατ' ἐκλογὴν χάριτος γέγονεν εἰ δὲ χάριτι, οὐκέτι ἐξ ἔργων, ἐπεὶ ἡ χάρις οὐκέτι γίνεται χάρις.

It is amazing that so many Natural Theologians think that they have figured out a way to mix grace and works together. But, no matter how hard they shake grace and works together, just like an oil and vinegar, given enough time, they will separate because they cannot be blended together.

Fourth, salvation in the Bible is based entirely on the person and work of Christ. His oath, His covenant, His righteousness, and His good works are the basis of salvation. Jesus paid it all!

Biblical Redemption is thus unique because it is by way of the vicarious substitutionary blood atonement of the Incarnate of Son of God. Jesus paid all the costs necessary to satisfy Divine Justice and to set us free from eternal condemnation and perdition. He lived the life we never lived and died the death we should have died. See my book, *Studies in the Atonement*, for the details of this most wonderful plan of salvation.

Fifth, biblical Redemption is Trinitarian. We are:

> Chosen by the Father,
> Purchased by the Son,
> Sealed by the Spirit,
> Blessed God Three in One!

Each member of the economical Trinity has a distinct role to play in salvation. Redemption is planned by the Father, accomplished by the Son, and applied by the Spirit. Any view of salvation that is not Trinitarian is not biblical. See my work, *The Trinity, Evidence and Issues*, for an exegetical defense of this position.

Sixth, biblical Redemption is monergistic (God working alone), not synergistic (God and man working together). This means that salvation is 100% of God. It is not a 50/50 deal between God and man. As Jonah confessed,

> Salvation is from YHWH. (Jonah 2:9)
> Hebrew: יְשׁוּעָתָה לַיהוָה
> Septuagint: σοι σωτηρίου τῷ κυρίῳ
> Latin Vulgate: *pro salute Domino.*

Matthew Henry comments,

> He concludes with an acknowledgment of God as the Saviour of his people: *Salvation is of the Lord;* it *belongs to the Lord,* Ps. 3:8. He is the *God of salvation,* Ps. 68:19, 20. He only can work salvation, and he can do it be the danger and distress ever so great; he has promised salvation to his people that trust in him. All the salvations of his church in general, and of particular saints, were wrought by him; he is the *Saviour of those that believe,* 1 Tim. 4:10. Salvation is still of him, as it has always been; from him alone it is to be expected, and on him we are to depend for it. Jonah's experience

> shall encourage others, in all ages, to trust in God as the God of their salvation; all that read this story shall say with assurance, say with admiration, that *salvation is of the Lord,* and is sure to all that belongs to him. [109]

Henry is not alone in his interpretation.

> In the words "salvation comes from the LORD," Jonah extolled the work of the Lord as Savior. Here also is an emphasis on the Lord's sole sovereignty in the area of salvation. No one else can provide in such a way, though Jonah already showed in v. 8 how one might reject God's offer. It is correct to say that this line may serve as the key verse in the book. Fretheim is possibly correct in pointing out that salvation does seem to be the key motif in the book, and this verse points to that motif. Salvation for the sailors is emphasized in chap. 1, for Jonah in chap. 2, for the Ninevites in chap. 3; and it is the objective of God's questioning of Jonah in chap. 4. Jonah recognized that he deserved death, not deliverance. He then knew, as we do, that no one deserves deliverance. It is an act of mercy by a gracious God. [110]

It doesn't matter how you cut it, *God saves sinners all by Himself.*
- He devised the plan of salvation from eternity past.
- Mankind was prepared for the Incarnation of the Divine Son of God by His appearance in human form in the Garden and throughout human history. The theophanies prepared the way for the coming of Messiah. See my book, *The Trinity*, for full documentation on this point.
- Jesus came, lived, died, rose again, and sat down at the right hand of the Father.
- He is now reigning as King of kings and Lord of lords until He has put all His enemies under His feet.
- One day the Messiah is coming back to this wicked world to stop the madness of sin, resurrect the dead, initiate the Day of Judgment, cast the wicked into eternal conscious punishment, and create a new earth in which the people of God will fulfill the original Creation Mandate found in Gen. 1:26-31.
- The eternal state of the saints will be filled with worship, art, music, science, architecture, theology, animal sciences, space exploration, etc. A New World is coming and it will be ushered in by the literal Second Coming of the Lord Messiah Jesus.

All For The Glory of God

Seventh, we must emphasize the biblical truth that the goal of all things including salvation is not the happiness of man, but the glory of God. Isaiah declared,

> Everyone who is called by My name, And whom I have created <u>for My glory</u>, Whom I have formed, even whom I have made. (Isa. 43:7)

כֹּל הַנִּקְרָא בִשְׁמִי וְלִכְבוֹדִי בְּרָאתִיו יְצַרְתִּיו אַף־עֲשִׂיתִיו:
πάντας ὅσοι ἐπικέκληνται τῷ ὀνόματί μου ἐν γὰρ τῇ δόξῃ μου ατεσκεύασα αὐτὸν καὶ ἔπλασα καὶ ἐποίησα αὐτόν

We were created to increase the acquired glory of God. We are saved from eternal damnation to increase the acquired glory of God. Everything God does is focused on increasing His glory.

> "Worthy art Thou, our Lord and our God, to receive glory and honor and power; for Thou didst create all things, and because of Thy will they existed, and were created." (Rev. 4:11)

Ἄξιος εἶ, ὁ κύριος καὶ ὁ θεὸς ἡμῶν, λαβεῖν τὴν δόξαν καὶ τὴν τιμὴν καὶ τὴν δύναμιν, ὅτι σὺ ἔκτισας τὰ πάντα καὶ διὰ τὸ θέλημά σου ἦσαν καὶ ἐκτίσθησαν.

Much of "Christian" evangelism is now totally man-centered. The question usually asked of unbelievers is, "Do you want happiness, health, and prosperity?" This reveals how man-centered the evangelical world has become.

God-centered Evangelism

Sinners need to be reminded that they exist for God's glory and that He does not exist for their happiness. The famous agnostic, David Hume, never understood the gospel that he loudly repudiated. He argued that since God existed "for the felicity of man," and, manifestly not all men are happy, then perhaps God did not exist. He falsely assumed that God existed to serve the needs of man and the greatest need of man was to be happy.

In his Anglican Arminian church background, he had been taught that God wants man to be happy, healthy, and wealthy. This is why Jesus came to earth. The gospel was presented to him as a means whereby we can be happy. Thus the beginning and end of the gospel message is the happiness of man.

If he had heard the true gospel of Sovereign grace that man exists to glorify God and that we are here on earth to serve Him, perhaps he would not have become so vile an unbeliever and enemy of Jesus Christ.

The "seeker-friendly" church phenomenon, the health and wealth TBN gospel, the emergent church, and emerging church movements are all man-centered. They cater to the felt needs of man and sacrifice the biblical gospel in the process.

The Biblical Message

We need to return to the biblical gospel that man is a rebel sinner who is under the wrath of Almighty God. His only hope is that God will somehow rescue him. God devised a plan by which He could be "just and the justifier of the one who has faith in Jesus" (Rom. 3:26). Wiersbe comments,

> God must be perfectly consistent with Himself. He cannot break His own Law or violate His own nature. "God is love" (1 John 4:8), and "God is light" (1 John 1:5). A God of love wants to forgive sinners, but a God of holiness must punish sin and uphold His righteous Law. How can God be both "just and the justifier"? The answer is in Jesus Christ. When Jesus suffered the wrath of God on the cross for the sins of the world, He fully met the demands of God's Law, *and also fully expressed the love of God's heart.* The animal sacrifices in the Old Testament never took away sin; but when Jesus died, He reached all the way back to Adam and took care of those sins. No one (including Satan) could accuse God of being unjust or unfair because of His seeming passing over of sins in the Old Testament time. [111]

Conclusion

The third pillar of the biblical worldview is its unique concept of Divine Redemption in which it was decreed by God the Father in eternity past, accomplished by God the Son in history, and applied today by God the Holy Spirit in the present.

> To the One in Three,
> And Three in One,
> Be all the glory
> Both now and forever more,
>   Amen!

Chapter Six

The Book of Ecclesiastes

The greatness of the Book of Ecclesiastes has been recognized by many. It exposes and destroys all humanistic hope that man can find truth, justice, morals, meaning, and beauty in life apart from and independent of God's revelation in Scripture. Its relentless logic has impressed unbelievers as well as believers, Jews as well as Christians.

The well-known novelist Herman Melville stated, "The truest of all books is Solomon's and Book of Ecclesiastes is the fine hammered steel of woe."[112] The author Thomas Wolfe declared, "the Book of Ecclesiastes is the greatest single piece of writing I have ever known, and the wisdom expressed in it the most lasting and profound."[113] Derek Kidner states, "Anyone who spends time with Book of Ecclesiastes (that least ecclesiastical of men) finds himself in the company of a highly independent and fascinating mind."[114]

The famous French theologian, Jacques Ellul, was one of twentieth century's most outspoken opponents of Natural Theology and Natural Law. He was motivated by his lifelong study of the Book of Ecclesiastes.

> I have read, meditated on, and prayed over *Book of Ecclesiastes* for more than fifty years. I have probably explored it more than any other book in the Bible. It has perhaps given me more than any other.[115]

Duane Garrett correctly points out that the Reformers, Puritans, and many great Evangelical leaders of the past viewed the Book of Ecclesiastes as an apologetic against unbelief by demonstrating that human reason cannot find meaning apart from God.[116] It is thus no surprise that such apologists as Francis Schaeffer used the Book of Ecclesiastes to show unbelievers that if we adopt their secular worldview, all meaning and morals are lost. The historic evangelical position was based on revealed theology and maintained *Sola Scriptura* as its foundational principle.

This is in sharp contrast to modern "evangelical" Natural Theologians who have avoided the Book of Book of Ecclesiastes. They are not stupid. Why would they draw attention to a Book in the Bible that destroys the very foundation of Natural Theology? Thus, whereas the Book of Ecclesiastes was historically viewed as an apologetic refutation of humanism, it has now been set aside as irrelevant.

A Difficult Book

Most modern people have trouble understanding the Book of Ecclesiastes. Iain Provan calls it "a difficult book." [117] J. Stafford Wright states that it is "one of the most puzzling books of the Bible." [118] Scott describes it as "the strangest book of the Bible."[119] Moore and Akin both feel that the Book of Ecclesiastes is "the most misunderstood book of the Bible."[120]

It is hard for modern Gentiles to understand ancient Jewish Wisdom literature because there are no modern literary parallels. The sarcasm, humor, and wit displayed in the book are out of sync with modern culture. As Murphy and Huwiler point out, "The Book of Ecclesiasteshas a distinct voice among the texts of the Bible."[121]

Book of Ecclesiastes and Proverbs

Perhaps the best way to understand the Book of Ecclesiastes is to compare it to the book of Proverbs. Both books are found within the poetry section of the Old Testament. The five poetical books of Job, Psalms, Proverbs, Book of Ecclesiastes, and Song of Songs deal with the practical issues of life instead of such things as prophecy, history, or theology. They are also called "Wisdom literature" because they seek to educate us about life and how to live it.

Although Proverbs and the Book of Ecclesiastes are both wisdom literature, they teach us about life in two totally different ways. Proverbs begins with the assumption that there is a personal God who gives meaning to all of life (Prov. 1:7). The Book of Ecclesiastes begins with the assumption that life without God is meaningless (Ecc. 1:16, 17).

- Proverbs begins with the assumption that there is a personal God who gives meaning to all of life (Prov. 1:7). The Book of Ecclesiastes begins with the assumption that life without God is meaningless (Ecc. 1:16,17).

- Proverbs begins *with* God and asks the question, "*How* should we live." The Book of Ecclesiastes begins *without* God and asks, "*Why* should we live?"

- Proverbs is positive in tone. The Book of Ecclesiastes is negative.

- Proverbs gives believers hope for tomorrow. The Book of Ecclesiastes denies unbelievers any hope for tomorrow.

- Proverbs promises us that life will have meaning if we begin with God (Pro. 1:1–7). The Book of Ecclesiastes warns us that life will be meaningless if we begin without God (Ecc. 1:2).

- Proverbs tells us that wisdom is more important than money (Pro. 3:13–18). The Book of Ecclesiastes tells us that money is more important than wisdom (Ecc. 10:19; 1:17, 18).

- Proverbs assures us that a good reputation is important (Pro. 22:1). The Book of

Ecclesiastes tells us that it is meaningless (Ecc. 6:2).

In many other ways, the Book of Ecclesiastes reveals that without God, nothing in life will have any meaning or significance. It teaches this by being the "mirror reflection" or opposite of Proverbs.

The Hermeneutics of the *Book of Ecclesiastes*

The hermeneutical principle of the "passage of full mention" is another key to understanding the message of the Book of Ecclesiastes. This principle refers to an interesting phenomenon of Scripture. In addition to scattered references throughout the Bible to a specific biblical concept, sometimes there is a seminal passage in Scripture where that specific truth is developed in depth. For example, Isa. 40 is the "passage of full mention" on the transcendence of God, 1 Cor. 15 is the "passage of full mention" on the bodily resurrection, Rom. 4-5 is the "passage of full mention" on the doctrine of justification.

When confronted by Natural Theology, we must ask, "Is there a "passage of full mention" in Scripture where God specifically addresses the foundational idea upon which Natural Theology is based?" We are not asking if Scripture specifically addresses this or that *modern* expression of this foundational concept. That would be a violation of cultural context.

All forms of humanistic theology are based on the fundamental idea that *man starting from himself, in himself, and by himself, apart from and independent of God and His revelation in the Bible, can discover truth, justice, morals, meaning, and beauty, through human reason, experience, feelings, or faith.* Is this foundational issue ever addressed in Scripture? Yes.

The Book of Ecclesiastes is the Scriptural "passage of full mention" in which the Creator of the universe addresses the foundational principle of all Natural theologies. In the Book of Ecclesiastes the one true God destroys any hope whatsoever that man is the Origin of truth, justice, morals, meaning and beauty. The Book of Ecclesiastes establishes the divine truth that if we begin with *man*, we will end with complete and total *meaninglessness*.

When we turn to see how "Evangelical" Natural theologians and philosophers have handled the Book of Ecclesiastes, what do we find? Ninety nine times out of a hundred, they completely ignore the Book. They do not even refer to it at all! Like the proverbial ostrich, they stick their head in the sand and pretend that it does not exist. They know that if they attacked the inspiration and canonicity of Ecclesiastes, they would be fired from the Evangelical schools or churches were they are employed.

Liberal Attacks on the Book of Ecclesiastes

When we turn to Roman Catholic and liberal Protestant Natural theologians and philosophers, we find that they attack the inspiration and canonicity of Ecclesiastes. Why are they so hostile to this Book? They recognize the threat that this biblical Book poses to their worldview. If the Book of Ecclesiastes is inspired, then God has declared all Natural Theologies "Meaningless! Utterly meaningless!"

This is why the Book of Ecclesiastes has been relentlessly attacked since the rise of Western European Natural Theology. They correctly see that the Book of Ecclesiastes is a dagger aimed at the very heart and soul of Natural theology. John Gill, the great Hebrew scholar, documented that the most consistent of all Natural theologians, the Deists, were united in their rejection of the Book of Ecclesiastes.[122]

After spending several years reading all the rationalistic arguments against the Book of Ecclesiastes, I have come to the conclusion that they are worthless and wicked. They do not disprove the inspiration or canonicity of the Book. Most of the arguments today were originally given by German rationalists in the 18th or 19th centuries and are hopelessly out of date. For example, they ignore all the archeological and textual discoveries since that time.

Authorship

Theological rationalists erroneously assume that if they can disprove (sic) that King Solomon was the author of the Book of Ecclesiastes, the book's inspiration is automatically refuted. Albert Barnes noted in his day, "modern critics have indeed alleged that Solomon could not have written it."[123]

The apostate assumption is gratuitously accepted today by all liberals. They assume that it was *impossible* for King Solomon to write the Book of Ecclesiastes.[124] Liberal commentaries simply wave aside the idea that Solomon wrote the book. Lange pointed out that the philosophers in his day did all in their power to destroy the Book of Ecclesiastes.[125]

Why are theological rationalists so desperate to overthrow the Book of Ecclesiastes? What is it about the Book that makes them so afraid? Stop and ask yourself, "If the smartest man who ever lived tried to find meaning in life, apart from and independent of God's special revelation in Scripture, through human reason and experience and, in the end, concluded that without Divine Revelation life has no meaning, is the basis of all humanistic thought in jeopardy? The only possible answer is, "Yes!"

This is why theological rationalists expend so much energy attacking the Book of Ecclesiastes. It destroys all hope that unregenerate man can find truth without God, morals without Scripture, and meaning without revelation. Hengstenberg comments,

> ...the soulless, spiritless, vulgar Rationalism has been capable of little sympathy with the book. A Th. Hartman gave most open expression to his antipathy to it. He describes it as "the work of a morose Hebrew Philosopher, composed when he was in a dismal mood and in places thoroughly tedious."[126]

In terms of authorship, several facts are agreed upon by all. First, both Jewish and Christian traditions identify Solomon as the author. F. C. Cook comments,

> This Book is placed, in the most ancient Jewish and Christian lists, between the other two Books (Proverbs and the Song of Songs) attributed to Solomon, and the constant tradition of the Jewish and Christian Churches has handed down Solomon without question as the author.[127]

Second, rationalists have argued that the vocabulary, geographical references, theme, and personal comments of the author demonstrated that Solomon could not be the author, because the book had to be written many centuries after Solomon died. But, conservative scholars have refuted these arguments one by one by showing that the vocabulary, geographical references, theme, and personal comments of the author were indeed possible in Solomon's day. They have also argued that Solomon was the only author who had the depth and breadth of knowledge to have written it.[128]

> In summary, though many scholars deny Solomonic authorship because of the supposed lateness of the language of the Book of Ecclesiastes, recent studies have called into question the validity of their linguistic evidence and reopened the possibility of identifying the unnamed author with Solomon. Since the evidence is inconclusive, the following commentary assumes the traditional view that Solomon was the human author. However, regardless of who wrote it, whether Solomon or a later Jewish sage, the presence of this book in the Bible indicates that it is God's Word.[129]

> Some modern scholars have argued that the philosophical cast of the book and its many distinctive words point to a postexilic date. However, the linguistic arguments have all been satisfactorily answered by conservative scholars, and a pre-exilic date is fully justified. It is likely the book was composed near the end of Solomon's reign, perhaps in his last decade (940–930 B.C.).[130]

Since the book itself does not name Solomon as the author, the issue of authorship is not tied to its inspiration. The authorship of the book is not mentioned elsewhere in Scripture. Thus, if Solomon did not write it, its inspiration is not threatened. Some conservative commentators have held to the inspiration of the Book of Ecclesiastes but not to Solomon's authorship.[131]

Inspiration

Its inspiration was never questioned in either the Jewish or Christian traditions. The authors of the New Testament utilized it as Scripture.[132] Just because you do not like its message is not sufficient to reject its inspiration. For the biblical Christian, the Book of Ecclesiastesis is inspired Scripture.

> The book, entitled Koheleth, or Book of Ecclesiastes, has ever been received, both by the Jewish and Christian Church, as written under the *inspiration* of the Almighty; and was held to be properly a part of the sacred canon.[133]

Date of Composition

The exact date when the Book of Ecclesiastes was written remains an open question. Unlike Isaiah, the book nowhere ties its composition to a particular king. A book based upon the teachings of Solomon could have been written long after his death. Editorial updates that modernized the vocabulary and spelling in the text could have been done several times without threatening that the book is a faithful summary of Solomon's belief system.[134]

The Original Text of Book of Ecclesiastes

We are happy to report that "The Hebrew text is in good condition."[135] The LXX and other translations are accurate for the most part. The fragments found in the Dead Sea Scrolls are generally identical. Leupold concludes, "The fact remains that we have in this book, as ordinarily, a good Hebrew text." [136]

Place in Canon

First, its relationship to the Old Testament as a whole is best described as follows.

5 Basic Law		5 Basic Prophecy
9 Pre-exile history	5 Personal life	9 pre-exile prophecy
3 Post- exile history	(Book of Ecclesiastes)	3 post exile prophecy

Second, the five Wisdom books have been described as the "Second Torah." The differences between the first and second Torahs are profound. The first "Torah" (Gen.-Deut.) reveals the divine laws that govern the external universe. The second "Torah" (Job-Songs) reveals the laws that govern the internal universe. This second Torah has been viewed in three different ways.

> a. Literary style: There is a great amount of poetry in these five books. Thus some commentators have labeled this section of the canon as Poetical Books.
> b. Focus: This second Torah is intensely personal in tone. Your personal relationship to God, your neighbor, you wife, and others is the focus.

Chapter Six The Book of Ecclesiastes

c. Law: This Torah gives us the laws that govern true spirituality, such as prayer and praise.

Third, its relationship to the other Wisdom books:

- Job: the problem of Evil. How do I cope with evil when it happens to me?
- Psalms: the practice of Prayer. How do I pray to the Lord?
- Proverbs: the way of Wisdom. How will a wise person treat others?
- Book of Ecclesiastes: the meaning of Life. How can we have meaning in life?
- Song of Songs: the happy marriage. How can I have a happy marriage?

Fourth, its relationship to the New Testament: The NT parallel to the Book of Ecclesiastes is found in 1 Cor. 15:12-20, 32. Paul's use of such key words as "vain," "profitless," etc. and his relentless logic that if Messiah has not been bodily raised from the dead, life has no meaning are all clear echoes of the Book of Ecclesiastes.

> Now if Messiah is preached, that He has been raised from the dead, how do some among you say that there is no resurrection of the dead? But if there is no resurrection of the dead, not even Messiah has been raised; and if Messiah has not been raised, then our preaching is **vain**, your faith also is **vain**. Moreover we are even found false witnesses of God, because we testified against God that He raised Messiah, whom He did not raise, if in fact the dead are not raised. For if the dead are not raised, not even Messiah has been raised; and if Messiah has not been raised, your faith is **profitless**; you are still in your sins. Then those also who have fallen asleep in Christ have perished. If we have hoped in Messiah in this life only, we are of all men most to be pitied. If from human motives I fought with wild beasts at Ephesus, what does it **profit** me? If the dead are not raised,
> "Let us eat and drink, for tomorrow we die." (1 Cor. 15:12-19, 32)

Literary Style

Book of Ecclesiastes is a mixture of several different styles, of which Hebrew poetry is only one type.

> Some have supposed that the Book of Ecclesiastes is a poem. That some poetic lines may be found in it, there is no doubt; but it has nothing in common with poetic books, nor does it exist in the hemistich form in any printed edition or MS. yet discovered. It is

plain prose, and is not susceptible to that form in which the Hebrew poetic books appear.[137]

Garrett comments, "Due to a testimony to the stylistic complexity of Book of Ecclesiastes, scholars are not even able to agree on whether the book is predominately prose or poetry."[138] Murphy and Huwiler agree, "Translators do not agree on which parts of the book are poetry and which are prose."[139]

Pagan Sources for the Book of Ecclesiastes?

Once the theological rationalists rejected the divine inspiration of the Book of Ecclesiastes, they had to explain the obvious greatness of the book. They retreated to the old argument that whenever anything of greatness appeared in Israel, it had to come from the pagans around them. The Jews were incapable of being original, unique or great in their ideas. Thus they always borrowed their ideas from the brilliant Gentile thinkers in the pagan world around them. Ellul comments,

> The third presupposition of commentators has to do with their certainty that Book of Ecclesiastes is not based on authentic Hebrew thought, but rather derives from one of the surrounding cultures. When scholars make this hypothesis the center of their research, presupposing a foreign origin for the book, they plunge into very dubious waters.[140]

Modern Natural theologians disagree as to the sources of the Book of Ecclesiastes. This alone should cast doubt on the entire enterprise of trying to find Gentile sources for Jewish ideas.

> Duane Garrett: Egyptian instructional literature (with a fair amount of influence also coming from Babylonian and other sources.[141]
>
> William P. Brown: The Babylonian Gilgamesh Myth.[142]
>
> Murphy: Egyptian, Canaanite-Phoenician, Greek sources.[143]

After surveying the arguments that the Book of Ecclesiastes came from Aramaic, Phoenician, Greek, Egyptian, or Babylonian sources, Jacques Ellul concluded, "The diversity of theories is amazing...Typically, we find as many different possibilities as we have scholars."[144]

He examined the pagan source materials that supposedly were parallels to the Book of Ecclesiastes and concluded, "I remain rather skeptical of these parallels."[145] Prof. Barton's conclusion should be repeated, "there is even less trace in Qohleth of Greek philosophical, than of Greek linguistical influence."[146]

The idea that the Jews were incapable of original or inspired ideas is a subtle form of anti-Semitism that eventually produced the Holocaust. It is time to call "source theories" what they really are: racial prejudice and hate speech.

Finally, Hengstenberg points out that one of the goals of the author of the Book of Ecclesiastes was to warn the people of God not to adopt the philosophies of the surrounding pagan nations.

> At all periods in which the powers of this world have weighed oppressively on the people of God, the temptation has been peculiarly strong to approve and adopt the worldly wisdom which prevailed amongst the surrounding heathen nations. The danger lay very near of coming, in that manner, to terms with the world, and seeking thus to be on equal footing with it…the author utters his warning in chap. vii. 25. 26; he further admonishes the Israelites to offer energetic resistance to its attackers themselves. In chap. Xii.12, he warns them against familiarizing themselves with worldly literature. [147]

The "pagan source theory" contradicts the very purpose of the Book of Ecclesiastes. As such, it is useless as well as false.

The Epistemology of the Book of Ecclesiastes

How the author tried to find meaning without God is important. He tried rationalism and empiricism, and they both failed to find meaning or morals.

The Idealism of Rationalism

Rationalism is the attempt to discover meaning and morals through the fallen mind or reason of man. The rationalist believes that if he uses such philosophic tools as logic and discourse, he could discover final answers to the ultimate questions of life. It does not matter if we are talking about pagan or "Christian" rationalists. For both of them, the real is the rational and the rational is the real. Man's reason is the measure of all things.

Solomon diligently studied the Natural theology and philosophy of his day to see if he could, through them alone, discover truth and meaning.[148] He "talked to himself" about the meaning of life, *not* to God. He applied his "mind" to find the meaning of life. He never once gave a "Thus says YHWH" or cited the Torah as his authority. His rationalism is expressed in the verses below.

> **Book of Ecclesiastes 1:13 And I set my mind to seek and explore by wisdom concerning all that has been done under heaven.**

Book of Ecclesiastes 1:16 **I said to myself, "Behold, I have magnified and increased wisdom** more than all who were over Jerusalem before me; and **my mind has observed a wealth of wisdom and knowledge."**

Book of Ecclesiastes 1:17 And **I set my mind to know wisdom and to know madness and folly.**

Book of Ecclesiastes 7:25 **I directed my mind to know, to investigate, and to seek wisdom and an explanation, and to know the evil of folly and the foolishness of madness.**

Book of Ecclesiastes 8:9 All this I have seen and **applied my mind** to every deed that has been done under the sun wherein a man has exercised authority over *another* man to his hurt.

The Hope of Empiricism

Empiricism is the attempt to find meaning through the five senses. Since philosophy failed to produce anything, he turned to the sciences. This is another reason why Solomon could be the author.

> And Solomon's wisdom surpassed the wisdom of all the sons of the east and all the wisdom of Egypt for he was wiser than all men, than Ethan the Ezrahite, Heman, Calcol and Darda, the sons of Mahol; and his fame was *known* in all the surrounding nations. He also spoke 3,000 proverbs, and his songs were 1,005. And he spoke of trees, from the cedar that is in Lebanon even to the hyssop that grows on the wall; he spoke also of animals and birds and creeping things and fish. (1 Kings 4:30-34)

The author looked at the world around him and tried to find meaning on the basis of what he saw with his own eyes. The epistemological impact of the following verses should be noted.

Book of Ecclesiastes 2:13 And **I saw** that wisdom excels folly as light excels darkness.

Book of Ecclesiastes 4:1 Then **I looked** again at all the acts of oppression which were being done under the sun. And behold *I saw* the tears of the oppressed and *that* they had no one to comfort *them*; and on the side of their oppressors was power, but they had no one to comfort *them.*

Book of Ecclesiastes 8:17 and **I saw** every work of God, *I concluded* that man cannot discover the work which has been done under the sun. Even though man should seek laboriously, he will not discover; and though the wise man should say, "I know," he cannot discover.

Book of Ecclesiastes 9:11 **I again saw** under the sun that the race is not to the swift, and the battle is not to the warriors, and neither is bread to the wise, nor wealth to the discerning, nor favor to men of ability; for time and chance overtake them all.

Book of Ecclesiastes 4:1 Then **I looked** again at all the acts of oppression which were being done under the sun. And behold *I saw* the tears of the oppressed and *that* they had no one to comfort *them*; and on the side of their oppressors was power, but they had no one to comfort *them*.

Book of Ecclesiastes 4:7 Then **I looked** again at vanity under the sun.

Book of Ecclesiastes 1:14 **I have looked** all the works which have been done under the sun, and behold, all is vanity and striving after wind.

Book of Ecclesiastes 2:24 There is nothing better for a man *than* to eat and drink and tell himself that his labor is good. This also **I have looked**, that it is from the hand of God.

Book of Ecclesiastes 3:10 **I have seen** the task which God has given the sons of men with which to occupy themselves.

Book of Ecclesiastes 3:16 Furthermore, **I have seen** under the sun *that* in the place of justice there is wickedness, and in the place of righteousness there is wickedness.

Book of Ecclesiastes 3:22 And **I have seen** that nothing is better than that man should be happy in his activities, for that is his lot. For who will bring him **to see** what will occur after him?

Book of Ecclesiastes 5:13 There is a grievous evil *which* **I have seen** under the sun: riches being hoarded by their owner to his hurt.

Book of Ecclesiastes 5:18 Here is what **I have seen** to be good and fitting: to eat, to drink and enjoy oneself in all one's labor in which he toils under the sun *during* the few years of his life which God has given him; for this is his reward.

Book of Ecclesiastes 6:1 There is an evil which **I have seen** under the sun and it is prevalent among men-

> Book of Ecclesiastes 7:15 **I have seen** everything during my lifetime of futility; there is a righteous man who perishes in his righteousness, and there is a wicked man who prolongs *his life* in his wickedness.
>
> Book of Ecclesiastes 8:9 All this **I have seen** and applied my mind to every deed that has been done under the sun wherein a man has exercised authority over *another* man to his hurt.
>
> Book of Ecclesiastes 8:10 So then, **I have seen** the wicked buried, those who used to go in and out from the holy place, and they are *soon* forgotten in the city where they did thus. This too is futility.
>
> Book of Ecclesiastes 10:5 There is an evil **I have seen** under the sun, like an error which goes forth from the ruler--
>
> Book of Ecclesiastes 10:7 **I have seen** slaves *riding* on horses and princes walking like slaves on the land.

The author concluded that, without God, science was just as meaningless as philosophy. Ellul pointed out that,

> For all their phenomenal devices, modern scientists find themselves faced with more and more insoluble enigmas. The more science advances, the more it discovers how much we don't know. So scientists today are not much better off than Qohelet when he declares that science amounts to a chasing after wind. Since we cannot grasp ultimate reality, each step we take shows us a vaster horizon. It shows how far we are from the boundary of possible knowledge. A chasing after wind.[149]

The Realistic Conclusion of the Author

As an apologetic against Natural Theology and philosophy, the author of the Book of Ecclesiastes put himself in the shoes of the typical humanist who assumes that he can find meaning and morals without God. He then proved that if we begin only with man, all meaning will be lost. Jacques Ellul's acerbic comments are insightful,

> What shall we say about all the writers who use the well-known rhetorical tactic of presenting the opinion of their adversaries as their own, in order to let the reader gradually discover how impossible that opinion is? Such a text requires a reading on a second level. The historian and the exegete never venture out onto the shifting ground. But I believe all of Book of Ecclesiastes requires

such a second-level interpretation. The thing that has most surprised me in the majority of Book of Ecclesiastes commentators was their extraordinary knowledge of Hebrew, coupled with the superficiality of their thought. Some of them know Hebrew better than the author of Book of Ecclesiastes himself; they know other ancient languages, Babylonian and Egyptian culture, and offer us an impressive bibliography. But their thinking is inconsistent and their theology empty. In brief, their utter lack of comprehension of the text stems from a total lack of interest and research into this area.[150]

Kidner saw the same apologetic thrust of Book of Ecclesiastes as Ellul saw.

> For so famous a thinker the search must naturally begin with wisdom, the quality most highly praised in his circle. But he says nothing of its first principle, the fear of the Lord, and we can assume that the wisdom he speaks of is (as his method demands) the best thinking that man can do on his own...So Qoheleth is taking wisdom with proper seriousness as a discipline concerned with ultimate questions, not simply a tool for getting things done.[151]

The author of the Book of Ecclesiastes demonstrates that both rationalism and empiricism, the two main epistemologies of Natural Theology, *cannot* discover meaning in life. In Ecc. 8:17 he concluded,

> man **cannot discover** the work which has been done under the sun. Even though mankind should seek laboriously, he **will not discover** it; and though the wise man should say, "I know," he **cannot discover** it.

The word מָצָא, translated "discover" in the passage above, is found 450 times in the Old Testament. When used of intellectual pursuits, it means to seek out the truth or meaning of something by diligently searching it out.

The author now states with absolute clarity that mankind הָאָדָם "cannot discover" the meaning of life. He repeats the word "cannot" in this verse and throughout the Book of Ecclesiastes to emphasis the absolute *inability* of man, apart from and independent of God, to discover truth, justice, morals, meaning or beauty. Dr. Walvoord comments,

> Solomon closed his treatment of the enigma of contradictions in divine retribution much as he had concluded his discussions on the significance of adversity and prosperity (7:1-14) and on the significance of righteousness and wisdom (7:15-29), namely, by acknowledging man's ignorance of God's ways (cf. 7:14b, 28a).

> After searching diligently (**I applied my mind**; cf. 1:17; 8:9) **to** gain **wisdom** and observing **man's** many activities, he concluded that man is ignorant of God's work (the phrases **all that God has done** and **what goes on under the sun** are synonymous). In emphatic terms, repeating the
> negative three times (v. 17) and the verb "comprehend" twice —**no one can comprehend . . . man cannot discover . . . he cannot really comprehend**—Solomon said that no one can understand God's ways (3:11; cf. Isa. 55:9; Rom. 11:33) **even if** he expended all his energies or were **wise** and claimed he could.[152]

Other commentators agree.

> The person who has to know everything, or who thinks he knows everything, is destined for disappointment in this world. Through many difficult days and sleepless nights, the Preacher applied himself diligently to the mysteries of life. He came to the conclusion that "man cannot find out the work that is done under the sun" (v. 17; see 3:11; 7:14, 24, 27–28). Perhaps we can solve a puzzle here and there, but no man or woman can comprehend the totality of things or explain all that God is doing. Historian Will Durant surveyed human history in his multivolume *Story of Civilization* and came to the conclusion that "our knowledge is a receding mirage in an expanding desert of ignorance."[153]

> He also relies only on the power of human reason, stating seven times that he "communed with my own heart." In essence, the writer consciously ignored special revelation to find out if life holds any meaning apart from insights provided by God. Given this framework, the book makes an important contribution. It resonates with the emptiness we all feel when alienated from God and demonstrates that apart from a personal relationship with Him, life is meaningless indeed. The Teacher's conclusions also remind us that, while nature does witness to God's existence, and human experience commends a moral lifestyle, only a living Word from God can pierce the darkness in which we live. Reason apart from revelation is powerless to provide mankind with valid spiritual hope.[154]

This is also stated in Ecc. 7:14, "man **cannot discover** anything *that will be* after him." Or, again in Ecc. 7:23-24,

> I tested all this through wisdom, *and* I said, "I will be wise," but it was far from me. What has been is remote and exceedingly mysterious. **Who can discover it?**

Dr. Michael Eaton comments, "*Who can discover?* is a rhetorical question. The answer is, generally speaking, no-one." [155] The standard reference works agree,

> Even Solomon with all his God-given wisdom could not understand all that exists, how God manages it, and what purposes He has in mind. He searched for the "reason [scheme] of things" but found no final answers to all his questions.[156]

> Who can find it out? Here the rhetorical question is the equivalent of a negative statement, "nobody can find it out." Find out is to discover by means of observing and reflecting. It is a key verb not only in the subsection to follow, but also in much of the remainder of the book. The intention of this question and that in 6.12 are not very different.[157]

> Simply stated, wisdom was beyond his human reach. *that which is* (מַה־שֶּׁהָיָה) refers to all things, "reality" according to Fox and Bezalel Porten's interpretation.[158]

The Key Phrases in the Book

There are phrases that are repeated that help us understand the Book of Ecclesiastes.
1. The writer used the phrase "under the sun" (תַּחַת הַשֶּׁמֶשׁ) twenty-nine times and the phrase "on the earth" (עַל־הָאָרֶץ) nine times. What was the author saying when he used these phrases?

> The society which Qoheleth addressed was an earthly- a secular one imprisoned by this world, Its view was bounded by the horizons of this world...Such a condition accounts for the frequent reoccurrence of the phrase *under the sun*. This was the area of concern for Qoheleth's audience and he chose to meet his audience on their own ground to reveal the vanity of a self-contained world, of a purely secular order.[159]

> Qoheleth writes from concealed premises, and his book is in reality a major work of apologetic...Its apparent worldliness is dictated by its aim: Qoheleth is addressing the general public whose view is bounded by the horizons of this world; he meets them on their own ground, and proceeds to convict them of its inherent vanity. This is further borne out by his characteristic expression "under the sun",

> by which he describes what the NT calls "the world...His book is in fact a critique of secularism and of secularized religion.[160]
>
> Qoheleth's phrase *under the sun*, which is a common expression in the Book of Ecclesiastes (twenty-nine times) and one that appears nowhere else in the OT. Qohelet thus restricts his remarks to terrestrial human activity and work.[161]
>
> If we look at the world without God...If with the atheist, we lay aside the idea of God...the mysteries of the world..remain...without solution.[162]

Leupold correctly sees that the words "under the sun" are the key to understanding the purpose, theme, and argument of the book.

> "under the sun" Few interpreters have understood it rightly; hardly any have applied it consistently. In it lies the corrective for the extravagant views that Koheleth seems to utter. It must always be borne in mind that the use of this phrase the author rules out all higher values and spiritual realities and employs only the resource and gifts this world offers. The use of this phrase is equivalent to drawing a horizontal line between earthly and heavenly realities and leaving out of consideration all that is above that line, that is to say, all higher values.[163]
>
> ...the correct appreciation of this phrase is one of the major safeguards of the message of the entire book. ...Each time the phrase occurs it is as though the author had said, "Let us for the sake of argument momentarily rule out higher things." ...The proper evaluation of this phrase removes a number of difficulties of interpretation. Time and again the author presents what would normally have been regarded as a very extreme utterance, if not rank heresy. But the presence of the little phrase: "under the sun" always says in effect, "What I claim is true if one deals with purely earthly values." [164]

2. The word "vanity" or "meaningless" (הֶבֶל) appears thirty-seven times and is intensified in the phrase, "Vanity of vanities!" or "Meaningless! Utterly Meaningless!" (הֲבֵל הֲבָלִים).

> The repletion of the word Hebel, like the repetition of the word "holy" in Isa, 6, intensifies the nature and comprehensiveness of the meaningless. Absolute meaningless, utter meaningless, of all things![165]

> 'All is vanity.' In the terms we use today the summing up could be: 'Utter futility...utter futility! The whole thing is futile.'[166]

> Hebel means "absurd" in the sense of meaningless.[167]

> ...the main point of the book is to demonstrate the futility of life apart from God (3:12; 12:13-14)."[168]

> ...the thesis which forms the subject of his treatise: "Vanity of vanities; All is vanity." Man's labor is profitless; nature and human life repeat themselves in monotonous succession, and all must fall ere long into oblivion. Nothing is new, nothing is lasting.[169]

> The book addresses two principle questions. The first issue is whether human experience is meaningful, controllable, and predictable. The author suggests that it is not. People are unable to put meaning into life, to discern a coherent pattern in their existence, or to control or even know what will happen to them. The only certainty in life is death...life has no meaning.[170]

> Eaton attempts to interpret the Book of Ecclesiastes as essentially an apologetic work. He observes that much of the book does not take God into account and is characterized by
> gloom and pessimism. He argues that when God is introduced, however, the "under-the-sun" terminology drops out and the Teacher speaks of the joy of man (2:25; 3:12; 5:18, 20; 9:7; 11:7–9) and the generosity of God (2:26; 3:13; 5:19). Like earlier Protestant scholars, he asserts the book to be evangelistic and apologetic: "What, then, is the purpose of the Book of Ecclesiastes? It is an essay in apologetics. It defends the life of faith in a generous God by pointing to the grimness of the alternative."[171]

Rejoice, Know, Remember

When we arrive at Ecc. 11:9, the fog suddenly disappears and the sun shines through the humanistic despair of the meaninglessness of life. Young people are suddenly *commanded* to *"Rejoice!"* Hengstenberg comments bear repeating,

> At a time when dark discontent had got the mastery over the minds of men, the Spirit of God exhorts them through the writer through this book to enjoy cheerfully divine gifts, admonishing them, however, in order to prevent carnal misunderstandings, to keep in view the account they will have one day to give to the Holy God, of all their doings: he warns them to remember their Creator, who

alone has the power to render their life prosperous and happy. In depicting the joylessness of the age, he shows how fitting it is to enter betimes on this path of self-surrender to the Creator, to consecrate even the bloom of youth to Him.[172]

The Hebrew word mf (rejoice) is a qal imperative and is thus emphatic.

> Cheerfulness, here, is not merely permitted: it is commanded, and represented as an essential element of piety.[173]

It appears for the first time in the Book of Ecclesiastes as the answer to the gloom and doom of existential meaninglessness. But, on what grounds are young people now commanded "Rejoice?" The author now gives a second command: *Know* that God will bring you to judgment for all these things.

The word יָדַע (know) is also a qal imperative. You must now *rejoice* because you *know* that your life has meaning and significance because it is important to *God*, who is the "measure of all things." Leupold explains,

> The "know thou" that follows is certainly to be more than a dead awareness. It must mean a knowledge that possesses and controls the heart. It implies that a man must actually reckon with this fact…The command implies simply: Do all your enjoying in such a way that you regulate it by the thought of the last judgment. For that the *last* judgment is referred to and not such visitations as may come when living already in this life is distinctly indicated by the article: God will bring you into *the* judgment" (bam-mishpat); not into various judgments, but into the one great judgment.[174]

If we begin with man as the "measure of all things," life will be meaningless. But the author now brings God, the Day of Judgment, and eternity into perspective. Since we are going to be held accountable by God for what we think, say and do, then they evidently have eternal significance and meaning!

But, on what grounds does God have the right to hold you accountable on the Day of Judgment? The third command is found in 12:1: "*Remember* now your Creator in the days of your youth." Kidner comments,

> At last we are ready—if we ever intend to be—to look beyond earthly vanities to God, who made us for Himself. The title Creator is well-chosen…to remember Him is no perfunctory or purely mental act: it is to drop our pretence of self-sufficiency and commit ourselves to Him.[175]

Once you interpret life from "*above* the sun" or heaven, then life makes sense. Leupold correctly points out,

> 12:1a gives the absolutely essential foundation of true joy: "And remember your Creator while you are young." To "remember" certainly implies more than to recall that there is a Creator. It surely means to let that remembrance shape conduct, for He is to be remembered as "Creator." As such, being the Author of our being, He has complete and absolute claims upon us. These we should acknowledge by our surrender to Him.[176]

What about all the liberals who claim that the Book of Ecclesiastes is only a skeptical work written by someone who had lost his faith in God? How can they handle the dramatic change of perspective from "under the sun" to "from heaven" that begun in 11:9? Leupold points out that the liberals simply dismiss the entire passage as a later interpolation.

> The more critical extreme criticism does not approve of the reference to the Creator here, being of the opinion that neither the thought nor the expression fits into the context (e.g. *Galling*). One might expect such a view as far as the critical approach is concerned, Since he is of the opinion that the entire book moves on a low level of thought, every touch of higher values must of necessity be deleted.[177]

The Book changes its tone and thrust once the author has demonstrated that life without God is life without meaning. He then gives the divine revelation that life has meaning because God gives it meaning.

The Theme of the Book of Ecclesiastes:

In the light of its apologetic purpose, Franz Delitzsch correctly saw that "the Book of Koheleth is...proof of the power of revealed religion."[178] Dr. Larry Richards hit the nail on the head when he said,

> (1) Twenty-nine times the writer used the phrase "under the sun" to define the limits he chose for his search. Only data which the senses can test and probe would be considered. Nothing from beyond this space-time universe would be considered. Nowhere in the Book of Ecclesiastes is Moses or Scripture or any form of revelation mentioned. Verse 13 of chapter 1 illustrates the limits that Solomon set for himself:

"I devoted myself to study and to explore by wisdom all that is done under heaven."

(2) The second key phrase appears seven times and reflects the same limitation. Solomon said that, "I thought in my heart" or "thought to myself" in reaching his conclusions. His methodology was empirical, but all the data he gathered was evaluated by the standard of his own intelligence. In this book Solomon recognized no higher wisdom than his own; he never looked beyond the conclusions unaided intelligence can draw. The third key word appears 34 times! It is "meaningless," a term translated in other versions as "vanity" or "emptiness." Solomon's determined effort to make sense of human life led him to the same tragic conclusion of many modern philosophers. Life is absurd. There is no meaning or purpose in human experience. There may be fleeting joys. But ultimately, above the doorway through which men are born into this world and the doorway through which they exit is written the same phrase: "Meaningless, meaningless, everything is meaningless."[179]

The well known commentators, Murphy and Huwiler, conclude,

> The book addresses two principle questions. The first issue is whether human experience is meaningful, controllable, and predictable. The author suggests that it is not. People are unable to put meaning into life, to discern a coherent pattern in their existence, or to control or even know what will happen to them. The only certainty in life is death...life has no meaning.[180]

The Outline of the Book

The structure of the book has remained a great controversy. The humanists rearrange the contents to fit their preconceived notions, even deleting the sections that do not fit with their fanciful interpretations. Literary critics show off their "genius" by using various visual aids such as weave patterns or geometric forms. Dr. Walvood comments,

> The view that the Book of Ecclesiastes consists of a combination of the contradictory views of three men (a skeptic, a writer of wisdom, and a believer)—a view common among critics at the beginning of the 20th century—has been largely abandoned. And the unity of the book, at least its thematic unity, has been generally affirmed. However, there is still no general consensus that the book follows a logical development or argument. Many scholars see the book as a

loose collection of wisdom sayings similar to the Book of Proverbs. Other scholars see a connected argument only in the first part of the book (Ecc. 1-6) and a collection of practical exhortations in the second part (chaps. 7-12).[181]

We found many outlines that are clear, concise, and useful. But we have chosen Walvood's and Zuck's outline as one of the best.

I. Introduction: The Futility of All Human Endeavor (1:1-11)
   A. Title (1:1)
   B. Theme: The futility of human effort (1:2)
   C. General support: The futility of human effort demonstrated from nature (1:3-11)
      1. Thesis: No ultimate profit in human labor (1:3)
      2. Proof: Ceaseless, wearisome rounds (1:4-11)
II. The Futility of Human Achievement Empirically Demonstrated (1:12-6:9)
   A. Personal observations on the futility of human achievement (1:12-2:17)
      1. Futility of human achievement shown by personal investigation (1:12-15)
      2. Futility of human wisdom (1:16-18)
      3. Futility of pleasure-seeking (2:1-11)
      4. Futility of a wise lifestyle (2:12-17)
   B. The futility of human labor empirically demonstrated (2:18-6:9)
      1. Labor's fruits may be squandered by someone else (2:18-26)
      2. Labor cannot alter God's immutable, inscrutable providence (3:1-4:3)
      3. Labor is often motivated by inappropriate incentives (4:4-16)
      4. Labor's fruits may sometimes not be enjoyed (5:1-6:9)
III. The Limitations of Human Wisdom Empirically Demonstrated (6:10-11:6)
   A. Introduction: Everything is immutably and inscrutably foreordained (6:10-12)
   B. Man cannot fathom the plan of God (chaps. 7-8)
      1. Man's ignorance of the significance of adversity and prosperity (7:1-14)
      2. Man's ignorance of the significance of righteousness and wisdom (7:15-29)
      3. Man's ignorance of the enigma of divine retribution (chap. 8)
   C. Man does not know what will happen (9:1-11:6)
      1. No one knows what will happen to him (9:1-10)
      2. No one knows whether his wisdom will succeed (9:11-10:11)
      3. Criticism is risky in view of one's ignorance of the future (10:12-20)
      4. Work diligently despite ignorance of the future (11:1-6)
IV. Conclusion: Live Joyously and Responsibly in the Fear of God (11:7-12:14)
   A. Call to live joyously and responsibly (11:7-12:7)
      1. Enjoy life because the darkness of death is coming (11:7-8)

    2.   Enjoy life in your youth, remembering that God will judge (11:9-10)
    3.   Live responsibly in your youth for old age and death are coming (12:1-7)
B.   Final advice in view of the futility of all human endeavor (12:8-14)
    1.   Reiteration of the theme: The futility of all human endeavor (12:8)
    2.   The peculiar authority of this book (12:9-12)
    3.   Final advice: Fear God and keep His commandments (12:13-14)[182]

Conclusion

In the light of the Book of Ecclesiastes, what should be our judgment of Natural Theology and Natural Law? If we follow the Word of God, then we must condemn them as apostate thinking. The Book of Ecclesiastes is the passage of full mention in Scripture that directly refutes the idea that man is the Origin of truth, justice, morals, meaning, and beauty, i.e. the measure of all things. God declares all forms of Naturalism as:

> Meaningless!
> Utterly Meaningless!
> Absolutely Meaningless!

Our rejection of Natural Law and Natural Theology is based on the three pillars of Job, Genesis, and Book of Ecclesiastes. Creation, Fall, and Redemption, which are the core beliefs of the biblical worldview, rest securely on these three books of the Bible. They are immutable and transcendent in truth and power.

To God alone belongs the glory!

Chapter Seven

Biblical Theism

Introduction

The first application of the biblical worldview is to question, "What is God?" Is God a he, she or it? Is God a personal being or an impersonal force? Are there more gods than one? Is God finite or infinite? Does God know nothing, anything, some things or everything? What can God do and not do?

Natural theologians assume that the attributes of God falls within the domain of philosophy, not the Bible. Autonomous man, starting only with himself, by himself, and through himself, apart from and independent of any Revelation, can discover God's attributes through human reason, experience, feelings or faith. Man does not really *need* the Bible *per se* to figure out God. "Just give us until tomorrow and we will figure God out," is their motto.

A History of Failure and Heresy

The history of Natural Theology is littered with fruitless attempts and numerous heresies. They have tried and utterly failed to identify and define God's attributes apart from and independent of Special Revelation. It seems that "tomorrow" never came!

In one debate, the natural theologian asserted, "We do not really need the Bible to discover the attributes of God. Philosophy can do a better job than simply sitting around reading Bible stories. The attributes of God is a subject far beyond and above the limited IQs of the primitive authors of the Bible. Scripture is OK for salvation, but deficient for such deep subjects."

I pointed out that the entire debate was dependent upon the Bible. "To discuss the attributes of God is stupid if we are not taking about the God of the Bible. Plato's "god" was an abstract principle and Aristotle believed in many gods. The philosophers could not agree on anything about the gods. Nothing! Zero! Nada!"

Bad Attitudes

This attitude comes out most clearly when the subject is whether or not "God" knows the future. The failure of philosophy is apparent the moment you point out that you must first define the word "God" before you debate what this "god" can and cannot know.

Most natural theologians begin by assuming a limited god. Thus they are arguing in a circle when they ask, "Does a limited god have unlimited knowledge?" They end where they began, a god created in their own image and likeness!

"Does God know the future?" cannot be answered until you first define who and what "God" is. To ask if "X" knows this or that is fruitless if you cannot first define "X."

Natural theologians spend their time arguing over whether "God" (not defined) can know if Pat will mow his lawn next Tuesday. If God does know the future, is Pat "truly free" not to mow his lawn next Tuesday? They assume that in order for Pat to be "truly free," God cannot and must not know what Pat will or will not do next Tuesday. In order for Pat to be "truly free," God must be "truly bound."

Of course, since natural theologians and philosophers begin with the classic Greek pagan concept of libertarian "free will," it does not surprise us in the least that they end up with a limited finite pagan god, much like Zeus. "Garbage in, garbage out" can be written over their abortive attempts to answer the question of whether God knows the future.

The Bible Reveals the Truth

In this chapter we will demonstrate that the Bible gives us final answers to such ultimate questions because it is God's self-disclosure of what He is, does and knows. God tells us in Scripture that He knows all of the future and that His knowledge is infallible and certain because the future is "fixed" by His eternal decrees.

A skeptical professor at a local university asked me one day, "Why did God allow evil?" I responded, "Because He wanted to."

This answer stunned him. No other Christian had given him such a blunt answer. He asked, "Where did you get that answer?" I responded, "In the Bible, Romans 9. Let us read it together." We sat side by side and read about the Potter and the clay. The skeptic had never read this passage before and he was visibly moved by the power of what Paul wrote.

"But what if I don't like the idea that God does what He wants to do?" "Then I will tell you something else that God may want to do: Cast you into hell for all eternity." "Are you saying that GOD determines whether or not I end up in hell?" "Yes. You are nothing more than a lump of ordinary clay and He can make you a vessel fitted for hell if He so chooses. Your destiny has already been decided by God before He created the universe." My answer utterly destroyed his self-confidence and pride. He had assumed that he determined what God could or could not do while the reverse was true.

"But, I am happy to tell you there is something else God may want to do." "What?" "God may want to open your heart to the gospel; give you repentance and faith; make you his child; forgive your sins through the merits of Christ and take you to heaven at death. God may decide to save you instead of damn you. But, don't make a mistake about this one point: Your destiny is in the hands of almighty God and you should go to Him for salvation."

The skeptic was shaken by these biblical truths. I do not know the end of that story as he did not come back to teach the next school year. I would not be surprised if he rushed up to me one day and shouted, "God did not want to damn me but to save me! I am now a Christian by His grace!"

An Essential Christian Doctrine

It is amazing that we must once again defend the omniscience of God since it is enshrined in every creed of Christianity since the first century. No historic creed has ever confessed that God is ignorant of the future.

The concept that the God of the Bible knows everything and that "everything" means EVERYTHING, including the future, is the historic Christian position. The idea that God does not know the future in its entirety has always been a tenet of every major heresy condemned by all churches. It is amazing to us that the doctrine of God's knowledge has once again been cast into controversy by the vaunted claims of natural theologians and philosophers who pretend to be "Evangelical Christians".

We must remember that heresies do not simply vanish into thin air once they are repudiated by the Christian Church. They reappear under a new name in the next generation. Thus the purity of the Gospel, like political freedom, is something that must be fought for in each new generation.

Is the question of whether God knows the future an "ivory tower" issue, such as how many angels can dance on the head of a pin? No. Our only confidence in the future turning out as God has promised in His Word is that He knows "end from the beginning." The basis of the inspiration of Scripture, the sufficiency of the atonement, and our hope of heaven all rely upon God's infinite knowledge of the future.

The Main Issues

The central issues and questions are as follows:

- Does God control the future or does the future control God?
- Does God's Will determine what man does or does man's will determine what God does?
- Does God respond to man's decisions or does man respond to God's decisions?
- Do God's decrees precede or follow man's actions?
- Who acts first and who follows?
- Is God a knee-jerk deity or the sovereign Lord of heaven and earth?
- Is there a place in space or time where we can draw a line and say that God's knowledge starts or ends there?
- Is the future a safe hiding place to escape the omniscient eye of the Maker of heaven and earth?

The only basis of our salvation and hope of heaven rests on the biblical and historic Christian view that God is infinite in all His attributes *including* His knowledge. Thus the salvation of your immortal soul depends on your answer to these questions because God's attributes stand or fall together. As we will see, once you deny that God knows the future, all the other "omni" attributes fall like dominos.

PART I
PRINCIPLES OF APPROACH

As we begin our study of the extent of the knowledge of God, we must emphasize that we are not referring to our knowledge of God. Instead, we are referring to God's knowledge of himself and His Creation.

The first question that comes to mind is *why* did God create the universe? Natural Theology has come up with all kinds of silly answers, such as "God was lonely." God has revealed in Scripture that He created the universe *for His glory*.

Everyone who is called by My name, And whom I have created for
My glory, Whom I have formed, even whom I have made. (Isa. 43:7)

כֹּל הַנִּקְרָא בִשְׁמִי וְלִכְבוֹדִי בְּרָאתִיו יְצַרְתִּיו אַף־עֲשִׂיתִיו׃

πάντας ὅσοι ἐπικέκληνται τῷ ὀνόματί μου ἐν γὰρ τῇ δόξῃ μου κατεσκεύασα αὐτὸν καὶ ἔπλασα καὶ ἐποίησα αὐτόν

Notice the three verbs "called," "created," and "made." The *Pulpit Commentary* points out,

> **I have created ... formed ... made him** (comp. ver. 1) "The three verbs describe the process of formation from the first rough cutting to the perfecting of the work" (Cheyne) The third verb would, perhaps, be best translated. "I have perfected," or "I have completed (him)" All three acts—creation, formation, and completion—are done by God for his own glory (comp. Prov. 16:4)[183]

Did God create the universe for His glory? Yes. Then He must have known and ordained that it would glorify Him in the future. This is also revealed in Isa. 43:21

The people whom I formed for Myself **will** declare My praise.

עַם־זוּ יָצַרְתִּי לִי תְּהִלָּתִי יְסַפֵּרוּ׃

λαόν μου ὃν περιεποιησάμην τὰς ἀρετάς μου διηγεῖσθαι

The text plainly states that the people whom He created for His glory "**WILL**" in the future declare the praise of God. This is also stated in Isa. 29:23.

> They **will** sanctify My name; Indeed, they **will** sanctify the Holy One
> of Jacob, And they **will** stand in awe of the God of Israel.

This future praise and worship is *predicted* because it is *foreknown*. Prediction without foreknowledge is not possible. Why would God create a universe for His glory if He did not know that it would in the future increase His acquired glory?

The question, "Does God know the past, the present, *and the future* of the Creation or is its future somehow 'closed' to God?" This needs to be analyzed further.

- Is God by His very nature *incapable* of knowing the future?
- Thus the problem lies in some *defect* within the nature or being of God?
- Are we saying that even if God really *wanted* to know the future that He is not *able* to do so?
- That even if God really, really tried hard with all of His power to know the future, He would fail because He was *not* powerful enough?
- Thus, He is not REALLY omnipotent as well as not really omniscient?

- What if other beings in the universe can know the future, doesn't this make God *less* in power and glory than those who can know the future?

Note: The Adventist "Open View" theologian, Richard Rice, argued that while the Seventh Day Adventist prophetess Ellen G. White knew the future, God did not. Was she therefore *greater* than God?

- What if the devil was capable of knowing and predicting the future?
- What about fortune tellers and psychics?
- What if they can predict the future?
- Wouldn't they be greater than a god who could not know the future?
- If we say that God could know the future, but that He decided not to know some of it, doesn't He have to know what He does not want to know before He can choose not to know it?
- Does He roll the dice and let Lady Luck decide what He can and cannot know in the future?
- If God chooses not to know the future of the universe, is this not a form of Deism?
- Is God so heartless and cruel that He does not *care* what will happen to His creatures in the future?
- Does this mean that God makes no plans or provision for the future pain and suffering of His creatures because they were *unforeseen* to Him?
- That He made no plans to overcome future evil because He did not know it would appear?
- What if we say that the problem is not in the nature of God but in the nature of the future itself?
- That the future of the universe is totally random and chance-based?
- That there are an infinite number of possible universes that could come into existence on the basis of pure chance and luck?
- That not even God can know which possible universe will actually exist?
- If we say that chance decides which possible universe happens, is not Chance the GOD above God?
- Or, do we say that God does know *some* of the future, but not all of it?
- That He knows the "main points" of the future, but not the dirty details?
- What if He decided not to know the future "free-will" decisions of angels and men?
- But isn't the universe so interconnected that what men and angels choose to do affects the rest of the universe?
- Is it really possible to isolate the decisions of men and angels from the motives, means, and results of those decisions?
- Are we really to believe that the decisions of men and angels do not cause ripples in the space/time continuum?
- That the effects of "free will" decisions do not set in motion domino affects all around them?

Beyond The Intellect of Man

By this time you realize that the question of whether God knows part of or all of the future by choice or nature is far beyond the finite capacity of man's limited mind. Thankfully, God is not silent! He has revealed the answer to us in Scripture.

False Assumptions Cloud the Issue

It is thus very important that anyone who is going to discuss this issue "come clean" about the presuppositions he is bringing to the discussion. The failure to reveal the hidden principles that contextualize theological issues results in much confusion and self-contradiction.

For this reason, we are going to lay out the principles that will guide us in our study of the extent of the knowledge of God. To make them absolutely clear, we will contrast our principles with those of Natural Theology.

The Biblical View	Natural Theology
God's self-disclosure in Holy Scripture is the only way we can have true knowledge of the extent of God's knowledge (1 Cor. 1:18–2:16)	Autonomous human reason unaided by divine revelation can discover the nature and extent of God's knowledge.
Thus the extent of God's knowledge is the sole domain of special revelation, and must be decided by Scripture alone (Sola Scriptura: 1 Cor. 4:6)	Thus the nature and extent of God's knowledge is **not** the sole domain of special revelation.
The only method by which we can ascertain the teaching of Scripture on God's knowledge is the historical, grammatical, exegesis of relevant texts.	Philosophic reflection and argumentation are more important than biblical exegesis.
We must distinguish between primary and secondary texts. "Primary texts" are those passages that have the extent of God's knowledge directly in view. "Secondary texts" are those passages that do not have God's knowledge in direct view but may by inference bear on the subject. Secondary texts must be interpreted in the light of the teaching found in the primary texts. Secondary texts cannot negate, overthrow or contradict the teaching found in primary texts.	There is no need to resort to such distinctions. Secondary texts are just as valid for proof texting as are primary texts.
The speculations of philosophy (Christian or pagan) that either contradict or go beyond the teaching of the primary biblical texts must be rejected as spurious. "Let God be true and every man a liar" (Rom.	The speculations of philosophy (Christian or pagan) may modify any aspect of divine revelation that is not in conformity to the opinions of the great philosophers.

3:4)	
Humanistic philosophy is built on the false doctrine of the autonomy of human reason. Scripture tells us that this is why philosophy never found God (1 Cor. 1:21)	If man is "truly free," then he must not be limited by divine revelation. Man's autonomous reason is sufficient to discover the nature and extent of God's knowledge.
The incomprehensibility of God means that we will not be able to explain fully the "whys" and "hows" of the knowledge of God.	We can modify any aspect of the nature and extent of God's knowledge that we cannot fully explain. If we cannot explain "how" God can know something, then we can deny that he knows it.

The chart above reveals the presuppositions that guide most discussions of God's knowledge. If one begins with the assumption of human autonomy, i.e. that fallen man can by his depraved and finite reason alone determine what God can or cannot know, then he will eventually end up reducing God to what *man* can or cannot know. In effect, he ends up making a god in his own image.

The "How" Questions
On the other hand, if we begin with God's self-disclosure in Scripture, then we can have the certitude of absolute truth. Does this mean that we will be able to explain fully to everyone's satisfaction "how" God can know such things as the future? No. Does this bother us? No. Since Scripture is the Revelation of an Infinite Mind and man has only a finite and depraved intellect, then the finite mind of man will not be capable of an infinite understanding of what is revealed by God. This is why Scripture tells us that many of the truths it reveals go beyond the finite capacity of the human mind to understand or explain (Rom. 11:13; Eph. 3:19; Phil. 4:7; etc.) Once you take the "mystery" out of Christianity, it becomes just another boring man-made religion.

Not a "Cop Out"
Is our appeal to the incomprehensibility of God a "cop out" - as some humanistic theologians have charged? No. The doctrine of the incomprehensibility of God is the clear teaching of Scripture, and we have yet to see any humanistic theologian attempt to refute the exegetical evidence for it.

Those who reject revealed truth because it does not "make sense" to them eventually end up in some form of atheism. Indeed, the highest conceit of man is to demand "how" and "why" Scripture is true before accepting it (Rom. 9:19–20) It reveals a commitment to the humanistic principle: *Man is the measure of all things—including God.*

Clark Pinnock As An Example
One example of this is Clark Pinnock. In the book, *Predestination and Free Will*, Pinnock uses the typical humanistic buzzwords and cliches such as "the demands of reason," etc., to indicate that *human reason unaided by Divine Revelation is the Origin of truth and meaning.*

Pinnock condemns those who appeal to the incomprehensibility of God (p. 143) Instead, he offers a "rational hypothesis to explain sovereignty and freedom" that will satisfy "the requirements of intelligence" (p.144) His "rational hypothesis" will "require us to rethink aspects of conventional or classical theism" (p. 144) But how do we know that his "rational hypothesis" is true? He refers to his "intuition" and "reason" that can "sense" what it is true (p.150) Thus, he is perfectly "rational" to say, "I stand against classical theism" (p. 151)[184]

This is how you can spot a humanist. He will use such phrases as:

> It seems to me that...
> I think that...
> It is only rational that...
> Intelligent people understand that...
> Before the Bar of Reason...
> My intuition tells me...
> Common sense tells me that...
> It is only reasonable that...
> I do not see how...
> It is not comprehensible to me that..., etc.

Biblical theologians do not accept the humanistic principle of human autonomy. They are committed to the opposite proposition: *God is the measure of all things—including man.* Without Divine Revelation, we can never know God.

> To the Law and to the Testimony! If they do not speak according to
> this Word, they have no dawn light. (Isa. 8:20)

With these brief words of introduction, we will now examine the Scriptures to see the self-disclosure of God concerning what He knows.

PART II
THE EXTENT OF GOD'S KNOWLEDGE

If the authors of Scripture, under Divine inspiration, believed that God's knowledge could not be limited by anything, but was absolute Omniscience, how would they communicate that idea to their readers? This question must be answered before we even pick up the Bible. If we do not answer it, then we do not know what to look for and what to expect to find in Scripture. The following list reveals what we need to look for when we open the Bible.

- The Vocabulary of God's Knowledge
- The Fact of God's Knowledge
- The Extent of God's Knowledge
- The Primary Texts
- The Secondary Texts

The Vocabulary of God's Knowledge

If the authors of Scripture believed that God has infinite knowledge of Himself and the world He created, we would expect to find them using those Hebrew and Greek words which would indicate to their readers that God is capable of understanding, comprehending, and knowledge. In other words, we would expect to find that the God revealed in Scripture is a God of knowledge, not a god of ignorance.

Old Testament Vocabulary

In the Hebrew language there are several words that are mean knowledge, understanding and comprehension.

A. The word יָדַע is the most common word for understanding and knowledge in the Hebrew Scriptures. It is used of man's knowledge and understanding hundreds of times. It is also applied to God to indicate that He has true knowledge of Himself and the world He created for His glory. (See: Exo. 3:7, 19–20; 2 Sam. 7:20; 1 Kings 8:39; Job 23:10; Psa. 31:7, 40:9, 69:5, Jer. 1:5, etc.)

B. The word בִּין is used to describe God's knowledge in Job 11:11, 28:23; Psa. 5:1, 33:15, 139:2. The wicked deny that God "takes notice" of their sin in Psa. 94:7b.
"Neither shall the God of Jacob *notice it*": לֹא־יָבִין אֱלֹהֵי יַעֲקֹב

C. The word דֵּעָה is used in 1 Sam. 2:3 in the phrase, "Yahweh is a God of knowledge" (אֵל דֵּעוֹת יְהוָה) The wicked used this word when questioning whether God knows anything. "How doth God know?" (Psa. 73:11a) אֵיכָה יָדַע־אֵל :

D. The word חָזָה is used in Psa. 11:4,7 and Psa. 17:2 to indicate that God "sees" all things.

E. Another word for "consider," "behold," and "see" is רָאָה. It is applied to God's knowledge in Gen. 29:32, 31:42; Exo. 3:7, 4:31; Psa. 9:14, 10:11, 25:18,19, 84:10, 119:153, 159. The wicked deny in Psa. 94:7 that God really sees anything.
"Yet they say, YHWH *shall not see*". יֹאמְרוּ לֹא יִרְאֶה־יָּהּ

F. In Job 34:25, we told that God "takes knowledge of" (יַכִּיר) the works of man.

G. The Psalmist declared in Psa. 147:5, "His understanding is infinite." רַב־כֹּחַ לִתְבוּנָתוֹ אֵין מִסְפָּר :

H. The biblical authors referred to "the eyes" of God to indicate that He sees all things. Nothing escapes His omniscient sight.

> For the eyes of YHWH run to and fro throughout the whole earth. (2 Chron. 16:9)

> For my eyes are upon all their ways; they are not hid from my face, neither is their iniquity concealed from my eyes. (Jer. 16:17)

> The eyes of YHWH, which run to and fro throughout the whole earth. (Zech. 4:10)

The authors of the Hebrew Scriptures used every word in their vocabulary to affirm that God has knowledge. The only ones who deny or question this are the wicked.

New Testament Vocabulary

When we turn to the New Testament Hebrew Scriptures, the same pattern is followed. The common Greek words for knowledge, understanding, and comprehension are applied to God without hesitation.

A. The common Greek verb for "knowing" is γινώσκω. It is applied to God in Lk. 16:15; John 10:15; 1 Cor. 3:20; Gal. 4:9; 2 Thess. 2:19; 1 Thess. 3:20 and 1 John 3:20.
B. The noun γνῶσις is used for God's knowledge in Rom. 11:33, where we are told that God's γνῶσις is incomprehensible.
C. In Acts 15:18, God's knowledge (γνωστα) is described as eternal (απο αἰῶνος)
D. Two different Greek words are used in the New Testament to signify God's foreknowledge of the future. The noun πρόγνωσίς (foreknowledge) is used in Acts 2:23 and 1 Pet. 1:2. The verb προγινώσκω (to foreknow) is used in Rom. 8:29; 11:2 and 1 Pet. 1:20.
E. In Greek, the word for intellect or mind is νοῦς. It is used of God in Rom. 11:34 and 1 Cor. 2:16.
F. The Greek verb οἶδα means "to know" and is used of God in 2 Cor. 11:11; 12:3 and 2 Pet. 2:9.
G. The noetic sense of "seeing" is expressed by the Greek word βλέπω and is used in Mat. 6:6 to refer to God's seeing us wherever we are.
H. The authors of the New Testament, like the authors of the Old Testament, used every word that existed in the language of their day to convey the idea that God knows Himself and the world He made without limitation.

The Fact of God's Knowledge

The nouns and verbs used for God's knowledge in both the Old and New Testaments are sufficient to establish its factuality beyond all doubt. This doctrine played a significant role in the life of the believer. In her prayer, Hannah states in a matter of fact manner,

> "YHWH is a God of knowledges."
> (1 Sam. 2:3)
>
> אֵל דֵּעוֹת יְהוָה
> θεὸς γνώσεων κύριος

Notice that in both the Hebrew (דֵּעוֹת) and the Greek (γνώσεων) text, the word "knowledge" is actually in the plural. This indicates that Yahweh is the God of "*knowledges;*" i.e. all knowledge. Notice also that the Septuagint emphasizes that God is the Sovereign Lord (κύριος) of all knowledge.

Hanah argues in her prayer that because God is "a God of knowledges," there is no GOD like Him (v. 2.) To her the very idea that God was ignorant of anything including the future acts of angels and men would have been blasphemous. How could He judge the world if He were ignorant? (vs. 3–10)

> "*For* Jehovah is a God of omniscience." The plural "knowledges" (דֵּעוֹת) indicates that God knows and is acquainted with every individual thing, that, as He is raised above every created thing, and thus present with all things and creatures, so they are present and known to Him; and thus it expresses the thought that the concrete

> For Jehovah hears such words; He is *"a God of knowledge"* (*Deus scientiarum*), a God who sees and knows every single thing. The plural דֵּעוֹת has an Intensive signification. [186]
>
> In ver. 3 she appeals to God's omniscience, "for Jehovah is a God of knowledges," the pl. being intensive, and signifying every kind of knowledge. [187]

Throughout the Psalms, God is addressed as the One who knows all things. In Psa. 139 David said in verse 2,

> You know when I sit down and when I rise up; You understand my thoughts from afar.

אַתָּה יָדַעְתָּ שִׁבְתִּי וְקוּמִי בַּנְתָּה לְרֵעִי מֵרָחוֹק׃

In verse 6, David concludes,

> Such knowledge is too wonderful for me;
> It is too high, I cannot attain to it.

[פְּלִיאָה] דַעַת מִמֶּנִּי נִשְׂגְּבָה לֹא־אוּכַל לָהּ׃

ἐθαυμαστώθη ἡ γνῶσίς σου ἐξ ἐμοῦ ἐκραταιώθη
οὐ μὴ δύνωμαι πρὸς αὐτήν

Several comments are in order.

First, God's knowledge is directly in view. Thus, this is a primary passage of full mention on the subject of the extent of God's knowledge.

Second, this passage is very significant because the focus is on God's knowledge of the future. BEFORE an idea or a word proceeds from man, God knows all about it. Walvoord and Zuck correctly point this out.

> The Lord (**You** is emphatic in Heb.; cf. v. 13) knew every move he made; the two opposites of sitting and rising represent all his

> actions (this is a figure of speech known as a merism; cf. vv. 3, 8) God knew not only David's actions; He also knew his motivations (**thoughts**; cf. v. 17) **Afar evidently refers not to space but to time.** [188]
>
> The daily activities of the psalmist were also thoroughly **familiar** to the Lord. The opposites of **going out** in the morning and **lying down** at night represent the whole day's activities (another merism; cf. vv. 2, 8) But the one sample that epitomizes God's omniscience is in verse 4. Before the psalmist could frame **a word on** his **tongue,** the LORD was thoroughly familiar with what he was about to say. (The Heb. for "word" is millâh and the similar-sounding word for **completely** is kūllāḥ) [189]

Third, the extent of it is revealed by contrasting it with the limited mind of man. God's knowledge is "too high", i.e. beyond the capacity of man's finite mind to understand. David's initial response to this staggering knowledge was that he was troubled. Like many who respond to the fact of God's omniscience, he thought it was confining, that God had besieged him and cupped His **hand** over him.

Moreover, this kind of **knowledge** was out of David's control—it was **too wonderful for** him. The word "wonderful" is in the emphatic position, at the beginning of the sentence. On the meaning of "wonderful" as "extraordinary or surpassing," In other words divine omniscience is **too** high for humans to comprehend (also cf. comments on 139:14)

Even though David could not explain "how" or "why" God knows all things, this did not make the doctrine odious to him. Instead, it caused David to fall at God's feet in worship, awe, and praise.

The New Testament is just as committed to the fact of God being a God of all knowledges. When Paul encountered a situation which exceeded his capacity to understand, he would rest in the fact that ὁ θεὸς οἶδεν "*God knows*" (2 Cor. 12:3) Paul makes it clear that God knows even when we do not. See also 2 Cor. 11:11 where Paul appeals to the fact that ὁ θεὸς οἶδεν "God knows."

The Attributes of God's Knowledge

The attributes of God's knowledge are directly addressed in both Testaments. Instead of sitting in a dark room trying to figure out what God can or cannot know by our own limited intelligence, why not turn to the light of Scripture?

Perfect in Knowledge

First, God's knowledge is תָּמִים *"perfect"* according to Job 37:16.

> The wondrous works of *Him who is perfect in knowledge.*
>
> הֲתֵדַע עַל־מִפְלְשֵׂי־עָב מִפְלְאוֹת תְּמִים דֵּעִים׃

The perfection of God's knowledge means that it is not deficient in anything for

> he who is perfect is not lacking in anything.
> τέλειοι καὶ ὁλόκληροι ἐν μηδενὶ λειπόμενοι
> (James 1:4)

God's knowledge is thus *complete* and *nothing need be added to it.* This means that God's knowledge is *self-existent* and *independent* of anything outside of His own divine nature. He does not need to use logic or the scientific method to discover Truth. His knowledge is one, unified, single, perfect vision of all things from the end to the beginning of the Creation from and to all eternity. Paul tells us that God is not in need of anything because He is perfect in every respect (Acts 17:25)

He Does Not Need Our Information

Because God's knowledge is perfect, He is not in need of any information from us.

> Can anyone teach God knowledge, Seeing He judgeth those that are high? (Job 21:22)
>
> הַלְאֵל יְלַמֶּד־דָּעַת וְהוּא רָמִים יִשְׁפּוֹט׃
>
> πότερον οὐχὶ ὁ κύριός ἐστιν ὁ διδάσκων
> σύνεσιν καὶ ἐπιστήμην αὐτὸς δὲ φόνους
> διακρινεῖ

In order for God to judge man on the Day of Judgment, He has to have perfect knowledge of all things. This is why God is not in need of someone to give Him counsel, which is information and advice (Rom. 11:34)

> Who has known the mind of the Lord?
> Τίς γὰρ ἔγνω νοῦν κυρίου;
>
> Who has become his adviser?
> ἢ τίς σύμβουλος αὐτοῦ ἐγένετο;

It Does Not Increase or Decrease

Since His knowledge is perfect, it cannot increase or decrease. It is complete and whole. He does not have to investigate to find out anything.

He sees iniquity *without investigation.*
(Job 11:11)

וַיַּרְא־אָוֶן וְלֹא יִתְבּוֹנָן׃

For *He does not have to wait for the results of a judicial investigation* to regard a man.(Translation K&D, Job II:255–256) (Job. 34:23)

כִּי לֹא עַל־אִישׁ יָשִׂים עוֹד לַהֲלֹךְ אֶל־אֵל בַּמִּשְׁפָּט׃

He will break mighty men *without inquiry* and puts others in their place. (Job 34:24)

יָרֹעַ כַּבִּירִים לֹא־חֵקֶר וַיַּעֲמֵד אֲחֵרִים תַּחְתָּם׃

But don't we have to tell God in prayer what we need? If we don't tell Him, how will He know what we need or want? The purpose of prayer is not to inform God of your needs. He knows what you need and what you are going to say BEFORE you say it. Prayer is for our benefit, not God's information.

Your *Father knows* what you need *before you ask him.* (Mat. 6:8)

οἶδεν γὰρ ὁ πατὴρ ὑμῶν ὧν χρείαν ἔχετε <u>πρὸ τοῦ ὑμᾶς αἰτῆσαι αὐτόν</u>

Jamieson, Fausset, and Brown comment:

> [God] needs not to be *informed* of our wants, any more than to be *roused* to attend to them by our incessant speaking. What a view of God is here given, in sharp contrast with the gods of the heathen![190]

It Is Infinite

Since His knowledge is perfect, it is no surprise to us to find that it is *infinite* according to Psa. 147:5.

His understanding is *infinite.*

לִתְבוּנָתוֹ אֵין מִסְפָּר

Being "infinite" means that we cannot place any limitations on His knowledge. There is no "cutting off" place where we can say that His knowledge begins or ends.

It Is Eternal

Since it is infinite, God's knowledge is *eternal.* In Acts 15:18, James reminded the counsel that the inclusion of the Gentiles into the church did not catch God by surprise. God had known (γνωστα) everything from eternity (ἀπ' αἰῶνος)

> Nothing could be more germane to St. James's argument than thus to show from the words of Amos that God's present purpose of taking the Gentiles to be his people was, like all his other works, formed **from the beginning of the** world (comp. Eph. 1:9, 10; 3:5, 6; 2 Tim. 1:9, etc.) [191]

God does not have to wait until the end to see what will happen like we do. He knows "the end from the beginning" (Isa. 46:10) A. T. Robertson comments,

> There is no occasion for surprise in the story of God's dealings with the Gentiles as told by Barnabas and Paul. God's eternal purpose of grace includes all who call upon his name in every land and people (Isa. 2:1; Mic. 4:1) This larger and richer purpose and plan of God was one of the mysteries which Paul will unfold in the future (Rom. 16:25; Eph. 3:9) James sees it clearly now. God is making it known (ποιων ταυτα γνωστα [poiōn tauta gnōsta])[192]

It Is Immutable

Being perfect, infinite and eternal, God's knowledge is *immutable* (Mal. 3:6; James 1:17) Because it is immutable, God cannot make a mistake; He cannot lie; He does not change His mind.

> God is not a man, that he should lie; neither the son of man, that he should change His mind: hath he said, and shall be not do it? Or hath he spoken, and shall he not make it good?
> (Num. 23:19)

> And also the Strength of Israel will not lie nor repent: for he is not a man, that he should change His mind. (1 Sam. 15:29)

These Old Testament passages teach us a great truth we can live by and die by. D. A. Carson emphasizes that,

> V29 offers us a description of God as one who *does not lie* (unlike Saul!) nor *change his mind.* God may in mercy delay punishment, or give men and women opportunities to change their minds in repentance; but he does not change his mind about his purposes and plans. God had determined that the future of Israel would be in the hands of a *better* man, David (28) Later readers, no doubt in

> very different circumstances, could take comfort and assurance from the fact that their God made them promises, and his promises were absolutely true and certain.[193]

The New Testament is just as clear on this point.

> The hope of eternal life that God, *who cannot lie*, promised before the world began. (Tit. 1:2)

> In the same way, when God wanted to make the *unchangeable character of his purpose* perfectly clear to the heirs of his promise, he guaranteed it with an oath so that by these two *unchangeable* things, in which it is *impossible for God to prove false*, we who have taken refuge in him might have a strong encouragement to take hold of the hope set before us. (Heb. 6:17–18)

Several comments should be made on the passages above. First, the authors of Scripture repeatedly emphasize that God is not a man and thus His knowledge is not limited or flawed as man's knowledge. This is stressed in other passages as well.

> But YHWH said unto Samuel, "Do not look on his countenance, or on the height of his stature; because I have refused him: for *YHWH does not set as a man sees; for a man looks on the outward appearance, but YHWH looks on the heart.* (1 Sam. 16:7)

> Do You have eyes of flesh? or do You see as man sees? Are Your days as the days of man? Are Your years as man's days, that You have to inquire after my iniquity, and search after my sin? (Job 10:4–7)

> For My thoughts are not your thoughts, neither are your ways My ways, saith YHWH. For as the heavens are higher than the earth, so are My ways higher than your ways, and My thoughts than your thoughts (Isa. 55:8–9)

The main reason why humanists are always trying to limit the knowledge of God is to bring God down to the level of man. They have forgotten God's stern rebuke,

> You thought that I was altogether such a one as yourself: But I will reprove you, and set them in order before your eyes. (Psa. 50:21)

Since God's knowledge is absolute and unlimited, He is incapable of lying. Notice that Heb. 6:17–18 clearly links together God's immutability and omniscience in such a way that you cannot have one without the other. Thus God's knowledge is *infallible* and cannot err in any sense.

It Is Clear, Distinct, Certain, and Orderly

Since God's knowledge is perfect in all aspects, it is *clear* instead of unclear, *distinct* instead of vague, *certain* instead of uncertain, and *orderly* instead of chaotic. Why?

> For God is not *a God* of confusion but of harmony/peace.
> (1 Cor. 14:33)
>
> οὐ γάρ ἐστιν ἀκαταστασίας ὁ θεὸς ἀλλὰ εἰρήνης.

It Is Infallible

Is God's knowledge an "iffy" thing that may or may not pan out as the future unfolds? Does the *infallibility* of God's knowledge mean that the future must *necessarily* happen as He knows it? In order for the future *necessarily* to happen as God sees it, must it be *certain, fixed, preordained and predetermined* from eternity? Is anything left to luck or chance?

How can we answer such deep questions? *Sola Scriptura*! Scripture alone can give us God's answers to such questions. Why?

First, human reason is not adequate to come up with an answer, because the world with all its philosophic reasoning and logic never knew the true God according to 1 Cor. 1:21.

> the world through its wisdom did not know God.
>
> οὐκ ἔγνω ὁ κόσμος διὰ τῆς σοφίας τὸν θεόν

The word "not" (οὐκ) is taken out of its normal word order and placed first in the phrase in order to make it emphatic that the world through human philosophy NEVER, EVER knew the true God. Jamieson, Fassuet, and Brown are right on target with their comment.

> The deistic theory that man can by the light of nature discover his duty to God, is disproved by the fact that man *has* never discovered it without revelation. All the stars and moon cannot make it day; that is the prerogative of the sun. Nor can nature's highest gifts make the moral day arise; that is the office of Christ. [194]

The classic Evangelical commentators agree with them.

> Christians must abandon human philosophy's appeal to rationalism and rely on revelation if we are to resolve our differences and maintain our essential unity in Christ. [195]

> All the valued learning of this world was confounded, baffled, and eclipsed, by the Christian revelation and the glorious triumphs of the cross. The heathen politicians and philosophers, the Jewish rabbis and doctors, the curious searchers into the secrets of nature,

were all posed and put to a nonplus. This scheme lay out of the reach of the deepest statesmen and philosophers, and the greatest pretenders to learning both among the Jews and Greeks. When God would save the world, he took a way by himself; and good reason, for *the world by wisdom knew not God,* v. 21. All the boasted science of the heathen world did not, could not, effectually bring home the world to God. In spite of all their wisdom, ignorance still prevailed, iniquity still abounded. Men were puffed up by their imaginary knowledge, and rather further alienated from God.[196]

In spite of the highly sophisticated discussion of natural theology by the Stoics and Epicureans on 'the nature of the gods', that intellectual world did not know God.[197]

Paul quoted Isaiah 29:14 in 1 Corinthians 1:19, proving that God has written a big "0—Failure!" —over the wisdom of men. In his address on Mars' Hill, Paul dared to tell the philosophers that Greek and Roman history were but "times of this ignorance" (Acts 17:30)[198]

These words might be written as an epitaph on the tomb of ancient philosophy, and of modern philosophy and science so far as it assumes an anti-Christian form (Luke 10:21) Human wisdom, when it relies solely on itself, may "feel after God," but hardly find him (Acts. 17:26, 27)[199]

With all its "wisdom," the world was not able to find God or salvation. When we trace human history, we discover a record of man gaining more and more knowledge, but less and less real wisdom, especially about spiritual matters. Review Rom. 1:18–32 to see how the world turned from God. God's plan was so simple and unique that it seemed to be foolishness to the world! God saves those who believe what He says about His Son.[200]

Knew not God (οὐκ ἔγνω [ouk egnō]) Failed to know, second aorist (effective) active indicative of γινωσκω [ginōskō], solemn dirge of doom on both Greek philosophy and Jewish theology that failed to know God. Has modern philosophy done better? There is today even a godless theology (Humanism) "Now that God's wisdom has reduced the self-wise world to ignorance" (Findlay)[201]

Second, Paul warns us that speculative theology, in which you try to figure out God by your own intellect instead of going to Scripture, produces nothing but pride and conceit.

> Now these things, brethren, I have in a figure transferred to myself
> and Apollos for your sakes; that in us ye might learn, "*Do not go
> beyond what is Written,*" that no one of you should be puffed up for
> the one against the other. (1 Cor. 4:6)
>
> Ταῦτα δέ, ἀδελφοί, μετεσχημάτισα εἰς ἐμαυτὸν καὶ Ἀπολλῶν δια
> ὑμᾶς, ἵνα ἐν ἡμῖν μάθητε τὸ Μὴ ὑπὲρ ἃ γέγραπται, ἵνα μὴ εἷς ὑπὲρ
> τοῦ ἑνὸς φυσιοῦσθε κατὰ τοῦ ἑτέρου.

If the authors of Scripture believed that the future, including the decisions and works of man, is already *fixed, certain, preordained* and *predetermined,* and that at the same time, man is *accountable* to God for his thoughts, words and deeds, how would they convey that idea to their readers? By what vocabulary? By what exegesis?

What if we find that they held to the *certainty* and *necessity* of the future and that man was *accountable* at the same time? Just because pagan Greek philosophy taught that man is not accountable if his actions are predetermined, are we to throw the Bible in the trash and follow the philosophers instead of Scripture?

Back to the Bible

To answer the questions stated above, all we have to find is just *one* passage in the Bible where the acts of a man were both predetermined and accountable at the same time. Why? If Divine predetermination and human accountability are both revealed in Scripture, then in principle both truths are *compatible*; i.e. *not contradictory.*

This is why the historic Christian view is sometimes called the "compatibility" view and the contrary views are called the "contradictory" views. If the authors of Scripture believed and taught that Divine predetermination and human accountability were compatible truths because God understood how they were compatible even though man does not, on what grounds can those who claim to be Christians state that the two doctrines are incompatible and thus inherently contradictory to God as well as man? On what grounds do they limit God's ability to understand what He has revealed in Scripture?

First, did the authors of Scripture ever describe the future, including the acts of man as "certain," "necessary," "determined," "fixed," "foreordained" or "appointed?" Did they ever say that the future "must" happen? Is the future "certain?" Or is it up to the roll of the dice in a cosmic crap game?

The Exodus Prediction

> And He said unto Abram, *Know for certain* that your seed *hall* be
> sojourners in a land that is not theirs, and they *shall* serve them;
> and they *shall* afflict them four hundred years; And also that nation,
> whom they shall serve, I *will judge:* and afterward they *shall* come
> out with great substance. (Gen. 15:13–14)

The passage above is remarkable in that it gathers all the decisions and acts of all the people involved in the move to Egypt, the enslavement and oppression of the Jews, the coming of Moses and the events leading to the Exodus. God told Abraham that all these things were "certain" to happen. The use of "shall" and "will" instead of "may" or "might" reveals that all these future things would happen just as God said they would.

If these future events were *certain* to happen, then Abraham's knowledge of them would likewise be *certain.* You cannot have certain knowledge of that which is fundamentally uncertain. Thus God told Abraham that he could count on this prediction of future events coming true.

The Story of Joseph

That this is what Moses understood is clear from his account of Joseph in Genesis chapters 38–50. The decision of his brothers to beat him and then sell him into slavery, the slave masters taking him to Egypt instead of another country, the false rape charge made by Potiphar's wife, his prison experience, his rise to Pharaoh's side and the decision of Jacob to move to Egypt; were all these decisions and acts of all the people involved autonomous; i.e. were they independent of God? Can we really describe them in terms of mere coincidence and luck? Was Joseph just unlucky when he experienced bad things and lucky when he experienced good things? Was it merely by chance that the jailer liked him? Was it really a mere coincidence that Pharaoh made him second to himself? Instead of sitting around speculating, let us turn to the testimony of Joseph to see what he believed.

> But as for you, you thought to do evil against me; *but God meant it unto good*, to bring to pass, as *it is* this day, to save many people alive. (Gen. 50:20)

Can words be clearer? Did not Joseph believe that God planned *everything* including what his brothers did to him in order to save many people from starvation? Did he believe that *everything* that happened to him happened *necessarily as part of God's plan?* Why did Potiphar like Joseph? Moses tells us,

> And his master saw that YHWH was with him, and that YHWH *caused* all that he did to prosper in his hand. (Gen. 39:3)

> עֹשֶׂה יְהוָה מַצְלִיחַ בְּיָדוֹ׃ וַיַּרְא אֲדֹנָיו כִּי יְהוָה אִתּוֹ וְכֹל אֲשֶׁר־הוּא

> ᾔδει δὲ ὁ κύριος αὐτοῦ ὅτι κύριος μετ' αὐτοῦ καὶ ὅσα ἂν ποιῇ κύριος εὐοδοῖ ἐν ταῖς χερσὶν αὐτοῦ

According to Moses, "Yahweh caused" (Heb. יְהוָה מַצְלִיחַ Gk. ποιῇ κύριος) everything Joseph did to prosper. Joseph believed that God was in control of the entire situation.

But did the belief that God planned the whole thing in any way lessen, negate or reduce the responsibility of all those involved? No. The brothers admitted that their decisions and actions that led to selling Joseph into slavery were wicked and evil. They knew that they were responsible for what they did. They knew that they deserved punishment.

> So shall you say unto Joseph, Forgive, I pray you now, *the transgression of your brothers, and their sin, for what they did unto you was evil.* And now, we beg you, forgive the transgression of the servants of the God of your father. And Joseph wept as they spoke unto him. (Gen. 50:17)

Joseph agreed that they had intended to do evil to him. BUT everything they did was also part of a bigger picture, the sovereign purpose and plan of God. As Joseph looked back at his life with all its ups and downs, he saw the hand of God behind it all.

David and the Philistines

> And David inquired of YHWH, saying, "Shall I go up against the Philistines? *Will You deliver them into my hand?*" And YHWH said unto David, "Go up; for *I will certainly deliver* the Philistines into thy hand." (2 Sam. 5:19)

What was going to happen when David entered into battle with the Philistines? Was there the possibility that the Philistines would win and David would lose? Was it only up to the decisions of all the men involved and to Lady Luck as to who would decide to run away in defeat? Could things turn out in any different way? Or was the future battle "certain" to happen just as God said, because God would see to it? Did God interfere in the affairs of men to determine who would win the battle? Was the final outcome of the battle already "certain" before David left camp? The passage is quite clear that David's victory was already certain and "in the bag" before he picked up his spear.

Death Awaits You

> YHWH had showed me that he *shall certainly die.* (2 Kings 8:10)

Hazael wanted to know if he would in the future recover from his illness. He asked the prophet of YHWH and was told that he "shall certainly die." But was this already set in stone? Could not something happen that would heal Hazael? Or was his death already *certain*? It was as certain as God lives.

The Babylonian Captivity

> The king of Babylon shall *certainly* come and destroy this land, and shall cause to cease from thence man and beast. (Jer. 36:29)

> Thus says YHWH, "This city shall *certainly* be given into the hand of the army of the king of Babylon, and he shall take it. (Jer. 38:3)

> But seek not Beth-el, nor enter into Gilgal, and pass not to Beer-sheba: for Gilgal shall *certainly* go into captivity, and Beth-el *shall come* to nought. (Amos 5:5)

> For thus Amos said, "Jeroboam *shall die* by the sword, and Israel shall *certainly* be led away captive out of their own land. (Amos 7:11)

> Israel shall *certainly* go into captivity. (Amos 7:17)

Were the invasion of Babylon and the captivity *certain* to happen in the future? Couldn't the king suddenly decide not to invade Israel? Wasn't there the possibility that Israel would defeat the Babylonians? No. It was already *certain* before the Babylonians climbed into their chariots.

Would Jeremiah Die?

> For I will *certainly* deliver you, and you *shall not* fall by the sword. (Jer. 39:18)

How could God guarantee Jeremiah that the future would turn out as He said it would? Was it really "certain" and already "fixed" that Jeremiah would not die? Could some Babylonian soldier suddenly decide to run his sword through Jeremiah? No. God would interfere and see to it that Jeremiah would not be harmed.

Future Events Already Appointed

> For the vision is yet for the appointed time; It hastens toward the goal, and it will not fail. Though it tarries, wait for it; For it will certainly come, it will not delay. (Hab. 2:3)

Since the captivity has been "appointed" by God, it will *certainly* come to pass in the future in exactly the way God said it would happen. If future events could turn out differently than the vision stated, then God would be guilty of telling *a lie.*

Are Future Events Fixed?

> He answered them, "It is not for you to know what times or seasons *the Father has fixed* by His own authority. (Acts 1:7)

> εἶπεν δὲ πρὸς αὐτούς, Οὐχ ὑμῶν ἐστιν γνῶναι χρόνους ἢ καιροὺς οὓς ὁ πατὴρ ἔθετο ἐν τῇ ἰδίᾳ ἐξουσίᾳ

The disciples asked Jesus if the Old Testament prophecy of a future restoration of Israel was to be fulfilled at that time.

> And so when they had come together, they were asking Him, saying, "Lord, is it at this time You are restoring the kingdom to Israel?" (Acts 1:6)

Οἱ μὲν οὖν συνελθόντες ἠρώτων αὐτὸν λέγοντες, Κύριε, εἰ ἐν τῷ χρόνῳ τούτῳ ἀποκαθιστάνεις τὴν βασιλείαν τῷ Ἰσραήλ?

Jesus answered that the timing of the fulfillment of a future restoration of Israel was none of their business and He was not going to reveal them the timing of that prophecy. But lest they give up hope that Israel would be restored, He went on to state that the future was already been "fixed" by the Father. Thus the "times and seasons" in focus were *future* χρόνους ἢ καιροὺς and cannot be limited to the present situation as some heretics have proposed.

The word ἔθετο is a second aorist middle indicative of τίθημι and emphasizes the sovereignty of the Father over the *future* times and seasons. The standard Greek Lexicons document that the word is used in several senses in secular and biblical literature. One of its clear meanings is to fix, set in place, destine, appoint or pre-determine something or someone by your own authority.

> Friberg: God's designed self-activity *to arrange,*
> *establish, fix* (AC 1.7; 2C 5.19; 1T 1.12)
> UBS: appoint, destine; arrange.
> Thayer: *to set, fix, establish* (Latin *statuo*)
> BDAG: mid. w. acc. *fix, establish, set.*

In terms of how Luke uses the word when man "fixes" something or someone, in Acts 12:4, King Herod by his own authority "fixed" Peter in prison. In Acts 19:21, Paul "fixed" his resolve to go to Jerusalem with such firmness that no one could dissuade him otherwise.

When we turn to passages where God or Messiah is said to "fix" things or people, in Acts 20:28, Luke tells us that the elders were "fixed," (i.e. "set over" or "appointed") over the church by the authority of Christ. In 1 Cor. 12:18, the Holy Spirit by His own authority "fixes" each believer in the Body of Christ with a specific function. In 1 Cor. 12:28, by His own authority Christ "fixed" various offices in the church.

Then in a very significant passage, 1 Thess. 5:9, Paul states,

> For God has not destined us for wrath, but for obtaining salvation
> through our Lord Jesus Christ,
>
> ὅτι οὐκ ἔθετο ἡμᾶς ὁ θεὸς εἰς ὀργὴν ἀλλὰ εἰς περιποίησιν σωτηρίας διὰ τοῦ κυρίου ἡμῶν Ἰησοῦ Χριστοῦ

Paul clearly states that God has by His own authority not "destined," (i.e. "fixed") believers for wrath but salvation. In order to be emphatic about this, Paul takes the word "not" (οὐκ) out of its normal word order and places it first at the head of the phrase. But is the "wrath" in the passage a reference to present or future wrath? The context is absolutely clear that Paul has in mind the *future* wrath of Christ when He returns to judge the world (v. 2)

God has by his own authority "fixed" or "destined" the future in such a way that believers will not suffer "the Wrath of the Lamb" (cf. Rev. 6:16) when He returns to judge the world in righteousness. The "Prince of Preachers," Matthew Henry comments,

> If we would trace our salvation to the first cause, that is God's appointment. Those who live and die in darkness and ignorance, who sleep and are drunken as in the night, are, it is but too plain, *appointed to wrath;* but as for those who are of the day, if they watch and be sober, it is evident that they are *appointed to obtain salvation.* And the sureness and firmness of the divine appointment are the great support and encouragement of our hope. Were we to obtain salvation by our own merit or power, we could have but little or no hope of it; but seeing we are to obtain it by virtue of God's appointment, which we are sure cannot be shaken *(for his purpose, according to election, shall stand),* on this we build unshaken hope, especially when we consider, (2.) Christ's merit and grace, and that salvation is by our Lord Jesus Christ, who died for us. Our salvation therefore is owing to, and our hopes of it are grounded on, Christ's atonement as well as God's appointment: and, as we should think on God's gracious design and purpose, so also on Christ's death and sufferings, for this end, *that whether we wake or sleep* (whether we live or die, for death is but a sleep to believers, as the apostles had before intimated) *we should live together with Christ* live in union and in glory with him forever. And, as it is the salvation that Christians hope for to *be for ever with the Lord,* so one foundation of their hope is their union with him. [202]

In Acts 1:7 Jesus is emphatic that the details of the future times and seasons were already fixed, set, appointed, ordained, and destined by the Father by His own authority. The fact that the disciples would not be told the future did not mean that the future was not known and fixed by God. Paul even preached this truth to the heathen philosophers on Mars Hill.

> For he *has fixed a day* when he is going to judge the world with justice through a man he has appointed (Acts 17:31)

> καθότι ἔστησεν ἡμέραν ἐν ᾗ μέλλει κρίνειν τὴν οἰκουμένην ἐν δικαιοσύνῃ ἐν ἀνδρὶ ᾧ ὥρισεν, πίστιν παρασχὼν πᾶσιν ἀναστήσας αὐτὸν ἐκ νεκρῶν.

The Day of Judgment has already been "fixed" by the Father. It is an inescapable and unavoidable appointment that we must all keep. But is there not the possibility that something could happen that God did not foresee and that would cancel or change the Day of Judgment? No. It is "set in stone" and cannot tarry or be overthrown.

The word "fixed" is a translation of the Greek verb ἔστησεν. It is an indicative aorist active 3rd person singular of ἵστημι. According to the Lexicons it means:

> Friberg: of time *set, appoint* (AC 17.31)
> UBS: fix (a day of judgment)
> Thayer: *to appoint* (cf. colloquial English *set*): ἡμέραν, Acts 17:31.
> BDAG: to set/fix ***a time*** a period of time ἡμέραν
> (s. ἡμέρα 3a) Ac 17:31.

The way it was used in secular and biblical literature means that the future Day of Judgment has been pre-determined and set in concrete by God. As Matthew Henry put it,

> There is a day appointed for this general review of all that men have done in time, and a final determination of their state for eternity. The day is fixed in the counsel of God, and cannot be altered; but it is his there, and cannot be known. A day of decision, a day of recompense, a day that will put a final period to all the days of time.[203]

Other commentators agree:

> A day fixed by God, they were told, was at hand, in which God would **judge the world in righteousness**, and in which they themselves would be judged also. And the certainty of this was made apparent by the fact that he who was ordained to be Judge was raised from the dead, and so ready to commence the judgment. The time for immediate action was come; God's revelation had reached them.[204]

> God did set the day in his counsel and he will fulfil it in his own time. **Will judge** (μελλει κρινειν [*mellei krinein*]) Rather, is going to judge, μελλω [*mellō*] and the present active infinitive of κρινω [*krinō*]. Paul here quotes Psa. 9:8 where κρινει [*krinei*] occurs.[205]

> From one man he made every nation of humanity to live all over the earth, *fixing the seasons of the year and the boundaries they live in* (Acts 17:26)[206]

> ἐποίησέν τε ἐξ ἑνὸς πᾶν ἔθνος ἀνθρώπων κατοικεῖν ἐπὶ παντὸς προσώπου τῆς γῆς, ὁρίσας προστεταγμένους καιροὺς καὶ τὰς ὁροθεσίας τῆς κατοικίας αὐτῶν

If man were free in the Greek ideal of absolute human autonomy, then he would be absolutely free to choose when and where he lives. But Paul says that the time and place of your birth and your habitation is something that God determines and appoints before you were ever born.

The Greek word προστεταγμένους is a perfect passive participle accusative masculine plural of προστάσσω. It means that the time and place of your birth, life, and death were not only known by God but also pre-determined by God from all eternity.

> That he is the sovereign disposer of all the affairs of the children of men, according to the counsel of his will (v. 26): *He hath determined the times before appointed, and the bounds of their habitation.* See here, (1.) The sovereignty of God's disposal concerning us: he *hath determined* every event, *horisas,* the matter is fixed; the disposals of Providence are incontestable and must not be disputed, unchangeable and cannot be altered. (2.) The wisdom of his disposals; he hath *determined* what was *before appointed.* The determinations of the Eternal Mind are not sudden resolves, but the counterparts of an eternal counsel, the copies of divine decrees. *He performeth the thing that is appointed for me,* Job 23:14. *Whatever comes forth from God was before all worlds hid in God.* (3.) The things about which his providence is conversant; these are time and place: the times and places of our living in this world are determined and appointed by the God that made us. [1.] *He has determined the times* that are concerning us. Times to us seem changeable, but God has fixed them. *Our times are in his hand,* to lengthen or shorten, embitter or sweeten, as he pleases. He has appointed and determined the time of our coming into the world, and the time of our continuance in the world; our time to be born, and our time to die (Eccl. 3:1, 2), and all that little that lies between them- the time of all our concernments in this world. Whether they be prosperous times or calamitous times, it is he that has determined them; and on him we must depend, with reference to the times that
> are yet before us. [207]

> The apostle here opposes both Stoical Fate and Epicurean Chance, ascribing the *periods* and *localities* in which men and nations flourish to the sovereign will and prearrangements of a living God.[208]

> *He himself fixed beforehand* correctly translates the force of the Greek participle which describes action that took place before he *created* and *made them live.* In some languages it is impossible to translate *beforehand* without indicating specifically what event is

being referred to; therefore "before he created them he decided when and where they would live."[209]

Are Future Events Going to Happen Necessarily?

Did anyone ever do anything that was "necessary" for him to do according to the preordained plan and purpose of God? This question is so important that only special revelation can answer it.

> *Was it not necessary* for the Messiah to suffer these things, and to enter into his glory? (Luke 24:26)
>
> <u>οὐχὶ ταῦτα ἔδει</u> παθεῖν τὸν Χριστὸν καὶ εἰσελθεῖν εἰς τὴν δόξαν αὐτοῦ;

Certain questions come to mind.

- Was it *necessary* for Judas to betray Christ?
- For the Romans to deliver Him to death?
- For the Jewish leaders to demand His death?
- For the soldier to pierce His side with a spear?
- Did all the choices of everyone involved take place *necessarily*?
- Was it all mere coincidence?
- Was there a chance that He would not have been arrested, tried, tortured and crucified or did those things have to done by all those involved because it was *necessary*?
- If they did things because they had to; i.e. it was *necessary*, were they held accountable to God for what they did?

The present text and the next one answer these questions.

> Brothers, *it was necessary for the Scripture to be fulfilled*, which the Holy Spirit spoke long ago through the mouth of David about *Judas*, who was the guide to those who arrested Jesus (Acts 1:16)
>
> Ἄνδρες ἀδελφοί, <u>ἔδει πληρωθῆναι τὴν γραφὴν</u> ἣν προεῖπεν τὸ πνεῦμα τὸ ἅγιον διὰ στόματος Δαυὶδ <u>περὶ Ἰούδα</u> τοῦ γενομένου ὁδηγοῦ τοῖς συλλαβοῦσιν Ἰησοῦν,

Luke tells us that all the choices and decisions of man that came together to cause the death of Messiah, including the decision of Judas to betray the Lord, were done *necessarily*.

> Explaining and showing that *it was necessary* that the Messiah *should suffer*, and *to rise again from the dead* (Acts 17:3)

> διανοίγων καὶ παρατιθέμενος ὅτι τὸν Χριστὸν <u>ἔδει παθεῖν</u> καὶ
> <u>ἀναστῆναι ἐκ νεκρῶν</u> καὶ ὅτι οὗ τός ἐστιν ὁ Χριστός [ὁ] Ἰησοῦς ὃν
> ἐγὼ καταγγέλλω ὑμῖν.

Was Messiah's death at the hands of sinners a matter of bad luck, a chance happening, a mere coincidence? No. All these things happened because it was *necessary* for them to take place. They were part of God's eternal plan of the ages.

Are Future Events Ever Predetermined?

Do the biblical authors say that someone ever chose to do something that God *predetermined* that he should chose to do it?

> For the Son of man is going away, *as it has been predetermined: but how terrible it will be for that man by whom He is betrayed!* (Lk. 22:22)
>
> ὅτι ὁ υἱὸς μὲν τοῦ ἀνθρώπου κατὰ τὸ <u>ὡρισμένον</u> πορεύεται, πλὴν
> οὐαὶ τῷ ἀνθρώπῳ ἐκείνῳ δι' οὗ παραδίδοται.

When Judas chose to betray the Lord, was his choice *predetermined by God*? If Luke was inspired by God to write his Gospel account, then we have to accept the fact that he clearly stated that Judas' betrayal was something that God predetermined.

But, we hasten to add, lest anyone foolishly think that this meant that Judas was not responsible for his actions, Luke adds, "Woe unto that man through whom He is betrayed."

There is no indication in the text to suggest that Luke had a problem believing that the choices and actions of Judas were predetermined by God and that he was responsible for his choices at the same time. These two were compatible and not contradictory.

> Him, being delivered up by the *predetermined* counsel and foreknowledge of God, you by the hand of lawless men did crucify and slay (Acts 2:23)
>
> τοῦτον τῇ <u>ὡρισμένῃ</u> βουλῇ καὶ προγνώσει τοῦ θεοῦ ἔκδοτον διὰ
> χειρὸς ἀνόμων προσπήξαντες ἀνείλατε

The men who crucified the Lord did not know that what they did was predetermined by God before time began. *They are responsible for what was predetermined for them to do.* Peter did not give any indication that he was bothered with these revealed truths. They were compatible in his eyes.

What About Predestination?

If the biblical authors believed that the future was predetermined, we would expect them to use such words as "predestination." Did they ever use such terminology when describing the future acts of men?

> For of a truth in this city against thy holy Servant Jesus, whom You did anoint, both Herod and Pontius Pilate, with the Gentiles and the peoples of Israel, were gathered together, *to do whatsoever thy hand and thy council predestined to come to pass* (Acts 4:27–28)
>
> ποιῆσαι ὅσα ἡ χείρ σου καὶ ἡ βουλή [σου] προώρισεν γενέσθαι.

Do you really believe that every word in the Bible is God's Word? Then, regardless of how you feel about it, you have to accept the fact that such words as "predestination," "foreordained," "destined," "election", "foreknown", and "predetermined" are found in the Bible.

Those who had a hand in putting to death the Son of God are held accountable for what they did and, at the same time, what they did was predestined by God from eternity that they should do it. The text cannot be dismissed by saying that God *knew* that they would do it. The word προώρισεν means to predestine or predetermine that certain things will be done in the future.

Must the Future Happen?

Does the Bible ever say that the future acts of a man "must" happen?

> From that time began Jesus to show unto His disciples, that He *must go* to Jerusalem, and *suffer many things* of the elders and chief priests and scribes, and *be killed*, and the third day *be raised up* (Matt. 16:21)

Jesus "must" go, suffer, die and be raised. Why? It was the Father's plan for Him to die on the cross. The same statement is repeated in Mark 8:31.

What about "end times" predictions? Will the future events happen because they *must* happen?

> And you are going to hear of wars and rumors of wars. See to it that you are not alarmed. *These things must take place;* but that's not the end (Matt. 24:6)

The decisions and actions of men that are predicted in Matt. 24 "must" happen as God says they will happen.

Is the Future Open to Change?

If the future were open to change, then the Bible could *not* describe future events as happening necessarily. But if it does speak of future events as necessarily happening, then this is clear indication that the writers believed that the future was fixed.

Acts 23:11, "*You must testify* in Rome"

Acts 27:24, "You *must* stand before the emperor"

Paul was told that God had decided that he was going to witness to Caesar in Rome. The future had already been fixed and predetermined. Not even a shipwreck could prevent Paul's trip to Rome.

Paul was immortal until he had completed his destiny. These are but a few of the passages in the Bible that speak of future events, including the acts of man, as things that "must" happen.

Are Future Events "Destined" By God?

> When the Gentiles heard this, they began rejoicing and glorifying the word of the Lord. Meanwhile, *all who had been destined to eternal life believed.* (Acts 13:48)
>
> ἀκούοντα δὲ τὰ ἔθνη ἔχαιρον καὶ ἐδόξαζον τὸν λόγον τοῦ κυρίου καὶ ἐπίστευσαν <u>ὅσοι ἦσαν τεταγμένοι εἰς ζωὴν αἰώνιον·</u>

Luke clearly states that those who had been "destined to eternal life" believed. Their decision to believe is something that God "destined" them to do. This is in contrast to the destiny of reprobates.

> They keep on stumbling because they disobey the Word, as *they were destined to do* (1 Pet. 2:8)
>
> καὶ λίθος προσκόμματος καὶ πέτρα σκανδάλου· οἳ προσκόπτουσιν τῷ λόγῳ <u>ἀπειθοῦντες εἰς ὃ καὶ ἐτέθησαν.</u>

We have to deal with what Peter says in this verse without violating the grammar and syntax of the Greek text. He says that those who decided to disobey the Lord were "destined" to do this. Paul said the same thing in Rom. 9:22 when he referred to reprobates as "vessels of wrath prepared for destruction." Jude says the same thing in Jude 4.

We realize that this is Christianity for the tough-minded and that weak and obstinate sinners cannot accept the plain teaching of these Scriptures. They will not bow before God in humility.

I was once told by a well-known Natural Theologian, "I will become an atheist before accepting the kind of god described in those verses." I replied, "But you are already an atheist now because you have already denied the existence of the God described in these Scriptures!" He became quite angry and sullen and has refused to talk to me again.

Are Future Events "Ordained" and "Preordained?"

Do the authors of the Bible ever trace man's decisions and actions back to God's preordination?

> And Absalom and all the men of Israel said, "The counsel of Hushai the Archite is better than the counsel of Ahithophel. *For YHWH had ordained to defeat the good counsel of Ahithophel, to the intent that YHWH might bring disaster upon Absalom* (2 Sam. 17:14)

This passage is remarkable. It answers the questions, "Why did Absalom and all the men of Israel *choose* not to listen to Athithophel when he was clearly the wisest counselor in their midst? Why did they *choose* to take Hushai's advice instead?" The text states that God caused them to choose Hushai because *He had ordained* to defeat Absolom. *They chose what He ordained them to choose.*

When one Natural Theologian asserted to me, "God is a gentleman, Bob, and thus He would never interfere with man's free will," I took him to this passage because God only not interfered with the "free will" choices of Absalom's advisors, but He did so to bring them to destruction. Thankfully, this passage exploded his little idol of "free will," and he is no longer a rationalist!

It Is Incomprehensible to Man

Since God's knowledge is perfect, infinite, eternal and immutable, it is no surprise that it is also *incomprehensible*. It is beyond our capacity to understand or to explain how God can know the end of eternity at the beginning of eternity. But this is what the Bible teaches.

> Have you not known? Have you not heard, that the everlasting God, YHWH, the Creator of the ends of the earth, fainteth not, neither is weary? That *His understanding is incomprehensible?* (Isa. 40:28)

> O how deep are God's riches, wisdom and knowledge! *How impossible to explain his judgments or to understand his ways!* (Rom. 11:33)

When the humanists in Augustine's day objected to the Gospel by saying, "I will not believe until I understand," Augustine replied, "I believe in order that I may understand."

Secondary Texts

The Wicked and God's Knowledge

Today, many natural theologians and philosophers question and even openly deny the fact of God's omniscience. They boast that they are on the "cutting edge" of modern theology. But they are merely following in the footsteps of people whom the Bible describes as "the wicked."

> Is not God in the height of heaven? Look also at the distant stars, how high they are. And you say, *"What does God know? How He can judge through thick darkness? Clouds are a hiding place for Him, so that He cannot see;* and He walks on the vault of heaven." (Job 22:12–13)

The passage rebukes the arrogance of thinking that God is so transcendent that He cannot know what is happening on earth. It ridicules the idea that darkness and clouds can prevent God from seeing what is happening on earth.

> And they say, "*How does God know? And is there knowledge with the Most High?*" Behold, these are the wicked. (Psa. 73:11–12)

Notice that the challenge is given to explain "how" God knows. Since no one can fully explain how God knows *anything*, much less *everything*, the wicked go on to question whether God has any knowledge at all.

> And they say, "*YHWH does not see. Nor does the God of Jacob pay heed.*" (Psa. 94:7)

The denial of God's knowledge is used as a reason for not being afraid of the judgment of God. He will not take notice of our sin, so don't worry about it.

> Why do you say, O Jacob, and assert, O Israel, "*My way is hidden from YHWH. And the justice due me escapes the notice of my God?*" (Isa. 40:27)

Some people in Isaiah's day cast doubt on the knowledge of God by claiming that their sins were "hidden" from God, and thus He did not "take notice" of them. Who are these people who question the fact of God's knowledge? The prophets? No. The righteous? No. Those who love the Lord? No.

In each context where the knowledge of God is questioned, it is always the *wicked* who cast doubt on God's knowledge. They are the ones who demand that the righteous tell them "how" and "why" God knows things. When the righteous fail to do so, this is used as the basis to reject revealed truth.

I have been judged and criticized severely for saying that those who deny the omniscience of God are wicked people and not Christians at all. But I am merely following Scripture and if that offends the politically correct theologians of today, they can go pound sand! I will obey God while they obey their master.

The wicked today are just as bold in casting doubt on God's knowledge. They have ransacked the Bible for texts which indicate to them that God is ignorant on some things such as the future. They use the following secondary texts to contradict the clear teaching of the primary texts.

Does God Know Where You Are?

> Then YHWH God called to the man, and said to him, "Where are you?" And He said, "Who told you that you were naked? Have you eaten from the tree of which I commanded you not to eat?" (Gen. 3:9, 11)

These passages indicate to humanistic theologians that God was ignorant not only of the whereabouts of Adam and Eve, but also of their sin. They assume that the questions God asked revealed His ignorance. Is this really what is taught in this passage? Are not the questions asked for *man's* sake so that he might confess his sin? This is the historic Jewish and Christian understanding of the text.

If this secondary text could overthrow the knowledge of God, it would mean that God has no *present* knowledge of where we are and no *past* knowledge of what we have done. Prayer would be useless, and the Judgment Day impossible.

Some natural philosophers have attempted to use this passage to prove that God cannot know the future. Why they do this is beyond us. The passage is clearly speaking of the *present* whereabouts of Adam and his *past* transgression. God did not ask, "Where will you be tomorrow? What will you do tomorrow?" He asked, "Where are you? What have you done?" If these questions were interpreted literally, God would not know our past or present! You can see why the wicked would love this idea, as they think they will escape accountability for the evil they do and the heresies they teach.

Does God See You?

> And YHWH came down to see the city and the tower, which the sons of men had built. (Gen. 11:5)

It is claimed by natural theologians that this passage proves (sic) that God was ignorant of what man was going to do in the future. Thus, He had to travel down to earth to see what was going on. If taken literally, it would not only deny the omniscience of God, but also His *omnipresence*. In order to find out what was going on, God had to leave heaven and travel to earth in order to gain knowledge. He would not be present everywhere, but would be a creature of time and space.

Once again, it is knowledge of the *past* and *present* that is in view. God did not go down to see what they *were* going to do, but what man *had* done and *was* doing at that time. This is why the historic Jewish and Christian interpretation has always pointed out that the passage is anthropomorphic in nature. Early revelation described God as if He were a man and had to travel from place to place. When Natural theologians try to make literal what is metaphorical, they err, not knowing the Scripture nor the power of God. They would overthrow all the primary texts which clearly teach that God is omnipresent as well as omniscient (cf. Psa. 139:7–12)

Prayer would be a stupid ritual because unless God happened to pass by at the time you were praying; He would not know that you were praying. Once again Natural Theology ends up with Zeus or Jupiter.

Sodom and Gomorrah

> And YHWH said, "The outcry of Sodom and Gomorrah is indeed great, and their sin is exceedingly grave. I will go down now, and see if they have done entirely according to the outcry, which has come to Me; and, if not, I will know.
> (Gen. 18:20–21)

Once again, if taken literally, the omnipresence of God as well as His omniscience would be denied. God had to go and see if the rumor He had heard was true. And, if He discovered that it was not true, then He would know it. But does God really have to travel to the site of sin to know about it? Does He have to investigate rumors? No. Such primary texts as Job 11:11 state that

"He sees iniquity *without investigating.*"
(יִרְאֶה־אָוֶן וְלֹא יִתְבּוֹנָן:)

Does God Know Our Hearts?

"…now I know that you fear God."
(Gen. 22:12)

If taken literally, not until Abraham passed the test did the angel of YHWH (a theophany of the Son of God) know the spiritual condition of Abraham's heart. Yet, there are dozens of primary passages which state that God and Messiah know the spiritual condition of the hearts of man.

You alone *know the hearts of all the sons of men.* (1 Kings 8:39)

God sees not as man sees, for man looks at the outward appearance, but YHWH *looks at the heart.* (1 Sam. 16:7)

Some Natural theologians and philosophers have used this passage to prove (sic) that Abraham changed the future. They assume that when God told Abraham to kill his son, that is what God had ordained to happen in the future, but Abraham's obedience changed the future.

The absurdity of this interpretation is obvious from the fact that, while Abraham was going up one side of the mountain, a ram was climbing up the other side to be the substitute sacrifice (v. 13) God provided the ram because:

(a) He never decreed that Isaac would be killed;
(b) He knew that Abraham would discover that the most precious person in his life was God, not his son;
(c) A ram would be sacrificed instead of Isaac.

Failed Expectations?

What more was there to do for My vineyard that I have not done in it? Why, when I expected it to produce good grapes did it produce worthless ones? (Isa. 5:4)

It is claimed that this passage teaches that God was ignorant that Israel was not going to bear good fruit. His expectations were not met because He did not know the future. If taken literally, it would portray a pathetic, impotent god! This poor god is constantly frustrated by unforeseen events that fail to meet his expectations. But this interpretation would contradict dozens of primary passages that clearly establish the omniscience of God. In the same book, Isaiah says that God "declares the end from the beginning" (Isa. 46:10) Thus, whatever Isa. 5:4 means, it cannot be twisted to contradict what the author elsewhere clearly teaches.

Is God Absent-Minded?

> Their sin I will remember no more. (Jer. 31:34)

If taken literally, this text suggests to some philosophers that God can forget the past. But does God have lapses of memory like we do? Or is this verse to be interpreted in some other way? The word "anthropomorphic" simply means that God sometimes spoke of himself as if he were a man. Thus he had a hand and an eye. In this passage, our debt to God is "forgotten," i.e. counted no longer against us in a forensic or legal canceling of it.

There are dozens of primary texts that indicate that God never "forgets" the past in the sense of a lapse of memory. The Day of Judgment would be impossible without God's omniscient knowledge of the past with all of its sins.

The word "remember" is used in its *judicial* sense, that God will not legally hold our sins against us because the Messiah took the punishment for those sins in our place (Isa. 53:4–6)

It Never Entered God's Mind

> And they built the high places of Baal that are in the valley of Ben-hinnom to cause their sons and their daughters to pass through the fire to Molech, which I had not commanded them
> nor had it entered My Mind that they should do this abomination,
> to cause Judah to sin. (Jer. 32:35)

Some natural theologians have used this text to prove that God was ignorant of the future human sacrifices that would take place in the valley of Ben-hinnom. They claim that it never entered His mind that such a future abomination would take place. It took Him by complete surprise! But is this really what the passage is saying? No. The passage is simply stating that God never told them to kill their children and that *it never crossed His mind to tell them to do so*. The Hebrew grammar is clear on this point.

To Know Is To Love

> You only have I known among the families of the earth. (Amos 3:2)

If taken literally, some have urged that God admits that His knowledge is limited to the nation of Israel and He is ignorant of other nations. Yet, is not the word for "known" (יָדַע) used for the *love relationship* between a man and his wife (Gen. 4:1)? Is not Israel described as the "wife" of Yahweh? Is not God here speaking of His special love relationship to Israel? Yes.

The Day of Judgment

> Then I'll tell you plainly, "I never knew you. Get away from me, you
> evildoers!" (Matt. 7:23)

If we take these words literally, then Christ on the Day of Judgment will admit that He was ignorant of the existence of many people. Yet, if Christ were here admitting that He was ignorant of them, on what basis did He send them to hell? He says to them, "Get away from me, you evildoers!"

Evidently, Jesus knows of their sin and will send them to hell for it. Doesn't the context indicate that Jesus was using the Hebrew meaning of the word "know?" Thus, He never had *a personal love relationship* with these people.

Does God Repent?

What about the passages where God is said in the King James Version to "repent?" (Gen. 6:6–7; Exo. 32:14; Jud. 2:18; 1 Sam. 15:11, 35; 2 Sam. 24:16; 1 Chron. 21:15; Psa. 106:45; Jer. 26:19; Joel 2:13; Amos 7:3, 6; Jonah 3:9–10; 4:2) Do these passages prove that the future is unknown to God? Do they prove that God changes His "mind" (i.e. eternal decrees) about the future?

First, if we take the King James Version translation and give it a literal interpretation, it would appear that God "repented" of **sin.** This would not bother the Natural philosopher, Stephen Davis, associate professor of philosophy at Claremont College. He has argued that God can sin, lie, and even break His own promises! Luckily for us, He has not done these things so far.[210]

But is this what these passages mean? Is there a GOD above God to whom He is accountable? To whom does God repent and whose forgiveness does He seek? The Bible clearly states in many places that "God *cannot* lie" (Num. 23:19: Tit. 1:2) He *cannot* even be tempted to sin, much less be guilty of sin (James 1:13) Thus whatever the KJV meant by the word "repent," the translators did not mean to imply that God sins and therefore needs repentance.

Second, the KJV is not consistent in its translation of the Hebrew word וַיִּנָּחֶם as "repent." Elsewhere in Genesis it is translated:

> And Isaac brought her into his mother Sarah's tent, and took
> Rebekah, and she became his wife; and he loved her: and
> Isaac *was comforted* after his mother's death (Gen. 24:67)

> And in process of time the daughter of Shuah Judah's wife died; and
> Judah *was comforted*, and went up unto his sheepshearers to
> Timnath, he and his friend Hirah the Adullamite. (Gen. 38:12)

> Now therefore fear ye not: I will nourish you, and your little ones.
> And he *comforted* them, and spake kindly unto them. (Gen. 50:21)

Obviously, the word "repent" would not fit into the other places in Genesis where the Hebrew word is found. It is translated "to comfort." This reveals that the Hebrew word is an *emotive* term signifying *a change in feelings or emotion.* Gen. 6:6 is a good example.

> And it repented YHWH that he had made man on the earth, and it
> grieved him at his heart. (KJV)

וַיִּנָּחֶם יְהוָה כִּי־עָשָׂה אֶת־הָאָדָם בָּאָרֶץ וַיִּתְעַצֵּב אֶל־לִבּוֹ׃

Modern translations render the word וַיִּנָּחֶם as follows:

1. RSV: was sorry
2. NKJ: was sorry
3. NRS: was sorry
4. NASB: was sorry
5. Moffat: was sorry
6. Torah: was saddened
7. Taylor: broke his heart

Why have modern translators changed "repented" to such an emotive word as "sorry?" There are good reasons for what they did.

First, there is a parallelism in the Hebrew text that indicates what the word וַיִּנָּחֶם means. The parallel word is וַיִּתְעַצֵּב and is correctly translated "was grieved." Thus the word וַיִּנָּחֶם refers to the emotions or attitude of God, not His plans or intellect.

If this is true, then we would expect to find the ancient translations rendering the Hebrew word וַיִּנָּחֶם as an emotive term.

- The Septuagint: angry (ἐνεθυμήθη possibly from θυμόω)
- Targum Neofiti 1: regret
- Targun Pseudo-Jonathan: regret
- Syriac: grieve
- Arabic: grieve
- Latin Vulgate: regret (paenituit)

Keil and Delitzsch's comment on Gen. 6:6 is worth repeating.

> The force of יִנָּחֶם "it *repented* the LORD," may be gathered from the explanatory יִתְעַצֵּב, "it grieved Him at his heart." This shows that the repentance of God does not presuppose any variableness in His nature or His purpose, In this sense God never repents of anything (1 Sam. 15:29), "quia nihil illi inopinatum vel non praevisum accidit" (Calvin) The repentance of God is an anthropomorphic expression for the pain of the divine love at the sin of man, and signifies that "God is hurt no less by the atrocious sins of men than if they pierced His heart with mortal anguish" (Calvin)[211]

The natural theologians and philosophers should have resisted the temptation to "twist" the Scriptures "to their own destruction." (2 Pet. 3:16)

If the authors of Scripture believed that "x" will *certainly* happen in the future, they would express that idea by saying that "x" *shall* or *will* happen. They would use "shall" and "will" because they are the *language of certitude.* They could strengthen that idea by saying that "x" shall or will *surely* or *certainly* happen in the future.

If they went one step further and used *the language of necessity*, they would say that "x" *must* happen in the future. Thus if "x" *shall* and *must* happen in the future, then future events are both *certain* and *necessary.*

If they believed that the future events are neither certain nor necessary, they would avoid using such language as "shall," "will," and "must." To say that they used the language of certitude and necessity but did not believe in them is make them into fools or liars.

Can Man Change the Future?

Some Natural theologians have ransacked the Bible in a desperate attempt to find passages in the Bible where man changed the future. If man can change the future, then the future is neither known nor already decided by God. Instead, it is open to contingency (luck and chance) and closed to Divine determinism.

Why someone would choose to believe that the universe is open to Lady Luck but closed to the Lord is beyond us.

One such passage is 1 Sam. 23:6–13. The story is quite simple. David had fled to the city of Keilah. When David found out that Saul was planning to march to Keilah, he sought the Lord for guidance. Should he go or stay at Keilah? If he stayed at Keilah, would the men of Keilah turn him over to Saul? The Lord said that if he stayed, they would betray David. Thus he fled the city and escaped Saul.

When God told David that if he stayed at Keilah, he would die, does this mean that God had *predicted* that this would happen? Some Natural theologians say, "Yes, God had planned that David would in fact die at Keilah. But, when David ran away, he changed the future. His escape changed God's plans and decrees." There are several errors at the core of the humanist argument.

First, in the context, the subjects of God's knowledge, His eternal plans or decrees, and the nature of future events is not addressed. The passage has to do with *personal guidance* in the light of future possibilities *from the standpoint of David*. Thus this is not a primary passage, but a secondary text.

Second, in terms of literary genre, 1 Sam 23 is a historical narrative. A first year seminary student knows that it is hermeneutically precarious to establish a doctrine on historical narratives.

Third, when we think about the future, all we can do is *imagine the possibilities from our viewpoint* because we do not know the actualities of what will in fact happen. But God is not so limited. He knows the actualities as well as all the possibilities because He knows and has always known what will take place from the beginning of time to the end.

Since man does not know what the future holds, he can only know the future in terms of what can *possibly* happen according to his understanding. He does not know future actualities. Therefore, the future is "open" to man in the sense that he can imagine many different future possibilities. The humanists make the fatal error of assuming that God is limited like man when it comes to the future.

The fourth fatal error is that the humanist assumes that *what is possible to man is actual to God.* It is this assumption that controls their interpretation of 1 Sam 23. For example, if I ask God, "Lord, if I stand in front of an oncoming bus and it runs me over, will I die?" If the Lord replies, "Yes, you will die." Does this mean that God was *predicting* that the future *actually* was for me to be run over by a bus, or were my question and His answer *hypothetical scenarios?*

Hypothetical scenarios refer to all the *possible* situations that *I* can *imagine* that could happen, *given the proper circumstances.* If a bus runs over me, given certain hypothetical circumstances, I will die. If David remains at Keilah, given certain hypothetical circumstances, he will die.

The humanist at this point assumes that since my being run over by a bus is a *possible* future event *to me*, this means that God had actually ordained it to happen, that when I chose not to get run over by that bus, I changed the future and then God had to change His eternal decree.

The fifth reason is interesting. When the humanists bring up this passage, they always neglect to quote 1 Sam 23:14 which says,

> And David abode in the wilderness in the strongholds, and remained
> in the hill-country in the wilderness of Ziph. And Saul sought him
> every day, but *God did not deliver him into his hand.*

The reason that Saul at Keilah or anywhere else did not kill David was not due to David changing the future, but to *the intervention of a Sovereign God.*

Lastly, this passage does not refute the omniscience of God, but rather establishes it. The only grounds on which David could ask God about possible future scenarios is that he assumed that God knew all things.

Is the Future Open to Infinite Possibilities?

Is it possible for God to lie? For God to make a mistake? To break His promise? Is it possible that in the future God could become the devil and the devil become God? Can the devil win in the end? The humanist, given his worldview, must believe that all these things are possible.

Anyone who says that the future is open to infinite possible worlds, would have to go down the same path of apostasy as Stephen Davis and Clark Pinnock.

According to the biblical worldview, it is *impossible* for God to lie (Tit. 1:3) God cannot fail to keep His word (Num. 23:19) He *cannot* deny His own nature (2 Tim. 2:13) The Lord will win, not the devil (Rev. 20:10) *The impossibility of God becoming the devil or lying is only possible because the future is NOT open to contingency (luck and chance) Only in a predetermined universe can we say that some things are NOT possible.*

Figurative Language

We have no problem handling these secondary texts because Scripture sometimes speaks to us in "figurative language" (John 16:25) Paul tells us that he spoke "in human terms" (Rom. 3:5) Why? "I am speaking in human terms because of the weakness of your flesh" (Rom. 6:19) Thus, he did not hesitate to "speak in terms of human relationships" (Gal. 3:15)

This is not a "cop out." Orthodox theologians have biblical precedent to interpret these secondary texts as the use of the *figurative language of human terminology.* Because we would have to go to Sodom to see if it were as bad as we have heard, God is pictured in this figurative sense as doing so.

Changes in Revelation

We must also point out that a *change in special revelation* in which God commands someone to do something and then, from our perspective, "changes His mind" and tells him not to do it, does not biblically imply any change in the eternal plans of God. He sometimes tests the hearts of men so that *they* might know where they are spiritually.

As we already pointed out, when God commanded Abraham to kill Isaac, this does not mean that He had ordained that Isaac would die by his father's knife. Thus God had a ram going up the one side of the mountain while Abraham and Isaac went up the other. The ram was already provided as the substitute sacrifice because God NEVER intended His command to be carried out. He wanted Abraham to know that God must have first place in his life, not Isaac.

When God *revealed* to Moses, "I am going to destroy Israel," and then Moses offered to die instead, from the perspective of man, it would appear that God changed His mind and decided not to destroy Israel (Exo. 32:10f)

But God never intended to destroy the Jewish people because He had already predicted the coming of the Messiah. God was not going to invalidate hundreds of messanic prophecies by wiping out the Jewish people. *A change in revelation does not imply a change in God's mind or eternal decrees.*

The same point can be made about God's threat to destroy Ninevah (Jonah 3) They repented under the *preaching* of the prophet (Matt. 12:41) Today we preach, "Turn or burn! Repent or perish!" This does not mean that God has decreed us to burn and perish, but rather that if we do not repent, that will be our doom.

Summary

The God who is there is not silent about the fact and nature of His knowledge of Himself and the universe He created for His glory. Philosophers may question or even deny revealed truth but they cannot overthrow it.

The Extent of God's Knowledge

Did the authors of Scripture believe that God's knowledge was infinite in its extent and that nothing was closed to the knowledge of God? How would they convey this idea to their readers? By what vocabulary?

Given these questions, we would expect to find them using the same general format they followed when teaching any revealed truth. They usually give us *general statements* which directly teach the truth, which are then illustrated by *specific* examples.

General Statements about The Extent of God's Knowledge

Does the Bible state specifically and directly that God knows *everything*? Is this the understanding of the authors of Scripture? If they believed that God did *not* know everything, then we would expect them to state this in a clear manner. Let us turn to the Word of God for our answer.

HANNAH'S CONFESSION OF FAITH

We have already seen that Hannah's use of the plural דֵעוֹת indicates that Yahweh is the God of all knowledge, whatever kind it is.

YHWH is a God of knowledges (1 Sam. 2:3)

When someone says, "The knowledge of the future is a kind of knowledge that God cannot know," he is violating Hannah's clear confession of faith.

PSALM 139

Psalm 139 is a passage of full mention on the extent of God's knowledge. David says to Yahweh, "You know everything" (v. 4) Then he lists all the things that God knows, including his future thoughts and words before they even enter his mind.

v. 1 O YHWH, You have *searched me* and *known me*.

לַמְנַצֵּחַ לְדָוִד מִזְמוֹר יְהוָה חֲקַרְתַּנִי וַתֵּדָע׃

κύριε ἐδοκίμασάς με καὶ ἔγνως με

v. 2, You *know* when I sit down and when I rise up; You *understand* my thoughts from afar.

אַתָּה יָדַעְתָּ שִׁבְתִּי וְקוּמִי בַּנְתָּה לְרֵעִי מֵרָחוֹק׃

σὺ ἔγνως τὴν καθέδραν μου καὶ τὴν ἔγερσίν μου σὺ συνῆκας τοὺς διαλογισμούς μου ἀπὸ μακρόθεν

v. 3, You *scrutinize* my path and my lying down.

אָרְחִי וְרִבְעִי זֵרִיתָ וְכָל־דְּרָכַי הִסְכַּנְתָּה׃

τὴν τρίβον μου καὶ τὴν σχοῖνόν μου
σὺ ἐξιχνίασας καὶ πάσας τὰς ὁδούς
μου προεῖδες

v. 4, Even before there is a word on my tongue, Behold,
O YHWH, *You know everything.*

כִּי אֵין מִלָּה בִּלְשׁוֹנִי הֵן יְהוָה יָדַעְתָּ כֻלָּהּ׃

ὅτι οὐκ ἔστιν λόγος ἐν γλώσσῃ μου
ἰδού κύριε <u>σὺ ἔγνως πάντα τὰ ἔσχατα</u>
v. 5, You have enclosed me behind and before, and laid Your

hand upon me.

אָחוֹר וָקֶדֶם צַרְתָּנִי וַתָּשֶׁת עָלַי כַּפֶּכָה׃

καὶ τὰ ἀρχαῖα σὺ ἔπλασάς με καὶ ἔθηκας
ἐπ᾽ ἐμὲ τὴν χεῖρά σου

v. 6, Such knowledge is too wonderful for me; It is too high,
I cannot attain to it.

(פְּלִיאָה) [פְּלִיָּה] דַעַת מִמֶּנִּי נִשְׂגְּבָה לֹא־אוּכַל לָהּ׃

ἐθαυμαστώθη ἡ γνῶσίς σου ἐξ ἐμοῦ ἐκραταιώθη
οὐ μὴ δύνωμαι πρὸς αὐτήν

The Psalmist uses every word and phrase in the Hebrew language to indicate the infinite extent of God's knowledge. The passage above is so clear and distinct on the infinite extent of God's knowledge that we have never seen any attempt by those who limit God's knowledge to explain it away. They simply ignore it and proceed with their philosophic speculations.

IS GOD'S UNDERSTANDING INFINITE?

Instead of sitting around and pooling our ignorance on the subject, what has God revealed about this question in Scripture?

> Great is our Lord, and mighty in power; *His understanding is infinite* (Psa. 147:5)

גָּדוֹל אֲדוֹנֵינוּ וְרַב־כֹּחַ לִתְבוּנָתוֹ אֵין מִסְפָּר׃

μέγας ὁ κύριος ἡμῶν καὶ μεγάλη ἡ ἰσχὺς αὐτοῦ καὶ τῆς συνέσεως
<u>αὐτοῦ οὐκ ἔστιν ἀριθμός</u>

In the context, God's glory is revealed by His omniscience because,

> He counts the number of the stars;
> He calls them all by *their* names.

מוֹנֶה מִסְפָּר לַכּוֹכָבִים לְכֻלָּם שֵׁמוֹת יִקְרָא׃

ὁ ἀριθμῶν πλήθη ἄστρων καὶ πᾶσιν
αὐτοῖς ὀνόματα καλῶν

The universe may be vast and immeasurable to man, but it is only a finite speck of dust to the Almighty. He knows its measurements because He made it.

In v. 5, the Psalmist gives a poetic contrast between the finite universe and the infinite nature of God. Yahweh is "great" (Heb. גָּדוֹל Gk. μέγας) He is a "mega" God, and not a finite deity like the heathen worship.

God is "great" for two reasons:

1. He is *omnipotent in power* because He is "abundant in strength." His power has no limits. There is nothing that is beyond the power of God to accomplish.

2. He is *omniscient in knowledge* because, as Leupold correctly translates the Hebrew phrase, "There is no limit to His understanding." [212]

The words in v.5, אֵין מִסְפָּר, mean that God's "knowledge" or "understanding" cannot be numerically quantified as the stars can. There is no number which can represent God's knowledge because it is infinite in nature; hence, there is no limit to it or on it. The classic commentator Delitzsch points out,

> To His understanding there is no number; i.e. in its depth and fullness it cannot be defined by any number. What a comfort for the church as it traverses its ways, that are often so labyrinthine and entangled! Its Lord is the Omniscient as well as the Almighty One. [213]

In his commentary on the Psalms, Moll states,

> He has assigned a number to the stars which men cannot count (Gen. 15:5) This means that, in creating them, He called forth a number determined by Himself. It is also said that He calls them all by name; i.e. that He knows and names them according to their special features, and employs them in His service according to His will, in conformity with the names which correspond to such knowledge. The Omniscience and Omnipotence of God are thus presented at once to the soul. The greatness of God (v. 5) with respect to might (Job 37:23) corresponds to the fullness of His understanding (Psa. 145:3), which no number can express. The same Lord who, with infinite power and unsearchable wisdom, rules the stars in their courses, rules also the world of man. [214]

The prophet Isaiah followed the Psalmist in using the same word לִתְבוּנָתוֹ for God "understands" when he declared,

> Have you not known? Have you not heard? The everlasting God, Jehovah, the Creator of the ends of the earth, fainteth not, neither is weary; *there is no searching out of his understanding.* (Isa. 40:28)

The Septuagint is emphatic in its translation. It uses the word φρονήσεως as the Greek equivalent for the Hebrew לִתְבוּנָתוֹ. Thus the translators were stressing that God's way of thinking; i.e. *how* He knows all things, is incomprehensible to man.

> καὶ νῦν οὐκ ἔγνως εἰ μὴ ἤκουσας θεὸς αἰώνιος ὁ θεὸς ὁ κατασκευάσας τὰ ἄκρα τῆς γῆς οὐ πεινάσει οὐδὲ κοπιάσει <u>οὐδὲ ἔστιν ἐξεύρεσις τῆς φρονήσεως αὐτοῦ</u>

The Apostle John declared his understanding of the extent of God's knowledge in language that is hard to dismiss.

> If our hearts condemn us, God is greater than our hearts and *knows everything*. (1 John 3:20)
>
> ὅτι ἐὰν καταγινώσκῃ ἡμῶν ἡ καρδία, ὅτι μείζων ἐστὶν ὁ θεὸς τῆς καρδίας ἡμῶν καὶ <u>γινώσκει πάντα.</u>

In the context, John follows David in describing God as the "mega God" because He is greater (μείζων) than us; i.e. He is omnipotent. Then he adds that not only is God greater in power than we are, but He is also greater in knowledge because He knows all things. There is nothing in the context to indicate that we should limit "everything."

The author of Hebrews is picturesque as well as transparent in his view of the extent of God's knowledge.

> No creature can hide from him. Everything is naked and helpless before the eyes of the one to whom we must give an account. (Heb. 4:13)
>
> καὶ <u>οὐκ ἔστιν κτίσις ἀφανὴς ἐνώπιον αὐτοῦ, πάντα δὲ γυμνὰ καὶ τετραχηλισμένα τοῖς ὀφθαλμοῖς αὐτοῦ,</u> πρὸς ὃν ἡμῖν ὁ λόγος.

The author of Hebrews speaks of God's knowledge first in the negative and then in the positive. He first says that there is nothing in the universe that is closed to God's sight. There is no creature great or small, *not even man*, that escapes the omniscient eye of the Creator.

Second, "all things" are open to God's sight. How else could God "work all things together" for our good and His glory (Rom. 8:28)? How could He be "working all things after the counsel of His will" (Eph. 1:11) if He did not know what was going to happen next? This passage is so comprehensive and all-encompassing, that we cannot limit the Mind of God in any sense. How then can some claim that the future is *closed* to His sight?

AN OMNISCIENT MESSIAH

The divine nature of the God/man at times revealed itself while He was on earth. In the following places the divine attribute of omniscience was applied to Him.

> But Jesus did not trust himself unto them, because *He knew all things.* (John 2:24)

> αὐτὸς δὲ Ἰησοῦς οὐκ ἐπίστευεν αὐτὸν αὐτοῖς διὰ <u>τὸ αὐτὸν γινώσκειν πάντας</u>

Note the use of the infinitive γινώσκειν. The divine nature of the Messiah was at all times omniscient.

> ...and *didn't need anyone to tell him what people were like. For he himself knew what was in every person.* (John 2:25)

> καὶ ὅτι <u>οὐ χρείαν εἶχεν</u> ἵνα τις μαρτυρήσῃ περὶ τοῦ ἀνθρώπου· αὐτὸς γὰρ <u>ἐγίνωσκεν τί ἦν ἐν τῷ ἀνθρώπῳ.</u>

We must remember that John is writing after Christ ascended to heaven. The ascended Messiah knows the spiritual condition of the hearts of all men because He is omniscient. In Rev. 2:23, the ascended Christ says,

> I am the one who searches minds and hearts. I will reward each one of you as your works deserve.

> ἐγώ εἰμι ὁ ἐραυνῶν νεφροὺς καὶ καρδίας, καὶ δώσω ὑμῖν ἑκάστῳ κατὰ τὰ ἔργα ὑμῶν.

Christ uses the same phraseology found in the Old Testament where it describes the omniscience of Yahweh (Psa. 7:9; Jer. 11:20, 17:10)

> Now we know that *you know everything* and do not need to have anyone to ask you questions. Because of this, we believe that you have come from God (John 16:30)

> νῦν οἴδαμεν ὅτι <u>οἶδας πάντα</u> καὶ οὐ χρείαν ἔχεις ἵνα τίς σε ἐρωτᾷ· ἐν τούτῳ πιστεύομεν ὅτι ἀπὸ θεοῦ ἐξῆλθες.

In the context, the disciples had come to realize that Jesus was not simply a man with limited human knowledge like themselves, but He was God as well as man and thus He was omniscient in His divine nature (John 20:28)

> He said to him a third time, "Simon, son of John, do you love me?" And Peter was deeply hurt that he had said to him a third time, "Do you love me?" So he said to him, "Lord, *You know everything.* You know that I love you!" (John 21:17)

> λέγει αὐτῷ τὸ τρίτον, Σίμων Ἰωάννου, φιλεῖς με; ἐλυπήθη ὁ Πέτρος ὅτι εἶπεν αὐτῷ τὸ τρίτον, Φιλεῖς με; καὶ λέγει αὐτῷ, <u>Κύριε, πάντα σὺ οἶδας</u>, σὺ γινώσκεις ὅτι φιλῶ σε. λέγει αὐτῷ [ὁ Ἰησοῦς], Βόσκε τὰ πρόβατά μου.

Peter inverts the normal word order by putting the word πάντα ("all") first to emphasize that Christ knows ALL in an absolute sense. There is no way in the context to escape the truth of Peter's confession. Jesus the Christ, the Son of the living God, Second Person of the Holy Trinity, knows ALL things.

Specific Illustrations

GOD'S KNOWLEDGE OF HIMSELF

- His eternal plans for man and the universe: 2 Kings 19:25; Jer. 29:11–12; Acts 1:7.
- His future works are known to Him from eternity: Acts 15:18.
- Exhaustive knowledge of each member of the Trinity of the other members of the Godhead: Mat. 11:27; John 7:29, 8:55, 17:25; 1 Cor. 2:10–11.

GOD'S KNOWLEDGE OF THE SPACE/TIME UNIVERSE

- All of history, the end from the beginning: Isa. 46:10.
- Extends to the ends of the earth: Job 28:24.
- Sees everything under the heavens: Job 28:24.
- All possible events in the future: Isa. 48:18–19; Ezk. 37:3; Mat. 11:21–23.
- When a sparrow falls to the ground: Mat. 10:29.
- He speaks of future events as if they already happened: Rom. 4:17; 8:30.
- The number and names of the stars: Psa. 147:4.
- All creatures: Heb. 4:13.
- When He will judge the world: Mat. 8:29; Acts 17:31; Rev. 14:7, 15.
- He foresees the future: Gal. 3:8–9.
- He foreknows the future: Acts 2:23; Rom. 8:29; 1 Pet. 1:2, 18–20.

GOD'S KNOWLEDGE OF MAN

- All men: 2 Sam. 7:20; Psa. 33:13; Jer. 15:15.
- The hearts of all men: 1 Sam. 16:7; 1 Kings 8:39: Psa. 7:9; 17:2; 26:2; 139:2; Jer. 11:20; 12:3; 17:10; Lk. 16:15; John 2:24; 21:17; Acts 1:24; Rom. 8:27; Rev. 2:23.
- When a man will be born and when he will die: Job 14:5: 21:21; Psa. 31:15; Mat. 26:18, 45; Mk. 14:35, 41; John 2:4; 7:6, 8, 30; 8:30; 12:27; 13:1; Acts 17:26.
- Man's ways: Job 23:10; 34:21.
- Man's thoughts: Psa. 139:2; Ezk. 11:5; Heb. 4:12.
- Man's meditations: Psa. 5:1.
- Man's works: Job 34:25; Psa. 33:15; Matt. 16:27.
- Man's sorrows: Gen. 29:32; 31:42; Exo. 3:7; 4:31; Psa. 25:18–19; 31:7; 119:153.
- Every word man speaks: Jer. 17:16.
- A man's future: Exo. 3:19–20; Jer. 18:22–23.
- How many hairs are on his head: Matt. 10:30.
- The folly of man: Psa. 69:5.

Chapter Seven Biblical Theism

- The wrongs of man: Psa. 69:5.
- The wickedness of man: Gen. 6:5.
- Our future needs and prayers before we ask: Mat. 6:8.
- Every intent of the thoughts of man's heart: Gen. 6:5; Heb. 4:12.
- The shame of man: Psa. 69:19.
- What man is made of: Psa. 103:14.
- Man's actions: Psa. 139:2–4.
- All about a man before he is born: Jer. 1:5.

What about the future acts of man, good and evil? Does God know the future decisions and acts that we will do? The Scripture illustrates that God knows the good and evil that we will do from all eternity and even declares it in prophecy. The following is but a few samples of the *hundreds* of passages in which God reveals what men will think, say and do in the future:

- All the evil things that Joseph's brothers, Potiphar's wife and others would do to him would place him where he could save his family from starvation: Gen. 50:20.
- Pharaoh would not obey Moses: Exo. 7:3–5.
- Nebuchadnezzar would destroy Tyre: Ezek. 26:1–14.
- Nebuchadnezzar would conquer Egypt: Ezk. 30:10.
- Nebuchadnezzar would conquer Judah: Jer. 25:9.
- Judah's captivity would last seventy years: Jer. 25:11.
- Babylon would fall in seventy years: Jer. 25:12.
- Cyrus would rebuild Jerusalem: Isa. 44:28–45:1.
- Judas would betray Jesus: Psa. 41:9; Lk. 22:21–22; John 6:64; 13:18, 19, 21, 26, 27.
- Peter would deny Him three times: Mat. 26:34.
- The Jews, the Romans, Herod, and Pontius Pilate would murder Jesus: Acts 4:27–28.

Summary

We have examined in some detail what the authors of Scripture said about the nature and extent of God's knowledge. We found them saying what they would have to say in order to convey the idea that God's omniscience is absolute and unlimited by anything past, present or future.

Those who disagree have a great task set before them. If the authors of Scripture believed that God did NOT know the past, present or future, how would they express that idea to their readers? By what vocabulary? By what illustrations? The heretics will have to come up with multiple, clear, primary biblical passages that clearly state, "He does NOT know everything" or, "I YHWH do NOT know."

Let them follow the same procedure as we have followed and marshal their exegetical evidence. They will have to produce primary passages in which the knowledge of God is clearly in focus and that knowledge is specifically limited. Let us now turn to those who deny the omniscience of God.

PART IV
FALSE VIEWS

There are so many clear biblical passages on the perfection of God's knowledge that one wonders how anyone who had ever read the Bible could come up with the ideas that God does not know everything, that His knowledge is dependent upon something outside of Himself, that He is learning new things every second or that His knowledge does not effectually cause whatsoever comes to pass. Jonathan Edwards, the greatest intellect that America ever produced, comments,

> One would think it wholly needless to enter on such an argument with any that profess themselves Christians: but so it is; God's certain Foreknowledge of the free acts of moral agents, is denied by some that pretend to believe the Scriptures to be the Word of God.[215]

There are three clear tests of any view of the nature and extent of God's knowledge. Does this view strengthen or weaken the biblical and evangelical doctrine of:
1. the verbal, plenary, inerrant, infallible inspiration of the Bible?
2. the substitutionary blood atonement of Christ on the cross?
3. Divine Providence over all things?

While there are many other test doctrines that could also be applied to this subject, these three are sufficient to doom any heretical or deviant view. Why? Any view of God which destroys His Word, casts doubt on Christ's atonement, and rebels against Divine Providence cannot be of God, but comes from Satan.

All the false views listed below fail the three tests listed above. For example, in the book, *Battle of the Gods*, you will find nearly 300 pages refuting pagan finite godism, Process Theology and philosophy, neo-processian views and "moral government" theology. Since each of the false views listed below should receive a detailed refutation and this far exceeds the limits of this book, we can only summarize in brief the chief problems with each view. See the resource guide at the end of the syllabus for further study.

The History of False Views

THE ANCIENT POLYTHEISTIC WORLD

The ancient pagans did not believe in one infinite/personal God who was Maker of heaven and earth. Instead, they believed that the universe was eternal, and that there were multiple gods and goddesses who were finite; i.e. limited in nature, power and knowledge.

In this pagan worldview, the gods fought among themselves for preeminence. There was no concept of the universe being ruled by one sovereign, infinite God who filled heaven and earth. The chaos of the gods allowed a certain view of man's powers and abilities to develop.

The pagan worldview taught that man was *autonomous* in an absolute sense. He was totally and absolutely "free" and even the gods could not violate this freedom. The Greek philosophers were the first to articulate the idea that man had a "free will" and that no one, not even a god, could violate it. The Greek philosopher Epictetus wrote,

> Not even Zeus himself can get the better of my free will.[216]

> Who can any longer restrain or compel me, contrary to my own opinion? No more than Zeus.[217]

In a contingent (i.e. chance-driven) universe in which no one was in control, not even the gods, man was totally free to be or do whatever he wanted. Man was even free to become a god if he so chose. Nothing was beyond the ability of man.

The pagan philosophers claimed that man had to be "free" in order for man to be responsible for his actions. If his choices and actions were in any way the result of what other people or even the gods themselves decided, then man was not really free.

The Greek philosophers demanded that man must be autonomous in order for man to be responsible because they assumed that *man was the measure of all things including his responsibility*. They understood the word "responsibility" to mean response-ability.

Man's responsibility was thus limited by two things: ignorance and inability.
   a. If he did not know about something, then he could not be held responsible for doing it.
   b. If he did not have the power to do something, he could not be held responsible for not doing it.

There was no concept in the pagan worldview that man's responsibility meant *accountability to his Creator who would one day judge him*. Thus the pagan concept of man's autonomous "free will" was possible only in the context of that pagan polytheistic worldview.[218]

ATHENS VERSUS JERUSALEM

When pagans first professed to be "Christians," some of them retained much of their pagan worldview. It was not long before they realized that the biblical worldview did not have room for the pagan concept of man's absolute free will.

The choice they faced was whether they should abandon or modify the biblical worldview to make room for the pagan concept of man's freedom or should they abandon the pagan concept of man and submit to revealed truth?

The rest of church history is the story of those who tried to mix the oil of the biblical worldview with the water of the pagan worldview and those who saw that such an attempt was useless. In the end, just as the oil and the water will separate, any attempt to marry Christ with Baal will fail.

The biblical authors did not buy into the pagan polytheistic worldview or its doctrine of human autonomy. They taught that man was created by God to bear His image. Therefore human responsibility meant that man was *accountable* to God for whatever God told him to know, be or do. *God was the measure of man's accountability. Man's ignorance and inability had no bearing on the issue.*

WHAT ABOUT THE HEATHEN?

Natural "evangelical" theologians and philosophers such as Pinnock and Sanders do not believe that the heathen will go to hell. They argue that that if someone has never heard the gospel, he cannot believe. Thus his ignorance and inability are valid *excuses* why God should not condemn him to hell. We have given a full refutation to this view elsewhere and can only summarize it here.[219]

First, as to whether or not the heathen have an excuse, the Apostle Paul in Romans 1:20 states that they are *"without excuse."* In case he was not understood, he repeated the dramatic words *"without excuse"* in Romans 2:1.

Humanistic theologians and philosophers will present all kinds of *excuses* why the heathen should not be thrown into hell. When we point them to clear Scripture that says that they are "without excuse," they usually respond, "But…they do have good excuses." It does not seem to dawn on them that they have directly contradicted the Word of God.

Second, they are operating on a false definition of human responsibility. They are assuming the pagan worldview in which man is the measure of all things including his responsibility.

To the extent that man knows and is capable, to that extent he is responsible. But the biblical worldview teaches that man is responsible in the sense that he is *accountable* to an Authority and Power higher than himself.

> For all of us must appear before the judgment-seat of Christ, so that *each one may give an account* of the things *done* in the body, according to what he has done, whether *it be* good or evil. (2 Cor. 5:10)
>
> τοὺς γὰρ πάντας ἡμᾶς φανερωθῆναι δεῖ ἔμπροσθεν τοῦ βήματος τοῦ Χριστοῦ, ἵνα κομίσηται ἕκαστος τὰ διὰ τοῦ σώματος πρὸς ἃ ἔπραξεν, εἴτε ἀγαθὸν εἴτε φαῦλον.
>
> No creature can hide from him. Everything is naked and helpless before *the eyes of the one to whom we must give an account.* (Heb. 4:13)
>
> καὶ οὐκ ἔστιν κτίσις ἀφανὴς ἐνώπιον αὐτοῦ, πάντα δὲ γυμνὰ καὶ τετραχηλισμένα τοῖς ὀφθαλμοῖς αὐτοῦ, πρὸς ὃν ἡμῖν ὁ λόγος.

One way to spot a humanistic thinker is to ask, "Is human responsibility defined in terms of man's ability and knowledge or is it defined in terms of one's accountability to his Creator?" When someone says that man's ability and knowledge limit his responsibility, you are talking with a humanist.

If he or she says that man's responsibility is defined by accountability to God, you are dealing with a biblical theist. On the Day of Judgment, man will not be seated on the throne judging God but God will judge every thought, word and deed of man.

IGNORANCE IS NO EXCUSE

In the biblical worldview, man fell into ignorance through sin at the Fall of Adam. Thus ignorance of one's duty to God and man is no excuse before God. This is why in Lev. 4 and Num. 15, if you sinned *in ignorance*, it was still viewed as a sin by God and you still had to offer a sacrifice to atone for that sin. Indeed, Christ will return one day,

> In flaming fire taking vengeance on *those who do not know God*. (2 Thess. 1:8)

> ἐν πυρὶ φλογός, διδόντος ἐκδίκησιν τοῖς μὴ εἰδόσιν θεὸν

On the Day of Judgment, people will be held accountable to God for what they did not know and for what they did know but disobeyed. They are sometimes called sins of omission and sins of commission. This is why the heathen go to hell even though they did not know the gospel. Their ignorance does not negate their accountability to God (Psa. 9:17) Paul put it this way,

> For all who have sinned apart from the Law will also perish apart from the Law: and all who have sinned under the Law will be judged by the Law. (Rom. 2:12)

> ὅσοι γὰρ ἀνόμως ἥμαρτον, ἀνόμως καὶ ἀπολοῦνται, καὶ ὅσοι ἐν νόμῳ ἥμαρτον, διὰ νόμου κριθήσονται·

It does not matter if you had or did not have the teaching of the law of God, if you sin, you will perish. Those who sinned without having a Bible will perish as certainly as those who had a Bible and failed to obey it.

INABILITY IS NO EXCUSE

In the biblical worldview, man fell into spiritual inability through sin at the Fall of Adam. Although man is now a sinner, he still has the responsibility to be as holy and perfect as God (Matt. 5:48; 1 Pet. 1:16) In the following texts, notice the *vocabulary of inability* used by the authors of Scripture:

> No man *can* come to me unless the Father who sent me draws him. (John 6:44)

> So he said, "This is why I told you that no man *can* come to me unless it be granted him by the Father. (John 6:65)

> That's why the mind that is set on the flesh is hostile toward God. It refuses to submit to the authority of God's Law because *it is powerless to do so*. (Rom. 8:7)

> Those who are under the control of the flesh *can't* please God. (Rom. 8:8)

> A person who isn't spiritual doesn't accept the things of God's Spirit, for they are nonsense to him. *He can't understand them because they are spiritually evaluated.* (1 Cor. 2:14)
>
> No man *can* say, "Jesus is Lord," except by the Holy Spirit. (1 Cor. 12:3)

Just because *you are not free* to come to Christ, submit to God's Law, confess Christ as Lord or live a perfect and sinless life because *your will is powerless*, does not mean that you will not be held accountable to God. It is because of sin that you are not able to do these things.

BIBLICAL HISTORY

Lastly, if we go through biblical history and look to see if ignorance or inability ever let anyone "off the hook" before God, we find that this *never* happened.

Were there ignorant people at the Flood, the Tower of Babel, Sodom and Gomorrah, the conquest of Canaan, the Exodus and the Exiles? Yes. Did their ignorance or inability qualify them to escape the judgment of God? No. Did not Jesus say that the Judgment Day will be like those events? Yes. "As it was in the days of…so shall it be. …" *Then ignorance and inability are not valid excuses before God.*

When a humanist responds, "But my god would not condemn ignorant people," respond back to them, "You are right! *Your god* would not do that. But this is the real problem. You have created a false god in your own image. Since *you* would not condemn the heathen, neither can your god. You are assuming that man is the measure of all things, including God."

THE CLASH OF WORLDVIEWS

Francis Schaeffer used the following illustration to point out that there is room in the biblical worldview for only *one* absolute free will. Imagine that you were shipwrecked on a deserted island. Since no other person was on the island, you had absolute freedom to do what you wanted because there was no one to interfere with that freedom. You did not need to wear clothes if you did not want to. You picked any fruit you wanted. You went where you wanted. But one day, another person was shipwrecked on the island. All of a sudden, you were no longer absolutely free to do as you please. What if he wanted to eat the same fruit that you wanted? What if he wanted you to pick it for him? What if he wanted you to wear clothing? In the end, only one of you can be free.

In the same way, in the biblical worldview, God is the only One with absolute free will.

> But our God is enthroned in the heavens: *He does whatever He pleases.* (Psa. 115:3)
>
> And all the inhabitants of the earth are reputed as nothing; and *He does according to his will* in the army of heaven, and among the inhabitants of the earth; and none can stay his hand, or say unto him, "What doest thou?" (Dan. 4:35)

Chapter Seven Biblical Theism

DO YOU BELIEVE IN FREE WILL?

A "Christian" humanist once asked me, "Do you believe in free will?" I replied, "Yes. *God* has an absolute free will to do with you and me as it pleases Him."

The humanist was obviously surprised by my answer. He replied, "I don't mean God's free will, I mean *man's* free will." I then asked, "Shouldn't we first begin with God and then proceed to man? Where does the Bible begin?" "Oh," said the humanist, "I see your trick. If we begin with God, then He will end up with an absolute free will and man is limited. Well, I refuse to begin with God because *man* must not be limited — not even by God." "This," I said, "is the real issue. As a biblical theist, I begin where the Bible begins, "In the beginning *God*" and as a humanist, you begin where pagan philosophy begins: "In the beginning man."

AN IRRECCONCILIBLE CONFLICT

Many pagan philosophers, such as Jean Paul Sarte, saw the issues clearly:[220]

> If the biblical worldview is true, then God is the only One with an absolute free will and man is limited by God. If the pagan worldview is true, then man is the only one with an absolute free will and God or the gods are limited by man. It is impossible to reconcile the pagan worldview with the biblical worldview.
>
> In the Bible, God is eternal, infinite and unlimited. The universe was created by God and is limited by Him. In the pagan worldview, the universe is eternal and the gods are finite and thus limited by the universe. Man is unlimited and totally free—even from the gods.
>
> Monotheism and polytheism cannot be reconciled. Neither can the concepts of man which developed out of them. I must choose between the two. It is either one or the other. There is no middle ground.
>
> If I choose the pagan worldview of human autonomy in which I am absolutely free, then I must deny that the God of the biblical worldview exists. If He exists, I am limited. If He does not exist, then I am free. If I choose the biblical worldview, then I must submit to the Lordship of Christ over all of life.

While this train of thought is understood by many secular philosophers, some "Christian" natural philosophers and theologians have tried in vain to reconcile the pagan worldview with the biblical worldview. But their attempts have always failed because they always begin as their fundamental starting point with the pagan idea that man has to be totally free and unlimited in the classic Greek philosophic sense of absolute human autonomy. They never begin with God or His revelation. But if you begin with man, you will never end with God.

FAILED ATTEMPTS AT SYNERGISM

Throughout church history there have been people who tried to blend together in some kind of synergistic system the pagan worldview of autonomous man with the biblical world view of a Sovereign God. They have always ended in failure because Christ and Satan will never walk together hand in hand. In the end, there can be only one.

> Stop becoming unevenly yoked with unbelievers. What partnership can righteousness have with lawlessness? What fellowship can light have with darkness? What harmony exists between Christ with Belial, or what do a believer and an unbeliever have in common? What agreement can a temple of God make with idols? (2 Cor. 6:14–16)

No one will be able to reconcile two radically different worldviews because we cannot serve two Masters. We will always end up hating one of them and serving the other. Either we choose the sovereign God of the Bible or the autonomous man of pagan philosophy.

GNOSTICS, MANICHAEANS, MARCIONITES, AND VALENTIANS

The heresies which plagued the early Church such as Gnosticism, Manichaeanism, Marcionism and Valentianism all taught that God had to be limited in knowledge and power in order for man to be absolutely free. God could not know the future as this would limit man's freedom. The early Christian creeds where explicitly written to exclude from the Church those who limited God's knowledge or power.

THE RENAISSANCE

The "Age of Reason" has incorrectly been contrasted to the "Age of Faith." The battle has never been between reason and faith *per se* but between *human reason* and *Divine revelation*. It takes a great deal of faith to believe that man is totally free. It also takes faith to bow before Scripture. Thus the issue is not faith, but the Object of our faith: either God or man.

THE SOCINIANS AND UNITARIANS

The *Socinians* not only denied the Trinity and the inspiration of the Bible, they also denied that God knew the future and that God's foreknowledge guaranteed that future events would necessarily happen according to God's decrees.

From the Socinians came the *Unitarians* who claimed that God did not choose to know all of the future. He chose not to know the future free acts of man.

JEHOVAH'S WITNESSES, MORMONS, AND OTHER CULTS

The idea that God does not choose to know the future free acts of man was picked up by such Arian cults as the Watchtower, and also by polytheistic cults like the LDS Mormons.

The main problem with this argument is that not only is it absolutely unbiblical, but also plainly idiotic. In order for God to choose what future events He wants to know and what future events He does *not* want to know, He has to first know them *all*.

If A through Z is going to happen in the future, in order for God to select b, g, l, r, s and t as things He does not want to know, He first has to know them. Otherwise, His knowledge becomes a haphazard, chance-driven, cosmic crap game, and Lady Luck is really the Supreme God. To think that God's knowledge is decided by the roll of the dice would not inspire us to worship God!

PROCESSIANISM

Alfred North Whitehead was one of the most vicious heretics and anti-Christs of the 20th century. He claimed that the God of the Bible was the devil and that Christianity with its concept of sin was one of the worst things that ever happened to humanity and that Jesus was not very intelligent. When asked if he read the Bible, he responded that he preferred reading Plato.

He taught that God was the soul of the world and the world was God's body. The two were in an eternal bi-polar relationship. You can't have one without the other. God could not know the future because it was open to unlimited possibilities. God was evolving, and in the end the heavens and the earth would beget God. [221]

With such sheer blasphemy and anti-Christian bigotry, one would not expect anyone to call him a "Christian" theologian and philosopher. But Natural Christian philosophers and theologians refer to him as a "Christian" thinker whose "insights" are valuable.

If you think that we are too severe in our condemnation of Whitehead and the processianism that he invented, Ronald Nash had this to say,

> To its critics, Process Theology is the most dangerous heresy presently threatening the Christian Faith. Process theology does not eliminate pagan ideas from the faith, its critics argue. Rather, Process thought is a total capitulation to paganism. Here there is no middle ground ...A being who is not essentially omnipotent or omniscient, who is not the sovereign and independent Creator, is neither worthy to receive our worship nor to bear the title "God." [222]

Some of Whitehead's followers included Charles Hartshorne, Schubert Ogden, David Griffin, Norman Pittenger, H. P. Owen, John Cobb, Jr., Nelson Pike, L. McCabe, and Lewis Ford. They have attacked Christianity and the Bible with great vigor. No wonder Bruce Demarest concluded,

> A former student of Whitehead reported that the master once commented that Christian orthodoxy could not be reconciled with his philosophy. Moreover, Brown, James, and Reeves acknowledge that Process Theology bears affinities with Theravada Buddhism, the thought of Heraclitus, the Unitarian Socinus, and the idealist philosophies of Hegel, Schelling, and T. de Chardin. By its own admission, then, Process Theology represents a departure from a

theology that broadly could be called biblical and historic Christianity.[223]

NEO-PROCESSIANISM IN NEO-EVANGELICAL CIRCLES

In neo-evangelical circles, one finds the heretical theories of Whitehead taught by such people as Clark Pinnock, Richard Rice, Gregory Boyd, Stephen Davis, Bruce Reichenbach, Gordon Olson, H. Roy Elseth, George Otis, Jr., and many others.[224]

Neo-processians are absolutely dogmatic that their god *cannot* know the future. But while their god does not know or ordain the future, they think that they and others *can* know the future!

Richard Rice is a Seventh Day Adventist and was faced with the rude reality that while he could deny that God knew the future and still keep his job at an SDA university, if he dared to deny that Ellen G. White knew the future, he would soon be collecting unemployment checks. Thus in the first edition of his book, he argued that while God did not know the future, Ellen G. White did! Need we say more?

CHRIST DID NOT DIE FOR YOU OR YOUR SINS

What are the implications of process thought? If God does not know the future, did He know that Christ would die? Elseth, Rice and others say, "No. God did not know that Jesus would die on the cross."

Does Jesus know the future? "No, he does not know the future." If God and Jesus do not know the future, particularly the free acts of man such as his sins, then did Jesus know of you and die for your sins when He hung on the tree? "No. God and Jesus did not know of you or your sins because they were in the future."

We have engaged in arguments with processians who deny that Jesus knew of or died for our sins. Yet, they are still running around in "evangelical" circles claiming to be fellow Christians.

Although it is not politically correct today to question people's profession of faith, anyone who denied that Jesus knew us and died for our sins on the cross has denied the biblical Gospel and is under the anathema of God (1 Cor. 15:3–4; Gal. 1:8).

DRIFTING INTO MORMON THEOLOGY

It is interesting to note that when the Mormons responded to Beckwith's book, *The Mormon Concept of God*, they were delighted that he had abandoned the historic orthodox view of omniscience and was moving over to *their* way of thinking. They then applauded Clark Pinnock for adopting the Mormon doctrine of the Openness of God![225] Thus, when we complain that Middle Knowledge and Process Theology are doctrines found in the cults and in the occult, we have good reason to say this.

My old friend, Dr. Carl F. Henry, in a powerful chapter entitled, "The Stunted God of Process Theology," sums up why Biblical theists are so hard on Process Theology.

> Orthodox Christians, both Protestant and Catholic, deplore the way in which process thinkers reject the supernatural, spurn the objective reality of the Trinity, disavow the miraculous, and

repudiate a Word of God mediated solely through Christ. They object to the elimination by most process theologians of Christ as the mediator through whom alone God speaks His word. Process theologians also assail the traditional instance on divine decrees and election, on *creation ex nihilo*, on miraculous redemption and on biblical eschatology. In place of divine decree and foreordination, process thinkers stress divine persuasion; they subordinate history and eschatological finalities broadly to the endless love of God. So great is the gulf between the two systems of theology that both can hardly lay claim to the title "Christian." [226]

THE COUNTER-REFORMATION

The Pope did not sit idly by while half of Europe walked out of his church and into the freedom of the gospel. He launched a counter-Reformation movement whose goal was to recapture nations and individuals who had become Protestants. The Society of Jesus (or the Jesuits) was given the task of retaking countries that had been won over by the preaching of the Reformers. They used two methods to overcome Protestantism. [227]

First, they kidnapped, raped, sodomized, tortured, murdered and made war on Protestants to force them to return to popery. The Jesuits, during the Thirty Years War and in the Inquisition, slaughtered several million Protestants. (See *Foxe's Book of Martyrs* for the details.)

Second, they invented doctrines that would undercut the four foundational truths of the Reformation: salvation is by *grace alone*, through *faith alone*, in *Christ alone*, according to *Scripture alone*.

The Origin of Molinism

According to *all* the standard reference works, a Jesuit priest named Luis de Molina invented the idea that God's decisions (i.e. decrees) in eternity are in response to what He foresees us initiating in the future. In this way, Molina could undercut the Reformation doctrines of the absolute necessity and efficacy of God's grace. It is interesting to note that his book on the subject was dedicated to the Inquisition of Portugal, where the Jesuits murdered many people.

Does God reward us with the decree of salvation on the basis of what He foresaw we would do by our own power? Thus, He decreed to save us because He foresaw that we would repent and believe? Is God's grace given in response to what we will do before (and thus without) His grace? Does He love us because He foresaw that we would first love Him? Does He choose us because He foresaw that we would first choose Him? Molina's end result is that God's decree to save us is a *reward* for what God foresaw we would do by our own power.

Many Catholic theologians were horrified by what Molina invented and labeled it as nothing more than a modern twist on the old Pelagian heresy. They almost succeeded in getting one Pope to condemn it as heresy.

Opposition to Molinism died down once it was seen that it deceived ignorant Protestants quite easily. Jesuit universities in Protestant countries made a point of indoctrinating Molinism into those Protestants who foolishly chose to be educated by them.

As these Jesuit-trained Protestants rose to prominence in Evangelical circles, they in turn introduced the Jesuit doctrine of Molinism in Protestant circles. But knowing that the average Protestant was suspicious of anything coming from the bloodthirsty Jesuits who had murdered their forefathers, it was decided to rename the doctrine "Middle Knowledge" instead of "Molinism" in an attempt to hide its Jesuit origins. But a rose by any other name still smells the same.

A few Protestant supporters of Molinism such as William Lane Craig have admitted the Jesuit origin of the doctrine and even warned that Molina had defective views of grace.[228] His honesty and openness on such issues is commendable. But the vast majority of those who teach it either ignorantly or deceptively hide its historical origins.

HOW TO UNDERCUT THE GOSPEL

Molina saw that the best way to undercut the gospel of grace alone was to deny that we are spiritually incapable of pleasing God. Instead, he put forth the old Greek humanist idea that man is totally and absolutely free from the effects of Adam's Fall into sin and guilt. Man's "free will" is thus not in bondage to sin, and the freedom of the will remains unimpaired. Molina emphasized the *unrestrained* freedom of the will.

We once again are confronted with an *a priori* commitment to a pagan worldview in which man is autonomous. We searched in vain for any substantial exegetical evidence put forth by Molina to *prove* that man is autonomous. He merely assumes that this is true and proceeds from there.

THE FATAL ERROR

This is the fatal error with all those who follow Molina. Such "Christian" humanistic philosophers as Alvin Plantinga [229] and William Lane Craig, [230] and those who follow them, naively assume the pagan doctrine of human autonomy as their starting point. They *assume* that if God predetermines the future, then man is not responsible.

A WORD OF CLARIFICATION

We must stop for a moment and emphasize that when we point out that some philosopher or theologian within "Evangelical" circles is a humanistic thinker and is teaching a pagan worldview, this does not mean that we are judging his heart. A philosopher or theologian can be a good father or mother, kiss babies, pet dogs, etc., but be a pagan in his worldview at the same time. Just because someone professes that he is "saved" does not mean he is on his way to heaven. The Apostle of Love questioned the profession of faith of many people in his day (1 John 2:4)

Being "saved" is no guarantee that you do not have pagan ideas floating around in your head. We are using Scripture to judge if a man's philosophy or theology is humanistic. We have no interest in judging people's hearts. God will do that on the Day of Judgment (1 Cor. 4:1–5)

PROBLEMS WITH MIDDLE KNOWLEDGE

The problems with the doctrine of "Middle Knowledge" are so profound and extensive that any committed Christian who loves the Lord and obeys Scripture can have nothing to do with it.

NOT A BIBLICAL OR APOSTOLIC DOCTRINE

The first problem that the supporters of Middle Knowledge face is that it is not a part of apostolic and historic Christianity. In Jude 3, we are told:

> ... to continue your vigorous defense of *the faith that was passed down to the saints once and for all.*
>
> ἔσχον γράψαι ὑμῖν παρακαλῶν ἐπαγωνίζεσθαι <u>τῇ ἅπαξ παραδοθείσῃ τοῖς ἁγίοις πίστει.</u>

Biblical theologians have always believed and taught that if a doctrine is *new*, then it is *not* true. If it is true, then it will not be new. The Reformers spent a great deal of time and energy tracing their doctrines in church history all the way back to the first century. Why did they do this? They had two reasons that weighed heavily on their mind.

First, from Jude 3, it is obvious that "the Faith;" i.e. the body of doctrines that constitutes biblical Christianity, was delivered once and for all of time in the first century in the teachings of Jesus and the Apostles (Eph. 2:20; 3:4–5) The Christian Church is to defend the doctrines given by the Apostles (Acts 2:42) If the Apostles did not teach a doctrine, it does not constitute a part of "the Faith."

Second, Jude used the aorist tense when he used the word παραδοθείσῃ (delivered) to emphasize the finality of the Faith. When it comes to doctrine or morals, there will be no "new" revelations after the New Testament. The principle of *Sola Scriptura* means that what we believe and how we live are to be determined by Scripture *alone*.

This understanding works well when we deal with the Book of Mormon, the Divine Principle or the visions of Ellen White. They cannot be accepted because they teach new doctrines that were not a part of biblical and historic Christianity.

It is a wonder to us that some of those involved in the Middle Knowledge doctrine will refute Mormonism by pointing out the recent origins of Smith's doctrine and then turn around and say that the fact that the doctrine of Middle Knowledge is of recent origin has no bearing on the issue! Hypocrisy has no limits!

What should we do with doctrines such as Middle Knowledge that have appeared only in recent church history? All the Protestant and Roman Catholic reference works that deal with the history and origin of the doctrine of Middle Knowledge confirm that it was invented by a Jesuit priest named Luis de Molina as part of the counter-Reformation, as discussed earlier.

IN PRINCIPLE NOT IN SCRIPTURE

Since Molinism (or Middle Knowledge) is clearly of recent origin, it is not a part of "the Faith once for all delivered to the saints." *Thus it cannot in principle be found in Scripture because the authors of the Bible died many centuries before Molina invented the doctrine.*

How then can some of those who teach the false doctrine of Molinism claim to find it in the Bible? By reading it back into biblical texts and thereby committing the hermenutical fallacy of *eisegesis*.

Most of those who teach this Jesuit doctrine will usually give "rational" arguments instead of any hard exegesis. Being humanists in their thinking, they assume that whatever they can come up with by "thinking" about it, has to be true. They will talk endlessly about someone doing this or that in the future. There is no need to bring a Bible to their lectures. Frank Beckwith provides a good example of this procedure.

FRANK BECKWITH'S PROOFS FOR MIDDLE KNOWLEDGE

In his discussion of the Omniscience of God in his book, *The Mormon Concept of God*, how does Beckwith *prove* that the Jesuit doctrine of Middle Knowledge is true?[231]

First, he uses two illustrations: Pat mowing the lawn on Tuesday and Jim marrying Kim. That's it! Does he bring up a single verse of Scripture? No. Why not? As all humanistic thinkers, he assumes that *he* is autonomous. Thus *he* can come up with the truth *without* special revelation from God. He assumes that if he can think of this or that hypothetical situation, which seems to *his* mind to prove Middle Knowledge, then it is automatically true. His eventual conversion to Roman Catholicism is not a surprise.

What Beckwith and other Molinists fail to understand is that although stories and illustrations may clarify a doctrine, they can never establish its truthfulness. They are great at spinning stories and illustrations by the dozens. But until they come up with solid exegetical evidence for their position, we are not interested. Speculative theology has always ended in heresy.

Second, while Beckwith never quoted from Scripture, he did quote the "guru of Evangelical Middle Knowledge," Dr. William Lane Craig. But Craig's citation does not contain any Scripture either. But that does not bother Beckwith or many others because, to some of them, Craig's words are just as authoritative as Scripture.

Since Molinism was specially invented by the Jesuits to convert Protestants, it is interesting to note that Beckwith and several other Molinists have converted to Roman Catholicism! Their apostasy is tacit proof that our criticism of Molinism is not only accurate, but prophetic.

QUESTIONS FOR MOLINISTS

1. Are God's decisions or decrees in eternity determined by what He sees will happen in the future?
2. Thus, is God's foreknowledge prior to and hence the origin of God's decrees?
3. Or, is what will happen in the future determined by what God decided or decreed in eternity?
4. Thus, are God's decrees prior to His foreknowledge; i.e. is what He foresees what He has decreed shall happen?
5. Did God decree to create the universe because He first saw that it would be created?
6. Or was the universe created because God decreed it?
7. Which came first, the decree to create or the divine foreknowledge of creation?
8. Did the future universe limit God's knowledge?
9. Is God's knowledge dependent or independent of the future universe?
10. Is His knowledge derived or deduced?
11. Is time the same for God as it is for us?
12. Does God "look into the future" like a man looking through a telescope?

Chapter Seven   Biblical Theism

13. Does God really have "foreknowledge" or is that word anthropomorphic?
14. Does God control the future or does the future control God?
15. Is the past, present and future the same for God as it is for man?
16. Is God's will determined by what man will do?
17. Or does God's will determine what man will do?
18. Is God free?
19. What kind of freedom does He have?
20. Is He free to sin, to lie, to fail, etc.?
21. Is God's will limited by His nature, thus He cannot sin?
22. Can man interfere with God's free will?
23. Does man's "free will" triumph over God's free will?
24. Or shall God's will be done on earth as it is in heaven?
25. Is it "My will be done" or "Thy will be done?"
26. In the finite universe God created for His glory, how many ultimate free wills can there be?
27. Does man have a "free will?"
28. Does the Bible ever discuss the subject of man's free will?
29. Can you give even one passage where this is done?
30. Is man free to be perfect and sinless?
31. Can you choose to be sinless today?
32. If not, why not?
33. Is man free to be omnipotent and omniscient?
34. Can God ever interfere with man's free will?
35. Does the decree of inspiration follow foreknowledge; i.e. did God will to inspire the book of Romans (or any other Scripture) because He first saw Paul writing it?
36. Did the authors of the Bible write their books because God willed it or did He will it because He saw them writing them?
37. Is man's free will perfect and infallible?
38. Or is it imperfect and fallible?
39. If man's free will is imperfect and fallible, then how can the Bible be perfect and infallible?
40. If God cannot interfere with man's free will, what prevented Paul or any other author of the Bible from putting mistaken ideas and contradictory information in it?
41. Did God violate the free wills of the authors of Scripture and allow them to write only what He wanted them to write?
42. Did God will that Christ would die because He first saw that He would die?
43. Or did Christ die because God willed it?
44. Was the betrayal and execution of Christ necessary?
45. Did all the events and choices of the men involved in the atonement have to happen the way they happened?
46. Could Judas have decided at the last moment not to betray Jesus and thus abort the atonement?
47. Were Herod or Pilate free to let Jesus go and derail the atonement?
48. What prevented the soldiers from breaking the bones of Christ?

The Bible, Natural Law, and Natural Theology: Conflict or Compromise?

49. Were the death of Christ and all the choices and acts of the men that made it transpire part of God's eternal predetermined plan for history?
50. Did they do what they did because God planned it?
51. Was the death of Christ a fluke or an accident that was not in God's plans?
52. Was the atonement something God decided to do in order to make something good come out of the death of Christ, which He foresaw would happen but did not ordain to happen?
53. Was Peter certainly going to deny the Lord three times or was it possible for him not to do it even though Christ predicted it?
54. Has God fixed, appointed, predestined or ordained the times and seasons?
55. In prophecy, is God telling us what He definitely knows will happen in the future?
56. Or, is there an element of chance or luck concerning the future that means that it does not necessarily have to come true?
57. Does God love us because He first saw us loving Him?
58. Does God choose us because He first saw us choosing Him?
59. Did God will to give us grace because He first saw us repenting and believing?
60. Which is right?

Biblical View	Molinistic View
As many as were ordained to eternal life believed.	As many as believed were ordained to eternal life.
You did not choose Me but I chose you.	I chose you because you first chose Me.
If the Lord wills, we will go to a city and make a profit.	If we go to a city and make a profit, then the Lord wills it.
I will come to Rome, if God wills it.	If I go to Rome, then God wills it.
Man proposes but God disposes.	God proposes but man disposes.
God works in man the willing and the doing	Man works in God the willing and the doing.
God's will determines the casting of the lots.	The casting of the lots determines God's will.

61. Where in the Bible is human autonomy clearly taught?
62. Is the "freedom" spoken of in Scripture a moral work of Christ in which He sets us free from the penalty, power and presence of sin?
63. Where in the Bible is the absolute freedom of human autonomy discussed or taught?

64. Is salvation a reward for what God sees we will do in the future?
65. Is damnation a punishment for what God sees we will do in the future?
66. Does man have "natural powers" to repent and believe?
67. After the Fall, was man's will affected by sin? In what ways?
68. Can we please God by our own natural powers?
69. Can the saints in heaven sin?
70. If not, are they free?
71. In the eternal state, is there a chance that someone will sin and start the whole mess over again?
72. Should we begin with God or man in our worldview?
73. In your worldview, is it possible for Christ to die all over again?
74. Do you believe that the future is open to chance and luck?
75. Does the future hold infinite possibilities?
76. Was the time/space universe created as one?
77. Can we separate time from space?
78. Do you believe that time is eternal but space created?
79. If time is eternal, is God eternally "in" time or is time eternally "in" God?
80. Is God therefore dependent upon time for His existence?
81. If God is dependent upon time for His existence, is time the true GOD above God?
82. What about the heathen?
83. Are there any valid excuses the heathen can give God as to why He cannot throw them into hell?

CONCLUSION

In this brief study of the nature and extent of God's knowledge, we have demonstrated that the historic Christian view is in line with the clear teaching of Scripture.

God knows *all* things, including the *future*. His foreknowledge is certain and infallible because it flows from His eternal decrees. The Bible describes the wicked as the only ones who deny or limit God's knowledge.

Today, it is necessary to warn God's people that false teachers have arisen who will deny "the faith once for all of time delivered to the saints." But we must follow the Apostle Paul who said,

> Let God be true even if this makes everyone a liar. (Rom. 3:4)

μὴ γένοιτο· γινέσθω δὲ ὁ θεὸς ἀληθής, πᾶς δὲ ἄνθρωπος ψεύστης.

Chapter Eight

Biblical Anthropology

Humanism and the Death of Anthropology

The second issue that natural theologians assure us is something that only human reason can explore and explain is the origin and nature of man. The Bible was written a time long ago and is of little use in developing the discipline of anthropology. But, this is not true at all. As we shall see, the Bible not only reveals final answers about God, but it also reveals final answers about man.

The Day "Essence" Died, Humanistic Views of Man Died

The greatest mega-shift in Western philosophy was the collapse of essentialism and the triumph of existentialism. "Essentialism" or "ontology" was the long-held Western belief in and search for the "essence" or "nature" of the "being" of reality as a whole or the objects around you. Once you discovered the "essence" or "nature" of the "being" of something, then you understood its "meaning."

The Greek philosophers fought over how and where to find the "essence" or "nature" of "being" and whether the external form of something indicated its true essence/nature/being. Plato pointed "up" to the World of Ideas and claimed that the essence or meaning of something was "up there" somewhere and could be retrieved by rationalism. Aristotle pointed to the object and said that its meaning is not "up there" but "in there," i.e. in the object. He postulated that we need to "grasp" its meaning/essence/nature "inside" of it empirically.

Subsequent Western philosophers believed that, instead of the meaning or nature of things being "up there" or "in there," meaning was in the mind of man and in the object at the same time. We are born with "innate" ideas in the brain and when they come into contact with the inner essence or nature of something, they connect and knowledge happens. Thus meaning is "in here" and "in there" at the same time.

As time went by, it became obvious to everyone that there was no agreement as to what ideas were innate or even how to define the words "innate" and "ideas." Thus the "essence" or "nature" of things still remained out of reach.

The End of the Road

Modern Philosophers concluded that meaning, essence, nature, and being were only in the mind of man, i.e. "in here." Things in and of themselves did not have any meaning, essence, nature or being. We impose or project our own meaning upon the world around us. Kant was the greatest of the German philosophers who abandoned any idea of meaning being "out there" somewhere. Meaning was produced by the categories of the mind.

It wasn't long before Western philosophers realized that if meaning, essence, nature, and being were only in the mind of man, and there was no agreement as to how they got there or how to define any of the key terms, the whole thing was stupid and a waste of time. No one was able to discover the meaning, essence, nature or being of reality as a whole or in the object themselves.

The humanist attempts to find meaning, essence, nature or being "out there" objectively in "Nature" or subjectively "in the mind" collapsed. Secular philosophers concluded that those old Greek ideas did not exist except as figments of the mind. And, even if they did exist, no one knew how to define or find them. Thus the knowledge of them is impossible. And, if no one can know them, why waste time talking about them?

The Mystery of Substance

The word "substance" is a good example of this failure of definition. What is the "substance" of something? Is it accessible to us? Can we pick some up and look at it? How do we gain knowledge of it? What is the "substance" of substance? No one knows. In the end, Western humanism could not define what it is or how to know it. Thus the word "substance" lost all meaning, and remains only as a psychological term used to manipulate people emotionally.

Essentialism collapsed and Existentialism was born. It taught that all we can know is what exists in front of us for the moment. What is, *is*. That is all we can say. There is no "higher" or "inner" meaning or "essence" to things. There is no "substance" behind or beneath things that reveal to us their true "meaning." Humanism's attempt to find meaning in life was just as futile as attempting to jump over your own shadow. What you see - is what you get.

So What?

What does this have to do with anthropology? Modern philosophy no longer believes that we should try to discover the "essence" or "nature" of the "substance" of "mankind". What makes man *man* is no longer a politically correct question. There is no such thing as a permanent, continuing "human nature" that makes man distinct from other life forms on the planet. Man *qua man* is a pipe dream. The day Essentialism died, anthropology died with it. When God died, man died.

The Myth of Human Nature

Natural Law philosophers tell us that there is a "substance" out there called "human nature" that is the "seat" of "reason" and the "place" where natural laws exist and can be discovered. [232] They have been so successful in indoctrinating Western people with the idea that they have a "human nature," that, whenever anyone questions the validity of it, panic and anger ensues. Maybe you think you have a "human nature." Since I never found one lying around somewhere, I don't have one myself.

Most Western humanists still teach that "human nature" is some "thing" that each "normal," "rational" or "civilized" man and woman supposedly possesses. How, when, where, why, and, from what or whom, they got "it," is not agreed upon. But, "it" contains mystical and magical intrinsic "faculties" or innate "powers" that were given to them before or after conception. No one knows where they came from. Who or what gave them these faculties or powers has never been agreed upon. It is "just there."

Women, Children and Slaves

For thousands of years, Natural Law taught that women, children, slaves and the "barbarian" races did not have a "human nature." Their "inner nature" was animal, sub-human. More on that issue later.

Amazing Super-Powers

The Greek philosophers idealized these mysterious divine "faculties" in that they viewed them as perfect, autonomous, immutable, and self-sustaining. What affected one faculty did not necessarily affect the others. They came together as a "package deal" in that they all contained the same *perfect* powers in the same amounts. They are so magical as to be defined as "divine" in some sense. Dr. Jean Porter, one of the most articulate natural theologians today, pointed out,

> This is a striking theological idea and a potentially powerful social and political claim. If reason is in some sense divine, if the rational person therefore shares in the dignity and authority of God, then this implies that the rational person should have authority within the community.[233]

These "faculties" include such *divine* "powers" as reason, feelings, innate ideas, conscience, free will, etc. They were "mechanical" in nature because they worked automatically. They were "autonomous" because they worked regardless if the gods (or God) existed or not. They did not depend upon the gods (or God) for their creation or maintenance.

Unity, Dignity, and Human Nature

Originally, the Stoics taught that this "thing" called "human nature" was what made male Greek citizens distinct from animals and the rest of the world. Without it, the unity and dignity of Greek men disappeared.

Since "human nature" depended upon gender, ethnic, civic, and rational qualifications, what did the Greeks do with non-citizens, unborn babies, newborn babies, the mentally handicapped, mentally diseased or damaged people, slaves, the elderly, women, etc? The Greeks "exposed" or "disposed" of them because they did not have a "human nature." Infant girls and physically defective baby boys were put out with the trash!

Modern Natural Law

Modern Natural Law theorists claim that all people, regardless of race or rank, have a "human nature." But, how do they deal with the reality that not all people are "rational," or "civilized?" After all, drug addicts are "addicts" because they do not have a "free will" when it comes to their dependence on drugs. Demon-possessed people do not have a "free will", but are under the control of the devil. What about babies born with brain damage? The brains of adults can be injured or become diseased.

Can people lose their "human nature?" What about mentally ill people who no longer manifest reason, consciousness, or free will? Are they still "human?" Where is the evidence that they have a "human nature?"

J. P. Moreland and William Craig understand that when they claim that all people have a good and perfect "human nature," mentally handicapped children, people with brain injuries, etc. don't seem to fit their claim. To overcome this reality, they create an alternate reality.

> First, there is what can be called **Aristotelian rationality**. In this sense, Aristotle called man a *rational* animal. Hence, *rational* refers to a being with *ratio*—a Latin word referring to the ultimate capacity or power to form concepts, think, deliberate, reflect, have intentionality (mental states like thoughts, beliefs, sensations that are *of* or *about* things.) Humans are rational animals in that, by nature, they have the powers of reason...humans are rational even if through defect (e.g. being a defective newborn) they cannot exercise that power, because the power of reason is possessed simply in virtue of having a human nature. It is important to distinguish between having a power and being able to exercise or develop it. [234]

In their fantasy world, all people are born with perfect and immutable powers such as reason, conscience, free will, innate ideas, etc. Some people do not manifest these powers because they do not "exercise" them! How they can believe such nonsense is beyond us.

Secular Humanism's Love of Death

Secular humanists today abort infants, kill born unwanted or defective babies, euthanize mentally or physically challenged people, and assist the suicide of the elderly because they classify them as "non-persons," i.e. non-humans or sub-humans.

We must keep in mind that the Nazi Natural Law theologians redefined Jews, Gypsies, and homosexuals as "sub-humans" and liquidated them by the millions. In the 20th century, Marxists redefined certain social groups as "non-persons" and slaughtered hundreds of millions of people. Abortion has slaughtered millions of babies on the grounds that they are not "persons," but only "tissue." Ideas *do* have consequences.

Romanticism

Modern Law theorists romanticize that all people start out life with the same exact perfect faculties at conception. If we delete any of these divine powers or faculties from the essence or substance of "human nature," the entire concept collapses. Thus we have to gratuitously assert that every human being, from Adam to the last baby born, has the same exact identical "human nature" that all other people have and that everyone has exactly the same perfect powers!

Unless we can get into a time machine and travel back to the Garden of Eden or move forward in time to Armageddon, such claims are impossible to verify. The idea of an ideal, static, perfect "human nature" possessed by all human beings is thus a leap-of-faith statement rooted in some kind of psychological "wish fulfillment."

Pelagius' Old Heresy

Christian theologians must remember that the issue of whether man is born with a good, perfect, and sinless "human nature" was the central controversy between Augustine and Pelagius. The Western Church declared at the Council of Orange that Pelagius was teaching heresy and that man did not have a good and perfect nature. We sin because we *are* sinners.

The issue resurfaced at the Reformation in the debate between Luther and Erasmus. Is man born with a perfect free will or is his will in bondage to his sinfulness inherited from Adam? Erasmus wrote *The Freedom of the Will* while Luther wrote *The Bondage of the Will*. Old controversies don't fade away but are revived from time to time under different names.

Modern Natural Law theologians are guilty of teaching the heresy of Pelagianism when they claim that all people are conceived or born with a perfect and good "human nature." On this basis, they assert that all people "naturally" seek the good because "human nature" is good. The idea that some people seek evil and do not want the truth, but rather love lies, does not fit into their Natural Law theories.

Is Man Naturally Good or Evil?

Pope John Paul in his encyclical *Fides et Ratio* defined "human nature" in the following ways.

> Reason is by its nature orientated to truth and is equipped moreover with the means necessary to arrive at truth (no. 94). Humans are by nature truth-seekers, pausing to ask why things are as they are (no. 3). Humans seek to know the truth about personal existence, about life, and about the Creator, for man has been created as the one who seeks after truth (nos. 5 and 28).[235]

Pelagius would have agreed with the Pope's definition of human nature. Jean Porter admits that Catholic Natural Law theorists "consistently say that human depravity cannot destroy our knowledge of the natural law. Because the natural law is grounded in human nature, knowledge of it cannot be wholly lost so long as human beings continue to exist."[236]

What if "human nature" is now evil and in bondage to sin (Rom. 3:10-18)? What if people "naturally" prefer the darkness rather than the light (John 3:19-20)? What if man does not "naturally" seek God but rather "naturally" rejects God (Rom. 3:11)? What if fallen man no longer has the "natural" ability to repent of his sins or believe the gospel (John 6:44 cf. Rom. 8:7; 1 Cor. 2:14; 12:3)? What if man is sinful "by nature" (Eph. 2:3)? How can it be the Source or Origin of "natural" laws, truth, justice, morals, meaning or beauty? It can't.

The Origin of Human Nature

While we are discussing the concept of "human nature," who invented the idea of a "human nature" that has all these wonderful perfect, magical, divine, ideal powers? How can all people have these god-like powers when only a few people exercise them some of the time? Is the idea of "human nature" innate, universal, intuitive, and self-evident? If so, how come the majority of mankind throughout history never heard of or believed in it? Where did the idea of "human nature" originate? When? Where? By whom?

I realize such questions are upsetting to natural law theologians because they strike at the very foundation of their theory. But we must become epistemologically self-conscious by asking why we believe what we believe, and, if it is a valid idea, it will withstand scrutiny.

Zeno of Citium

The idea of "human nature" was invented by a pagan Greek philosopher by the name of Zeno of Citium.[237] He wrote a book entitled, "Concerning Human Nature" in which he claimed that "within" each rational and civilized male Greek citizen there was a divine "spark" (i.e. "soul") that existed apart from and independent of the body. Since it was *divine*, it had the attributes and powers of the gods. These divine powers are "faculties."

Zeno went on to found the Stoic school of philosophy. Other Greek philosophers adopted his idea of "human nature" and today it is the Western humanistic secular basis for the unity and dignity of man. He was also the inventor of Natural Law theory that was based upon his concept of human nature. The two ideas have been intrinsically bound to each other from that day forward.[238]

Natural Law Based Upon Human Nature

It may be a surprise that the historical origins of Natural Law theory and the idea of human nature can be traced back to the pagan Greek philosophy of Stoicism. But this is acknowledged by all general reference works. A few modern scholars have attempted to dig further back in Greek philosophy to find the roots of Zeno's thinking. But that Stoicism is the mother of the heresy of "Natural Law" is clear.

Howard Kainz, one of the most well-known modern natural theologians today, stated, "Natural law in the strict sense and as an explicit theory emerged, as we shall see, with the Stoics."[239] The great Nicholas Wolterstoff correctly pointed out the independence of these two Stoic ideas.

> From its beginnings among the Stoics of antiquity, the natural law tradition of ethical theory has undergone many transformations…It is from human nature as such that they propose to derive ethical principles; and it is their claim that these are not only knowable, but in good measure actually *known*, by every rational adult human being whatsoever.[240]

Dr. Jean Porter pointed out that the connection between the classic Greek concepts of "human nature" and Natural Law theory is now problematic.

> Both Kark Rahner and Bernard Lonergan argued that this account of natural law is inadequate because it represents a "static" and "classical" view of human nature.[241] …what we require…the development of a natural law grounded in human nature.[242]

The Rationality of Human Nature

Does "human nature" exist in some physical, ontological or metaphysical sense? No. Is it observable? No. Can we examine it? No. Can we access it in any sense? No. Do we really know anything about it? No. Yet, natural theologians and philosophers insist that it *must* exist for their various natural law theories to work. They also assert that "human nature" has to be *good* or how else can we say that *all* men seek the good *by nature*? It has to be *rational* or how else can we define man as a "rational animal" *by nature*. It has to be *free* or how else can we say that all men have *free will* by *nature*?

The denial of the existence, rationality, and validity of the Stoic idea of a static, perfect, divine "human nature" pulls the rug out from under the feet of all Western humanistic schemes to find truth and morals without God. One of the Natural Theology's key presuppositions has unsolvable problems!

Natural law theorists claim that "human nature" is universal, innate, static, immutable, and perfect in all respects because it *has* to exist in order to have a *secular* basis for the unity and dignity of man.

Why Accept It?

Why should we accept Zeno's view of man? Natural theologians tell us that the alternative is too horrifying to consider. Without "human nature," there can be no Natural Law. Without Natural Law, there can be no natural rights! Without natural rights, woman's rights, child rights, and even international law becomes impossible. This is the abyss that modern humanists are desperately trying to avoid.

In this game of philosophic poker, the secular philosophers "came to reject the basic claim that there is an unchangeable human nature from which moral norms can be derived."[243]

The "romantic" idea of a perfect, good, and universal human nature in the hearts of all people is crumbling to pieces today. Dr. Porter pointed out in her second book on natural law that secular philosophers are now arguing that,

> We have no direct access to human nature, and our attempts to understand it are bound to be conditioned by our own cultural and even personal presuppositions, which are likely to determine our sense of what counts as natural...the idea of a fixed human nature is suspect because it fails to take account of the socially constructed, radically contingent character of all communal practices and moral norms.[244]

The Catholic philosophers cast a spell upon Western man that lasted a thousand years. Western philosophers blindly accepted the ideas of "human nature" and "Natural Law." But now the spell has been broken and people are awakening to the truth that the "emperor has no clothes," and that those old Stoic ideas are bankrupt.

Human Rights and Natural Rights

The Western concepts of "natural rights," "human rights," "women's rights," and "child rights," found in various United Nations declarations, were based upon the Western Natural Law tradition.[245] As long as Europe dominated the world, it imposed these ideas on the rest of the world. But "the day of the white man" has passed and there are now calls for such Western ideas as "Natural Law," "human nature," and "natural rights" to be cast aside as legacies of European colonialism.

This situation came to a head in 1999 when several non-Western UN representatives called into question the Western concepts of "natural rights." The reaction was swift and brutal. Western humanists warned, "If you abandon the concepts of "Natural Law," there is no *secular* basis for the "rights" of man." But the damage was done because the "cat" was now out of the bag.

But What About The Bible?

Since the Bible is important to those who claim to be a "Christian" in some sense or the other, we are warranted to ask, "Is Zeno's concept of "human nature" found in the Bible?" After over thirty years of reading the Bible in the original languages, we have yet to find it mentioned anywhere.

Some "Christian" Natural Law theorists state that the Apostle Paul believed in Stoicism and put it into his Epistles.[246] But they never give a detailed exegetical demonstration of their claim. It is just another empty assertion.

Other theorists claim that "the image and likeness of God" (Gen. 1:28) can be interpreted as a reference to Zeno's concept. But, since the book of Genesis was written long before Zeno was born, the timing is wrong. The cultural context of Genesis is not the same as the context of Zeno.

The meaning of "the image and likeness of God" in Genesis is interpreted by Moses in the immediate context as man "taking dominion" over the earth. It *never* has any ontological or metaphysical meaning anywhere in Scripture.

Their Misuse of Scripture

This brings up a huge problem. Whenever natural theologians cite the Bible in defense of their ideas, they begin by *assuming* their particular version of Natural Law as the framework within which Scripture is to be interpreted! They begin by *assuming* as true what they have yet to prove true. They are rowing with only one oar and end up going in circles. Dr. Jean Porter admitted,

> Their reading of Scripture was itself shaped by wider assumptions about the natural law, which were in turn formed by a multifaceted tradition of reflection on the natural law.[247]
>
> ...they employ their overall concept of the natural law as a framework for interpreting Scripture as a moral document.[248]

This is why it is unwise to take for granted their interpretation of Scripture. They read the Bible through the lens of Natural Law instead of seeking to understand the text in light of its grammar, syntax, and historical context. They read modern ideas back into ancient biblical texts without hesitation. As we will demonstrate in a later chapter, they seem incapable of accurately quoting the text of Scripture but add and subtract words as they please.

How Then Can Man Have Unity and Dignity?

Since the Bible does not teach the idea of "human nature," on what basis can we believe in the unity and dignity of mankind? In the biblical world view, the unity and dignity of mankind rests upon Creation, Fall, and Redemption.

Bible-based Christians agree with modern humanists that a *secular* basis for the unity and dignity of man is impossible. All secular attempts to find a basis for the unity and dignity of man have failed. The only basis left for the unity and dignity of man is a *religious* basis found in the Bible alone. With Scripture, man has unity and dignity. Without the Bible, man is dead.

Creation

In terms of Creation, man-as-image-bearer-of-God is the basis of his dignity and meaning. Paul told the Greeks that man was "one" because God created man and providentially ruled where and when he is to be born, live, and die (Acts 17:25f). If you delete man's relationship to his Creator, man is only an animal and has no dignity or rights. Even capital punishment for murder is just according to the Bible because man is the image bearer of God.

> Whoever sheds man's blood, By man his blood shall be shed, For in the image of God He made man. (Gen.9:6)

As Larry Richards pointed out,

> **Capital punishment.** The text quotes God as commanding capital punishment for murder. The reason given is that God made man in His own image. It is important to understand that the death sentence is neither retribution, nor simply preventative. Because we bear God's image, each human being is irreplaceable. Every human life is so significant that no penalty less than death provides an adequate measure of its value. Only by decreeing capital punishment as a penalty for murder can society affirm the ultimate worth and value of each individual citizen. [249]

Once you deny the Creator-creature relationship between God and man, murder loses all meaning because all is meaningless. James, the half brother of Jesus, tells us that we "ought" not curse people with our tongue.

> With it we bless *our* Lord and Father; and with it we curse men, who have been made in the likeness of God. From the same mouth come *both* blessing and cursing. My brethren, these things ought not to be this way. (James 3:9-10)

> ἐν αὐτῇ εὐλογοῦμεν τὸν κύριον καὶ πατέρα καὶ ἐν αὐτῇ καταρώμεθα τοὺς ἀνθρώπους τοὺς καθ' ὁμοίωσιν θεοῦ γεγονότας, ἐκ τοῦ αὐτοῦ στόματος ἐξέρχεται εὐλογία καὶ κατάρα. οὐ χρή, ἀδελφοί μου, ταῦτα οὕτως γίνεσθαι.

In his commentary on James, Peter Davids tell us that,

> The idea that man was made in God's image refers to Gn. 1:26 LXX (καθ' ὁμοίωσιν; cf. Gn. 9:6; Sir. 17:3; Wis. 2:23; 2 Esd. 8:44; Clem. *Hom.* 3:17, which have the same concept with different vocabulary). But it is important to realize that this fact was used in Jewish traditions to reject the cursing of men: *Mek.* on Ex. 20:26; *Gn. Rab.* 24:7–8 on Gn. 5:1; Sl. Enoch 44:1; 52:126; Sipra on Lv. 19:18. The connection is simply that one cannot pretend to bless the person (God) and logically curse the representation of that person (a human). Likewise, the angry curse upon a person while liturgically blessing God makes moral and logical nonsense from James's theological standpoint. [250]

The biblical basis of "oughtness" is rooted in its doctrine of man-as-image-bearer. The only basis for the ethical treatment of men and animals is the doctrine of Creation. Once you deny Creation and replace it with a secular "nature-without-God," there is no way to discover what we ought and ought not to do.

The Radical Fall of Man

In terms of the Fall, Paul proclaimed to the Greek philosophers that man was sinful and that God has fixed a Day of Judgment at the end of history when each person must give an account to Him (Acts 19:30-31 cf. 2Cor. 5:10). God's Revealed Law will judge all mankind, *not* some "Natural Law" found in "nature." (Acts 17:30-31).

Redemption

In terms of Redemption, God calls all sinners to repent and to believe the Gospel (Acts 17:30). The salvation of the soul through regeneration and the salvation of the body through resurrection is the focus of redemption (Acts 17:31-34).

The Bible knows nothing of a secular "human nature" or its god-like powers or faculties. Man-as-image-bearer (Gen. 1:26-27) received *revealed* Laws from his Creator (Gen. 2:15f). Thus the biblical basis for the unity, dignity, worth, meaning, and significance of man is founded on the *revealed* truth that man was created to glorify God (Isa. 43:70; 1 Cor. 10:31). No Jew or Christian in the Bible ever believed in "human nature." This is why the Bible does not mention such "faculties" or "powers" as "reason" or "free will."

Biblical Christians Cheered

Biblical Christians cheered when they saw the non-Western president of the UN call for the rejection of such Western *secular* concepts as "human nature," "natural rights," and "the rights of man," because the Bible is the only basis upon which such rights can be sustained. The sooner non-Christians understand that without the Bible the rights of man cannot be sustained, the sooner they will be willing to listen to the Gospel. As long as they think they can have truth and morals *without God,* they will turn a deaf ear to the Gospel. When natural theologians defend a *secular* basis (i.e.

without God or His Word) for truth, justice, morals, meaning, and beauty, they do biblical Christianity a disfavor and give unbelievers a reason *not* to accept Christ.

The Babylonian Captivity of the Church

The Greek concept of "human nature" entered Christendom when Greek philosophy overwhelmed the Biblicism of the early church. It is now an essential element in Catholic Natural Theology and neo-Protestant Natural Theology. This explains why natural theologians and philosophers went into panic mode when the humanistic concepts of "human nature" and "human rights" were attacked by secular humanists. B. F. Skinner's book, *Beyond Freedom & Dignity*, was a shot heard in the secularized church as well as around the world.[251]

Skinner has won the day so far as state education is concerned. The only ones who still believe in "natural rights" based on "Natural Law" and "human nature" are Catholics and erstwhile Protestants. Western secular humanists have abandoned these Greek ideas and moved on to post-modernism.

Man is Dead

If modern secular anthropologists no longer believe there is such a thing as "human nature," what do they teach at the local junior college or university? Anthropology has now been reduced to:

> **Zoology**: Man is only a primate. Thus "man" does not exist as a separate category. This is why there are so many TV programs focusing on lemurs, chimpanzees, and orangutans. "See, man is only one primate among many," says the humanist on National Geographic or Nature cable TV programs.
>
> **Psychology**: Man is only one self-conscious animal among other animals. This is why there is such a desperate search to find some animal somewhere that is self-aware. Gorillas, dolphins, and other animals are often portrayed as self-conscious animals just like man. "See, man is not really unique!"
>
> **Sociology**: Marxism and socialism are popular in Western education today because man is understood only in terms of sociological units and relationships. Humanists have given up trying to define what man *is*. Instead, they discuss man as a social animal interrelating and interacting with each other as a troop of primates. This why there is a flood of TV programs describing the social interactions of meerkats, lemurs, monkeys, etc. "See, people are only the same as meerkats!"

Western education no longer believes that there is any truth to find, any morals to follow, and any meaning to life. This is all true once you reject the God who is there and is not silent. With God, all these things are possible. Without God, all is meaningless.

Chapter Eight Biblical Anthropology

O Happy Day!

Biblical Christians rejoiced to see that secular and religious humanism are now officially D.O.A. The inerrant, propositional Revelation given to us in Scripture is the only Light in a world of philosophic darkness and despair. It is either God's way or the highway!

Existentialists such as Paul Sartre openly admitted that without God, life has no meaning, no morals, no truth, and no justice. In contrast, natural theologians deny this and try their best to give unbelievers the vain hope that they can have morals and meaning *without* God. What does the Bible say on this issue?

The Book of Ecclesiastes

First, as we have already established, in the Book of Ecclesiastes, the smartest man who ever lived stated thirty seven times that, without God, *all of life is meaningless*. This is the theme of the book from the very beginning.

> "Meaningless!
> Meaningless!"
> says the Teacher.
> "Utterly meaningless!
> Everything is meaningless."
> (Ecc. 1:2 NIV)

The classic exegetical commentaries on Ecclesiastes agree on this point.

> After identifying himself as the author, Solomon declared most emphatically that everything is futile or **meaningless.** Five times in this one verse he used *he_bel*, the Hebrew word for "meaningless." Four of those times are in a twofold repetition of a Hebrew superlative construction which the KJV renders "Vanity of vanities" and the NIV renders **Meaningless! Meaningless! And Utterly meaningless!** As indicated in the *Introduction's* "Theme and Purpose," he used this metaphorical term throughout the book to refer to what is without real substance, value, permanence, significance, or meaning. Here at the outset he applied this to **everything,** by which he meant all human endeavors, as is obvious from verse 3 and his argument throughout the book. [252]

> He now starkly sets forth the theme of his book in a manner befitting the theme itself: "Everything is meaningless."[253]

> The major theme of Ecclesiastes is the pointlessness of human activity...The expression still endures today to point out to many the meaningless of life without God. [254]

> **Vanity.** This traditional KJV rendering of a key word in this book is correctly translated by the NIV as "meaningless." Solomon's search for meaning in life apart from God and divine revelation was futile. Like modern existential philosophers, Solomon concluded that life is meaningless. How good to know that God's revelation of Himself and His purposes give a meaning to your life and mine which can be found in no other source.[255]
>
> LIFE IS MEANINGLESS: THE PROBLEM (1:1–11) *1:1–11 "Nothing matters! All is meaningless!"* Solomon began his discourse on life by declaring, "Everything is meaningless" (1:2; see 12:8; Ps. 39:5–6). He illustrated this meaninglessness from the realms of nature (1:1–7) and human experience (1:8–11). Sunrises and sunsets come and go. The winds blow and the rivers flow, but for no apparent purpose. The human experience could be summarized as, "Been there, done that!"[256]

God warns us that if we try to interpret life without His revelation in Scripture, life will be meaningless.

Second, not only does "without God" mean "without meaning," it also means "without hope." In Eph. 2:12, (ἐλπίδα μὴ ἔχοντες καὶ ἄθεοι ἐν τῷ κόσμῳ) and 1 Thess. 4:13, (οἱ μὴ ἔχοντες ἐλπίδα), the Apostle Paul emphatically states that those who are "without God" are, as a direct result, "without hope." As Dr. Wiersbe pointed out in his commentary on 1 Thess. 4:13,

> **Revelation: We Have God's Truth (1 Thes. 4:13, 15a)** How can mortal man penetrate beyond the grave and find assurance and peace for his own heart? From Old Testament days till the present, mankind has tried to solve the riddle of death and the afterlife. Philosophers have wrestled with the question of immortality. Spiritists have tried to communicate with those who have gone beyond. In our modern world, scientists have investigated the experiences of people who claimed to have died and returned to life again. They have also studied occult phenomena, hoping to find a clue to the mystery of life after death. Paul solved the problem when he wrote, "For this we say unto you by the Word of the Lord" (1 Thes. 4:15). We Christians need not wonder about death or life after death, for we have a revelation from God in His Word. Why substitute human speculation for divine revelation? God gave Paul a special revelation concerning the resurrection and the return of Christ (see 1 Cor. 15:51–54). What Paul taught agreed with what Jesus taught (John 5:24–29; 11:21–27). And God's revelation is based on the historic fact of Christ's resurrection. Since our Savior has conquered death, we need not fear death or the future (1 Cor.

15:12ff). The authority of God's Word gives us the assurance and comfort we need. [257]

Other commentators agree.

> *Those who have no hope* is literally "the others" or "the rest, who do not have hope." These are the same group of people whom Paul has just called "those outside" (v. 12), that is, those who are not members of the Christian community. The contrast is not between kinds or degrees of grief, but between two groups of people; that is, Christians, who have reason to hope, and non-Christians, who do not. [258]

> **Who have no hope.** Only believers have *hope* of life after death. The speculations and surmisings of pagan philosophy do not amount to a hope. [259]

In Eph. 2:13, Paul gives us a very startling view of what life is like "without God."

> Remember that at that time you were: separate from Messiah, excluded from citizenship in Israel, and foreigners to the covenants of the promise, without hope, (ἐλπίδα μὴ ἔχοντες) and without God in the world. (ἄθεοι ἐν τῷ κόσμῳ)

A.T. Robertson and other commentators point out that Paul was emphatic that if you are "without God," then you are "without hope" for anything.

> **Having no hope** (ἐλπιδα μη ἐχοντες [*elpida mē echontes*]). No hope of any kind. In Gal. 4:8 οὐκ [*ouk*] (strong negative) occurs with εἰδοτες θεον [*eidotes theon*], but here μη [*mē*] gives a more subjective picture (I Thess. 4:5). **Without God** (ἀθεοι [*atheoi*]). Old Greek word, not in LXX, only here in N.T. Atheists in the original sense of being without God and also in the sense of hostility to God from failure to worship him. See Paul's words in Rom. 1:18–32. "In the world" (ἐν τῳ κοσμῳ [*en tōi kosmōi*]) goes with both phrases. It is a terrible picture that Paul gives, but a true one. [260]

> **having no ... hope**—beyond this life (1Co 15:19). The CONJECTURES of heathen philosophers as to a future life were at best vague and utterly unsatisfactory. They had no divine "promise," and therefore no sure ground of "hope." Epicurus and Aristotle did not believe in it at all. The Platonists believed the soul passed through perpetual changes, now happy, and then again miserable; the Stoics, that it existed no longer than till the time of the general burning up of all things. [261]

> *(4) Hopeless: "having no hope"* This follows very naturally, for the Christian's *hope* is based on the divine *promise*. Accordingly, since in the earlier period the covenant-promise had not been revealed to the Ephesians, as has just been indicated, hence they also lacked hope: solid, firmly-anchored assurance of salvation. Such hope is one of God's most precious gifts, and is mentioned alongside of faith and love (1:15, 18; cf. I Cor. 13:13). It is knowledge of God's promise plus confidence with respect to its fulfillment (cf. II Cor. 1:7). It is the proliferation of faith. It amounts to the conviction that all things will be well, even when all things seem to be wrong (Rom. 4:18). It never disappoints, because it, too, like faith and love, is a divine gift (Rom. 5:5).
> In their state of unbelief the Ephesians had lacked this hope. Instead, they had been filled with fear and despair. The Greek and Roman world of Paul's day was, indeed, a *hopeless* world. [262]

> The readers had no hope and (5) were without God "in the world" (RSV). The phrase "in the world" characterizes both conditions (TEV *you lived in this world*; also TNT; NEB is good: "Your world was a world without hope and without God"). *Hope* probably has the broadest sense possible; it is doubtful that it is restricted to "hope in the Messiah," as some think (see "without hope" also in 1 Thes. 4.13). *You lived…without hope* may be expressed as "you lived without anything good to look forward to" or "you lived without being able to imagine that any good would come to you." *Without God* here means that though pagans have their own gods they do not have the knowledge of and relation with the one true God, the God of Israel; there is no implication in the Greek word that God abandoned or rejected them. *You lived…without God* may be expressed as "you lived without knowing God" or "…without being related to God." [263]

The choice is simple. Without God as the Origin of truth, justice, morals, meaning, and beauty, all is meaningless!

How Sad

This is what makes us so sad when we see religious humanists pick up the baton where the secular humanists dropped it. Natural Theology and Natural Law boldly proclaims,

> Just give us until tomorrow and we will discover truth, justice, morals, meaning, and beauty *independent of and apart from God and the Bible.* Man starting only from himself, by himself, through himself, can discover these things autonomously through human reason, experience, feelings or faith. Yes, we can!

How sad! Just when unbelievers finally admit that without the God of the Bible and the Bible of God there is no truth, justice, morals, meaning or beauty, "Christian" humanists come along and give them comfort and aid! What makes this so disconcerting is that they do so in the name of helping unbelievers to believe! But, believe in what? To believe in *themselves*!

The Need for Biblical Anthropology Today

The present crisis in Western philosophy underscores that it is time to boldly proclaim God's view of man as revealed in Scripture. Why waste time on the failed attempts of Zeno, Plato, Kant or Sartre? Why whip a dead horse?

The Bible reveals much about man because it was written to explain the Creation, Fall, and Redemption of man. Man qua man must be understood in the context of these three pillars of Special Revelation or man ceases to be man.

What Is Man?

One of the most profitable studies of Scripture is to examine the questions asked in the Bible. One of the most interesting questions is found in Psa. 8:4. The KJV translated it: "What is man, that thou art mindful of him? and the son of man, that thou visitest him?" The KJV's translation is inadequate at best. The Hebrew text is:

מָה־אֱנוֹשׁ כִּי־תִזְכְּרֶנּוּ וּבֶן־אָדָם כִּי תִפְקְדֶנּוּ׃

We translate it as follows:

> What is weak and wicked humanity,
> that You should take any notice of him?
> Or the child of a human being,
> that You should care about him?

First, there are three regular words for "man" in Hebrew. The first word, אָדָם, is a non-generic term for "people" in general. The second word, אִישׁ, is gender specific for males. The third word, אִשָּׁה, refers to females.

David does not use any of these words in his first question: מָה־אֱנוֹשׁ. He uses the rare word אֱנוֹשׁ. This word stresses the *weakness* and *sinfulness* of people. Since the Semitic root of the word means sickness and illness.

> the basic emphasis would be on man's weakness or mortality, a connotation permitted by some contexts, particularly those that emphasize man's insignificance (e.g., Psa 8:4 [H 5]; Job 7:17)... Man's insignificance in view of the vastness of the universe is set forth in the question, "What is man?" (Psa. 8:4)...The word vAna, reminds man of his transience and of his lowly position before the Almighty. [264]

> The Heb. word here is אֱנוֹשׁ which emphasizes man's mortality and weakness. David is stunned that the all-powerful Creator should exalt such puny beings by caring for us and by giving us dominion over His earth. [265]

The way God asks this question is very important. Man is not viewed in the *abstract* but as he is in the *real* world. What is weak, pathetic, perverted, and wicked man? Why would God take any notice of such an evil creature? Why would God have compassion on the children of such wicked and weak people? Why?

The Humanistic Question

In sharp contrast to Psa. 8:4, the humanists ask, "What is perfect and ideal man?" They do not begin with man's weakness or wickedness but with some abstract concept of an ideal, good, and perfect "human nature." This is why they refer to man's "reason" as if it were a perfect, infallible, and inerrant guide to truth and morals. Man's "will" is always assumed to be free of any depravity or moral bias. It is perfectly free in an *ideal* sense.

The Realism of the Bible

Biblical anthropology is the only worldview that has a *realistic* view of man. The Bible does not even hide the "warts and moles" of the patriarchs, the prophets, and the apostles. They are described as "crooked sticks" that God used to draw straight lines. Noah had a drinking problem. Abraham lied his way out of problems. Jacob was a con man. David had a problem with lust. Peter was a coward. Paul lost his temper. We could go on and on.

I. The Creation

In our chapter on the biblical concept of Creation we learned the following things:

1. The universe does not begin with the impersonal, but with the personal because it begins with the personal Creator.
2. Man is not in contradiction of his own existence. His personality is reflective of the personal Creator who made him. This means that all humanistic views which reduce man to the level of an animal or a machine must be viewed as erroneous.
3. Because man was created in the image of God, we must view man as a unique creature who stands outside of and apart from the rest of the Creation. Indeed, God placed man over the earth to rule as His vice-regent (Gen. 1:26–29).
4. Man stands outside of the cosmic machine. Any world view which traps man in "nature" is false. Man stands outside of and over Creation as its prophet, priest and king. He is not an animal or a machine but the unique image bearer of God.
5. We can speak of the unity and dignity of mankind only because all of humanity ultimately came from Adam and Eve. The different races are simply genetic variations on the descendants of Adam and Eve. The unity and dignity of man depend upon the Adam and Eve model of creation. We can speak of "mankind" because we all came from Adam and Eve.
6. This is in stark contrast to some humanistic ideas of evolution which view each race of man as evolving from different primates. If this is true, then one race could claim to be superior over the other races. Slavery could be justified because there is no such thing as "mankind."

7. Because man is God's image bearer, he is a responsible moral agent who will be held accountable by God for his thoughts, words and deeds on the Day of Judgment at the end of history.
8. While animals are not viewed in the Bible as responsible moral agents because they do not have immortal souls, man is viewed as responsible. This means that all views of man which negate his accountability must be rejected.
9. The Christian view does not accept any chemical, environmental, societal or economical determinism. Man is not the victim of his circumstances. He will be held accountable for what he thinks, says and does.
10. Only on the basis of the Bible can man have any meaning.

II. The Fall

The Bible tells us that at the very beginning of human history man fell into a state of sin and guilt. The radical Fall of man is viewed by the biblical authors as being a real event in space-time history (Rom. 5:12ff; 1 Cor. 15:21ff). It is never viewed as a myth. It was an actual event which you could have witnessed with your own eyes.

The original sin was not sex. It was open rebellion against God's *revealed* Law, not some kind of "natural law" derived from the world. Man attempted to become his own god (Gen. 3:5).

Self-deification is one way in which man tries to be autonomous, i.e. independent from God. This is always the goal of apostate thought. Indeed, the history of philosophy is nothing more than man's attempt to escape God and His revealed Law.

In his temptation, Satan told man three lies:

1. You can be whatever you want to be.
This lie denies that man is a finite being and is thus limited. Just as man is not a bird and thus cannot flap his arms and fly away, neither is he autonomous. We can be only what God has made us to be.

2. You can know whatever you want to know.
This denies that man's understanding is finite. But man and his thoughts are finite and, hence, cannot obtain an infinite comprehension of anything. We can know only what God has made us capable of knowing.

3. You can do whatever you want to do.
In this lie man is told that he can be his own law-giver. He does not have to obey God's revealed Law, but he can make up his own laws. Unbelief is man's rebellion against God and His revealed Law.

God, Evil and You

The biblical account of man's radical fall into sin gives us a key to understanding life. The world that now exists is not to be viewed as "normal." This means that death is not normal. Sin is not normal. Evil is not normal. Man is now subnormal. His problem is not his humanity but his depravity. Man's problem is not that he is finite but that he is a sinner (Eph. 2:1–3).

The old saying, "To err is human but to forgive is divine," is built on the humanistic assumption that man's problem is his humanity. But this is not true. Adam and Eve were created righteous and sinless at the Beginning. Jesus Christ was a real human being but He was also sinless. After the Resurrection, believers will be sinless. "Humanness" does not automatically mean sinfulness.

Once you equate "humanness" with sinfulness, you arrive at the basis of the liberal denial of the inspiration of Scripture. They usually argue in this way: "Since "to err is human," and the Bible was written by humans, this means that the Bible *has* to have errors. The errors and contradictions in the Bible only prove its humanness."

This argument fails to take into account man's original righteousness and his subsequent Fall into sin and guilt. It also does not take into account God's sovereignty in assuring that the Bible was created errorless through fallen human instruments. The Living Word and the Written Word are both errorless and sinless (2 Cor. 5:21). Man's problems are fundamentally moral in nature and not physical, environmental or social.

III. Redemption

According to Scripture, God did not leave man in a state of sin and guilt. As we demonstrated in the book, *Studies in the Atonement*, the triune God of Father, Son and Holy Spirit worked together to provide a salvation for sinners.[266]

God the Father planned salvation from eternity past (Eph. 1:4). God the Son entered history and died on the cross for the sins of His people (1 Cor. 15:3, 4). And God the Holy Spirit takes what Christ accomplished according to the plan of the Father and applies it to the people of God (Eph. 4:30).We are Chosen by the Father, Purchased by the Son, and Sealed by the Spirit, Blessed God Three in One!

God's wondrous plan of Redemption began in eternity past and secures eternity future for His people. Jesus Christ has entered history and through His life, death and resurrection has created a new humanity which will one day enjoy a new earth which has been returned to its original paradise condition (2 Pet. 3:11–13).

The Christian View of Man

The Biblical world view interprets all of life in terms of three basic ideas:

1. The Creation of the universe out of nothing.
2. The radical Fall of man into sin and depravity.
3. The Redemption accomplished by Christ.

In Christian philosophy, we refer to these three principles as Creation, Fall and Redemption. They are the basis of all Christian thinking. This is why they are introduced at the very beginning of the Bible in Genesis 1–3. The remainder of Scripture is only a development and application of these three concepts to all of life. Just like a three legged stool, remove one of these principles and Christianity falls. A Scriptural self-image begins with an application of Creation, Fall and Redemption to mankind.

Creation

First, in terms of Creation, man is not to be viewed as an animal or machine but as a unique creature created in the image of God. As such, man is to be viewed as something wonderful and not as junk.

Man has been invested by his Creator with certain inalienable rights which no one, not even the state, should violate. Man is a free moral agent who has not been programmed deterministically by anything in the world around him. This means that man is accountable to God for his actions and faces a Day of Judgment at the End.

When you look in a mirror you can say to yourself,

> I have been created in the image of God and thus I have worth, significance, meaning and dignity. God has commanded me to exercise the talents He gave me for His glory and to take dominion of the world around me. (Gen. 1:27f)

The Fall

In terms of the Fall, when we look in the mirror, we see ourselves as sinners who have rebelled against the God who made us. Adam was given the choice of either obeying or rebelling against God. In Genesis 3, he followed the slander of Satan and rebelled against God and plunged the entire human race into guilt and depravity. This means that we are sinners by constitution and sin comes as naturally to us as breathing (Rom. 5:12–19).

The radical Fall explains the darker side of man's actions. How can such wonderful creatures, beautifully constructed by God with such great potential, do such horrible things? Where does human evil come from? Why do men do the evil they do? When you look into a mirror you can say to yourself,

> I am a rebel sinner in need of God's grace and forgiveness. I have broken God's laws and deliberately transgressed His commandments. I will one day stand before God on the Judgment Day to give an account for every thought, word, and deed. I cannot save myself because I am incapable of doing good works, repenting of my sins or believing the Gospel.

Redemption

The third concept by which the Scripture interprets all of life is the concept of Redemption through the merits of Messiah alone. As we demonstrated in the book, *Studies in the Atonement*, God did not leave man in the state of sin, guilt, misery and condemnation. Instead, He sent His Son to do a work of redemption by which not only man but also planet earth will be redeemed from the evil consequences of the Fall (John 3:16; Rom. 8:19–22).

Salvation or redemption is not to be viewed in terms of absorption or annihilation. When God saves an individual, that person will not be absorbed into God's essence or being. As redeemed individuals we will exist for all eternity.

The atonement is the payment of the price demanded by Justice in order to set us free from the just condemnation of our sins. Christ Jesus has done all that is necessary for our salvation. Our responsibility is simply to receive His wonderful work of salvation (John 1:12). Thus salvation is 100% by the grace of God and it is not based on human merit, performance or work (Eph. 2:8, 9).

Not only is the soul of man redeemed so that after death he can live in the presence of God in heaven, but his body will be redeemed at the Resurrection (1 Thess. 5:23). Thus man and his world are to be redeemed and purified by the Creator through the saving work of Jesus Christ.

God's plan of salvation gives us the solution to the problem of evil. Evil is going to be assessed, brought to judgment, and then quarantined in a place called hell where it can never again affect the rest of the universe. All of the evil consequences of sin will be eradicated by God's work of redemption. Planet earth will be purified by fire from all the effects of Adam's fall into sin (2Pet. 3).

The work of Messiah is thus the final answer to the problem of evil. Evil will be dealt with either by redemption or judgment. Messiah Jesus has triumphed over sin and will one day bring the universe back into its original harmony and beauty (Col. 1:18–20).

If you are a Christian, when you look in the mirror, you can say to yourself,

> I am a child of God through faith in the atoning work of Jesus the Messiah. I have been saved by grace alone, through faith alone, through the person and work of Messiah alone. He is my Savior and my God. I now trust in Him for all things and live only to please Him.

Biblical Self-Image

The Christian position on man involves three foundational concepts: We are wonderfully created in the image of God, terribly marred and twisted by the Fall and marvelously redeemed by the atonement of Christ. Any anthropology which does not take into account the threefold state of man in terms of Creation, Fall and Redemption is not a biblical perspective.

The threefold biblical view of man's nature in which he is viewed as an image-bearer, a sinner, and a saint provides us with a sufficient basis not only to develop a proper self-image but also to develop a free society.

Checks and Balances in Government

The authors of the American Constitution believed that man was a sinner and thus he needed a system of checks and balances for government to work. They believed that power corrupts and that absolute power corrupts absolutely. Therefore no branch of the government is to gain the supremacy over the other branches of the government. By a system of checks and balances, totalitarianism and tyranny can be prevented in this great land.

Capitalism and the Bible

Compassionate Capitalism and the free market system developed out of the biblical view of man. A planned economy has always led to utter disaster. Countries which have gone into Marxism cannot even feed themselves. Without the free economies of the West, these countries would have gone down in ruin years ago.

The only hope of humanity is to return to the Christian view of man and to the principles of form and freedom, dignity and worth that have been generated by the biblical worldview. The only alternative is totalitarianism which treats man only as a thing.

Summary

The healthiest self-image is the one derived from Scripture because it describes man as he really is. Thus there is no contradiction between what we experience in life and what we find in the Bible. Man and his world are understandable only if we look at them from the perspective of Creation, Fall and Redemption. Any other world view is doomed to fail.

Humanism and Human Life

Humanism teaches that man is the result of a chance-governed evolutionary process in a closed system wherein God or any act of God is excluded in principle. God is not so much refuted as He is defined out of existence. Since there is no infinite reference point which could possibly give meaning or significance to any particular, human life has no intrinsic value, dignity, freedom or meaning.

While human life, like animal life, has no intrinsic value or dignity, it can have "acquired worth" in terms of its utility or function. When a person's utilitarian worth is over, so far as the state is concerned, that person no longer has any "right" to life.

The "privilege of life" can be withdrawn by the state at will. Because human life has no intrinsic worth, it is perfectly proper, if deemed for purposes of utility, to abort unborn babies, murder babies already born, to put to death those who are sick, handicapped, disabled or old.

The following points are usually argued by humanists to demonstrate that it is perfectly proper to do away with human beings if it is deemed "useful" to society.

1. Economic considerations may lead to the termination of "useless" lives. This "useless" person may be the child of a welfare mother. It is cheaper to kill that child than to give additional financial aid for the care and education of that child. One of the reasons Planned Parenthood and its abortion mills were created was for the killing of poor, non-white babies.

2. People who are "miserable" may be terminated. The argument is usually given that this person has a "miserable life" due to the fact that they are handicapped or that they may possibly experience pain in the future.

    What this argument really means is that those around them will feel "miserable" when they have to care for or look at the individual. Thus physical deformity as well as disability is usually looked upon as viable grounds for abortion or mercy killing.

3. Children who are "unwanted" can be killed. This killing may take place before they are born, which is abortion or after they are born, which is infanticide. Pagan judges have upheld both forms of murder.

4. Inconvenient pregnancies can be terminated at will. Human life has no intrinsic worth and if this child will be inconvenient because it will interfere with your career or personal pleasure, then it is perfectly proper to kill that baby.

5. The "right to life" is not absolute. There are no inalienable rights given by a divine Creator to anyone because there is no God. Rights are given by the state and can be withdrawn by the state at will.

6. Over-population necessitates the killing of worthless human beings. This means that the unwanted, the handicapped, the terminally ill, or the elderly should be encouraged to take their own life or they should be forced into suicide clinics where their life will be forcibly taken from them. Death pills or suicide pills should be made available to anyone who wishes to take his life. Nationalized health programs always produce "death panels" made up of government officials who decide if you live or die.

7. In the future there will be food and fuel shortages, which mean that the state will have to "liquidate" unnecessary "assets," i.e. people.

8. The few (i.e. the poor, the sick and the elderly) should be willing to sacrifice for the many (i.e. the wealthy, healthy and young). They should be willing to go to suicide clinics so the rest of us can enjoy life.

9. If someone wants to die, doctors should be willing to perform this task. Physicians should become doctors of death as they did in the Third Reich.

10. People who can no longer make any contribution to society are to be viewed as

"parasites" and since they do not produce any goods or services, they should be "terminated." This is what communist countries have practiced for years. Life is cheap where there is no God.

Summary

Without the basis of the God of the Bible, human life loses all dignity and worth. Man is reduced to an animal and is treated as such. Man was created in the image of God. Thus every human being from the moment of conception to death has *intrinsic* worth and inalienable rights. The intrinsic worth and dignity of man is immutable and cannot be affected by a lack of "acquired worth" or "economic considerations." The utility of a person has no bearing whatsoever on the issue of the worth of man-as-the-image-bearer-of-God.

The sanctity of human life is clearly taught in Scripture. Killing human beings because they are in the way of personal pleasure or affluence is murder. Only the God who gave life has the right to order the death of anyone. This is why Christians believe in capital punishment and are against abortion at the same time. While God has ordered capital punishment in certain cases (Gen. 9:6), He has condemned the killing of the innocent (Exo. 20:13).

The Sanctity of Life Declaration
1. Genetic experimentation on fertilized human eggs is morally wrong and should be illegal because the destruction of such eggs is the killing of human life. Some techniques used to overcome infertility are immoral and should be made illegal. When fertilized human eggs are washed down the sink, this is the murder of innocent human beings.
2. It is morally wrong and should be illegal to experiment on the human DNA code to predetermine the race, sex or physical characteristics of human beings. Human beings should not be genetically programmed or "bred" as is done with cattle. We have already seen how Hitler's dream of breeding a "super-race" ended.
3. Abortion is morally wrong and should be made illegal except where the life of the mother is threatened. Even though the case where the life of a mother is threatened is exceedingly rare, yet the biblical principle would be to preserve the life of the mother as opposed to the life of the child.
4. All acts of infanticide in which babies are murdered either through active or passive means are immoral and should be made illegal regardless of what economic or other considerations are made.

    Active means of infanticide include choking the child to death, stabbing the child in the heart, cutting the brain or poisoning the child. Passive usually means placing the child in a closet or in a container and allowing the child to die slowly and excruciatingly through starvation and dehydration. Some have cried for days before they died a horrible death. If someone killed a dog this way, it would be viewed as a crime. How then can human babies be killed this way without criminal charges? Have we come to the place where to kill a dog is more heinous than the murder of precious little babies?
5. All so-called "mercy killing" is morally wrong and should remain illegal. It is nothing more than murder regardless if it is done through passive or active means.
6. Active or passive euthanasia is morally wrong and should be made illegal. To encourage the elderly to commit suicide is to aid and abet murder.

7. Medical care should not involve age limits or "useful life" standards. To deny medical care to someone because they are no longer viewed as being "useful" is nothing but murder.
8. Suicide should not be legalized. Suicide clinics or "death pills" should not be forced on or offered to the elderly.
9. The state should not have any "final solution" for "undesirables." This is exactly what Hitler did to Jews, gypsies and other ethnic and racial groups which they deemed as "undesirables."
10. There should be no program of "liquidation" of those who think or teach differently than the state. The Gulags of the Soviet Union and the gas chambers of the Nazis both resulted in death for anyone who thought or taught differently than state policy. This is immoral and should remain illegal.

Summary

The end result of humanism is death while biblical Christianity brings life and light through the Gospel. Humanism brings man down to the level of an animal while Christianity lifts him up to be the image bearer of God. While Christians promote life,
humanists are the merchants of death.

Chapter Nine

A Biblical Philosophy of Science

Introduction

The rationale, basis, function, and nature of "science" is something that natural philosophers and theologians have staked out as the sole domain of human reason and experience and thus we do not need any information from Special Revelation, i.e. the Bible. But, must we "put away our Bibles" when it comes to science? Are science and the Bible like oil and water, i.e. you cannot mix the two? Humanists assume this to be true. But, is this really true?

Lots of Questions

There are many questions about "science" that have to be answered before we can evaluate the different views of science that are in the world today.

- What is the origin, nature, means, methods, and purpose of science?
- Can it explain everything, most things, a few things or nothing?
- Does it have any limits or can it do and be everything?
- Does science deal with absolute truth or are its theories relative to the surrounding culture and times?
- What are its foundational faith-based principles, presuppositions, and assumptions?
- What kind of faith is it based upon? Arbitrary faith, blind faith, cultural faith, etc.?
- Why did science come into existence?
- How, where, when, and through whom did the idea of science arise?
- Does the universe really need an explanation?
- If so, what kind of explanation?
- Is a rational, empirical or mystical interpretation the right one?
- Is the universe actually explainable? In its entirety? Or are there things in the universe that are mysteries, i.e. not explainable in nature?
- Or is the universe chance-driven and thus not explainable in nature?
- Is science actually a psychological phenomenon? Is it the projection of man's futile attempt to deal with his fear and insecurity by projecting order and purpose onto a meaningless and chaotic universe?

- Or is the universe orderly in and of itself?
- Does everything in the universe have a purpose, function, and place?
- If the universe is meaningless and purposeless in nature because it is the result of a random combination of chance plus time plus energy plus matter, on what grounds do we think that it is capable of explanation?
- Is history guided by irrational forces?
- Why does man assume he can explain the world around him?
- How can we justify the existence and enterprise of science?
- Is science actually religious in nature?
- How and in what ways?
- Why have the hard sciences fallen on such hard times today?

These kinds of questions are the focus of the philosophy of science. Humanists usually disguise their *philosophy* of science by pretending that science is *factual*. But, don't be deceived. What secular humanists call "science" is actually 99% a mixture of philosophy and religion.

When someone says, "I believe in science," he actually means that he believes in a religion called *scientism*.[267] The following dialogue has taken place many times in a university setting. The unbeliever has rejected the Bible and the gospel because he "believes in science."

Unbeliever: I don't believe in God. I believe in science. Christian: What is this "science" in which you believe? Unbeliever: What do you mean?

Christian: Where can I find this "science?" Does it have a physical address or an email address? What is the telephone number for science? Where is its headquarters? Who is the head of it? Does it pay taxes? Does it have a mission statement or manifesto?

Unbeliever: Science does not have a physical address or an email or a website. By "science" I mean what we know by observation and experimentation.

Christian: So, you admit that "science" does not exist *per se*. The word "science" is a symbol for what some people, some of the time, in some cultures, believe about the world. The word "science" is what current religious and philosophic ideas are dominant in a society. Each society creates its own science.[268]

Unbeliever: But "science" is based on objective facts. It is objective and neutral.

Christian: That's what some people have said some of the time. But, one man's science is another man's superstition. Western "science" simply means Western cultural consensus. If 51% of people who call themselves "scientists" vote for an idea, is it "science" or politics? Scientific theories change all the time. Larry Laudan has documented how Western science has radically changed its view of reality over thirty times.[269]

Unbeliever: But science is not just mob rule! It is not consensus, but fact.

Christian: Have you read Kuhn's work?[270]
Unbeliever: What are you talking about? Science is an agreed upon body of knowledge supported by observation and experimentation.
Christian: Your definition of science is just one *belief* among a vast number of different philosophies of science. It is called "realism" and was invented by the philosophy of Logical Positivism. Many scientists today hold to other views of science such as anti-realism.
Unbeliever: Are you saying that "science" is relative to its cultural context?
Christian: You got it! Does the sun revolve around the earth or does the earth revolve around the sun? Science first taught one and then the other. Is the world flat? At one time science taught that it was. Do atoms really exist or is the atom paradigm only a convenient fiction? Newton's science taught that an object's mass does not depend upon its velocity, while Einstein's science taught the opposite. Scientists evangelize each other and try to convert each other to their position. Young scientists are told that they have to believe in what passes as "scientific orthodoxy" at the time. Take the global warming theory. If a scientist refused to convert to this faith-based theory, he was punished in various ways, such as being fired from his job or by losing his government funding.
Unbeliever: I thought science was based on inductive reasoning.
Christian: The so-called "scientific method" of inductive reasoning is laden with *a priori* ideas that are gratuitously accepted. If you do not accept those presuppositions, then all the induction is no more than circular reasoning.[271]
Unbeliever: If this is true than all hope for truth and meaning is lost!
Christian: If you mean that if we start with *man* as the Origin and measure of truth, then, yes, all is meaningless.[272] But I have good news for you. If we begin with the God of the Bible as the Origin and Measure of all things, including truth, justice, morals, meaning, and beauty, then we can have all those things. Humanistic science is sinful man's attempt to explain the world without God. It can't be done. Biblical science begins with God and then explains the world in terms of its relation to Him. Unless we start with "In the beginning God created the heavens and the earth," all is meaningless.

A brief review of ancient Greek philosophy would be helpful to understand the roots of humanistic ideas about science.

PART ONE

ANCIENT GREEK PHILOSPHY
The philosophers of Greece supposedly based their ideas on human reason and experience, and

they prided themselves on being "rational" in all things. From the very beginning of recorded history, the word "rational" referred to what psychologically "felt" right to the majority of people in a given culture. To the Greeks, the idea that the world was a flat plane "felt" rational. The idea that the world was a round sphere would have been deemed "irrational" in that day.

Science at one time taught that the sun revolved around the earth; that astrology could predict the future; the spontaneous creation of life; that disease was healed by bleeding the patient; light is unaffected by gravity; etc., etc. Thus what is "rational" is relative to the dominant social beliefs at that time.

The Duckbilled Platypus

The duckbilled platypus is a good example of the psychology of rationality. When the first explorers of Australia returned to Europe, they reported the existence of a weird animal that had the bill of a duck, webbed feet, fur, laid eggs, and suckled its young. The scientists of Europe pronounced it a fraud and that such a creature could not rationally exist. They considered it a sick joke.

Then explorers returned to Australia and brought back the skins of the animal as proof. But the scientists declared the skins of the platypus to be a clumsy fraud created by sewing together body parts from different animals. It was stated in universities across Europe that it was not "rational" that such a creature could exist. The real is the rational and the rational is the real. If something is "unthinkable," then it does not exist.

The explorers had to bring a live duckbilled platypus back to Europe, and only when the scientists were forced to watch it swimming around did they grudgingly admit it must be real. The "irrational" was the real, and rationality once again showed one of its weaknesses as a philosophy.

Greek Rationality

Besides the invention of the psychological term "rational," other philosophical ideas developed by Greek philosophy are still with us today. Zeller, one of the more astute humanists of our day, states in his standard work on the pre-Socratic philosophers,

> From Greek Philosophy, however, the whole of European philosophy has descended. For the ideas which the Romans express in their philosophic literature were not original, but were taken from the Greeks, clothed in the Latin language and passed on to the medieval and modern world.[273]

Most modern philosophers, such as Alfred North Whitehead, have admitted their indebtedness to Greek philosophy. On numerous occasions Whitehead proudly proclaimed that "philosophy only repeats Plato!" He assumed that the closer we get to Greek philosophy and the farther we depart from Christianity, the better off we will be philosophically and morally.[274]

Greek Philosophy and Secular Humanism

Greek philosophy is also important because it represents secular humanism in full bloom. The Greeks attempted to explain the existence and form of the universe and the uniqueness of man solely on the basis of human reason, intuition, experience, and faith. They developed their philosophies from themselves, by themselves, and upon themselves without any reliance on divine revelation. Again, Zeller comments,

> It was the Greeks who won for man freedom and independence of philosophic thought, who proclaimed the autonomy of reason."[275]

Zeller goes on to define what he meant when he said "freedom" and "independence." He meant "freedom" and "independence" *from* God. It did not matter if one is considering the being, attributes, sovereignty, salvation, works, law, or revelation of God, man must be "free" of God or he is not "really" and "truly" free.

First, as Zeller states, the Greek philosopher was free "to live life as he pleased" because he was "free" from "ethics founded on religious authority."[276] This has always been the great goal of man since his Fall into sin and rebellion in the Garden. Man must be "free" to be his own lawgiver and judge. God and His Law must go if man is to be free.

Second, the Greek philosopher was free "to behave as he pleased" because he was "free" from "a religion based on revelation."[277] If man is to be a truth-maker, law-maker, and god-maker, he cannot be limited by the Bible or any other divine revelation. Truth, justice, morals, meaning, and beauty must be decided by what *man* thinks or feels about it. The concept of a God who reveals absolute truth or morals is clearly repugnant to Zeller.

Religion, philosophy, and science by human reason alone (not by Revelation) was the basis of Greek thought and is still the basis of all apostate thought. "Freedom" to apostate man always means freedom *from* the God who made him. If man is not free in this absolute sense, he is not "truly" free.

Human Autonomy

When Zeller spoke of "the autonomy of reason," he meant that the Greeks did not think that they were dependent on the gods or God for their existence, knowledge, or ethics. They assumed that they could "go it alone" *without* God because they were "autonomous," i.e. independent *from* God. They did not need God or His grace or revelation.

The philosophic doctrine of human autonomy is the very soul and substance of all humanistic thought. But, can man really "go it alone" by relying solely on his own finite and corrupt reason, intuition, and experience? Is truth or morality possible if man begins by rejecting God and His revelation and relying only on himself?

When the Rubber Meets the Road

Let us examine the Greek philosophies to see if they were able to produce anything of lasting worth. After all, if man's reason, intuition, and experience are *really* sufficient, then *surely* the Greek thinkers would have come up with a philosophy that was both believable and livable. But, if after thousands of years in which humanistic thinkers have had all the time and resources needed to produce something, they have in reality produced nothing — then evidently man's reason, intuition, and experience are not really self-sufficient or autonomous after all.

After all the exaggerated claims about human reason, intuition, and experience, if man fails to "go it alone," then this calls for a radical change in the way that truth, justice, morals, and beauty can be discovered and known.

To trace Greek philosophy from the pre-Socratic period to Aristotle requires us to examine their development of the four main divisions of philosophy:

1. *Metaphysics:* The science of Being. What really exists? What is "reality"? What lies behind or beneath reality?
2. *Epistemology:* The science of Knowledge. Can we know what exists? How can we know it? Is it possible to "know" anything?
3. *Ethics:* The science of Morals. What is "good" and "evil?" Can we discern good from evil? How do we do this? Are there moral absolutes or is everything relative?
4. *Aesthetics*: The science of Beauty. What are "beauty" and "ugliness?" Are there absolute standards by which we can discern and judge whether something is "beautiful"? How can we discover them?

Metaphysics
The Pre-Socratics

With the appearance of a slave-based society, a leisure class appeared in Greek society. People had the freedom and time to sit around and try to figure out final answers to the ultimate questions of life. Where did we come from? How did we get here? Why are we here? What are we to do? Where are we going?

Thales is considered to be the earliest of the Greek philosophers. The main question which Thales addressed was, "What is ultimate reality?" i.e. "Of what is it composed or made?"

Thales assumed many things that he never questioned. They were faith-based assumptions that he did not question or prove. His philosophy grew out of and rested upon these assumptions. For example, he gratuitously assumed that ultimate "reality" was "One," not "Many." This is the doctrine of Monism, which states that there is no *qualitative* distinction between gods, men, animals or things. All is One and One is All. They are all part of "what is." They are all "One."

This is in stark contrast to the Biblical idea that God is distinct *qualitatively* and *quantitatively* from the universe. The Biblical doctrine of Creation means that God and the creation are *two* totally different things. They are *not* "One." We are not a part of God or one with God or an emanation from God. While the Greeks, Hindus, Buddhists, and all monists believe that "All is One," the Bible teaches that "All is Two."

Since Thales assumed that everything was eventually and ultimately "One," he wanted to know the identity and nature of this "One" thing that composed all of reality. This "One" made up the existence of the world. Thales also gratuitously assumed that whatever this "One" thing was:

1. It was a material substance,
2. It could be perceived by the five senses of man.
3. It was as eternal as the world of space and time.

Earth, Air, Fire, Water

In other words, the "One" substance, which made up everything, was something man could touch, taste, see, feel, or hear. Thales chose WATER as the "One" ultimate eternal substance which made up all of reality. Ultimate reality was "One" and this "One" was WATER.

After Thales asked what is the identity and nature of the "One" basis of reality, other philosophers put forth their own answers. At first, they assumed along with Thales that this "One" was a material substance perceivable by the five senses.

Heraclitus chose FIRE as ultimate reality. Anaximenes proposed that AIR was the "One." Empedocles and Aristotle topped them all by stating that reality was composed of a combination of EARTH, AIR, FIRE, and WATER!

If you are tempted to think that these philosophers were just plain stupid, you must realize that their idea that EARTH, AIR, FIRE, and WATER made up reality is still with us today. The psychological theory that there are four basic personality types (sanguine, phlegmatic, choleric, melancholic) is a modern version of the Greek idea of EARTH, AIR, FIRE, and WATER!

Idealism

Once the Greek philosophers had exhausted all the material substances open to sense perception that they thought were qualified to be the "One," some of them decided that it was "rational" to believe that the "One" must be a material substance that was *not* perceivable by the senses. This "substance" lay "behind" or "beneath" earth, air, fire, and water. Although it could not be seen, touched, heard, tasted, or smelled, it existed anyway.

Anaximander was first to propose this step toward abstract idealism. He stated that "APEIRON" underlay all of reality. It is difficult to translate this word, but it seems to refer to a material substance lying behind or below all things as a "ground of being."

Pythagoras was the philosopher who took the next step. He believed that a material substance could not be the "One" of reality, regardless of whether it could be perceived by the senses or not. Reality was actually something abstract. It was a "Number."

This step in philosophy opened the door to Idealism, which believes that "ideas" or "numbers" are more real than material substances. This led to the classic contrast between "mind" and "matter" in Greek thought.

The Greek philosophers finally came to the conclusion that the "One" that made up ultimate reality was *not* a material substance open to sense perception. It was an "idea" or a "number" that could be perceived only by the mind apart from the senses.

One or Many?

This led philosophers to consider further questions concerning the "One" that supposedly made up reality. Was this "One" one or many in *quality* or *number?* Was this "One" at *rest* in an *unmovable* and *static* sense or was it in *constant flux* or *motion?*

Democrates put forth the idea that reality was "One" in quality but "many" in number, while Empedocles stated that the "One" was many in quality but one in number! Parmenides felt that reality was "One" in both quality and number. The "One" was ultimate. All else was illusion. This idea is the basis of such eastern religions as Hinduism.

Monism and Pluralism

Thus from the Greeks came the conflict between the monists and pluralists. Yet, they both assumed that reality was "One" and that it was eternal. No real distinction lay between things in this life. They all existed as part of "One" world, and man could discover the nature of the "One" by reason alone.

Being or Becoming?

Another conflict that arose centered in the debate between Parmenides and Heraclitus. Was the "One" that composed all of reality in a state of *being* or was it in the process of *becoming?*

Heraclitus championed the position that there is no "being," but all is "becoming" in a dynamic process of constant change. "No one steps in the same river twice" was Heraclitus' slogan. Everything was in flux. Thus absolute knowledge of truth or morals was impossible because everything is constantly changing. What seems "permanent" is illusory. Nothing is fixed, perfect or immutable, not even the gods.

Heraclitus never realized that he had only succeeded in refuting himself. If "Nothing is true in an eternal immutable sense" is true, than Heraclitus' ideas are not true either! If he is wrong, then he is wrong. If he is right, then he is wrong. Either way, he is wrong!

Parmenides taught that there is no "becoming," but that all is "being." Thus everything is static, fixed, and immutable in the sense of immovable. His disciple Zeno tried to demonstrate by several famous paradoxes such as an arrow in flight that motion is an illusion. What is "real" is permanent. Change and movement are illusory.

The pre-Socratic period ended in a classic stalemate between Heraclitus' "becoming" and Parmenides' "being." They could not solve the contradictions between the two.

Plato

Plato was the first philosopher to attempt a synthesis between the two systems of Parmenides and Heraclitus. He began by assuming by faith that ultimate reality was "One," that it was eternal, and that man could discover its identity on the basis of his reason alone.

The Platonic solution was to place "being" on top of "becoming" like a sandwich. Plato's "World of Ideas" with its "Idea of the Good" took on all the attributes of Parmenides' being. It was eternal, static, immutable, and transcendent. Heraclitus' world of flux became the "World of Matter" that Plato defined as "non-being." It had all the attributes of Heraclitus' "becoming."

But, merely laying Being (Mind) on top of Becoming (Matter) did not bring them into contact with each other. No knowledge of this world was possible as long as "matter" and "mind" remained isolated from each other.

In order to overcome this problem, Plato invented the concept of a finite god who exists between the World of Ideas and the World of Matter. This "Demiurge" was not omnipotent, omniscient or sovereign. The Demiurge molded formless matter according to the patterns he saw in the World of Ideas without any idea of what he was making or what the future of it would be. Thus Plato's god was not infinite in knowledge or power. He did not exist prior to or independent of reality. He was a finite part of a finite world. As such, he could not know the future of what he made.

But, even with a Demiurge, Plato never solved the problem that what was knowable and what was real belonged only to the World of Ideas. The World of Matter remained unknowable and only reflected the ideas or patterns that molded it.

The Platonic system only satisfied philosophers for a brief time. Skeptics eventually took over Plato's Academy and ended up teaching that no true knowledge of anything was possible. Thus no absolute morals were possible. This is the logical conclusion of all philosophic systems that begin with the assumption of human autonomy. When man begins only with himself, from himself, and by himself, he will always end in skepticism and relativism.

Aristotle

Even though he had been a disciple of Plato, Aristotle saw that Plato had not really solved the problems of meaning and knowledge. As a matter of fact, he had merely relocated them. For example, instead of explaining the meaning of the chair in front of him, Plato pointed up to the idea of "chair-ness," which supposedly resided in the "World of Ideas." But, merely shuffling the chair from "here" to "there" hardly constitutes an explanation!

In his *Metaphysics,* Aristotle put forth fourteen arguments that refuted Plato's system. Plato was too idealistic and rationalistic in that he did not explain matter, he merely defined it away! Rearranging Parmenides' "being" and Heraclitus' "becoming" into a dichotomy did not resolve anything. But, like all the philosophers before him, Aristotle assumed Monism and human autonomy. Instead of Plato's dual world, Aristotle had one world composed of a mixture of "form and matter," "mind and matter" or "essence and matter."

"Matter" was pure potential and "mind" was pure actuality. There was an Ultimate Cause unto which all things were being attracted. This produced the motion involved in moving from potential to actual. In this way, Aristotle hoped to blend together Parmenides' "being" with Plato's "mind" and Heraclitus' "becoming" with Plato's "matter."

The fatal flaw in Aristotle's reasoning was that the "form" of something did not have to be consistent with its "essence." Thus, the knowledge of particulars becomes impossible. Only universals were knowable in the last analysis. Once again no knowledge of this world was really possible.

Aristotle believed in many finite gods who were neither omniscient nor omnipotent and were only a part of the process of potentiality becoming actuality. These gods did not know the future. Since Aristotle's gods could only know universals, they could not know particulars. They were incapable of knowing you or your future.

Epistemology

The Pre-Socratics

The early philosophers were empiricists, and restricted knowledge to what was perceivable by the five senses. When this went nowhere, they turned to rationalism that relied only on ideas in the mind. Further refinements such as idealism, materialism, realism, etc. flowed out of the basic conflict between Parmenides and Heraclitus.

The radical problem was that they all assumed that man could "go it alone," i.e. he is autonomous. The doctrine of human autonomy doomed all their philosophies to ultimate relativism and skepticism.

Plato

Since Plato was a rationalist, he did not believe that all knowledge came from the senses. Man actually already knew everything because he had pre-existed his birth in the World of Ideas. He had "fallen" into a physical body. This fall was a bad thing because it made man forget all he knew. But, as man *reasoned*, he could "remember" or "recollect" the ideas that existed in the "World of Ideas." While the Demiurge god was not omniscient, Plato felt that man was!

Aristotle

Aristotle championed empiricism against the rationalism of Plato. But, like Plato, he still assumed monism and human autonomy. In his theory of knowledge, Aristotle taught that we can "abstract" or "grasp" the "essence" or meaning of an object logically. Thus Aristotle placed knowledge not in things "as they are" but in their "essence." Matter (i.e. form) was still unknowable. Aristotle's system as well as Plato's was eventually abandoned. Skepticism and relativism triumphed once again.

Ethics

The Pre-Socratics
Not having any authority higher than their own finite reason, the pre-Socratic philosophers could not generate any ethical absolutes that were infinite or universal. But, this did not stop them from *calling* their ideas universal, intuitive, and self-evident.

The fact that the philosophers had *conflicting* ideas did not seem to bother them. But, how can two contradictory ideas, that were mutually exclusive, be universal, intuitive, and self-evident at the same time? If one idea is "universal, intuitive, and self-evident," then how could the opposite idea also be "universal, intuitive, and self-evident?" Due to this "Law of Non-Contradiction" they cannot both be all of those things.

Universal, Intuitive, Self-evident
One way to solve the problem that your ideas were not really "universal, intuitive, and self-evident" even when you *pretended* they were, was to claim that your ideas were "universal, intuitive, and self-evident" among men who were rational, cultured, and of good will. Your ideas were "universal, intuitive, and self-evident" among those people who were superior in intellect or class. Anyone who thought differently did not really count as they were obviously inferior to you. In this way you could exclude women, children, non-whites, and third world "savages."

They based their ideas on the consensus of their society. No one else matters to them. Whenever you hear or read philosophers claiming that their ideas are "universal, intuitive, and self-evident," they are guilty of *racism*, *classism*, and *snobbery*. They are also hypocritical since they ignore contradictions between themselves of their same class.

Plato
Socrates and Plato tried to create absolutes on the basis of their own subjective and personal conceptions of the "idea" of the "Good." Everything that conformed to their idea of "Good" was good. Anything that contradicted their idea of the "good" was "evil." How convenient!

The main problem with this line of reasoning was this question: How could Plato or Socrates prove that their subjective, personal, culturally-limited, and finite idea of what was "good" was *better* than someone else's idea of what is "good?" To Socrates, homosexuality was both natural and good. We tend to excuse this side of Socrates because it reflected the consensus of Greek society at that time.

In the end, Socrates never refuted Thrasymachus's argument that "Might Makes Right." Socrates' and Plato's own finiteness relativized any absolutes they tried to make.

Aristotle
Aristotle abandoned Plato's attempt to generate absolutes by an arbitrary concept of "the idea" of "the Good." In its place he taught that ethics was a sliding scale of pleasure and pain and not an

issue of absolutes. What was "good" would be attracted to the Ultimate Cause to which all things were moving. But, this attempt to have "relative" and "mutable" morals failed.

Aesthetics

To the Greek philosophers, ideal perfection was the standard of beauty. Imperfection was ugliness. This is why they painted and sculpted perfect bodies for the gods, man, and animals, set in the background of a perfect nature. For example, the nude male body was pictured in its ideal form without imperfections of any kind because it was, in their mind, the pinnacle of ideal perfection. It was not until much later that the female body was likewise judged perfect ideal beauty.

The dogma of human autonomy ultimately led humanists to the idea that, "Beauty is in the eye of the beholder." Since man was the measure of all things, this includes both beauty and ugliness. In the end, this idea lead to the destruction of any hope of objective standards of beauty and ugliness. One man's beauty was another man's ugliness.

Summary

In the end, each philosopher was contradicted by the philosophers who followed him. Nothing was permanently established as certain or absolute. The Greeks failed to produce a philosophy or worldview that was *believable* or *livable*, i.e. they could not live what they believed.

We should not be surprised by this fact. Humanistic thought always fails in the end because its foundational commitment to human autonomy renders it incapable of success. When finite man starts only with his own reason, feelings or experience, he will always end in skepticism (no knowledge is possible) and relativism (no morals are possible). After all the exaggerated claims of man's independence from divine revelation, when the "rubber met the road," human reason, intuition, and experience led man down a blind alley.

PART TWO

Humanistic Science

The history of humanistic science has always followed the history of Natural Philosophy. As the philosophic worldview of society changed, science changed along with it. In this sense, humanistic science is a "tag along" because it always follows the ever-changing wind of philosophic fads. Like a chameleon that changes its color to match the color of its background, science has changed and adapted to whatever dominant worldview is in vogue at the time. It is thus relative, not absolute.

The Golden Age of Greece

Humanistic "science" was first developed by the Pre-Socratic philosophers who assumed the validity of the pagan dogma of human autonomy, i.e. "man is the measure of all things." They assumed that man was the Origin of truth, justice, morals, meaning, and beauty; that man could understand the universe by reason alone, apart from and independent of any special revelation from God.

At the beginning, some Greek philosophers such as Heraclitus believed that their observation of "Nature" was the way to obtain knowledge of the world around them. Hence, the word "science" originally meant "knowledge from observation."

These early philosophers believed that if something could not be experienced by the five senses, it did not exist. This position was later revived in modern times under the name "empiricism" and the Vienna School of Positivism. Scientism and realism are modern expressions of this ancient theory.

Monism

Another mega-shift took place in Greece around the same time. In addition to human autonomy, the Greeks now adopted the religious doctrine of Monism, borrowed from Orphic mysticism, which taught, "All is One." The "Many" diversities around us do not really exist even if that is what our eyes told us. All is ONE, not four.

Note: Monism is the basis of Eastern religions such as Hinduism and Buddhism. This is why modern science has returned full circle to its roots in Eastern mysticism.

Once Monism became an article of faith in Western philosophy, everything could be viewed as being a "uni-verse," i.e. unity out of diversity. A "uni-versity" is supposed to bring all knowledge together in one grand theory. Since humanism begins with man instead of God, it has not and, indeed, cannot generate a grand theory that encompasses all things. This is why modern universities teach there is no truth to discover, no morals to live by, no justice to implement, and no meaning to life.

The Theory of Atoms

In contrast to drifting off into idealistic non-material "Being," philosophers such as Leucippus, Democritus, and Epicurus believed that the universe was composed of very small material "atoms." They were the material "stuff" that made up all four elements.

"Atoms" were invisible and thus could *not* be observed by the five senses. They could not be defined and their existence was accepted by *faith alone*. Although they could not be seen or felt, "atoms," whatever they were, were said to be the basic building block of the universe. They were a paradigm or model of what reality was as expressed on a piece of paper. The diagram of an atom reflected what was out there in the world although no one had ever seen or touched an atom.

These "atoms" were little particles of matter like very small marbles or beads. Each atom was an exact replica of the universe complete with a central sun called a nucleus and planets rotating around it called electrons and neutrons. Each micro atom was only a miniature version of the macro universe! This model was neat and tidy and felt "rational."

The religion of Atomism was later rejected by Aristotle, but resurrected in the 17th century and is still taught in most high school science classes to this day. When your high school teacher showed you a plastic model of an atom, did he or she tell you that it was only one scientific "model" among many? It is actually a religious myth from ancient Greece.

Quantum Mechanics

When college students take their first class in quantum mechanics, they discover that "atoms" do not really exit. They are only a "model" or picture of what philosophers in the past imagined lay "beneath" the visible universe. No one has ever seen any little atomic micro-universes. No nuclei, electrons or protons were observed. Instead of little pieces or particles of matter, like tiny pebbles, ultimate reality was now defined in terms of "sub-atomic" elements composed of magnetic energy fields.

By this time your head should be reeling with the realization that what you thought in high school was "science" was oversimplification, poor models, and even ancient religious dogma. In defense of the atom theory, realists point out that the theory led to the development of the atom bomb and nuclear power. Thus the theory *worked*.

Some people assume that something is true if it works. But anti-realists rightly point out that the atom idea is only one possible explanation for such things. After all, we can go to the moon using Newton's physics or Einstein's physics. While they contradict each other, we can make it to the moon using either one of them.

Realists argue that while it is true that no one has ever seen atoms, they have left "tracks" in cloud chambers.[278] But there are other scientists who can explain these so-called "tracks" without using the theory of atoms.

Plato's Academy

When Plato set up his famous Academy, over the door was written that only those who knew geometry could enter. He was referring to the "plane" geometry invented by some Greek scientists and philosophers who believed that the uni-verse was a flat plane with four corners. They had no concept of a round earth or uni-verse.

Astrology

This is why the astrologers such as Ptolemy assumed that whatever stars he saw over him in the Greek night sky would the same ones that everyone one else saw. The idea that people could be living on the other side of a round planet and thus see a different night sky with different stars in view never occurred to him.

Ptolemy is the father of modern astrology. He assumed that you were born under a certain astrological signs on a specific date because everyone is living on the same flat plane. Your "sign" assumes you were born in Greece! Since I have dealt at length with astrology elsewhere, I refer you to that resource. [279]

Ptolemy was also the father of "plane" geometry, which taught that sides of a triangle are never parallel and parallel lines never intersect. These ideas are the theorems, i.e. faith commitments, of plane geometry. All calculations are based upon such ideas.

SMSG's Universe

When I was a tenth grade high school student, I was selected by Yale University to become part of its Student Mathematics Study Group (SMSG). Edward Begle introduced us to Einstein's round earth and a bubble universe in which sides of a triangle are ultimately parallel and all parallel lines ultimately intersect. Given the curvature of the surface of the earth, every line is actually bent as it follows the curvature of the planet. It is actually impossible to draw a straight line!

Imagine a large soap bubble floating in the air in front of you. As you move your head from side to side, you see little flashes of light sparking on its surface. Now take away the soap film that made up the bubble's skin but leave behind the sparkles of light. All you now see is a sphere of dancing sparkles of light that is expanding outward as you watch it. That was the universe according to SMSG!

Modern Math

We also learned that modern mathematics no longer assumes the validity of ancient Greek ideas of mathematics. Most people do not understand that the Greeks developed a "base ten" mathematical model because they had ten fingers! But, what happens if we move over to a different base? For example, if we adopt a base two model instead of a base ten numeric system, one plus one now equals one-zero instead of two!

Another new approach we learned is that mathematical equations cannot "prove" anything because they are only *translations* from one language to another. Just because you can translate a sentence from the English language into a mathematical meta-language, this is no different than translating English into French or German. This is why I am unimpressed by natural theologians who think they have proven a theory because they can put it into the form of a mathematical equation. Big deal! They are only *translating* their theory, not proving it.

Aristotle

Aristotle was the first humanist philosopher who divided "science" into categories such as biology, zoology, physics, theology, etc. He followed the pre-Socratics in utilizing observation as his basic methodology to discover reality. He believed that earth, air, fire, and water were the four basic elements that made up the world.

Based on his observation that the sun rose in the East and set in the West, Aristotle taught geocentrism, i.e. the earth was the center of the universe and the sun, moon, and stars revolved around it. This became a scientific faith-dogma for over a thousand years. It could not be questioned.

Note: Since no one at that time had gone into outer space and looked back and saw the shape of the earth or its relationship to the planets, moon and sun, was a "geo" or "helio" view of earth the result of observation or were they both nothing more than mere speculation? They were both statements of what humanist man *believed* at that time.

Thomas Aquinas

When the official natural philosopher and theologian of the Roman Catholic Church, Thomas Aquinas, adopted the philosophy of Aristotle, geocentricism became part of Roman Church dogma. This explains why there was such a violent reaction when Copernicus and Galileo taught heliocentricism, i.e. the earth revolved around the sun. If the sun were indeed the center of the universe, this would threaten the very foundation of Aristotelian Natural Philosophy and Theology, and, by logical extension, the foundation of Catholic teaching.

The Copernican Revolution

The issue that faced Copernicus was not science versus religion but *religion masquerading as science versus organized religion*. Aristotelian science taught that the sun revolved around the earth. This was based on the observation that the sun rose and set. But Copernicus boldly stated that observation was not a guide to truth. The sun does not really rise or set. Your eyes are deceiving you.

It took a hundred years for the heliocentric model to triumph over Aristotle's geocentricism. But, after the work of Johannes Kepler, the battle was over. Science changed its worldview once again.

The Rise of Rationalism

Once modern science discarded observation, the way was open for speculations based solely on an abstract concept of human "Reason." Science was now following Rationalism, which had become the dominant worldview during the Renaissance. The real was the rational and the rational was whatever *felt real* to you.

Descartes' "reason" told him that invisible corpuscles made up the mechanistic world in which we lived. Spinoza drew up a mathematical model for the universe in which everything could be reduced to an equation. Rationalistic science reigned supreme. It supposedly dealt in absolutes deduced from self-evident, intuitive, universal truths.

Science was now viewed as a rational enterprise that could explain everything. Nothing was beyond its reach. "Miracles" were mysteries that science had not yet explained. Scientists were little gods in white coats running around pontificating on everything. Since they were objective and neutral in their work, their speculations and theories were accepted as "facts" regardless of the amount of empirical evidence to support them.

Note: Science now faced the conflict between induction and deduction. Some scientists arrogantly called induction "the" scientific method. This claim was first refuted by the philosopher David Hume and later by Karl Popper.[280]

Isaac Newton

Isaac Newton's worldview of the universe as a vast machine running according to immutable mechanical laws became dominant as it fit in with the rationalist dream that everything had a "rational" explanation. This is why Darwin's theory of evolution became an overnight success - even though there were no hard facts to support it. The "missing links" that he promised would show up, have never appeared!

Genetics renders Darwin's belief that acquired characteristics could be passed on to one's descendents not only obsolete but absurd. The "survival of the fittest" is a joke. While we smile at Darwin's claim that primate-man lost his tail by sitting on it, the theory of evolution still remains a religious dogma of scientism.

Empiricism Takes Over

When Empiricism dislodged Rationalism, science adapted to the change in worldview and became empirical in nature. If a word or statement could not be empirically verified or falsified in the laboratory, it was meaningless according to the Vienna School of Logical Positivism. Since such words as "God," "soul," or "angel" are not empirically verifiable, they were simply dismissed as meaningless. Religion was not refuted *per se*. It was simply defined out of existence.

Laboratory experiments became the rage until people caught on to the fact that scientists began with a theory in mind and then set up experiments that would validate it. When they did not get the results they expected, they tossed those results out and kept trying until they got what they wanted. For example, whenever an experiment demonstrates that the universe is actually only thousands of years old instead of billions of years, it is dismissed because it contradicts the dogma of the old earth. The test results that support a young earth are thrown into the trash.

Empiricism collapsed when its self-refuting nature became obvious. *It could not be empirically verified that things needed to be empirically verified!* Thus the principle of empiricism was itself meaningless according to its own foundational principle! Humanistic philosophers and scientists were once again adrift in the abyss of the unrelated.

This was the same problem with the principle of induction. *It itself could not be validated by induction! It depended on deductions drawn from a priori ideas such as the uniformity of nature, human autonomy, etc.*

Note: Any scientific theory that successfully refutes itself is doomed.

Einstein Rides to the Rescue

Albert Einstein's "theory of relativity" was another Copernican Revolution in the philosophy of science. His ideas forever changed the way we look at the world. He combined his love of music with his Talmudic heritage and blended them with the philosophy of Spinoza and ended up with a unified field of knowledge that he called "the theory of relativity." His view of the world was as dynamic as Newton's was mechanical.

The phrase "theory of relativity" is unfortunate because Einstein did not believe in moral or physical relativism. Einstein's scientific laws were as rigid, immutable, and absolute as Newton's. The speed of light in a vacuum is the same everywhere in the universe. There is no such thing as chance or free will because everything, including the thoughts and choices of man, are determined. His faith-based presuppositions were written in concrete.

One surprising element in Einstein's worldview that is not well-known is that he believed that science and religions were compatible. Max Jammer explains,

> Einstein never conceived of the relating between science and religion as an antithesis. On the contrary, he regarded science and religion as complementary to each other or rather as mutually depending on each other, a relating that he described by the metaphor quoted above, "Science without religion is lame, religion without science is blind." [281]

The reason why science and religion are compatible is that science itself springs from *a priori* religious ideas. Einstein stated,

> Speaking of the spirit that informs modern scientific investigations, I am of the opinion that all the finer speculations in the realm of science spring from a deep religious feeling, and that without such feeling they would not be fruitful. I also believe that, this kind of religiousness, which makes itself felt today in scientific investigations, is the only creative religious activity of our time. The art of today can hardly be looked upon at all as expressive of our religious instincts. [282]

When faced with having to "prove" his belief that the speed of light in a vacuum is the same everywhere in the universe, Einstein retorted, "God does not play at dice." Jammer comments,

> Einstein's persistent objection to the new quantum mechanics, on the grounds that "God does not play at dice," was, at least to some extent, religiously motivated. [283]

Where did he obtain his ideas of the unity of nature, the rationality of the universe, unrestricted determinism, and the denial of free will? All these concepts are faith-based religious dogmas he derived from Spinoza's pantheistic, philosophic religion.[284] Einstein declared his love of and dependence upon the religious and philosophic concepts of Spinoza on many occasions.

Chapter Nine A Biblical Philosophy of Science

The Search for the Impossible

One great example of scientific religious dogma is what Jammer describes as Einstein's "indefatigable tenacity in searching for a unified field theory."[285] Like most past humanists, Einstein believed that man was the Origin of truth, justice, morals, meaning, and beauty. He really *believed* that someone, somewhere, somehow, some time would create a unified theory of knowledge that explained EVERYTHING. [286] He spent his entire life trying to produce a theory that encompassed all things.

While some humanists today have abandoned the search for a unified field of knowledge, it still resurfaces now and then and creates great excitement at the possibility. One example is the work of Stephen Hawking.[287] He created a world in his mind in which God *could not* exist. His rejection of God was not intellectual but emotional.

Quantum Mechanics

Einstein's unified field theory began to fall apart as Quantum mechanics attacked the basis of the theory of relativism by rejecting his doctrine of unrestricted determinism.[288] Heisenberg demonstrated that Einstein's laws did not work when applied to sub-atomic elements. Heisenberg's famous "principle of indeterminacy" demonstrated that we could not know the position, speed, or direction of sub-atomic particles because the moment we tried to view or measure them, we alter their position, speed, and direction.

Stop and think for a moment. Humanists had always assumed that they could KNOW ultimate reality by observation and experimentation. But, if Heisenberg was right, then they CANNOT know reality, because the moment they try to observe it or experiment to know it, they alter it! Thus, the universe is ultimately *unknowable*.

Einstein realized that his Spinozian belief in unrestricted determinism was the foundation of his theory of relativity, and tried his best to refute Heisenberg. But, as Jammer correctly saw, "Einstein failed to disprove Heisenberg's indeterminacy relations." [289]

Einstein's worldview fell apart as his assured "laws" of science were no longer viewed as absolute or true. They were only sentences written on a piece of paper. Quantum Mechanics now rendered Einstein just as obsolete as Newton had done to Aristotle.

Constant Change

As we have pointed out, science tags along with contemporary religious philosophy and Natural Theology tags along with science, in that it always adopts whatever secular view of science is in vogue at the time.

- Medieval Roman Catholic Natural Theology based its arguments on the philosophy of Aristotle via Thomas Aquinas. Today many Catholic philosophers (and a few erstwhile Protestant philosophers) still yearn for the "good old days" when Aquinas was the dominant worldview.[290]

- When Newton displaced Aquinas, Protestant Natural Theologians, particularly in Great Britain, shifted their theoretical base to Newtonian physics. The world was one vast machine like a watch. This is why there were so many arguments from the watch to the Watch Maker.
- When Einstein displaced Newton, Protestant Natural theologians, British ones taking the lead once again, simply switched their theoretical base over to his Theory of Relativity.
- When Quantum Mechanics displaced Einstein, a few Natural Theologians once against had to shift their theoretical base to a new mystical, Eastern worldview.

When you build your worldview on the shifting sand of popular opinion instead of upon the solid rock of Scripture, your views will change from day to day as you try to keep up with the ever-changing culture around you. Being "relevant" can be exhausting.

Time and Eternity

This is particularly true of Einstein's concept of the relationship between time and eternity. Roman Catholic theology traditionally based its understanding of time and eternity on Aquinas who had "Christianized" Aristotle's view. Most modern Catholic theologians have yet to move on in their worldview.

Since Protestant theologians are always trying to be "relevant," they have been faster to adopt whatever is in fashion at the time. But, they are usually twenty five years behind the secular world. By the time they adopt a new worldview, the world has already moved on to newer ideas.

With the advent of Einstein's physics, a shift took place in Natural Theology. Aquinas and Newton were "thrown under the bus" and Einstein was now enthroned.

Post-Modern "Christian" Theologians

This is the key to understanding the writings of such scholars as Whitehead, Hartshorne, Torrance, Pannenberg, Boyd, Sanders, Rice, etc.[291] They abandoned Newton and moved over to Einstein's view of time and eternity. But, their dependence on the theory of relativity is a sign of spiritual weakness, not strength. They are violating the biblical command not to conform to this world (Rom. 12:1-2).

Evangelical theologians often fail to understand that Process Theology, Neo-Processianism, the Open View of God, etc. are nothing more than versions of Einstein's theories. The origins of such heresies are philosophic in origin and nature, *not* biblical. This is why you can cite Scripture after Scripture to them that clearly refute their heresies but they remain unmoved. Their faith-based doctrines are from Einstein, not God.

What is particularly absurd, is that "evangelical" rationalists, such as J. P. Mooreland and William Lane Craig, do not accept Einstein's doctrine of unrestricted determinism. They still cling to the old pagan Greek idol of "free will." Their attempt to deny the foundation of Einstein's unified field of knowledge (i.e. determinism), but, at the same time, adopt his view of time and eternity will not survive the test of time or consistency.[292] They will learn the bitter truth that you cannot have your cake and eat it too!

The Black Hole of Existentialism

After the demise of Rationalism and Empiricism, Existentialism took the philosophic world by storm. Man's attempt to build a unified field of knowledge of the universe was now abandoned as not only impossible, but *delusional*. The humanistic hope that man could be the Origin of truth, justice, morals, meaning, and beauty *died*. Everything became relative and subjective. There was no objective truth to believe, no morality to live by or beauty to admire. All was meaningless, including science.

Existentialism revealed that scientific objectivity and neutrality were illusions. Everything was relative, including math and logic. There were no absolutes or order behind the scenes, not even the so-called "laws" of science. The crisis was indeed great as the motivation for and the basis of humanistic science was now destroyed.

Relativism has always been the inner cancer eating away at the soul of humanism. If I am the Origin of truth and you are the Origin of truth, and yet we end up with contradictory "truths," either I am right and you are wrong or we are both wrong! We cannot both be right - unless truth is relative, i.e. there is no truth.

Public Indoctrination or Education?

In the 1960's the public school system aggressively taught existential relativism. All is meaningless and without significance. That generation was excited to learn there were no absolutes in the bedroom. Anything goes! If it feels good, do it! Make love, not war! Turn on, tune in, drop out!

The artists caught on quickly and modern anti-art soon became the norm. A crucifix in a jar of urine was viewed as art. The line between pornography and modesty was erased. In film, murder without guilt and sex without meaning was the new art.

Relativism then moved on to the factory. It did not make any real difference if you made a good car or a shoddy one. It is all relative in the end and without meaning. People no longer took pride in their work because it had lost all meaning. We should work to live, not live to work.

It then moved to politics. Political "science" died. Politicians could now say something, deny they said it, and later boast that they had said it. What they said was relative to the audience at hand.

Medicine was relativized and doctors were called upon to murder unborn and newly born babies, children with physical or mental defects, the mentally disturbed, and, finally, the elderly. They now became merchants of death.

The Last Idol to Fall

The last vestige of the old Newtonian worldview to succumb to the killer virus of relativism was science. Once humanists took relativism to its logical conclusion, science died. It no longer had any absolute value or meaning. Science was not good or evil. It just was.

This downward process is why students today are not interested in protesting wars or becoming chemists. It all means nothing. Personal peace and affluence are the only values today. We have finally arrived at the end of the yellow brick road of humanism and the Emerald city was only a mirage.

How Did We Destroy Ourselves?

How did we get in such a mess? By falling prey to the humanist dream that man, starting only from himself, by himself, with himself, could understand the world around him without special Revelation from God. Any progress the West made in scientific knowledge came from those early scientists who believed that the Bible was the basis for the existence and necessity of science.

Francis Schaeffer traced this line of despair and then challenged humanists to turn back to the Bible as the only basis of science.[293] In contrast, Natural Theologians, i.e. religious humanists, do not call secular humanists to turn to the Bible. Instead, they pick up the torch dropped by secular humanists and continue to dream the impossible dream that man is the Origin of truth, justice, morals, meaning, and beauty.

The Alternatives

Some scientists could not tolerate Existentialism and moved over to "new" worldviews and "new" epistemologies. Following the Beatles and the hippie drug culture of the 1960s, some scientists abandoned Western secular philosophy entirely and moved their theoretical base over to New Age forms of Hinduism and Buddhism. The findings of modern physicists, particularly in the field of quantum mechanics and Heisenberg's principle of indeterminacy, have raised serious doubts about the scientific validity of materialism's understanding of the nature of reality. [294]

Many young physicists have adopted Eastern idealism, which assumes reality to be "mind," and denies the existence of "matter!" There is a growing fascination with Taoism or Buddhism which have become a popular religious framework for modern physics. [295]

Why? The sterile character of Western materialism has driven people into the seductive arms of Shiva. The pendulum has begun to swing from the extreme of materialism to the extreme of idealism.

Dr. Bernard Ramm foretold this shift toward idealism in modern physics in 1953. His prophetic words are worth considering:

> Both Nevius and Hocking believe that the current shift in physics from the older Newtonian physics to the new relativity and atomic physics is seriously damaging to the naturalistic program...If the contentions of such men as H. Weyl, A. Compton, J. Jeans, W. Carr, A. Eddington, and F. Northrop are correct, then it is conceivable that

> fifty years of science will see an abandonment of the naturalistic program by the scientists...The slight breeze in the direction of idealism may turn to prevailing winds. [296]

People familiar with modern physics know today Eastern idealism is fearless and aggressive.[297] Materialism is vulnerable, because it is beset by a simplistic and reductionistic methodology that renders it philosophically unacceptable.[298]

The Tao of Physics,[299] *The Dancing Wu Li Masters,*[300] *Instant Physics,*[301] and a host of other books have signaled the shift to Eastern philosophy. But, since Hinduism and Buddhism were not capable of developing a theoretical basis for science in the East, how could it provide a basis for science in the West? The attempt to find a basis for science in Eastern Mysticism will fail because the Eastern denial of material reality renders science delusional.

Second, those who did not move toward the East, went in the direction of Linguistic Analysis in which everything is reduced to semantics. They have concluded that a scientific "law" expresses someone's personal and subjective culturally-bound perception of what he or she thinks is reality. But, one person's reality is another person's fantasy. Thus, linguistics has not been able to generate an intellectual basis for science.

Summary

Humanistic science has tried every possible method to find an intellectual basis of and motivation for science. It has followed Western philosophy into the abyss of the unrelated. In the end it has fallen into the black hole of Existentialism and lost any hope or meaning.

This gives the biblical Christian a window of opportunity to remind the heathen that God has made foolish the philosophy of this world 1 Cor. 1:20). It is by the Bible alone that science can have any meaning or significance. Let us now turn to the Biblical view of science.

PART II

The Bible and Science

The humanists have done a great snow job in obscuring the relationship between science and the Bible. They want you to believe that science is against the Bible and the Bible is against science. Thus there is a natural antagonism between religion and science. They claim that religion is based on faith while science is based on facts. They usually bring up the Scopes Monkey trial and then mock Christians as ignorant baboons.

First, the truth is that *humanistic* science and the Bible are enemies because humanism (i.e. scient*ism*) is itself a *religion*. Since the Humanist Manifesto I and II both state that humanism is a *religion*, the underlying conflict is between the *religion* of humanism and the *religion* of the Bible. Don't let them bully you on this issue.

Second, humanists presuppose the classic Greek philosophic dichotomy in which reality is divided into a lower and upper level.

<u>mind</u>	<u>essence</u>	<u>grace</u>	<u>freedom</u>	<u>faith</u>
matter	form	nature	nature	reason

<u>belief</u>	<u>noumenal</u>	<u>religion</u>	<u>faith</u>	<u>sacred</u>
knowledge	phenomenal	science	facts	secular

By framing philosophic issues within these dichotomies, humanists have already rigged the issue. You must object to these dichotomies because they are *a priori* religious ideas that contradict the Bible. I simply refuse to be pigeonholed into these dichotomies.

Third, humanists like to pretend that they are neutral and objective and that their theories come from their observation of brute facts. In reality, they presuppose a host of unproven faith-assumptions such as human autonomy, ontological thinking, evolution, brute facts, Monism, etc., and these presuppositions control their perception and interpretation of the world. To ask proof for the so-called method of induction is "to cry for the moon" according to Frank Ramsey.[302]

Humanistic scientists begin with blind faith in certain presuppositions that they use to build their worldview. Their philosophy of science is derived from their worldview. Their so-called "scientific theories" are applications of their philosophy of science, which were derived from their worldview based entirely on faith assumptions. The following diagram may help. You move up from faith to scientific theories.

↑ false scientific theories

false philosophy of science

false philosophic worldview

false presuppositions

faith assumptions

Fourth, the development of science did not take place in the non-Christian pagan world because humanistic worldviews could not provide a sufficient theoretical basis of or motivation for science.

- The Greeks believed that the world came out of chaos, that chance and luck control it, and that it will one day fall back into chaos.
- Eastern humanists denied material reality.
- African and Meso-American cultures were based on mythological cosmologies that could not generate science.

Chapter Nine A Biblical Philosophy of Science

The Biblical Philosophy of Science

As with all things, science must be understood in the context of Creation, Fall, and Redemption.

Science in the Light of Creation

First, the biblical doctrine of Creation gives us the only basis of and motivation for science. The Christian knows from his Bible that he can pick up a rock and ask, "What is the meaning of this rock? What is its purpose? What function does it have in the environment? How can I use it to benefit mankind? How can I glorify God through this rock?"

Humanism cannot answer any of these questions because it begins with the faith assumption that there is no Creator who made the rock with meaning and purpose. It cannot give us any reason why the rock should be used to benefit mankind. What if there is a rare slug that lives under that rock?

I know from the Bible that all things, including the rock, have objective meaning because it was given meaning by the Creator.

> YHWH has made everything with its own purpose in mind. (Pro. 16:4)

כֹּל פָּעַל יְהוָה לַמַּעֲנֵהוּ וְגַם־רָשָׁע לְיוֹם רָעָה׃

The Hebrew text is clear that,

> ...all is made by God for its purpose, i.e. a purpose premeditated by Him, that the world of things and of events stands under the law of a plan, which has in God its ground and its end.[303]

> Everything in God's design has its own end and object and reason for being where it is and such as it is; everything exhibits his goodness and wisdom, and tends to his glory.[304]

God told Adam to pick up a rock, a plant, or an animal and try to understand its divine meaning and purpose. How can we use these things to benefit mankind and to glorify Him? Man was to use his capacity to reason within the context of Revelation, not outside of it or in opposition to it. Logic, like fire, is good in its place. But once logic, like fire, runs wild, it destroys all there is including itself.

The biblical worldview of Creation teaches us the following points that provide the philosophic framework for the existence and value of science. These points were already discussed in previous chapters on Creation.

- Man was created by God. Thus he did not evolve from lower animals.

- God made man unique in that he is the image bearer of God.
- No animal was created to bear God's image.
- Man has intrinsic dignity, worth, and significance because he is the image bearer of God.
- Man is more valuable and important than animals. Thus animals serve the existence and benefit of man as well as the glory of God.
- God commanded man to take dominion of the earth. Thus man has the responsibility to take dominion over the animals and the earth itself.
- God commanded man to name the animals and to take care of the garden, which means that science began in the Garden of Eden as a command of God to man.
- In naming the animals, man used observation and his mind to come up with names that reflected the nature of the animal named. The Hebrew concept of naming someone or something was significant (eg. Gen. 17:5; 28:19). We must not confuse it with the modern practice of giving arbitrary and meaningless names.
- Since everything has a divine purpose and a meaning, man is responsible to discover the purpose and meaning of everything.
- The basis of science is the Genesis Cultural Mandate to take dominion of the earth.
- Man has the responsibility to be a good steward of the planet because he will have to answer to God for what he did with it.

Second, in the Biblical worldview, science is man's fallible attempt to understand the divine purpose and meaning of things, how to use that knowledge to take dominion over them, and then to use them for the glory of God and the benefit of mankind.

Third, science is limited to taking dominion over the earth. It cannot answer the following ultimate questions:

- Does the universe exist, or is it an illusion?
- Did the universe have a beginning?
- Will it have an end?
- How long did it take for the universe to come into existence?
- How old is the universe?
- Why does it exist as opposed to not existing?
- Why does the universe have a uniform structure capable of prediction?
- Is man to be viewed as separate from other life forms on the planet?
- Is man only an animal, or is man a "higher" form of life?
- Is man's existence and comfort more important than the existence and comfort of animals?
- Does man have intrinsic purpose, meaning, significance, dignity, and worth?
- Is man more important than plants and animals?
- Does man have the right to alter his environment?
- Does man have the right to consume and control animals?

- Are there moral absolutes?
- Does man have an immortal soul?
- Is the soul conscious after death?
- Does it go to heaven or hell, or is it reincarnated into another body?

One example is light. Science cannot explain what it is. Some say it is composed of particles and others say it is composed of energy waves. They have each created tests that confirm their theory. According to the Bible, science should take dominion over electricity and use it for benefit of mankind and the glory of God. [305]

Fourth, the Bible reveals absolute answers to the questions above.

- The universe exists.
- It had a beginning.
- It will have an end.
- It took six days for God to bring the universe into existence.
- The universe is between six to ten thousand years old.
- It exists for the glory of God.
- The universe has a uniform structure capable of prediction.
- Man to be viewed as separate from all other life forms on the planet.
- Man is not an animal, but a "higher" form of life.
- Man's existence and comfort are more important than the existence and comfort of animals.
- Man has intrinsic purpose, meaning, significance, dignity and worth.
- Man is more important than plants and animals.
- Man has the right to alter his environment.
- Man has the right to consume and control animals.
- Man has an immortal soul.
- Man is conscious after death.
- He ends up in hell or heaven.
- Reincarnation is not true.
- There are revealed moral absolutes.

Fifth, the Biblical worldview begins with God (Gen. 1:1) and everything is defined in terms of its relationship to that God, who is the measure of all things.

God

Miracles

Angels

Demons

Man

Morals

Meaning

Animals

Plants

Things

Sixth, the humanistic worldview begins by denying the existence of the infinite/personal Creator revealed in the Bible. Once there is no God, there begins a downward spiral that reduces everything in the end to the level of meaningless "things." Once God is dead, man is dead; meaning is dead; everything is dead, including science.

No Meaning Means No Morals

This is why humanistic science cannot generate any values or morals. It has never been able to generate an "ought" from what "is." Because of this, humanism cannot distinguish between evil and good science. It cannot judge that inventing a bomb that will kill all life is evil or that inventing a cure for cancer is good. It is all one and same.

Seventh, only Creation gives us two essential ideas that make science possible.

1. The universe is intrinsically intelligible, understandable; it can be organized, altered, and controlled because it was created by the infinite mind of a God of order, not confusion. The pagans always assumed that the universe was ultimately *mysterious* in nature and thus not really intelligible. It is a waste of time to try to figure things out because there is nothing to figure out.
2. Man was created by God with the mental capacity to understand, relate, alter, and control the world around him because he was created in the image of God.

What good would an intelligible universe be if the brain of man was not wired by the Creator to understand it? A universe not quite intelligible or a man not quite intelligent enough to understand it would be a bridge broken at either end.

Humanism is the bridge broken at both ends. This is why modern animal rights groups commit terrorism. They do not believe that "man" exists. We are only one species of primates that got in control of the world because we evolved a thumb. Man-ape does not have any rights that the other life forms on the planet do not share. Man-ape is not special with special rights over and above other animals. Given the history of man-ape, he should go extinct for the good of the world. If we have to kill millions of people to save one bald eagle, so be it. Human life is no more important or sacred than the toad squashed under the wheels of a truck on Route 66.

Science in the Light of the Fall

The implications of man's radical Fall into sin and guilt are important. The pre-lapsarian world of man and his environment were totally different from the post-lapsarian world in which we now live. The Bible records that God placed various curses upon the environment as part Adam's punishment (Gen. 3:17f; Rom. 8:20-22). Divine judgments such as the Flood, the destruction of Sodom, etc. were catastrophic in nature. Thus the humanistic dogma of uniformitarianism, which teaches that everything has always been the same, is erroneous.

Man was radically altered by the Fall. Every aspect of his thoughts and life was corrupted and polluted by sin. All of psychology and sociology is aberrant in nature and not normal because man is not normal. He is a fallen creature in rebellion against his Creator.

It is important to remember the Fall because Natural Theology and Natural Law presupposes that man's "mind" and "will" escaped totally or to a great extent the effects of the Fall. Man's "Reason" is still inerrant and his will is still "free"! These are the hidden assumptions upon which humanists view man as the measure of all things.

Science In the Light of Redemption

In the 1960's, Star Trek gave young people the hope that mankind would one day ultimately overcome nationalism and become a united earth under a one-world government. Man would cast off materialism and capitalism. This is why the crew were never seen being paid money or spending money. Everyone worked for the common good and their needs were met. No one was interested in getting rich.

Star Trek also pictured all religions, even alien ones such as Spock's, as equally valid. It did not matter what you believed as long it did not hurt anyone but yourself. But, did the humanists who created the TV series have any *basis* for their *utopian* hopes? None whatsoever! Given the history of mankind, there is no reason to believe that man can change himself or his environment for the better.

Utopian Dreams

Where did the producers of Star Trek get their *utopian* hopes? They borrowed them from the biblical doctrine of Redemption. The Bible *alone* gives us a sound basis for utopian hopes for human nature and the earth. Paradise was lost, but one day it will be regained! Man will be perfect in a perfect world once Messiah comes back.

When King Messiah returns to this world, human history as we know it will be brought to its preordained conclusion. The resurrection of the body and the Day of Judgment will encompass all of humanity (Matt. 25:31-46). The old earth will be purged by fire and a new earth with a new atmosphere will be created (2 Pet. 3:3-15). The elect will be recreated incapable of sin (1 John 3:2) and, as a result, there will be no pain, sickness, suffering, death or crime for all those things will have passed away (Rev. 21:4).

The Biblical View of Aesthetics

Most Christians understand that the Bible has much to say about ethics, but they seem unaware that it also has a lot to say about aesthetics. Prof. Caverno in his excellent article on beauty in *The International Standard Bible Encyclopedia* begins his discussion with this comment.

> That the Bible is an ethical book is evident. Righteousness in all the relations of man as a moral being is the key to its inspiration, the guiding light to correct understanding of its utterance. But it is everywhere inspired and writ in an atmosphere of aesthetics. Study will bring out this fact from Genesis to Revelation. The first pair make their appearance in a garden where grew "every tree that is pleasant to the sight" (Gen 2:9), and the last vision for the race is an abode in a city whose gates are of pearl and streets of gold (Rev 21:21). Such is the imagery that from beginning to end is pictured as the home of ethics--at first in its untried innocence and at last in its stalwart righteousness. The problem will be to observe the intermingling of these two elements--the beautiful and the good--in the whole Scripture range.[306]

The extensive vocabulary of Hebrew words for beauty found in the Old Testament is astounding. God is described as "beautiful" (Psa. 27:4). Thus His House of Worship was filled with works of art "for the glory of God and for beauty's sake." (Exo. 28:2, 40; 2 Chron. 3:6).

The word "beauty" was used by Solomon more than any other writer. He described the husband and wife in the Song of Songs as calling each other "beautiful" at least fifteen times. This is one of the keys to a happy marriage.

We are also warned that physical beauty will not last, but will fade away with time (Pro. 31:30). Thus your relationship to your mate must not be based upon external beauty but upon the inner beauty of a godly character (1 Peter 3:1-6).

Beautiful jewelry, clothing, crowns, buildings, etc, are described as "beautiful" (ex. Isa. 3:18). There is nothing wrong with surrounding yourself with beauty.

After several years of studying this issue, the following is a brief summary of the biblical view of aesthetics.[307]

Aesthetics in the Light of Creation

The biblical account of Creation supplies us with the only valid basis for a proper understanding of the Origin, existence, function, and explanation of beauty and the art that expresses it. Thus art is not a meaningless fluke of a meaningless chance-driven evolutionary process. It is a reflection of the image of God in man.

Man's aesthetic being is patterned after God's aesthetic being. Animals and machines do not produce or appreciate art. But man, as God's image-bearer, is both an art-maker and an art-appreciator. Art is part of human existence from the very beginning because it is based on the Creator-creature relationship.

Man as image-bearer was given a Creation Mandate in Genesis 1:28–30. Man's art was intended to be a vital part of his obedience to this Mandate. Humanism tries vainly to provide a mandate for art or science.

After the work of Creation was finished, God looked over all He had made and pronounced it טוֹב i.e. the creation was *beautiful* as well as perfect. The intrinsic goodness of the Creation means that no art medium is intrinsically evil. No combination of sounds, forms, colors or textures is intrinsically evil.

This is why Christian artists must take their stand against the idea that matter (ex. the human body) is intrinsically evil. There is no biblical reason to put diapers or leaves on nude statutes! No combination of tones or colors is intrinsically evil or demonic.

Christian art should reflect the original Creation in all of its beauty, form, harmony and goodness. For example, David composed musical compositions that celebrated Creation by using the mediums of poetry, song, and instrumental music (Ps. 8; 19; 89; 100, etc.). Franz Joseph Haydn's *Creation* is another good example of an artistic display of the beauty of the original creation.

The biblical doctrine of Creation supplies us with the only valid basis upon which to explain the origin, existence, function and diversification of color. The theory of evolution can never explain why a black cow eats green grass and produces white milk.

The Bible reveals that color is here in all of its diversification simply because God likes color. Beauty is thus ultimately in the eye of *the Beholder*—the Creator God. He is the original artist who is the aesthetic pattern for man who was created in God's image.

When we look at the world of color and form that God created (such as a beautiful sunset), we must confess that God is the great Painter. When we examine the shape of the mountains, the different forms of animal and plant life, and the human body, we know that God is the great Sculptor.

When we read in Scripture that in heaven God surrounds Himself with angelic and human choirs; that angelic choirs sang their heavenly music at Creation and the birth of Christ; that the stars sing for joy; that God made musical instruments in heaven to be played continuously before

Him; that God commanded man to worship Him through music, we know that He is the great Musician (Rev. 5:8; 14:1–3; Luke 2:13, 14; Job 38:7; Ps. 30:4; 33:3).

Ideal Geometric Form

One interesting feature of biblical aesthetics is the geometric form that symbolized perfection. While the Greeks thought that the circle represented perfection and the Egyptians thought that the pyramid form was perfection, the Bible always pictured perfection in terms of a rectangle.

The Ark, the Tabernacle, the Temple, the Heavenly Jerusalem, the rebuilt temple of Ezekiel, etc., were all rectangles, not circles or pyramids. God revealed rectangle blueprints to Noah, Moses, and Ezekiel. Since He is the Great Architect, what is the significance of the rectangle as opposed to the circle or pyramid?

When we examine the literary forms within Scripture, we find beautiful poetry, prayer, prose, praise and proclamation. Thus we must confess that God is the great Poet and Writer.

Art is not for art's sake. It exists for God's glory for He is here and is not silent. The little bird singing in the forest, where and when no human ear can hear it, is still beautiful because God hears it. The desert flower, where and when no human eye can see it, is still beautiful because God sees it.

Aesthetics in the Light of the Fall

The radical Fall of man into sin and guilt supplies us with the only valid basis to understand the origin and existence of ugliness, evil, pain, suffering, chaos, war, pain, sorrow, and death. What is now is not what originally was.

Since the Fall polluted every aspect of man's being, the aesthetic aspect of the image of God in man was corrupted by sin. Man's aesthetic abilities are now used *against* God instead of for God. Thus we find the rise of apostate art which finds its climax in idolatry where the art object is worshiped as God. Idolatry reveals that man now worships the creature instead of the Creator (Rom. 1:18–25).

Biblical art should reflect the ugliness of man that sin has caused. It should reveal the misery, agony, and pain of sin, death, and hell. It should point to the ultimate despair of a life without God. It should portray the horror of hopeless sinners in the past who were the recipients of the great judgments of God against sin. The Flood or the destruction of Sodom should be depicted by art.

Art should supply the mediums through which the people of God can express their own despair, conviction of sin, confusion, pain, discouragement, etc. We need "songs in the night," songs when loved ones die, songs of confession of sin. The Psalms supply us with many examples of this kind of art (Psa. 51, etc.)

The Christian artist should aesthetically surpass the pessimistic existentialist artist when it comes to portraying the despair, ugliness and hopelessness of sin. The doctrine of total depravity as taught in such places as Rom. 3:9-19 is more realistic and frightening than anything the humanists can come up with. We need aesthetically to confront man with the ugliness and horror of his rebellion against God and with the reality of divine judgment against sin.

Aesthetics in the Light of Redemption

The biblical doctrine of Redemption gives us the only basis for artistic portrayals of truth, justice, meaning, morals, and beauty. We should reclaim every square inch of this world for Christ. Every thought and talent is to be redeemed unto God's glory for all of life is to be lived for Him (I Cor. 10:31; II Cor. 10:5). All of culture is to be conquered for Christ. Even though sin makes it impossible to attain total perfection in this life, Christians are given the Spirit of God to execute this Mandate as much as possible in all of culture.

It is from the Bible we get the idea that the good will ultimately triumph over evil; that justice will established and injustice punished. Christians know from the Bible that they "will live happily ever after" through the merits of the person and work of Messiah.

When Jesus returns and creates a new earth, the Elect will fulfill the original Creation Mandate given to Adam. Our wildest dreams cannot comprehend the wondrous art, science, and philosophy that shall be produced by the glorified saints in the eternal state. Redemption supplies us with the only valid basis for Christians going into the arts. It is through grace alone and Christ alone that we escape apostate art such as the veneration of idols and icons.[308] Redeemed sinners respond aesthetically to God because the image of God is renewed within them (Eph. 4:24; 5:18, 19).

The arts should be viewed as:

- Obedience to the Creation Mandate (Gen. 1:28).
- Obedience to the Mission Mandate (Matt. 28:19, 20).
- The stewardship of God-given talents (Matt. 25:14–30).
- Worship, praise, rest, recreation, prayer, and confession (ex. Psa. 19; 23; 51; 90; 100).
- The edification of the saints.
- The evangelism of sinners.

Christian art should at times reflect the great moments in the history of redemption, the thanks, prayer, and praise of redeemed sinners, and the saints' desire for sinners to be saved. Again, many of David's Psalms are artistic expressions of thankfulness to God for salvation (Ps. 103, etc.).

Christian art should portray the following:

- God exists and has communicated to man.
- There is hope, love, meaning, truth, etc.
- The beauty and dignity of Christ.
- There is order behind the chaos of life. God is still in control.
- The beauty that will be in the new creation.
- That good will ultimately triumph over evil.
- That the righteous will be vindicated and the wicked punished.

Christian artists engaged in evangelism should attempt to push sinners to despair in order to drive them to Christ. We should reveal both the ugliness of sin and the beauty of salvation. In this sense every artist is an evangelist to a lost, sick, and dying world, for every Christian is scripturally called upon to evangelize his world for Christ (Matt. 28:19-20). This means that the Christian artist should viewed himself or herself as a prophet, priest and king to the people of God.

- As a prophet, he should protect the people of God from idolatry.
- As a priest, he should lead people to worship of God alone through the arts.
- As a king, he should provide for the aesthetic needs of the people of God and protect them from apostate art which leads to idolatry.

Perhaps it would be helpful to see that art has various functions. The following describes some of these functions. A given piece of art may have one, some, or all of these functions:

- "Cool" art: art aimed at creating a distinct mood, impression or emotion on those exposed to the art. *Example:* Psalm 150.
- "Hot" art: art aimed at communicating truth to the intellect. This can be called "message art." *Example:* Psalm 1 and Proverbs.
- "Reflective" art: art which expresses and reflects the mood and emotional state of the artist. *Example:* Psalm 51.
- "Aesthetic" art: art aimed purely at the aesthetic sense of man. It is "beautiful" without being cool, hot or reflective. It is for entertainment purposes. This is art for beauty's sake. *Example:* the artwork in the tabernacle and temple (Exod. 25; II Chron. 3:6).
- "Enrichment" art, i.e. the "hidden art" of daily life: flower arrangements, table settings, attention to the selection of color of different foods, etc. This is art in which every home should be involved.

Closing Questions on Aesthetics

1. *Is it proper to distinguish between secular and religious art?* Answer: Yes/No. Yes, if you mean the distinction between art which portrays a biblical or "religious" event or scene and art which has a non-religious subject as its focus. There is a difference between a picture showing Noah's Flood and one showing a country picnic. No, if you mean that only religious art is "Christian art." Christian art is not restricted to events in biblical history, for the entire world is God's world (Ps. 24). Also, all art is "religious" in the sense of being either apostate or God-glorifying or somewhere in between. There is no "secular" art in the sense of "neutral" art.

2. *Can a Christian artist create art to entertain people?* Answer: We are to glorify God and to *enjoy* Him forever. Entertainment and recreation are legitimate creature necessities and, therefore, legitimate fields of work for the Christian. Those who are negative and suspicious of entertainment reveal a hidden strain of Platonic thinking.

3. *Should we judge a work of art on the basis of the life style of the artist?* Answer: No, just as we can take a crooked stick and draw a straight line, even so wicked men and women can produce beautiful art.

4. *Can a Christian artist create "cool," reflective, or aesthetic art or must he restrict himself to portraying and conveying the gospel through "hot" art?* Answer: The Christian is not restricted to any one particular function or form of art. A still life painting of a bowl of fruit

is just as "Christian" as a painting of the crucifixion if it is done for God's glory. The artist is not restricted to "hot" art.

5. *Is "good" art determined on the basis of the intent of the artist or on the amount of biblical truth it conveys?* Answer: The quality of a work of art is not determined solely on the basis of the intent of the artist or the clarity of its message. A Christian artist can produce poor art even though he did it for God's glory and tried to convey the gospel.

6. *How do we judge the quality of art?* Answer: By such aesthetic standards as:
    a. Technical excellence: Does the artist have the technical ability to do superior work in his medium of choice?
    b. Validity of style and medium: Is the medium the appropriate one to the style?
    c. Intellectual content: Is the artist's worldview clearly expressed in the art?
    d. The integration of content and vehicle: Are the two united in making one statement?
    e. The difference between art and pornography. The portrayal of the nude body is art when done to glorify God in His creation of the human body.
    f Pornography is the portrayal of the nude body to simulate sexual lust and immorality.

Conclusion

Many humanists today believe that "science" is a curse that has brought us Global warning, nuclear energy, and other environmental disasters. We should all go back to living in a grass hut; walking around looking for vegetables and fruit to eat; living without electricity or cars.

The Bible alone gives us the only theoretical foundation for science and the arts. It alone provides us with a reason why they should exist and why we should do them. Humanism cannot provide us with any rationale or motivation for either one.

> To God alone belongs all the glory!
> Great things He has done.

Chapter Ten

The Failure of Definition

The insurmountable problem facing natural theologians is their inability to define who they are, what they do, how they do it, what they hope to accomplish, and why they bother to do it. In order to define the nature, origin, function, methodology, and goal of "Natural Theology," "Natural Religion," "Natural Law," and "Natural Apologetics" they have to define the adjective "natural" and the nouns "nature," "theology," "law," and "apologetics" solely through human reason, experience, feelings and faith apart from and independent of God and the Bible. But this is where everything collapses into ruins.

Nature

Let us begin with the most important noun. What is the meaning of the word "Nature?" It is the key term from which they derive the words "natural," "unnatural," and "naturally." Why do some authors write "Nature" while others write "nature?" Does the meaning change when the "n" is capitalized? If so, how does it change the meaning of the word? Is "Nature" visible or invisible, material or ideal, objective or subjective? Is man inside "Nature" as a part of it or man outside of "Nature?" Is "Nature" something inside man or something he projects onto the world around him? Is "nature" controlled and predetermined by fate, the gods, devils, etc. or does chance and luck determine the future of "Nature?"

I have asked natural theologians and philosophers these questions for many years but they have never given me any clear answers. Some of them have even admitted that they do not have any answers to give me! There are no agreed upon definitions for any of their key terms. Yet, they still believe in "nature" or "Nature" even if they cannot define it. The failure to define what they talking about renders all their work meaningless.

"Evangelical" natural theologians, philosophers, and apologists often cheat at this point. They make the claim that they are able to generate truth and morals apart from and independent of the Bible solely on the basis on their own reason, experience, feelings or faith. Yet, when I ask them for clear definitions of their key terms, they start quoting the Bible! If you use the Bible to prove that you do not need to use the Bible, something is wrong!

Natural

Since no one knows what the word "Nature" or "nature" means, you do not need a degree in rocket science to understand that they cannot define the adjective "natural." Does the word "natural" only refer to good things or can evil things be "natural" as well? Does the word "natural" describe what *is* or what *ought* to be? If something is "natural," is it beautiful or ugly?

Theology

It is amazing to us that natural theologians never define the word "theology." What is the meaning of "theology?" Where did the word originate? Why does the Bible never use the word? The Bible has prophets, apostles, priests, and pastors but not one "theologian." Why is that?

A Brief History Lesson

The word "theology" was invented by Aristotle as one of the "sciences" that man creates through rational reflection. The idea of "divine revelation" in which God tells man what to believe and how to live never crossed his mind. In its historic and classical sense, "theology" is a humanistic enterprise built solely on human reason, experience, feelings or faith apart from and independent of God and the Bible. "Theology" is *man's* speculations *about* God instead of an exposition of what God has *revealed* about Himself.

Is Theology a Science?

Natural theologians have always been desperate to be accepted as a "science" by unbelievers. This has led them to adopt rationalism, empiricism, mysticism or fideism as the basis of their theology. Once they adopt such apostate epistemologies, it is no surprise that they end up denying Revelation in the name of Reason.

Law

Given their failure to produce an agreed-upon definition of the words "nature," "natural," "unnatural," and "theology," it should not be a surprise to find that natural theologians have also failed to define the key word "law." What is the exact meaning of the word "law?"

Some natural theologians use the capital "L" when they write the word "Law." Do they intend to signify that the meaning of "Law" is different from "law?" Are there absolute, universal, self-evident, intuitive, transcendent, and eternal "laws" floating around somewhere in the universe? If so, how do we find them? How do we abstract them from trees or mountains? Should we study animal behavior to derive these "laws"?

"Natural" laws must be accessible and definable if we are going to apply them to society as civil law. Since everyone disagrees over what is or is not a "natural law," how do we determine who is right? If we appeal to the Bible as the "higher law" by which we judge "natural laws," then the basis of "natural law" is overturned.

Are there are relative, limited, culturally-conditioned "laws?" How can the same word "law" be used for both absolute and relative rules of behavior? Is the word "law" only a cloak for personal opinion and prejudice?

Are there *natural* laws-without-God, *moral* laws-without-God, *civil* laws-without-God, *scientific* laws-without-God, logical laws-without-God, and *aesthetic* laws-without-God? Are these laws in "matter" or only "in" "mind?" Natural theologians have utterly failed to agree on any answers to these questions.

The Laws of Logic

Aristotle assumed that the "laws" of logic "existed" somewhere out there in the universe, (i.e. in Nature). But, if so, in what sense do they "exist?" Do they have any metaphysical or material existence? Can we find them in the stars or in the rocks and trees around us? Where are they?

The First Move

The attempt to find these "laws" in "matter" failed. So, natural theologians retreated from "matter" to "mind." Once the "Laws of logic" were reduced to the mind of man, they were pronounced "rational" instead of "material."

The Second Move

The Don Quixote quest to find the laws of logic in the external world of Nature or in the internal world of the mind failed. Once again, natural theologians were forced to move the laws of logic.

Today, the "laws" of logic are said to be *linguistic* in nature and reflect the "nature" of human language. They have now retreated from matter to mind to language! Each time the laws have been moved, they have retreated further and further away from reality. Like a helium balloon cut free from its string, the laws of logic have floated away out of the reach of man.

The Last Move

An interesting twist has recently occurred in humanistic circles that may surprise Christians. Some logicians have announced that there is an extraterrestrial Origin for the laws of logic! This is the latest step in humanism's flight from reality. They would rather believe that little gray men in UFOs brought these "laws" to earth than to bow before Divine Revelation. Truly Paul was inspired when he wrote, "They became futile in their speculations, and their foolish heart was darkened. Professing to be wise, they became fools." (Rom. 1:21-22)

Eastern Rejection

On what basis do natural theologians claim that their "laws" of logic are valid? They assert that Aristotle's "laws" are universal, intuitive, and self-evident. If Aristotle's laws were universal, then all men in all cultures throughout all of history would have heard of and believed in them. But, as we have already pointed out, Eastern philosophies and religions do not believe in Aristotle's "laws" of logic. Many non-Western cultures, philosophies, and religions do not believe in these ancient Greek laws of logic.

Since belief in these laws is manifestly not universal, then they are not self-evident or intuitive. But natural theologians and philosophers do not let those facts get in the way of claiming Aristotle's laws are "universal, self-evident, and intuitive." It seems to me that they use these words to psychologically manipulate people.

Not Mentioned in the Bible

Are Aristotle's laws of logic mentioned in the Bible? No. Did the prophets, the apostles or Jesus ever appeal to them as the basis of truth and morals? No.

If the prophets, apostles, and Messiah never appealed to these "laws" as the basis of truth or morals, what does this mean? Since they did not refer to these laws of logic, how should Christians view them? If you are a Christian, you cannot avoid these questions and their implications.

Theism

Natural theologians have failed to define their other key words as well. When they say they want to prove "theism," what do they mean by that word? Is it really possible to define theism-without-God? Does "theism" refer to the God of the Bible or some vague idea of some kind of god or goddess? Does Zeus fit the meaning of "theism?" What about polytheism, pantheism, etc.? Does the "theism" they are attempting to prove include the "gods" of Islam and modern Judaism as well as Christianity? Is the "god" they hope to find at the end of a chain of their arguments, the biblical God as distinct from the demon god of Islam?

Some natural theologians admit that all they hope to "prove" through "reason" is some vague form of "theism." Others claim to be able to prove the existence of the God of the Bible. Some claim that Natural Religion and Natural Theology form the basis of Christianity while others deny this. Who is right?

The Words "Reason" and "Rational"

Some natural theologians say that they can prove that their notion of "theism" is "rational," i.e. in line with the demands of something they call "Reason." Others like Kierkegaard claim that the proof of their brand of theism is irrationality!

What does the word "reason" mean? Some natural theologians write "Reason" while others write "reason." Does using a capital "R" mean something? Why do they capitalize the "r?" Have they abstracted the fallible ability of some people some of the time to think and made it into an ideal, infallible, romantic, omniscient, and omnipotent "Reason?" Is this why they capitalized the "r"?

Which Is the Basis of the Other?

Chapter Ten The Failure of Definition

Does "reason" justify "Reason" or does "Reason" justify "reason?" If "reason" justifies "Reason," are we arguing in a circle? Do "reason" and "Reason" stand before the "bar" of a yet higher authority over them? Is there an authority higher than "Reason," to whom it must bow? On what basis do they assume that the "rational" is always good and not evil? Hitler felt that the Holocaust was the "rational" solution to the Jewish problem.

Not in the Bible

Why does the word or concept of "Reason" never appear in the Hebrew and Greek text of Scripture? No. Did the prophets and apostles ever appeal to "Reason" as the basis of truth or morals? No. Since the prophets and apostles never claimed to be "rational" or "irrational," why should Christians rush around trying to prove to unbelievers that Christianity is "rational"? Did Paul say that the *revealed* Gospel was "foolishness" according to Greek philosophy (1 Cor. 1:23)? Yes. Why then do natural theologians argue that the gospel is not "foolishness" but "rational?" Are they violating Scripture?

Is Irrational the Opposite of Rational?

Is the word "rational" a logical or psychological term? One clue would be the meaning of the word "irrational." Since it is the opposite of "rational," they are bound together. But, what *feels* "rational" to one man may *feel* "irrational" to another man. Is it possible that what natural theologians mean by the word "rational" is only the psychological *feeling* of "certainty"?

Certainty and Doubt

Do our "feelings" of certitude ride up and down an emotional scale all day long? Is "certitude" more psychological than logical or metaphysical? Do our "feelings of certitude" depend more on blood sugar than on syllogisms? Is it possible to "feel" certain that something is "rational" in the morning, but, by noon "feel" that it "irrational?"

Since the word "doubt" is often used as the opposite of the word "certain," isn't it also a psychological term? We "doubt" something when we *feel* uncertain or uneasy about it. If "certainty" and "doubt" are both psychological terms, does this mean that the words "rational" and "irrational" are only psychological terms as well?

The Problem

When I begin to push for precise definitions of these key terms, I usually get a blank stare. "Oh," one natural theologian responded, "the word 'rational' means 'rational.' It means what it means." He could not define any of his words.

We surveyed hundreds of Natural Theology books written by Catholics and neo-Protestants alike. Very few attempted to define their key words with any precision. They usually assumed that their readers would pour into those terms whatever cultural meaning was in their heads. By avoiding precise definitions of the key terms in their arguments, their arguments would have an *appearance* of validity because the readers would pour into those words what they already believed.

A Brief history of The Middle Ages

A "mega-shift" takes place when a fundamental change occurs in the foundation or basis of thought and life. For example, Thomas Aquinas caused a mega-shift in European thought and life by abandoning Platonic mysticism and replacing it with Aristotelian empiricism. The conflict between Platonic and Aristotelian forms of Christianity led to the Great Schism between Greek and Latin Christendom.[309]

The shift in worldview from Plato to Aristotle had far reaching consequences that are still with us today. Through the labors of Thomas Aquinas, the Medieval Roman Catholic Church became dependent upon the humanistic philosophy and theology of Aristotle.

Some neo-evangelicals have claimed that Aquinas was the first "Protestant" or "Evangelical" theologian. Norman Geisler lists R. C. Sproul, John Gerstner, Stuart Hackett, and Arvin Vos as joining him as self-declared Thomists.[310] To his credit, he also admits that Aquinas' Natural Theology was vigorously rejected by Schaeffer, Van Til, Henry, Clark, Carnell, and Holmes.[311]

After spending 176 pages extolling Aquinas as "evangelical," on the last page (p. 177) Geisler admits that Aquinas taught things he could not accept:

- The divine authority of the Church of Rome (and the pope)
- The supremacy of Aristotle's philosophy
- The Apocrypha as part of Scripture
- The transubstantiation of the bread and wine in the Mass
- Baptismal regeneration
- Human life begins forty days after conception for males and eighty days for females
- The number and nature of the sacraments

We would also add that Aquinas taught praying to and the veneration of Mary and the saints, the veneration of relics, pictures, and statues, putting to death those who disagreed with Rome's theology, the Catholic doctrine of justification by works, it is not necessary to hear of or believe in Jesus or his Gospel to go to heaven, the existence of purgatory and limbo, etc.[312] Aquinas mixed works with faith and grace with merit in his view of salvation. His understanding of justification was erroneous. In short, he taught a false gospel condemned by Gal. 1:8.

Despite the attempts of those on the payroll of the Acton Institute to prove that the Reformers followed Aquinas, they have never produced a single passage where Calvin, Luther, et al, based their doctrine on the authority of Aquinas or his Summa. The Reformers consistently judged Aquinas by Scripture and never appealed to his authority as the basis of truth and morals. The anti-

Protestant Catholic councils such as Trent quoted Aquinas as their authority to reject the Reformation gospel but also to torture and murder Protestants.

The Islamic Influence

Aquinas derived his philosophy from the works of such Muslim philosophers as Ghazali and Averroes. They, in turn, derived their ideas from the pagan Greek philosophy of Aristotle.[313] Their arguments for Islam and against Christianity were drawn from the pagan Greek concepts of the autonomy, self-sufficiency, and dominance of human "reason."

A Muslim Philosophic Jihad

The Roman Catholic Church faced a philosophic Jihad that threatened to overwhelm the intellectual life of Europe. Catholic theologians and philosophers had no answers to the "rational" arguments of the Muslim apologists. Obviously, a "Catholic" answer had to be found that could counter the Muslim influence in academia.

The Muslims had intimidated the Catholics and made them feel inferior because, while the Muslims appealed to an idealistic Aristotelian human "Reason" as the basis of their doctrines, all the Catholics had was blind "faith" in the dogmas of Rome. Thus the conflict was between Islamic "Reason" versus the Catholic "Faith." Framing the conflict as "reason or faith" is still with us today.

If You Can't Beat Them, Join Them!

The answer came from an unlikely source. A monk, whose nicknamed was "the dumb ox," came up with the solution. Aquinas suggested that the best way to deal with Islam was to abandon Catholic blind "faith" and adopt Aristotle's "Reason!" Thus Aquinas abandoned the dogmatic faith of popery and adopted the same pagan philosophic worldview as the Muslim apologists. He embraced the Aristotelian dogma of the autonomy of human reason in which man is the "measure of all things" and the Origin of truth, justice, morals, meaning, and beauty.

It is no surprise that Aquinas' ideas were first officially condemned as heresy and viewed as undermining the authority of the papacy. But, after his death, the condemnation was removed and he was proclaimed the official philosopher of the Roman Catholic Church.

Aquinas took Aristotle's dichotomy of form/essence and turned it into the nature/grace dichotomy. He later refined it into the secular/sacred dichotomy that still plagues us today. It was thus Aquinas who opened the way for secular humanism to take over Western philosophy, science, ethics, art, politics, and theology. Like a malignant cancer, secularism cannot stop consuming all of life and culture until there is no sacredness left.

What is Happening Today?

This gives us a practical insight into the secular humanist's all-consuming lust to root out all sacred symbols from society. It can be a monument to the Ten Commandments, "In God we trust" on our coins or prayer before a football game. Any and all "sacred" things must be destroyed.

Secularism cannot tolerate these things. As Francis Schaeffer, Gordon Clark, Carl F. Henry, and many other well-known Evangelical scholars have pointed out, Thomas Aquinas is directly to blame for setting in motion the secularist vision of life.

Look Before You Leap

Protestants should "look before they leap" to embrace Aquinas' Aristotelian worldview. Aquinas' "Natural" Theology and "Natural" Law are only pseudo names for "Secular" Theology and "Secular" law! Last time I checked, "without God" means "*without God.*"

Besides being an oxymoron, "Natural" (i.e. Secular) theology and "Natural" (i.e. Secular) Law are only religious forms of secular humanism. Natural (i.e. Secular) theology and Natural (i.e. Secular) Law both attempt to find final answers *without* God (i.e. they are God-less) or His Word (i.e. they are Bible-less) solely on the basis of "Nature" (i.e. man's reason, experience, feelings, and faith), apart from Christ (i.e. they are Christ-less).

The attempt to find God-without-God, and to find morality-without-God has always been a failure according to the Bible (I Cor. 1:21). Once Aquinas let religious humanism out of Pandora's Box, it unleashed great evils upon the earth.

His Last Testimony

One year before his death in 1274, Aquinas had an experience that shook the foundations of his theology. His contemporaries described it as a religious or mystical experience in which he encountered God in a powerful way. As a result of this experience, Aquinas declared, "All my work is as worthless as straw!" He renounced his philosophical work and refused to write one more page of Natural Theology, Natural Philosophy or Natural Law! [314]

It is amazing to us that while erstwhile Evangelicals are rushing to embrace the Natural Law and Theology of Aquinas, he repudiated it as worthless straw. Since he rejected it himself at the end of his life, shouldn't this put a question mark over his theology? We think so.

A Muslim Crisis

The Muslim philosophers and apologists followed Aristotle's reasoning that the world had to be eternal. But this did not sit well with Muslim theologians who pointed out that the Qur'an clearly taught that the world was created. When the philosophers were accused of heresy, they devised a trick or ruse to avoid the charge.

The Muslim philosophers and apologists divided philosophy into a dichotomy in which something can be true according to "Reason" and, at the same time, be false according to "Faith." The reverse could also be true. Thus it was the Muslims who set up the original false dilemma of "Reason or Faith" as the only two options before us. Then they demanded that people must choose either one or the other. By "Reason" they meant the classic pagan concept of man as the Origin of truth and thus the measure of all things. By "Faith" they meant *blind* Islamic faith.

They went on to restrict "knowledge" to that which comes from human Reason, which rested on "facts." "Belief" came from human faith, which rested on religious authority. While "reason" tells us what we "know," faith tells us what we "believe."

By this ploy, when the Muslim apologists were asked if the world was created or eternal, they answered, "While Reason tells me that it is eternal, Faith tells me that it was created." They *knew* that the world was eternal and they *believed* that it was created at the same time! Knowledge came from reason, not from faith.

Aquinas' Natural theology

Since Thomas Aquinas was the first (and greatest) of Western attempts to produce a "Christian" version of Aristotle's Natural Theology, how did he define his key words? He simply followed Aristotle's definitions as given in the *Metaphysics*.

To Aquinas, Aristotle was the unquestioned authority on the meaning of all these terms. Indeed, Aristotle's *Metaphysics* was the "Bible" of Medieval Roman Catholic Natural Theology. Since Aquinas adopted the worldview of Aristotle, he accepted his definitions without question. J. P. Mooreland and William Craig acknowledge that, "The English term *substance* has many different meanings associated with it. Likewise, there have been different uses of the term in the history of philosophy."[315]

Almost every philosopher acknowledges that Thomas Aquinas' Natural Theology was a Christian version of Aristotle's humanistic philosophy. [316] Even the fanatical natural theologian Dudziszewski admitted,

> There is much for a Christian to complain of in Thomas Aquinas and I speak as one who loves him. Some of the obstacles may result from his having borrowed a subscriptural ontology from pagan philosophers...his reliance upon pagan sources seems to lead him into misinterpretation of Scripture itself.[317]

This is why Aquinas' "Catholic" doctrines depended more on Aristotle than on the Bible. For example, his view of the Eucharist came directly from Aristotle's "form and essence" dichotomy.

Protestant natural theologians as well as Catholic theologians adopt the traditional view of Aristotle/Aquinas on "inner nature" and "substance." [318] Moreland and DeWesse use such phrases as "inner nature" that reflect Plato's universalism and Aristotle's empiricism. They parrot Aristotle's definitions as modified by Aquinas. If Aristotle said it, that settles it, they believe it! They are so committed to the pagan concept of "substance, that they boldly state, "God is a substance."[319] We note that they did not cite one Scripture to support their position that "God is a substance."

The statement "God is a substance" will surprise most Christians because Jesus said "God is spirit" (John 4:24) and that a spirit does *not* have "flesh and bones" (Lk. 24:39). The moment we reduce God to "substance," He is no longer spirit, i.e. without substance.

To say that God is a *spiritual* substance does not help us either. Since the word "substance" (like "nature," "essence," "meaning," "reason," "rational," etc.) means *anything* and *everything*, it means *nothing*.

Aristotle and the Catholic Mass

Aristotle taught that all things were a combination of external form and internal essence. The real "inner nature" or "meaning" of an object was its "essence," not its external physical form. The form of something did not have to conform to its essence. It could look like one thing but actually be something else.

The Eucharist had the external "form" of bread. It looked, smelled, felt, and even tasted like bread. You would gain weight if you ate too much of it. But, according to Aquinas, its inner "essence" or "nature" was changed by the priest into the living flesh of Christ.

The communion wine may look and taste like wine and you could even get drunk on it, but its "inner nature," (i.e. its "essence" or "substance") was the living blood of Jesus. This is why the Roman Catholic Church made Aquinas their official philosopher. Many of their doctrines depended on the Aristotelian formulations given by Aquinas.

This explains why so many Protestants who adopt Natural Theology end up converting to Roman Catholicism. [320] Once they adopted Aristotle's pagan philosophy of "inner nature" and "substance," they were philosophically prepared to accept Roman Catholicism. Natural Theology was correctly described by the Puritans as a Trojan Horse in which the pope was hiding! Its purpose has always been to replace *Sola Scriptura* with *sola ratione*. [321]

Why The Reformation Happened

The Reformation happened partly because Aristotle's philosophy had become passé in Europe. Occam's Realism was now the cultural consensus of the day. If something looked, smelled, felt, and tasted like bread, it was bread. If it tasted like wine and you got drunk if you drank too much of it, it was wine. The Mass was nonsense.

The moment you say that the "inner nature" or "essence" of something need not correspond to its external form, no knowledge of the world around you is possible. The "form" lying in the bed next to you may look like your wife, but its true "inner nature" or "essence" could be something else!

Aristotle's Geocentrism

Aquinas taught Aristotle's doctrine that the earth was the center of the universe. The sun, moon, and stars rotated around the earth. If Aristotle said it, that settled it, Aquinas believed it! This is explains why there was such a violent reaction to Copernicus' idea that the sun was the center of the universe and the earth revolved around it.

The Medieval Catholic Church was built upon the worldview of Aristotle. The Catholic natural theologians clearly understood that a "domino" effect would happen if Aristotle's geocentrism was rejected. If Aristotle and Aquinas were in error on this fundamental point, how many other Catholic doctrines would also be in error? Of course, they were right and the falling dominos led eventually to the Reformation.

Nature Moves Inside

Philosophy took a major leap with Descartes and Leibniz. The "nature" of something was no longer "out there," "beneath there," "up there" or "in there." "Nature" was now "in here," i.e. in the mind of man as well as "in there," in the object. The word "Nature" described some vague kind of *correspondence* between the mind of man and objects in the world. Ideas were magically innate, self-evident, universal, and intuitive in the mind of man. Of course, no one could define what those terms meant but they were psychologically useful to manipulate the naïve masses.

The correspondence theory did not last long. How the inner "nature" or "essence" of things in the world "corresponded" to some kind of Platonic "innate" ideas in the mind could not be explained or demonstrated. If ideas were innate in the mind, why don't we all have the same ideas? How did this correspondence work? No one knew for sure.

And the Beat Moved On

Western philosophers eventually abandoned the idea that the "inner nature" of things, i.e. their meaning, essence, or substance, was "in there," i.e. in the object. Instead, "Nature" was now moved totally into the mind of man. Our minds *projected* meaning, essence, substance, and order upon the chaos around us. We create the world we see around us.

This is why modern philosophy is divided into pre and post Emmanuel Kant. His epistemology forever reshaped the history of modern philosophy. The fourteen categories of the mind created "Nature." We impose order, number, texture, color, sound, etc. onto the indefinable sensations (*ding ah sich*) coming into us. The "inner nature" or "meaning" of things is in our mind alone.

Existentialism

The next step was obvious to Jean Paul Sartre. If the "inner nature," "meaning," "essence," and "substance" of things, individually or corporately viewed, is not "out there," "beneath there," "up there," or "in there," but, only "in here," then it is *nowhere*! There is no such thing as "nature," "substance," "meaning," "being," "essence," etc. *Existence* is all there. What is, *is*. That is all we can say.

The birth of Existentialism meant the death of Western metaphysics, epistemology, ethics, and aesthetics. This is why secular education today teaches that there is no truth to find in philosophy, no knowledge in epistemology, no morality in ethics, and no beauty in aesthetics.

Since Aristotle's and Aquinas' beliefs such things as "reason, "free will," "human nature," "substance, etc. are not part of the biblical worldview, the secular abandonment of such beliefs did not panic Bible-based Christians. But it did throw natural theologians and philosophers into hysteria. Their worldview was falling to pieces before their eyes.

Instead of a "Back to the Bible" movement, natural theologians launched a "Back to Aquinas" movement in the late 20th century and early 21st century. Dr. Norman Geisler was the one who spearheaded the movement and was later joined by Sproul, Moreland, Craig, etc.[322]

Nature Loses its Meaning

When Western culture abandoned Aristotle's philosophy, it no longer served as the philosophical glue that held together Western cultural consensus. Once the consensus disappeared, all the definitions that depended on that consensus disappeared as well.

The attempt to attach the meaning of such terms as "theism" to whatever is the consensus at the moment is how modern natural theologians define their terms.[323] This is a sad commentary on the power of relativism in religious communities.

This also explains why appeals to "common sense" collapsed. What made "sense" to the "common" man changed whenever the consensus of his culture changed. "Common sense" said that the earth was the center of the universe and the sun revolved around it. Our eyes saw the sun rise and set. When the consensus changed over to a heliocentric worldview, it now made "sense" to the "common" man that the earth revolved around the sun. It did not matter that this contradicted what he saw with his own eyes.

Relative Natural Law

Even "Natural Law" changed as the cultural consensus changed. British and American Natural Law philosophers (such as Thomas Hobbes) followed Aristotle and Aquinas in defending slavery and the subjugation of women. Natural theologians attacked Wilberforce, Spurgeon, Whitfield, and other evangelicals who sought to free the slaves and give women equal rights. [324]

Natural Law philosophers proclaimed that "common sense" and "Nature" were absolutely united in defending slavery and the subjugation of women. The "inner nature" of women proved they could not be treated as equals. The "inner nature" of black slaves was animal and not human at all. Their "external form" may look human, but their "inner nature" was beast. Thus slavery based on race and the rape and murder of hundreds of thousands of Africans were justified by appeals to Aristotle and Aquinas.

What happened when the political situation changed and the slaves were set free? The cultural consensus changed and Natural Theology and Natural Law theorists abandoned their original position and announced that "common sense" and "Nature" were now in favor of the abolition of slavery and the emancipation of women.

The conceit, haughtiness, and triumphalism of modern day proponents of Natural Theology and Natural Law require us to remind them of their past support of slavery, the subjugation of women, British Colonialism, American Manifest Destiny, the genocide of Native Americans and other races. How can "Natural Law" give us absolutes when it changes from generation to generation?

I know that such questions are unsettling to natural theologians and philosophers. But these questions must be answered or Natural Theology, Natural Law, and Natural Apologetics go down the drain as a waste of time.

The "nature" of Nature

Modern natural theologians are nostalgic for the good old days when Aristotle's philosophy was the cultural consensus.[325] If "Nature" refers to the world that is empirically experienced, then what do we mean when we talk about the "inner nature" of things? For example, the "nature" of man is invisible to the eye. All we see are individual people. No one has ever seen, touched, heard, or smelled "human nature." It supposedly lies "behind," "beneath" the man or woman that we see in front of us. This "nature" is the invisible "ground of" of visible man and is intangible. This is why modern philosophy denies there is such a thing as "human nature."

The same holds true for all other particular things. If our knowledge is limited to the empirical, then we cannot know the universal "nature" of dogs, fish, rocks, trees, man, etc. Plato said that we must have universals if we want to have knowledge. But, whoever saw or touched a universal? We cannot pick them off trees like apples!

If truth, justice, morals, meaning, and beauty are objectively "out there" somewhere in "Nature" waiting for us to discover, particular things cannot give us any way to know them because empiricism cannot generate universals. Schaeffer told us at L'Abri over and over again that no matter how high you pile finite experiences, they won't magically morph into universals just because you want them to! Empirical experience is finite experience and thus it cannot generate universal knowledge. No experience carries within itself its own interpretation. Interpretations of experience always come from outside experience.

The Good, the Bad, and the Ugly

The other problem that confronted modern secular humanists is that when they looked at "Nature," they saw a very cruel and chaotic world. We see and experience the good, the bad, and the ugly in "Nature!" The idealistic and romantic idea of the "noble savage" and the tame, majestic lion was pure fantasy.

Another problem that surfaced was when you followed a chain of finite effects back to their finite causes you are still only dealing with finite things. It seemed "rational" to the majority of mankind for the majority of history that finite effects lead back to finite deities, not the infinite personal God of the Bible. How can we argue from finite things to one infinite Being? The idea of monotheism never crossed the minds of the ancient philosophers. Even Aristotle believed in many gods and goddesses!

If it is valid to argue from the good we experience to a good god, then it is equally valid to argue from the evil we experience to an evil god. This is why Natural Religions have always been polytheistic in believing in good and evil gods.

"Nature" is filled with conflict and chaos. This indicated to purveyors of "Natural Religions" that there must be many conflicting deities fighting each other. One deity sends a storm and another one tries to stop it. And, since the male/female matrix is found in "Nature," then most "Natural Religions" concluded that these finite deities were male and female as well.

The Chaos of the Words

The Medieval meaning of the words nature, natural, theology, law, etc. depended on an Aristotelian consensus in society. Once this consensus was broken, the terms, like helium balloons, whose strings have been cut, floated away into meaninglessness. To see how confusing and contradictory key words like "nature" became, ask yourself the following questions: "What is the *nature* of the *nature* of *Nature*? Do we all *naturally* know it by *nature*? Is it discoverable by *natural*, *unnatural*, or *supernatural* methods?"

The Psychology of Nature

It gets even more complicated when we realize that the word "natural" is a *psychological* term. Ever since the "back to nature" movement that developed during the Renaissance, Western people assumed that whatever is "natural' is automatically good and right. TV ads pitch "natural" vitamins and "natural" cures because the word "natural" has the psychological power to manipulate the naive. Products are better because they are "natural."

Same Sex Marriage

During 2007, a political controversy arose over whether to legalize same sex marriage. Since same-sex acts were no longer illegal due to sodomy laws being ruled unconstitutional in most states, modern humanists argued that same sex marriage should no longer be illegal.

Secular natural theologians and philosophers argued: "What is *natural* sex? If heterosexual sex feels *natural* to you, then it is *natural*. In the same way, if gay sex feels *natural* to you, then gay sex is *natural*. On what basis can either group claim that what feels *"natural"* to them is the *only* meaning of what is *"normal?"* In "Nature," animals have gay sex as well as heterosexual sex. Thus, isn't gay sex both *natural* and *normal*? Ergo, same sex marriage should be legalized."

Various Catholic and Neo-Protestant Natural theologians went on national radio and TV programs and boasted that they could prove, without any reference to God or the Bible, solely on the basis of "Nature" and "Reason," that same sex acts and same sex marriage should be illegal because they were "unnatural," i.e. not "normal." They invoked "reason," "experience," and "common sense" as proving their position.[326]

These theologians assumed that there was enough Christian cultural consensus left to provide a psychological edge to their arguments, but, they were living in the past. They did not realize that Western culture had moved to a new consensus that was relativistic. Whatever feels "natural" to you is "normal" to you.

Both liberal and conservative natural theologians cannot define the words "natural," "unnatural," or "normal" because they cannot define the word "Nature." The attempt of Natural Religion, Natural Theology, and Natural Law to derive what is "normal" from "Nature" is useless. Without the Bible, there is no way to condemn homosexuality and same-sex marriages. Once you lay aside the Bible, then what *is*, is right. You cannot get an "ought" from an "is." No matter how much you want to get morality from matter, it will not happen.

Christians would have made a better case if they had pointed out that according to the Bible, marriage belongs in the sphere of the family and not the spheres of the state or the church. The state cannot define marriage because it does not have the divine right to do so. Marriage is not a sacrament of the Church because it is not a "church" institution. Gen. 2 and Heb. 13:4 declare that marriage is a creation institution that is valid for all of mankind. It is not a "Christian" institution.

The failure to define the words "natural" and "unnatural" doom all their ethical judgments. I will never forget a natural apologist on a CA Christian radio program debating a homosexual on marriage. He claimed that he could condemn homosexuality solely on the basis of "reason" apart from and independent of God and the Bible. I waited to see how he was going to pull that rabbit out of his hat as I had heard him the week before make the claim that he could condemn abortion solely on the basis of "reason" and he had only succeeded in making himself look like a fool.

A sharp gay guy called the program and pushed the Christian host to prove that homosexuality was wrong without recourse to God or the Bible. The natural apologist had only one "rational" argument: gay sex was "unnatural." That was his big argument.

The gay responded that sex with a man was "natural" because in "Nature" dogs and other animals do it, gay sex felt "natural" to him, and sex with a woman would feel "unnatural" to him. The natural apologist did not have a good answer to these arguments. He repeated the charge that gay sex was "unnatural" because it was "unnatural" to him.

Things really heated up when the gay pushed the apologist to prove that gay sex was "unnatural." This is when things fell apart. The apologist meekly replied that Paul in Rom. 1 calls it "unnatural." After all his boasting that he could condemn homosexuality solely on rational grounds apart from and independent of the Bible, in the end, he was quoting the Bible! What a bummer! This is what results from failing to define you terms. Once you claim that if something feels "natural" to you, it is OK to do it, you have just validated every sexual perversion known and unknown.

Nature Becomes Man

Four things became clear to Western philosophers.

1. There are no objective truths, morals, or laws "out there" in "Nature."
2. Even if they were "out there" in "Nature," we have no way to epistemologically dig them out so we can know them.
3. The search for meaning has led nowhere.
4. All is meaningless.

Faced with these four realities, Natural Theology retreated from the external world of "Nature" to the internal world of "human nature." Truth, justice, morals, meaning, and beauty are not "out there" among the birds and trees but "in here," i.e. in the mind of man.

Natural theologians now looked *within themselves* to find truth, justice, morals, meaning, and beauty. But, which aspect of "human nature" should be abstracted, idealized, romanticized, and deified as the Origin? They disagreed on which part of "human nature" is the Origin and Measure of all things.

- Some chose their reason and became rationalists.
- Some chose their experience and became empiricists.
- Some chose their feelings and became mystics.
- Some chose their faith and became fideists.

Natural Theology Is a Myth

There is no "Natural Theology" in a monolithic sense. There are only competing Natural Theolog*ies* that contradict each other on metaphysics, epistemology, ethics, and esthetics. There is no consensus among them on the meaning of the word "God." The kinds of Natural Theologies that exist today include: Christian, Muslim, liberal, conservative, Catholic, Orthodox, Protestant, Process, neo-Process, New Age, Arminian, Reformed, and Open View.

Since they each define their terms in a relativistic way, they can use the same arguments developed by opposing theologies. This is why Protestant Natural theologians use the Muslim Kalam argument even though they admit that the word "God" does not mean the same in Islam as it does in Christianity. If the Kalam argument were valid, then Islam is true and Christianity false. But, if we redefine all the key terms according to our own subjective belief system, we can pretend it is valid for all religions.

What They Do Have in Common?

Modern Natural Theologies only have one thing in common: their hostility to *Sola Scriptura*, which they denounce as "bibliolatry." They are absolutely irate at the very idea that the Bible *alone* is the *final* and *ultimate* authority over what we should believe and how we should live. Why? They believe that *man* (*not* God) is the Origin of truth, justice, morals, meaning. Beginning only with their own reason, experience, feelings or faith, they can produce truth, justice, morals, meaning, and faith *without God and His Revelation*.[327]

This is why Biblical Christians are happy that the authors of the Bible never used such philosophical concepts and terms to define God, the world or man. If they had tied the Bible to the philosophical fads of their day, the Bible would not be the inerrant Word of God for *today*. Those who attach their religion to the wagon of whatever philosophic fad is in vogue at the time have guaranteed that their religion will be obsolete tomorrow.

Conclusion

The convoluted history of the contradictory and relative meaning of the terms thrown around by Natural Theology, Natural Law, Natural Apologetics leave us high and dry. Natural theologians dream the impossible dream of defining God-without-God; morality-without-God; aesthetics-without-God; the universe-without-God; man-without-God; meaning-without-God; justice-without-God. Isaiah's comment is most *apropos* at this point.

Chapter Ten   The Failure of Definition

To the Law and to the Testimony!
If they do not speak according to this Word,
it is because they have no light.

Chapter Eleven

Natural Law

> A great number of people are continually talking of the Law of Nature; and then they go on giving you their [personal] sentiments about what is right and what is wrong; and these sentiments, you understand, are so many chapters, and sections of the Law of Nature...[The "Natural Law" consists] in so many contrivances for avoiding the obligation of appealing to any external standard, and for prevailing upon the readers to accept of the author's sentiment or opinion as a reason, and that a sufficient one, for itself.[328]
>
> Jeremy Bentham

Introduction

The Foundation of Natural Law

Humanism is without question the philosophic foundation of all Natural Law theories. This is why it does matter if the particular theory is pagan or Christian, objective or subjective, rationalistic or mystical. They are all based on the assumption that man, starting solely from himself, by himself, through himself, only with the resources within himself, is the Origin and Measure of truth, justice, morals, meaning, and beauty, apart from and independent of God and the Bible. Natural Law has manifested itself in both secular and religious forms.

Secular Humanism

Secular Humanism is theoretical atheism because it assumes that man can discover truth and morals without God. Not only are God and the Bible not necessary for truth and morals, but belief in God and the Bible stands in the way of man's upward and onward evolution. Religion is a social and a psychological illness that must be rooted out of modern life in order for mankind to progress. Its political expression as found in the Soviet Union, North Korea, China, Cuba, and other Marxist societies, has demonstrated that secular humanism cannot generate truth without God or morals without God. The oppression of all freedom is the end result.

Religious Humanism

Religious Humanism is practical atheism. It is the heartfelt conviction that there is spiritual virtue in finding a foundation for truth and morals in some place other than God and the Bible. It does not matter if the foundation is external Nature or internal human nature. As long as the Origin of truth and morals is not God and His Word, the religious humanist is happy.

In an unholy and perverted alliance, religious humanists have become the "priests" of secular humanists who become depressed and afraid that because they have thrown out God and the Bible, they threw out truth and morals.

Secular Humanist: "Now that I have thrown out God and the Bible, I am afraid and depressed that truth and morals are no longer possible."

Religious Humanist: "There, there, Dear, don't you worry! Cheer up because I will help you to think of a way in which you can have truth and morals without God or the Bible. We are actually doing God a favor by deleting Him and the Bible from Law, Religion, Theology, Philosophy, Science, and Apologetics. God wants us to build a unified field of knowledge without Him or His Scripture. Be comforted with the thought that there are no philosophic consequences to denying the existence of the God of the Bible. You can live a happy and virtuous life *without* God."

Naturalism

Naturalism is another word for Humanism. It has both secular and religious forms and emphasizes that "Nature" is the mine out of which humanists can dig the ore of truth and morals. It does not matter if "Nature" is conceived of as the external world of matter or the interior world of mind. Natural Law, Natural Religion, Natural Theology, and Natural Apologetics are supposedly dug out of the mine of "Nature."

The following chart shows the theoretical relationship between humanistic disciplines. Humanism is the foundation of Naturalism, which is the foundation of Natural Law. It is the foundation of Natural Religion, which is the foundation of Natural Theology. It in turn is the foundation of Natural Apologetics.

Natural Apologetics

Natural Theology

Natural Religion

Natural Law

Naturalism

Humanism

The theoretical links between these disciplines supply us with the pedagogical order in which we will discuss them. Since we have already dealt with humanism and naturalism in Part One, we will begin with an analysis of the theory of Natural Law.

Standard Definitions

Although the standard reference works do not agree in their definitions of "Natural Law," there are several common ideas associated with the theories.

> Along with his concept of natural theology, Aquinas developed the concept of natural law. Human beings, by their own reason, can gain knowledge of the ethically good without reference to God's revelation.[329]
>
> ...those absolute and universally value imperatives that are innate in the reason of every individual and necessarily come into consciousness with the development of the mind...a means of emancipation from the supernatural ontology of revelation.[330]
>
> a law or rule of action that is implicit in the very nature of things.[331]
>
> What is right is inherent in our human nature and that is known to us intrinsically.[332]
>
> a body of law derived from nature and binding upon human society...discernable...by right reason...but not directly revealed.[333]
>
> Natural law: common to all people...fundamental to human nature.[334]
>
> The validity of natural law...even if we were to suppose...that God does not exist or is not concerned with human affairs.[335]
>
> Natural law was the rational principles governing the universe. Because it is rational it can be known and obeyed by reasonable men.[336]
>
> **natural moral law** consists in true moral principles grounded in the way things are and, in principle, knowable by all people without the aid of Scripture.[337]
>
> **natural moral law** – the notion that there are true, universally binding moral principles knowable by all people and rooted in creation and the way things are made.[338]

Mortimer Adler in his monumental work, *The Great Ideas*, traced the history of Natural Law theory back to ancient Stoic Greek philosophy where "the laws of nature are often conceived of expressing an inherent rationality in nature itself." [339] He goes to state,

> "Nature" was not viewed as dead matter but a living sentient Being with intelligence and feelings. This led in ancient times to the worship of Nature." [340]

This ancient Greek paganism has come down to in such terms as "Mother Nature" and is worshipped by Wicca and other modern pagan cults as Gaia.

No Clear Definition

Modern philosophers have pointed out that there has never been a commonly agreed upon definition of "Natural Law" because there has never been any agreed upon definition of the key words "nature," "natural," and "law."[341] The different theories that call themselves "Natural Law" differ on *essential* things as the nature, origin, substance, method, and goal of "Natural Law." The well-known natural law theorist, Dr. Howard Kainz, was honest enough to admit that when you examine the Natural Law theories of...

> Aristotle, Plato, the Stoics, Aquinas, Surez, Hobbes, Locke, Grotius, Pufendorf, and Kant...there are major differences in the approaches and presuppositions and tenets, so that it would seem to be oversimplifying and misleading to talk about multiple applications of "the" natural law...One thinks of the various "natural law" movements taking place now...which have by no means tried to arrive at a consensus about what is meant by natural law, or about which theory offers the best expression of natural law.[342]

The German scholar Erik Wolf in 1955 counted over 120 conflicting definitions of the words "nature" and "law."[343] We stopped counting after we identified over 200 conflicting definitions. One dictionary had 36 different definitions of the word "nature!" Is "reason" a part of "nature" or "nature" a part of "reason"? Is "nature" out there, up there, in there, in here, etc.? No knows for sure.

Many modern natural law theorists, especially "Evangelical" ones, are not as honest as Kainz. They pretend that Aquinas' Medieval understanding of Natural Law is the "traditional" view. But, as Dr. Jean Porter pointed out,

> I speak of traditional versions or accounts of the Natural law, rather than of one traditional theory of the natural law, because there have been a number of such accounts. The most familiar of these is the version that emerged in early Catholic theology and was subsequently was incorporated into official Catholic teachings...this

version presupposes a definite idea of human nature and offers a natural law comprised of definite, stringent moral precepts.[344]

However, medieval interpretations of the natural law are significantly different from most later versions, including the influential "new natural law" theory of German Grisez and John Finnis.[345]

The widely influential "new natural law" theory developed by German Grisez and John Finnis might seem to offer a counterexample to this claim. However, this theory is explicitly distinguished from "old" natural law theories by the fact that it does not attempt to derive moral conclusions from observations about human nature.[346]

Even Stephen Grabill is forced to admit,

it is already possible to differentiate two types of natural-law theories within late medieval scholasticism, each proposing distinct moral ontologies: a realist theory of natural law, represented by-- among others--Thomas Aquinas and Duns Scotus, and a nominalist theory of natural law, represented by – among others- Willaim of Occam and Pierre d'Ailly. Thus given the scope and importance of these developments, it is simply improper to speak of any *single* "classical and Christian," or even "medieval" natural-law tradition.[347]

While the older Natural Law theorists pretended that there were objective laws "out there" inherent in the material universe, modern theorists, like Hobbes, argued that "Nature supplies no pattern for the good state."[348] The Protestant apostate, Budziszewski, brushed aside all these essential differences and pretended that the different theories of Natural Law did not disagree over fundamental ideas,

Some people think that there cannot be a natural law simply because there *is* more than one theory about it. After all, if the natural law is made up of objective moral principles that everyone knows, shouldn't all of us have the same theory about it? This is not a convincing argument because the different theories of natural *do* agree about its basic content. What they disagree about are *secondary* things, such as where the knowledge of it comes from.[349]

Budziszewski's answer is ignorant at best and deceptive at worse. First, he admits that there *are* conflicting theories of "Natural Law." Anyone who is familiar with the history of Natural Law theories cannot deny this reality.

Dr Carl F. Henry, perhaps the most profound Evangelical thinker of the 20th Century, commented,

> Natural law theorists- reaching back to and before the pre-Socratics have themselves at times disagreed over the precise content of natural law. It has been invoked to defend freedom and slavery, hierarchy and equality.[350]

Second, Budziszewski claims that disagreements over the nature, origin, attributes, methodology, ontology, number, and identity of these so-called "Natural laws" are "secondary things!" Last time we checked, metaphysics, epistemology, ethics, and aesthetics are *primary* things, not secondary.

Third, he dismisses this objection because he asserts that *all* theories have the *same* content. He does not document this claim. He merely asserts it.

Classic "Catholic" versions of Natural Law supported slavery, wars of aggression and conquest, the Inquisition, the murder of hundreds of thousands of Protestants, genocide of non-Europeans, and the subjugation of women. They also condemned masturbation, the use of contraception for birth control, and oral sex between a husband and wife as "unnatural." All non-Catholic marriages were condemned as illegal.[351]

Fourth, he gave what must be called a "lame duck argument" to support his claim that his view of Natural Law was intuitive and self-evident to all men.

> You know, don't you, that nothing can both *be* and *not be* in the same sense at the same time?"[352]

Budziszewski asserts that Aristotle's "law" of contradiction is an idea that is "intuitive, self-evident, innate, and universal" to all human beings in all ages and cultures. He counts upon the ignorance of his readers who do not know that, while this "law" is a part of Western cultural consensus due to the influence of Aquinas, it is *not* a part of Eastern cultural consensus. A Hindu or Buddhist has no problem ignoring Aristotle's "rule" of logic.

Budziszewski knows that most of his readers have been indoctrinated with such Catholic ideas their entire life. Western people assume the law of contradiction to be true because that is all they know. Thus they will not notice that he has just run a con-game on them. But those who know the history of ideas are not deceived by such shell and pea games.

The Root Problem

Budziszewski foolishly assumes that there are brute "laws" in "Nature" that somehow, someway "just there." He assumes that the "laws" of logic are "just there" in "Nature" and that all men and women *automatically* know them.

But, were these "laws" known *before* Aristotle? No. Do children *automatically* know and obey these laws? No. Is it not the case that a child's imagination often involves things that can both "be" and "not be" at the same time? The "monster under the bed" comes to mind.

If all human beings *innately* know Aristotle's Greek "laws of logic" from conception, why do we have to teach courses on logic? Why don't all students earn an "A" on the subject? As someone who has taught logic, I know that most people do not know of or obey the "rules" of Western Greek logic!

Despite the tricks of Budziszewski and his "Evangelical" followers, the fact remains that Natural Law theorists have never agreed among themselves on the *fundamental* issues of the origin, nature or content of "natural laws."

Natural Law a Myth

"Natural Law" is thus a myth in that there is no historic monolithic form, school or agreed-upon definition of "Natural Law." Since "Natural Law" has no definite meaning and has been used to support and refute such things as slavery, it means nothing.

The trick of modern Natural Law theorists is to cite Aristotle's definitions of key terms without informing their readers that they no longer believe in Aristotle's worldview. For example, while Aristotle claimed to find *objective* laws in the *material* world of earth, air, fire, and water (i.e. "Nature"), modern Law theorists find *subjective* laws in the *mind* of man (i.e. "reason as nature"). They have shifted the laws from "matter" to "mind." Who today accepts Aristotle's world view in which the sun revolves around the earth?

Why the Flag of "Natural Law" Is Still Waved Today

The phrase "Natural Law" has become an emotive term that is used to psychologically manipulate people. It is like a flag waved at a football game. It has more to do with psychology than metaphysics, and, like Pavlov's dogs, many Western people still genuflect when they hear the words "Natural Law."

The raw truth is that the phrase has evolved in meaning from generation to generation as it followed the philosophic and cultural consensus of the meaning of such words as "Nature," "natural," "law," "substance," "meaning," and "essence." The reason for this "paralysis of definition" is that there has never been any agreed-upon authority by which a definition could be created. Each philosopher defined it according to his or her own personal epistemology and the definitions were free to move with cultural consensus. How convenient!

No Consequences

One of the greatest problems with Natural Law theory is that breaking a *law* is supposed to have *physical or legal* consequences. But nothing happens when you break natural "laws." Old

Catholic "Natural Law" used to teach that if you masturbated, you would go blind. Are you blind yet? Are people put in jail for using contraception?

For this reason, modern natural law theorists have now dumped the word "law" and replace it with the word "principle." This is why Dr. Kainz pointed out that Modern Natural Law theorists such as Grisez and Finniss, argue that the word "law" is used only in an *analogical* or *metaphorical* way and should not be understood as an ontological term.[353]

The Greeks

At the beginning, Aristotle and the Greek philosophers defined "Natural Law" as composed of those objective and absolute "laws" of truth, justice, morals, meaning, and beauty found intrinsically within the material universe that some men some of the time were able to abstract from Nature and by which they were able to construct a worldview that told them what to believe and how to live as individuals and as city states. Why or how these intrinsic "laws" of truths and morals are in "Nature," no one knew. Who or what put them there was not discussed. There are "just there." My dear friend and mentor, Dr. Van Til, explains,

> The "natural man" assumes that he can and must interpret himself and the facts of the universe without any reference to the God who is actually there. The "natural man" assumes that the facts of the space-time world are not what Christ, speaking for the triune God, says they are. For the "natural man" the facts are just there. They are contingent, i.e. not pre-interpreted by God. The "natural man" assumes that there is a "principle of rationality," including the laws of logic, i.e. the law of identity, the law of excluded middle and the laws of contradiction which is, like the facts," just there. The facts he speaks of he assumes to be non-created facts. There is no "curse" that rests upon nature because of man's sin. The "natural man" assumes that he himself, being "just there," can relate the space-time facts which are "just there" by means of a "principle of rationality" that is "just there" to one another or that if he cannot do this, no one can.[354]

How we dig 'laws" out of the material universe was never agreed upon by the Greeks. Human reason, experience, feelings and faith were all chosen as the method by which man could discover the objective laws that govern all of life. Why, how, and through whom these laws were autonomous, (i.e. they exist apart from and independent of the gods), was never explained. Why these laws were valid regardless if the gods did not exist was never demonstrated.

> The idea that natural law might be valid and binding even if God did not exist had been suggested before Grotius. For example, by Robert Bellarmine and other scholastics. But Grotius made this point more explicitly and forcibly, and is frequently credited with

> the groundbreaking proto-modern attempt to disengage natural law
> from the question of the existence of a Divine Legislator.[355]

Since they used the "natural" laws of logic to prove other "natural" laws, in the end, it was one vast circular argument. The early Greek philosophers assumed that they could pick absolute laws off the trees like apples or dig them out of the ground like potatoes because they are "just there."

The Revolving Door of Logic

Western forms of logic are like a revolving door that cannot work on its own. It has a pin on the bottom and one on the top that rests in a solid frame work. The door cannot simply revolve on its own but is dependent on the frame in which it is set. In the same way, Aristotle's Greek "laws" of logic must be "set" in a frame work that will enable them to work. Western Humanism's assumption that the laws of logic are "brute" facts, i.e. they are "just there," leaves the revolving door lying on its side, useless.

Philosophic Slogans

How did the Greeks know when they found one of these autonomous laws-without-God in Nature? It would be "obvious" to them because it would be "universal, self-evident, and intuitive." That is all that was needed to be said. Just intoning these slogans was sufficient proof in and of itself.

Now, when they said that an idea was "universal, self-evident, and intuitive," they did not mean that *all* men and women in all places throughout all of time knew of and believed in those ideas. No, the Greeks restricted the words "universal, self-evident, and intuitive" to the cultural consensus among *rational, civilized, white, Greek males* who were citizens. If an idea was true to them, then it was "universal, self-evident, and intuitive." Truth by cultural consensus is the basis of natural law theory.

Most Natural theologians invoke the word "universal" as a justification for what they believe but then define it away. The classic work by Chadbourne on Natural Law is marred by this trick. He assets that his ideas are 'universal, intuitive, and self-evident" to "every civilized man"[356] who lives "in the highest forms of society."[357] If you disagree with him, then you are an uncivilized ignorant savage!

Women and Slaves

Women, children, slaves, and the non-white "barbarian" races were not viewed as "rational" or "civilized." They were not included in the word "universal." Whether or not the majority of mankind throughout history ever heard of or believed in these "universal" ideas did not matter. As long as the upper class of Greek citizens, i.e. the white male philosophers and politicians, believed in those ideas, they were universal, self-evident, and intuitive. Others need not apply.

Modern Cliches

Modern Natural theologians and Natural Law theorists use such clichés as "normal people," "rational man," "civilized man," "rational mind," "moral intuition," and "rational thought," etc. in order to exclude the vast majority of mankind. They assert that their ideas are "universal, self-evident, and intuitive" to "rational," "normal," and "civilized" people. What if you do not buy into their ideas? Obviously, the problem is with *you*, not their ideas. *You* are intellectually deficient, not the idea.

The Bible is for Stupid People

This is why some Natural theologians put down those who believe in the Bible as "stupid." Car washers, dog walkers, checkout clerks, ditch diggers, maids, janitors, etc. are not smart enough to be Natural theologians. The Bible is written for those types of people. High IQ people do not need the Bible because they can figure out things on their own. This is why elitism, pride, and conceit have always plagued Natural Law theorists.

The Bible

The philosophic slogans "universal, self-evident, intuitive" never appear once in the Bible. No author of the Bible ever claimed in fact or principle that his teachings were "universal, self-evident, and intuitive." As we have demonstrated in other books the prophets, priests, people, apostles, and Messiah Yeshua based truth and morals upon "Thus says YHWH," i.e. Revelation. Their favorite phrase was "as it is written."

A Classic Fallacy

Natural Law theorists who still claim to be "Christian," (in some sense or the other), feel the emotional need to find Natural Law theory somewhere in the Bible. But it does not take them long to realize that the Torah and the Gospel are not natural but *supernatural* in origin. There are no clear biblical passages that explicitly teach any theory of "Natural Law." Thus another approach had to be adopted.

First, Natural theologians and Natural Law theorists *assume* the traditional dichotomy between "general revelation" and "special revelation." Since such terminology is *theological* terminology developed in Medieval Scholastic Catholic theology and not from Scripture *per se*, we need to ask ourselves if such language is valid? Western philosophers have always loved dichotomies.

Plato:	mind/matter
Aristotle:	form/essence
Aquinas:	nature/grace
Rousseau:	nature/freedom
Kant:	phenonmenal/noumenal

298

The theological dichotomy between "general" and "special" revelation is an extension or application of the "nature/grace" and "secular/sacred" dichotomies.

<u>special</u> = <u>sacred</u> = <u>grace</u> = <u>mind</u>
general = secular = nature = matter

If we do not adopt pagan Greek dichotomies, why are we using them to describe divine revelation? Furthermore, how can they both modify the noun "revelation" when that word does not have the same meaning in each phrase?

How can the noun "revelation" be *both* verbal and non-verbal? If it can mean anything and everything, it means nothing. It seems to us that the medieval theologians who invented this dichotomy based it on the nature/grace dichotomy. This is an issue that needs to be discussed.

Second, "Christian" law theorists *assume* that their particular theory of "Natural Law" and "General Revelation" are one and same thing. In this way, they can cite all the passages in the Bible that teach "general revelation" as if they proved their personal relative idea of "Natural Law." Budziszewski gratuitously asserts, "I have defended the view that natural law is general revelation."[358]

This "categorical fallacy" is the foundation of J. Daryl Charles' work, *Retrieving the Natural Law*.

> The present volume represents an attempt to focus on human moral intuitions that, like wisdom, are universal, and thus part of what theologians call "general revelation" and "common grace."[359]

Given this erroneous assumption, Charles cites such biblical passages as Psa. 19; Rom. 1 and 2 as if they referred to his personal view of "Natural Law."[360] But this error is typical of Natural Law theorists in general. They fail to define terms and thus habitually commit the "fallacy of equivocation" and the "categorical fallacy."

Natural Law is Not General Revelation

Upon examination, it is clear that General Revelation is *not* Natural Law. The following chart summarizes the differences between the two.

The Differences between Natural Law and General Revelation

General Revelation	Natural Law
Activity of God	Activity of Man
Began at Creation.	Began in Greece with Zeno of Citium.
Universal: throughout the entire universe.	Western Europe and America.
Continuous, seven days a week, 24 hours a day.	Some of the time by some men.

Two things witnessed:
  a. the attributes of God
  b. the sinfulness of man
Origin: God's immediate self-revelation.
Non-verbal witness.
Renders all men without excuse
Does not reveal the way of salvation.
	Two issues discussed:
	  a. the existence of gods
	  b. the problem of evil
	Origin: man's reason, experience, feelings or faith.
	Philosophic discourse.
	Does not render all men without excuse.
	Gives conflicting ways of salvation.

After his analysis of whether Natural Law should be identified with General Revelation, the great Dutch theologian Berkouwer, concluded, "the identification of general revelation and natural theology is *an untenable position.*"[361] His book on General Revelation is one of the greatest theological works of the twentieth century.

Paul tells us that General Revelation is *God's* activity in that "GOD made it evident to them," i.e. the Gentiles (Rom. 1:19).

> For God made it evident to them.
> ὁ θεὸς γὰρ αὐτοῖς ἐφανέρωσεν

The verb ἐφανέρωσεν is an indicative aorist active 3rd person singular. The word ὁ θεὸς is *emphatic*. God and *God alone* is the One who is revealing Himself. The point Paul is making is that the unbelief of the pagan Gentile world is not God's fault. He is revealing Himself in the Creation around twenty four hours a day seven days a week. The problem is that man's depravity does not allow God's revelation to get through. Paul states that men "suppress the truth in unrighteousness" (τῶν τὴν ἀλήθειαν ἐν ἀδικίᾳ κατεχόντων) (Rom. 1:18). Dr. Wiersbe comments,

> The word translated "hold" in Rom. 1:18 can also be translated "hold down, suppress." Men knew the truth about God, but they did not allow this truth to work in their lives. They suppressed it in order that they might live their own lives and not be convicted by God's truth. The result, of course, was refusing the truth (Rom. 1:21–22), and then turning the truth into a lie (Rom. 1:25). Finally, man so abandoned the truth that he became like a beast in his thinking and in his living. [362]

The universality of man's condemnation is based upon the universality of God's General Revelation. God has revealed Himself to every human being who ever existed, is existing now, and will ever exist. He is now revealing Himself (ἐφανέρωσεν) to all people everywhere at the same time. *Universal condemnation rests upon universal revelation.*

Chapter Eleven   Natural Law

The endless variety of relativistic forms of "Natural Law" theory cannot be equated with general revelation because they are not universal but *limited* to specific people, places, individuals, cultures, religions, and times. Until Natural theologians can teach every human being who ever lived, is living now, and shall ever live in the future, their theories are not universal.

Another important difference is that the different theories of Natural Law represent the *failure* of sinful man to accept the light of General Revelation. This is why Natural Law theories cannot be the foundation of ethics.

The Light of the World

Jesus said that He was the "Light of the world" (John 9:5). His incarnation was described by John as Light "coming into the world" (ἐρχόμενον εἰς τὸν κόσμον) (John 1:9). Even though the Light that entered the world had the potential of "enlightening" every man, it failed to do so. What was the cause of the failure of all human beings to embrace the Light of the world?

First, John tells us that there was nothing wrong with the Light. It was not defective in any sense. It was brightly shinning.

Second, the problem is rooted in the fact that man is spiritually blind and thus *cannot* comprehend (οὐ κατέλαβεν) the light!

> And the light shines in the darkness, but the darkness <u>did not comprehend it</u>. (John 1:5)
>
> καὶ τὸ φῶς ἐν τῇ σκοτίᾳ φαίνει καὶ <u>ἡ σκοτία αὐτὸ οὐ κατέλαβεν</u>.

The light is shining, but man does not comprehend it. Why? Man's spiritual depravity *blinds* him to the Light. Our love of darkness blinds us to the Light.

> And this is the judgment, that the light is come into the world, but men loved the darkness rather than the light; for their deeds were evil. For everyone who does evil hates the light, and does not come to the light, lest his deeds should be exposed. (John 3:19-20)
>
> αὕτη δέ ἐστιν ἡ κρίσις ὅτι τὸ φῶς ἐλήλυθεν εἰς τὸν κόσμον καὶ ἠγάπησαν οἱ ἄνθρωποι μᾶλλον τὸ σκότος ἢ τὸ φῶς· ἦν γὰρ αὐτῶν πονηρὰ τὰ ἔραγα πᾶς γὰρ ὁ φαῦλα πράσσων μισεῖ τὸ φῶς καὶ οὐκ ἔρχεται πρὸς τὸ φῶς, ἵνα μὴ ἐλεγχθῇ τὰ ἔργα αὐτοῦ·

Paul said that the "natural man" is *not* capable of understanding spiritual things.

> But a natural man does not accept the things of the Spirit of God; for they are foolishness to him, and he cannot understand them, because they are spiritually appraised. (1 Cor. 2:14)

ψυχικὸς δὲ ἄνθρωπος οὐ δέχεται τὰ τοῦ πνεύματος τοῦ θεοῦ, μωρία γὰρ αὐτῷ ἐστιν καὶ οὐ δύναται γνῶναι, ὅτι πνευματικῶς ἀνακρίνεται·

Is Man Really Blind?

The foundational assumption of all Natural Law theories is that man is *not* really blind. He *can* and *does* "comprehend" and "understand" the light of general revelation. He is *not* so wedded to his sin that he refuses to see the Light. But John, Jesus, and Paul said that the light is shining but unregenerate man cannot and will not comprehend it *because* he is spiritually blind.

> And even if our gospel is veiled, it is veiled to those who are perishing, in whose case the god of this world has <u>blinded the minds of the unbelieving</u>, that they might not see the light of the gospel of the glory of Christ, who is the image of God. (2 Cor. 4:3-4)

εἰ δὲ καὶ ἔστιν κεκαλυμμένον τὸ εὐαγγέλιον ἡμῶν, ἐν τοῖς ἀπολλυμένοις ἐστὶν κεκαλυμμένον, ἐν οἷς ὁ θεὸς τοῦ αἰῶνος τούτου ἐτύφλωσεν τὰ νοήματα τῶν ἀπίστων εἰς τὸ μὴ αὐγάσαι τὸν φωτισμὸν τοῦ εὐαγγελίου τῆς δόξης τοῦ Χριστοῦ, ὅς ἐστιν εἰκὼν τοῦ θεοῦ.

Natural Law theorists claim that man *does* comprehend the light because he is *not* really blind. So, you will have to choose whom you are going to believe. The prophets, apostles, and the Messiah said that unregenerate man *cannot* "comprehend" (ἡ σκοτία αὐτὸ οὐ κατέλαβεν) or understand (οὐ δύναται γνῶναι) general revelation because their mind has been blinded (τούτου ἐτύφλωσεν τὰ νοήματα). Natural law theorists say the exact opposite. Whom are you going to believe?

In the Beginning There Was Nature

Originally, "Nature" was the objective, external, material, universe just "out there." Who, what or how these "laws" were put into Nature was not agreed upon. But these intrinsic autonomous laws governed the gods as well as man.

External Nature

The external, objective, material universe "out there" all around us was assumed to be the meaning of the word "Nature" for some time. But, in time, this meaning was abandoned. The meaning of "Nature" shifted from "matter" to the internal, subjective, non-material "mind" of man, i.e. human reason.

Internal Nature

When "Nature" morphed into the subjective "reason" of man, the laws were longer "out there" but "in here," i.e. within the mind of man. As we saw in our chapter on biblical anthropology, this is when the idea of "human nature" was invented for the first time. Internal natural laws needed a "container" or "box" within man. "Human Nature" was invented to be the "seat" or box into which natural laws could be placed and then discovered later on. [363]

Natural Rights and Slavery

We must remind the reader that for thousands of years Natural Law theories did not extend natural rights to all people. British and American Natural Law philosophers (such as Thomas Hobbes) followed Aristotle and Aquinas in defending slavery, the subjugation of women, wars of conquest, genocide, etc. They proclaimed that slavery was in accord with the "laws" of Nature, reason, and common sense. [364]

Natural Law philosophers believed and taught that "Nature," "reason," and "common sense" supported slavery and the subjugation of women. The "inner nature" of women proved they were not equal to men and should not be allowed to vote. The "inner nature" of slaves was animal. Their "external form" may look human, but their "inner nature" was pure beast. Thus slavery based on race and the rape, murder, and enslavement of millions of Africans was justified by appeals to Aristotle's and Aquinas' Natural Law theories. Dr. Anyabwile, whose work on the roots of race-based slavery is outstanding, documents that,

> The institution of slavery with all its inhuman brutality demanded a psychologically satisfying justification. The panacea offered by proslavery adherents involved the denial of the African's humanity...the African had no soul, was the result of human-ape intercourse, was sub-human or at least a lower species of humanity, was uneducable and uncivilized, and so on.[365]

The well-known commentator Prof. Dr. H. Moule noted in his commentary on Philemon,

> Meanwhile the law and usage of slavery had the support of philosophic theory, which maintained an aboriginal and essentially natural place of slavery in the order of human life. Plato, in his ideal Commonwealth, gives slavery ample room, and the master who kills his slave, though regarded as a wrongdoer, is visited with only a *ceremonial* purification. Aristotle, in the opening pages of his "Polity," discusses the relation of slave to master as one of the foundations of society. He defines the slave as a being who is by *nature* the property of another; who is and has nothing outside that fact; who is merely, as it were, his master's limb, and extension of his master's physical organism, with other one function of capacity to do his master's pleasure. In short, he is a human being devoid of all personal rights...they are formidable words indeed; exactly fitted to supply a supposed intellectual justification for usages of pitiless cruelty in the field of real life...It is important to point out by

the way how totally absent from the teaching of the Old Testament is the Aristotelian view of slavery.[366]

Relative Natural Law

Ernest Van den Haag correctly pointed out that "natural law" has been used to support and condemn the same position. It can evidently mean all things to all men.

> Just as some philosophers inferred from natural law that slavery is wrong, others, particularly in antiquity (Aristotle among them), found that slavery is justified by natural laws. Just as some will deduce from natural law that women are equal to men and ought to be treated as equals other concluded that women are inferior and should be subordinated to men. Similarly, capital punishment can be opposed or supported on natural law grounds.[367]

The root problem is pointed out by Alan Richardson.

> Natural law theorists have tended to defend the *status quo* since it presumably is based on the nature of things.[368]

Natural Law theorists have *always* defended the *status quo* in society. They *have* to do so because they have *already* declared the *status quo* as self-evident, intuitive, necessary, absolute, and universal. If they admitted that they were wrong and that "nature" now dictates the *opposite* view, how can they escape the charge of *arbitrary* natural law? They *can't* change because it would nullify the entire premise of natural law itself. As Leslie Stephens pointed out "Nature is a word contrived in order to introduce as many equivocations as possible into all theories, political, legal, artistic or literary, into which it enters."[369]

What happened when the *status quo* changed, women were allowed to vote, and the slaves set free? The cultural consensus changed and, all of a sudden, Natural Law theorists abandoned their original position and announced that "Nature," "reason," and "common sense" *now* supported the abolition of slavery and the emancipation of women. George Hunsinger explains,

> Barth rejected the idea of an unmediated and unconditioned moral law to which human beings has universal access, even in their fallen state. What is regarded as "natural law" is always at bottom a cultural construct. From the standpoint of Christian ethics, it can offer no reliable basis for knowing what is right, nor can it offer any firm and clear basis for making ethical decisions, natural law theory posits an autonomous ground of ethical reflection completely separate from divine revelation. Christian ethics cannot build on this basis, Barth argued, because no such basis exists on which to build.[370]

The only way to counter the conceit, haughtiness, and triumphalism of modern day Natural Law theorists is to remind them of their past support of race-based slavery, the subjugation of women, British colonialism, American Manifest Destiny, the genocide of Native Americans and other races. Lest we forget, the history of Natural Law is not glorious because it usually supported the denial of rights to many people.

Colonial America

This exposes the ugly side of Colonial America. We have conveniently forgotten that the "natural rights" found in the Declaration of Independence, Constitution, Bill of Rights and other documents from that period did *not* extend to women, children, slaves or Native Americans. Not even all white males had these rights. Only landholders were allowed to vote!

When modern natural theologians pine for the "good old days" of Colonial America, I cringe. It means the suppression of women and the enslavement of non-whites. It means slave ships, whips, shackles, auction blocks, rape, murder, selling of children, forced labor, torture, sending small pox infected clothing to Indian Reservations, and other horrors. No, they were not the "good old days." The historical reality is that Natural Law did not give natural rights to all people. It always fought against extending rights to all people.

The Abolitionist Preachers

It took preachers with a Bible in one hand and a gun in the other to abolish slavery and to extend rights to all people regardless of race or creed. The leaven of Scripture finally worked its way through society and brought an end to slavery. The Civil War was not the beginning, but the end of that process.

There was one American church denomination that was always opposed to slavery. Susan B. Anthony (1820-1906) commented in one of her fiery speeches,

> The Scotch Covenanters or Reformed Presbyterians is the only evangelical church in all the nominally free states of the North that can consistently claim freedom from all sanction of, or compromise with slavery, "the sum of all villainies." The Old Scotch Covenanters refuse church fellowship not only to slave-holders, but to churches that fellowship slave-holders. [371]

Natural Law Theories Today

Divergent Natural Law theories have returned with a vengeance today. Like the mythical Phoenix, they spring from the ashes of their past refutations. They have been resurrected by no longer anchoring natural laws in objective external laws found in the material universe. They have given up that attempt. Einstein and Quantum Mechanics have forever killed it off. Ned Wisnefske comments,

> To listen to an account of natural theology in the modern period is to hear the story of the demise of a way of thinking, until in the end natural theology is left for dead. The story begins in philosophy with the "world-destroying" Kant, drags on through a century of scientific achievements which rubbed out the hand of God from nature, and ends with Barth's "Nein!" – the repudiation of natural theology by theology itself. Isn't it odd, then that natural theology is again with us? …What is it about natural theology that it was not finished off by even the most influential and resolute thinkers?[372]

Wisnefske explains modern Naturists have redefined the phrase "Natural Law" to refer to some subjective aspect of the inner non-material mind of man. Some choose human reason, feelings, experience, faith or common sense. The word "Nature" has been demoted to "nature."

Catholic Natural Law

Since Aquinas wrote Aristotle's Natural Law theory into the theology of Roman Catholicism, Catholic theologians and philosophers have never stopped defending it. The Greek doctrine is so enshrined within Catholicism that if they were to abandon it, Catholicism would collapse into ruins.

During the Renaissance, Catholic Natural Law fought two wars. The secular humanists on the left sought to delete God from the world and the Reformers on the right sought to delete Catholicism from the Church.

Secular Humanism

Secular Humanism has, for all practical purposes, ended the power of the papacy over Catholic Europe. Only 2% of European Catholics attend weekly Mass. The Pope did not even have enough influence to force the European Common Market to include a statement that Christianity was an important element in European history. Abortion and easy divorce have increased in direct proposition to the loss of Rome's influence on the culture of Europe.

The Reformation Mega-shift

The Reformation was a reaction to and rebellion against the form/essence dichotomy of Greek philosophy that had become the official position of the Roman Church. The Reformation was thus a mega-shift against the Catholic/Islamic/Aristotelian worldview.

> In the aftermath of the Protestant of the Reformation, and due in part to the reaction of Luther and other Reformers to scholastic or Thomistic philosophy, development of natural-law theory was primarily the province of Catholic thinkers.[373]

Luther said that Aquinas went to hell like all the pagans before him! Aristotle and the other pagan philosophers were in error and we should reject them. Calvin and the other Reformers dismissed the "schoolmen," i.e. followers of Aquinas, as heretics and fools.

> Luther and Calvin (the differences between them on this point are not significant) argued that natural theology was blind apart from the Word of God: Nature presented human beings with a hidden God.[374]

While all this is true, the Reformers reminded their followers that they had only begun to jettison all their inbred Catholic doctrines. While they had left Rome, Rome has not completely left them. For example, they still retained such Catholic doctrines as the perpetual virginity of Mary!

It is thus no surprise that at times they lapsed into the language of Natural Law and Natural Theology by way of habit and education. Their motto "Always Reforming" clearly indicated that they understood that they did *not* have the time to root all Catholic teaching out of their thinking. It was left to their heirs to continue to purify theology of Catholic heresies.

Modern Revival of Natural Law

The Roman Catholic Acton Institute in Grand Rapids, headed by Father Sirico, has played a major role in the modern revival of Natural Law theory in Protestant circles. It funded various Protestants as well as Catholics to write books in defense of Natural Law. It also sponsored seminars introducing Natural Law in many Protestant schools. Stephen Grabill's work, *Rediscovering the Natural Law in Reformed Theological Ethics*, is an example of the influence of the Acton Institute. In his introduction, Grabill writes,

> I also wish to express my appreciation to the Acton Institute where I have been employed throughout the process of writing this book. The Institute provided assistance through the dissertation itself and through its subsequent revision into the current form. I thank its president. Father Robert Sirico, and executive director Kris Mauren, personally for their support of this project.[375]

Grabill describes himself on the back cover of his book as, "a research scholar in theology at the Acton institute." He incorrectly asserted that "the Reformers inherited the natural-law tradition from their late medieval predecessors without serious question."[376] He misrepresented the historical record deliberately in order to trick Reformed people into accepting natural theology and rejecting *Sola Scriptura*.

We admit that there were times when the Reformers lapsed into the European cultural consensus created by Catholic Natural Law. Grabill's conclusion is worth repeating. But Scripture, not Aquinas, was the rule of faith.

> Calvin, Vermigli, and the Reformed scholastics all share the conviction that Scripture is the cognitive foundation (*principium cognoscendi*) of theology and that moral arguments can be based on axioms derived from that *principium*. Consequently, they recognize the existence of a natural knowledge of God that is present in the natural order and discernible with in conjunction with or apart from Scripture. This knowledge, however has no saving efficacy and merely serves to render all people to be "without excuse" for their moral infractions.[377]

Grabill bases his conclusion on scattered remarks here and there, usually taken out of context. However, the Reformers did not actually defend Aquinas' Natural Theology as part of their systematic theology.

Most importantly, instead of dividing life into the mind/matter, form/essence, reason/faith, nature/grace, and secular/sacred dichotomies of pagan and Catholic philosophy, the Reformers brought *all of life* under the divine authority of Scripture. What we believe and how we live is to be decided by God through Special Revelation *alone*. All of life is sacred and under the rule of Scripture. There is no secular realm where the Lordship of Christ and the Bible are irrelevant. Therefore, Natural Law without Scripture is blind.

The Reformers unified all of life by bringing it under the Lordship of Christ by putting all things under the objective absolute authority of Scripture. It became the basis of their theology, philosophy, science, the arts, law, government, and ethics. The Lordship of Christ was applied to all of life and every square inch of earth was claimed for Christ alone.

We must also point out that one searches in vain in the writings of Luther or Calvin for any passages in which they appealed to Aquinas or his *Summa* as their authority for doctrine or morals. The Creeds of the Reformation nowhere appeal to Aquinas or his Natural Theology as their authority. The only ones appealing to Aquinas are the anti-Reformation Catholic Creeds such as Trent.

The Eyes of Lady Justice

The Swiss Reformers symbolized *Sola Scriptura* by changing the symbol of Lady Justice. The pagans always pictured Lady Justice as being blindfolded. But the Swiss took off her blindfold and had her point her sword to the open Bible at her feet. Revealed Law was the only way for a nation to have moral laws. "Natural" (i.e. secular) law was a fraud.

Instead of the Catholic/pagan doctrine of "Natural" Law, the Reformers saw society being regulated according to the Revealed Laws found in the Bible. Justice was no longer blind and in the dark, but now she stood in the blazing light of the Word of God.

Our Evangelical Fathers

The heirs of the Reformation, such as the Puritans, rebelled against the pagan dogma of the self-sufficiency of human reason. Instead of looking to man's reason or man's faith as the Origin and measure of all things, including God, the Puritans taught that we should look outside of ourselves to God's Word alone for the final answers to truth, justice, morals, meaning, and beauty. Their doctrine of *Sola Scriptura* was the answer to the Greek dogma of *sola ratione*.

The Great Awakening

One of the themes of Jonathan Edwards' Great Awakening was the insufficiency of human reason and general revelation.[378] Princeton theologians such as Archibald Alexander argued against the exaltation of human reason above the authority of Scripture.

> We must unequivocally deny to reason the high office of deciding at her bar what doctrines of Scriptures are to be received and what not.[379]

Instead of bowing before the idol of reason, Alexander stressed that we must,

> insist that all opinions, pretensions, experiences, and practices must be judged the standard of the Word of God.[380]

Evangelical scholars such as Schaeffer, Henry, Clark, Ellul, Van Til, Berkouwer, etc., followed the lead of the Reformers in rejecting Natural Law and Natural Theology.[381] They taught that God, instead of man, was the Origin of truth, justice, morals, meaning and beauty; Revelation was the final authority instead of human reason or faith; Jesus is Lord – not Plato, Aristotle, Whitehead, etc. Francis Schaeffer's comments on Aquinas are representative of the historic Evangelical view of Aquinas.

> Aquinas held that man had revolted against God and thus was fallen, but Aquinas had an incomplete view of the Fall. He thought that the Fall did not affect man as a whole but only in part. In his view the will was fallen or corrupted but the intellect was not affected. Thus people could rely on their own human wisdom and this meant that people were free to mix the teachings of the Bible with the teachings to the non-Christian philosophers.[382]

> Among the Greek philosophers, Thomas Aquinas relied especially on one of the greatest, Aristotle (384-322 B.C.). In 1263 Pope Urban IV had forbidden the study of Aristotle in the universities. Aquinas managed to have Aristotle accepted so the ancient non-Christian philosophy was re-enthroned.[383]

> This opened the way for people to think of themselves as autonomous and the center of all things.[384]

Aquinas opened Pandora's Box when he introduced Aristotle's dogma of the autonomous reason. It led to the rise of rationalism. Francis Schaeffer explained it this way.

> A rationalist is someone who thinks that man can begin with himself and his reason plus what he observes, without information from any other source, and come to final answers in regard to truth, ethics, and reality...No one stresses more than I that people have no final answers in regard to truth, morals or epistemology without God's revelation in the Bible. This is true in philosophy, science, and theology. Rationalism can take a secular or theological form. In both, the rationalist thinks that on the basis of man's reason, plus what he can see about him, final answers are possible. My books stress that man cannot generate final answers from himself. First, even without the Fall, man was finite and needed the knowledge God gave him (revelation). Second, on this side of the Fall this is even more necessary.[385]

Bernard Ram explained,

> Just as Scripture was the supreme source of revealed truth so Aristotle was the supreme source of our natural knowledge. Thomas repeatedly calls him "The Philosopher," and cites him as possessing full authority. To be with Aristotle was to be with the truth, and to be against Aristotle was to be against the truth...He Christianized Aristotle and Aristotelianized Christianity.[386]

J. I. Packer pointed out that, despite loud affirmations, Aquinas's five "proofs" for the existence of God are not logical.

> All arguments for God's existence, all expositions of the analogy of being, of proportionality and of attribution, as means of intelligently conceptualizing God, and all attempts to show the naturalism of theism, are logically loose. They state no more than possibilities (for probabilities are only one kind of possibility) and can all be argued against indefinitely. They cannot be made watertight, and if offered as such they can be shown not to be watertight by anyone who knows any logic. This will damage the credit of any theology that appears to be building and relying on these arguments.[387]

Norman Geisler

Dr. Norman Geisler was the first to openly break with the historic Evangelical position on Aquinas. In his book defending Thomas Aquinas, he stated that since the previous generation of Protestant apologists, such as Carl Henry, Francis Schaeffer, Van Ti, etc. were now dead, the time was now ripe for him and other secret Thomists to come "out of the closet."[388]

Geisler was right. If these Jesuit-trained Thomists would have revealed their beliefs while these past great Evangelical scholars were alive, they would have been run out of evangelical circles. The great Evangelical philosophers and theologians such as Van Til, Gordon Clark, Carl F. Henry, Francis Schaeffer, Ellul, etc. all rejected Natural Theology and Natural Law. They understood that the doctrine of *Sola Scriptura* was the basis of the Reformation. Any doctrine that was not compatible with *Sola Scriptura* was neither Protestant nor Reformed.

Back to Rome

Norman Geisler represented a new generation of "neo-Protestants" (Carl F. Henry's terminology) that had received their higher education from Catholic universities such as Notre Dame, Marquette, Fordham, etc. They were all indoctrinated by their Jesuit professors into Catholic Natural Law, Natural Religion, Natural Theology, and Natural Apologetics. "Nature" took the place of Scripture. *Sola scriptura* was replaced with *sola ratione*.

As "Evangelical" schools, such as Wheaton, Baylor, BIOLA, Azusa, Messiah, Regent University, Dallas Seminary, etc. hired Jesuit-trained theologians and philosophers, they changed from their original Bible-centered education to a new curriculum that was based on Catholic Natural theology, Law, philosophy, and apologetics.[389] This has led to "evangelical" professors and their students converting to Roman Catholicism while in "evangelical" colleges and universities!

Reformed Law Theory

The Reformed colleges and seminaries were the last to abandon *Sola Scriptura* and to enshrine Humanistic Naturalism. Westminster Theological Seminary is an example of this degeneration.

Francis Schaeffer was educated by C. Van Til and Gordon Clark at Westminster Theological Seminary (Philadelphia, PA). Van Til's letter to his student Schaeffer is indicative of their rejection of Natural Theology.

> I think you will agree then, that no form of natural theology has ever spoken properly of the God who is there. None of the great Greek philosophers, like Plato and Aristotle, and none of the great modern philosophers, like Descartes, Kant or Kierkegaard and others, have ever spoken of the God who is there. The systems of thought of these men represent a repression of the revelations of the God who

is there. However, no man has, from a study and of the facts of nature by means of observation and ratiocination, ever come to the conclusion that he is a creature of God and that he is a sinner in the sight of God, who, unless he repents, abides under the wrath of God. [390]

Dr. John Frame was a professor at Westminster Theological Seminary at both the Philadelphia and California campuses. His insight on the whether the ideas of "Nature" or "Natural Law" are found in the Bible is significant.

So the biblical view of the natural world is intensely personalistic. Natural events come from God, the personal Lord. He also employs angels and human beings to do his work in the world. But the idea that there is some impersonal mechanism called 'nature' or 'natural law' that governs the universe is absent from the Bible. So is the notion of an ultimate 'randomness,' as postulated by some exponents of quantum mechanics. [391]

Prof. Frame's comment is in sharp contrast to the new "Natural Law" professors at Westminster Seminary (CA).

David VanDrunen

Grabill listed a number of modern Natural Law theorists including Dr. David VanDrunen.[392] When I heard that Westminster Theological Seminary (CA) had hired him as a faculty member, I purchased his book *Aquinas and Natural Law* and corresponded with him concerning his views.

He was educated by the Jesuits in Natural Theology and Natural Law. It was thus no surprise to find that he, like Grabill, was on the payroll of the Catholic Acton Institute. The Institute even published his second book! VanDrunen's relationship to this Roman Catholic organization is very disturbing.

Guilt by Association?

One defense given by WTS professors was to pretend that our objections to VanDrunen were based solely upon "guilt by association."[393] They admitted that some of their teachers have:

- graduated from Catholic universities,
- taught at Catholic universities,
- dedicated their books to Catholic scholars and priests,
- been members of Catholic societies and institutions,
- received money from the Catholics,
- books published by Catholic publishers,
- written books that are used in Catholic schools.

They assured us that none of the above should concern Reformed Christians. Who are they kidding? We are not so naïve as to believe that a true-blue Protestant at a Catholic university would be allowed to preach the Reformation truths of grace *alone,* faith *alone*, Christ *alone*, Scripture *alone*.

The issue is not just their associations and financial ties to Catholic institutions, but the fact that these professors are teaching and defending *Catholic* Natural Law, Natural Religion, Natural Theology, and Natural Apologetics, therefore leading many astray.

The End of Van Til's Apologetic

When CA Westminster Seminary hired David VanDrunen, this signaled the final end of Van Til's presuppositional apologetics at WTS and the rise of Catholic thought at what once was the premier Reformed Seminary. Like Grabill, VanDrunen in his introduction to his book, thanked his Jesuit teachers for their counsel and Catholic financial support while writing his book.[394] Eric Landry introduced VanDrunen to the WTS community with the following words.

> Orthodox Presbyterian theologian David VanDrunen, presents a positive case for engaging non-Christians in the public square by utilizing the insights of natural law.[395]

VanDrunen sets forth his case for Natural Law in an insightful article:

> But when Christians face a moral impasse in the public square, what is the proper way to proceed in order to attain some measure of agreement among the different parties? In this article, I point to the idea of natural law as an answer to this question."[396]

> It seems to me that one of the best ways for Christians to make natural law arguments is to begin with these general truths that most people would not dispute and then attempt to show by use of wisdom and appeals to common sense how more particular on controversial actions would or would not be consistent with these general moral truths.[397]

Knowing that I had uncovered VanDrunen's connection to the Catholic Acton Institute, and once this book was published, the WTS alumni would feel nervous about throwing Van Til, Gordon Clark, John Murray, and Francis Schaeffer "under the bus," VanDrunen tried to prove (sic) from Scripture that we do not need to go to the Bible for truth and morals.

> Romans 2:14-15 speaks of the law of God being written on people hearts, such that even those without access to the law revealed in Scripture are held accountable to God through their consciences. Many prominent Christian theologians have identified natural law

as the standard for civil law and government, including not only medieval theologians such as Thomas Aquinas but also reformers, such as John Calvin.[398]

> God has inscribed the natural law on the heart of every person (Rom. 2:14-15), and all people know the basic requirements of God's law, even if they suppress that knowledge (Rom. 1:19, 21, 32).[399]

> ...the law of God still written on all people's hearts.[400]

If Natural Laws are indeed written on every human heart (i.e. part of "human nature"), how is it that the vast majority of mankind throughout human history never heard of, believed in or practiced them? Furthermore, is this a correct interpretation of this passage?

VanDrunen modified his claim to "most every unbeliever...most people...most unbelievers...most Christians" believe is true and moral.[401]

Notice that he went from "all" to "most." He should have said "few" instead of "most" because Natural Law depends upon whatever the relative cultural consensus says is true and moral at the time. Most Christians would have trouble basing their faith on these shifting sands.

Michael Horton

WTS professor Michael Horton felt the need to support hiring Prof. VanDrunen by giving more arguments in favor of Natural Law. He began by asking a question.

> How can we say that God cannot be truly known at least in a saving way, unless one has been exposed to the Christian Scriptures?[402]

He tried to prove from the Bible that it is not necessary to prove things from the Bible! Of course, by going to the Bible to prove that we do not need the Bible is to prove we need the Bible! He also cites Rom. 2:15 as a proof text.

> Gentiles have the moral law indelibly written on their conscience (2:15). Not only do they know the second table (duties to neighbors); they know the first table as well (duties to God).[403]

> There is a genuine revelation of God in nature. Who can deny the wisdom behind the obvious design and order inherent in the cosmos, without which science could not even begin its investigation? It is obvious that all of this is the execution of a marvelous architect, and this communicates real knowledge of God to everyone.[404]

But he does not mean the external objective "Nature" found in the material universe. By "Nature" he means

> reason, common sense, or the obvious characteristics of human anatomy will be recognized to the extent that it reveals God as the source. [405]

If man's "reason" and "common sense" are sufficient for truth and morals, apart from and independent of God and His Word, then Horton correctly asks,

> How much does one have to know to be saved? [406]

This gets to the heart of the Reformation doctrines of *Sola Scriptura*, the necessity of hearing of and believing in the biblical gospel for salvation, the lost condition of the heathen, etc. Horton's answer will shock most WTS graduates.

> We are not God and we do not have any list of propositions in scripture to which assent is required in order to qualify as saving faith. [407]

His answer would have shocked Machen, Van Til, Clark, Schaeffer, etc.. It also flies in the face of Rom. 10:9-10.

> If thou shall confess with your mouth that "Jesus is Lord," and shall believe in your heart that "God raised him from the dead," thou shall be saved for with the heart man believes unto righteousness; and with the mouth confession is made unto salvation.

A proposition is a statement of fact the meaning of which is either true or false. The proposition "Jesus is LORD (i.e. YHWH)" requires one to believe in the deity of Jesus the Messiah. Either He was or was not God manifested in the flesh. The proposition "God raised him from the dead" requires one to believe that Jesus was raised bodily from the dead. He is either physically alive or dead. Dr. Horton clearly understands that he is going against the historic position of Reformed Theology that saving faith is composed of *three* things:

> (1.) *knowledge* of the core propositional statements of gospel,
> (2.) *intellectual assent* to those propositional statements, and
> (3.) *personal trust* in Christ.

Horton reduces saving faith to personal faith or commitment to Jesus.

> Although we have plenty of propositions about the person and work of Christ, these merely serve to give definition to the person in whom we place our trust. It is trust in Christ, not the number of true propositions we hold, that is the empty hand that receives the treasures of God's kingdom.[408]

Once knowledge and assent are deleted from saving faith, the door is open to the Catholic doctrines of "invincible ignorance" and "felicitous inconsistency."

Roman Catholic Doctrines

The Roman Catholic doctrine of "invincible ignorance" simply says that the heathen can make it to heaven without ever hearing of or believing Jesus Christ and his Gospel if they lived a good life according to their conscience, i.e. Natural Law. According to the new Catholic Catechism, even atheists can make it to heaven.

The doctrine of "felicitous inconsistency" refers to non-Christians who have heard of Christ and his gospel but, reject them both. They can still be saved if they have lived a good life according to what Natural Law tells them in their hearts.

The new Catholic Catechism even says that Muslims who deny the Trinity, the deity of Christ, etc. – can still make it to heaven if they lived a life consistent with the Natural Law written in their conscience. Horton comments,

> We may hold doctrines that, if taken to their logical conclusion, would obscure or even deny the gospel, yet by "felicitous inconsistency," as our older theologians expressed it, embrace Christ and all his benefits.[409]

Rejecting clear Scripture, Natural Law theologians always points to *themselves* as the Origin of truth, justice, morals, meaning, and beauty. Human reason, common sense, etc, thus become the "measure of all things," including the fate of those who have never heard of Christ and His gospel or those who knowingly reject them both.

PART TWO

The Arguments for Natural Law

Many different arguments have been set forth to prove the validity of Natural Law. Most of these arguments are pure nonsense, as they are based on racial prejudice and cultural conceit. Other arguments are based on hearsay and anecdotal evidence and when examined, fall to pieces. Only two arguments survive from century to century. First, it is asserted that mathematics proves that we can get truth from "Nature." Second, it is claimed the Bible teaches Natural Law.

SECTION ONE

Chapter Eleven   Natural Law

Does Mathematics Prove Natural Law?

Natural Law theorists have argued that mathematics is a clear example of "natural laws" that are innate, self-evident, intuitive, and universal. [410] It is still used by some Catholic and Evangelical theorists today.

The controversy whether math is the product of *nature* or *nurture* was hotly debated at the beginning of the twentieth century. After a great deal of debate, secular philosophers abandoned the idea that the "laws" of mathematics are innate ideas that are a part of "human nature. People are not born with the innate idea that 1+1=2.

The History of Numbers

We must begin with the history of numbers. Why? We are so familiar with using 1, 2, 3, 4, 25, 100, 1,000, etc., that it will be a surprise to most people to learn that for most of human history such numbers did not exist. If you would have said or written 1, 2, 3, or given simple mathematical equations such as 1+1=2 to the authors of the Bible, they would not have had the slightest idea of what those numbers meant.

Arabic Numbers

Today we refer to these numbers as "Arabic numbers." While the introduction of these numbers in Western culture can be traced back to Arab merchants, they did not invent them *per se*. The Arabs found different numbers used in different cultures as they traveled around Asia and the Middle East. For example, they found the number 0 in India. These numbers were introduced in Europe in the twelfth century AD, but it took centuries before they came into common use.

It is interesting to note that Catholic Natural Law theorists and natural theologians condemned the use of Arabic numbers as heresy and championed the continued use of the Roman numeral system (I, II, III, IV, etc.). Modern natural law theorists accept a view of math that the earlier theorists rejected.

Ancient Middle Eastern Cultures

The earliest written records reveal that ancient Middle Eastern cultures such as the Assyrians did not have any concept of *abstract* numbers, i.e. they never discussed numbers in and of themselves in an abstract sense. For example, there were no words for "million" or "billion" in any of the ancient languages.

Any "counting" done in ancient cultures was always done in terms of *concrete* notations. These notations were based on the idea of a one on one *correspondence*. For example, they would use a stone to represent a sheep. When they wanted to know how many sheep they had, they pulled out their leather bag and looked to see if there was a correspondence between the stones and the sheep. They would also sometimes cut notches on a wooden staff to correspond to the number of sheep.

The Babylonians took a pointed stick and made impressions in a tablet of wet clay to represent how many objects they wished to record. The Egyptians used hieroglyphics of animals and other objects to represent amounts. For example, the amount of "one hundred thousand" was represented by the picture of a bird.

Most ancient cultures used their ten fingers to correspond to objects. This is the basis of our own "base ten" system. Some cultures did not use a base 10 system. For example, the Sumerians used 60 as their base.

Moses and the Torah

Since Moses was the author of the first five books of the Bible, it is interesting to note that although he was well-educated in the Egyptian method of keeping track of objects, he never used it in the Pentateuch, and neither did he use the Assyrian, Hittite, or Babylonian systems in the Torah. The Jews in Moses' day had words to correspond to numbers of things. These words were treated like any other Hebrew word.

one	echad
two	senayim
three	salos
four	arabaa
five	hames
six	ses
seven	seba
eight	smoneh
nine	tesa
ten	eser
hundred	meah
thousand	eleph
ten thousand	rebabah

Similarly, when we write a check today, on the second line we write out the amount in words instead of Arabic numbers. While the Ancient Hebrews had words to correspond to things, they did not have any numbers. For example, in the Genesis account of Creation, Moses gives us a record of what God did on "day one," "day two," "day three," etc.

When Moses wanted to record large amounts, he would write it out word for word. For example, while we would write 930 in Arabic numbers, Moses would write "nine hundred and thirty" [תְּשַׁע מֵאוֹת שָׁנָה וּשְׁלֹשִׁים] (Genesis 5:5). The Hebrew word that represented the highest amount recorded in the Old Testament was ten thousand. That was the largest number in the Hebrew language.

Large Numbers

What about such huge numbers as "million" or "billion?" Did ancient cultures have any concept of very large numbers? No. They could only conceive of an amount that was sitting in front of them. We have no evidence that they had a concept of such abstract concepts as billion, trillion, or anything higher.

The concept of "million" was actually invented by an Italian banker 600 years ago when he ran out of words to represent the amount of money in his bank. A French banker invented the concept of a "billion" in 1500. Such words as trillion and quadrillion are also of recent origin. They represent modern advances in abstract mathematics.

The Biblical Authors

Did the biblical authors ever run out of words to express quantify things? Yes. When Joseph tried to keep track of how much he had stored up during the seven good years, Genesis 41:49 says that he eventually ran out of words to express it [לִסְפֹּר כִּי־אֵין מִסְפָּר]. The Egyptians even had a hieroglyphic of a man throwing up his hands in despair to represent an amount for which they did not have a word.

Did the biblical authors ever use the letters of the Hebrew alphabet to represent numbers? No. They used words for amounts, not numbers. Did the authors of the New Testament ever use the letters of the Greek alphabet to represent numbers? No. Was it even possible for them to place hidden numeric codes in the writings? No.

The New Testament followed the Old Testament in using words instead of numbers: one = eis, two = duo, three = treis, etc. Even in Revelations 13:18, the "mark of the beast" is written out in the Greek words "six hundred sixty-six" [ἑξακόσιοι ἑξήκοντα ἕξ].

The historical facts are clear that it was simply not possible for Moses, the prophets, or the apostles to use Arabic numbers in their writings. There is simply no archeological or literary evidence that the pre-exilie Jews ever used the letters of the Hebrew alphabet to represent numbers. The burden of proof is on anyone who says otherwise.

Jesus and the Apostles

Enough has been demonstrated to prove that mathematics was unknown to the authors of the Bible.[411] Since no ancient culture ever found the truths of mathematics in "Nature," the claim of Natural law theorists that mathematics is universal, self-evident, intuitive, and innate falls to the ground is destroyed.

SECTION TWO

Biblical Arguments

While the theory of Natural Law was invented by Aristotle and clearly attempts to discover laws-without-God, some "Christian" Natural Law theorists have attempted to justify it Biblically.

Self-refuting

If you go to the Bible to justify Natural Law, you have refuted yourself at the outset. Thus only a few Protestant Natural Law theorists have set forth passages from the Bible that supposedly teach the idea that we can find in Nature-without-God laws-without God that give us truth-without God and morals-without God.

The General Revelation Argument

As we have already pointed out, natural theologians and philosophers have assumed, like *Budzszewski*, that general revelation and Natural Law are identical. This fundamental fallacy of equivocation led them to cite biblical passages where "general revelation" is mentioned as if those passages likewise proved (sic) Natural Law.[412]

Biblical Passages

There are only a few specific biblical passages that have been cited as proving the concept of Natural Law. We will examine these passages to see if they clearly teach Aristotle's doctrine.

I Cor. 11:14
Does "Nature" Teach Us Truth and Morals?

Some Natural theologians have quoted the words "nature doth teach thee" from 1 Cor. 11:14 (KJV) as a proof text that the Bible teaches that "Nature" is the Origin of truth, justice, morals, meaning, and beauty.[413]

> Naturalist: "We can derive truth and morals from Nature apart from and independent of God and the Bible."
> Theist: "I don't think the Bible teaches that."
> Naturalist: "Yes it does! Paul stated "Nature" teaches us truth and morals in 1 Cor. 11:14."
> Theist: "I think you are misinterpreting the passage. Did you check out the Greek word translated "nature"? Did you exegete the passage carefully?"
> Naturalist: "No need to do so. I am a Christian philosopher. I don't do exegesis. My reason tells me what the passage means."

The "quote and run" method employed by Natural theologians is reminiscent of how Jehovah's Witnesses abuse the Bible. Since they cite the words "nature doth teach thee" and then run off without any attempt to exegete the verse, it falls upon us to point out that they are guilty of "twisting" the Scriptures (2 Pet. 3:16). The text reads as follows:

> Doth not even nature itself teach you, that, if a man have long hair, it is a shame unto him? (1 Cor. 11:14)

> οὐδὲ ἡ φύσις αὐτὴ διδάσκει ὑμᾶς ὅτι ἀνὴρ μὲν ἐὰν κομᾷ ἀτιμία αὐτῷ ἐστιν?

In the immediate context, Paul appeals to "φύσις" as "teaching" two things:

(1.) It is shameful for men to have long hair and women short hair.
(2.) It is appropriate for women to have long hair and men short hair.

First, the issue of hair styles does not fall under the categories of "truth and morals." To have long or short hair is hardly a matter of immorality. The length of your hair is a *relative* issue found in *cultural* fads and styles. Natural theologians are making a categorical fallacy when they claim that the passage has in view absolute truth and morals.

Second, the chapter division is in error. Paul actually began to discuss such cultural issues as food, drink, hair styles, and head coverings in 1 Cor. 10:23-33.

> All things are lawful, but not all things are profitable. All things are lawful, but not all things edify. *Therefore*, let no one seek his own *good*, but that of his neighbor. Eat anything that is sold in the meat market without asking questions for conscience' sake; FOR THE EARTH IS THE LORD'S, AND ALL IT CONTAINS. If one of the unbelievers invites you and you want to go, eat anything that is set before you without asking questions for conscience' sake.
> But if anyone says to you, "This is meat sacrificed to idols,"
> do not eat *it*, for the sake of the one who informed *you* and for conscience' sake; I mean not your own conscience, but the other *man's*; for why is my freedom judged by another's conscience? If I partake with thankfulness, why am I slandered concerning that for which I give thanks? Whether, then, you eat or drink or whatever you do, do all to the glory of God. Give no offense either to Jews or to Greeks or to the church of God; just as I also please all men in all things, not seeking my own profit but the *profit* of the many, so that they may be saved.

Paul states in 1 Cor. 10:29 that Christians have the "freedom" to adopt or not to adopt cultural customs. See Paul's exposition of "Christian Liberty" in such places as Rom. 14 and Gal. 5.

The attempt to read absolute morality into this passage has caused much confusion. When Paul said, "All things are lawful," did he mean, "All *moral* things are lawful?" Did he mean that it is now lawful for Christians to kill, steal, rape, etc.? Do we have the "freedom" to violate absolute morality? I don't think any sane person would say so.

Paul clearly has in view the lawfulness and freedom of Christians to engage in relative *cultural* practices or styles, i.e. "All *cultural* things are lawful." Whether you have long hair or short hair is not an issue of truth or morals. A piece of cotton on your head will not determine whether God hears your prayer! He has in view relative customs of a society.

Also, in 1 Cor. 10:29, Paul clearly has in view the conscience of *unbelievers*, not believers. If an unbeliever feels that a certain custom is important to him, then, in order to win him to Christ, the Christian is free to conform to that custom. For example, if you are in a culture where male prostitutes wear long hair and female prostitutes wear short hair, then, while long or short hair is not a moral issue to you, for the sake of the unbeliever, don't look like a prostitute!

Natural theologians have made the fatal mistake of reading Western, European, post-Renaissance scientific ideas into this first century text. It was impossible for Paul to know of the Newtonian world view in which there are mechanical "natural laws" inherent in "Nature." Thus Paul could not mean "natural laws" when he wrote "nature." Any interpretation which claims that Paul is talking about "laws inherent in nature" is eisegesis and not exegesis.

The Greek word φύσις, translated "nature" in the KJV, referred to the cultural customs of the society in which they lived. As Matthew Henry pointed out, "custom is in a great measure the rule of decency."[414] Every culture legislates what is "natural" and "unnatural," i.e., what is against custom or in conformity to custom. Calvin comments:

> Paul again sets nature before them as a teacher of what is proper. Now he means by 'natural' what was accepted by common consent and usage at that time, certainly as far as the Greeks were concerned. For long hair was not always regarded as a disgraceful thing in men. Historical works relate that long ago i.e., in the earliest times, men wore long hair in every country. But since the Greeks did not consider it very manly to have long hair, branding those who had it effeminate, Paul conceded that their custom, accepted in his own day, was in conformity with nature. The word "nature" refers to what was culturally acceptable.[415]

The great Charles Hodge pointed out:

> The form which these feelings assume is necessarily determined in a great measure by education and habit. The instinctive sense of propriety in an eastern maiden prompts her, when surprised by strangers, to cover her face. In a European it would not produce that effect. In writing, therefore, to eastern females, it would be correct to ask whether their native sense of propriety did not prompt them to cover their heads in public. The response would infallibly be in the affirmative. It is in this sense the word nature is commonly taken here.[416]

It was for this reason that the great J. Meyer said, "The instinctive consciousness of propriety on this point had been established by custom and had become nature."[417] This understanding of the word "nature" was held by such early commentators as Chrysostom.[418] Ellingworth and Hatton point out, "Paul's use of the word translated *nature* reflects both the culture in which he lived and his Christian convictions."[419] The *Expositor's Greek Testament* defines the word "nature" as "social sentiment."[420] Lenski defines it as "the custom in vogue in their midst."[421] Meyer emphasized that the hair styles and coverings "had been established by custom and had become nature."[422]

This understanding conforms to the context of the passage and the line of argumentation that Paul is using. After a lengthy discussion, Thiselton comments,

> One of the most discriminating discussions of φύσις in this particular verse comes from Schrage. He compares its use here with the

occurrences of the term in Rom 1:26; 2:14. To be sure, he observes, unlike the Stoics Paul does not hear "the voice of God from nature" as some competing or alternate source to scripture. In contrast to Cicero, φύσις as "nature" is characterized by "ambivalence and relativity" of a kind unlike the concept among the Stoics. In Paul's sense of the term, "natural" need not refer to a structure inherent in creation but may include "the state of affairs surrounding a convention" or the quality, property, or nature *(Beschaffenheit)* of male or female gender and the order, or arrangement, or system of things as they are *(die Ordnung der Dinge)*. Unless we take fully into account "the ambivalence of 'natural,'" we shall find insoluble problems with such historical counterexamples as the custom of Spartan warriors of wearing shoulder-length hair. Paul simply appeals to "how things are" or "how things are ordered" in the period and context for which he is writing. Judiciously Schrage cites Calvin: "Now he means by 'natural' what was accepted by common consent and usage at that time.... For long hair was not always regarded as a disgraceful thing in man." [423]

Matthew Poole concludes,

> Interpreters rightly agree, that this and the following verses are to be interpreted from the customs of the countries; and all that can be concluded from the verse is, that it is the duty of men employed in divine ministrations, to look to behave themselves as those who are to represent the Lord Jesus Christ, behaving themselves with a just authority and gravity that belong to his ambassadors, which decent gravity is to be judged from the common opinion and account of the country wherein they live. Nothing in this is a further rule to Christians, than that it is the duty in praying and preaching, to use postures and habits that are not naturally, nor according to the customs of the place they live, uncomely and irreverent as looked upon. [424]

The pagan Greek concepts that there is something "out there" called "Nature;" that it has intrinsic laws and truths in it; that man can solely discern them through human reason, apart from and independent of divine revelation, is not found in the Hebrew Old Covenant Scriptures or the Greek New Covenant Scriptures.

The *Oxford Dictionary of Jewish Religion* states, "The concept of nature as a system operating according to fixed laws of its own derives from Greek philosophy rather than the Bible." [425] The *New Catholic Encyclopedia* agrees with this fact. [426] The *International Standard Bible Encyclopedia* comments,

> "Nature" in the sense of a system or constitution does not occur in the Old Testament...The later conception of "nature" came in through Greek influences.[427]

The attempt to cite 1 Cor. 11:14 as a proof text for the pagan concept of Natural Law is a complete failure.

Rom. 2:15
Is The Law Written on the Hearts of All Men?

There is only one biblical text that is used by *all* Natural Law theorists and theologians. It has become a mantra that is chanted as if merely reciting the words is all that is needed. No exegesis is ever given. That text is Rom. 2:15. While they think it is their strongest text, it is actually their greatest weakness.

> in that they show the work of the Law written in their hearts, their conscience bearing witness, and their thoughts alternately accusing or else defending them,
>
> οἵτινες ἐνδείκνυνται τὸ ἔργον τοῦ νόμου γραπτὸν ἐν ταῖς καρδίαις αὐτῶν, συμμαρτυρούσης αὐτῶν τῆς συνειδήσεως καὶ μεταξὺ ἀλλήλων τῶν λογισμῶν κατηγορούντων ἢ καὶ ἀπολογουμένων,

The Natural Law theorist interpretation has three basic propositions.

1. The text is *universal* in scope, i.e. has all men in view.
2. The word "law" referred to "natural laws" found either in Nature-nature or nature-reason.
3. These "natural laws" are written in the hearts of all men.

As we shall demonstrate, all three propositions are absolutely erroneous.

Without Excuse
In the first two chapters of Romans, Paul argued that some Gentiles do not have the Torah revealed to them. Yet, they are "without excuse" (εἰς τὸ εἶναι αὐτοὺς ἀναπολογήτους). When they stand before God on the Day of Judgment, they will not be able to escape the wrath of God (1:18) by giving the excuse that God failed to provide them with any revelation.

These Gentiles may not have the light of Torah, but they had the light of the Creation around them. In other words, the light is brightly shinning and the music is playing loudly but these Gentiles suppressed (κατεχόντων) the witness of Creation and worshipped the Creation instead of the Creator (Romans 1:25).

Chapter Eleven Natural Law

The Basis of God's Condemnation

God's condemnation rests upon the fact of man's ungodliness and unrighteousness (1:18) and inherited depravity from Adam (5:12-21). Thus the presence or absence of Torah does not determine the condemnation of sinners. We are "born in sin and conceived iniquity" (Psa. 51:5); we are "already perishing" (ἀπολλυμένοις) from the moment we are conceived (1 Cor. 1:18); we are "dead in trespasses in sins" (Eph. 2:1-2). Nowhere does Paul say that Creation tells us the way of salvation. While it is sufficient for condemnation, it is not sufficient for salvation.

All Natural Religions Condemned

Paul's description of the "Natural Religions" of the Gentile world is graphic and condemnatory (1:18-32). All Natural Religions are idolatrous because they are not the result of man's search for God but man's flight from God. No sinner seeks the true God and thus no sinner understands God.

> There is none who understands [God],
> There is none who seeks for God. (Rom. 3:11)
>
> οὐκ ἔστιν ὁ συνίων,
> οὐκ ἔστιν ὁ ἐκζητῶν τὸν θεόν.

The word "not" (οὐκ) is taken out of its regular word order and placed first to *emphasize* that absolutely no one understands God because absolutely no one seeks God. Sinful man only seeks gods made in his own image who will condone his sin.

> It is clear that the argument which intends to demonstrate the universality of sin builds up to a climax. ..The picture he draws is dismal: no one is righteous; in fact, no one understands his deplorable condition. And no one is even trying to understand, is even searching for God, the Source of all wisdom and knowledge. But are there no exceptions? Paul answers, "There is no one ...no one ...no one ...no one ...not even one."[428]

The Fate of the Heathen

What will happen to those who never had Torah? Will they perish and end up in hell? Can they give some kind of excuse to avoid punishment for their sins? Paul emphatically states,

> For all who have sinned without the Torah will also perish without
> the Torah; and all who have sinned under the Torah will be judged
> by the Torah (Rom. 2:12)
>
> ὅσοι γὰρ ἀνόμως ἥμαρτον, ἀνόμως καὶ ἀπολοῦνται, καὶ ὅσοι ἐν
> νόμῳ ἥμαρτον, διὰ νόμου κριθήσονται·

Paul leaves no loopholes to escape divine judgment. Regardless of whether you have or do not have the Torah, you *will* perish in your sin. The Gentiles and the Jews who do not hear of and believe in Jesus Christ and His gospel will most surely perish in their sins and end up in the eternal conscious torment of Gehenna. [429]

The Torah

What was the Torah ("Law") mentioned by Paul in Chapter two? As Ridderbos and other N.T. scholars have pointed out, "the Torah," ὁ νόμος is not to be reduced to the Ten Commandments or natural law. Yet, this is what most Natural Law theologians assume to be true.

The Two Tablets Error

Natural Law theologians usually make the mistake of thinking that the Decalogue was recorded on two different stone tablets with some of the laws written on the first tablet and the rest on the second. They have debated for centuries how to divide up the Ten Commandments. Are they divided evenly with five on one tablet and five on the other or did the first tablet have four and the second six commandments? As Prof. Meredith Kline demonstrated, both tablets had all Ten Commandments on them. One copy was for YHWH and the other copy for Israel. [430]

Torah Encompassed All of Life

The "Torah" Paul had in mind encompassed *all* that God had revealed through Moses in the Old Covenant Scriptures.[431] For the Jew, the Torah encompassed all of life and judged what was right and what was wrong. The Torah judged how to cut your hair, what to eat, how to dress, how to deal with aggressive animals, how to deal with adultery, what was the right kind of mate to marry, how to raise children, the proper way to go to the bathroom, etc., etc. All of life was under Torah. John Murray comments,

> The law referred to is definite and can be none other than the law of God specified in the preceding verses as the law which the Gentiles do not have, the law the Jews did have and under which they were, the law by which men will be condemned in the day of Judgment.[432]

The failure of Natural Law theologians to understand the Jewish nature of Paul's idea of Torah was the result of presupposing the Greek dichotomy between secular and sacred. They reduced Torah to "sacred" laws in order to make room for secular laws-without-God drawn from Nature-without-God. This is why they never understood why the Torah judged such things as menstruation.

The purpose of the Torah was to tell Israel how to live. It sat in judgment of what they thought, said, and did. It either accused or excused their behavior in all of life. Thus no Jew checked his own reason, feelings, experience or faith to see how to cut his hair or what to eat (Prov. 3:5-6). The Torah decided such issues. There was no "secular" side of life where Torah did not apply.

The Function or Work of Conscience

Paul emphatically stated that some Gentiles do *not* have the Torah (ἔθνη τὰ μὴ νόμον ἔχοντα) to guide them (Rom. 2:14). Note that there is no definite article before ἔθνη. This is very important because the Natural Law theologian assumed that all Gentiles *do* have the Torah but from a different source, namely from Nature, Revelation.

> Theist: A "Gentile" by definition is someone who does *not* have the Torah to guide him in all of life.
>
> Naturalist: No! The Gentiles *do* have natural Law. They just get it from Nature, not Revelation.
>
> Theist: No! Paul states twice in Romans 2:14 that Gentiles do *not* have the Torah (τὰ μὴ νόμον ἔχοντα). He is not saying that they have a Torah-without-God through Nature-without-God. In 2:12, he states that those who sin "without Torah" (ἀνόμως ἥμαρτον), will perish "without Torah" (ἀνόμως καὶ ἀπολοῦνται). If they have the Torah, how can he say that Gentiles sin and will perish *without* it?

Paul is stating that the "conscience" in the heathen takes the place of the Torah by sitting in judgment of what he thinks, says, and does. It attempts to guide the heathen in all of life. His conscience either accuses him of doing the wrong thing or commends him for doing the right thing. Instead of the Torah, the heathen has a "conscience." Meyer points out,

> their moral nature, with its voice of conscience commanding and forbidding, supplies to their own Ego the place of the revealed law possessed by the Jews. [433]

The classic commentator, Robert Haldane, put it this way,

> We have here a distinction between the *law* itself, and the *work* of the law. The work of the law is the thing that the law doeth, -- that is, what it teaches about actions, as good or bad. This work, or business, or office of the law, is to teach what is right or wrong.[434]

An Exegesis of Rom. 2:14-16

With these insights on the context, let us now exegete Rom. 2:14-16. First, we must exegete verses 14, 15, and 16 because they are only one sentence wrongly divided into three verses. Natural Law theologians do not seem aware of this.

> For when Gentiles who do not have the Torah culturally do the things of the Torah, these, not having the Torah, are a torah to themselves, in that they show the work of the Torah written in their hearts, their conscience bearing witness, and their thoughts alternately accusing or else defending them, on the day when, according to my gospel, God will judge the secrets of men through Messiah Jesus.

ὅταν γὰρ ἔθνη τὰ μὴ νόμον ἔχοντα φύσει τὰ τοῦ νόμου ποιῶσιν,οὗ
τοι νόμον μὴ ἔχοντες ἑαυτοῖς εἰσιν νόμος· οἵτινες ἐνδείκνυνται τὸ
ἔργον τοῦ νόμου γραπτὸν ἐν ταῖς καρδίαις αὐτῶν, συμμαρτυρούσης
αὐτῶν τῆς συνειδήσεως καὶ μεταξὺ ἀλλήλων τῶν λογισμῶν
κατηγορούντων ἢ καὶ ἀπολογουμένων,ἐν ἡμέρᾳ ὅτε κρίνει ὁ θεὸς τὰ
κρυπτὰ τῶν ἀνθρώπων κατὰ τὸ εὐαγγέλιόν μου διὰ Χριστοῦ Ἰησοῦ.

Second, we have to deal with the persistent and pernicious *misquotation* of this passage by Natural Law theologians. Please notice that Paul does not say "the Law written on the hearts of all men" but "*the work* of the Torah written in their hearts."

Catholic and Protestant Natural Law theorists alike consistently drop out the words "the work of" and pretend that Paul wrote "the law written on the hearts of all men." The Protestant theologians should have known better. Perhaps they were following the precedent set by Catholic naturalists.

J. Daryl Charles
...the inner witness of the "law written on the heart." [435]

Because it is in the heart of each person and established by reason, the natural law is therefore universal in its precepts, possessing an authority that extends to all men..it is "immutable and permanent throughout the variations of history...it cannot be destroyed or removed from the heart of man." [436]

...there is a law "written on the heart" of every human being. [437]

J. Budzszewski

On the tablets of the heart a law is written indeed, the same for all men (as Thomas Aquinas said) not only as to rectitude but as to knowledge. [438]

natural law is general revelation. [439]

St. Paul spoke of "a law written on the heart."[440]

Jean Porter

For the scholastics, the "one everlasting and immutable law" is nothing other than the law to which Paul refers in Romans 2:14, which is written on the hearts of the men and women of the nations, through which they judge what is good and evil, and in terms of which they will themselves be judged on the last day. [441]

VanDrunen

God has inscribed the natural law on the heart of every person (Rom. 2:14-15), and all people know the basic requirements of God's law, even if they suppress that knowledge (Rom. 1:19, 21, 32). [442]

Michael Horton

Gentiles have the moral law indelibly written on their conscience (Rom. 2:15). Not only do they know the second table (duties to neighbors); they know the first table as well (duties to God). [443]

J. P. Mooreland and William Lane Craig

God has written his moral law upon all men's heart, so that they are morally responsible before him (Rom. 2:15). [444]

Third, Natural Law theologians not only delete the words "*the work of*" but add the words "*on the hearts of all men.*" But, Paul did *not* write "on the hearts of all men" but "in *their* hearts" (ἐν ταῖς καρδίαις αὐτῶν). Is he referring to *all* people?

Not All Men

In the context, Paul does not have in view all men but only *those* Gentile pagans who do not have the written Torah. The pronoun "their" refers only to some Gentiles. *The text is not universal in scope.* Paul does *not* include Jews in this text. Lenski explains,

> Jews cannot be included, for they are under the Mosaic code. The Greeks are also excluded ... because the Greek is a pagan he is not necessarily included...Also those who sin and perish "without any law" (v.12) are excluded...This interpretation will not be accepted by those who think that all Gentiles are here referred to. But Paul had looked around in this wicked world a bit. It still contains men who have no conscience at all, who in no way respond even to an inner law...Yes, ἔθνη without the article is correct. [445]

Paul is not speaking *universally* of *all* mankind. First, Paul divides humanity into two groups: those who have the revealed Torah and those who do not have it. Thus he is not speaking about all human beings.

Second, the word "Gentile" in verse 14 does *not* have the definite article because Paul was not making a universal statement about all Gentiles. Some Gentiles *have* heard Torah and thus cannot be grouped together with those who never heard Torah. John Murray comments: "the reason is that there are some Gentiles who did have the law and on that account did not belong to the category of which he is speaking."[446]

Meyer points out that the lack of the definite article before the word "Gentiles" means that what Paul was saying must,

> not be understood of the *Gentiles collectively*...for this must have been expressed by the article,,, and the putting of the case ὅταν ....ποιῇ with respect to the heathen generally would be in itself untrue – but Paul means rather *Gentiles among whom the supposed case occurs.*[447]

Fourth, in Rom. 2:15, the Greek word ἔργον ("work") is an accusative neuter singular and the Greek word γραπτὸν ("written") is also an accusative neuter singular. The case, gender, and number of the two words grammatically mean that the "WORK" of the Torah is what is "WRITTEN" in the hearts of the Gentiles who do not have the Torah. *Thus the Torah is not written in the heart per se*. There is something *else* in the hearts of the heathen that functions *in the place of* the Torah.

Fifth, the word τοῦ νόμου ("the Torah") is a masculine singular and cannot modify an accusative neuter singular. The syntax and grammar of the Greek text forbids saying it was written in the heart. The "work" of the Torah is what *functions* in the hearts of the heathen *in the place* of the Torah.

What is the meaning of the word τοῦ νόμου in this text? In the context, it clearly means the revealed Torah that the Jews possessed. The attempt of Natural theologians to interpret τοῦ νόμου as some nebulous natural law violates every hermeneutical principle known. John Murray emphatically states, "Paul does not say that the law is written upon their hearts."[448]

Since Paul says that there is something in the heart of the heathen that does the same work that the Torah does for the Jews, what is the work of function of the Torah?

The Work of Torah

We don't have to guess the answer. Paul clearly tells us that "the conscience" (ἧς συνειδήσεως) does the work that the Torah does. The classic commentators agree that *the work of the Torah* is what Paul had in view. The exegetical commentators who pay attention to grammar and syntax agree.

> Not the law itself (Wolf, Koppe, &c.): for the Ten Commandments are not formally written in their heart. [449]

> They *had the work of the law.* He does not mean that work which the law commands, as if they could produce a perfect obedience; but that work which the law does.[450]

> As the etymology of the word, both in Greek and in English (from Latin) implies, conscience is a *knowledge along with* (or shared with) the person. It is that individual's inner sense of right and wrong; his (to a certain extent divinely imparted) moral consciousness viewed in the act of pronouncing judgment upon himself, that is, upon his thoughts, attitudes, words, and deeds, whether past, present, or contemplated. As the passage states, the resulting *thoughts* or

judgments are either condemnatory or, in certain instances, even commendatory.[451]

Paul was not saying that God's specific revelation to Israel through Moses was intuitively known by pagan peoples. He was saying that in a broad sense what was expected of all people was not hidden from those who did not have the revelation given to Israel. Their own conscience acknowledged the existence of such a law. Thrall suggests that Paul was saying that in the pagan world the conscience performed roughly the same function as the law performed in the Jewish world. [452]

Paul describes the moral process which takes place in the heart of man after a good or bad act; the conscience, συνείδησις, sits in judgment, and pronounces the sentence in God's name according to the law; the διαλογισμοί are the several moral reflections and reasonings which appear as witnesses testifying and pleading in this court of conscience, and are often conflicting, since the sinful inclinations and passions interfere and bribe the witnesses; the object of the χατηγορεν, or πολογεσθαι, is the moral action which is brought before the tribunal of the conscience. The χα indicates that the conscience finds more to accuse than to excuse. This judicial process, which takes place here in every man's heart, is a forerunner of the great judgment at the end of the world. [453]

The Biblical Concept of the Conscience

The word English word "conscience" carries a great deal of cultural and philosophical baggage that has been collected down through the centuries. Natural Law theorists naively assume that the word refers to the Stoic idea of an infallible divine faculty resident in "human nature." They do not define or defend their assumption. They simply assume that is what the word means.

The biblical concept of the "conscience" has *nothing* to do with Stoicism. The Hebrew Old Testament never refers to the "conscience." There isn't even a Hebrew word for it. No one in the Torah ever appealed to it as an inner judge of right and wrong. Since Jews had the Torah, they did not *need* a conscience.[454]

In the New Testament, the word never appears in the Gospels and is never referred to by Jesus or the Twelve. In the Epistles, the Greek word συνείδησις simply means "joint" ,συν . "knowledge" (είδησις) and has no ontological reality. It simply meant to be *sincere* in what you say and do. This is why it is used as the opposite of lying in Rom. 9:1.

> I am telling the truth in Christ, I am not lying, my sincerity bears me witness in the Holy Spirit,
>
> Ἀλήθειαν λέγω ἐν Χριστῷ, οὐ ψεύδομαι, συμμαρτυρούσης μοι τῆς συνειδήσεώς μου ἐν πνεύματι ἁγίῳ,

Barclay and Nida point out that the word,

> Conscience may be variously translated, depending upon the particular set of associations connected with certain terms or phrases—for example, "my heart," "my innermost," "that which speaks within me," or "the voice in my heart." [455]

In Acts 23:1 Paul said,

> And Paul, looking intently at the Council, said, "Brethren, I have lived my life with a perfectly good conscience before God up to this day."
>
> ἀτενίσας δὲ ὁ Παῦλος τῷ συνεδρίῳ εἶπεν, Ἄνδρες ἀδελφοί, ἐγὼ πάσῃ συνειδήσει ἀγαθῇ πεπολίτευμαι τῷ θεῷ ἄχρι ταύτης τῆς ἡμέρας.

Newman and Nida analyze the word συνειδήσει ("conscience") in this text to mean "in my heart I have no serious questions about my whole life before God."[456] Vincent's *Word Studies in the New Testament* defined συνειδήσει in the following way.

> In scripture we are to view conscience, as Bishop Ellicott remarks, not in its abstract nature, but in its practical manifestations. Hence it may be *weak* (1 Cor. 8:7, 12), unauthoritative, and awakening only the feeblest emotion. It may be *evil* or *defiled* (Heb. 10:22; Tit. 1:15), through consciousness of evil practice. It may be *seared* (1 Tim. 4:2), branded by its own testimony to evil practice, hardened and insensible to the appeal of good. On the other hand, it may be *pure* (2 Tim. 1:3), unveiled, and giving honest and clear moral testimony. It may be *void of offence* (Acts 24:16), unconscious of evil intent or act: *good*, as here, or *honorable* (Heb. 13:18). The expression and the idea, in the full Christian sense, are foreign to the Old Testament, where the testimony to the character of moral action and character is borne by external revelation rather than by the inward moral consciousness.[457]

As Walvoord and Zuck point out, the post-lapsarian conscience of man,

> is not an absolutely trustworthy indicator of what is right. One's conscience can be "good" (Acts 23:1; 1 Tim. 1:5, 19) and "clear" (Acts 24:16; 1 Tim. 3:9; 2 Tim. 1:3; Heb. 13:18), but it can also be "guilty" (Heb. 10:22), "corrupted" (Titus 1:15), "weak" (1 Cor. 8:7, 10, 12), and "seared" (1 Tim. 4:2).
> All people need to trust the Lord Jesus Christ so that "the blood of Christ" might "cleanse [their] consciences" (Heb. 9:14). [458]

When Natural theologians interpret the word συνειδήσει as a reference to the pagan Greek concept of a divine faculty resident in "human nature," they are guilty of reading pagan ideas back into Scripture. Scripture should be interpreted while standing on Mt. Zion, not Mt. Olympus.

The Biblical Concept of Regeneration

The final proof that Paul is not saying that the Torah is written in the hearts of all men is that all other references in Scripture to the Law being written in the heart refers to the work of *regeneration*.

> But this is the covenant which I will make with the House of Israel after those days," declares the LORD, "I will put My Torah within them, and on their heart I will write it; and I will be their God, and they shall be My people. (Jer. 31:33)

The members of the New Covenant will all be forgiven of their sins and regenerate. The Reformed Theologian W. G. Shedd comments,

> He is not speaking of that writing of the law in the human heart which is effected in regeneration, alluded to in Jer. Xxxi.33, 34; Heb. X. 16, 17; 2 Cor. Iii.3.[459]

Dr. Warren Wiersbe comments,

> **Regeneration: a new covenant (Jer. 31:31–40)**
> Any plan for the betterment of human society that ignores the sin problem is destined to failure. It isn't enough to change the environment, for the heart of every problem is the problem of the heart. God must change the hearts of people so that they want to love Him and do His will. That's why He announced a New Covenant to replace the Old Covenant under which the Jews had lived since the days of Moses, a covenant that could direct their conduct but not change their character. Jewish history is punctuated with a number of "covenant renewals" that brought temporary blessing but didn't change the hearts of the people. The Book of Deuteronomy records a renewal of the covenant under Moses, before the people entered the Promised Land. In addition, before he died, Joshua led the people in reaffirming the covenant (Josh. 23–24). Samuel called the nation to renew their vows to God (1 Sam. 12), and both Hezekiah (2 Chron. 29–31) and Josiah (2 Chron. 34–35) inspired great days of "revival" as they led the people back to God's Law. The fact that the blessings didn't last is no argument against times of revival and refreshing. When somebody told Billy Sunday that revivals weren't necessary because they didn't last, the

evangelist replied, "A bath doesn't last, but it's good to have one occasionally." A nation that is built on spiritual and moral principles must have frequent times of renewal or the foundations will crumble. But the New Covenant isn't just another renewal of the Old Covenant that God gave at Sinai; it's a covenant that's new in every way. The New Covenant is *inward* so that God's Law is written on the heart and not on stone tablets (2 Cor. 3; Ezek. 11:19–20; 18:31; 36:26–27). The emphasis is *personal* rather than national, with each person putting faith in the Lord and receiving a "new heart" and with it a new disposition toward godliness.[460]

The classic commentators agree.

God's New **Covenant** will involve an internalization of His Law. He **will put** His **Law in their minds** and **on their hearts,** not just on stones (Ex. 34:1). There will be no need to exhort people to **know the LORD because they will** already **all know** God (cf. Isa. 11:9; Hab. 2:14). God's New Covenant will give Israel the inner ability to obey His righteous standards and thus to enjoy His blessings. Ezekiel indicated that this change will result from God's bestowal of the Holy Spirit on these believers (cf. Ezek. 36:24-32). In Old testament times the Holy Spirit did not universally indwell all
believers. Thus one different aspect of the New Covenant is the indwelling of the Holy Spirit in all believers (cf. Joel 2:28-32).[461]

The character of the new covenant: "I (Jahveh) give (will put) my law within them, and write it upon their heart." בְּקִרְבָּם is the opposite of נָתַן לִפְנֵיהֶם, which is constantly used of the Sinaitic law, cf. 9:12, Deut. 4:8; 11:32, 1 Kings 9:6; and the "writing on the heart" is opposed to writing on the tables of stone, Ex. 31:18, cf. 32:15f., 34:8, Deut. 4:13; 9:11; 10:4, etc. The difference, therefore, between the old and the new covenants consists in this, that in the old the law was laid before the people that they might accept it and follow it, receiving it into their hearts, as the copy of what God not merely required of men, but offered and vouchsafed to them for their happiness; while in the new it is put within, implanted into the heart and soul by the Spirit of God, and becomes the animating life-principle, 2 Cor. 3:3.[462]

A covenant written on hearts. The Lord then made an amazing announcement: "The day will come … when I will make a new covenant with the people of Israel and Judah" (31:31). This covenant would be unlike the present Mosaic covenant (31:32), in that God would "write" it on his people's hearts (31:33). It would bring about a new kind of relationship with God and a permanent remission of sin (31:34). [463]

In the Old Testament, whenever God wrote His Torah on someone's heart, this meant he was *regenerated* by a work of the Spirit of God. This is clearly the O.T. precedent. Did Paul ignore this precedent and change the meaning to some kind of vague "natural" law in the hearts of all men? One way to answer this question is to ask if he utilized Jer. 31:31 elsewhere in his writings. Yes, he did. In 2 Cor. 3:3 Paul contrasted the Old and New Covenants is several ways.

> being manifested that you are a letter of Messiah, cared for by us, written not with ink, but with the Spirit of the living God, not on tablets of stone, but on tablets of human hearts.
>
> φανερούμενοι ὅτι ἐστὲ ἐπιστολὴ Χριστου διακονηθεῖσα ὑφ' ἡμῶν, ἐγγεγραμμένη οὐ μέλανι ἀλλὰ πνεύματι θεου ζῶντος, οὐκ ἐν πλαξὶν λιθίναις ἀλλ' ἐν πλαξὶν καρδίαις σαρκίναις.

In a clear paraphrase of Jer. 31:31, Paul clearly interprets God writing on the "tablets of human hearts" as the work of regeneration. Hendriksen explains,

> "Not on tablets of stone but on tablets of human hearts." The first contrast of writing materials is that of ink and Spirit; the second is between stone and human hearts. We Would have expected Paul to indicate the dissimilarity of Paper and hearts, but instead he introduces the word *stone*. He takes the second contrast from the prophecies of Ezekiel (11:19; 36:26), where God removes the people's heart of stone and gives them a new heart of flesh and a new spirit within them.
> Further, through Jeremiah God tells the people of Israel that he will put his law within them and write it on their hearts (31:33). As God had written his law on tablets of stone (Exod. 31:18; 32:15; Deut. 9:10–11) in Old Testament times, so he would write his law on the hearts and minds of his New Testament people. Paul contrasts the Old Testament law, which remained external, with the New Testament law, which functions internally. In effect, Paul intimates that the Old Testament covenant has become obsolete and the New Testament covenant, inaugurated by Jesus and the coming of the Holy Spirit, is now operative (compare Heb. 8:13). [464]

If, as the Natural Law theologians assume, Paul in Rom. 2:15 is saying that all men have a natural law written on their hearts, then to be consistent with Jer. 31:31f, then all men are regenerate, forgiven, and on their way to heaven! Based on these arguments, we must conclude that their attempt to twist Rom. 2:15 into a proof text for Natural Law is erroneous.

The Law of the Mind: Rom. 7:23

Natural theologians also cite Rom. 7:23 as another proof text for Natural Law.

> but I see a different law in the members of my body, waging war against the law of my mind, and making me a prisoner of the law of sin which is in my members.

> βλέπω δὲ ἕτερον νόμον ἐν τοῖς μέλεσίν μου ἀντιστρατευόμενον τῷ νόμῳ τοῦ νοός μου καὶ αἰχμαλωτίζοντά με ἐν τῷ νόμῳ τῆς ἁμαρτίας τῷ ὄντι ἐν τοῖς μέλεσίν μου.

They seize upon the phrase "the law of my mind" and interpret it to mean "the natural law that is discovered in my reason." Jean Porter argued,

> The interpretation of the natural law as reason, or as tantamount to the most fundamental principles of practical reason, is undergirded by even more impressive scriptural support. As we have already noted, this interpretation is supported by appealing to Paul's claim that the nations are given their own law through reason (Rom. 2:12-16) and to his more obscured reference to the law of the mind (identified with reason), which wars with the law of the flesh (identified as human tendencies toward sinfulness, which are innate, given our fallen condition: Rom. 7:23).[465]

Huguccio of Ferrara, the canon lawyer, defended Catholic Natural Law theory by arguing,

> Concerning this natural law, the Apostle says, "I see another law in my members, which opposes the law of the mind," that is to say, the reason, which is called law, just as has been said.[466]

Natural Law theologians are clearly guilty of the well-known Pelagian heresy by their misinterpretation of Rom. 7:14-25.

1. Paul was describing the inner struggles of *unregenerate* natural man.
2. The struggle was between the natural "reason" and the sinful "flesh" of man.
3. Reason is here described as "the law of the mind," i.e. the natural law that is found in the mind of all men innately.
4. Thus Paul is saying that in the heart of all men there is a struggle going on between doing what we all know by reason (nature) is the right thing to do and doing what our lusts tempt us to do.

This heretical interpretation is based upon an *a priori* adoption of Natural Law theory as the framework within which Scripture is to be interpreted. The naturalists go to Plato and other Greek philosophers and use them to interpret this passage. They ignore any Old Testament (i.e. Jewish) background and do not take into account the entire passage, its context and what Paul says elsewhere on the same subject.

First, the change in the tense of the Greek verbs beginning in verse 14 clearly demonstrates that Paul is finished with his conversion story and is now moving on to the *present* struggles he encounters *as a regenerate child of God*.

Second, the word "law" (νόμος) appears six times in this section.

> v. 14 the Law   ὁ νόμος
> v. 16 the Law   τῷ νόμῳ
> v. 22 the Law of God   τῷ νόμῳ τοῦ θεοῦ
> v. 23 a different law   ἕτερον νόμον
> v. 23 the law of my mind   τῷ νόμῳ τοῦ νοός μου
> v. 23 the law of sin   τῷ νόμῳ τῆς ἁμαρτίας

Third, in verse 1, Paul begins by stating,

> I am speaking to those who know the Torah.
> γινώσκουσιν γὰρ νόμον λαλῶ

The word γινώσκουσιν is a present active participle and indicates that their knowledge of Torah was not a dead past event but a present living reality. The word is taken out of its normal word order and placed first to emphasize that they *really* knew Torah.

Fourth, what Torah did these people know in such a dynamic manner? He clearly cites from the Ten Commandments and even uses the word "commandment" (vs. 8f) as a synonym for Torah.

> What shall we say then? Is the Torah sin? May it never be! On the contrary, I would not have come to know sin except through the Torah; for I would not have known about coveting if the Torah had not said, "You shall not covet." (Rom. 7:7).

Paul does not have in mind some nebulous Greek natural law that was found "out there" in "Nature" or "in" the mind (reason) of man. He has in view the written Torah.

Fifth, in verses 14 and 16, the word ὁ νόμος refers to the revealed Torah. What is his attitude toward Torah?

> He viewed it as spiritual (v. 14)
> He agreed with it. (v. 16)
> He viewed it as good (v. 16)
> He wanted to obey its commandments (v. 19)
> He joyfully concurred with it in the inner man (v. 22)

It was the governing principle of his mind (v. 23)

In the next section of the Epistle, Paul states that the unregenerate or natural man hates God and His revealed Torah and cannot submit to it.

> because the mind set on the flesh is hostile toward God; for it does not subject itself to the Torah of God, for it is not even able *to do so*; (Rom. 8:7)
>
> διότι τὸ φρόνημα τῆς σαρκὸς ἔχθρα εἰς θεόν, τῷ γὰρ νόμῳ τοῦ θεοῦ οὐχ ὑποτάσσεται, οὐδὲ γὰρ δύναται·

The "mind of the natural man" (τὸ φρόνημα τῆς σαρκὸς) is hostile (ἔχθρα) toward God (εἰς θεόν) and the revealed Torah of God (νόμῳ τοῦ θεοῦ). That is why the natural man is spiritually *incapable* of submitting to it (οὐδὲ γὰρ δύναται).

The claim of Natural theologians that in Rom. 7:23 Paul was describing the operations of natural law in the reason of all unregenerate men and women is absurd. It would contradict what Paul went on to say in the next section. The natural man does *not* delight in and *concur with* the Law of God.

The "law" in the mind of the Apostle Paul was the *revealed* Torah. That he could not keep it perfectly was his shame. That remaining sin in his heart tempted him to disobey it was his pain. With his mind he delighted in Torah, agreed with its commandments, and wanted to keep them. But, while he was dead to sin in the legal sense of justification (7:1f), sin was not dead to him.

> The conflict here graphically described between a self that "desires" to do good and a self that in spite of this does evil, cannot be the struggles between conscience and passion in the *unregenerate,* because the description given of this "desire to do good" in Rom 7:22 is such as cannot be ascribed, with the least show of truth, to any but the *renewed.*[467]

> Now the apostle states that he delights in God's law according to his "inner being." When he uses such phraseology he is not copying Plato or the Stoics. He is not expressing a contrast between man's rational nature and his lower appetites. With Paul the inner man is the one that is hidden from the public gaze. It indicates *the heart.* It is here that a new principle of life has been implanted by the Holy Spirit. By means of this implantation the sinner has become a *new* man, a person who is being daily transformed into the image of Christ. In this connection study such passages as II Cor. 4:16; Eph. 3:16; Col. 3:9, 10.[468]

In my exposition of the biblical doctrine of regeneration, I concluded my exegesis of Rom. 7 in the following words.

> Paul is speaking of the normal Christian life. This passage is not speaking of the unregenerate or of the backslidden saint. Does not Paul use the present tense through the passage in obvious distinction to the use of the past tense in vs 9–13? Does not v. 22 reveal the heart of the believer? Will not all true believers confess their inability to live a perfect life which is bemoaned in vs. 15, 16–24? Does not the conclusion found v. 25 reveal that Paul is discussing the Christian life? Nowhere in the text do we read that the believer is struggling with two *natures*. All we find is a believer struggling with *sin*. This sin is said to "indwell" him (v. 17). It is said to be present in whatever he does even when he does good (v. 21). But Paul does not lay the sin-problem in the Christian life on the presence of an "old man" but rather he views the Christian himself as the problem. *I* am carnal, sold under sin. For that which *I* do *I* allow not; for what *I* would, that *I* do not; but what *I* hate, that I do (vs. 14, 15). O wretched man *that I am* (not wretched old man in me), who shall deliver *me* from the body of this death (vs. 24)? The end of v. 25 renders any higher life or deeper life interpretation of this passage impossible. It has been rightly said that Romans 7 keeps us from inferring too much from Romans 6. [469]

Once again Natural theologians twist the Scriptures. Their inability or unwillingness to quote it correctly, interpret it in its context, observe the grammar and syntax of the text, deal with the original languages, and interact with the Jewish background and literature make them unreliable guides in spiritual matters.

SECTION THREE

Biblical Evidence against the Natural Law Theory

First, no prophet or apostle ever taught any theory of Natural Law. They never appealed to "Nature" or "natural laws" as the basis of truth and morals.

Second, the prophets and apostles did not know of, believe in, teach or follow Aristotle's "laws" of logic that supposedly were part of the "natural law" written on the hearts of all men, i.e. part of "human nature."

Classical natural logicians claim that Aristotle's natural "laws" of logic are necessary, self-evident, universal, intuitive, self-explanatory, and undeniable.[470] Yet, they have been denied. Even Brooks and Geisler admit, "True, there are other kinds of logic...non-Aristotelian logic." In response, they simply assert that Aristotle's laws "are necessary and undeniable."[471] Just saying something is "necessary" and "undeniable" does not prove that it is. If wishes were horses, beggars would ride!

Third, the fact that stares us in the face is that the Biblical authors *under divine inspiration* violated Aristotle's so-called natural laws of logic.

- Aristotle taught that arguments from silence (*ad ignorantiam*) were invalid. Yet, biblical authors did not accept or follow that "natural law." In Isa. 8:20 and Heb. 7:14, the authors argued from silence.

- Appealing to authority (*ad verecundiam*) is a violation of Aristotle's natural "laws" of logic. Yet, the biblical authors appealed to the authority of God, Scripture, prophets, apostles, and Messiah as the basis of truth and morals (Isa. 7:7; 1 Cor. 15:3-4).

- The historical origin or age of an idea (*ad annis*) is not a valid argument according to Aristotle. Yet, Jude declared that if a doctrine was not part of the apostolic "faith once for all of time delivered unto the saints" (Jude 3), it is a false doctrine.

- Aristotle claimed that appeals to or threats of force (*ad baculum*) are not valid. Yet, the Bible is filled with threats of hell and damnation if you reject its message (Deut. 4:26; Mat. 3:7; Lk. 13:3, 5).

- Appeals to the misery (*ad misericordiam*) of someone are not valid according to the natural "laws" of Aristotle. Yet, 1 John 3:17 and many other passages in Scripture violate this so-called "law" of logic.

We could give many more examples of "illogical" arguments in the Bible. The reason Natural theologians become upset when we point out these things is that they want Christianity to be "rational" in the eyes of unbelievers. But, instead of Christianizing rationality, they have rationalized Christianity!

Chapter Eleven Natural Law

Who Elected Aristotle God?

Why should we let the heathen tell us what is or is not "rational?" Who elected Aristotle God? And why should we worry about "fitting in" with their heathen ideas of rationality? The prophets, apostles and Messiah never claimed to be "rational." Why should we bother? Stop and think for a moment.

- In 1 Cor. 1:18-25, did the apostle Paul deal with the issue of how Jews and Greeks viewed the Gospel?
- From his experience, did Paul say that unbelieving Jews viewed the Gospel as a "stumbling block" that prevented them from becoming followers of Yeshua?
- Did he suggest that we should delete from the Gospel those elements that are "stumbling blocks" to Jews?
- Should we alter our message to fit in with what the Jews tell us is acceptable to them?
- From his experience, when Paul preached the message of the cross to Greek philosophers, did they view the gospel as "rational" or "foolishness?"
- Did he suggest that we should alter the Gospel to avoid the charge of "foolishness," i.e. irrationality?
- Did Paul try to "fit in" with what the Greeks defined as "rational?"
- Did he continue to preach the same message to both Jews and Greeks regardless of why they rejected it?

We are not embarrassed in the least with the "repent or perish" and "turn or burn" message of the Bible because it is *true*. It really doesn't matter to us how many hoops the heathen want us to jump through in order to gain their respect. In the end, the message of the cross *will be* a stumbling block and foolishness to unbelievers because they are wicked and they do not seek God (Rom. 3:10f).

Theist: "Why are so you anxious that the heathen view the Gospel as "rational" instead of "foolishness?" Naturalist: "If I want them to listen to me, I have to be "rational" in their eyes." Theist: "The end does not justify the means!"

Third, the Bible is *exclusive* and not inclusive when it comes to the knowledge of God's laws. Psa. 147:19-20 is a classic example of this truth.

> He declares His words to Jacob, His statutes and His ordinances to Israel. He has not dealt thus with any nation; And as for His ordinances, they have not known them. Praise YHWH!

מַגִּיד [דְּבָרוֹ] [וּדְבָרָיו] לְיַעֲקֹב חֻקָּיו וּמִשְׁפָּטָיו לְיִשְׂרָאֵל׃
לֹא עָשָׂה כֵן לְכָל־גּוֹי וּמִשְׁפָּטִים בַּל־יְדָעוּם הַלְלוּ־יָהּ׃

The Psalmist uses poetic parallelism to emphasize the *exclusive* nature of the Torah revealed to God's covenant people. He first states this in *positive* form and then in *negative* form.

First, he states in the positive that God's "words," "statutes," and "ordinances" were *revealed* to the nation of Israel. The three terms are synonyms in that they all refer to the Torah revealed trough Moses. Torah comes from Revelation and is not derived from "Nature."

Second, but saying this in the positive does not negate the claim of Natural Law theory that the same Torah was "written on the hearts of all men, nations, and cultures." The Psalmist goes on to stress the *exclusive* nature of the Torah by denying that it has been revealed anywhere else to anyone. Princeton's A. J. Alexander in his classic commentary on the Psalms pointed out,

> This revelation to Israel is peculiar and exclusive...The last clause declares the other nations ignorant not only of *his* laws or judgments, but any that deserve the name."[472]

The Puritan David Dickson stated that the Psalmist in this Psalm argues that,

> Where the word of God in his Scriptures is not laid open... the people there live in deadly darkness."[473]

Matthew Henry commented,

> For his distinguishing favor to Israel, in giving them his word and ordinances, a much more valuable blessing than their peace and plenty (v. 14), as much as the soul is more excellent than the body. Jacob and Israel had God's statutes
> and judgments among them. They were under his peculiar government; the municipal laws of their nation were of his framing and enacting, and their constitution was a theocracy.
> They had the benefit of divine revelation; the great things of God's law were written to them. They had a priesthood of divine institution for all things pertaining to God, and prophets for all extraordinary occasions. No people besides them went upon sure grounds in their religion.
> 1.   Now this was a preventing mercy. They did not find out God's statutes and judgments of themselves, but *God showed his word unto Jacob,* and by that word he made known to them his *statutes and judgments.* It is a great mercy to any people to have the word of God among them; for *faith comes by hearing* and reading that word, that faith without which it is impossible to please God. A distinguishing mercy, and upon that account the more obliging: "He hath not dealt so with every nation, not with *any* nation; and, *as for his judgments, they have not known them,* nor

are likely to know them till the Messiah shall come and take down the partition-wall between Jew and Gentile, that the gospel may be preached to every creature.'' Other nations had plenty of outward good things; some nations were very rich, others had pompous powerful princes and polite literature, but none
were blessed with God's statutes and judgments as Israel were. Let *Israel* therefore *praise the Lord* in the observance of these statutes. *Lord, how is it that thou wilt manifest thyself to us, and not to the world! Even so, Father, because it seemed good in thy eyes.*[474]

Conclusion

The Stoic theories of "Nature," "human nature," "reason," "conscience," and "Natural Law" have been weighed in the balance of Scripture and have been found wanting. They are *anti*-biblical as well as *un*-biblical. Therefore, they are *heretical* in nature and are based upon Pelagian and pagan views of God, man, and the world.

It is also increasingly clear that all the various Natural Law theories are not "rational" in any sense of the word. They cannot agree on any common definitions among themselves. There are as many definitions of "nature" as theorists.

So many conflicting theories fly under the banner of "Natural Law" that the entire enterprise is of little social worth. For example, one natural law theorist approves sodomy and the next condemns it. One theory condemns the use of contraception and another approves it. Chaos thus reigns in Natural Law circles.

Arbitrary natural law always leads to tyranny, not freedom. We are embarrassed by the irrational attempts by Natural Law theorists to make the Gospel rational and palatable to the heathen. Their failed attempts have the opposite effect, making Christianity a mockery to the contemporary, thinking irreligious.

We cannot accept the vaunted claims of Natural Law theorists that man, not God, is the Origin of truth, justice, morals, meaning, and beauty; that man, not God, is the "measure of all things." Only when sinners give up their vain attempt to find meaning *without* God will they find meaning *in* God.

To God alone be all the glory!

Chapter Twelve

Natural Religion

Introduction

"Natural Religion" is based upon "Natural Law." If "Nature as nature" or "nature as reason" can give us truth and morals apart from and independent of God and the Bible to create a society with just laws, then why can't we also derive from them religious truth to create one true religion apart from and independent of God and the Bible? If human reason is sufficient for the one, surely it is sufficient for the other. A "Natural" religion is thus supposedly derived from either objective Nature "out there" or subjective human nature (i.e. reason, feelings or faith) "in here." Either way, it is religion-without-God.

The First Problem

In the history of the world, no "natural religion" ever discovered or developed a concept of or theory of "Natural Religion." If the theory of "Natural Religion" is self-evident, universal, and intuitive, why didn't some natural religion ever discover it? The reason is quite simple. "Natural Religion" is a unique Catholic theory developed by Medieval Natural Theology. It is based upon Catholic concepts, without which it is incomprehensible. It is thus a relative Western European concept reflective of Europe's Catholic cultural consensus.

The Second Problem

The second problem that confronts us is that there are no agreed upon common definitions for the key words in "Natural Religion." Even the *New Catholic Encyclopedia* admits that "the vagueness and ambiguity of terms such as "nature" and "natural" make it difficult to define."[475]

If you thought trying to construct a common definition for the words "nature," "natural," and "reason" was hopeless, just try to construct a common definition for the word "religion" that is agreeable to everyone. It is easier to nail Jell-O to the wall than to define the word "religion!"

The Word "Religion"

The word "religion" has such a convoluted and torturous history that modern secular philosophers have thrown up their hands in despair and abandoned all hope of crafting a common definition agreeable to all. Several examples will help us to see the difficulties at hand.

Religion: Belief in God?

Does the word "religion" imply or require belief in one or more deities? No. Pantheism, Northern Buddhism, and the "mind science" cults do not believe in any gods whatsoever, yet, we all call them "religions."

Religion: Belief in the Supernatural?

Does the word "religion" imply belief in the supernatural, miracles, revelations, absolutes, universals, angels, demons, heaven, hell, etc.? No. Atheism is a religion. So is Marxism. Even the *Humanist Manifesto I* states that humanism is a religion! The word "religion" evidently can mean anything and everything and thus it means *nothing* to modern secularists. For our purposes the word "religion" refers to any belief system or worldview that tells people what to believe and how to live.

Natural Religion: a Myth

There is no monolithic theory of "Natural Religion" out there somewhere roaming around but there are many different *conflicting* theories that go by that name with each natural theologian defining it according to his or her own personal tastes and prejudices.

The Main Flaw

This is the main flaw in the present flood of books defending "Natural Religion." They will refer to "Natural Religion" as if "it" were a unified field of knowledge with concrete ideas. They assume we know what they are talking about. Thus they avoid any discussion of how to define the word "religion."

Common Nonsense Philosophy

Some natural theologians claim to believe in Scottish "Common Sense" philosophy. They claim to have absolute faith that the common man in the street has a better grasp on reality (i.e. "sense") than those who live in the ivory towers of academia. Yet, they never defer to the "common man" for his definition of the word "religion."

Countless surveys have been taken of how "common" people understand the word "religion." Without fail, they always define it as belief in God, miracles, angels or some organized religion such Christianity or Islam. When asked if atheism is a religion, they almost always say, "No."

Why don't those who believe in "Common Sense" adopt the "common sense" definition of "religion" held by the common man? Because they know it is pure nonsense! UFO's, reincarnation, astrology, Big Foot, etc, also make "sense" to modern common man! Do you feel comfortable with putting "God" in the same list of "common sense" beliefs as little gray aliens from outer space?

A Common Error

Most natural theologians gratuitously believe that "Natural Theology" and "Natural Religion" are synonyms for each other, but they are different in several crucial respects and should not be confused.

First, Natural Religion and Natural Theology differ in terms of *contact with biblical ideas*. "Natural Religions" developed in *total* isolation from *any* exposure to *biblical* ideas. No Jew or Christian ever stepped ashore on that land. No Jewish or Christian businessman or missionary ever visited that land. For example, North, Central, and South America, parts of southern Africa and Asia, Australia, and other geographically isolated lands were never penetrated with Middle Eastern biblical ideas or literature until modern times. In contrast, "Natural Theologies" developed through interaction with biblical ideas.

Second, they differ in terms of *timeframe*. "Natural Religions" were possible only as long as the isolation of the religion lasted. Once a "Natural Religion" came into contact with biblical ideas, it adopted some of those ideas and became a natural theology. For example, Hinduism absorbed and adapted to biblical ideas after contact with Christian missionaries.[476]

Given the modern technology of mass publishing and distribution of religious literature, hundreds of thousands of missionaries going around the world, religious radio and TV religious programs beamed by satellite throughout the world, no religion today can develop in total isolation from biblical ideas. Thus the study of "Natural Religion" is the study of *ancient* cultures that were geographically isolated from Middle Eastern ideas.

Third, they differ in terms of *starting points*. A "Natural Religion" begins at ground zero without any biblical concepts of God, creation, man, the universe, history, progress, law, sin, salvation, miracles, resurrection, science, theology, atonement, scripture, revelation, linear history, end of history, heaven, hell, logic, proof, evidence, cause and effect, etc. A Natural Theology begins with biblical and Western ideas. For example, it asks, "What evidence is there that the "God" of the Bible exists?"

Fourthly, they differ in *context*. The context of a Natural Religion was Gentile by race and pagan by faith. The context of a Natural Theology is Western European, Judeo-Christian culture.

Lastly, Natural theologians cannot develop a "Natural Religion" because they are so saturated with biblical ideas that it is impossible to root all of them out of their thinking. Those biblical ideas color the way they look at the world by projecting and imposing a grid of meaning upon human experience.

The Design Argument

In order to see how biblical ideas have influenced the way Western people look at the world, two examples will now be given. The first example is the biblical idea of "design." The Bible teaches that an orderly God created an orderly world in which everything has a purpose and meaning.

YHWH has made everything for its own purpose...
(Prov. 16:4)

כֹּל פָּעַל יְהוָה לַמַּעֲנֵהוּ

The classic commentaries point out that the text clearly states that everything has meaning because everything was *designed* by God for a specific purpose.

Jehovah hath made everything for its end.
The noun מַעֲנֶה here signifies, not "answer," as in ver. 1, or in 15:1, 23; but in general that which corresponds with the thing, the *end* of the thing. The suffix refers back to the "all, all things." The Vulgate renders "*propter semet ipsum*," but this would have לְמַעֲנוֹ. [See critical notes. BERTHEAU, KAMPH., DE W., N., S., M., *etc.*, agree with our author in the interpretation which is grammatically most defensible, and doctrinally least open to exception. An absolute Divine purpose and control in the creation and administration of the world is clearly announced, and also the strength of the bond that joins sin and misery [477]

Everywhere else מַעֲנֶה means answer (*Venet.* προς πόκρισιν ατο), which is not suitable here, especially with the absoluteness of the כֹּל; the Syr. and Targ. translate, *obedientibus ei*, which the words do not warrant; but also *propter semet ipsum* (Jerome, Theodotion, Luther) give to 4b no right parallelism, and, besides, would demand לְמַעֲנוֹ or לְמַעֲנֵהוּ. The punctuation לַמַּעֲנֵהוּ, which is an anomaly (cf. כַּגְּבִרְתָּהּ, Isa. 24:2, and בְּעָרֵינוּ, Ezra 10:14), shows (Ewald) that here we have, not the prepositional לְמַעַן, but ל with the subst. מַעֲנֶה, which in derivation and meaning is one with the form מַעַז abbreviated from it (cf. מַעַל, מַעַר), similar in meaning to the Arab. *ma'anyn*, aim, intention, object, and end, and mind, from *'atay*, to place opposite to oneself a matter, to make it the object of effort. Hitzig prefers לְמַעֲנֶה, but why not rather לְמַעֲנֵהוּ, for the proverb is not intended to express that all that God has made serve a purpose (by which one is reminded of the arguments for the existence of God from final causes, which are often prosecuted too far), but that all is made by God for its purpose, i.e., a purpose premeditated by Him, that the world of things and of events stands under the law of a plan, which has in God its ground and its end, and that also the wickedness of free agents is comprehended in this plan, and made subordinate to it.[478]

The Lord hath made all things for himself. So the Vulgate, *propter semetipsum*; and Origen ('Præf. in Job'), δι'ἑαυτόν. That is, God hath made everything for his own purpose, to answer the design which he hath intended from all eternity (Rev. 4:11). But this translation is not in accordance with the present reading, לְמַעֲנֵהוּ, which means rather "for its own end," for its own proper use. Everything in God's design has its own end and object and reason for being where it is and such as it is; everything exhibits his goodness and wisdom, and tends to his glory. Septuagint, "All the works of the Lord are with righteousness."[479]

This biblical concept led to the Western idea that *everything is part of a great and grand design*. Nothing is meaningless because nothing is purposeless. There are no accidents or random events. Nothing is the result of blind luck. Chaos and confusion are not real. There is a reason why things happen. All things can be understood and explained.

What does this mean? Because Western man believed that everything was designed with a purpose in mind, they looked in "nature" for these "designs." They assumed what they what they going to find *before* they found it.

The West Was Right

From a biblical point of view, Western man was right to use the biblical idea of design and on that basis to invent modern science! Science developed in the West because of the influence of biblical ideas. Even Alfred Whitehead admitted this.

The Heathen Were Wrong

In contrast, Asian, American, and African "natural religions" did not begin with the biblical concept of design. They saw meaningless cycles of chaos and chance all around them. Thus they never looked for or found any "designs" in "nature."

While this does not negate the wonderful advances in technology that developed in ancient pagan cultures such as China or Egypt, this does reveal why these advances did not lead to a unified concept of science. The biblical idea of Creation was missing from these ancient mythologies and this prevented any coherence.

The Fundamental Error of Paley

This is the fundamental error of Paley's arguments for Natural Theology. When a Western man finds a watch on the ground, his mind has already been influenced by the biblical idea of design. He picks up the watch and asks, "Who made this? Where did it come from? What is its meaning and purpose?" He does this because he already assumed that things do not just happen. The watch *must* have an explanation for existing because it is a part of a grand *design*. It has a *meaning* that he can discover.

Someone from an ancient natural religion that never had any biblical idea of design would not ask those questions. He would simply pick up the watch and stick it in his hair as an ornament. It would never cross his mind to ask who made it or what was its meaning or purpose.

Modern Atheism: a Christian Heresy

Western Atheism is a Christian heresy because it could not exist apart from and independent of God and the Bible. An atheist must first *assume* what he wants to deny in order to deny it.[480] Without God and the Bible, he can neither deny nor affirm anything. For example, atheists dismiss miracles on the grounds that, since everything can be understood and explained, there *must* a good explanation for all so-called miracles.

> Theist: "What about the miracle of Jesus walking on the water?"
> Atheist: "Everything is understandable and explainable. Thus a miracle is simply something that science has yet to explain. I have a good explanation for the "miracle" you mentioned. Either it did not happen or he was walking on a sand bar and the water was only up to his ankles. Thus it only *looked like* he was walking on water."
> Theist: "On what grounds do you assume that everything, including miracles, can be understood and explained by man?"
> Atheist: "Everything is explainable because there is a reason for everything."
> Theist: "But that is an idea that came from the Bible! Without the Bible, there is no reason to believe that the universe is understandable and explainable."

Modern atheism collapses if you exorcize from it all biblical ideas. Several more examples will illustrate what we are saying.

History, Progress, and the End of the World

The biblical view of "history" is that it had a "beginning," it is "progressing" positively toward a predetermined "end," and will reach a climax at the end of time.[481] The idea that history is going somewhere is *biblical* thinking.

In this light, it is clear that such Western theories as evolutionism and Marxism are Christian heresies because they are both based upon the biblical idea that "history" is moving ever upward and onward, i.e. there is a positive *progress* in history.

Evolution is moving ever upward and onward and thus animals are getting *better* with each new generation. Hegel, Darwin, Marx, and Lenin built their philosophies on the biblical idea that history is progressing toward a good end.

Again, if you removed the biblical concept of "progress" from Hegel's philosophy, it would collapse. The biblical concept of progress is what drives the dialectic from thesis to antithesis to synthesis.

If you removed the biblical idea of progress from "Star Trek," its optimistic utopian future of humanity would collapse. This is even why Western fairy tales end with the words, "and they lived happily ever after." At the "end" of history, the wicked will be punished and the righteous vindicated. The good will triumphed over the evil. Justice will finally have its day. Thus good people will live happily ever after.

In contrast, ancient "natural religions" did not have an optimistic view of "history" in which we are moving toward a better world. They had no concept of "history" and hence did not think that "it" was going somewhere. Things are not progressing toward a better world but going around and around in ceaseless meaningless cycles. Justice will not have its day, and evil often triumphs over good, and *that is just the way it is*.

The Fundamental Error of Aquinas

From these examples, we can see the foundational error of Aquinas' Five Proofs for the existence of God. His arguments begin and end with key biblical concepts without which the arguments cannot function. They used to "make sense" to Western man because he had been conditioned to think that way by two thousand years of Christian influence, but they don't work anymore.

Why His Arguments Don't Work Anymore

Modern Natural theologians are often mystified why their "rational" arguments produce so few converts. In a post-modern world, where crucial biblical concepts have been stripped from the conscious mind of modern man, the old arguments of Aquinas have become meaningless. They have gone the way of Aristotle's geocentric universe. This is why Natural theologians spend 99.9% of their time "preaching to the choir," i.e. speaking to *Christian* audiences. They shore up the faith of Christian people by giving them arguments based on what they *already* believe.

Natural Religion: Common Definitions

The definitions of "Natural Religion" found in dictionaries and encyclopedia are inadequate at best. *Webster New International Dictionary* defined it as,

> a religion validated on the basis of human reason and experience apart from miraculous or supernatural revelation.[482]

Chadbourne defines it:

> Natural religion, as generally defined, is what can be learned of God and of relations to Him without the Bible.[483]

Such vague definitions confuse Natural Theology with Natural Religion. We offer the following definition of what the phrase "Natural Religion" means in most Western discussions: *In those pagan cultures, totally isolated from any contact with Jews, Christians, the Bible or any of its ideas, thinking (i.e. "rational") men and women, were able, solely through their observation of and reflection on Nature or on their own reason, to discover true religious concepts, about God, the world, and man, that were self-evident, intuitive, and universal.*

We admit that most defenders of the idea of "Natural Religion" do not state this definition. But, it seems to us, to be what they are assuming as their working definition.

The Judgment of History

The various theories of Natural Religion are one thing and whether they actually *worked* in the real world is another. After an extended study of "natural religions," Jonathan Edwards, perhaps the greatest intellect America ever produced, concluded,

> He that thinks to prove that the world ever did, in fact, by wisdom know God, that any nation upon earth or any set of men, ever did, *from the principles of reason only without assistance from revelation, find out the true nature and true worship of the deity*, must find out some history of the world entirely different from all the accounts which the present sacred and profane writers do give to us, or his opinion must appear to be a mere guess and conjecture of what is barley possible, but what all history assures us never was really done in the world.[484]

In order to see if Natural Religions ever discovered any biblical ideas apart from the Bible, in the "Bellflower Lectures" (www.faithdefenders.com) we examined in great detail the pre-Christian religions of North, Central, and South America, sub-Sahara Africa, and Asia because they developed their religions apart from and independent of any contact with Biblical people or ideas. The only resources these pre-Christian pagans had:

- Nature-nature, i.e. the world around them.
- Nature-reason, i.e. their reason, experience, feelings, conscience, and faith.

What did we find? The religions that developed in *total* isolation from biblical religion, people, and ideas were, *without exception*, wicked, vile, degraded, violent, idolatrous, and perverted. The human sacrifices and cannibalism of Native American religions is so well-documented by the mass graves of their victims that they can no longer be denied..

The "natural religions" of Southern Africa and Asia were just as evil as the Mayan and Aztec were blood thirsty. Archeologists and anthropologists have destroyed the romantic and idealistic Renascence myths of the "noble savage." He never existed except in Jean-Jacques Rousseau's world of fantasy. This is why Natural theologians never document the "glories" of pagan religions and keep definitions and history as vague as possible.

Nature Worship

We must also point out that "Natural Religions" often ended in Nature worship.[485] Once you believe that "Nature" is teaching you and guiding you, it takes on *intelligence* and *will*, i.e. it becomes a god or goddess. "Mother Nature" is called "mother" for a reason. Chadbourne's romantic language about "Nature" borders on idolatry.

> We reverently enter the temple of nature, that we may there read the character of the builder. Its walls, we believe, were not piled by chance; its cunning adjustments are not the sporting of the elements. [486]

Did any "natural" religion in the history of the world ever discover even *one* biblical concept? No. We challenge anyone to find biblical monotheism, creation *ex nihilo*, the unity and dignity of man based upon Creation, the radical Fall of man into sin, vicarious atonement, salvation by grace alone, a day of judgment at the end of history, the resurrection of the body, etc. in pagan religions that had absolutely no contact with biblical ideas.[487]

Roman Catholic Missionaries

On one hand, we are thankful for the Catholic missionaries who carefully documented the *horrors* of the "natural religions" they encountered in a "first contact" context. But, on the other hand, the Catholic theologians that followed them blended these pagan religions with Catholicism and produced Catholic/pagan hybrids. For example, the local Aztec gods and goddesses were renamed to honor the saints and Mary. Pagan feasts became Catholic festivals. Various modern popes have acknowledged this historical reality.

Catholic Natural theologians absorbed the local paganism and then regurgitated it as cultural Catholicism. This is why they were always more successful in gaining converts than Evangelical missionaries who called for complete separation from and repudiation of all pagan ideas, gods, ceremonies, and festivals. While the Catholics absorbed paganism, the Protestants renounced it.

In this light, it should not be surprising that Catholicism teaches that the heathen are able to discover enough truth from "nature" to be saved without ever hearing of or believing in Jesus Christ and His Gospel. A working definition of the Roman Catholic doctrine would be as follows: *In those pagan cultures, totally isolated from any contact with Jews, Christians, the Bible or any of its ideas, thinking (i.e. "rational") men and women, were able, solely through their observation of and reflection on Nature or on their own reason, to discover true religious concepts, about God, the world, and man, that were self-evident, intuitive, and universal, unto salvation without hearing of or believing in Jesus Christ and His gospel.*

The Catholic Church calls this concept the "doctrine of invincible ignorance." As already noted, the Catechism of the Catholic Church defines it as follows:

> Those who, through no fault of their own, do not know the Gospel of Christ or his Church, but who nevertheless seek God with a sincere heart, and, moved by grace, try their actions to do his will as

they know it through the dictates of their conscience, those too many achieve eternal salvation.[488]

The Catechism specially applies its doctrine to the Muslims.

The Church's relationship with the Muslims. the plan of salvation also includes those who acknowledge the Creator, In the first place amongst whom are the Muslims; these profess to hold the faith of Abraham, and together with us they adore the one, merciful God, mankind's judge on the last day. [489]

It also applies this doctrine to the Jews as well as the Muslims.[490] Thus salvation is possible not only for those who *never heard* the Gospel but also to those *who reject* it. The Jews crucified Jesus because they rejected His deity, miracles, teachings, atonement, resurrection, ascension, session, and return. The Muslims also knowingly deny the deity and atonement of Jesus and the Holy Trinity. Yet, they too can go to heaven according to the Catechism despite their rejection of Christ and His gospel.

Protestant Liberalism

During the 1920's, most mainline Protestants adopted the Catholic doctrine as part of their liberalism. This doctrine was renamed "inclusivism" as opposed to "exclusivism." They defined the doctrine as: *In those pagan cultures, totally isolated from any contact with Jews, Christians, the Bible or any of its ideas, thinking (i.e. "rational") men and women, were able, solely through their observation of and reflection on Nature or on their own reason, to discover true religious concepts, about God, the world, and man, that were self-evident, intuitive, and universal, unto salvation without hearing of or believing in Jesus Christ and His gospel.*

Historic Evangelical Theology

Historically, Evangelical theologians believe that the heathen could *not discover* enough truth to be saved. The heathen must hear of and believe in Jesus Christ and His Gospel to be saved.[491] Their working definition is as follows: *In those pagan cultures, totally isolated from any contact with Jews, Christians, the Bible or any of its ideas, thinking (i.e. "rational") men and women, were not able, solely through their observation of and reflection on Nature or on their own reason, to discover true religious concepts, about God, the world, and man unto salvation, without hearing of and believing in Jesus Christ and His Gospel salvation is not possible.*

The Present Shift

With the collapse of the Evangelical commitment to the inerrancy and authority of Scripture during the 1980s, the theological current began to move toward the Catholic view of the heathen.

Neo-Protestants (using Carl Henry's term) such as Robert Schuler, Clark Pinnock, John Sanders, etc. have called it "The wideness of God's mercy" view. [492]

Protestant Apostates

Those Protestants who converted to Romanism became quite vocal about the salvation of the heathen. One example would be Peter Kreeft, who was raised in an Evangelical home but later renounced the gospel and joined the Catholic Church. He became a professor at Boston (Catholic) College.

Despite the fact that he was an apostate Protestant, InterVarsity Press published some of his books. InterVarsity Press was at one time was a Protestant evangelical publisher, but now publishes many Catholic authors.

Ronald Tacelli, a fellow professor at Boston College, joined with Kreeft and together they wrote *Handbook of Christian Apologetics*.[493] It was published by IVP and was widely used as a textbook in "Evangelical" colleges, universities, and seminaries such as BIOLA that had abandoned their Protestant heritage.

Kreeft wrote several other books including *Ecumenical Jihad*, published by St. Ignatius Press.[494] This book is significant because, together with his *Handbook*, they give us a modern presentation of the Catholic position on the fate of the heathen.

Ecumenical Jihad

Kreeft states, an "explicit knowledge of the incarnate Jesus is not necessary for salvation." [495] In his book, *Ecumenical Jihad*, he states that he had an out-of-body experience, during which he saw Muhammad, Buddha, Confucius, and other pagans in heaven worshipping at the feet of Mary. She (not Jesus) is the unifying force in heaven. In another books he pictured Socrates and other pagan philosophers worshipping at the feet of Mary in heaven.

What about the Reformers such as Calvin, Luther, *etc*? Kreeft did *not* see them in heaven. He leaves his readers with the distinct impression that they are roasting in hell. So much for ecumenical love fests!

How does he *prove* that it is *not* necessary to hear of or believe in Jesus to be saved? He argued, "Abraham, Moses, and Elijah, for instance, had no such knowledge, yet they were saved."[496]

Since this is a standard argument used by many Natural theologians to prove (sic) that Natural Religion is sufficient for salvation, we will stop and examine it.

First, the issue in focus is the eternal fate of those who NEVER had *any* special revelation. We have in focus those who only had Nature-nature or nature-reason. Thus to bring up people in Old Testament times who *had* special revelation is a *false analogy*. Abraham, Moses and Elijah were saved because they believed the special revelation given to them in their day.

Second, it is also logically invalid to being up people who existed *before* the birth of Jesus as if biblical theists argue that people who lived *before* Jesus of Nazareth was born had to believe in

Him. Thus Kreeft created a "straw man argument" that he could knock down with ease. Kreeft goes on to argue,

> Socrates (or any other pagan) could seek God, could repent of his sins, and could obscurely believe in and accept the God he knew partially and obscurely, and therefore he could be saved.[497]

His statement is a flat contradiction of Scripture. Socrates (or any other pagan) never knew God (1 Cor. 1:21) because he never sought God (Rom. 3:10-21).

The Biblical View

Biblical theists have always followed the teaching of the Bible concerning the eternal destiny of the heathen. The biblical doctrine is as follows: *In those pagan cultures, totally isolated from any contact with Jews, Christians, the Bible and any of its ideas, no one was able, solely through his observation of and reflection on Nature or on their own reason, to discover any true religious concepts of God, the world, man, sin, and salvation. Without hearing of and believing in Jesus Christ and His Gospel, no salvation is possible.*

The biblical view has always been the historic Evangelical doctrine of "the lost condition of the heathen." It is the basis of the Mission Mandate (Matt. 28:19-20) and the necessity and urgency of preaching the Gospel to all nations (Lk. 14:23).

Historically, the lost condition of the heathen was the motivation behind the great missionary movements in the eighteenth, nineteenth, and twentieth centuries. Great missionary leaders such as William Carey, Adonanium Judson, Amy Carmichael, Hudson Taylor, and David Livingston all believed that the heathen needed to hear the Gospel in order to be saved. Hundreds of millions of "third-world" Christians worship at the feet of Jesus today due to the doctrine of the lost condition of the heathen.

In sharp contrast, the doctrine that the heathen do not need to hear of and believe in the Gospel message to be saved has damned hundreds of millions to an eternity in hell. The liberal view, popularized by Pearl S. Buck and others destroyed missions in the early 1920's. If the heathen are saved through their own "Natural Religion," why bother preaching to them? They are going to heaven anyway.

The Catholic/liberal view denies the necessity for evangelism and missions. It was sown in compromise, fertilized by contextualization, and has produced the bitter fruit of damnation. Nothing good ever came of it and nothing good will ever come of it.

The Bible and Natural Religion

What is the *biblical* view of the religions developed by the Gentiles and what will be the eternal destiny of those who never heard the Gospel? We recognize that there will be many Natural theologians and philosophers who really don't care what the Bible teaches. But their condemnation is just, and they will learn by their own painful experience what it means to fall into the hands of an angry God!

The Context of the Question

The subject of the heathen usually arises in the context of witnessing. The unbeliever attempts to escape the Gospel call to repentance and faith by hurling what he thinks is an unanswerable objection to Christianity: "But what about the heathen? Are you telling me that all those innocent people are going to hell? Even when they didn't have a chance?"

Evidently, to many non-Christians the damnation of the heathen serves as a challenge to Christianity as well as an escape hatch from the claims of the Gospel. The unbeliever is hoping that you will agree with him that he can make it to heaven *without* believing in Jesus. If so, then there is *no* necessity or urgency for him to repent of his sins and accept the Lordship of Christ.

Stop and think for a moment about the unbeliever and his desperate need of salvation. When Natural theologians agree with him that it is *not* necessary to believe in Jesus to go to heaven, they confirm him in his unbelief and, on the Day of judgment, the blood of his damnation will be on their hands (Acts 20:26 cf. Ezk. 3:18-19).

The Coils of Liberalism

The Liberal takeover of the major denominations flooded colleges and seminaries with the teaching of universalism. Hell was only an empty threat. God is too loving and man is too good for hell to exist. Since I have dealt with universalism in another book, [498] I will not go into the heresy of universalism any further.

Some neo-evangelicals are now propagating the heresy of semi-universalism in which any sincere heathen who "lives up to the light he has" will be saved. They argue that God is too loving to damn those who "never had a chance." For example, the so-called "Open View of God" heresy does not teach the lost condition of the heathen. Neither do they usually believe in the eternal conscious torment of the damned in hell. Most of them choose annihilation as the fate of the few unbelievers who will be condemned on the Day of Judgment. [499]

PART ONE

Asking the Right Questions

In theology, it is very important that you ask the right questions. If you fail to ask the right questions, you will not get the right answers. The key with the heathen issue is to frame the question in such a way as to force Natural theologians *to go to the Bible* for the answer. They will try to avoid this at all costs and instead frame the question in terms of what feels "rational" to them. But, ask them the following questions:

- Does the Bible teach that saving faith involves *knowledge* of certain propositional statements given in Scripture, *intellectual assent* to those propositions, and *personal commitment* to Christ?
- Is there a body of doctrines that must known and believed in order to the saved according to the Bible?

- According to the Bible, is faith in Jesus Christ always part of the salvation process or can someone skip over faith and repentance and still experience salvation?
- Is justification *by* faith or *without* faith according to the Bible?
- Can a sinner be saved from hell according to the Bible even when he consciously *rejects* Jesus Christ?
- On what grounds can a sinner claim admittance to heaven according to Scripture?
- Does the Bible say that the Gentiles dwell in darkness or light?
- Is there any other name under heaven by which we can be saved?
- Does the Bible teach that is it necessary to hear of and believe in Jesus Christ and His Gospel to be saved from hell and go to heaven at death?

As we have already demonstrated in our chapter on the Book of Job, the Bible describes the Gentiles as living in "pitch black darkness."[500] While Natural theologians assume that the Gentiles have the light of Natural Law to guide them, the Bible says they have no light.

The Same Old Tired Arguments

Those who "feel" that it is only "rational" to believe that the heathen can be saved apart from and independent of the Gospel have a few stock arguments that they repeat over and over again.

1. If a sinner is sincere in whatever religion he believes in and he lives up to the light he has, it would be unjust for God to condemn him to hell.

2. If a sinner never heard the Gospel, this means that he never had a chance to be saved. Therefore it would be unjust for God to condemn someone who never had a chance.

3. We are condemned if and when we reject Jesus Christ and His Gospel. It is obvious that those who have never heard of the Gospel cannot be condemned for rejecting it! Therefore it would be unjust for God to condemn the heathen.

Categories of Unbelief

The issue can be further clarified by observing that all unbelievers without exception can be placed into one of the following categories which describe the circumstances of their unbelief.

1. *Ignorance*: The geographic area in which the unbelievers live is so remote that the Gospel message has never penetrated it. The unbelievers have absolutely no opportunity to hear the Gospel even if they wanted to do so.

2. *Neglect*: The Gospel has penetrated the area and is present and available, but some unbelievers neglect to hear or study it. Thus they are still ignorant of the Gospel and are not saved due to their neglect.

3. *Nominal acquaintance*: The Gospel is vaguely understood but there is no true saving belief in it.

4. *Conscious rejection*: The unbeliever denies or rejects the Gospel and clings to his own pagan ideas and religion.

5. *Nominal acceptance*: The unbeliever professes to accept the Gospel and to

believe in Jesus Christ but this profession is false. This is where 90% of professing Christendom must be placed.

Now, the question of the heathen concerns only the first case where sinners are ignorant of the Gospel because there is absolutely no opportunity to hear it. The Scriptures are very clear that if we neglect, deny or only nominally accept the Gospel, we cannot be saved "for how shall we escape if we neglect so great salvation" (Heb. 2:3)?

Who Qualifies as a Heathen?

Another point that should be made is that the proper definition of "heathen" is *any and every unbeliever*. We must not allow people to assume that the word "heathen" refers only to the primitive peoples of the Third World. The secular unbelievers who live in New York City or London are just as "heathen" just as much as a Hindu or an Australian bushman.

A Biblical Response

One way to bring this truth home to the unbeliever who challenges the Gospel with the heathen question is to respond in the following manner: Unbeliever: "But, what about the heathen?" Theist: "Well, what about *you*? You will not be saved unless *you* believe in Christ." Unbeliever: "I don't mean *me*. I am referring to the heathen, i.e., those who never heard the gospel." Theist: "Why should *they* concern you? The issue is that *you* are one heathen who has heard the Gospel. Now what are *you* going to do about it? Are you trying to avoid the issue of your sin by bringing up an irrelevant question? The real question is, "What about *your* eternal fate?"

The basic and foundational issue in the heathen question is whether or not the Scriptures view ignorance due to neglect or to the absence of the Gospel as constituting sufficient grounds for salvation, and whether or not the lack of faith constitutes unbelief as well as the rejection of faith.

PART TWO

Principles of Approach

With these introductory remarks in mind, let us begin our study of this subject by setting forth several opening principles which shall guide us in our study.

Principle I: *The Scriptures alone can tell us of the eternal destiny of all those who do not believe in the person and work of Christ as presented in the Biblical Gospel.* We must strive to bring every thought into conformity to the Holy Scriptures. Our faith must be Biblical from beginning to end.

Principle II: *We must be careful to avoid the four typical humanistic approaches to this issue.*

1. The Natural theologian who is a *rationalist* thinks that his reason or logic can tell him where the heathen go at death. He usually begins his position by saying, "I think that...." "It is only logical that...." "The only intelligent answer is...."

2. The Natural theologian who is an *empiricist* thinks that stories and testimonies which relate human experience will decide the issue. They usually will tell some groundless story which is incapable of verification about some heathen somewhere who supposedly worshipped the true God without actually knowing who or what He really was or who had angels or Jesus appear to him in dreams or visions. They usually begin their position by saying, "Have you heard the story about...."

3. The Natural theologian who is a *mystic* will trust his subjective emotions or feelings to tell him the truth. They usually begin their position by saying, "I feel that...." "My heart tells

me..."

4. The Natural theologian who is a *fideist* will trust the creeds and confessions of his faith such at the New Catholic Catechism. They usally begin their position by saying, "I believe..." "My faith says that.." "The Creed says..."

Principle III: *Defend God at all costs.*

Whatever God does is right and just. "Shall not the Judge of all the earth do right?" (Gen. 18:25). God is not unjust or unloving because He casts the wicked into hell. He is sovereign in His wrath as well as in His grace. Some people defend man at all costs even to the degradation of God. "But let God be true and every man a liar" (Rom. 3:4).

Principle IV: *Never tone down a Biblical doctrine because it offends people.*

The Gospel itself is offensive to unbelievers. Should we abandon it because the unregenerate think it foolish? The disciples came to the Lord Jesus and told Him that He had offended the Pharisees. His reaction shows us the proper attitude when the truth offends people.

> Then his disciples came, and said to Him, "Don't you know that the Pharisees were offended, after they heard this saying?" But He answered and said, "Every plant, which my heavenly Father has not planted, shall be rooted up. Let them alone: they are blind guides of the blind. And if the blind guide the blind, both shall fall into the ditch." (Matt. 15:12–14)

Jesus did not beg the Pharisees to forgive Him because He offended them. He goes on to offend them even more by calling them "blind guides."

Principle V: *Take one step at a time.*

There are many issues involved in the heathen question and each one has to be answered before you can come to a final conclusion.

Principle VI: *Determine in your spirit to believe whatever God says in His Word.*

We must be careful that we approach the heathen issue with an open mind and a humble heart in utter submission to the authority of Scripture.

PART THREE

With these opening principles given, we will now set forth the central propositions of the biblical position.

Proposition I: *All men are sinners and in need of salvation.*

This first proposition is so basic to the Christian Gospel that it is damnable heresy to deny it. Carefully read Romans 1–3, for you will find in this passage a full exposition of the just condemnation of God which rests universally upon all men "for all have sinned" and "the wages of sin is death" (Rom. 3:23; 6:23).

Proposition II: *General Revelation is not sufficient for salvation.*

Universal Witness, (i.e. "general revelation"), is God's immediate non-verbal self-revelation in the Creation and in the hearts of some heathen (Rom. 1:18–28; 2:14–15). While it is sufficient to condemn the heathen because it leaves them "without excuse" (Rom. 1:20), the Scriptures never speak of it as being sufficient to save them.

It must be further pointed out that the Bible teaches that no sinner has ever lived up to the light he has. The heathen suppress and reject the light of creation and worship the creature instead of the Creator (Rom. 1:18, 21–25, 28). Thus there never has been and there never shall be a sinner who lives up to all the light he receives from Universal Witness (Rom. 3:10–18).

Proposition III: *The fact of judgment is determined on the basis of the legal status of the person in question.*

Because all men are sinners in the sight of God, all men are under the wrath of God (Rom. 3:23). The doctrine of original sin involves the imputation of Adam's sin to all mankind. This imputation is followed by the condemnation of God and the judgment of death (see Psa. 51:5; 58:3 cf. Rom. 5:12–21; 1 Cor. 15:22).

We sin because we *are* sinners. What we *are* determines the *fact* of judgment. Thus it is wrong to teach that we are lost *if* and *when* we reject Christ. The Gospel is preached to those who are *already* lost and perishing (1 Cor. 1:18). You are condemned to hell because of what you are, i.e., a sinner. The heathen are condemned because of what they are, i.e., they are sinners. Therefore, they are under God's wrath.

When an unbeliever asks, "Are you saying that God is going to throw good people into hell just because they don't believe in Jesus?" We respond, "No one is righteous, no not one. There are no good people. We all deserve to go to hell."

Proposition IV: *The degree of punishment is determined on the basis of the light and life of the person in question.*

Because God is just, there will be degrees of punishment in hell. All sinners in hell will be *perfectly* miserable but not *equally* miserable. In determining the degree of punishment in hell, our Lord takes into account the words (Matt. 12:26, 37) and works (Matt. 16:27; Rev. 20:11–15; 22:12) of sinners. Disobedience and unbelief due to ignorance do not deliver one from punishment for ignorance of the Law is no excuse (Lev. 5:17). But sins done in ignorance will not receive as much punishment as sins done consciously in violation of known law.

> And that servant, which *knew* his lord's will, and prepared not himself, neither did according to his will, shall be beaten with *many* stripes. But he that *knew not*, and did commit things worthy of stripes, shall be beaten with *few* stripes. For unto whomsoever much is given, of him shall be much required: and to whom men have committed much, of him they will ask the more (Luke 12:47–48)

The more you know, the more responsible you are to live up to that light. The greater the responsibility, the greater will be the reward or punishment.

Certain cities were liable to more severe divine punishment because they actually saw and heard the Christ, and yet, rejected Him.

> Verily I say unto you, *It shall be more tolerable* for the land of Sodom and Gomorrah in the day of judgment, than for that city (Matt. 10:15)

> Then began he to upbraid the cities wherein most of his mighty works were done, because they repented not: Woe unto thee, Chorazin! woe unto thee, Bethsaida! for if the mighty works, which

> were done in you, had been done in Tyre and Sidon, they would have repented long ago in sackcloth and ashes. But I say unto you, *It shall be more tolerable* for Tyre and Sidon at the day of judgment, than for you. And thou, Capernaum, which are exalted unto heaven, shalt be brought down to hell: for if the mighty works, which have been done in thee, had been done in Sodom, it would have remained until this day. But I say unto you, *That it shall be more tolerable* for the land of Sodom in the day of judgment, than for thee. (Matt. 11:20–24)

The writer of the Hebrews speaks of some unbelievers receiving more punishment than others.

> How much severer punishment do you think he will deserve who has trampled underfoot the Son of God, and has regarded as unclean the blood of the covenant by which it was sanctified, and has insulted the Spirit of grace? (Heb. 10:29)

The sin of the Pharisees was made greater by their contact with Christ (John 15:22). While the fact of judgment is determined by what we are, i.e., our nature, the degree of punishment is determined on the basis of the amount of true knowledge we have received and the quality of life that we lived (Rom. 2:3–6). Degrees of punishment in hell reveal that hell is not annihilation but eternal torment.

Proposition V: *The explicit teaching of Scripture is that the only way to escape the wrath of God is to believe in the Lord Jesus Christ.*

> Turn to Me, and be saved, all the ends of the earth; For I am God, and there is no other. (Isa. 45:22)

> He who believes in the Son has eternal life; but he who does not obey the Son shall not see life, but the wrath of God abides on him. (John 3:36)

> I am the door; if anyone enters through Me, he shall be saved, and shall go in and out, and find pasture. (John 10:9)

> I am the door; if anyone enters through Me, he shall be saved, and shall go in and out, and find pasture. (John 14:6)

> And there is salvation in no one else; for there is no other name under heaven that has been given among men, by which we must be saved. (Acts 4:12)

> whom God displayed publicly as a propitiation in His blood through faith. *This was* to demonstrate His righteousness, because in the forbearance of God He passed over the sins previously committed;

> for the demonstration, *I say*, of His righteousness at the present time, that He might be just and the justifier of the one who has faith in Jesus. Since indeed God who will justify the circumcised by faith and the uncircumcised through faith is one. (Rom. 3:25–26, 30)

> For no man can lay a foundation other than the one which is laid, which is Jesus Christ. (1 Cor. 3:11)

> For there is one God, *and* one mediator also between God and men, *the* man Christ Jesus, (1 Tim. 2:5)

Proposition VI: *All non-Christian religions are condemned in Scripture because:*
1. They are idolatrous (Rom. 1:25).
2. They are not the fruit of man's search for God but man's rejection of God (Rom. 1:18–24).
3. They actually give worship to Satan and his demons (1 Cor. 10:19–22).
4. They all fail to find God (1 Cor. 1:18–31).

Proposition VII: *The absence of special revelation does not in any way relieve the heathen from perishing.*

The fact that they die physically reveals that God views and treats them as sinners. Thus they face an eternity in hell.

> For there is no respect of persons with God. *For as many as have sinned without law shall also perish without law; In the day when God shall judge the secrets of men by Jesus Christ according to my gospel.* (Rom. 2:11–12, 16)

> *For all* have sinned, and come short of the glory of God. (Rom. 3:23)

> Wherefore, as by one man sin entered into the world, and death by sin; and so death passed upon *all men*, for that *all have sinned.* (Rom. 5:12)

> For the wages of sin is death; but the gift of God is eternal life through Jesus Christ our Lord. (Rom. 6:23)

Proposition VIII: *The Scriptures teach that all unbelievers will be cast into the lake of fire when Jesus returns in glory and power* (see Matt. 25:41, 46; Rev. 21:6). The Bible tells us about the fate of those who do not know God.

> And to you who are troubled rest with us, when the Lord Jesus shall be revealed from heaven with his mighty angels, In flaming fire taking vengeance *on them that know not God, and that obey not the gospel* of our Lord Jesus Christ: *Who shall be punished with*

> *everlasting destruction from the presence of the Lord, and from the glory of his power*; When he shall come to be glorified in his saints, and to be admired in *all them that believe* (because our testimony among you was believed) in that day. (2 Thess. 1:7–10)

Proposition IX: *Unbelievers must hear or read of the Lord Jesus Christ through human instrumentality in order to be saved.*

The Gospel does not come to us from angels, visions or dreams. God has committed unto the Church the privilege and responsibility of spreading the Gospel.

> Go therefore and make disciples of all the nations, baptizing them in the name of the Father and the Son and the Holy Spirit, teaching them to observe all that I commanded you; and lo, I am with you always, even to the end of the age.
> (Matt. 28:19–20)

> Whoever will call upon the name of YHWH will be saved. How then shall they call upon Him in whom they have not believed? And how shall they believe in Him whom they have not heard? And how shall they hear without a preacher? And how shall they preach unless they are sent? Just as it is written, "How beautiful are the feet of those who bring glad tidings of good things!" However, they did not all heed the glad tidings; for Isaiah says, "YHWH, who has believed our report?" So faith *comes* from hearing, and hearing by the word of Messiah. (Rom. 10:13–17)

Proposition X: *God will always send the Gospel by a human instrumentality to those who have been ordained to eternal life.*

Cornelius is a good example of how God will send the Gospel to His elect. The angel that came to Cornelius did not give him the Gospel. The angel told Cornelius to send for Peter so that Cornelius would hear the Gospel and be saved.

> And he showed us how he had seen an angel in his house, which stood and said unto him, Send men to Joppa, and call for Simon, whose surname is Peter; *Who shall tell you words, whereby you and all your house shall be saved* (Acts 11:13–14)

Cornelius obeyed the angel and when Peter came and preached the Gospel, then, and not until then, was Cornelius saved (Acts 10:44–48). He was a moral, God-fearing man (Acts 10:1–2). Yet, he was *not* saved until the Gospel came and he placed his faith in Jesus Christ. It should also be pointed out that God told Paul to continue preaching at Corinth because the elect were in the city (Acts 18:9–10 and 2 Tim. 2:10).

Proposition XI: *If salvation is possible through ignorance or neglect of the Gospel, then Jesus Christ died in vain, i.e., for nothing.*

His death was necessary and a mockery if salvation can be obtained by any other manner than by believing Him. "I do not frustrate the grace of God: for if righteousness come by the law, then Messiah is dead in vain." (Gal. 2:21)

Proposition XII: *A survey of the history of redemption reveals that ignorance, neglect and nominal acquaintance or acceptance were never sufficient grounds to deliver anyone from the just wrath of God against sin.*

A. *The Flood*:

Man sinned (Gen. 6:1–5, 11–13) and God's judgment came upon him for his sin (Gen. 6:6–7, 13, 17). Only the believer Noah and his family were delivered from God's wrath (Gen. 6:8–10, 14–16, 18–22).

Question: *Were there any ignorant, sincere and neglectful people in Noah's day? What happened to them?* If we asked Noah about the fate of all unbelievers in his day regardless if they were ignorant or neglectful, what would he say? Is the flood a pre-picture of the judgment Day at the second coming of Jesus Christ? (Matt. 24:37–39; 2 Pet. 2:5, 9). Since all the heathen (unbelievers) without exception perished under the flood waters of God's wrath, what does this tell us about God's judgment on unbelievers when Christ returns? All unbelievers will perish regardless if they are ignorant or neglectful.

B. *The Tower of Babel*:

Man sinned and God's judgment came upon him (Gen. 11). This judgment took two forms. First, human language was diversified. Second, the human race was scattered.

Question: *Were there any sincere, ignorant or neglectful people working on the tower? What happened to them?* Is it not the case that the two major reasons why some men are ignorant of the Gospel corresponds exactly to God's two judgments, i.e., different languages and mankind scattered over the face of the earth? Thus is not man's ignorance an extension of God's judgment against sin? If so, is it possible to view ignorance as the basis of the heathen's salvation seeing that such ignorance is part of God's judgment against unbelievers?

C. *Sodom and Gomorrah*:

Man sinned (Gen. 18:20–21; 19:1–9) and God's judgment came upon him (Gen. 19:10–11; 23–29). Only the believer Lot and his two daughters were delivered from the fire and brimstone.

Question: *Were there any sincere, ignorant, and neglectful people living in these cities? What happened to them?* Abraham said that "the judge of all the earth shall do right" (Gen. 18:25). *What did God do with all the unbelievers in Sodom and Gomorrah?*
If we asked Abraham and Lot about the eternal fate of all unbelieving sinners, what would they say? Is the destruction of these cities a preview of the coming destruction on the Day of Judgment? (Luke 17:28–30; 2 Pet. 2:5–9; Jude 7). What significance does this have on the heathen question?

D. *The History of God's People. 1. God's Judgment upon Egypt at the time of the Exodus.*

Were there any sincere, ignorant, and neglectful Egyptians? Were they saved from the judgment plagues of God? Were only the firstborn of these who believed God's Word safe from the angel of death, or did the angel pass over any houses where the people were sincere, ignorant, or neglectful?

2. *God's Commandment to Israel.* Was idolatry allowed in Israel? What was the penalty for idolatry? (Deut. 18) *Was there any difference in the sight of Torah whether the idolater was sincere, ignorant, or neglectful (Lev. 5:17)?* If sincere or ignorant idol worship saved one from the judgment of God, would this make true worship meaningless because it was not necessary for salvation? How would Moses answer the question of the heathen?

3. *God's Destruction of the Canaanites. To what fate did God assign the heathen Canaanites?* (Josh. 9:24, etc.). *Were there any sincere, ignorant or neglectful Canaanites? What happened to*

them? How would Joshua answer our question?

4. *God's Deliverance of Rahab.* Was Rahab a Canaanite? Why was she delivered while the rest of her people were destroyed? (Josh. 2:8–13). Were the only ones delivered from destruction those who believed in Jehovah? How would Rahab answer our question?

5. *God's View of the Nations.* How did Israel view the idolatrous nations around them (Psa. 9:17)? What happens to those who do not bow to Jehovah (Psa. 2:11–12)?

6. *The Conversion of Ruth (see Ruth).* How, and why, did Ruth join the people of God? Does she not serve to show how Gentiles were saved in Old Testament times? How could they be saved? How would Ruth answer the heathen question?

E. *Jonah and Nineveh (see Jonah).*

Were there any sincere, ignorant, or neglectful people in Nineveh? What fate had God assigned them? Why did the judgment turn away? How would Jonah answer the question of the heathen?

F. *Messiah Jesus*

Did He ever claim to be the only way of salvation? (John 14:6). What did He call false religious leaders? (John 10:8). Did He state that only faith in Him will deliver one from the judgment of God? (John 3:16, 36). How would He answer if we ask Him about the heathen?

G. *The Apostles.*

Did they teach that only faith in Christ saves? (Acts 4:12; 10:43; 16:31; Rom. 5:1; 10:9–13). Did they ever teach that there is no salvation outside of the Gospel? (Rom. 10:14–17). Is Christ the only Mediator between God and man? (1 Tim. 2:5). How would they answer the question of the heathen?

H. *Missions.*

Are we commanded to preach the Gospel to all men (Mark 16:15–16)? Why? Do they need it? *If the ignorant and sincere can be saved as long as they don't hear the Gospel, do missionaries actually damn more than they save?* Would it not be cruel to introduce the Gospel to ignorant people? If men were not already lost and without hope, would missions make any sense?

Part III

Finally, there are sound Biblical answers to those who think God is unjust in condemning the heathen.

I. *How dare anyone accuse God of being unjust in whatever He does!* The Apostle Paul rebukes such a rebellious attitude in Romans 9:11–24.

If the righteous judge of all the earth has revealed in His Word that all the heathen will be cast into the lake of fire (Rev. 20:15), who is the man that can condemn God for doing so?

II. *Sincerity in living up to some of the light we have received will only make us a candidate for further light as it did for Cornelius in Acts 10.* But Cornelius had to be saved through the Gospel given by a human messenger (Acts 11:14). Not even the angel could tell Cornelius the Gospel. Sincerity is not enough.

III. *As sinners, the only thing we deserve is God's eternal wrath in hell.* The Bible does not teach that God owes us anything or that we even deserve a chance to be saved. It teaches that we don't in any sense deserve to be saved. Salvation is by GRACE. This means that God does not owe anyone anything (Rom. 4:1–5). God does not have to save anyone at all. It is all of grace.

Conclusion

The Bible is absolutely clear on three points:

> No other god (Exo. 20:3)
> No other name (Acts 4:12)
> No other way (John 14:6)

With few exceptions, modern Natural theologians deny these cardinal biblical concepts. They believe and teach that any god by any name will do because there are many ways to heaven. While God says that the heathen are "without excuse" (Rom. 1:20 cf. 2:1), they are determined to give them such excuses as: "We did not know. We did not have a chance. We are too good to be damned. It isn't fair. God is too good to damn us." But God will shut the mouths of all unbelievers on the Day of Judgment (Rom. 3:19). No unbelievers will escape the just wrath of God Almighty.

> And do you suppose this, O man...that you will escape the judgment of God? (Rom. 2:3)

> And the kings of the earth and the great men and the commanders and the rich and the strong and every slave and free man, hid themselves in the caves and among the rocks of the mountains; and they said to the mountains and to the rocks, "Fall on us and hide us from the presence of Him who sits on the throne, and from the wrath of the Lamb; for the great Day of their wrath has come; and who is able to stand?" (Rev. 6:15-17)

Chapter Thirteen

Natural Theology

No Common Definition

Natural theologians have never agreed on the meaning of the words "natural" and "theology" or the phrase "Natural Theology." Since the meaning of the words has changed each time the cultural consensus changed, there is no historical or philosophical continuity of meaning. Thus the words "natural theology" are vacuous and quite meaningless.

Why then do they use the words "Natural Theology"? It has become a psychological tool to manipulate ignorant people. It invokes a time long ago when there was a Christian consensus in our culture. The phrase is a slogan waved like a flag to inspire faith in church people.

What is "Theology?"

First, as we already stated, "theology" is not a biblical word or idea. It is nowhere found in the Hebrew or Greek text of the Bible. No prophet or apostle every called himself a "theologian" or described their preaching as "theology." To discover the origin and meaning of theology, we must examine pagan philosophy.

Second, as we have pointed out, the pagan philosopher Aristotle was the author of the word and its meaning. According to him, "theology" is a humanistic-based science like biology or astronomy. It is a word created by combining two different words: logos and theos. The word "Theo-logy" means man's study of divine things. Man is the Origin and measure of theology and it has nothing to do with revelation. The "attributes" of the gods refers to what qualities and powers *man* attributes to or projects onto the gods.

Natural Theology

Since theology is a humanistic enterprise and begins and ends with man, what is "Natural Theology?" Only a vague definition is possible. Prof. William P. Aston defines Natural Theology as, "the enterprise of providing support for religious beliefs by starting from premises that neither are nor presuppose any religious beliefs."[501]

How can you provide support for religious ideas if you do not start with those ideas in mind? T. H. L. Parker in *Baker's Dictionary of Theology*, defined it as:

> *Theologia naturalius* as it is now understood is a theology constructed irrespective of revelation. In its pure form it has never

existed within the church, which is clearly committed to revelation in some degree. [502]

Parker acknowledges that Natural Theology changes in meaning and he can only take a "snapshot definition" of what it is at the moment he is writing about it. He is right on target. William Hordern explained it this way,

> Ever since Thomas Aquinas there has been a distinction between natural and revealed theology. Natural theology means man's philosophical study of religious questions. Natural theology is all that man can learn about God, immortality, and such questions by the use of reason alone. It appeals to facts and theories that are available to any rational man. It can be summed up quickly by saying that natural theology represents man's search for God; revealed theology represents God's search for man.[503]

Hordern brings perhaps the best of the definitions, and properly defines Natural Theology by contrasting it to Revealed Theology. Natural Theology is what *man* says, and Revealed Theology is what *God* says.

Natural Religion

Natural Theology is built upon Natural Religion, which, in turn, is built upon Natural Law. They all stand or fall together. The definitive work on the history of Natural Theology was written by Clement C. J. Webb.

> For we may, I think, take it as agreed that Natural Theology must stand in the closest possible relation to Natural Religion; that it must denote the reasoned and articulated account of what is implied in the existence of natural religion.[504]

As we have previously demonstrated, the foundation of all the various Natural Law and Natural Religion theories is humanism, i.e. man is the Origin and Measure of all things, including God. They in turn are the two pillars upon which Natural Theology rest.

Its Link to Roman Catholicism

The great Dutch theologian Berkouwer documents that Natural Theology is the historic position of Roman Catholicism.

> Since the Middle Ages, Roman Catholic theology has without a moment's regret defended the right and the possibility of natural theology. She has not simply used it as a non-essential appendix to her theology, but has made it an organic part of her system of

> doctrine. Moreover, it is clear that this is not simply the hobby of Roman Catholic *theology*, but that the Roman *church* considers it of great importance. This is at once apparent in the decisions of the Vatican Council when it emphasized the natural knowledge of God as a *rational* knowledge and carefully distinguished it from the knowledge of faith.[505]

Dr. Bernard Ramm explained that Natural Theology cannot be understood properly apart from the Roman Catholic denial of the radical effects of the Fall. Thomas Aquinas had a weak view of the Fall and saw man, not as dead in his trespasses and sin, but as only weakened and sick.

> According to this position human nature was complete before God graced it with original righteousness. Therefore after the entry of sin and the fall of man human nature is still complete even though deprived of original righteousness. Certainly shadows have fallen over it. Man is depraved to the extent that he needs God's revelation to learn the way of salvation, and God's grace to trust the Savior. But this yet leaves a large territory in which the human mind is competent. It may create a true philosophy (Aristotle); it may prove the existence of God; it may demonstrate the immortality of the soul; it may create a system of ethics based upon natural laws; and it can prove the divine origin of the Roman Catholic Church.[506]

> The Roman Catholic position is that the general revelation of nature may be so read by man apart from Christ and apart from grace that he can prove that God is, and know some of his attributes.[507]

It is should thus be no surprise that when Protestants fall into the heresy of Natural Theology, it often leads them back to Rome. The ancient heresy of Pelagianism lies at the bottom of all "natural" theologies because Natural theologians assume that *man* has the final answers within himself and that he is good enough to discover them on his own without any information from God.

Our Definition

Natural Theology is fallen man's humanistic attempt to define God without God and to define theology without God. Starting from only from himself, by himself, through himself, within himself, on the sole basis of human reason, experience, feelings or faith, the natural man attempts to go from:

- the finite to the infinite,
- the visible to the invisible,

- the material to the spiritual,
- the temporal to the eternal,
- chaos to order,
- non-life to life,
- meaninglessness to meaning,
- the impersonal to the personal,
- nature to God,
- what is to what ought to be.

In order to produce a valid Natural Theology you cannot presuppose, start with, or proceed in your arguments with any biblical beliefs or terms that would compromise your arguments. If you presuppose, start with or proceed with the very religious beliefs you are trying to prove, your arguments are no longer "objective" and "neutral." You are arguing in a circle, going nowhere fast.

Of course, the claim of objectivity and neutrality is an old rationalist canard that has been abandoned in modern times by most secular philosophers and scientists. The only place in the world today where the myths of neutrality and objectivity still exist is in the halls of Christian academia. But then, they are always at least fifty years behind the world!

The Impossible Task

What should make us hesitate to embrace the ever-changing relative world of Western, European, Natural Theologies, is that Christians are absolutely incapable of producing a valid non-Christian Natural Theology! Why? They are so hopelessly saturated with Biblical ideas that they CANNOT think without using Biblical categories. They are *in* the Biblical Box and cannot think *outside* of that Box.

In order for Natural Theology to be authentically "Natural," it must be developed **outside** the Box of Biblical ideas.

Natural Theology   X   Biblical Ideas
Natural Religion   X

Inside the Box are *Biblical* ideas that:
- must not contaminate nor pollute the mind;
- cannot be presupposed;
- cannot be a part of any argument;
- cannot play a role at any point in any chain of arguments;
- cannot show up at the beginning or the end;
- cannot be the source of any key terms.
- cannot influence anyone in anything at any time.

The fact that faces us is that Western, European, Christian Natural Theologians couldn't produce an authentic "Natural" Theology even if their life depended upon it! The only thing a Christian can produce is a "Christian" Theology. Thus the arguments developed by Western, European, "Christian" Natural Theologians such as Thomas Aquinas, William Paley, Charles Hodge, William Lane Craig, J. P. Moreland, Norman Geisler, R.C. Sproul, etc. are *irrelevant* because they presuppose and utilize Biblical ideas from beginning to end. They are incapable of being either objective or neutral.

Beware of Old Canards

One way that modern Natural theologians avoid having to define or defend their ideas is to claim that their arguments are "misunderstood." They assume that if you are intelligent and sincere, you will "naturally" understand what they were saying. Thus you will "naturally" agree with them because their arguments are intuitive, self-evident, and universal. Carl F. Henry explains,

> One distressing feature of Thomism is the repeated claim by its exponents that its critics misrepresent or improperly understand the argument and draw wrong inferences from rejoinders. Does Thomas claim that the proofs are logically demonstrative or merely existentially undeniable? (There is much to commend the view that Aquinas opposed Augustine's arguments as based on harmony and beauty and sought to replace them with strict proof, i.e., logical demonstration; otherwise Thomas is not Aristotelian and his distinction between philosophy and revelation fails.) Does he use or avoid the principle of sufficient reason? Are the proofs to be considered several correlative arguments or simply one comprehensive argument? (Thomas says the first proof is more obvious. Does he claim that each singly is valid, or that taken cumulatively they are demonstrative?) On and on run the differences among Thomistic interpreters, each claiming to champion the authentic Thomas. [508]

Western, European, "Christian" Natural Theologians were born into the Biblical Box; grew up in the Box; were educated in the Box; married in the Box; raised their children in the Box; earned their living in the Box; worshiped in the Box; loved the Box; defended the Box. *There is no way they can think outside of the Box even if they wanted to do so.*

Dialogue on Natural Theology

Natural theologian (NT): Did you see my new book, *Rational Christianity*?
Biblical theologian (BT): Yes.
NT: What did you think?
BT: I didn't believe a word of it.
NT: But didn't I demonstrate the existence of God and solve the problem of evil?
BT: No. You failed on both counts.

NT: Why?

BT: "Natural Theology" is like the cereal "Grape Nuts," which is neither grapes nor nuts. Likewise, "Natural Theology" is neither "natural" nor "theology." Do you *really* believe that *you* proved the existence of God and solved the problem of evil by human reason alone, apart from and independent of Scripture, through Nature alone? You have to be kidding!

NT: I really believe that I have developed a rational basis for Christianity.

BT: I submit that you cannot do this because you are so influenced by Biblical ideas that you cannot intellectually function without using those Biblical ideas. You were born in a Biblical box and cannot get out of that box.

NT: But I can pretend that I am not in the Box.

BT: Like a kid pretending to ride a horse by riding a broomstick? Fat chance!

NT: What I mean is that I can think outside the Biblical Box.

BT: I don't think so.

NT: Sure I can! If I abandon the Biblical Box and move over to a non-Christian Box like the Greek Philosophers, then I can think outside the Christian Box. I will adopt the ideas of Thales, Socrates, Plato, Aristotle, and other philosophers. They will be my mentors. Then, beginning with those pagan ideas, I will intellectually argue my way out of their pagan box all the way back to the Biblical Box.

BT: Now, let me get this straight. You intend to defend the Biblical Box by first *abandoning* it? Then you will move over to some pagan box and adopt their pagan ideas? And you really think you can make your way back to Jesus starting with some pagan philosophy?

NT: Yes.

BT: You are crazy! It is impossible for you to think outside the Biblical Box. Take for example the goals of your book listed on the back cover:

    (1.) To prove the existence and attributes of God,
    (2.) to solve the problem of evil,
    (3.) by human reason alone.

The words "prove," "existence," "God," "solve," "problem," "evil," "reason," and "Nature" all have *Christian* meanings. If you are trying to think outside the Biblical Box, you have already failed. Take the word "God." Which "God" are you trying to prove? The pantheistic god of Hinduism? The finite gods of the Greeks? What kind of "God" are you hoping to find at the end of your arguments? As a Christian, don't you mean the God of the Bible?

NT: Yes. I am trying to prove the existence of the Christian God.

BT: Then you are still thinking in the Biblical Box! Instead of trying to prove the existence of the Biblical God, you should simply say that you are trying to find out if "X" exists. You will not know what "X" means until you arrive at the end of your arguments. You may end up with a god or gods that are not like the Christian God at all.

NT: Are you saying that a Christian is *incapable* of producing Natural Law, Religion, Theology and Apologetics?

BT: Yes! The only person who is capable of producing an authentic "Natural" Theology is a "natural" unregenerate man or woman who has never heard of any Biblical ideas such as: The Jewish God; The Christian God; natural revelation; special revelation; inspired Scriptures (the Bible); monotheism; an infinite and personal God; the spiritual non-material nature of God; infinite nature of God; omnipotence of God; omniscience of God; omnipresence of God; holiness of God; grace of God; the Trinity; "Nature;" the universe; the universe is not eternal; the finite nature of the universe; the universe had a beginning; Creation *ex nihilo*; Design; Cause and effect motif; the creation of man; the unity of mankind; the dignity of man; Adam and Eve; the Fall of man into sin and guilt; original sin; the sinful nature of man; the Law of God; the Ten Commandments; salvation; atonement; prophets; apostles; fulfillment of prophecy; the Messiah; Jesus; etc.

NT: Aren't you being too picky?

BT: No. All the terms used by Western, European, Christian, Natural Theologians are Biblical or Christian terms. Thus they would have to abandon all these terms in order to think outside the Box. But can you really do this? I don't think so. For example, when you claim to prove the "existence" of "God," you have in mind the Biblical "God" and not some other deity. When you use the word "existence," you understand it in the Biblical sense of an infinite, spiritual, non-material, non-spatial, non-temporal existence. Or, are you referring to a god made out of a coconut husk with mother-of-pearl eyes and teeth? I don't think so!

NT: But the Bible gives us many examples of Natural Theology in such places as Psa. 19, Acts, 17, and Rom. 1. The Bible is filled with Natural Theology.

BT: I hate to pop your balloon, but you are guilty of a categorical fallacy. General Revelation is not the same as Natural Theology. Thus when you appeal to verses that speak of *God's* General revelation as if they prove *man's* Natural Theology, you are in error. Let me explain what I mean.

1. "General revelation" in the Bible is *God's* immediate non-verbal revelation to all men all the time in all places in all generations. It is immediate, universal, and constant. All men are without excuse because God is personally confronting all men at all times in all places.
2. The light is shinning and the music is playing all the time but sinful man shuts his eyes and plugs his ears so that he does not see the light or hear the music. Notice that Psa. 19:1 says that "the *heavens* are telling the glory of God." It does not say that natural *man* is telling the glory of God!
3. In contrast to God's immediate, universal General revelation, Natural Theology is the human activity of a few White, Western, European, Christian philosophers trained in Western logic and philosophy. Since only a few people in the West have ever read their books, how can it be said the *all* men everywhere throughout all of history are without excuse because of what they write?
4. I have examined every Biblical passage put forward by Natural Theologians and did not find a single command, precept or example of Natural Theology in the Bible! There was no need for it because the authors of the Bible had a revealed Torah and Gospel.

NT: If what you say is true, how can you prove to non-Christians that Christianity is *rational*?
BT: Why should we let the heathen make hoops for us to jump through? We are not circus dogs! The prophets and apostles were more interested in being *faithful* than rational. Besides, rationalism is a refuted philosophy, and even philosophy in general has resoundingly failed down through the centuries. The Bible tells me ahead of time that the gospel is *foolishness* to philosophy (1 Cor. 1:22). Dr. Robert Reymond was right on target when he commented,

> Natural theology does not square with the actual apologetic activity of the early church as we find it depicted in the book of Acts. The natural theologian maintains that it is not right to ask skeptics to believe in Christ on the basis of scriptural authority before they had had a chance to consider the evidence supportive of the Christian claims. But does the unbeliever posses some independent criterion of verification which can and should authenticate the truth of Christian revelation in advance of faith? I think not. Otherwise, we must conclude that Dionysius the Areopagite, who believed in Christ simply on the basis of Paul's testimony prior to any investigation into what Paul proclaimed, was the biggest fool on Mars's Hill that day in A.D. 50 (Acts 17:22-3), and that the most intelligent men there were those who determined to hear Paul again on some subsequent occasion! No, the missionary efforts of Peter, Stephen, Philip, and Paul never urged lost men to do anything other than to repent of sin and bow in faith before Jesus Christ. When they debate, they draw their arguments from the Scriptures (Acts 17:2; 18:28). They never imply that their hearers may legitimately question
> the existence of the Christian God, the truth of Scripture, or personal commitment. Never do they suggest by their appeal to the evidence of God's presence and benevolence (Acts 4:9-10; 14:17; Rom. 1:20-21) that they are endeavoring to erect a "probability construct." They went forth into the world not as professional logicians and philosophical theologians but as preachers and witnesses, insisting that repentance toward God and faith in Jesus Christ are the sinner's only proper responses to apostolic witness.[509]

NT: But you have to have a *common ground* with unbelievers such as human reason and rationality. What do you do with people who do not believe in the Bible?
BT: Yes, we do have "common grounds" with all people via Creation, Fall, and Redemption. But not the humanistic common grounds you submit. The prophets never changed their message of "Thus says YHWH." The Apostles preached the Word to Jews and Gentiles who rejected the Bible. They too paid the price for confronting the world with the command to

repent of their sins and believe in Jesus Christ. Show me in the Old or New Testament where the authors of Scripture taught your "common ground" idea.

NT: When Paul met with the Greek philosophers on Mars Hill, he used pagan philosophy as the common ground between him and the unbelievers.

BT: I think you haven't read that passage in some time and have forgotten what Paul actually said to the Greeks. I have my Bible here and I want you to show me where Paul appealed to the Greek concept of "reason" or "rationality" as the basis of his message.

NT: I don't have the time to hold Bible studies.

BT: This is what I always find with you guys. You will cite a biblical passage and then run away from it as fast as you can. For example, you are using the Bible to prove that you don't need to use the Bible. I have a problem with that.

NT: I don't need the Bible myself but I cite it for your sake. If you look at the beginning of Acts 17, you will find that Paul argued from Reason that Jesus was the Christ.

BT: Misquoting and misinterpreting the Bible doesn't really help your position. The verse actually says that Paul "argued with them *from the Scriptures.*" It is erroneous that you dropped out the words "from the Scriptures."

NT: Wait a minute. Let me look up the verse because Mooreland, Craig, Geisler, Koukl, and Beckwith say that Paul clearly referred to human Reason as the judge of whether Jesus was the Messiah. You are saying that Paul was appealing to the Bible as the judge. One of you is mistaken.

BT: Don't ever trust Natural theologians to quote the Bible accurately - much less interpret it in accordance with sound hermeneutics.

NT: I heard from a professor at my seminary that you are a Barthian.

BT: Oh, another red herring argument! Van Ti, Clark, Henry, Schaeffer, and I all rejected Barth's liberalism. But this does not mean that he was wrong on *everything*. That is a logical fallacy. Carl F. Henry explained that Barth was right on this issue.

> Not only had modernism, like Thomism, replaced God by man as a theological starting point but, as Karl Barth protested, it had also in effect deified man himself. It recognized no point of reference outside man in establishing theological truth. Its main speculative ally, philosophical idealism, wholly forfeited the unconditionally transcendent, and depicted the divine Spirit as immanent in all men. Modernism in principle therefore forsook theology for anthropology and for humanism.[510]

> Barth was doubtless right in rejecting natural theology. For the Protestant Reformers the "natural theology" elaborated from the universe by the scholastics was a pagan distortion of the revelation in the creation. God's revelation in created reality results not in theological truth but rather in the unregenerate man's

> misconception of God and, in view of the sinner's revolt against light, inevitably in a pagan notion of God. Only special redemptive revelation remedies this predicament. Paul declares that man "holds down the truth [general revelation] in unrighteousness"; through his sinful response he, in fact, transforms it into idolatrous alternatives. Brunner puts the contrast succinctly: "Biblical and natural theology will never agree; they are bitterly and fundamentally opposed" [511]

NT: We have moved beyond Barth today. I have developed in my book a rational Natural Theology that proves the existence and nature of God apart from biblical revelation.

BT: The only person who can develop an authentic Natural Theology by reason only, through Nature alone, is a pagan who has never had any contact with any Biblical ideas whatsoever. In other words, only someone *totally* outside of the Biblical Box can develop a pure Natural Theology. You were born and raised in the Biblical Box and are incapable of freeing yourself from biblical ideas.

The Bible and Natural Theology

> Christianity came into the world as a revealed religion: it was given to the world by Christ as a doctrine of redemption and salvation and love, not as an abstract and theoretical system, and He sent His Apostle to preach, not occupy professor's chairs. Christianity was "the Way", a road to God to be trodden in practice, not one more philosophical system added to the systems and schools of antiquity. The Apostles and their successors were bent on converting the world, not on excogitating a philosophical system. [512]

The above statement by the great Medieval scholar, Frederick Copleston, is a healthy reminder that biblical Christianity did not seek to win the approval of the world by conforming the Gospel to whatever unbelievers felt was "rational" at the time. The prophets and apostles boldly proclaimed the everlasting Gospel and confronted unbelievers with the clarion call to repent of their sins and bow in submission to Jesus Christ. They were prophets and apostles, not philosophers or theologians.

Avery Dulles in his definitive work, *The History of Apologetics,* documents that in 1 Cor. 1-2, Paul,

> exhibits his distrust of Greek Wisdom and his well-founded fear that philosophy...could corrupt the faith of new converts. In the early chapters of this letter Paul draws a sharp contrast between two modes of religious knowledge, the one consisting of human wisdom, the other of obedience to divine revelation. For Paul, the

> first leads only to pride and delusion...Paul does not wish to support his preaching by any philosophical argumentation but solely by the power of the Holy Spirit, who gives fecundity to the preaching of the revealed word (1 Cor. 3:6). [513]

The truths of the Gospel were not conformed to different times or audiences (Rom. 12:1-2). There was only *one* Gospel and any attempt to change it was anathema. There **are** three NT passages that demonstrate this point with absolute clarity.

First, Paul warned that any attempt to tamper with the message of the cross would result in the judgment of God.

> I am amazed that you are so quickly deserting Him who called you by the grace of Christ, for a different gospel; which is really not another; only there are some who are disturbing you, and want to distort the gospel of Christ. But even though we, or an angel from heaven, should preach to you a gospel contrary to that which we have preached to you, let him be accursed. As we have said before, so I say again now, if any man is preaching to you a gospel contrary to that which you received, let him be accursed. (Galatians 1:6-9)

Walvoord and Zuck comment,

> Paul's astonishment was over an almost inconceivable turn of events— the Galatian believers were in the process of turning away (**deserting,** *metatithesthe,* as in a military desertion) from the truth. Part of the apostle's amazement was because it was happening **so quickly** after his last visit to them, or so soon after the false teachers began their insidious work. The departure was not simply from a system of theology but from God Himself, **the One who** had **called** them **by the grace of Christ** (the dominant theme of the epistle). In exchange they were embracing **a different gospel,** one that was false. Paul insisted that a gospel of legalism which adds work to faith is not the same kind of gospel that he preached and by which they were saved. It was actually an attempt **to pervert the gospel of Christ.** And Paul was aware of the fact that at the very time he was writing this epistle the false teachers were at work troubling or **throwing** the Galatians **into confusion** (cf. Acts 15:24; 20:29-30).1:8. To emphasize the fact that the true **gospel** of the grace of God cannot be changed, Paul first stated a hypothetical case. **If** he (a divinely called apostle) **or an angel** (a heavenly messenger) were to alter the gospel message—a highly improbable situation—then **let him be** accursed or **eternally condemned** (*anathema*). **1:9.** In this verse Paul seemed to repeat himself, but he actually advanced his thought. Paul and Barnabas had given a warning of judgment

when they had preached to the Galatians. Now Paul repeated it. A zealous champion of the purity of the gospel of grace, Paul said it again: **If anybody** were **preaching** a different **gospel** (which the false teachers were), he would come under God's eternal judgment. It is not difficult to understand why Paul reacted so strongly, because the Judaizers were impugning the Cross; for if works were necessary for salvation, then the work of Christ was not sufficient (cf. 2:21). Furthermore a great deal is at stake for lost people. When the gospel message is corrupted, the way of salvation is confused and people are in danger of being eternally lost. [514]

The second passage is from 2 Corinthians.

But I am afraid, lest as the serpent deceived Eve by his craftiness, your minds should be led astray from the simplicity and purity *of devotion* to Christ. For if one comes and preaches another Jesus whom we have not preached, or you receive a different spirit which you have not received, or a different gospel which you have not accepted, you bear *this* beautifully. (2 Cor. 11:3-4)

Garland's comment on this passage is notable.

Paul never names his opponents but continually refers to them only indirectly, "if someone comes." Barrett comments that these rivals merely come, while Paul, as an apostle, is sent (see 1 Cor 1:17). But Paul also describes his first visit as "coming" but with a distinct difference: When I came to you, brothers, I did not come with eloquence or superior wisdom as I proclaimed to you the testimony about God. For I resolved to know nothing while I was with you except Jesus Christ and him crucified. I came to you in weakness and fear, and with much trembling. My message and my preaching were not with wise and persuasive words, but with a demonstration of the Spirit's power, so that your faith might not rest on men's wisdom, but on God's power. (1 Cor 2:1–5) The opponents came with eloquence, a swaggering boldness, and persuasive words that proclaimed a testimony about themselves rather than Christ. Not only did they trespass on Paul's allotted field, but they sowed that field with the tares of a false gospel. Their preaching is false—a different Jesus, Spirit, and gospel—that can only lead Christians away from Christ. This gospel apparently places greater emphasis on Human standards as valid criteria for evaluating others, on rhetorical showmanship, on racial heritage, and on ecstatic visions. [515]

The third passage deals with Paul's public rebuke of Peter, who had "adapted" the gospel in order to be "relevant" to his target audience. While Paul agreed that Christians can personally "adapt" to such innocent cultural mores as clothing, food or hair styles (1Cor. 10:23-11:16), this was not what Peter had done. Paul charged that Peter and others were "not straightforward about the truth of the gospel" (Gal. 2:14). He had tried to mix works with grace in order to appease his audience.

> But when I saw that they were not straightforward about the truth of the gospel, I said to Cephas in the presence of all, "If you, being a Jew, live like the Gentiles and not like the Jews, how *is it that* you compel the Gentiles to live like Jews? We *are* Jews by nature, and not sinners from among the Gentiles; nevertheless knowing that a man is not justified by the works of the Law but through faith in Christ Jesus, even we have believed in Christ Jesus, that we may be justified by faith in Christ, and not by the works of the Law; since by the
> works of the Law shall no flesh be justified. But if, while seeking to be justified in Christ, we ourselves have also been found sinners, is Christ then a minister of sin? May it never be!" (Gal. 2:14-17)

Dr. Wiersbe commented,

> Paul was right in ignoring the "spiritual positions" of the people mentioned in v. 6. Even the best leaders can make mistakes, and Paul cites Barnabas and Peter as examples. After the Jerusalem conference, Peter had visited the Gentile church at Antioch where Paul and Barnabas were still ministering (Acts 15:35). In Acts 10, God had clearly revealed to Peter that no foods or peoples were unclean; but the apostle fell back into legalism just the same. When he first came to Antioch, Peter mingled with the Gentiles and ate with them; but after some visitors came from Jerusalem, he withdrew himself and put up the old Jewish barriers again. Even Barnabas fell into the trap (v. 13), amazing his missionary companion, Paul. The reason was fear (v. 12); for "the fear of man brings a snare" (Prov. 29:25, NKJV). Peter and Barnabas were not walking uprightly. What we believe determines how we behave. Because Peter and Barnabas were confused about spiritual truth, they were unable to walk a straight line. The "truth of the Gospel" is not only something for us to defend (v. 5), but it is also something for us to practice (v. 14). In vv. 14–21 we have a summary of the rebuke Paul gave to Peter. Certainly Paul said more than this, but the following digest summarizes the matter very well: "You are a Jew," said Paul to Peter, "but you used to live like the Gentiles, with no barriers between you and other Christians. Now you want the

> Gentiles to live like Jews, doing what you did not even do yourself!" The "we" in vv. 15–17 refers, of course, to the Jews. "We Jews have had special privileges and may not be guilty of Gentile sins; but we are saved the same way they are!" We would expect Paul to say, "They must be saved the way we are," but he reverses the order. Salvation did not mean that Gentiles had to become like Jews, but that the Jews had to go to the level of the condemned Gentiles! "We are justified—given a right standing before God—by faith in Jesus Christ," argues Paul. "The works of the law will never justify a man. Was any Jew ever saved by keeping the law? Of course not!" In vv. 17–18, Paul showed Peter the folly of going back to the Law. "You say you have been saved by faith in Christ. Well, if you go back to the Law, you are confessing that you are still a sinner needing to be saved and that Christ did not save you. In fact, you are saying that your faith in Christ made you a sinner again, and that makes Christ the minister of sin!" To turn back to the Law denies the work of Christ on the cross. "You preached the Word to the Gentiles yourself," Paul went on, referring to Acts 10, "but now you have changed your mind. You preached salvation by faith; now you preach salvation by law. You are building up the very things you once tore down, which makes you a sinner, because you tore down something that God wanted to keep standing." In other words, Paul showed Peter the inconsistency of his actions and his beliefs. "The Law is not a way of life, Peter; it is a way of death. The Law kills us (v. 19) that the Gospel might raise us up again. A Christian is not someone who is trying to obey an outward law. A Christian is one who has the living Christ within. By faith, I am united to Christ forever. When He died, I died; when He arose, I arose with Him. He lives out His life through me as I walk by faith—this is the Christian life! It is not a set of rules and regulations. To go back to the Law is to frustrate (make empty) the grace of God! If the Law is God's way of salvation, then Christ died in vain!" Neither Galatians nor Acts records Peter's response, but we know that Paul's rebuke accomplished its purpose. In fact, one of the last admonitions Peter wrote was that believers should read Paul's letters to find God's truth about this present age (2 Peter 3:16–18). [516]

Many today have fallen into the same error of Peter. The "seeker church," "emergent church," "emerging church," and "New Perspective on Paul" all seek to be "relevant" to post-modern unbelievers by "adapting" the gospel to the felt needs of whatever target audience they have in mind. But, in their haste to be "relevant," they have thrown the baby out with the bathwater and jettisoned core concepts of the gospel that render what they are preaching a *false* gospel.

Natural Theology: a False Gospel

The different and divergent "gospels" preached by all the various schools of Natural Theology are false gospels and fall under the condemnation of Scripture. At the bottom of each of these false gospels is a works-based view of salvation in which unregenerate sinners can merit truth and morals by being sincere and rational. Despite the clear testimony of Scripture, natural theologians believe that the natural man has a good heart that seeks God; wants the truth; and understands spiritual things.

The Carrot and the Stick

In order to motivate a plow horse to keep moving, farmers would sometimes tie a carrot on the end of a stick and place it just beyond the reach of the animal. The poor beast would keep trotting toward the carrot he saw in front of him, never quite reaching it. In the same way, Natural theologians put the carrot of truth in front of non- Christians and promise them that if they keep running toward the truth, they will eventually reach it. But, no matter how sincere or intelligent the unbeliever, he or she will never reach the truth without God's revelation.

Paul's Example

This is why the Apostle Paul refused to use philosophic arguments in his preaching. *If you can argue someone into believing, then someone smarter than you can argue them out of believing.* If your "faith" is based on philosophic reasoning instead of the revealed Word of God, it is a bogus faith. Paul reminded the Corinthians,

> And my message and my preaching were not in persuasive words of philosophy, but in demonstration of the Spirit and of power, that your faith should not rest on human philosophy, but on the power of God.
>
> καὶ ὁ λόγος μου καὶ τὸ κήρυγμά μου οὐκ ἐν πειθοῖ[ς] σοφίας [λόγοις] ἀλλ' ἐν ἀποδείξει πνεύματος καὶ δυνάμεως, ἵνα η πίστις ὑμῶν μὴ ᾖ ἐν σοφίᾳ ἀνθρώπων ἀλλ' ἐν δυνάμει θεοῦ.

Paul was rightfully concerned that when people are "converted" by sophisticated philosophic arguments, their faith would rest on those arguments. William Hendriksen comments,

> In the last verse of this section, Paul states his purpose for rejecting persuasive words and superior wisdom. He has come to the Corinthians to preach the gospel. And his preaching has resulted in their personal faith in God. Paul informs them that this gift of faith neither originates in nor is supported by human wisdom. If faith were of human origin, it would utterly fail and disappear. But faith rests on God's power that shields the believer and strengthens him to persevere (compare I Peter 1:5).
> God works faith in the hearts of the Corinthians through the preaching of Christ's gospel. He not only has given them the gift of faith but also has brought them to conversion. God commissions Paul to strengthen their faith by instructing them in the truths of

> God's Word. In brief, the Corinthians must know that faith rests not on human wisdom but on God's power. "Wisdom of men." Notice that Paul uses the plural noun *men* to illustrate that in Corinth many people are dispensing their own insight and wisdom. Man's discernment is temporal, faulty, and subject to change; God's wisdom is eternal, perfect, and unchangeable. When a Christian in faith asks God's for wisdom (James 1:5), he experiences the working of God's power. He rejoices in the salvation God has provided for him. [517]

I have seen many theologians and pastors fall away from the Faith in the last forty years. 1 John 2:19 tells us they never really belonged in the church to begin with. How did they come into the church at the beginning? They were often "converted" by Natural apologists who used philosophic arguments to convince them. Later on in life, these converts ran into a slick unbeliever who was smarter than the "Christian" philosopher who originally converted them to Christianity. They then converted to another belief or unbelief.

Saving Faith: a Work of the Spirit
Saving faith in the New Testament is the work of the Spirit of God, not the work of man. Since the heart of man is desperately wicked and hardened in sin (Gen. 6:5), only God can open the heart to the Gospel (Acts 16:14). Since the natural man will not and cannot seek God (Rom. 3:11), God has to seek man (Lk. 15:1-7). Since the mind of the unbeliever is blinded by Satan (2 Cor. 4:4), God has to open the mind (Eph. 1:18f).

Paul was confident that the conversion of the Thessalonians was real because it was produced by the power of God.

> for our gospel did not come to you in word only, but also in power and in the Holy Spirit and with full conviction. (1 Thess. 1:5)

Saving faith comes from hearing the Word of God, not hearing humanistic philosophic discourse. "So faith *comes* from hearing, and hearing of the word of Messiah." (Rom. 10:17)

The great Baptist preacher, Charles Spurgeon, had returned once again to Edinburgh. As he sat in his carriage outside the church where he was to preach, one of his critics stuck his head through the window and yelled, "I see some of your converts are back at the pub!" Without batting an eye, Spurgeon replied, "Aye, its true. They are mine - not the Lord's. Driver, move on."

Assurance: a Work of the Spirit
The New Testament is clear that the certainty or assurance that God exists, Jesus is the Messiah, the Bible is the Word of God, etc. is the *direct* work of the Holy Spirit (Rom. 8:16; 1 John 3:24). It is not the end conclusion of a long string of syllogisms. [518]

How did Peter come to full assurance (Heb. 10:22) that Jesus was the Messiah?

> And Simon Peter answered and said, "Thou art the Messiah, the Son of the living God." And Jesus answered and said to him, "Blessed are

you, Simon Barjona, because flesh and blood did not reveal *this* to you, but My Father who is in heaven." (Matt. 16:16)

Peter's assurance was not the end product of sophisticated philosophic arguments. No "flesh and blood" philosopher convinced him of the gospel. Hendriksen comments,

> In continuing his address to Peter, Jesus emphasizes that "flesh and blood," that is, merely human calculation, cogitation, intuition, or tradition, could never have produced in this disciple's heart and mind the insight into the sublime truth that he had just now so gloriously professed. On the expression "flesh and blood" see also N.T.C. on Gal. 1:16 and on Eph. 6:12. It was, says Jesus, "my Father who is in heaven" who had disclosed this truth to Simon Bar-Jonah and had enabled him to give buoyant expression to it. To this disciple, and to all those similarly minded, he, this Father in heaven, had "revealed" it (11:25, 26); and this not necessarily directly, by whispering something into the ear, but by blessing to the heart the means of grace, not the least of these means being the lessons which issued from the words and works of Jesus.[519]

Hendriksen is not alone in understanding the implications of what Jesus said. *The Pulpit Commentary* noted,

> **Flesh and blood**. This is a phrase to express the idea of the natural man, with his natural endowments and faculties. So St. Paul says (Gal. 1:16), "I conferred not with flesh and blood;" and "Our wrestling is not against flesh and blood" (Eph. 6:12). The Son of Sirach speaks of "the generation of flesh and blood" (Ecclus. 14:18). No natural sagacity, study, or discernment had revealed the great truth. None of these had overcome slowness of apprehension, prejudices of education, slackness of faith. No unregenerate mortal man had taught him the gospel mystery. **My Father which is in heaven**. Christ thus accepts Peter's definition of him as "the Son of the living God." None but the Father could have revealed to thee the Son.[520]

Peter's saving faith was supernatural in origin and nature. But, lest we think that he was unique and that the rest of us have to come to faith through human reasoning instead of revelation, Jesus said in Matthew 11:25-27,

> At that time Jesus answered and said, "I praise you, O Father, Lord of heaven and earth, that you have hid these things from the

> philosopher and the shrewd and have revealed them to babes. Yes, Father, for thus it was well-pleasing in your sight. All things have been handed over to Me by My Father; and no one knows the Son, except the Father; nor does anyone know the Father, except the Son, and anyone to whom the Son wills to real Him.

Who are the people that God has hid the truth from? Jamieson, Fausset, and Brown comment,

> **from the wise and prudent**—The former of these terms points to the men who pride themselves upon their speculative or philosophical attainments; the latter to the men of worldly shrewdness—the clever, the sharp-witted, the men of affairs. The distinction is a natural one, and was well understood.[521]

Salvation ultimately comes from the choice of God and not from the reasoning of man (Acts 13:48).

Human Reasoning in the Bible

The supposed goals of Natural Theology are to convert unbelievers and give assurance to believers by rationally demonstrating the existence of God and solving the problem of evil. But salvation and assurance are the work of the Holy Spirit in the heart and mind of man as he hears the Word of God. Nowhere in Scripture are salvation and assurance the result of man's *reasoning* or *speculation*.

The Greek word διαλογισμός and its cognates refers to man's ability to reason, speculate or rationally analyze things within himself and come to a conclusion based on his own opinion. Thayer defines it as "the thinking of a man deliberating with himself." Louw and Nida define it as,

> to think about something in a detailed and logical manner — 'to think about, to reason about, to ponder, reasoning; to think or reason with thoroughness and completeness - 'to think out carefully, to reason thoroughly, to consider carefully, to reason, reasoning.' διαλογίζομαι: διελογίζετο ἐν ἑαυτῷ 'he began to reason about this in himself' Lk 12.17; διελογίζετο ποταπὸς εἴη ὁ ἀσπασμὸς οὗτος 'she carefully considered what the greeting meant' Lk 1.29. διαλογισμός: ἐματαιώθησαν ἐν τοῖς διαλογισμοῖς αὐτῶν 'their reasoning became futile' (literally 'they became futile in their reasoning') Ro 1.21.[522]

Nowhere in Scripture is salvation or assurance based upon man's reasoning. They are always the result of the Spirit working with the Word, not independent of the Word.

We did an exhaustive study of all the passages in the Bible where someone "reasoned within himself" (ex. Mark. 2:6-8; LK. 5:22). Not once did "reasoning within yourself" ever produce faith or assurance. Those who "reasoned within themselves" were always *unbelievers*.

The Bible and Natural Theology

Throughout its long history, Israel never produced a single philosopher or theologian. Why not? They had infallible and inspired prophets. The New Testament Church did not produce a single philosopher or theologian either because it had an infallible Messiah and inspired apostles.

For example, the Bible nowhere refers to the "attributes" of God in the sense of the qualities or powers man attributes to God. Nowhere in the Bible does man create God in his own image. It is the other way around. God reveals Himself personally to man and also reveals true ideas about Himself, the world, man, sin, salvation, society, etc. God is the Author of our faith, not man (Heb. 12:2).

The Greatest Natural Theologians

The three greatest expositions of Natural Theology were written by Chadbourne, *Lectures on Natural Theology*,[523] Paley, *Evidences of Christianity*,[524] and Balfour, *The Foundations of Belief*.[525] To their credit, unlike modern "evangelical" Natural theologians, they traced Natural Theology back to Greek philosophy and did not pretend that it came from the Bible.

The above philosophical works gave the most detailed and illustrative arguments in the history of Natural Theology and would still be the standard works on the subject, except that they were based on Newtonian science. They viewed the universe as a vast machine that was running smoothly according to absolute mechanical laws.

The reason these books are not reprinted today is that, although their arguments are still used, the worldview that supported those arguments is obsolete. "Nature" has moved from the world *outside* of man to the mind *inside* of man.

I fail to see how arguments based upon a mechanical view of the world are still valid after you no longer believe in a mechanical universe. Once Newton died, his arguments should have died with him.

This is what makes me suspicious about repeating the same arguments , but each time basing them on radically different scientific world views. An argument that "feels" valid regardless of its worldview is more psychology than metaphysics.

The Sham, the Smoke and Mirrors, the Shell and the Pea

I can honestly say that after forty years of reading and studying Natural Theology I never found a single argument that is valid and that takes me all the way to the God of the Bible. They all depended on a cultural consensus that no longer exists or on psychological manipulations that no longer work. Avery Dulles came to the same conclusion.

> Conventional apologetics is in the embarrassing position of answering questions that no one is asking any more. If the "Gentiles" against whom Thomas Aquinas wrote his *Summa Contra Gentiles* were interested even then in the arguments he formulates, their modern descendants are not; and therefore his modern descendants dare not repeat his arguments as they though they still spoke to the condition of our contemporaries. What is needed is an apologetic that will start with the Sitz im Leben of the twentieth-century thought, listen to its criticisms, and put forth the truth-claims of the gospel both forcefully and modestly...Christian theology still stands or falls with the claim to revelation.[526]

Conclusion

In their eagerness to appear "rational" to a sinful world Natural theologians have built their house on the shifting sands of cultural consensus instead of building on the Rock of Scripture. By doing so, they have relegated their arguments to eventual obsolescence. As for me and my house,

> Jesus loves me,
> This I know;
> For *the Bible* tells me so.

Chapter Fourteen

Natural Apologetics

Introduction

When supporters of Natural Religion address Christians, they call what they do "theology." When they address non-Christians, they call it "philosophy." But, regardless of whom they address, it is still some form of Nature-based religion.

The word "Natural" supposedly means that "Nature" not only supplies them with what to believe, but also how to defend those "natural" beliefs. It is one vast circular argument that begins and ends with subjective and relative assumptions and presuppositions of what constitutes "Nature." This is why Natural, Catholic, Classical or Evidential Apologetics is foundationally idolatrous. It bows before the shrine of man's reason (rationalism), experience (empiricism), feelings (mysticism), or faith (fideism).

> For they exchanged the truth of God for a lie, and worshiped and
> served the creature rather than the Creator, who is blessed forever.
> Amen. (Rom. 1:25)

The First Problem

The first problem with Natural Apologetics is that they have no commonly agreed upon definitions for such words as "Nature," "natural" or "Apologetics." As documented by Gordon Lewis [527] and Avery Dulles, [528] there have been *many* different and contradictory kinds of "Natural Apologetics," with each one claiming to be derived from "Nature" apart from and independent of the Bible. Each apologetic system is different because each apologist begins with a different definition of "Nature."

After over forty years of reading the works of natural apologists, it is apparent that they argue from Nature-nature, Nature-reason, common sense, transcendental cosmic principles, mystical insights, innate ideas, dreams and visions, or empirical evidence. They are fundamentally incompatible with each other and thus fight among themselves as to which one has the "true" understanding of "Nature" and "apologetics." The smart ones never define any of their terms because they know the moment they do so, they would have to defend those definitions.

Since "Natural" Apologists follow the philosophic fads of the day, they generally fall into four basic kinds: rationalism, empiricism, mysticism, and fideism. Their popularity depends on which humanistic world view was culturally dominant at the time. When Rationalism was popular, rationalistic apologetics were popular as well. When the culture moved over to empiricism, evidential apologetics became popular. When existentialism pushed aside both rationalism and empiricism, experience-based apologetics became the rage. The New Age Movement produced mystical apologetics found in Vineyard and Pentecostal circles. When the culture moved to a self-centered narcissistic world view in which personal health and wealth became the goals of life, some "health and wealth" evangelists and apologists became dominant in Christian media.

This explains why so many Bible-based churches are small and some "health and wealth" Charismatic Churches are packed with thousands of people. Biblical pastors teach that the glory of God (not the personal health and wealth of man) is the chief end of life. They preach sermons based on the Hebrew and Greek text of Scripture instead of a psychobabble message based on popular self-help clichés that promote a good self-image.

The World Loves Its own

Messiah pointed out in John 15:19 that the "world" (i.e. unbelievers), love those who are "of the world" and hate those who are of God.

> If you were of the world, the world would love its own; but because you are not of the world, but I chose you out of the world, therefore the world hates you.
>
> εἰ ἐκ τοῦ κόσμου ἦτε, ὁ κόσμος ἂν τὸ ἴδιον ἐφίλει· ὅτι δὲ ἐκ τοῦ κόσμου οὐκ ἐστέ, ἀλλ' ἐγὼ ἐξελεξάμην ὑμᾶς ἐκ τοῦ κόσμου, διὰ τοῦτο μισεῖ ὑμᾶς ὁ κόσμος.

One of the typical arguments for Natural Law is that non-Christians will accept it while they would reject the Bible. It can thus serve as "common ground" between Christians and non-Christians. But, if this "common ground" means *pagan* ground, Biblical Christians are forbidden by Scripture to accept it (2 Cor. 6:14-18).

In reality, all arguments that claim to build "common ground" with unbelievers by having the Christian first give up God and the Bible are only versions of the old canard "the ends justify the means." Yes, it is true that unbelievers love Natural Law. Why? It requires a Christian to abandon God, Jesus, and the Bible! It is of the world, by the world, and in the world. Thus while the secular world loves Natural Law, Natural Religion, and Natural Theology, it hates those who preach *sola scriptura*.

The Second Problem

All systems of Natural Apologetics gratuitously assume the two foundational dogmas of pagan Greek philosophy: human autonomy and the sufficiency of human reason

They assume that man is sufficient in and of himself to discover truth and morals without any reference to or dependence upon divine revelation. Since man is autonomous to find truth and morals, it is then gratuitously assumed that man is likewise autonomous to defend those beliefs.

Can Nature or Reason Justify Apologetics?

This creates a tremendous burden on so-called "Christian" natural apologists. Where, when, and how does "Nature" or "Reason" *justify* doing apologetics at all? *In other words, can Natural Apologists give any arguments drawn solely from "Nature" or "Reason" to justify apologetics as something we "ought" to do?*

Biblical Apologist (BA): Can I ask you something that has nagged me for years?

Natural Apologist (NA): Sure. What is it?

BA: The *Bible* tells me to do apologetics in 1 Pet. 3:15 and Jude 3 and that is *why* I do it. But you claim that you can discover truth and morals apart from and independent of the Bible through human reason alone. Right? NA: That is the general idea.

BA: Why do you do apologetics?

NA: The Bible tells me to defend my faith.

BA: That's the problem! How can you use the Bible to justify an apologetic that is supposedly independent of and apart from the Bible? It seems odd to me that you go to the Bible to justify your apologetics. Where in *Nature* do you find any justification to do apologetics?

NA: Let me get this straight. Are you asking me to justify apologetics on purely *rational* grounds *apart from and independent* of the Bible?

BA: Yes!

NA: I will have to think about that. Geisler, Craig, and Mooreland all quote the Bible to justify why they do apologetics. If I have to come up with *rational* reasons to do *Natural* Apologetics, this is going to be tough.

BA: I honestly think it is impossible to start with what "is" and prove that apologetics is something we "ought" to do. Haven't you noticed that liberal seminaries no longer teach apologetics? Once you throw the Bible under the bus, there is no reason to do apologetics. Hasn't apologetics divided families, destroyed community solidarity, promoted prejudice, and caused wars? "Reason" tells me to let people believe whatever they want to believe. Don't judge other people's beliefs. Live and let live!

NA: But I believe in doing apologetics!

BA: Then give me one "rational" reason drawn solely from "Nature" why you should do apologetics.

NA: I see the problem but I don't see a solution at this time.

BA: This is the profound problem facing Natural apologists. Why do apologetics at all? Why not stay home, watch TV, and chill out?

The Third Problem

Natural or Evidential apologists admit that they *begin* with *man,* not God. R. C. Sproul, John Gerstner, and Arthur Lindsley in their book, *Classical Apologetics*, not only admit that they begin with man and not with God, they give a detailed defense of the pagan Greek doctrines of human autonomy and the primary of human reason.

> From time immemorial all people have assumed that they must begin with thinking with themselves for there is no other place where *they* must begin.[529] If man were the starting point, we all would have this in common and thus an initial point of contact.[530]
> We must start with ourselves rather than God:
> 1. It is psychologically impossible for us to start with God (as it is impossible for God to start with us.)
> 2. It is logically impossible for us to start with God for we cannot affirm God without assuming logic and our ability to predicate.
> 3. It is logically impossible to show the rational necessity of presupposing God except by rational arguments.[531]
> That is, we admit the charge of autonomy...that we begin autonomously.[532]

Let us analyze the arguments above.
1. "From time immemorial" is a literary cliché that refers to the Golden Age of Greece (500-300 BC). Western humanists assume that "civilization" began in Greece with the pre-Socratic philosophers. The history of non-Greek cultures is irrelevant. This phrase is indicative of racism and Western prejudice.
2. As we have already documented, when humanists assert that "all people assume" this or that idea, they do not literally mean every human being who has ever lived, is living now or shall ever live. They mean some Western, European, white, Judeo-Christian, civilized men some of the time have assumed that idea is true. Notice that the authors do not document their claim of universality. They merely assert that "all people assume" the Greek philosophic concepts of human autonomy and the sufficiency of reason.
3. They assert, "there is no other place where *they* must begin." It seems they never picked up the Bible and read Gen. 1:1. Moses did not say, "In the beginning *man*" but "In the beginning *God*." The word "must" implies some kind of moral imperative to start with man instead of God. On what basis is it more moral to start with yourself instead of looking to divine revelation? They do not explain or defend their argument.
4. They give two reasons why Christians should adopt the pagan dogmas of human autonomy and the sufficiency of human reason.
    > First, "we all would have this in common." Just because something is a "common" belief does not make it true. The idea that the sun revolved around the earth was the "common belief" of most Europeans "from time

immemorial." When we lower belief in God to the level of Big Foot and UFOs, we haven't done God a favor!

Natural apologists will often argue that if we would all adopt the Medieval Catholic version of Natural Law, the world would be a beautiful place. But, the Catholic reign of terror that lasted a thousand years was hardly a paradise! We must remember all the Christians who were burned at the stake! Idealistic and utopian fantasies often appear in their writings.

Second, we need "an initial point of contact" with unbelievers and if they believe in themselves, then we should join them in that man-centered belief.

Note: I have always wondered why Christians have to give up their biblical beliefs and accept pagan doctrines. Why not tell the unbelievers that they need "an initial point of contact" with Christians by accepting the Bible? Why do *Christians* have to give up their beliefs and accommodate anti-Christian and unbiblical doctrines? Did Elijah on Mt. Carmel adopt the doctrines of Baal as his point of contact? Did Jesus adopt the doctrines of the Sadducees?

5. Their next argument is that it is "psychologically impossible for us to start with God."

I wish they would have explained what they talking about. Whose psychological system? Freud, Skinner, Glasser, etc.? How is it "psychologically impossible" to start with God seeing Moses did this in Gen. 1:1?

Note: Psychology is not a "science" *per se* because human behavior is *unpredictable*. Psychology has been correctly described as the shamanism and witchcraft of modern anti-Christian secularism. Are they saying that it is psychologically harmful to begin with God or that it is a sign of mental illness to look to the Bible as your starting point? This is the perverted psychology of Marx and Freud!

6. They assert that it is "psychologically impossible" for God to "start with man." What do they mean by this assertion? Since they claim to derive their knowledge of God from "Nature," apart from and independent of God and the Bible, where in Nature do we find a "psychology" of God? On what "rational" basis do they assert what God can or cannot "psychologically" do?

Note: Since God tells us in Num. 23:19 that He is *not* a human being, why should human psychology define what God can or cannot do? Where in the Bible do they find any support for their argument?

7. The authors now move from human psychology to Greek logic. They assert that it is "logically impossible" to deny human autonomy and the sufficiency of human reason for two reasons.

First, they state, "it is logically impossible for us to start with God for we cannot affirm God without assuming logic and our ability to predicate."

a. Some modern forms of psychology teach that we need to "affirm" ourselves and others in order to be mentally healthy. Why do the authors think that we need to "affirm" God? Does

God need our affirmation? He says that he does not need anything (Acts 17:25).

b. They state that we must assume Western Aristotelian logic in order to affirm God. Since affirming something or someone is a psychological concept, what does this have to do with logic? Logic supposedly deals with *validity*, not affirmation.

c. Since Job and Moses never heard of Aristotle and his rules of logic, how did they manage to write the early books of the Bible? They could not assume Aristotelian logic because it did not exist in their day.

d. Job and Moses did just fine without any knowledge of modern philosophic ideas of predication.

Second, they assert, "It is logically impossible to show the rational necessity of presupposing God except by rational arguments."

a. The authors do not define what they mean when they spoke of "rational necessity." The word "rational" can mean anything and the word "necessity" is just as hopeless. Are we once again in the realm of *psychology*? Does "rational necessity" refer to some kind of emotion-based *feeling* of necessity? Or, are they claiming that they can produce a chain of syllogism that necessarily ends with the God of the Bible in the conclusion? If so, they should produce their argument as soon as possible as no one has ever seen it.

b. Also, their argument only works if you *care* whether some pagan philosopher thinks you are "rational." But they cannot even agree among themselves what is "rational." As a *Christian*, I am concerned that what I believe is *biblical*. I honestly don't *care* if some pagan somewhere thinks I am "rational" according to his heathen philosophy. The smile of God is more important to me than the frown of man.

> For am I now seeking the favor of men, or
> of God? Or am I striving to please men?
> If I were still trying to please men, I would
> not be a bond-servant of Messiah (Gal. 1:10).

Note: God has declared human philosophy "foolishness" (1 Cor. 1:20) and "empty deception" (Col. 2:8). Why then should we adopt the "foolishness" and "empty deception" of the world as our "point of contact" with pagans? This is what Natural apologists want us to do. The book, *Classical Apologetics*, is therefore marred by gratuitous assumptions that cannot be derived from "Nature," no matter how many different ways you define it.

For example, why should we assume that Aristotle's "Unmoved Mover" is the God of the Bible? If the deities he had in mind when he developed his arguments to prove their existence and attributes are different from the God of the Bible, then his gods are idols.

Why do Catholic or "Classical" Apologists equate Aristotle's "Unmoved Mover" with God? The authors tell us, "Thomas [Aquinas] is quite right when he says that everyone understands this Unmoved Mover to be God."[533]

"Everyone?" Well, I for one do not accept that nonsense. And, even more to the point, after all their claim that they are so LOGICAL, they are using the formal fallacy of *argumentum ad populum*! Something is true because "everyone" agrees?

The truth is Aristotle was a polytheist and believed in many gods. The "Unmoved Mover" did not have the attributes of the triune personal/infinite creator God of the Bible. It was a dead philosophic abstract created by a pagan philosopher. It does not know that it exists or that we exist and cannot love anyone!

The Bible says that Aristotle "never found God." His "Unmoved Mover" did not know or care if we lived or died. If such a monstrosity is "God," I am atheist.

The end result of Catholicism's adoption of Aristotle's "Unmoved Mover" as their view of God led to the need to populate heaven with Mary and the saints who could care for us, hear our prayers, and solve our problems. God became a distant and cold abstract deity as He was reduced to Aristotle's pagan "Unmoved Mover."

Do the Arguments Work?

Some modern Natural Apologists are honest enough to admit that none of their theistic "proofs" actually prove the existence of the God of the Bible. R. Douglas Geivett admits that even if the Muslim Kalaam argument were valid, it still does not prove the existence of the God of the Bible. He quotes Draper, an agnostic philosopher, who said, "this argument does not get all the way to God's existence."[534]

William Dembski sheepishly admits that the arguments for "intelligent design" do not prove the existence of the God revealed in Scripture!

> Who is the designer? As a Christian I hold that the Christian God is the ultimate source of design behind the universe….But there's no way for design inferences based on features of the natural world to reach that conclusion.[535]

To his credit, T. David Beck admits that the argument "by itself, does not uniquely identify God in its conclusion."[536] Geoffrey Bromiley concluded that man,

> cannot attain from it [creation] to a knowledge of the true God, but only to ignorance and idolatry…sin constitutes a distorting veil which is removed only by the new work of saving grace. For the

sinner, therefore, natural theology serves only to condemnation: "They are without excuse." [537]

Useless Arguments

Stop and think about what Geivett, Beck, and Dembski admitted. If you follow the Yellow Brick road of Natural Apologetics all the way to the Emerald City, you will only find a false wizard behind the curtain! You will not find the one true living God. In this light, of what use are their arguments if they do not prove the existence of the God of the Bible? *A lesser god will always be a false god.*

The arguments used by Natural Apologists are false for the following reasons:

1. "The foundation in Roman Catholic natural theology is the conviction that we can have some knowledge of God "from the created things.""[538] The Roman Catholic Church was led astray by Natural Theology and is now a false and apostate church. What good did Natural theology ever do for them? It preaches a false gospel of a works and is filled with idol worship and vain superstitions.

2. Natural Theology is anti-biblical as well as unbiblical. Its use of Scripture is erroneous. For example, Sproul, Gerstner, and Lindsley interpret Rom. 1:19-21 as referring to man's knowledge of God that "is mediate, or inferential, indicating the rational power to deduce the necessary existence of the invisible from the perception of the visible." [539] But Paul has in view the *immediate self-revelation* of God that confronts all human beings all the time in all places and generations. Once it is granted that not all human beings are capable of "rational power" due to birth defect, injury, low IQ, and the aging process, it is clear that man's Natural Theology is not universal in scope and cannot be equated with the absolute universality of God's immediate self-Revelation.

3. They erroneously assume that *man's* Natural Theology is the same thing as *God's* General Revelation. [540]

4. The heresies of Deism and Unitarianism are the logical end result of rationalism. The apostasy of Clark Pinnock is a perfect example and warning of the ultimate destination of theological rationalism.

5. The prophets and apostles did not use such arguments. They practiced confrontation, not compromise (common ground).

6. Most natural theologians do not believe in a literal seven-day creation or in a young earth. Instead, they teach a day-age theory with some kind of theistic evolution, once again appealing to contemporary scientific theories.

7. They do not accept the radical Fall of man into sin and guilt, in particular, they do not take seriously the noetic effects of the Fall.

8. Their foundational dogmas of human autonomy and the sufficiency of human reason are Pelagian in nature and deny the biblical truth of total depravity.

9. They are u*seless* because they do not take us to the true God.

10. Since they are useless, they are *irrelevant*.

11. They assume antiquated world views such as Aristotle or Newton.
12. They depend on cultural consensus.
13. They follow the philosophic fads of the day.
14. They do not and cannot define their key terms such as "reason," "nature," etc.
15. They do not and cannot exegetically demonstrate that their concept of reason, nature, etc. is found in the Bible.
16. They are based upon the heresies of Natural Law, Natural Religion, and Natural Theology.
17. They are circular in nature. [541]
18. Their appeal to "common sense" is nothing more than the *ad populum* fallacy.
19. They are guilty of psychobabble arguments.
20. They ignore the biblical concept of mystery. For example, they cannot explain how the love of God and Christ surpasses all knowledge and rational comprehension (Eph. 3:19; Phil. 4:7).
21. They fail to take seriously God's condemnation of philosophy in Scripture.
22. They ignore, play down or deny the doctrine of the incomprehensibility of God.
23. They claim that the natural man *does* understand the things of God in contradiction of 1 Cor. 2:14.
24. They claim that the natural man does seek God in contradiction of Rom. 3:11.
25. They often end up denying the lost condition of the heathen, eternal conscious punishment in hell, a conscious afterlife, the inerrancy of Scripture, the omni-attributes of God, that God knows the future, that the Roman Catholic Church, Eastern Orthodoxy, the cults such as the Mormons are false and apostate churches.
26. They are based upon unbiblical and anti-biblical anthropologies.
27. They try to find common ground with unbelievers by adopting their non-Christian and unbiblical beliefs.
28. They avoid the offense of the cross by not confronting sinners with their sin and condemnation. "Common ground" is only a form of *compromise* and is clearly condemned in Rom. 12:1-2.
29. They cannot justify doing apologetics from reason alone drawn from nature alone.
30. They assume rationalism, empiricism, mysticism, or fideism as their epistemology. No prophet or apostle ever adopted these pagan epistemologies.
31. They assume pagan ideas as human nature, free will, conscience, and Reason.
32. They ignore Rom. 1:18f, which declares that sinful man rejects General Revelation and, as a result, produces only idolatrous religions that worship the creature rather than the Creator.

Conclusion

The same old, tired arguments that have been around since Aristotle continue to be recycled by giving them a fresh coat of paint in each new generation. Christianity is always the worse off when it adopts them. The more evidence they give, the less faith exists, the fewer

Christians there are, and belief in the Bible decreases. Natural Law, Natural Theology, and Natural Apologetics appear when the church is weak and apostasy strong.

God is GOD because *He* – not man- is the Origin of truth, justice, morals, meaning, and beauty. He is the Measure of all things, not man. To God alone belongs all the glory. Amen.

Chapter Fifteen

What the World Needs to Hear

Introduction

What does the world need to hear from the Christian Church? This question is the most important issue facing the Church today. If we lose our nerve and fail to tell the world what it needs to know, we have utterly failed God and will suffer the consequences on the Day of Judgment.

Please note that we did not ask what the world *wants* to hear. Unbelievers are only interested in one thing: *themselves*. They have no concern for the glory of God or the good of others. They are self-centered and their felt-needs revolve around what they want and what they think will make them happy. Personal peace, affluence, health, pleasure, and popularity constitute the core goals of unregenerate sinners.

If we pander to the felt-needs of sinners, we will be loved by the world and unbelievers will flock to hear us say what they want to hear. Paul described it this way,

> For the time will come when they will not endure sound doctrine; but *wanting* to have their ears tickled, they will accumulate for themselves teachers in accordance to their own desires; and will turn away their ears from the truth, and will turn aside to myths. (2 Tim. 4:3-4)

This point needs to be stressed today as we are confronted with mega churches that openly teach that we need to speak to the felt-needs of unbelievers. In the name of being "relevant," the gospel message has been eviscerated. William Hendriksen's comments are relevant to the 21st century church.

> **But, having itching ears, will accumulate for themselves teachers to suit their own fancies.** It is not the herald of the gospel that is at fault, but *the hearing* of the fickle men who make up the audience! They have ears that *are itching* (from a verb which in the active means *to tickle;* hence, in the passive, *to be tickled,* and thus *to itch,* fig. "to have an irritating desire"). Their craving is for teachers to suit their *fancies* or *perverted tastes* (see on II Tim. 2:22). So great is that hankering that they pile up teacher upon teacher. This reminds one of Jer. 5:31, "The prophets prophesy falsely ... and my people

love to have it so," and of Ezek. 33:32, "And lo, thou art unto them as a very lovely song of one who has a pleasant voice and can play well on an instrument; for they hear thy words, but they do them not." The people here pictured are more interested in something different, something sensational, than they are in sober truth. And when sober truth is presented (as it surely was by Ezekiel), they are not interested in the truth itself, but only in *the way* in which it is presented, the preacher's "style," "oratory," ... the preacher *himself,* his voice, bearing, looks, mannerisms. Here in II Timothy 4:3, 4 the emphasis is on the craving for fascinating stories and philosophical speculations: **and will turn away their ears from the truth, and will turn aside to the myths.** God's redemptive truth, which deals with sin and damnation, with the necessity of inner change, etc. (cf. II Tim. 3:15–17) they cannot stomach. They *turn away* (as in II Tim. 1:15) from it, and *turn aside* (as in I Tim. 1:6) to "the myths," those familiar old womanish myths mentioned earlier (see on I Tim. 1:4, 7; 4:7; Titus 1:14; cf. II Peter 1:16) or anything similar to them. There are always teachers that are willing to "scratch and tickle the ears of those who wish to be tickled" (Clement of Alexandria, *The Stromata,* I. iii).[542]

The classic commentators agree with Hendriksen.

> They would seek out (543lit. "heap up") **teachers,** of whom many are always available, who would tell them what they wanted to hear rather than face them with the truth (cf. Rom. 1:18-32). Such teachers merely "tickle the ear" so that they **turn** people **away from the truth** on the one hand and toward **myths** (*mythous;* cf. 1 Tim. 1:4) on the other. Paul's main focus in this passage was on the inclinations of the audience rather than, as was more his custom (but cf. 2 Tim. 3:6-7), the evil intent of the false teachers. For error to flourish both sides of the transaction must cooperate. 2

> Don't be surprised when people aren't interested in truth. People want to hear what they want to hear—as all too many politicians realize and go on to exploit. But Christian ministry isn't politics. It's presenting God's truth, even when people do not like it, for their benefit and possible salvation.[544]

The Choice Before Us

The choice presented by Paul is between telling the truth in an age when people do not want to hear it, or telling them myths that will make them happy and you popular. The world needs to hear the raw, undiluted truth of God's Word. What are some of the popular "myths" today that unbelievers want to hear?
1. They are "divine" in some way.

2. They possess a good "human nature."
3. No one can judge them, not even God.
4. They have within themselves all they need for their own truth and morals.
5. They have an absolute free will that even God cannot violate.
6. They are autonomous, i.e. independent of God and the Bible.
7. Their reason, experience, feelings and faith are sufficient for all things.
8. Man is the Origin of truth, justice, morals, meaning, and beauty.
9. Man is the measure of all things, including God.
10. Natural Law, Religion, Theology, and Apologetics.
11. They can be whatever they want to be.
12. They can do whatever they want to do.
13. They can know whatever they want to know.
14. They have infinite potential.
15. Ignorance is the problem and knowledge is the cure.
16. There is a secret to living the good life, and if they find it, they will be healthy and wealthy.
17. They need a good self-image.
18. We are all OK.
19. God is all love.
20. There is no day of judgment.
21. There is no hell to fear.
22. All people are good deep down.
23. There is no such thing as sin.
24. There are many ways to heaven.
25. Everyone will end up in heaven.
26. The heathen are not lost.

These myths represent the core of what is preached today in most mega-churches. They offer a smorgasbord of self-help psychobabble sermons that uplift and affirm people in their sin. The cross is not preached. Sin is not mentioned. Health and wealth are the promised blessings of salvation. Heaven is here and now and there is no hell to fear.

This is why Natural Law, Natural Religion, Natural Theology, and Natural Apologetics are humanistic in nature and come from by pagan philosophers. They do not come from Divine Revelation and are often in direct contradiction to it.

The Plain Truth

It is time once again to proclaim the truth, the whole truth, and nothing but the truth as revealed in Scripture. The world needs to hear the TRUTH, not myths and lies. They do not need to be told they don't need God. They already believe that! They don't want God or His Law/Word. They want to be their own law-giver and truth-giver.

Helpless Sinners

We are all helpless sinners in rebellion against the God who created us. We are not autonomous in any sense. We are in bondage to sin and do not have a free will. Sin has given us a moral bias or prejudice against the truth. The sufficiency of human reason is a lie. We cannot begin with the finite and move to the infinite. We cannot magically turn particulars into universals. What **is** cannot become what **ought** to be just because we want it to be so.

Only One True God

There is only one God, and He condemns all the false gods created by Natural Religion. Any "god" less than the Triune God revealed in Scripture is a false god. The "gods" of popery, orthodoxy, liberalism, cults, occult, Process theology, Open View of God, emergent and emerging movements are no more god than a wooden idol of Shiva.

Jesus Is The Only Way

Jesus is the only way to heaven. Sinners must hear of and believe in Jesus Christ and the gospel of salvation by grace alone, through faith alone, in Christ alone in order to be saved. If they do not hear the gospel, they will perish in their sins. Works-based "gospels," such as Roman Catholicism, Eastern Orthodoxy, the cults, and the occult are false gospels that lead millions of sinners to hell.

Begin At The Beginning

If we begin with the biblical doctrines of Creation, Fall, and Redemption, we can understand God, man, the world and how they are relate to each other. We have final answers to all the questions of life and death. But if we are ignorant, ignore or reject these three foundational biblical concepts, no absolute knowledge or morals is possible. Either we begin with God or we end in the abyss of the unrelated.

The Bible Is 100% Inspired

The Bible is the inerrant, infallible, written Word of God, inspired from Genesis to Revelation. Any theology that denies the full inspiration and inerrancy of Scripture is heretical and should be thrown out of all Christian churches and educational institutions.

The Holy Trinity

God is triune. The Holy Spirit is the third person of the Trinity, and is God. Jesus Christ is God as well as man. As God incarnate, He was born of a virgin, lived a sinless life, did many miracles, died for our sins on the cross, arose bodily from the dead on the third day, ascended to heaven, sat down at the right hand of the Father. He is now interceding for the saints and will return bodily and literally one day to this world. There will be a Day of Judgment when Jesus will judge all mankind and decide who enters eternal bliss or eternal torment. There will be a new heavens and a new earth where the saints will enjoy the new earth while all unbelievers will suffer eternal conscious torment in hell.

Conclusion

Chapter Fifteen   What the World Needs to Hear

The *biblical* Gospel is the only hope for mankind and must be preached in purity and power. No substitutions or adulterations can be allowed. In short, the world needs to hear what it does not want to hear: *the truth as it is in Jesus*.

To this end we send forth this work as a means whereby God, in mercy, may send us a New Reformation to turn the hearts and minds of men to bow in submission to the Written and Living Word of God.

> To God alone be all the glory
> in this world and in the next!
> Amen!

Bibliography

After four years of research at the Library of Congress on Natural Theology and Natural Law, the list of books consulted was thirty five pages in length. The publisher wisely told us to reduce that list to what we considered to be the most important works to consult.

Adler, Mortimer, *The Great Ideas*, (New York: Macmillan, 1992).

Anayabwile, Thabiti M., *The Decline of African American Theology*, (Downers Grove: IVP, 2007).

Aquinas in Dialogue, ed. Jim Fodor and Frederick Christian Bauserschmidt, (Oxford: Backwell, 2004).

Archer, Gleason, *Encyclopedia of Bible Difficulties*, (Grand Rapids: Zondervan, 1982).

Asimov's Biographical Encyclopedia of Science and Technology, (New York: Doubleday & C., 1882).

Aston, William P, *Perceiving God,* (Ithaca, NY: Cornell University Press, 1991).

Baker's Dictionary of Theology, (Grand Rapids: Baker, 1960).

Balfour, Arthur James, *The Foundations of Belief*, (NewYork: Longmans, Green, and CO, 1895).

Barnes, Albert, *The Bible Commentary*, (Grand Rapids: Baker, 2001).

Barton, George, *A Critical and Exegetical Commentary on the Book of Ecclesiastes*, The International Critical Commentary, (Edinburgh: T. & T. Clark, 1908).

Beacon Bible Commentary, (Kansas City: Beacon Hill, 1967).

Beckwith, Frank, The *Mormon Concept of God*, (Lewiston, NY: Edwin Mellen Press: 1991).

Berkouwer, G. C.: *General Revelation*. Grand Rapids, (W.B. Eerdmans Pub. Co., 1955).

Boyd, Gregory, *Trinity In Process* (New York: Peter Lang, 1992).

Bratcher, Robert G. and Nida, Eugene Albert: *A Handbook on Paul's Letter to the Ephesians*, (NY: United Bible Societies, 1993).

Brooks, Ronald & Geisler, Norman, *Come, Let Us Reason Together*, (Grand Rapids: Baker, 1990).

Brown, William P., *Ecclesiastes*, (Louisville: Knox, 2000).

Budziszewski, J., *Written on the Heart, The Case for Natural Law*, (Downers Grove: IVP, 1997).

-----------------------, *What We can't Not Know*, (Dallas: Spence, 2003).

Building a Christian Worldview, ed. W. Andrew Hoffecker (Phillipsburg, NJ: P & R, 1986).

Cambridge and Vienna: Frank P. Ramsey and the Vienna Circle (Vienna Circle Institute Yearbook), ed. Maria Galavotti, (Netherlands: Springer, n.d.).

Candlish, Robert S., *Commentary on Genesis*,(Grand Rapids: Zondervan, n.d.).

Capra, Fritjof, *The Tao of Physics: An Exploration of the Parallels between Modern Physics and Eastern Mysticism*, (Boston, MASS: Shambhala Publications, 1999).

Carson, D. A.: *New Bible Commentary: 21st Century Edition*. 4th ed., (Downers Grove: IVP, 1994).

-----------------, The *Gagging of God*, (Grand Rapids: Zondervan, 1996).

Chadbourne, P. A., *Lectures on Natural Theology or Nature and the Bible*, (New York: Putnam's Sons, 1867).

Charles, Daryl, Retrieving the Natural Law: A Return to Moral First Things, (Grand Rapids: Eerdmans, 2008).

Clark, Gordon H., *The Philosophy of Science and Belief in God*, (Jefferson, MD: Trinity Foundation, 1987).

----------------------, *Religion, Reason, and Revelation*, (Jefferson, MD: Trinity Foundation, 1987).

Clarke, Adam, *The Holy Bible, with a Commentary and Critical Notes*, (Nashville: Abingdon-Cokesbury Press, n.d.).

Copleston, Frederick, *Aquinas*, (NY: Penguin, 1991).

------------------------, *A History of Philosophy: Vol. Two, Part 1, Augustine to Bonaventure*, (New York: Image Books, 1962).

Craig, William Lane, *The Only Wise God* (Grand Rapids: Baker, 1987).

Céline Mangan, O.P., trans. The Targum of Job (Collegeville: The Liturgical Press, 1991).

Charles, J. Daryl, *Retrieving The Natural Law*, (Grand Rapids: Eerdmans, 2008).

Cosgrove, Michael, *The Essence of Man* (Grand Rapids: Zondervan, 1977).

Davids, Peter H.: *The Epistle of James: A Commentary on the Greek Text,* (Grand Rapids: Eerdmans, 1982).

Davis, Stephen, *Logic and the Nature of God*, (Grand Rapids, Erdmann, 1983).

DeWesse, Garrett and Moreland, J. P., *Philosophy Made Slightly Less Difficult*, (Downers Gove: IVP, 2005).

Dulles, Avery, *A History of Apologetics*, (Eugene, OR: Wipf & Stock, 1999).

Ellingworth, Paul; Nida, Eugene Albert: *A Handbook on Paul's Letters to the Thessalonians,* (NY: United Bible Societies, 1998).

Ellul, Jacques, *Reason for Being*, (Grand Rapids: Eerdmans, 1990).

Encyclopedia of Religion 2nd, ed. Lindsay Jones, (NY: Thomson/Gale, 2005).

Elseth, Howard Roy. *Did God Know?* (St. Paul, Minn: Calvary United Church, 1977).

Encyclopedia of Philosophy, ed. Borchet, (NY: Thomson & Gale, 2006).

Encyclopedia of Religion and Ethics, ed. James Hastings, (NY: Scribners, 1917).

Evangelical Commentary on the Bible, ed. Walter Elwell, (Grand Rapids: Baker, 1989).

Exell, Joseph, *The Biblical Illustrator,* (Grand Rapids: Baker, 1963).

Fausset, A. R., *Bible Dictionary*, (Grand Rapids: Zondervan, 1979).

Frame, John, *Doctrine of God*, (Harmony, NJ: P & R, 2002).

Freeman, James M.; Chadwick, Harold J.: *Manners & Customs of the Bible*. Rev. ed., (North Brunswick: Bridge-Logos, 1998).

Garret, Duane A., *Hosea, Joel.* (Nashville: Broadman & Holman, 2001).

------------------------, *Proverbs, Ecclesiastes, and Song of Songs*, (Nashville: Broadman, 1993).

Geisler, Norman, *Thomas Aquinas: An Evangelical Appraisal,* (Eugene, OR: Wipf and Stock Publishers, 2003).

Gibson, Edgar, C. S., The Book of Job (Minneapolis: Klock & Klock, 1978).

Gill, John, *An Exposition of the Old Testament*, (London: Collingridge, 1851).

Grabill, Stephen, *Rediscovering The Natural law in Reformed Theological Ethics,* (Grand Rapids: Eerdmans, 2006).

Gullberg, Jan, *Mathematics: From the Birth of Numbers*, (NY: Norton, 1997).

Habel, Norman, *The Book of Job*, (Philadelphia: Westminster, 1985).

Hall, A. Rupert *The Revolution in Science 1500-1750*, (London, Longman, 1983).

Hayes, Stephen R., *Noah's Curse: The Biblical Justification of American Slavery*, (New York: Oxford University press, 2002).

Hawking, Stephen, *A Brief History of Time*, (NY: Bantam Books, 1996).

Hendriksen, William, *Exposition of Ephesians, (*Grand Rapids: Baker, 1953).

---------------------------,*Exposition of the First Epistle to the Corinthians,* (Grand Rapids: Baker, 2001).

Hengstenberg, ,Ernest W. A., *Commentary on Ecclesiastes*, (Eugene, OR: Wipf & Stock, 1998).

Henry, Carl F., *The Biblical Expositor, The Living Theme of The Great Book, with General and Introductory Essays and Exposition for each Book of the Bible in Three Volumes*, (Philadelphia: Holman,1960).

-------------------, "Natural Law and a Nihilistic Culture," *First Things* (Jan. 1995).

-------------------, *God, Revelation, and Authority*, (Wheaton: Ill, Crossway Books, 1999).

Henry, Matthew: *Matthew Henry's Commentary on the Whole Bible: Complete and Unabridged in One Volume*, (Peabody: Hendrickson, 1996).

Holman's Old Testament Commentary, ed. Max Anders, author Steven J. Lawson, (Nashville: Holman, 2004).

Hordern, William, *A Layman's Guide to Protestant Theology,* (NY: Macmillan, 1957).

Hume, David, *Enquiry Concerning Human Understanding*, (London: Clarendon, 1966).

In Defense of Natural Theology: A Defense of Post-humean Assessment, by James F. Sennett (Editor), Douglas Groothuis, (Downers Grove: IVP, 2005).

International Standard Bible Encyclopedia, ed. James Orr, (Grand Rapids: Eerdmans, 1986).

Jamieson, Robert; Fausset, A. R.; Fausset, A. R.; Brown, David Brown, David: *A Commentary, Critical and Explanatory, on the Old and New Testaments,* (Oak Harbor, WA: Logos, 1997).

Jammer, Max, *Einstein and Religion*, (Princeton: Princeton University Press, 1999).

Kainz, Howard P., *Natural law: An Introduction and Re-examination*, (Chicago: Open Court, 2004).

Keil and Delitzsch: Commentaries on the Old Testament (Grand Rapids: Eerdmans, 1966).

Kelsey, George D., *Racism and the Christian Understanding of Man*, (NY: Scribner's Sons, 1965).

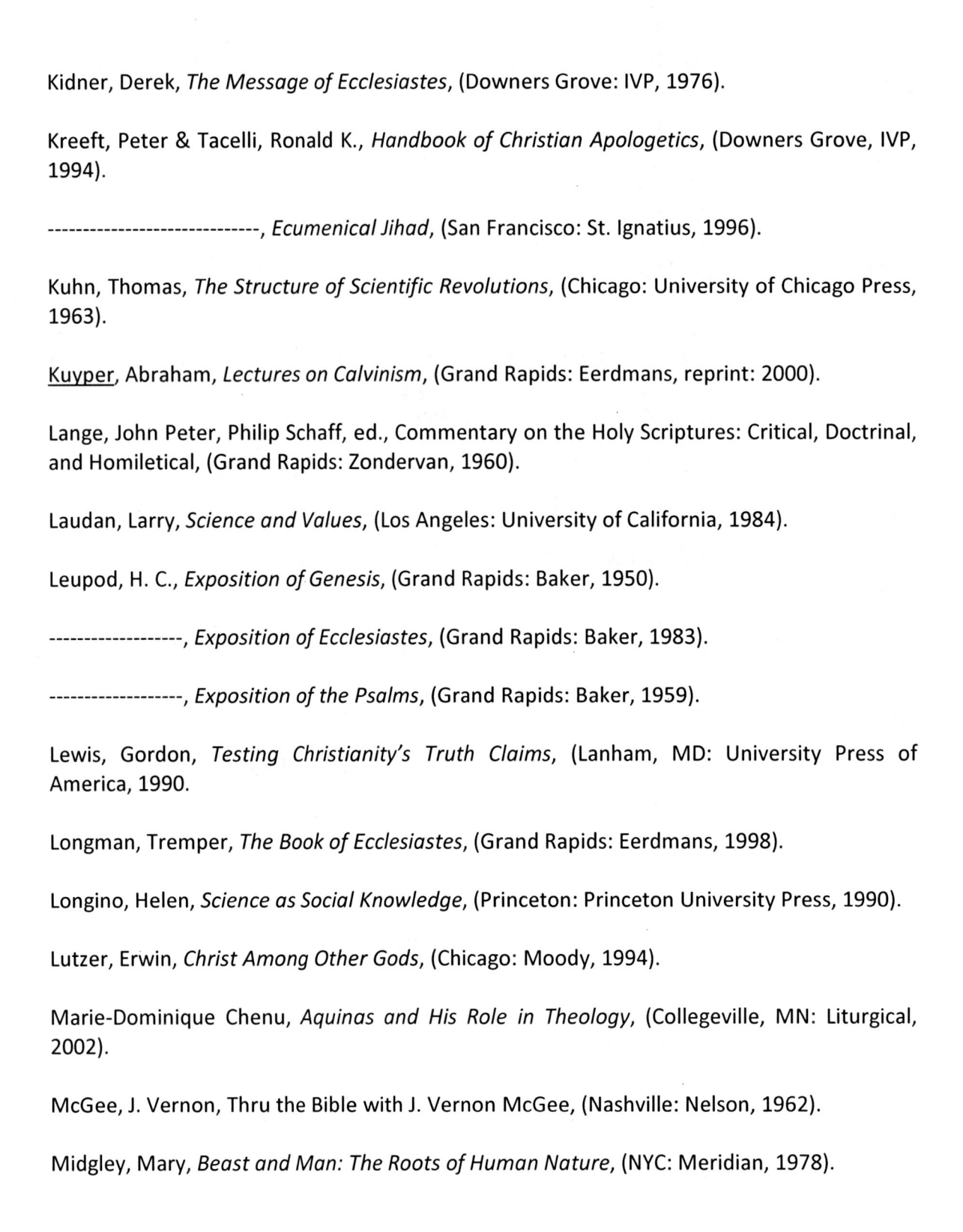

Kidner, Derek, *The Message of Ecclesiastes*, (Downers Grove: IVP, 1976).

Kreeft, Peter & Tacelli, Ronald K., *Handbook of Christian Apologetics*, (Downers Grove, IVP, 1994).

------------------------------, *Ecumenical Jihad*, (San Francisco: St. Ignatius, 1996).

Kuhn, Thomas, *The Structure of Scientific Revolutions*, (Chicago: University of Chicago Press, 1963).

Kuyper, Abraham, *Lectures on Calvinism*, (Grand Rapids: Eerdmans, reprint: 2000).

Lange, John Peter, Philip Schaff, ed., Commentary on the Holy Scriptures: Critical, Doctrinal, and Homiletical, (Grand Rapids: Zondervan, 1960).

Laudan, Larry, *Science and Values*, (Los Angeles: University of California, 1984).

Leupod, H. C., *Exposition of Genesis*, (Grand Rapids: Baker, 1950).

------------------, *Exposition of Ecclesiastes*, (Grand Rapids: Baker, 1983).

------------------, *Exposition of the Psalms*, (Grand Rapids: Baker, 1959).

Lewis, Gordon, *Testing Christianity's Truth Claims*, (Lanham, MD: University Press of America, 1990.

Longman, Tremper, *The Book of Ecclesiastes*, (Grand Rapids: Eerdmans, 1998).

Longino, Helen, *Science as Social Knowledge*, (Princeton: Princeton University Press, 1990).

Lutzer, Erwin, *Christ Among Other Gods*, (Chicago: Moody, 1994).

Marie-Dominique Chenu, *Aquinas and His Role in Theology*, (Collegeville, MN: Liturgical, 2002).

McGee, J. Vernon, Thru the Bible with J. Vernon McGee, (Nashville: Nelson, 1962).

Midgley, Mary, *Beast and Man: The Roots of Human Nature*, (NYC: Meridian, 1978).

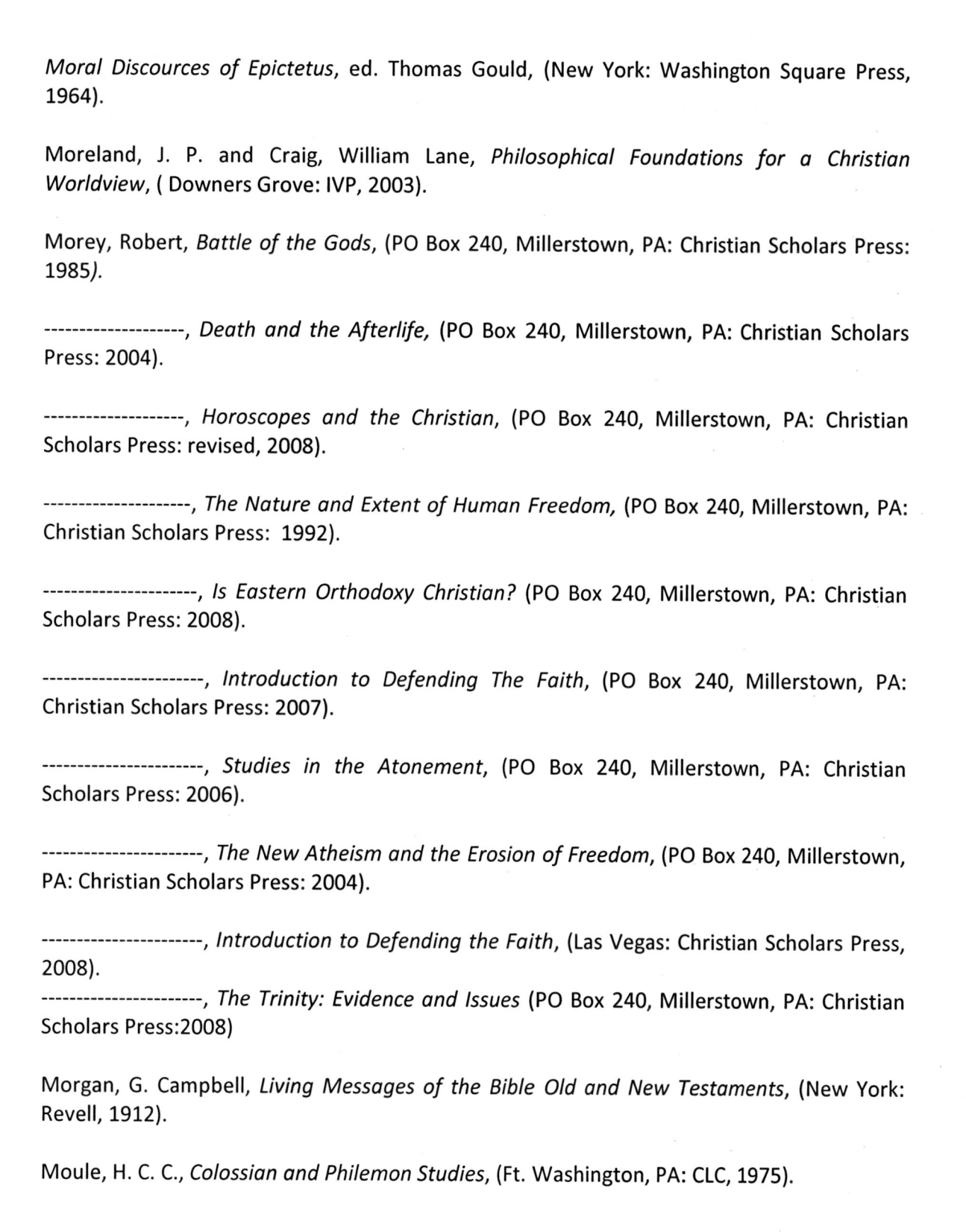

Moral Discources of Epictetus, ed. Thomas Gould, (New York: Washington Square Press, 1964).

Moreland, J. P. and Craig, William Lane, *Philosophical Foundations for a Christian Worldview*, (Downers Grove: IVP, 2003).

Morey, Robert, *Battle of the Gods*, (PO Box 240, Millerstown, PA: Christian Scholars Press: 1985*)*.

--------------------, *Death and the Afterlife,* (PO Box 240, Millerstown, PA: Christian Scholars Press: 2004).

--------------------, *Horoscopes and the Christian,* (PO Box 240, Millerstown, PA: Christian Scholars Press: revised, 2008).

--------------------, *The Nature and Extent of Human Freedom,* (PO Box 240, Millerstown, PA: Christian Scholars Press: 1992).

---------------------, *Is Eastern Orthodoxy Christian?* (PO Box 240, Millerstown, PA: Christian Scholars Press: 2008).

---------------------, *Introduction to Defending The Faith*, (PO Box 240, Millerstown, PA: Christian Scholars Press: 2007).

---------------------, *Studies in the Atonement,* (PO Box 240, Millerstown, PA: Christian Scholars Press: 2006).

---------------------, *The New Atheism and the Erosion of Freedom*, (PO Box 240, Millerstown, PA: Christian Scholars Press: 2004).

---------------------, *Introduction to Defending the Faith*, (Las Vegas: Christian Scholars Press, 2008).

---------------------, *The Trinity: Evidence and Issues* (PO Box 240, Millerstown, PA: Christian Scholars Press:2008)

Morgan, G. Campbell, *Living Messages of the Bible Old and New Testaments*, (New York: Revell, 1912).

Moule, H. C. C., *Colossian and Philemon Studies*, (Ft. Washington, PA: CLC, 1975).

Murphy, Roland and Huwiler, Elizabeth, *New International Biblical Commentary: Proverbs, Ecclesiastes, and Song of Songs*, (Peabody, Mass: Hendrickson, 1999).

Murphy, Roland E., *Ecclesiastes: Word Biblical Commentary*, (Dallas: Word, 1992).

Nash, Ronald, *On Process Theology*, (Grand Rapids: Baker, 1987).

New Bible Commentary, ed. D. A. Carson, A R. T. France, J. A. Motyer, and Gordon J. Wenham, (Downers Grove: IVP, 1994).

New Catholic Encyclopedia, (Washington, DC: Thomson/Gale, 2003).

New International Biblical Commentary: Proverbs, Ecclesiastes, and Song of Songs, (Peabody, Mass: Hendrickson, 1999).

Newman, Barclay Moon and Nida, Eugene Albert: *A Handbook on the Acts of the Apostles*, (NY: United Bible Societies, 1972).

Newport, John P., *Christianity and Contemporary Art Forms*, (Waco, TX: Word, 1970).

Noll, Mark A., *A History of Christianity in the United States and Canada*, (Grand Rapids: Eerdmans, 1992).

Ogden, Graham S. and Zogbo, Lynell: *A Handbook on Ecclesiastes*. NY: United Bible Societies, 1998).

Olson, Gordon C., *The Truth Shall Set You Free,* (Franklin Park, Ill: Bible Research Fellowship, 1980).

Oster, Blake, T. *Review of Books on the Book of Mormon 8/2*, (1996).

Otis, George, "The Foreknowledge of God," unpublished paper, (1941, n.p.).

Otto Zockler, *The Book of Job, Theologically and Homiletically Expounded*, Translated and Edited by Llewelyn J. Evans, (NY: Charles Scribner & Sons, 1872).

Parker, Joseph, *Preaching Through the Bible*, (Grand Rapids: Baker, 1961).

Paley's Evidences of Christianity, (NY: Carter & Brothers, 1882).

Provan, Iain, *Ecclesiastes: The NIV Application Commentary*, (Grand Rapids: Zondervan, 2001).

Packer, J. I., *God Who Is Rich in Mercy*, (Grand Rapids: Baker, 1986).

Pinnock, Clark, *A Wideness in God's Mercy*, (Grand Rapids: Zondervan, 1992).

Plantinga, Alvin C. *God, Freedom, and Evil* (Grand Rapids: Eerdmans, 1974).

Popper, Karl, *Conjectures and Refutations*, (London: Routledge, 1963).

Porter, Jean, *Natural & Divine Law*, (Grand Rapids: Eerdmans, 1999).

-----------------, *Nature as Reason,* Grand Rapids: Eerdmans, 2005).

Poythress, Vern Sheridan, *Redeeming Science: A God-Centered Approach*, (Wheaton, IL: Crossway, 2006).

Predestination and Free Will, eds. David Basinger and Randall Basinger (Downers Grove; IVP, 1986).

Ramm, Bernard, *Protestant Christian Evidences* (Chicago: Moody Press, 1966).

----------------------, *Varieties of Christian Apologetics*, (Grand Rapids: Baker, 1965).

Ramsey, Frank, *Philosophical Papers*, (Cambridge: Cambridge University Press, 1999).

Rawlinson, G., *Exposition of Job (The Pulpit Commentary)*, (McLean, VA: MacDonald, n. d.).

Reyburn, William David; Fry, Euan McG.: *A Handbook on Proverbs,* (NY: United Bible Societies, 2000).

Rice, Richard, *The Openness of God,* (Nashville TN; Review & Herald Pub., 1979).

Richards, Lawrence, O., *The Bible Reader's Companion*, (Wheaton: Victor Books, 1991).

--------------------------------, *The Teacher's Commentary,* (Wheaton: Victor Books, 1987).

Renick, Timothy, *Aquinas for Armchair* Theologians, (London: John Knox, 2002).

Robertson, A.T., *Word Pictures in the New Testament*, (Oak Harbor: Logos Research Systems, 1997).

Rookmaaker, Hans R., *Modern Art and the Death of a Culture*, (Downers Grove, IL: IVP, 1975).

Rothman, Tony, *Instant Physics: From Aristotle to Einstein, and Beyond*, (New York: Byron Preiss Publications, 1995).

Samuel Rolles Driver and George Buchanan Gray, *A Critical and Exegetical Commentary on The Book of Job*, (Edinburgh: T. & T. Clark, 1971).

Sanders, John, *No Other Name*, (Grand Rapids: Eerdmans, 1992).

Sarte, Jean Paul, *Being and Nothingness*, (New York: Washington Square Press, 1966).

Schaeffer, Francis, *The God Who Is There*, (Downers Grove, IL: IVP, 1968).

-------------------------, *Art and the Bible*, (Downers Grove, IL: IVP, 1974).

-------------------------, *How Should We Then Live?*, (Wheaton: Crossway Books, 1976).

Scott, Robert, *Proverbs, Ecclesiastes*, (Garden City: Doubleday, 1995).

Skinner, B.F., *Beyond Freedom & Dignity*, (Indianapolis: Hackett, 2002).

Smith, Billy K. and Page, Franklin S.: *Amos, Obadiah, Jonah*, (Nashville: Broadman & Holman Publishers, 2001).

Sorell, Tom, *Scientism: Philosophy and the Infatuation with Science*, (London: Routledge).

Sproul, R. C., Gerstner, John, and Lindsley, Arthur, *Classical Apologetics*, (Grand Rapids: Zondervan, 1984).

Stark, Rodney, *The Victory of Reason*, (New York: Random House, 2005).

Taylor James E., Introducing Apologetics (Grand Rapids: Baker, 2006).

The Columbia Encyclopedia, 6th ed., ed. Paul Lagosse, (New York: Columbia University Press, 2000).

The Catholic Encyclopedia, (Nashville: Thomas Nelson, 1987).

The Encyclopedia of Christianity, ed. Geoffery Bromiley, (Grand Rapids: Eerdmans, 2003).

The Expositor's Bible Commentary, ed. Frank Gaebelein, (Grand Rapids: Zondervan, 1991).

The Interpreter's Bible, (Nashville: Abington, 1954).

The International Standard Bible Encyclopedia, ed. James Orr, (Peabody, Mass: Hendrickson, 1996).

The Grace of God, The Will of Man, ed. Clark Pinnock, (Grand Rapids: Zondervan, 1989).

The New American Commentary, (Nashville: Broadman, 1994).

The New Bible Commentary Revised, (Downers Grove: IVP, 1970)

The Pulpit Commentary, (New York: Funk & Wagnalls, n.d.).

The Expositor's Bible Commentary, ed. Frank Gaebelin, (Grand Rapids: Zondervan, 1998).

The Encyclopedia Americana, (Danbury, CN: Encyclopedia Americana, 1998).

The New Encyclopedia Britannica, (Chicago: Encyclopedia Britannica, 1998).

The New Schaff-Herzog Encyclopedia of Religion, ed. Samuel Jackson, (New York: Funk & Wagnalls, 1910).

The Oxford Dictionary of Jewish Religion, ed. Werblowsky and Wigoder, (New York: Oxford University Press, 1997).

The Teachings of Modern Protestantism, ed. John White Jr. and Frank S. Alexander, (New York: Columbia University Press, 2007).

The Westminster Dictionary of Christian Theology, ed. Alan Richardson and John Brown, (Philadelphia: Westminster Press, 1983).

The Works of Jonathan Edwards, (Edinburgh: Banner of Truth, 1974).

Tise, Larry, *Proslavery: A History of the Defense of Slavery in America, 1701-1840*, (Athens, Georgia: University of Georgia, 1987).

To Everyone an Answer, ed. Beckwith, Craig, and Moreland, (Downers Grove: IVP, 2004).

Van den Haag, Ernest, "Not Above the Law," (*National Review* 43 (1991).

VanDrunen, David, *Law & Custom: The Thought of Thomas Aquinas and the Future of the Common Law*, (NY: Peter Lang, 2003), preface.

-------------------------, *The Biblical Case for Natural Law*, (Grand Rapids: Acton Institute, 2006).

Vincent, Marvin Richardson: *Word Studies in the New Testament* (Bellingham, WA: Logos, 2002).

Walvoord, John and Zuck, Roy, *The Bible Knowledge Commentary,* (Wheaton: Victor, 1985).

Web, Clement C. J., *Studies in The History of Natural Theology*, (Oxford: Claredon, 1915).

Webster's Third New international Dictionary, (Springfield, Mass: Merrian-Webster, 2002).

Wegner, Paul D., *The Journey from Texts to Translations*, (Grand Rapids: Baker, 1999).

Whybray, R. N., *Ecclesiastes: New Century Bible Commentary*, (Grand Rapids: Eerdmans, 1989).

Wiersbe, Warren W., *Be Satisfied*, (Wheaton, Victor Books, 1996).

-------------------------, *Wiersbe's Expository Outlines on the New Testament*, (Wheaton: Victor Books, 1997).

-------------------------, *The Bible Exposition Commentary,* (Wheaton: Victor Books, 1996).

-------------------------, *Wiersbe's Expository Outlines on the New Testament,* (Wheaton: Victor Books, 1997).

Wisnefske, Ned, *Our Natural Knowledge of God*, (New York: Peter Lang: 1990).

Willmington, H. L., *Wilmington's Bible Handbook,* (Wheaton: Tyndale, 1997).

Winthrop Jordan, *White Over Black: American Attitudes Toward the Negro, 1550-1812,* (Chapel Hill: University of North Carolina, 1968).

Wolf, Erik, *Das Problem der Naturrechtslebre*, (Karlsruhe; Muller, 1955).

Zeller, Edgar, *Outlines of Greek Philosophy*, (NY: Meridian Books, 1967).

Zukav, Guy, *The Dancing Wu Li Masters: An Overview of the New Physics,* (New York: Bantam Books, 1979).

EndNotes

[1] J. Vernon McGee, *Thru the Bible with J. Vernon McGee*, (Nashville: Nelson, 1962) pg. 581.

[2] *A New Rhythmical Version of the Book of Job, with Exegetical Notes and Addenda Containing Excursus on Difficult and Important Passages*, by Tayler Lewis. Reprinted in Lange, John Peter, Philip Schaff, ed., *Commentary on the Holy Scriptures: Critical, Doctrinal, and Homiletical*, Zondervan (Grand Rapids), 1960, pg. 1.

[3] One clear example is the journal *Philosophia Christi*, published by Biola University and the Evangelical Philosophical Society. Many of the theologians in this journal are not "evangelical" in any sense. Counter-Reformation Jesuit doctrines such as Molinism ("Middle Knowledge") are put forward as "Christian" doctrines. Such apostates as Stephen Davis, the "God can sin" and "God can lie" philosopher, are welcome to contribute articles and reviews. Liberals, Mormons, Catholics, etc. are allowed to teach their heresies.

[4] *Building a Christian Worldview*, ed. W. Andrew Hoffecker, (Phillipsburg: P & R, 1986) pg. xiii. We have a great respect for Hoeffecker and hope that our criticism of his historical approach is not interpreted as criticism of him personally.

[5] Carson, D. A.: *New Bible Commentary : 21st Century Edition*. 4th ed., (Downers Grove: IVP, 1994), S. Ro 12:1

[6] Kistemaker, Simon J. ; Hendriksen, William: *New Testament Commentary : Exposition of the First Epistle to the Corinthians*. Grand Rapids : Baker Book House, 1953-2001 (New Testament Commentary 18), S. 509

[7] Newman, Barclay Moon ; Nida, Eugene Albert: *A Handbook on the Acts of the Apostles*. New York : United Bible Societies, 993], c1972 (UBS Handbook Series; Helps for Translators), S. 332

[8] James E. Taylor, *Introducing Apologetics* (Grand Rapids: Baker, 2006), pg. 11.

[9] Ibid. pg. 10.

[10] Ibid. pg. 276.

[11] Ibid. pg. 276.

[12] *The Pulpit Commentary* (New York: Funk & Wagnalls, n.d.), pg. xl.

[13] Samuel Rolles Driver and George Buchanan Gray, *A Critical and Exegetical Commentary on The Book of Job*, (Edinburgh: T. & T. Clark, 1971), pg. xxv. See also, *Beacon Bible Commentary*, (Kansas City: Beacon Hill, 1967), pg. 2-21. *The Interpreter's Bible*, (Nashville: Abington, 1954) pgs. 878f.

[14] Ibid.

[15] Holman, *Old Testament Commentary*, ed. Max Anders, author Steven J. Lawson, (Nashville: Holman, 2004) pg. 3-4. Robert Alden, *The New American Commentary*, (Nashville: Broadman, 1993) pgs. 30-31.

[16] Taylor, ibid. pg. 12.

[17] Joseph Parker, *Preaching Through the Bible* (Grand Rapids: Baker, 1961) pgs. 375-376.

[18] G. Rawlinson, *Exposition of Job in The Pulpit Commentary* (McLean, VA: MacDonald Pub. Co., n.d.) 7:xiv.

[19] Gibson, Edgar C. S., *The Book of Job* (Minneapolis: Klock & Klock Christian Publishers, 1978), pg. 12.

[20] Céline Mangan, O.P., trans. *The Targum of Job* (Collegeville: The Liturgical Press, 1991), pg. 5.,

[21] For information on obtaining the audit materials on the Text and Canon of Scripture, http://www.faithdefenders.com.

[22] Gibson, pg. ix.

[23] Driver and Gray, ibid. pg. xix.

[24] Gibson, ibid. pg. xiv.

[25] Lewis, Ibid. pg. 29

[26] Ibid. pg. 20.

[27] Ibid. pgs. 17-18

[28] Ibid. pgs. 21-22.

[29] Otto Zockler, D. D., *The Book of Job, Theologically and Homiletically Expounded,* Translated and Edited by Llewelyn J. Evans, D. D., pg. 235.

[30] Ibid. pgs. 614-615.

[31] Joseph Exell, *The Biblical Illustrator* (Grand Rapids: Baker, 1963), pgs. 630-631.

[32] Alden, ibid. pg. 41.

[33] Holman, ibid. pgs. 7-8.
[34] Lewis, ibid. pg. 40.
[35] Ibid. pg. 41.
[36] Ibid. pg. 45.
[37] Rawlinson, ibid. pg. xviii.
[38] *In Defense of Natural Theology: A Defense of Post-humean Assessment*, by James F. Sennett (Editor), Douglas Groothuis (Editor), (Downers Grove: IVP, 2005).
[39] McGee, ibid. pg. 586.
[40] Rawlinson, ibid. pg. 85.
[41] Gibson, ibid. pgs. 18-19.
[42] Rawlinson, ibid. pg. iii.
[43] Gibson, ibid. pg. 28.
[44] Rawlinson, ibid. pg. 68.
[45] Gibson, ibid. pg. xii.
[46] Ibid. pg. xiii.
[47] Ibid. pg. xv.
[48] Beacon, ibid. pg. 48-49. (Rowley.)
[49] Gibson, ibid. pg. 89.
[50] Rawlinson, ibid. pg. 140.
[51] Rowley, ibid. pg. 70.
[52] Gibson, ibid. pg. 40.
[53] Beacon, ibid. pg. 48.
[54] Gibson, ibid. pg. 42.
[55] Reyburn, William David ; Fry, Euan McG.: *A Handbook on Proverbs*. New York : United Bible Societies, 2000 (UBS Handbook Series; Helps for Translators), S. 73
[56] Rowley, ibid. pg. 4.
[57] Ibid. pg. 207.
[58] Ibid. pg. xxvi.
[59] Ibid. pg. xv.
[60] Zockler, ibid. pg. 601.
[61] Parker, ibid. pg. 383.
[62] Keil and Delitzsch: *Commentaries on the Old Testament* (Grand Rapids: Eerdmans, 1966) Job, II:312.
[63] Ibid. II:313.
[64] It is sometimes hard for modern Western European Gentiles to understand what is going on in the ancient Jewish Bible. The Jewish humor, wit, and sarcasm go right over their heads. They don't get it!
[65] Rawlinson, ibid. pg. 615; Alden, ibid. pg. 368.
[66] Norman Habel, *The Book of Job*, (Philadelphia: Westminster, 1985) pgs. 520-521.
[67] Keil and Delitzsch, ibid. II:380.
[68] Parker, ibid. pg. 385.
[69] *The Biblical Illustrator*, ibid. pg. 596.
[70] Habel, ibid. pg.577.
[71] *The Expositor's Bible Commentary*, ed. Frank Gaebelin, (Grand Rapids: Zondervan, 1998), IV:1035.
[72] Ibid.
[73] *Pulpit Commentary*, ibid. pg.672.
[74] Holman, ibid. pg. 365.
[75] Keil and Delitzsch, ibid. II:380.
[76] Ibid. pg. 393.

[77] G. Campbell Morgan, *Living Messages of the Bible Old and New Testaments*, (New York: Revell, MCMXII), p. 18.

[78] Robertson, A.T.: *Word Pictures in the New Testament*. Oak Harbor : Logos Research Systems, 1997, S. 1 Co 1:21

[79] 3 Robert S. Candlish, *Commentary on Genesis,* (Grand Rapids: Zondervan, n.d.), p. 2.

[80] Ibid, p. 7.

[81] Ibid.

[82] Ibid, p. 5.

[83] Ibid, p. 6.

[84] Ibid, p. 14.

[85] Ibid, p. 4.

[86] Ibid.

[87] Ibid, p. 11.

[88] A. R. Fausset, *Bible Dictionary*, (Grand Rapids: Zondervan, 1979) p. 1310.

[89] *International Standard Bible Encyclopedia*, ed. James Orr, (Grand Rapids: Eerdmans, 1986), III:1174.

[90] Carl F. Henry, *The Biblical Expositor, The Living Theme of The Great Book, with General and Introductory Essays and Exposition for each Book of the Bible in Three Volumes*, (Philadelphia: Holman,1960), I:58.

[91] Keil and Delitzsch, *Commentaries on the Old Testament* (Grand Rapids: Eerdmans, n.d.), p. 46.

[92] Henry, Matthew: *Matthew Henry's Commentary on the Whole Bible : Complete and Unabridged in One Volume*. Peabody : Hendrickson, 1996, c1991, S. Ge 1:1.

[93] John Peter Lange, *Lange's Commentary on the Holy Scriptures* (Grand Rapids: Zondervan, 1960), I:71-72.

[94] Ibid, p. 71.

[95] Leupod, H. C., *Exposition of Genesis*, (Grand Rapids: Baker, 1950) pgs. 27f.

[96] The definitive work is Jan Gulllberg, *Mathematics: From the Birth of Numbers*, (NY: Norton, 1997).

[97] Henry, Matthew: *Matthew Henry's Commentary on the Whole Bible : Complete and Unabridged in One Volume*. Peabody : Hendrickson, 1996, c1991, S. Ho 6:1.

[98] Henry, Matthew: *Matthew Henry's Commentary on the Whole Bible : Complete and Unabridged in One Volume*. Peabody : Hendrickson, 1996, c1991, S. 1 Co 15:1.

[99] Spence-Jones, H. D. M. (Hrsg.): *The Pulpit Commentary: 1 Corinthians*. Bellingham, WA : Logos Research Systems, Inc., 2004, S. 484.

[100] Garret, Duane A.: *Hosea, Joel*. electronic ed. Nashville : Broadman & Holman Publishers, 2001, c1997 (Logos Library System; The New American Commentary 19A), S. 158.

[101] *New Bible Commentary*, ed. D. A. Carson, A R. T. France, J. A. Motyer, and Gordon J. Wenham, (Downers Grove: IVP, 1994), S. Gen. 3:9

[102] Keil, Carl Friedrich ; Delitzsch, Franz: *Commentary on the Old Testament*. Peabody, MA : Hendrickson, 2002, S. 1:62-63

[103] Spence-Jones, H. D. M. (Hrsg.): *The Pulpit Commentary: Genesis*. Bellingham, WA : Logos Research Systems, Inc., 2004, S. 104

[104] Robertson, A.T.: *Word Pictures in the New Testament*. Oak Harbor : Logos Research Systems, 1997, S. Ro 4:4

[105] Vincent, Marvin Richardson: *Word Studies in the New Testament*. Bellingham, WA : Logos Research Systems, Inc., 2002, S. 3:51.

[106] John Walvoord and Roy Zuck, *The Bible Knowledge Commentary,* (Wheaton: Victor, 1985), S. 2:453

[107] 7 Richards, Lawrence O.: *The Bible Readers Companion*. electronic ed. Wheaton : Victor Books, 1991; Published in electronic form by Logos Research Systems, 1996, S. 740

[108] 8 Wiersbe, Warren W.: *Wiersbe's Expository Outlines on the New Testament*. Wheaton, Ill. : Victor Books, 1997, c1992, S. 372

[109] 9 Henry, Matthew: *Matthew Henry's Commentary on the Whole Bible : Complete and Unabridged in One Volume*. Peabody : Hendrickson, 1996, c1991, S. Jon 2:1

EndNotes

[110] 10 Smith, Billy K. ; Page, Franklin S.: *Amos, Obadiah, Jonah*. electronic ed. Nashville : Broadman & Holman Publishers, 2001, c1995 (Logos Library System; The New American Commentary 19B), S. 252

[111] Wiersbe, Warren W.: *The Bible Exposition Commentary*. Wheaton, Ill. : Victor Books, 1996, c1989, S. Ro 3:21

[112] Quoted in: David Moore and Daniel Akin, *Book of Ecclesiastes, Song of Songs, (Holman Old Testament Commentary*, ed. Max Anders , Nashville, 2003), p. 1.

[113] ibid.

[114] Derek Kidner, *The Message of Book of Ecclesiastes*, (Downers Grove: IVP, 1976.), p. 11.

[115] Jacques Ellul, *Reason for Being*, (Grand Rapids: Eerdmans, 1990), p. 1.

[116] Duane Garrett, *Proverbs, Book of Ecclesiastes, and Song of Songs*, (Nashville: Broadman, 1993), p. 271.

[117] Iain Provan, *Book of Ecclesiastes*: The NIV Application Commentary, (Grand Rapids: Zondervan, 2001), p. 23.

[118] *The Expositor's Bible Commentary*, ed. Frank Gaebelein, (Grand Rapids: Zondervan, 1991), V:1137

[119] Robert Scott, *Proverbs, Book of Ecclesiastes*, (Garden City: Doubleday, 1995) Anchor Bible 18: p. 191.

[120] David Moore and Daniel Akin, *ibid*, p. 1.

[121] Roland Murphy and Elizabeth Huwiler, *New International Biblical Commentary: Proverbs, Book of Ecclesiastes, and Song of Songs*, (Peabody, Mass: Hendrickson, 1999), p. 159.

[122] John Gill, *An Exposition of the Old Testament*, (London: Collingridge, 1851), III:605.

[123] Albert Barnes, *The Bible Commentary*, (Grand Rapids: Baker, 2001), p. 87.

[124] George Barton, *A Critical and Exegetical Commentary on the Book of Book of Ecclesiastes*, The International Critical Commentary, (Edinburgh: T. & T. Clark, 1908). He states that it was "impossible" for Solomon to be the author (p.58).

[125] *Commentary on the Holy Scriptures*, ed. John Peter Lange, (Grand Rapids: Zonderan, 1960), Book of Ecclesiastes, p. 21.

[126] Ernest W. Hengstenberg, A Commentary on Book of Ecclesiastes, (Eugene, OR: Wipf & Stock, 1998) p. 33.

[127] Albert Barnes, *ibid, p.*1.

[128] ibid. pgs. 87f.

[129] Walvoord, John F. ; Zuck, Roy B.; Dallas Theological Seminary: *The Bible Knowledge Commentary : An Exposition of the Scriptures*. Wheaton, IL: Victor Books, 1983-c1985, S. 1:976

[130] Richards, Lawrence O.: *The Bible Readers Companion*. electronic ed. Wheaton : Victor Books, 1991; Published in electronic form by Logos Research Systems, 1996, S. 395

[131] Tremper Longman III, *The Book of Book of Ecclesiastes*, (Grand Rapids: Eerdmans, 1998), p. 4, gives a list of conservative scholars who not believe that Solomon wrote it. See also: Elllul, ibid, pgs. 16f.

[132] Eccl. 7:2; Mt. 5:3,4; Eccl. 5:2; Mt. 6:7; Eccl. 6:2; Luke 12:20; Mt. 6:19-84; Eccl. 11:5; John 3:8; Eccl. 9:10; John 9:4; Eccl. 10:12; Col. 4:6; Eccl. 12:14; 2 Cor. 5:10; Eccl. 5:1; 1 Tim. 3:15; James 1:19; Eccl. 5:6; 1 Cor. 11:10.

[133] Adam Clarke, *The Holy Bible, with a Commentary and Critical Notes*, (Nashville: Abingdon-Cokesbury Press, n.d.), III:799.

[134] Tremper Longman III, ibid, pgs. 9-11.

[135] *The Expositor's Bible Commentary*, ibid, p. V:1149. George Barton, *A Critical and Exegetical Commentary on the Book of Book of Ecclesiastes*, The International Critical Commentary, (Edinburgh: T. & T. Clark, 1908), pgs. 8f.

[136] H. C, Leupold, *Exposition of Book of Ecclesiastes*, (Grand Rapids: Baker, 1983) p. 23.

[137] Barnes, ibid.

[138] Duane Garrett, ibid., p. 271.

[139] Roland Murphy and Elizabeth Huwiler , ibid, p. 169.

[140] Ellul, ibid. pgs. 12-13

[141] Duane Garrett, ibid, p. 269.

[142] William P. Brown, *Book of Ecclesiastes*, (Louisville: KY: John Knox, 2000.), p. 1f

[143] Roland E. Murphy, *Book of Ecclesiastes: Word Biblical Commentary*, (Dallas: Word, 1992) vol. 23A, pgs. 1f.

[144] Ellul, ibid. p. 12.
[145] Ibid, p. 15.
[146] George Barton, ibid, pgs. 32f.
[147] Hengstenberg, ibid, p. 28.
[148] Adam Clarke, ibid, III:808.
[149] Ellul, ibid, p. 135.
[150] ibid, p. 12.
[151] Kidner, ibid, p. 31.
[152] Walvoord, John F. ; Zuck, Roy B. ; Dallas Theological Seminary: *The Bible Knowledge Commentary : An Exposition of the Scriptures*. Wheaton, IL : Victor Books, 1983-c1985, S. 1:997
[153] Wiersbe, Warren W.: *Be Satisfied*. Wheaton, Ill. : Victor Books, 1996, c1990, S. Ec 8:15
[154] Richards, Lawrence O.: *The Bible Readers Companion*. electronic ed. Wheaton : Victor Books, 1991; Published in electronic form by Logos Research Systems, 1996, S. 395
[155] *New Bible Commentary*, Editor D. A. Carson, (Downers Grove: IVP, 1994) S. Ec 7:23
[156] Wiersbe, Warren W.: *Be Satisfied*. Wheaton, Ill. : Victor Books, 1996, c1990, S. Ec 7:19
[157] Ogden, Graham S. ; Zogbo, Lynell: *A Handbook on Book of Ecclesiastes*. New York : United Bible Societies, 1998 (UBS Handbook Series; Helps for Translators), S. 263
[158] Longman, ibid, p. 200.
[159] *Evangelical Commentary on the Bible*, ed. Walter Elwell, (Grand Rapids: Baker, 1989), p. 433.
[160] *The New Bible Commentary Revised*, (Downers Grove: IVP, 1970), p. 570.
[161] Longman, ibid, p. 66.
[162] Franz Delitzsch, Commentary on the Song of Songs and Book of Ecclesiastes, (Grand Rapids, Eerdmans, n.d.), p. 179
[163] Leupold, ibid, p. 28.
[164] Ibid, pgs. 42-43.
[165] *Evangelical Commentary on the Bible*, ibid, p. 434.
[166] Kidner, ibid, p. 22.
[167] R. N. Whybray, *Book of Ecclesiastes: New Century Bible Commentary*, (Grand Rapids: Eerdmans, 1989), p. lix.
[168] Paul D. Wegner, *The Journey from Texts to Translations*, (Grand Rapids: Baker, 1999), p. 116.
[169] *The Pulpit Commentary*, ed. Deane, (New York: Funk & Wagnalls, n.d.), p. xviii.
[170] Roland Murphy and Elizabeth Huwiler, *New International Biblical Commentary: Proverbs, Book of Ecclesiastes, and Song of Songs*, (Peabody, Mass: Hendrickson, 1999), p. 159.
[171] Garrett, Duane A.: *Proverbs, Book of Ecclesiastes, Song of Songs*. electronic ed. Nashville : Broadman & Holman Publishers, 2001, c1993 (Logos Library System; The New American Commentary 14), S. 275
[172] Henstenberg, ibid, p. 240.
[173] Ibid. p. 242.
[174] Leupold, ibid, pgs. 270-271.
[175] Kidner, ibid, p. 100.
[176] Leupold, ibid, p. 273.
[177] Ibid, pgs, 273-274.
[178] Franz Delitzsch, Commentary on the Song of Songs and Book of Ecclesiastes, (Grand Rapids, Eerdmans, n.d.), p. 184.
[179] Richards, Larry ; Richards, Lawrence O.: *The Teacher's Commentary*. Wheaton, Ill. : Victor Books, 1987, S. 350
[180] Roland Murphy and Elizabeth Huwiler, *New International Biblical Commentary: Proverbs, Book of Ecclesiastes, and Song of Songs*, (Peabody, Mass: Hendrickson, 1999), p. 159.
[181] Walvoord, and Zuck, ibid., 1:978
[182] ibid, 1:978

EndNotes

[183] Spence-Jones, H. D. M.: *The Pulpit Commentary: Isaiah Vol. II*. Bellingham, WA: Logos Research Systems, Inc., 2004, S. 137

[184] *Predestination and FreeWill*, eds. David Basinger and Randall Basinger (Downers Grove, IL; InterVarsity Press, 1986) I document Pinnock's appeal to "reason" instead of Scripture in greater detail in my book, *Battle of the Gods*, Las Vegas: Christian Scholars Press: 2004)

[185] Lange, John Peter; Schaff, Philip; Erdmann, David ; Toy, C. H. ; Broadus, John A.: *A Commentary on the Holy Scriptures: 1 & 2 Samuel*. Bellingham, WA : Logos Research Systems, Inc., 2008, S. 65

[186] Keil, Carl Friedrich; Delitzsch, Franz: *Commentary on the Old Testament*. Peabody, MA: Hendrickson, 2002, S. 2:382

[187] Spence-Jones, H. D. M. (Hrsg.):*The Pulpit Commentary:1 Samuel*. Bellingham,WA: Logos Research Systems, Inc., 2004, S. 26.

[188] Walvoord, John F. ; Zuck, Roy B., *The Bible Knowledge Commentary : An Exposition of the Scriptures*. Wheaton, IL : Victor Books, 1983-1985, S. 1:891

[189] Ibid., S. 1:891

[190] Jamieson, Robert; Fausset, A. R.; Fausset, A. R.; Brown, David Brown, David: *A Commentary, Critical and Explanatory, on the Old and New Testaments*. Oak Harbor, WA: Logos Research Systems, Inc., 1997, S. Mt 6:8

[191] Spence-Jones, H. D. M. (Hrsg.): *The Pulpit Commentary: Acts of the Apostles Vol. II*. Bellingham, WA: Logos Research Systems, Inc., 2004, S. 3

[192] Robertson, A.T.: *Word Pictures in the New Testament*. Oak Harbor: Logos Research Systems, 1997, S. Ac 15:18

[193] Carson, D. A.: *New Bible Commentary: 21st Century Edition*. 4th ed. Leicester, England; Downers Grove, Ill., USA : Inter-Varsity Press, 1994, S. 1 Sa 15:1

[194] Jamieson, Robert ; Fausset, A. R. ; Fausset, A. R. ; Brown, David ; Brown, David: ibid., Logos Research Systems, Inc., 1997, S. 1 Co 1:21

[195] Richards, Lawrence O.: *The Bible Readers Companion*. electronic ed. Wheaton : Victor Books, 1991; Published in electronic form by Logos Research Systems, 1996, S. 757

[196] Henry, Matthew: *Matthew Henry's Commentary on the Whole Bible : Complete and Unabridged in One Volume*. Peabody : Hendrickson, 1996, c1991, S. 1 Co 1:17

[197] Carson, D. A.: *New Bible Commentary : 21st Century Edition*. 4th ed. Leicester, England; Downers Grove, Ill., USA : Inter-Varsity Press, 1994, S. 1 Co 1:17

[198] Wiersbe, Warren W.: *The Bible Exposition Commentary*. Wheaton, Ill. : Victor Books, 1996, c1989, S. 1 Co 1:10

[199] Spence-Jones, H. D. M. (Hrsg.): *The Pulpit Commentary: 1 Corinthians*. Bellingham, WA : Logos Research Systems, Inc., 2004, S. 7

[200] Wiersbe, Warren W.: *Wiersbe's Expository Outlines on the New Testament*. Wheaton, Ill. : Victor Books, 1997, c1992, S. 420

[201] Robertson, A.T.: *Word Pictures in the New Testament*. Oak Harbor: Logos Research Systems, 1997, S. 1 Co 1:21

[202] Henry, Matthew: *Matthew Henry's Commentary on the Whole Bible: Complete and Unabridged in One Volume*. Peabody: Hendrickson, 1996, c1991, S. 1 Th 5:6

[203] Henry, Matthew: *Matthew Henry's Commentary on the Whole Bible : Complete and Unabridged in One Volume*. Peabody: Hendrickson, 1996, c1991, S. Ac 17:22

[204] Spence-Jones, H. D. M. (Hrsg.): *The Pulpit Commentary: Acts of the Apostles Vol. II*. Bellingham, WA : Logos Research Systems, Inc., 2004, S. 62

[205] Robertson, A.T.: *Word Pictures in the New Testament*. Oak Harbor: Logos Research Systems, 1997, S. Ac 17:31

[206] Henry, Matthew: *Matthew Henry's Commentary on the Whole Bible : Complete and Unabridged in One Volume*. Peabody : Hendrickson, 1996, c1991, S. Ac 17:22

[207] Jamieson, Robert ; Fausset, A. R. ; Fausset, A. R. ; Brown, David ; Brown, David: *A Commentary, Critical and Explanatory, on the Old and New Testaments*. Oak Harbor, WA: Logos Research Systems, Inc., 1997, S. Ac 17:26

[208] Newman, Barclay Moon ; Nida, Eugene Albert: *A Handbook on the Acts of the Apostles*. New York: United Bible Societies, 993], c1972 (UBS Handbook Series; Helps for Translators), S. 341

[209] Stephen Davis, *Logic and the Nature of God*, (Grand Rapids, Erdmann, 1983) pgs. 88, 96.

[210] Keil and Delitzsch, ibid., Genesis I:139–140. See also Gleason Archer, *Encyclopedia of Bible Difficulties*, (Grand Rapids: Zondervan, 1982) pg 80–81.

[211] Frans Delitzsch, *Biblical Commentary on the Psalms*, (Grand Rapids, Mich.; Eerdmans, n.d.) vol. 3, pg. 400.

[212] H. H. Leupold, *Exposition of the Psalms*, (Grand Rapids: Baker Book House, 1959), pg. 989.

[213] Frans Delitzsch, *Biblical Commentary on the Psalms*, (Grand Rapids, Mich.; Eerdmans, n.d.) vol. 3, pg. 400.

[214] Carl Moll, *The Psalms, Lange's Commentary on the Holy Scripture*, (Grand Rapids: Zondervan, n.d.) vol. 9, pg. 671.

[215] *The Works of Jonathan Edwards* (Edinburgh:Banner of Truth, 1974) vol. I:30.

[216] *Moral Discources of Epictetus*, ed. By Thomas Gould, (New York: Washington Square Press, 1964), p. 7.

[217] ibid, p. 233.

[218] This point is documented by Royce Gruenler in his chapter in Nash's, *On Process Theology*, (Grand Rapids: Baker, 1987) pgs 330–356.

[219] Robert Morey, *Death and the Afterlife*, (Millerstown, PA: Christian Scholars Press, 2004), pgs 246–256.

[220] Jean Paul Sarte, *Being and Nothingness* (New York: Washington Square Press, 1966) pt. 4, ch.1.

[221] See my book, *Battle of the Gods*, (PO Box 640, Millerstown, PA 17062) for documentation of Whitehead's blasphemies.

[222] *On Process Theology*, ed. Ronald Nash (Grand Rapids: Baker, 1987) From the Introduction.

[223] ibid, p.27

[223] *Predestination & Free Will*, ed. David Basinger & Randall Basinger (Downers Grove IL; IVP, 1986); Richard Rice, *The Openess of God* (Nashville TN; Review & Herald Pub., 1979); Gregory Boyd, *Trinity In Process* (New York NY; Peter Lang); Stephen Davis, *Logic and the Nature of God*, ibid.; *Predestination & Free Will*, ed. David Basinger & Randall Basinger, ibid.; Gordon C. Olson, *The Truth Shall Set You Free* (Franklin Park, Ill: Bible Research Fellowship, 1980); Howard Roy Elseth, *Did God Know?* (St. Paul, Minn: Calvary United Church, 1977); George Otis, Jr., "The Foreknowledge of God," unpublished paper, 1941.

[225] Blake, T. Oster, *Review of Books on the Book of Mormon* 8/2 (1996): 99–146.

[226] *On Process Theology*, ibid. Pgs. 362–363.

[227] *The Catholic Encyclopedia* (Nashville: Thomas Nelson, 1987) p 396.

[228] William Lane Craig, *The Only Wise God* (Grand Rapids: Baker, 1987)

[229] Alvin C. Plantinga, *God, Freedom, and Evil* (Grand Rapids: Eerdmans, 1974)

[230] William Lane Craig, *The Only Wise God*, ibid.

[231] *Mormon Concept of God*, ibid. pgs. 12–13.

[232] Jean Porter in *Natural & Divine Law*, (Grand Rapids: Eerdmans, 1999) and later *Nature as Reason*, Grand Rapids: Eerdmans, 2005) argues that the Stoic concept of human nature is essential for Natural Law theories.

[233] Ibid, p. 157.

[234] Moreland and Craig, *Philosophical Foundations for a Christian Worldview*, ibid. p. 85.

[235] J. Daryl Charles, ibid, pgs. 41-42.

[236] Jean Porter in *Natural & Divine Law*, ibid, p. 171.

[237] Mary Midgley, *Beast and Man: The Roots of Human Nature*, (NYC: Meridian, 1978).

[238] Jean Porter in *Natural & Divine Law*, ibid, pgs. 66f.

EndNotes

[239] Howard P. Kainz, *Natural law: An Introduction and Re-examination*, (Chicago: Open Court, 2004), p. 1.

[240] *Natural & Divine Law*, ibid, p. 11.

[241] Ibid, p.31.

[242] Jean Porter, *Nature as Reason*, (Grand Rapids: Eerdmans, 2005), p. 107.

[243] *Natural & Divine Law*, ibid, p. 30.

[244] Jean Porter, *Nature as Reason*, ibid, p. 104.

[245] Ibid, p342f.

[246] Kainz, ibid, p. 87. "Paul may have been familiar with, and influenced by, Stoic notions of natural law."

[247] *Nature as Reason*, ibid, *p. 10.*

[248] *Natural & Divine Law*, ibid, p. 121.

[249] Richards, Lawrence O.: *The Bible Readers Companion*. electronic ed. Wheaton : Victor Books, 1991; Published in electronic form by Logos Research Systems, 1996, S. 30.

[250] Davids, Peter H.: *The Epistle of James : A Commentary on the Greek Text*. Grand Rapids, Mich.: Eerdmans, 1982, S. 146.

[251] 20 B.F. Skinner, *Beyond Freedom & Dignity*, (Indianapolis: Hackett: 2002).

[252] 21 Walvoord, John F.; Zuck, Roy B.; Dallas Theological Seminary: *The Bible Knowledge Commentary: An Exposition of the Scriptures*. Wheaton, IL: Victor Books, 1983-c1985, S. 1:979.

[253] 22. Garrett, Duane A.: *Proverbs, Ecclesiastes, Song of Songs*. electronic ed. Nashville: Broadman & Holman Publishers, 2001, c1993 (Logos Library System; The New American Commentary 14), S. 282.

[254] 23. Freeman, James M.; Chadwick, Harold J.: *Manners & Customs of the Bible*. Rev. ed.]. North Brunswick, NJ : Bridge-Logos Publishers, 1998, S. 337

[255] 24. Richards, Larry; Richards, Lawrence O.: *The Teacher's Commentary*. Wheaton, Ill.: Victor Books, 1987, S. 349.

[256] 25. Willmington, H. L.: *Wilmington's Bible Handbook*. Wheaton, Ill.: Tyndale House Publishers, 1997, S. 344.

[257] 26. Wiersbe, Warren W.: *The Bible Exposition Commentary*. Wheaton, Ill.: Victor Books, 1996, c1989, S. 1 Th 4:13.

[258] 27. Ellingworth, Paul; Nida, Eugene Albert: *A Handbook on Paul's Letters to the Thessalonians*. New York: United Bible Societies, 1994], c1975 (UBS Handbook Series; Helps for Translators), S. 94.

[259] 28. Vincent, Marvin Richardson: *Word Studies in the New Testament*. Bellingham, WA: Logos Research Systems, Inc., 2002, S. 4:40.

[260] 29. Robertson, A.T.: *Word Pictures in the New Testament*. Oak Harbor: Logos Research Systems, 1997, S. Eph 2:12.

[261] 30. Jamieson, Robert ; Fausset, A. R. ; Fausset, A. R. ; Brown, David ; Brown, David: *A Commentary, Critical and Explanatory, on the Old and New Testaments*. Oak Harbor, WA: Logos Research Systems, Inc., 1997, S. Eph 2:12.

[262] 31. Hendriksen, William; Kistemaker, Simon J.: *New Testament Commentary: Exposition of Ephesians*. Grand Rapids: Baker Book House, 1953-2001 (New Testament Commentary 7), S. 130.

[263] 32. Bratcher, Robert G. ; Nida, Eugene Albert: *A Handbook on Paul's Letter to the Ephesians*. New York : United Bible Societies, 1993 (UBS Handbook Series; Helps for Translators), S. 54.

[264] 33. TWOT Hebrew Lexicon

[265] 34. Richards, Lawrence O.: *The Bible Readers Companion*. electronic ed. Wheaton: Victor Books, 1991; Published in electronic form by Logos Research Systems, 1996, S. 352.

[266] 35. Robert Morey, *Studies in the Atonement*, (Millerstown, PA, PO Box 240, 17062: Christian Scholars Press, 2006). To obtain this book, go to www.faithdefenders.com.

[267] Tom Sorell, *Scientism: Philosophy and the Infatuation with Science*, (London: Rutledge, 1991).
[268] Helen Longino, *Science as Social Knowledge*, (Princeton: Princeton University Press, 1990).
[269] Larry Laudan, *Science and Values*, (Los Angeles: University of California, 1984)
[270] Thomas Kuhn, *The Structure of Scientific Revolutions*, (Chicago: University of Chicago Press, 1963). See also: A. Rupert Hall, *The Revolution in Science 1500-1750*, (London, Longman, 1983).
[271] Karl Popper, *Conjectures and Refutations*, (London: Routledge, 1963).
[272] Solomon, *The Book of Ecclesiastes*.
[273] Edgar Zeller, *Outlines of Greek Philosophy*, (NY: Meridian Books, 1967) pgs. 18-19.
[274] Robert Morey, *Battle of the Gods*, (Las Vegas: Christian Scholars Press, 2008).
[275] Zeller, ibid., p. 20.
[276] ibid.
[277] ibid.
[278] See the article on Wilson in Isaac Asimov, *Asimov's Biographical Encyclopedia of Science and Technology*, (New York: Doubleday & C., 1882).
[279] Robert Morey, *Horoscopes and the Christian*, (Las Vegas: Christian Scholars Press, revised, 2008).
[280] David Hume, *Enquiry Concerning Human Understanding*, (London: Clarendon, 1966), Book IV, section 4. Also: Popper, ibid.
[281] Max Jammer, *Einstein and Religion*, (Princeton: Princeton University Press, 1999), pgs. 68-69.
[282] Ibid, p. 32.
[283] Ibid, p. 58.
[284] Ibid, pgs. 46-58, 74, 81, 85, 92.
[285] Ibid, p. 57.
[286] Ibid, pgs. 46-58, 74, 81, 85, 92.
[287] Stephen Hawkins, *A Brief History of Time*, (NY: Bantam Books, 1996).
[288] Ibid, pgs. 53f.
[289] Ibid, p.53.
[290] See: Rodney Stark, *The Victory of Reason*, (New York: Random House, 2005) and J. Budziszewski, *Written on the Heart, The Case for Natural Law*, (Downers Grove: IVP, 1997).
[291] Ibid, pgs. 175f.
[292] Ibid, pgs. 259f.
[293] Francis Schaeffer, *The God Who Is There*, (Downers Grove: IVP, 1968).
[294] Bernard Ramm, *Protestant Christian Evidences* (Chicago: Moody Press, 1966), pp. 59, 60.
[295] Michael Cosgrove, *The Essence of Man* (Grand Rapids: Zondervan, 1977), p. 34.
[296] Ramm, ibid., p. 58.
[297] Guy Zukav, *The Dancing Wu Li Masters: An Overview of the New Physics* (New York: Bantam Books, 1979.)
[298] See my analysis and refutation of materialism in *Death and the AfterLife*, (Las Vegas: Christian Scholars Press, 2008).
[299] Fritjof Capra, *The Tao of Physics: An Exploration of the Parallels between Modern Physics and Eastern Mysticism*, (Boston, MASS: Shambhala Publications:1999)
[300] Guy Zukav , ibid.
[301] Tony Rothman, *Instant Physics: From Aristotle to Einstein, and Beyond*, (NY: Byron Preiss Publications, 1995)
[302] Frank Ramsey, *Philosophical Papers*, (Cambridge: Cambridge University Press, 1999. Most helpful was: *Cambridge and Vienna: Frank P. Ramsey and the Vienna Circle* (Vienna Circle Institute Yearbook), ed. Maria Galavotti, (Netherlands: Springer, n.d.).
[303] Keil, Carl Friedrich ; Delitzsch, Franz: *Commentary on the Old Testament*. (Peabody, Mass : Hendrickson, 2002, S. 6:242).
[304] Spence-Jones, H. D. M. (Hrsg.): *The Pulpit Commentary: Proverbs*. (Bellingham, WA : Logos Research Systems, Inc., 2004, S. 309)

[305] Gordon H. Clark, *The Philosophy of Science and Belief in God*, (Jefferson, MD: Trinity Foundation, 1987). See also: Abraham Kuyper, *Lectures on Calvinism*, (Grand Rapids: Eerdmans, reprint: 2000), chapter IV. And Vern Sheridan Poythress, *Redeeming Science: A God-Centered Approach,* **(Wheaton, IL: Crossway, 2006).**

[306] *The International Standard Bible Encyclopedia*, ed. Jsames Orr, (Peabody: Mass: Hendrickson, 1996) I:420.

[307] The biblical view of art has never received much attention. I am much indebted to my friends Francis Schaeffer and Hans Rookmaaker for their instruction on Christian art. To investigate this subject further, see:
- Abraham Kuyper, *Lectures on Calvinism*, (Grand Rapids: Eerdmans, reprint: 2000).
- Robert Morey, *Introduction to Defending The Faith*, (Las Vegas: Christian Scholars Press, 2007).
- John P. Newport, *Christianity and Contemporary Art Forms*, (Waco, TX: Word, 1970).
- Hans R. Rookmaaker, *Modern Art and the Death of a Culture*, (Downers Grove : IVP, 1975).
- Francis Schaeffer, *Art and the Bible*, (Downers Grove: IVP, 1974).

[308] Robert Morey, *Is Eastern Orthodoxy Christian?* (Las Vegas: Christian Scholars Press, 2008).

[309] I discuss the philosophic reasons behind the Great Schism in *Is Eastern Orthodoxy Christian?*, (Las Vegas: Christian Scholar's Press, 2008).

[310] Norman Geisler, *Thomas Aquinas: An Evangelical Appraisal,* (Eugene, OR: Wipf and Stock Publishers, 2003), p. 14.

[311] Ibid, pgs. 12-13

[312] For a layman's overview of Aquinas' theology, see:
- *Aquinas in Dialogue*, ed. Jim Fodor and Frederick Christian Bauserschmidt, (Oxfrod: Backwell, 2004);
- Marie-Dominique Chenu, *Aquinas and His Role in Theology*, (Collegeville, MN: Liturgical, 2002);
- Frederick Copleston, *Aquinas*, (NY: Penguin, 1991);
- Timothy Renick, *Aquinas for Armchair Theologians*, (London: John Knox, 2002)

[313] Frederick Copleston, *A History of Philosophy: Vol. Two, Part 1, Augustine to Bonaventure*, (New York: Image Books, 1962) gives an excellent overview of the influence of Muslim and Jewish philosophers upon Aquinas in pages 211-238. He states that this is now "common knowledge among historians." p. 211.

[314] I spent several years at the Library of Congress studying Natural Theology and Natural law. Only a few authors informed their readers that Thomas of Aquinas at the close of his life denounced his Summa as "worthless straw." The following documentation is sufficient to prove this fact.

　a) Martian Center at Notre Dame: (http://www.nd.edu/Departments/Maritain/etext/conway03.htm#VIII)
"The year 1273 was drawing to a close when the pen dropped from his hand, before reaching his fiftieth year. It was on St. Nicholas Day, the 6th day of December, and in that saint's chapel, that he had a long ecstasy while saying Mass; what was then communicated to him he never revealed, but from that hour "he suspended his writing instruments," as William de Tocco puts it. Mid-way in the treatise of the Sacrament of Penance, after finishing ninety Questions, of five hundred and forty-nine articles, he lapsed into silence. To every appeal made by superiors or brethren there came the same reply: "I can do no more". Fr. Reginald, his secretary and confidant, urged him to resume his task. "Father, why do you leave unfinished this great work, which you have undertaken for God's glory and the world's enlightenment?" But he could only draw the reply: "I can do no more. Such secrets have been communicated to me, that all I have written and taught seem to me to be only like a handful of straw." Canto X"

　b) Standford Enc. Of Phil: (http://plato.stanford.edu/entries/aquinas/)
"At Naples, he was given the task of elevating the status of the Dominican House of Studies. His writing continued until he had a mystical experience which made him think of all he had done as "mere straw."

　c) http://www.domestic- church.com/CONTENT.DCC/19980101/SAINTS/STTHOM.HTM
"At the end of his life, Saint Thomas stopped writing. He had a vision of Heaven and decided that compared to the great glory of God, his writing was 'like straw.'

　d) *World Book Encyclopedia*:
A1: 581; Thomas had a mystical experience in 1273 that caused him to stop writing. He said that all he had written seemed like straw compared with what he had seen this experience.

- e) *The Oxford Companion to Philosophy*:
  Thomas Aquinas dismissed his work as straw. (p. 43)
- f) *Routledge Encyclopedia of Philosophy*:
  1:333 "On or about 6 December 1273, while he was saying mass, something happened to Aquinas that left him weak and unable to go on writing or dictating. He himself saw the occasion as a special revelation. When Reginald of Piperno, his personal secretary and longtime friend, tried to persuade him to return to work on the Third Part of *Summa theologiae*, he said, "I can't." And when Reginald persisted, Aquinas finally said, "Everything I've written seems like straw by comparison with what I have seen and what has been revealed to me." ...all he had written seemed pale and dry."
- g) *Hasting's Encyclopedia of Religion and Ethics*:
  1:654 Thomas Aquinas stopped writing after his "ecstasy."

[315] J. P. Moreland & William Lane Craig, *Philosophic Foundations for a Christian Worldview*, (Downers Grove: IVP, 2003), p.214.

[316] Ibid, p. 215.

[317] J. Budziszewski, *Written on the Heart*, (Downers grove: IVP, 1997), p. 190.

[318] Garrett J. DeWesse and J. P. Moreland, *Philosophy Made Slightly Less Difficult*, (Downers Gove: IVP, 2005), p. 45.

[319] Ibid, p. 44.

[320] The 19th Century Oxford Movement that led so many Anglicans to embrace popery, was the end result of the rise of British Natural Theology. In modern times, Dudziszewski, Beckwith, Kreeft, etc, are Protestants who first adopted Natural Theology and then later converted to Romanism. Their rejection of the gospel is a sad but convincing reality that confronts all Natural theologians.

[321] J. P. Moreland, William Craig, Gregory Koukl, Frank Beckwith, Garrett DeWeese, etc. have attacked the doctrine of *sola scriptura* in numerous lectures and printed articles. For example, see: J. P. Moreland's speech before the Evangelical Theological Society, "How Evangelicals Became Over-Committed to the Bible and What Can be done about It," http://www.kingdomtriangle.com/discussion/moreland_EvangOverCommBible.pdf) or Koukl's article, *Is The Bible Sufficient?*, (www.str.org). He correctly calls his apologetic ministry, "Stand to Reason" instead of "Stand to Revelation" because he believes that human Reason is the Origin of truth and morals, not God or His Revelation.

[322] Norman Geisler, *Thomas Aquinas: An Evangelical Appraisal*, (Grand Rapids: Baker, 1992). In the introduction, Geisler admits that Evangelical scholars historically condemned Aquinas. But, now that so many of them have died, he felt the time was right to "come of the closet" and admit that he is a follower of Aquinas.

[323] *In Defense of Natural Theology*, ed. James F. Sennett and Douglas Groothuis, (Downers Grove: IVP, 2005). "In this volume we are using the term theism in the sense most prevalent in contemporary philosophy of religion..." (p. 9. n. 1). Their claim that the meaning of a word is decided by what 51% feel at the moment is the logical fallacy of *argumentum ad populum*.

[324] See Appendix One for the documentation.

[325] Rodney Stark, *The Victory of Reason*, (NY: Random house, 2005) is an example of those who yearn for the good old days of pre-Reformation Catholic Europe.

[326] See Koukl's website for such boasts (www.str.org).

[327] Garrett J. DeWesse and J. P. Moreland, *Philosophy Made Slightly Less Difficult*, (Downers Gove: IVP, 2005), pgs. 97-99.

[328] Cited by Howard P. Kainz, *Natural law: An introduction and Re-examination*, (Chicago: Open Court, 2004), p. 43.

[329] *The Westminster Dictionary of Christian Theology*, ed. Alan Richardson and John Brown, (Philadelphia: Westminster Press, 1983), p. 392.

[330] *The New Schaff-Herzog Encyclopedia of Religion*, ed. Samuel Jackson, (NY: Funk & Wagnells, 1910) VIII:83-84.

[331] *New Catholic Encyclopedia*, (Washington, DC: Thomson/Gale, 2003), 10:179.
[332] *The Encyclopedia of Christianity*, ed. Geoffery Bromiley, (Grand Rapids: Eerdmans, 2003), 703.
[333] *Webster's Third New international Dictionary*, (Springfield, Mass: Merrian-Webster, 2002), p. 1507.
[334] *The Columbia Encyclopedia*, 6th ed., ed. Paul Lagosse, (NY: Columbia University Press, 2000), p. 1971.
[335] *The New Encyclopedia Britannica*, (Chicago: Encyclopedia Britannica, 1998), 8:539.
[336] *The Encyclopedia Americana*, (Danbury, CN: Encyclopedia Americana, 1998), p. 791.
[337] Mooreland and Craig, *Philosophical Foundations*, ibid, p. 451.
[338] Ibid, p. 410.
[339] Mortimer Adler, *The Great Ideas*, (NY: Macmillan, 1992), p. 561. See also: *The Encyclopedia of Christianity*, ibid, 703; *The Encyclopedia Americana*, ibid, p. 791.
[340] *Encyclopedia of Religion* 2nd, ed. Lindsay Jones, (NY: Thomson/Gale, 2005), pgs. 6438-6441.
Encyclopedia of Philosophy, ed. Borchet, (NY: Thomson?Gale, 2006), 6:505-522.
Encyclopedia of Religion and Ethics, ed. James Hastings, (NY: Scribners, 1917), IV:201f.
[341] *Encyclopedia of Philosophy*, ibid, 6:505-52; *The Encyclopedia of Christianity*, ibid, pgs. 711f.
[342] Howard P. Kainz, ibid, p. xii.
[343] Erik Wolf, *Das Problem der Naturrechtslebre*, (Karlsruhe; Muller, 1955), p. 5.
[344] Jean Porter, *Natural & Divine Law*, ibid, p. 28.
[345] ibid, pgs. 25-26.
[346] Ibid, p. 27.
[347] Stephen Grabill, *Rediscovering The Natural law in Reformed Theological Ethics*, ibid, p. 57.
[348] *The Encyclopedia American,* ibid, p. 791.
[349] J. Budziszedwshi, *Written on the Heart: The Case for Natural Law*, (Downers grove: IVP, 1997), p. 65.
[350] Carl F. Henry, "Natural Law and a Nihilistic Culture," (*First Things* (Jan. 1995), p. 55.
[351] Jean Porter, *Natural & Divine Law*, ibid, p.190f.
[352] Budziszedwshi, ibid, p. 66.
[353] Kainz, ibid, pgs. 53f.
[354] *Cornelius Van Til's Letter to Francis Schaeffer*, (*Ordained Servant*, vol. 6 no. 4, Oct. 1997).
[355] Kainz, ibid, p. 33.
[356] P. A. Chadbourne, *Lectures on Natural Theology or Nature and the Bible*, (NY: Putnam's Sons, 1867), p. 18.
[357] Ibid, p. 21.
[358] Budziszedwshi, ibid, p. 210.
[359] J. Daryl Charles, *Retrieving The Natural Law*, (Grand Rapids: Eerdmans, 2008), p. 23.
[360] Ibid, p. 106.
[361] Berkouwer, G. C.: *General Revelation*. Grand Rapids : W.B. Eerdmans Pub. Co., 1955, S. 58.
[362] Wiersbe, Warren W.: *The Bible Exposition Commentary*. Wheaton, Ill. : Victor Books, 1996, c1989, S. Ro 1:18.
[363] *The Columbia Encyclopedia*, 6th ed., ed. Paul Lagasse, (NY: Columbia University Press, 2000) Natural law is "fundamental to human nature." (p. 1971).
[364] The documentation for Natural Law's defense of slavery is documented in the following works:
Thabiti M. Anayabwile, *The Decline of African American Theology*, (Downers Grove: IVP, 2007).
Stephen R. Hayes, *Noah's curse: The Biblical Justification of American Slavery*, (NY: Oxford University press, 2002).
George D. Kelsey, *Racism and the Christian Understanding of Man*, (NY: Scribner's Sons, 1965).
Mark A. Noll, *A History of Christianity in the United States and Canada*, (Grand Rapids: Eerdmans, 1992.
Winthrop Jordan, *White Over Black: American Attitudes Toward the Negro, 1550-1812*, (Chapel Hill: University of North Carolina, 1968).
Larry Tise, *Proslavery: A History of the Defense of Slavery in America, 1701-1840*, (Athens: University of Georgia, 1987.

[365] Thabiti M. Anayabwile, ibid, p. 101.
[366] H. C. C. Moule, *Colossian and Philemon Studies*, (Ft. Washington, PA: CLC, 1975), pgs. 288-289.
[367] Ernest Van den Haag, "Not Above the Law," (*National Review* 43 (1991), 25, 27.
[368] *The Westminster Dictionary of Christian Theology,* ibid, p. 393.
[369] *New Catholic Encyclopedia*, ibid, 10:194.
[370] *The Teachings of Modern Protestantism*, ed. John White Jr. and Frank S. Alexander, (NY: Columbia University Press, 2007), p. 177.
[371] Ibid, p. 133.
[372] Ned Wisnefske, *Our Natural Knowledge of God*, (NY: Peter Lang: 1990) p. 1.
[373] Kainz, ibid, p. 25.
[374] Ned Wisnefske, *Our Natural Knowledge of God*, ibid, p. 8.
[375] Stephen Grabill, *Rediscovering the Natural Law in Reformed Theological Ethics,* (Grand Rapids: Eerdmans, 2006), p. ix.
[376] Ibid, p. 3.
[377] ibid, p. 191.
[378] Thabiti M. Anayabwile, ibid, p. 24.
[379] Archibald Alexander, *A Sermon Delivered at the Opening of the General Assembly of the Presbyterian Church in the United States May 1808.*
[380] Ibid.
[381] Ibid, p. 4.
[382] Francis Schaeffer, *How Should We Then Live?,* (Wheaton: Crossway Books, 1976), p. 52.

[383] Ibid, p. 52.
[384] Ibid, p. 56.
[385] Francis Schaeffer, *The God Who Is There*, ibid, pgs 183-184).
[386] Bernard Ramm, *Varieties of Christian Apologetics*, (Grand Rapids: Baker, 1965), p. 90.
[387] J. I. Packer, *God Who Is Rich in Mercy*, (Grand Rapids: Baker, 1986) p. 13.
[388] Norman Geisler, *Thomas Aquinas: An Evangelical Appraisal*: (Eugene, OR: Wipf & Stock, 2003), Introduction.
[389] The hiring of Jesuit-trained professors is amazing. While this does not in and of itself mean that they teach Jesuit doctrine, it does mean we must examine their theology to see if they are in fact teaching what the Jesuits taught them. Indoctrination, not association, is our concern.

Reformed Theological Seminary:
Mark Futo is Professor of Old Testament, Academic Dean - Orlando. He received his M.A. and Ph. D. from The Catholic University of America.
Peter Lee also got his Ph.D. from The Catholic University of America and also is Assistant Professor of Old Testament at RTS.
Dr. John J. Yeo earned his Ph.D from the University of St. Michael's College in Canada:
Dr. William Davis (Adjunct) got his PhD from Notre Dame University. He teaches philosophy at RTS.

Westminster Theological Seminary:
In addition to VanDrunen, other Catholic educated professors who have taught at WTS:
Douglas Gropp: taught at Catholic University of America 1987-2007, currently teaching O.T.
Bryan D. Estelle: Associate Professor of Old Testament; Ph.D Catholic University of America. "He lectured in Hebrew at The Catholic University between 1997 and 2000. He is a member of the Society of Biblical Literature and the Catholic Biblical Association."
Richard Lints - Visiting Professor of Theology: M.A. University of Notre Dame, Ph.D. University of Notre Dame. "He has taught at the Yale Divinity School, Trinity College in Bristol England, and the University of Notre Dame."

Dordt Collge – (C. R. C.)

Mark Tazelaar -Professor of Philosophy. Ph.D., Loyola University
BIOLA University:
Michael Bauman: Ph.D. in Catholic Theology and literature from Fordham University.
Paul Copan: Ph.D. in Catholic philosophy from Marquette University.
Trinity Evangelical Divinity School
Bruce L. Fields, PhD - Doctor of Philosophy in New Testament from Marquette University.
Mark H. Senter III is chair of the Educational Ministries Department and professor of educational ministries at Trinity Evangelical Divinity School in Deerfield, Illinois: Doctor of Philosophy in foundations of education from Loyola University
Douglas A. Sweeney is associate professor of Church History and the History of Christian Thought and director of the Carl F. H. Henry Center for Theological Understanding at Trinity Evangelical Divinity School. He also served as an adjunct professor at Aquinas College in Nashville, Tennessee. Their catalog states: "Rooted in Catholic heritage, Aquinas College has a history founded on Dominican Tradition. Owned and administered by the Dominican Sisters of the Congregation of Saint Cecilia, the history of the College actually began its remote preparation with the establishment of the Saint Cecilia Congregation in 1860 at the request of Nashville's second bishop, James Whelan, O.P. "

[390] *Cornelius Van Til's Letter to Francis Schaeffer,* (*Ordained Servant*, vol. 6 no. 4, Oct. 1997).

[391] John Frame, *Doctrine of God*, (Harmony, NJ: P & R, 2002), p. 52-53).

[392] Grabill, ibid. p. 7. He also names Carl Braaten, Paul Helm, Arthur Holmes, Alister McGrath, Susan Schreiner and Daniel Weetberg. E. Calvin Beisner should have been mentioned.

[393] See: http://heidelblog.wordpress.com/2008/07/28/rome-and-wsc/.

[394] See: David VanDrunen, *Law & Custom: The Thought of Thomas Aquinas and the Future of the Common Law*, (NY: Peter Lang, 2003), preface.

..........................., *The Biblical Case for Natural Law*, (Grand Rapids: Acton Institute, 2006).

[395] Modern Reformation: vol. 15, No. 2, March/April 2006, p. 2.

[396] Ibid, p. 12.

[397] Ibid p. 14.

[398] Ibid, p.13.

[399] Ibid.

[400] Ibid.

[401] Ibid.

[402] Ibid, p. 4.

[403] Ibid p.6.

[404] Ibid.

[405] Ibid p. 7.

[406] Ibid p. 28.

[407] Ibid.

[408] Ibid.

[409] Ibid.

[410] Clement C. J. Web, *Studies in The History of Natural Theology*, (Oxford: Claredon, 1915), p. 35f.

[411] For further study of the history of math, see:
   Carl Boyer, *A History of Mathematics*, (NY: John Wiley & Sons)
   Patricia Lauber, *The Story of Numbers*, (NY: Random)
   The International Standard Bible Encyclopedia
   The Zondervan Pictorial Encyclopedia of the Bible
   The Encyclopedia Americana
   The Encyclopedia Britannica
   The Encyclopedia of Physical Sciences

[412] Budszewski (ibid, pg. 180) cites Psa. 19; 104; Acts 14:17 as general revelation passages that prove Natural Law. See also Porter, Grabill, VanDrunen, Horton, etc. They frequently misapply as well misquote biblical texts.

[413] J. Daryl Charles, ibid, p. 87. He traces the use of 1 Cor. 11 as an argument for Natural Theology all the way back to back to Tertullian!

[414] Matthew Henry, ibid. VI:560.

[415] John Calvin, *The First Epistle of Paul to the Corinthians*, (Grand Rapids: Eerdmans, 1968), p. 235.

[416] Charles Hodge, *Commentary on the First Epistle to the Corinthians*, (Grand Rapids: Eerdmans, 1965), p. 213.

[417] *One Volume New Testament Commentary*, (Grand Rapids: Baker, 1963)., n.p., comment on 1 Cor. 11:14.

[418] Thomas Edwards, *A Commentary on the First Epistle of Paul to the Corinthians*, (NY: Armstrong and Sons, 1886), p. 279.

[419] Ellingworth, Paul and Hatton, Howard, *A Handbook on Paul's First Letter to the Corinthians*. New York : United Bible Societies, 1995 (UBS Handbook Series; Helps for Translators), S. 251

[420] *The Expositor's Greek Testament*, ed. W. Nicole, (Grand Rapids: Eerdmans, 1967), II:873.

[421] R. Lenski, *The Interpretation of St. Paul's First and Second Epistles to the Corinthians*, (Minn: Augsburg, 1963), p. 435.

[422] *One Volume New Testament Commentary*, ibid.

[423] Thiselton, Anthony C.: *The First Epistle to the Corinthians: A Commentary on the Greek Text*. Grand Rapids, Mich. : W.B. Eerdmans, 2000, S. 844.

[424] Matthew Poole, *A Commentary on the Holy Bible*, (London: Banner of truth, 1969), III:577.

[425] *The Oxford Dictionary of Jewish Religion*, ed. Werblowsky and Wigoder, (NY: Oxford University Press, 1997), p. 496.

[426] *New Catholic Encyclopedia*, Ibid. 10:210.

[427] I.S.B.E., ibid.

[428] Hendriksen, William ; Kistemaker, Simon J.: *New Testament Commentary : Exposition of Paul's Epistle to the Romans*. Grand Rapids : Baker Book House, 1953-2001 (New Testament Commentary 12-13), S. 122 .

[429] Robert A. Morey, *Death and the Afterlife*, (PO Box 240, Millerstown, PA: Christian Scholars Press, 2004).

[430] Meredith Kline, *Treaty of the Great King*, (Grand Rapids: Eerdmans, 1963).

[431] I am indebted to two works of Herman Ridderbos: *Paul: An Outline of His Theology*, (Grand Rapids: Eerdmans, 1997) and *The Coming of the Kingdom*, (Nutley, NJ: P & R, 1962).

[432] John Murray, *The Epistle to the Romans*, (Grand Rapids: Eerdmans, 1965), p. 73.

[433] Heinrich August Wilhelm Meyer, *Critical and Exegetical Hand-Book to the Epistle to the Romans*, (Winona Lake, IN: Alpha Greek Library, 1980), p.92.

[434] Robert Haldane, *Exposition of the Epistle to the Romans*, (London: Banner of Truth, 1963), 91.

[435] J. Daryl Charles, ibid., p. 45. See also his article: "Returning to Moral first Things," Philosophia Christi, vol. 6, No. 1, 2004, pg. 61f. He consistently quotes Rom. 2:15 as "the law written on the heart."

[436] Ibid, p.102.

[437] Ibid, p. 158.

[438] J. Budziszewski, ibid., p. 109.

[439] Ibid, p. 210.

[440] J. Budziszewski, *What We can't Not Know*, (Dallas: Spence, 2003) p. 12.

[441] Porter, *Nature as Reason*, ibid, p. 327.

[442] Modern Reformation: vol. 15, No. 2, March/April 2006, ibid.

[443] Ibid p.6.

[444] Mooreland and Craig, *Philosophical Foundations*, ibid, p. 615.

[445] R. C. H. Lenski, *The Interpretation of St. Paul's Epistle to the Romans*, (Minneapolis: Augsburg, 1961), p. 163.

[446] John Murray, *The Epistle to the Romans*, (Grand Rapids: Eerdmans, 1965), p. 73.

[447] Heinrich August Wilhelm Meyer, *Critical and Exegetical Hand-Book to the Epistle to the Romans*, (Winona Lake, IN: Alpha Greek Library, 1980), p.92.

EndNotes

[448] John Murray, ibid, p. 74.

[449] Lange, John Peter ; Schaff, Philip ; Fay, F. R. ; Hurst, J. F. ; Riddle, M. B.: *A Commentary on the Holy Scriptures : Romans*. Bellingham, WA : Logos Research Systems, Inc., 2008, S. 101.

[450] Henry, Matthew: *Matthew Henry's Commentary on the Whole Bible : Complete and Unabridged in One Volume*. Peabody : Hendrickson, 1996, c1991, S. Ro 2:1.

[451] Hendriksen, William ; Kistemaker, Simon J.: *New Testament Commentary : Exposition of Paul's Epistle to the Romans*. Grand Rapids : Baker Book House, 1953-2001 (New Testament Commentary 12-13), S. 97.

[452] Mounce, Robert H.: *Romans*. electronic ed. Nashville : Broadman & Holman Publishers, 2001, c1995 (Logos Library System; The New American Commentary 27), S. 95.

[453] Lange, John Peter ; Schaff, Philip ; Fay, F. R. ; Hurst, J. F. ; Riddle, M. B.: *A Commentary on the Holy Scriptures : Romans*. Bellingham, WA : Logos Research Systems, Inc., 2008, S. 101.

[454] The KJV translates the Hebrew word ble (heart) is mistranslated "conscience" in a few places. When one Natural theologian demanded that ble be interpreted to mean the "conscience," I pointed him to Pro. 28:26, which says that whoever trusts in his ble is a fool. If he wants ble to refer to the conscience, then Scripture forbids us to trust the conscience!

[455] Newman, Barclay Moon; Nida, Eugene Albert: *A Handbook on Paul's Letter to the Romans*. New York : United Bible Societies, 1994 (UBS Handbook Series; Helps for Translators), S. 177.

[456] Newman, Barclay Moon ; Nida, Eugene Albert: ibid, S. 432.

[457] Vincent, Marvin Richardson: *Word Studies in the New Testament*. Bellingham, WA : Logos Research Systems, Inc., 2002, S. 1:655-656.

[458] Walvoord, John F.; Zuck, Roy B. ; Dallas Theological Seminary: *The Bible Knowledge Commentary : An Exposition of the Scriptures*. Wheaton, IL : Victor Books, 1983-c1985, S. 2:446.

[459] William Shedd, *A Critical Commentary on the Epistle of St. Paul to the Romans*, (Grand Rapids: Zondervan, 1967), p.48.

[460] Wiersbe, Warren W.: *Be Decisive*. Wheaton, Ill. : Victor Books, 1996, c1995 (An Old Testament Study), S. Je 31:31.

[461] Walvoord, John F. ; Zuck, Roy B. ; Dallas Theological Seminary: *The Bible Knowledge Commentary : An Exposition of the Scriptures*. Wheaton, IL : Victor Books, 1983-c1985, S. 1:1171.

[462] Keil, Carl Friedrich ; Delitzsch, Franz: *Commentary on the Old Testament*. Peabody, MA : Hendrickson, 2002, S. 8:282.

[463] Willmington, H. L.: *Willmington's Bible Handbook*. Wheaton, Ill. : Tyndale House Publishers, 1997, S. 394.

[464] Kistemaker, Simon J. ; Hendriksen, William: *New Testament Commentary : Exposition of the Second Epistle to the Corinthians*. Grand Rapids : Baker Book House, 1953-2001 (New Testament Commentary 19), S. 103.

[465] Jean Porter, *Natural & Divine Law*, ibid, pgs. 135-136.

[466] Cited by Jean Porter in *Nature as Reason*, ibid, p. 14.

[467] Jamieson, Robert ; Fausset, A. R. ; Fausset, A. R. ; Brown, David ; Brown, David: *A Commentary, Critical and Explanatory, on the Old and New Testaments*. Oak Harbor, WA : Logos Research Systems, Inc., 1997, S. Ro 7:19.

[468] Hendriksen, William ; Kistemaker, Simon J.: *New Testament Commentary : Exposition of Paul's Epistle to the Romans*. Grand Rapids : Baker Book House, 1953-2001 (New Testament Commentary 12-13), S. 235.

[469] Morey, Robert A.: *Studies in the Atonement,* (PO Box 240, Millerstown, PA: Christian Scholars Press, 2004), S. 133.

[470] Ronald Brooks & Norman Geisler, *Come, Let Us Reason Together*, (Grand Rapids: Baker, 1990), pgs. 14, 16.

[471] Ibid, p. 14.

[472] Joseph Addison Alexander, *The Psalms: Translated and Explained*, (Grand Rapids: Zondervan, n.d.) p. 559.

[473] David Dickson, *A Commentary on the Psalms*, (London: Banner of Truth, 1965), p. 525.

[474] Henry, Matthew: *Matthew Henry's Commentary on the Whole Bible: Complete and Unabridged in One Volume*. Peabody : Hendrickson, 1996, c1991, S. Ps 147:12.

[475] *New Catholic Encyclopedia*, ibid, 10:194.
[476] The evidence that contact with Christianity influenced changes in Hinduism can be found (6/24/08) at: http://www.acns.com/~mm9n/hindu/CH.htm and http://www.appiusforum.com/hinduism.html.
[477] Lange, John Peter; Schaff, Philip; Zuckler, Otto; Aiken, Charles: *A Commentary on the Holy Scriptures : Proverbs*. Bellingham, WA : Logos Research Systems, Inc., 2008, S. 154.
[478] Keil, Carl Friedrich ; Delitzsch, Franz: *Commentary on the Old Testament*. Peabody, MA : Hendrickson, 2002, S. 6:242-243.
[479] Spence-Jones, H. D. M. (Hrsg.): *The Pulpit Commentary: Proverbs*. Bellingham, WA : Logos Research Systems, Inc., 2004, S. 309.
[480] Robert Morey, *The New Atheism and the Erosion of Freedom*, (PO Box 240, Millerstown, PA: Christian Scholars Press, 2004).
[481] I explain the biblical view of history in: Robert Morey, *Introduction to Defending the Faith*, (PO Box 240, Millerstown, PA: Christian Scholars Press, 2004).
[482] *Webster's Third International Dictionary*, ibid., p.1507.
[483] P. A. Chadbourne, *Lectures on Natural Theology or Nature and the Bible*, (NY:Putnam's Sons, 1867), p. 24.
[484] Cited in Robert Reymond, *A New Systematic Theology of the Christian Faith*, ibid., p. 149.
[485] See the documentation given in *Encyclopedia of Religion*, ibid, pgs. 6438-6441 and in Mortimer Adler, *The Great Ideas*, ibid, p. 561.
[486] P. A. Chadbourne, *Lectures on Natural Theology or Nature and the Bible*, ibid, pgs. 44-45.
[487] In the lecture series, "The Bellflower Lectures on Natural Theology," I survey the natural religions of North and Central America, Sub-Sahara Africa, and Asia. (www.faithdefenders.com)
[488] *Catechism of the Catholic Church*, (Vatican: Libreria Editrice, 1994), Part One, Section 847.
[489] Ibid., Part One: Section 841.
[490] Ibid., Part one: Section 839-840.
[491] For the historic Evangelical view, see; Erwin Lutzer, *Christ Among Other Gods*, (Chicago: Moody, 1994); D. A. Carson, The *Gagging of God*, (Grand Rapids: Zondervan, 1996); Robert Morey, *Death and The AfterLife*, (PO Box 240, Millerstown, PA: Christian Scholars Press,, 2004).
[492] See also: Clark Pinnock, *A Wideness in God's Mercy*, Grand Rapids: Zondervan, 1992) and John Sanders, *No Other Name*, (Grand Rapids: Eerdmans, 1992).
[493] Peter Kreeft & Ronald K. Tacelli, *Handbook of Christian Apologetics*, (Downers Grove, IVP, 1994).
[494] Peter Kreeft, *Ecumenical Jihad*, (San Francisco: St. Ignatius, 1996).
[495] *Handbook of Christian Apologetics*, ibid p. 326.
[496] Ibid.
[497] Ibid, p. 328.
[498] Robert Morey, *Death and The Afterlife*, (PO Box 240, Millerstown, PA: Christian Scholars Press,, 2004).
[499] I deal with the "Open View" heresy in two books: *Battle of the gods*, (PO Box 240, Millerstown, PA: Christian Scholars Press,, 2004) and *The Nature and Extent of the Knowledge of God*, (PO Box 240, Millerstown, PA: Christian Scholars Press,, 2004).
[500] Job 38:2
[501] William P. Aston, *Perceiving God*, (Ithaca, NY: Cornell University Press, 1991) p.289.
[502] T. H. L. Parker in *Baker's Dictionary of Theology*, (Grand Rapids: Baker, 1960) p. 372.
[503] William Hordern, *A Layman's Guide to Protestant Theology*, (NY: Macmillan, 1957) p. 119.
[504] Clement C. J. Webb, *Studies in The History of Natural Theology*, ibid, p. 1.
[505] Berkouwer, G. C.: *General Revelation*,(Grand Rapids : W.B. Eerdmans Pub. Co., 1955, S. 62.
[506] Bernard Ramm, *Varieties of Christian Apologetics*, (Grand Rapids: Baker, 1965) p. 21.
[507] ibid, p. 22.
[508] Henry, Carl Ferdinand Howard: *God, Revelation, and Authority*. Wheaton, Ill. : Crossway Books, 1999, S. 2:113.

EndNotes

[509] Robert Reymond, *A New Systematic Theology of the Christian Faith*, ibid., p.150.

[510] Henry, Carl Ferdinand Howard: *God, Revelation, and Authority*. Wheaton, Ill. : Crossway Books, 1999, S. 2:120.

[511] Henry, Carl Ferdinand Howard: *God, Revelation, and Authority*. Wheaton, Ill. : Crossway Books, 1999, S. 2:88-89.

[512] Frederick Copleston, *A History of Philosophy*, Volume 2, Part 1, (NY: Image books, 1962), 27.

[513] Avery Dulles, *A History of Apologetics*, (Eugene, OR: Wipf & Stock, 1999), pgs. 11-12.

[514] Walvoord, John F; Zuck, Roy B. ; Dallas Theological Seminary: *The Bible Knowledge Commentary : An Exposition of the Scriptures*. Wheaton, IL : Victor Books, 1983-c1985, S. 2:590.

[515] Garland, David E.: *2 Corinthians*. electronic ed. Nashville : Broadman & Holman Publishers, 2001, c1999 (Logos Library System; The New American Commentary 29), S. 463.

[516] Wiersbe, Warren W.: *Wiersbe's Expository Outlines on the New Testament*. Wheaton, Ill. : Victor Books, 1997, c1992, S. 521

[517] Kistemaker, Simon J. ; Hendriksen, William: *New Testament Commentary : Exposition of the First Epistle to the Corinthians*. Grand Rapids : Baker Book House, 1953-2001 (New Testament Commentary 18), S. 76.

[518] Robert Morey, *Studies in the Atonement*, (Las Vegas: Christian Scholars Press, 2004), pgs. 265-279.

[519] Hendriksen, William; Kistemaker, Simon J.: *New Testament Commentary : Exposition of the Gospel According to Matthew*. Grand Rapids : Baker Book House, 1953-2001 (New Testament Commentary 9), S. 644.

[520] Spence-Jones, H. D. M. (Hrsg.): *The Pulpit Commentary: St. Matthew Vol. II*. Bellingham, WA : Logos Research Systems, Inc., 2004, S. 133.

[521] Jamieson, Robert ; Fausset, A. R. ; Fausset, A. R. ; Brown, David ; Brown, David: *A Commentary, Critical and Explanatory, on the Old and New Testaments*. Oak Harbor, WA : Logos Research Systems, Inc., 1997, S. Mt 11:25.

[522] Louw, Johannes P. ; Nida, Eugene Albert: *Greek-English Lexicon of the New Testament : Based on Semantic Domains*. electronic ed. of the 2nd edition. New York : United Bible societies, 1996, c1989, S. 1:350.

[523] P. A. Chadbourne, *Lectures on Natural Theology*, (NY: Putnam's Sons, 1867).

[524] *Paley's Evidences of Christianity*, (NY: Carter & Brothers, 1882).

[525] Arthur James Balfour, *The Foundations of Belief*, (NY: Longmans, Green, and CO, 1895).

[526] Avery Dulles, ibid, pgs. xiii-xiv.

[527] Gordon Lewis, *Testing Christianity's Truth Claims*, ibid. See his chart on page 286 where he contrasts different apologetic systems.

[528] *A History of Apologetics*, ibid.

[529] R. C. Sproul, John Gerstner, and Arthur Lindsley, *Classical Apologetics*, (Grand Rapids: Zondervan, 1984), p. 212.

[530] Ibid, p. 214.

[531] Ibid, p. 223-224.

[532] Ibid. p.231.

[533] Ibid, p. 267.

[534] *To Everyone an Answer*, ed. Beckwith, Craig, and Moreland, ibid, p. 76.

[535] Ibid, p. 94.

[536] Ibid, p. 104.

[537] *Baker's Dictionary of Theology*, ibid., p. 456.

[538] *Classical Apologetics*, ibid p. 44.

[539] Ibid.

[540] Ibid. The authors consistently equate General Revelation with Natural Theology without ever justifying this assumption.

[541] Gordon Clark, *Religion, Reason, and Revelation*, (Philadelphia: P & R, 1961), pgs 37-58. Clark's demonstration of the circular nature of Thomistic arguments has never been refuted. I cherish to this day his personal friendship and instruction in the things of God.

[542] Hendriksen, William; Kistemaker, Simon J.: *New Testament Commentary: Exposition of the Pastoral Epistles*. Grand Rapids: Baker Book House, 1953-2001 (New Testament Commentary 4), S. 311.

[543] Walvoord, John F.; Zuck, Roy B.; Dallas Theological Seminary: *The Bible Knowledge Commentary: An Exposition of the Scriptures*. Wheaton, IL : Victor Books, 1983-c1985, S. 2:758.

[544] Richards, Lawrence O.: *The Bible Readers Companion*. electronic ed. Wheaton: Victor Books, 1991; Published in electronic form by Logos Research Systems, 1996, S. 844.